Praise for *Essential C# 4.0*

D0570449

"It's essential!"

> —*Eric Lippert, Senior Engineer, Microsoft;*
> *coauthor,* Visual Studio Tools for Office 2007

"*Essential C# 4.0* continues the tradition of prior editions—the definitive work on C# the language and how to effectively code using it. This book covers all aspects of the language, from the basics to highly advanced topics; the reader doesn't just emerge understanding the language of C#, but emerges as a better developer.

> —*Troy Magennis, C# MVP and creator of HookedOnLINQ.com*

"I've been involved with C# since its earliest days and remember vividly a conversation with Anders Hejlsberg in which we discussed what C# didn't have when compared to C++ at the time. He spoke of simplicity and compact design but it was plain that C# didn't have the muscle to compete with C++ in those early days.

Here we are, almost a decade later, with the latest incarnation of C# ready to go and the difference is huge. The elegance of C# is still there but the power of the language has advanced by leaps and bounds. Now, C# is second to none and may be first among equals. An important aspect to remember is that C# is the language but it is the .NET framework that empowers our expression as developers. *Essential C# 4.0* presents both the language and the important aspects of that framework in a clear and concise manner that makes this book a great tool for learning the language and also covers aspects of general programming that are, well, essential."

> —*Bob Powell, C# MVP, www.bobpowell.net*

"*Essential C# 4.0* is a book that anyone who wants to be an expert C# programmer should own. It's a rare book that is on both my short list of books that I recommend for experts and my short list of books that I recommend for programmers new to C#."

> —*Peter Ritchie, President, Peter Ritchie Inc. Software Consulting;*
> *Microsoft C# MVP*

"Let Mark Michaelis serve as your guide from novice to expert C# developer. If you've never used C#, read this book carefully for a complete guided tour of the language. If you're already familiar with C#, you'll still find plenty to learn. Mark's coverage of the language is very complete, including the latest techniques in the C# 4.0 additions. This book is and will remain within easy reach. It's a ready reference that every C# developer should have handy."

—*Bill Wagner, Founder, SRT Solutions; Microsoft Regional Director; author of* Effective C# *and* More Effective C#

Essential C# 4.0

Essential
C# 4.0

■ Mark Michaelis

✦✦ Addison-Wesley

Upper Saddle River, NJ • Boston • Indianapolis • San Francisco
New York • Toronto • Montreal • London • Munich • Paris • Madrid
Capetown • Sydney • Tokyo • Singapore • Mexico City

Many of the designations used by manufacturers and sellers to distinguish their products are claimed as trademarks. Where those designations appear in this book, and the publisher was aware of a trademark claim, the designations have been printed with initial capital letters or in all capitals.

The .NET logo is either a registered trademark or trademark of Microsoft Corporation in the United States and/or other countries and is used under license from Microsoft.

Microsoft, Windows, Visual Basic, Visual C#, and Visual C++ are either registered trademarks or trademarks of Microsoft Corporation in the U.S.A. and/or other countries/regions.

The author and publisher have taken care in the preparation of this book, but make no expressed or implied warranty of any kind and assume no responsibility for errors or omissions. No liability is assumed for incidental or consequential damages in connection with or arising out of the use of the information or programs contained herein.

The publisher offers excellent discounts on this book when ordered in quantity for bulk purchases or special sales, which may include electronic versions and/or custom covers and content particular to your business, training goals, marketing focus, and branding interests. For more information, please contact:

U.S. Corporate and Government Sales
(800) 382-3419
corpsales@pearsontechgroup.com

For sales outside the United States, please contact:

International Sales
international@pearson.com

Visit us on the Web: informit.com/aw

Library of Congress Cataloging-in-Publication Data

Michaelis, Mark.
   Essential C# 4.0 / Mark Michaelis.
      p.   cm.
   Includes index.
   ISBN 978-0-321-69469-0 (pbk. : alk. paper)
   1. C# (Computer program language) I. Title.
   QA76.73.C154M5237 2010
   005.13′3—dc22
                              2009052592

ISBN-13: 978-0-321-69469-0
ISBN-10:   0-321-69469-4
Text printed in the United States on recycled paper at Edwards Brothers in Ann Arbor, Michigan.
First printing, March 2010

To my family: Elisabeth, Benjamin, Hanna, and Abigail.

You have sacrificed a husband and daddy for countless hours of writing, frequently at times when he was needed most.

Thanks!

Contents at a Glance

Contents

Contents of C# 4.0 Topics

Figures

Tables

Foreword

MARK MICHAELIS'S OVERVIEW OF THE C# language has become a standard reference for developers. In this, its third edition, programmers will find a thoughtful, well-written guide to the intricacies of one of the world's most popular computer languages. Having laid a strong foundation in the earlier editions of this book, Mark adds new chapters that explain the latest features in both C# and the .NET Framework.

Two of the most important additions to the book cover the latest tools for parallel programming and the new dynamic features found in C# 4.0. The addition of dynamic features to the C# language will give developers access to late-bound languages such as Python and Ruby. Improved support for COM Interop will allow developers to access Microsoft Office with an intuitive and easy-to-use syntax that makes these great tools easy to use. Mark's coverage of these important topics, along with his explanation of the latest developments in concurrent development, make this an essential read for C# developers who want to hone their skills and master the best and most vital parts of the C# language.

As the community PM for the C# team, I work to stay attuned to the needs of our community. Again and again I hear the same message: "There is so much information coming out of Microsoft that I can't keep up. I need access to materials that explain the technology, and I need them presented in a way that I can understand." Mark Michaelis is a one-man solution to a C# developer's search for knowledge about Microsoft's most recent technologies.

I first met Mark at a breakfast held in Redmond, Washington, on a clear, sunny morning in the summer of 2006. It was an early breakfast, and I like to sleep in late. But I was told Mark was an active community member, and so I woke up early to meet him. I'm glad I did. The distinct impression he made on me that morning has remained unchanged over the years.

Mark is a tall, athletic man originally from South Africa, who speaks in a clear, firm, steady voice with a slight accent that most Americans would probably find unidentifiable. He competes in Ironman triathlons and has the lean, active look that one associates with that sport. Cheerful and optimistic, he nevertheless has a businesslike air about him; one has the sense that he is always trying to find the best way to fit too many activities into a limited time frame.

Mark makes frequent trips to the Microsoft campus to participate in reviews of upcoming technology or to consult on a team's plans for the future. Flying in from his home in Spokane, Washington, Mark has clearly defined agendas. He knows why he is on the campus, gives his all to the work, and looks forward to heading back home to his family in Spokane. Sometimes he finds time to fit in a quick meeting with me, and I always enjoy them. He is cheerful and energetic, and nearly always has something provocative to say about some new technology or program being developed by Microsoft.

This brief portrait of Mark tells you a good deal about what you can expect from this book. It is a focused book with a clear agenda written in a cheerful, no-nonsense manner. Mark works hard to discover the core parts of the language that need to be explained and then he writes about them in the same way that he speaks: with a lucid, muscular prose that is easy to understand and totally devoid of condescension. Mark knows what his audience needs to hear and he enjoys teaching.

Mark knows not only the C# language, but also the English language. He knows how to craft a sentence, how to divide his thoughts into paragraphs and subsections, and how to introduce and summarize a topic. He consistently finds clear, easy-to-understand ways to explain complex subjects.

I read the first edition of Mark's book cover to cover in just a few evenings of concentrated reading. Like the current volume, it is a delight to read. Mark selects his topics with care, and explains them in the simplest possible terms. He knows what needs to be included, and what can be left out. If he wants to explore an advanced topic, he clearly sets it apart from the rest of the text. He never shows off by first parading his intellect at the expense of our desire to understand.

A centrally important part of this new edition of the book continues to be its coverage of LINQ. For many developers the declarative style of programming used by LINQ is a new technology that requires developing new habits and new ways of thinking.

C# 3.0 contained several new features that enable LINQ. A main goal of the book is to lay out these features in detail. Explaining LINQ and the technologies that enable it is no easy task, and Mark has rallied all his formidable skills as a writer and teacher to lay this technology out for the reader in clear and easy-to-understand terms.

All the key technologies that you need to know if you want to understand LINQ are carefully explained in this text. These include

- Partial methods
- Automatic properties
- Object initializers
- Collection initializers
- Anonymous types
- Implicit local variables (`var`)
- Lambdas
- Extension methods
- Expression trees
- `IEnumerable<T>` and `IQueryable<T>`
- LINQ query operators
- Query expressions

The march to an understanding of LINQ begins with Mark's explanations of important C# 2.0 technologies such as generics and delegates. He then walks you step by step through the transition from delegates to lambdas. He explains why lambdas are part of C# 3.0 and the key role they play in LINQ. He also explains extension methods, and the role they play in implementation of the LINQ query operators.

His coverage of C# 3.0 features culminates in his detailed explanation of query expressions. He covers the key features of query expressions such as projections, filtering, ordering, grouping, and other concepts that are central to an understanding of LINQ. He winds up his chapter on query expressions by explaining how they can be converted to the LINQ query method syntax, which is actually executed by the compiler. By the time you are done reading about query expressions you will have all the knowledge you need to understand LINQ and to begin using this important technology in your own programs.

If you want to be a C# developer, or if you want to enhance your C# programming skills, there is no more useful tool than a well-crafted book on the subject. You are holding such a book in your hands. A text such as this can first teach you how the language works, and then live on as a reference that you use when you need to quickly find answers. For developers who are looking for ways to stay current on Microsoft's technologies, this book can serve as a guide through a fascinating and rapidly changing landscape. It represents the very best and latest thought on what is fast becoming the most advanced and most important contemporary programming language.

—*Charlie Calvert*
  Community Program Manager,
  Visual C#, Microsoft
  January 2010

Preface

THROUGHOUT THE HISTORY of software engineering, the methodology used to write computer programs has undergone several paradigm shifts, each building on the foundation of the former by increasing code organization and decreasing complexity. This book takes you through these same paradigm shifts.

The beginning chapters take you through **sequential programming structure,** in which statements are written in the order in which they are executed. The problem with this model is that complexity increases exponentially as the requirements increase. To reduce this complexity, code blocks are moved into methods, creating a **structured programming model.** This allows you to call the same code block from multiple locations within a program, without duplicating code. Even with this construct, however, programs quickly become unwieldy and require further abstraction. Object-oriented programming, discussed in Chapter 5, was the response. In subsequent chapters, you will learn about additional methodologies, such as interface-based programming, LINQ (and the transformation it makes to the collection API), and eventually rudimentary forms of declarative programming (in Chapter 17) via attributes.

This book has three main functions.

1. It provides comprehensive coverage of the C# language, going beyond a tutorial and offering a foundation upon which you can begin effective software development projects.

2. For readers already familiar with C#, this book provides insight into some of the more complex programming paradigms and provides in-depth coverage of the features introduced in the latest version of the language, C# 4.0 and .NET Framework 4.

3. It serves as a timeless reference, even after you gain proficiency with the language.

The key to successfully learning C# is to start coding as soon as possible. Don't wait until you are an "expert" in theory; start writing software immediately. As a believer in iterative development, I hope this book enables even a novice programmer to begin writing basic C# code by the end of Chapter 2.

A number of topics are not covered in this book. You won't find coverage of topics such as ASP.NET, ADO.NET, smart client development, distributed programming, and so on. Although these topics are relevant to the .NET Framework, to do them justice requires books of their own. Fortunately, Addison-Wesley's .NET Development Series provides a wealth of writing on these topics. *Essential C# 4.0* focuses on C# and the types within the Base Class Library. Reading this book will prepare you to focus on and develop expertise in any of the areas covered by the rest of the series.

Target Audience for This Book

My challenge with this book was to keep advanced developers awake while not abandoning beginners by using words such as *assembly, link, chain, thread,* and *fusion,* as though the topic was more appropriate for blacksmiths than for programmers. This book's primary audience is experienced developers looking to add another language to their quiver. However, I have carefully assembled this book to provide significant value to developers at all levels.

- *Beginners:* If you are new to programming, this book serves as a resource to help transition you from an entry-level programmer to a C# developer, comfortable with any C# programming task that's thrown your way. This book not only teaches you syntax, but also trains you in good programming practices that will serve you throughout your programming career.

- *Structured programmers:* Just as it's best to learn a foreign language through immersion, learning a computer language is most effective when you begin using it before you know all the intricacies. In this vein, this book begins with a tutorial that will be comfortable for those familiar with structured programming, and by the end of Chapter 4, developers in this category should feel at home writing basic control flow programs. However, the key to excellence for C# developers is not memorizing syntax. To transition from simple programs to enterprise development, the C# developer must think natively in terms of objects and their relationships. To this end, Chapter 5's Beginner Topics introduce classes and object-oriented development. The role of historically structured programming languages such as C, COBOL, and FORTRAN is still significant but shrinking, so it behooves software engineers to become familiar with object-oriented development. C# is an ideal language for making this transition because it was designed with object-oriented development as one of its core tenets.

- *Object-based and object-oriented developers:* C++ and Java programmers, and many experienced Visual Basic programmers, fall into this category. Many of you are already completely comfortable with semicolons and curly braces. A brief glance at the code in Chapter 1 reveals that at its core, C# is similar to the C and C++ style languages that you already know.

- *C# professionals:* For those already versed in C#, this book provides a convenient reference for less frequently encountered syntax. Furthermore, it provides answers to language details and subtleties that are seldom addressed. Most importantly, it presents the guidelines and patterns for programming robust and maintainable code. This book also aids in the task of teaching C# to others. With the emergence of C# 3.0 and C# 4.0, some of the most prominent enhancements are:
  - Implicitly typed variables (see Chapter 2)
  - Extension methods (see Chapter 5)
  - Partial methods (see Chapter 5)

- Anonymous types (see Chapter 11)
- Generics (see Chapter 11)
- Lambda statements and expressions (see Chapter 12)
- Expression trees (see Chapter 12)
- Standard query operators (see Chapter 14)
- Query expressions (see Chapter 15)
- Dynamic programming (Chapter 17)
- Multithreaded programming with the Task Programming Library (Chapter 18)
- Parallel query processing with PLINQ
- Concurrent collections (Chapter 19)

These topics are covered in detail for those not already familiar with them. Also pertinent to advanced C# development is the subject of pointers, in Chapter 21. Even experienced C# developers often do not understand this topic well.

Features of This Book

Essential C# 4.0 is a language book that adheres to the core C# Language 4.0 Specification. To help you understand the various C# constructs, the book provides numerous examples demonstrating each feature. Accompanying each concept are guidelines and best practices, ensuring that code compiles, avoids likely pitfalls, and achieves maximum maintainability.

To improve readability, code is specially formatted and chapters are outlined using mind maps.

Code Samples

The code snippets in most of this text (see sample listing on the next page) can run on any implementation of the Common Language Infrastructure (CLI), including the Mono, Rotor, and Microsoft .NET platforms. Platform- or vendor-specific libraries are seldom used, except when communicating important concepts relevant only to those platforms (appropriately handling the single-threaded user interface of Windows, for example). Any code that specifically requires C# 3.0 or 4.0 compliance is called out in the C# 3.0 and C# 4.0 indexes at the end of the book.

Here is a sample code listing.

LISTING 1.17: Commenting Your Code

```
class CommentSamples
{
  static void Main()
  {
                          single-line comment
    string firstName; // Variable for storing the first name
    string lastName;  // Variable for storing the last name

    System.Console.WriteLine("Hey you!");

                   delimited comment inside statement
    System.Console.Write /* No new line */ (
        "Enter your first name: ");
    firstName = System.Console.ReadLine();

    System.Console.Write /* No new line */ (
        "Enter your last name: ");
    lastName = System.Console.ReadLine();

    /* Display a greeting to the console   }  delimited comment
       using composite formatting. */
    System.Console.WriteLine("Your full name is {0} {1}.",
        firstName, lastName);
    // This is the end
    // of the program listing
  }
}
```

The formatting is as follows.

- Comments are shown in italics.

  ```
  /* Display a greeting to the console
     using composite formatting. */
  ```

- Keywords are shown in bold.

  ```
  static void Main()
  ```

- Highlighted code calls out specific code snippets that may have changed from an earlier listing, or demonstrates the concept described in the text.

```
System.Console.Write /* No new line */ (
```

Highlighting can appear on an entire line or on just a few characters within a line.

```
System.Console.WriteLine(
    "Your full name is {0} {1}.",
```

- Incomplete listings contain an ellipsis to denote irrelevant code that has been omitted.

```
// ...
```

- Console output is the output from a particular listing that appears following the listing.

OUTPUT 1.4:

```
>HeyYou.exe
Hey you!
Enter your first name: Inigo
Enter your last name: Montoya
```

- User input for the program appears in italics.

Although it might have been convenient to provide full code samples that you could copy into your own programs, doing so would detract you from learning a particular topic. Therefore, you need to modify the code samples before you can incorporate them into your programs. The core omission is error checking, such as exception handling. Also, code samples do not explicitly include using System statements. You need to assume the statement throughout all samples.

You can find sample code and bonus mateial at intelliTechture.com/EssentialCSharp and at informit.com/msdotnetseries.

Mind Maps

Each chapter's introduction includes a **mind map**, which serves as an outline that provides an at-a-glance reference to each chapter's content. Here is an example (taken from Chapter 5).

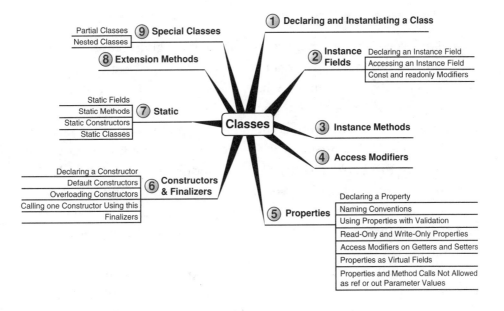

The theme of each chapter appears in the mind map's center. High-level topics spread out from the core. Mind maps allow you to absorb the flow from high-level to more detailed concepts easily, with less chance of encountering very specific knowledge that you might not be looking for.

Helpful Notes

Depending on your level of experience, special code blocks and tabs will help you navigate through the text.

- Beginner Topics provide definitions or explanations targeted specifically toward entry-level programmers.
- Advanced Topics enable experienced developers to focus on the material that is most relevant to them.
- Callout notes highlight key principles in callout boxes so that readers easily recognize their significance.
- Language Contrast sidebars identify key differences between C# and its predecessors to aid those familiar with other languages.

How This Book Is Organized

At a high level, software engineering is about managing complexity, and it is toward this end that I have organized *Essential C# 4.0*. Chapters 1–4 introduce structured programming, which enable you to start writing simple functioning code immediately. Chapters 5–9 present the object-oriented constructs of C#. Novice readers should focus on fully understanding this section before they proceed to the more advanced topics found in the remainder of this book. Chapters 11–13 introduce additional complexity-reducing constructs, handling common patterns needed by virtually all modern programs. This leads to dynamic programming with reflection and attributes, which is used extensively for threading and interoperability in the chapters that follow.

The book ends with a chapter on the Common Language Infrastructure, which describes C# within the context of the development platform in which it operates. This chapter appears at the end because it is not C# specific and it departs from the syntax and programming style in the rest of the book. However, this chapter is suitable for reading at any time, perhaps most appropriately immediately following Chapter 1.

Here is a description of each chapter (in this list, chapter numbers shown in **bold** indicate the presence of C# 3.0 or C# 4.0 material).

- *Chapter 1—Introducing C#:* After presenting the C# HelloWorld program, this chapter proceeds to dissect it. This should familiarize readers with the look and feel of a C# program and provide details on how to compile and debug their own programs. It also touches on the context of a C# program's execution and its intermediate language.
- ***Chapter 2—Data Types:*** Functioning programs manipulate data, and this chapter introduces the primitive data types of C#. This includes coverage of two type categories, value types and reference types, along with conversion between types and support for arrays.
- *Chapter 3—Operators and Control Flow:* To take advantage of the iterative capabilities in a computer, you need to know how to include loops and conditional logic within your program. This chapter also covers the C# operators, data conversion, and preprocessor directives.

- *Chapter 4—Methods and Parameters:* This chapter investigates the details of methods and their parameters. It includes passing by value, passing by reference, and returning data via a parameter. In C# 4.0 default parameter support was added and this chapter explains how to use them.

- *Chapter 5—Classes:* Given the basic building blocks of a class, this chapter combines these constructs together to form fully functional types. Classes form the core of object-oriented technology by defining the template for an object.

- *Chapter 6—Inheritance:* Although inheritance is a programming fundamental to many developers, C# provides some unique constructs, such as the new modifier. This chapter discusses the details of the inheritance syntax, including overriding.

- *Chapter 7—Interfaces:* This chapter demonstrates how interfaces are used to define the "versionable" interaction contract between classes. C# includes both explicit and implicit interface member implementation, enabling an additional encapsulation level not supported by most other languages.

- *Chapter 8—Value Types:* Although not as prevalent as defining reference types, it is sometimes necessary to define value types that behave in a fashion similar to the primitive types built into C#. This chapter describes how to define structures, while exposing the idiosyncrasies they may introduce.

- *Chapter 9—Well-Formed Types:* This chapter discusses more advanced type definition. It explains how to implement operators, such as + and casts, and describes how to encapsulate multiple classes into a single library. In addition, the chapter demonstrates defining namespaces and XML comments, and discusses how to design classes for garbage collection.

- *Chapter 10—Exception Handling:* This chapter expands on the exception-handling introduction from Chapter 4 and describes how exceptions follow a hierarchy that enables creating custom exceptions. It also includes some best practices on exception handling.

- *Chapter 11—Generics:* Generics is perhaps the core feature missing from C# 1.0. This chapter fully covers this 2.0 feature. In addition, C# 4.0 added support for covariance and contravariance—something covered in the context of generics in this chapter.

- *Chapter 12—Delegates and Lambda Expressions:* Delegates begin clearly distinguishing C# from its predecessors by defining patterns for handling events within code. This virtually eliminates the need for writing routines that poll. Lambda expressions are the key concept that make C# 3.0's LINQ possible. This chapter explains how lambda expressions build on the delegate construct by providing a more elegant and succinct syntax. This chapter forms the foundation for the new collection API discussed next.

- *Chapter 13—Events:* Encapsulated delegates, known as events, are a core construct of the Common Language Runtime. Anonymous methods, another C# 2.0 feature, are also presented here.

- *Chapter 14—Collection Interfaces with Standard Query Operators:* The simple and yet elegantly powerful changes introduced in C# 3.0 begin to shine in this chapter as we take a look at the extension methods of the new Enumerable class. This class makes available an entirely new collection API known as the standard query operators and discussed in detail here.

- *Chapter 15—LINQ with Query Expressions:* Using standard query operators alone results in some long statements that are hard to decipher. However, query expressions provide an alternative syntax that matches closely with SQL, as described in this chapter.

- *Chapter 16—Building Custom Collections:* In building custom APIs that work against business objects, it is sometimes necessary to create custom collections. This chapter details how to do this, and in the process introduces contextual keywords that make custom collection building easier.

- *Chapter 17—Reflection, Attributes, and Dynamic Programming:* Object-oriented programming formed the basis for a paradigm shift in program structure in the late 1980s. In a similar way, attributes facilitate declarative programming and embedded metadata, ushering in a new paradigm. This chapter looks at attributes and discusses how to retrieve them via reflection. It also covers file input and output via the serialization framework within the Base Class Library. In C# 4.0 a new keyword, dynamic, was added to the language. This removed all type checking until runtime, a significant expansion of what can be done with C#.

- *Chapter 18—Multithreading:* Most modern programs require the use of threads to execute long-running tasks while ensuring active response to simultaneous events. As programs become more sophisticated, they must take additional precautions to protect data in these advanced environments. Programming multithreaded applications is complex. This chapter discusses how to work with threads and provides best practices to avoid the problems that plague multithreaded applications.

- *Chapter 19—Synchronization and Other Multithreading Patterns:* Building on the preceding chapter, this one demonstrates some of the built-in threading pattern support that can simplify the explicit control of multithreaded code.

- *Chapter 20—Platform Interoperability and Unsafe Code:* Given that C# is a relatively young language, far more code is written in other languages than in C#. To take advantage of this preexisting code, C# supports interoperability—the calling of unmanaged code—through P/Invoke. In addition, C# provides for the use of pointers and direct memory manipulation. Although code with pointers requires special privileges to run, it provides the power to interoperate fully with traditional C-based application programming interfaces.

- *Chapter 21—The Common Language Infrastructure:* Fundamentally, C# is the syntax that was designed as the most effective programming language on top of the underlying Common Language Infrastructure. This chapter delves into how C# programs relate to the underlying runtime and its specifications.

- *Appendix A—Downloading and Installing the C# Compiler and the CLI Platform:* This appendix provides instructions for setting up a C# compiler and the platform on which to run the code, Microsoft .NET or Mono.

- *Appendix B—Full Source Code Listing:* In several cases, a full source code listing within a chapter would have made the chapter too long. To make these listings still available to the reader, this appendix includes full listings from Chapters 3, 11, 12, 14, and 17.

- *Appendix C—Concurrent Classes from* `System.Collections.Concurrent`: This appendix provides overview diagrams of the concurrent collections that were added in the .NET Framework 4.
- *Appendixes D-F: C# 2.0, C# 3.0, C# 4.0 Topics:* These appendices provide a quick reference for any C# 2.0, C# 3.0, or C# 4.0 content. They are specifically designed to help programmers quickly get up to speed on C# features.

I hope you find this book to be a great resource in establishing your C# expertise and that you continue to reference it for the more obscure areas of C# and its inner workings.

—*Mark Michaelis*
  mark.michaelis.net

Acknowledgments

NO BOOK CAN BE published by the author alone, and I am extremely grateful for the multitude of people who helped me with this one.

The order in which I thank people is not significant, except for those that come first. By far, my family has made the biggest sacrifice to allow me to complete this. Benjamin, Hanna, and Abigail often had a Daddy distracted by this book, but Elisabeth suffered even more so. She was often left to take care of things, holding the family's world together on her own. I would like to say it got easier with each edition but, alas, no; as the kids got older, life became more hectic, and without me Elisabeth was stretched to the breaking point virtually all the time. A huge sorry and ginormous Thank You!

Many technical editors reviewed each chapter in minute detail to ensure technical accuracy. I was often amazed by the subtle errors these folks still managed to catch: Paul Bramsman, Kody Brown, Ian Davis, Doug Dechow, Gerard Frantz, Thomas Heavey, Anson Horton, Brian Jones, Shane Kercheval, Angelika Langer, Eric Lippert, John Michaelis, Jason Morse, Nicholas Paldino, Jon Skeet, Michael Stokesbary, Robert Stokesbary, John Timney, and Stephen Toub.

In particular, Michael was a huge help in editing the technical content and serving as a sounding board as I was putting the material together, not to mention his invaluable friendship. I am also especially grateful to the C# MVPs (Nicholas and John), who know the language in certain areas second only to those on the C# team.

Eric is no less than amazing. His grasp of the C# vocabulary is truly astounding and I am very appreciative of his edits, especially when he pushed for perfection in terminology. His improvements to the C# 3.0 chapters were incredibly significant, and in the second edition my only regret was that I didn't have him review all the chapters. However, that regret is no longer. Eric painstakingly reviewed every *Essential C# 4.0* chapter with amazing detail and precision. I am extremely grateful for his contribution to making this book even better than the first two editions. Thanks, Eric! I can't imagine anyone better for the job. You deserve all the credit for raising the bar from good to great.

Like Eric and C#, there are fewer than a handful of people who know .NET multithreading as well as Stephen Toub. Accordingly, Stephen focused on the two rewritten multithreading chapters and their new focus on parallel programming. Stephen's feedback in combination with the changes that occurred between Beta editions caused me to ask Stephen to take a second look after I updated them based on his first review—he accepted. I truly can't imagine a better person to do the review. Thanks, Stephen! Thanks especially for putting up with me as I ramped up on the new API.

Paul and Robert were key technical reviewers for the second edition, and they painstakingly recompiled and executed each listing. This was a big effort and the errors you found were much appreciated, along with your suggestions.

Thanks to Scott Robertson at UCLA Extension for creating instructional materials for this book for university adoption.

Thanks to everyone at Addison-Wesley for their patience in working with me in spite of my frequent focus on everything else except the manuscript. Thanks to: Olivia Basegio, Sheri Cain, Curt Johnson, Joan Murray, and Brandon Prebynski.

Joan, thanks also for the weekly telephone calls to keep me on task during the second edition—well, for at least making me feel guilty when I wasn't on task. Thanks also for your willingness to put up with me for this third edition. I wish I could say that this time I made it less stressful for you, but I doubt I did. Thanks!

Thanks to Audrey Doyle. Anyone who can quote *The Chicago Manual of Style* has to be the right person to have on your team as the copy editor. The stuff she noticed and corrected made me wonder whether I am qualified to use email. Thanks especially for all the formatting help.

Prashant Sridharan, from Microsoft's Developer Division, was the one who got me started on this, and he provided me with an incredible jump-start on the material. Thanks, Prashant!

About the Author

Mark Michaelis recently started IntelliTechture, a software engineering and consulting company with high-end skills in Microsoft VSTS/TFS, BizTalk, SharePoint, and .NET. Mark also serves as a chief software architect and trainer for IDesign Inc.

Mark holds a BA in philosophy from the University of Illinois and an MS in computer science from the Illinois Institute of Technology. In 2007, Mark was recognized as a Microsoft Regional Director. Since 1996, he has been a Microsoft MVP for C#, Visual Studio Team System, and the Windows SDK. He serves on several Microsoft software design review teams, including C#, the Connected Systems Division, and VSTS. Mark speaks at developer conferences and has written numerous articles and books.

When not bonding with his computer, Mark is busy with his family or training for another triathlon (having completed the Ironman in 2008). Mark lives in Spokane, Washington, with his wife Elisabeth, and three children, Benjamin, Hanna, and Abigail.

▉ 1 ▪
Introducing C#

C# IS NOW A WELL-ESTABLISHED LANGUAGE that builds on features found in its predecessor C-style languages (C, C++, and Java), making it immediately familiar to many experienced programmers.[1] Part of a larger, more complex execution platform called the Common Language Infrastructure (CLI), C# is a programming language for building software components and applications.

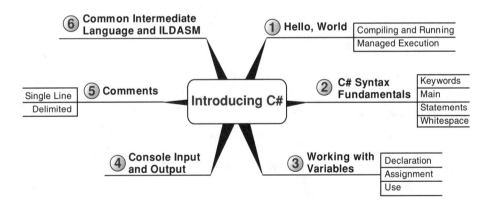

This chapter introduces C# using the traditional HelloWorld program. The chapter focuses on C# syntax fundamentals, including defining an entry point into the C# program executable. This will familiarize you with

---

1. It has now been more than ten years since the first C# design meeting.

the C# syntax style and structure, and it will enable you to produce the simplest of C# programs. Prior to the discussion of C# syntax fundamentals is a summary of managed execution context, which explains how a C# program executes at runtime. This chapter ends with a discussion of variable declaration, writing and retrieving data from the console, and the basics of commenting code in C#.

Hello, World

The best way to learn a new programming language is to write code. The first example is the classic HelloWorld program. In this program, you will display some text to the screen.

Listing 1.1 shows the complete HelloWorld program; in the following sections, you will compile the code.

LISTING 1.1: HelloWorld in C#[2]

```csharp
class HelloWorld
{
  static void Main()
  {
    System.Console.WriteLine("Hello. My name is Inigo Montoya.");
  }
}
```

■ NOTE

C# is a case-sensitive language: Incorrect case prevents the code from compiling successfully.

Those experienced in programming with Java, C, or C++ will immediately see similarities. Like Java, C# inherits its basic syntax from C and C++.[3] Syntactic punctuation (such as semicolons and curly braces), features (such as case sensitivity), and keywords (such as class, public, and void)

---

2. Refer to the movie *The Princess Bride* if you're confused about the Inigo Montoya references.
3. When creating C#, the language creators sat down with the specifications for C/C++, literally crossing out the features they didn't like and creating a list of the ones they did like. The group also included designers with strong backgrounds in other languages.

are familiar to programmers experienced in these languages. Beginners and programmers from other languages will quickly find these constructs intuitive.

Compiling and Running the Application

The C# compiler allows any file extension for files containing C# source code, but .cs is typically used. After saving the source code to a file, developers must compile it. (Appendix A provides instructions for installing the compiler.) Because the mechanics of the command are not part of the C# standard, the compilation command varies depending on the C# compiler implementation.

If you place Listing 1.1 into a file called HelloWorld.cs, the compilation command in Output 1.1 will work with the Microsoft .NET compiler (assuming appropriate paths to the compiler are set up).[4]

OUTPUT 1.1:

```
>csc.exe HelloWorld.cs
Microsoft (R) Visual C# 2008 Compiler version 4.0.20506.1
for Microsoft (R) .NET Framework version 4.0
Copyright (C) Microsoft Corporation. All rights reserved.
```

The exact output will vary depending on what version of the compiler you use.

Running the resultant program, HelloWorld.exe, displays the message shown in Output 1.2.

OUTPUT 1.2:

```
>HelloWorld.exe
Hello. My name is Inigo Montoya.
```

The program created by the C# compiler, HelloWorld.exe, is an **assembly.** Instead of creating an entire program that can be executed

---

4. Compilation using the Mono compiler, an open source compiler sponsored by Novell, is virtually identical, except that the compiler name is mcs.exe rather than csc.exe. Although I would very much have liked to place instructions for each platform here, doing so detracts from the topic of introducing C#. See Appendix A for details on Mono.

independently, developers can create a library of code that can be referenced by another, larger program. Libraries (or class libraries) use the filename extension `.dll`, which stands for Dynamic Link Library (DLL). A library is also an assembly. In other words, the output from a successful C# compile is an assembly regardless of whether it is a program or a library.

Language Contrast: Java—Filename Must Match Class Name

In Java, the filename must follow the name of the class. In C#, this convention is frequently followed but is not required. In C#, it is possible to have two classes in one file, and starting with C# 2.0, it's possible to have a single class span multiple files.

C# Syntax Fundamentals

Once you successfully compile and run the `HelloWorld` program, you are ready to start dissecting the code to learn its individual parts. First, consider the C# keywords along with the identifiers that the developer chooses.

■ BEGINNER TOPIC

Keywords

In order for the compiler to interpret the code, certain words within C# have special status and meaning. Known as **keywords** or **reserved words,** they provide the concrete syntax that the compiler uses to interpret the expressions the programmer writes. In the `HelloWorld` program, `class`, `static`, and `void` are examples of keywords.

The compiler uses the keywords to identify the structure and organization of the code. Because the compiler interprets these words with elevated significance, you can use keywords only under the specific rules identified by the language. In other words, programming languages require that developers place keywords only in certain locations. When programmers violate these rules, the compiler will issue errors.

C# Keywords

Table 1.1 shows the C# keywords.

TABLE 1.1: C# Keywords

abstract	add*	alias*	as
ascending*	base	bool	break
by*	byte	case	catch
char	checked	class	const
continue	decimal	default	delegate
descending*	do	double	dynamic*
else	enum	equals*	event
explicit	extern	false	finally
fixed	float	for	foreach
from*	get*	global*	goto
group*	if	implicit	in
int	interface	internal	into*
is	join*	let*	lock
long	namespace	new	null
object	on*	operator	orderby*
out	override	params	partial*
private	protected	public	readonly
ref	remove*	return	sbyte
sealed	select*	set*	short
sizeof	stackalloc	static	string
struct	switch	this	throw
true	try	typeof	uint

* Contextual keyword   *Continues*

TABLE 1.1: C# Keywords *(Continued)*

ulong	unchecked	unsafe	ushort
using	value*	var*	virtual
void	volatile	where*	while
yield*			

* Contextual keyword

After C# 1.0, no new keywords were introduced to C#. However, some constructs in these later versions use **contextual keywords,** which are significant only in specific locations. Outside these designated locations, contextual keywords have no special significance.[5] By this method, all C# 1.0 code is fully compatible with the later standards.[6] (Table 1.1 designates contextual keywords with a *.)

■ BEGINNER TOPIC

Identifiers

In addition to the keywords defined in C#, developers may provide their own names. Programming languages refer to these names as **identifiers** since they identify constructs that the programmer codes. In Listing 1.1, HelloWorld and Main are examples of identifiers. It is possible to assign a value to a variable and then refer to it later using its identifier. It is important, therefore, that the names the developer assigns are meaningful rather

---

5. For example, early in the design of C# 2.0, the language designers designated yield as a keyword, and Microsoft released alpha versions of the C# 2.0 compiler, with yield as a designated keyword, to thousands of developers. However, the language designers eventually determined that by using yield return rather than yield, they could ultimately avoid adding yield as a keyword because it would have no special significance outside its proximity to return.

6. There are some rare and unfortunate incompatibilities, such as the following:
   - C# 2.0 requiring implementation of IDisposable with the using statement, rather than simply a Dispose() method
   - Some rare generic expressions such as F(G<A,B>(7)); in C# 1.0, that means F((G<A), (B>7)) and in C# 2.0, that means to call generic method G<A,B> with argument 7 and pass the result to F

than arbitrary. A keen ability to select succinct and indicative names is an important characteristic of a strong programmer because the resultant code is easier to understand and reuse. In some rare cases, some identifiers, such as `Main`, can have a special meaning in the C# language.

■ ADVANCED TOPIC

Keywords

Although it is rare, keywords may be used as identifiers if they include "@" as a prefix. For example, you could name a local variable `@return`. Similarly (although it doesn't conform to the casing standards of C# coding standards), it is possible to name a method `@throw()`.

There are also four undocumented reserved keywords in the Microsoft implementation: `__arglist`, `__makeref`, `__reftype`, and `__refvalue`. These are required only in rare interop scenarios and you can ignore them for all practical purposes.

Type Definition

All code in C# appears within a type definition, and the most common type definition begins with the keyword `class`. A **class definition** is the section of code that generally begins with `class identifier { ... }`, as shown in Listing 1.2.

LISTING 1.2: Basic Class Declaration

```
class HelloWorld
{
  ...
}
```

The name used for the type (in this case, `HelloWorld`) can vary, but by convention, it should begin with a capital letter and a noun. If the name contains multiple words appended together, then each additional word should also begin with a capital letter. For this particular example, therefore, other possible names are `Greetings`, `HelloInigoMontoya`, `Hello`, or simply `Program`. (`Program` works especially if it is the class that contains the `Main()` method described next.) The CLI creators called this type of casing **Pascal casing** because of its popularity in the Pascal programming language. The alternative, **camel casing,** follows the same convention, except that the first letter is lowercase. Examples include `quotient`, `first-Name`, and `theDreadPirateRoberts`.

Generally, programs contain multiple types, each containing multiple methods.

Main

■ BEGINNER TOPIC

What Is a Method?

Syntactically, a **method** in C# is a named block of code introduced by a method declaration (for example, `static void Main()`) and followed by zero or more statements within curly braces. Methods perform computations and/or actions. Similar to paragraphs in written languages, methods provide a means of structuring and organizing code so that it is more readable. More importantly, methods avoid the need to duplicate code. The method declaration introduces the method and defines the method name along with the data passed to and from the method. In Listing 1.3, `Main()` followed by { ... } is an example of a C# method.

The location where C# programs begin execution is the **Main method,** which begins with `static void Main()`. When you execute the program by typing `HelloWorld.exe` at the command console, the program starts up, resolves the location of `Main`, and begins executing the first statement within Listing 1.3.

LISTING 1.3: Breaking Apart HelloWorld

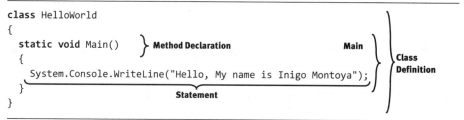

Although the Main method declaration can vary to some degree, `static` and the method name, `Main`, are always required for a program.

■ ADVANCED TOPIC

Declaration of the Main Method

Although it is possible to declare the Main method without parameters or a return type, C# supports specifying either one. Listing 1.4 shows the full declaration of the Main method.

LISTING 1.4: The Main Method, with Parameters and a Return

```csharp
static int Main(string[] args)
{
    ...
}
```

The args parameter is an array of strings corresponding to the command-line arguments. However, the first element of the array is not the program name but the first command-line parameter to appear after the executable name, unlike in C and C++. To retrieve the full command used to execute the program use System.Environment.CommandLine.

The int return from Main is the status code and it indicates the success of the program's execution. A return of a nonzero value generally indicates an error.

Language Contrast: C++/Java—main() Is All Lowercase

Unlike its C-style predecessors, C# uses an uppercase *M* for the Main method in order to be consistent with the Pascal-based naming conventions of C#.

The designation of the Main method as static indicates that other methods may call it directly off the class definition. Without the static designation, the command console that started the program would need to perform additional work (known as **instantiation**) before calling the method. (Chapter 5 contains an entire section devoted to the topic of static members.)

Placing void prior to Main() indicates that this method does not return any data (explained further in Chapter 2).

One distinctive C/C++ style characteristic followed by C# is the use of curly braces for the body of a construct, such as the class or the method. For example, the Main method contains curly braces that surround its implementation; in this case, only one statement appears in the method.

Statements and Statement Delimiters

The Main method includes a single statement, System.Console.Write-Line(), which is used to write a line of text to the console. C# generally uses a semicolon to indicate the end of a **statement,** where a statement comprises one or more actions that the code will perform. Declaring a variable, controlling the program flow, and calling a method are examples of statements.

Language Contrast: Visual Basic—Line-Based Statements

Some languages are line-based, meaning that without a special annotation, statements cannot span a line. Until Visual Basic 2010, Visual Basic was an example of a line-based language. It required an underscore at the end of a line to indicate that a statement spans multiple lines. Starting with Visual Basic 2010, many cases were introduced where the line continuation character was optional.

■ ADVANCED TOPIC

Statements without Semicolons

Many programming elements in C# end with a semicolon. One example that does not include the semicolon is a switch statement. Because curly braces are always included in a switch statement, C# does not require a semicolon following the statement. In fact, code blocks themselves are considered statements (they are also composed of statements) and they don't require closure using a semicolon. Similarly, there are cases, such as the using declarative, in which a semicolon occurs at the end but it is not a statement.

Since creation of a newline does not separate statements, you can place multiple statements on the same line and the C# compiler will interpret the line to have multiple instructions. For example, Listing 1.5 contains two statements on a single line that, in combination, display Up and Down on two separate lines.

LISTING 1.5: **Multiple Statements on One Line**

```
System.Console.WriteLine("Up");System.Console.WriteLine("Down");
```

C# also allows the splitting of a statement across multiple lines. Again, the C# compiler looks for a semicolon to indicate the end of a statement (see Listing 1.6).

LISTING 1.6: **Splitting a Single Statement across Multiple Lines**

```
System.Console.WriteLine(
    "Hello. My name is Inigo Montoya.");
```

In Listing 1.6, the original WriteLine() statement from the HelloWorld program is split across multiple lines.

Whitespace

The semicolon makes it possible for the C# compiler to ignore whitespace in code. Apart from a few exceptions, C# allows developers to insert whitespace throughout the code without altering its semantic meaning. In Listing 1.5 and Listing 1.6, it didn't matter whether a newline was inserted within a statement or between statements, and doing so had no effect on the resultant executable created by the compiler.

▪ BEGINNER TOPIC

What Is Whitespace?

Whitespace is the combination of one or more consecutive formatting characters such as tab, space, and newline characters. Eliminating all whitespace between words is obviously significant, as is whitespace within a quoted string.

Frequently, programmers use whitespace to indent code for greater readability. Consider the two variations on HelloWorld, as shown in Listing 1.7 and Listing 1.8.

LISTING 1.7: No Indentation Formatting

```
class HelloWorld
{
static void Main()
{
System.Console.WriteLine("Hello Inigo Montoya");
}
}
```

LISTING 1.8: Removing Whitespace

```
class HelloWorld{static void Main()
{System.Console.WriteLine("Hello Inigo Montoya");}}
```

Although these two examples look significantly different from the original program, the C# compiler sees them as identical.

■ BEGINNER TOPIC

Formatting Code with Whitespace

Indenting the code using whitespace is important for greater readability. As you begin writing code, you need to follow established coding standards and conventions in order to enhance code readability.

The convention used in this book is to place curly braces on their own line and to indent the code contained between the curly brace pair. If another curly brace pair appears within the first pair, all the code within the second set of braces is also indented.

This is not a uniform C# standard, but a stylistic preference.

Working with Variables

Now that you've been introduced to the most basic C# program, it's time to declare a local variable. Once a variable is declared, you can assign it a value, replace that value with a new value, and use it in calculations, output, and so on. However, you cannot change the data type of the variable. In Listing 1.9, `string max` is a variable declaration.

LISTING 1.9: Declaring and Assigning a Variable

```
class MiracleMax
{
  static void Main()
  {
          data type
          ⏜
      string max;
              ⏝
              variable
      max = "Have fun storming the castle!";

      System.Console.WriteLine(max);
  }
}
```

▪ BEGINNER TOPIC

Local Variables

A **variable** refers to a storage location by a name that the program can later assign and modify. *Local* indicates that the programmer **declared** the variable within a method.

To declare a variable is to define it, which you do by

1. Specifying the type of data which the variable will contain
2. Assigning it an identifier (name)

Data Types

Listing 1.9 declares a variable with the data type `string`. Other common data types used in this chapter are `int` and `char`.

- `int` is the C# designation of an integer type that is 32 bits in size.
- `char` is used for a character type. It is 16 bits, large enough for (nonsurrogate) Unicode characters.

The next chapter looks at these and other common data types in more detail.

■ BEGINNER TOPIC

What Is a Data Type?

The type of data that a variable declaration specifies is called a **data type** (or object type). A data type, or simply **type,** is a classification of things that share similar characteristics and behavior. For example, *animal* is a type. It classifies all things (monkeys, warthogs, and platypuses) that have animal characteristics (multicellular, capacity for locomotion, and so on). Similarly, in programming languages, a type is a definition for several items endowed with similar qualities.

Declaring a Variable

In Listing 1.9, `string max` is a variable declaration of a string type whose name is `max`. It is possible to declare multiple variables within the same statement by specifying the data type once and separating each identifier with a comma. Listing 1.10 demonstrates this.

LISTING 1.10: Declaring Two Variables within One Statement

```
string message1, message2;
```

Because a multivariable declaration statement allows developers to provide the data type only once within a declaration, all variables will be of the same type.

In C#, the name of the variable may begin with any letter or an underscore (_), followed by any number of letters, numbers, and/or underscores. By convention, however, local variable names are camel-cased (the first letter in each word is capitalized, except for the first word) and do not include underscores.

Assigning a Variable

After declaring a local variable, you must assign it a value before referencing it. One way to do this is to use the = **operator,** also known as the **simple assignment operator.** Operators are symbols used to identify the function the code is to perform. Listing 1.11 demonstrates how to use the assignment operator to designate the string values to which the variables max[7] and `valerie` will point.

---

7. I am not using max to mean the math function here; I'm using it as a variable name.

LISTING 1.11: Changing the Value of a Variable

```csharp
class MiracleMax
{
  static void Main()
  {
      string valerie;
      string max = "Have fun storming the castle!";

      valerie = "Think it will work?";

      System.Console.WriteLine(max);
      System.Console.WriteLine(valerie);

      max = "It would take a miracle.";
      System.Console.WriteLine(max);
  }
}
```

From this listing, observe that it is possible to assign a variable as part of the variable declaration (as it was for max), or afterward in a separate statement (as with the variable valerie). The value assigned must always be on the right side.

Running the compiled MiracleMax.exe program produces the code shown in Output 1.3.

OUTPUT 1.3:

```
>MiracleMax.exe
Have fun storming the castle!
Think it will work?
It would take a miracle.
```

C# requires that developers assign a local variable before accessing it. Additionally, an assignment returns a value. Therefore, C# allows two assignments within the same statement, as demonstrated in Listing 1.12.

LISTING 1.12: Assignment Returning a Value That Can Be Assigned Again

```csharp
class MiracleMax
{
  static void Main()
  {
    // ...
    string requirements, max;
    requirements = max = "It would take a miracle.";
```

```
        // ...
    }
  }
```

Using a Variable

The result of the assignment, of course, is that you can then refer to the value using the variable identifier. Therefore, when you use the variable max within the `System.Console.WriteLine(max)` statement, the program displays `Have fun storming the castle!`, the value of max, on the console. Changing the value of max and executing the same `System.Console.WriteLine(max)` statement causes the new max value, `It would take a miracle.`, to be displayed.

■ ADVANCED TOPIC

Strings Are Immutable

All data of type `string`, whether string literals or otherwise, is immutable (or unmodifiable). For example, it is not possible to change the string `"Come As You Are"` to `"Come As You Age"`. A change such as this requires that you reassign the variable to point to a new location in memory, instead of modifying the data to which the variable originally referred.

Console Input and Output

This chapter already used `System.Console.WriteLine` repeatedly for writing out text to the command console. In addition to being able to write out data, a program needs to be able to accept data that a user may enter.

Getting Input from the Console

One of the ways to retrieve text that is entered at the console is to use `System.Console.ReadLine()`. This method stops the program execution so that the user can enter characters. When the user presses the Enter key, creating a newline, the program continues. The output, also known as the **return,** from the `System.Console.ReadLine()` method is the string of text that was entered. Consider Listing 1.13 and the corresponding output shown in Output 1.4.

LISTING 1.13: Using System.Console.ReadLine()

```
class HeyYou
{
  static void Main()
  {
      string firstName;
      string lastName;

      System.Console.WriteLine("Hey you!");

      System.Console.Write("Enter your first name: ");
      firstName = System.Console.ReadLine();

      System.Console.Write("Enter your last name: ");
      lastName = System.Console.ReadLine();

      ...

  }
}
```

OUTPUT 1.4:

```
>HeyYou.exe
Hey you!
Enter your first name: Inigo
Enter your last name: Montoya
```

After each prompt, this program uses the System.Console.ReadLine() method to retrieve the text the user entered and assign it to an appropriate variable. By the time the second System.Console.ReadLine() assignment completes, firstName contains to the value Inigo and lastName refers to the value Montoya.

■ ADVANCED TOPIC

System.Console.Read()

In addition to the System.Console.ReadLine() method, there is also a System.Console.Read() method. However, the data type returned by the System.Console.Read() method is an integer corresponding to the character value read, or –1 if no more characters are available. To retrieve the actual character, it is necessary to first cast the integer to a character, as shown in Listing 1.14.

LISTING 1.14: Using **System.Console.Read()**

```
int readValue;
char character;
readValue = System.Console.Read();
character = (char) readValue;
System.Console.Write(character);
```

The System.Console.Read() method does not return the input until the user presses the Enter key; no processing of characters will begin, even if the user types multiple characters before pressing the Enter key.

In C# 2.0, the CLR designers added a new method called System. Console.ReadKey() which, in contrast to System.Console.Read(), returns the input after a single keystroke. It allows the developer to intercept the keystroke and perform actions such as key validation, restricting the characters to numerics.

Writing Output to the Console

In Listing 1.13, you prompt the user for his first and last names using the method System.Console.Write() rather than System.Console.Write-Line(). Instead of placing a newline character after displaying the text, the System.Console.Write() method leaves the current position on the same line. In this way, any text the user enters will be on the same line as the prompt for input. The output from Listing 1.13 demonstrates the effect of System.Console.Write().

The next step is to write the values retrieved using System.Console. ReadLine() back to the console. In the case of Listing 1.15, the program writes out the user's full name. However, instead of using System.Con-sole.WriteLine() as before, this code will use a slight variation. Output 1.5 shows the corresponding output.

LISTING 1.15: Formatting Using **System.Console.WriteLine()**

```
class HeyYou
{
  static void Main()
  {
      string firstName;
      string lastName;
```

```
        System.Console.WriteLine("Hey you!");

        System.Console.Write("Enter your first name: ");
        firstName = System.Console.ReadLine();

        System.Console.Write("Enter your last name: ");
        lastName = System.Console.ReadLine();

        System.Console.WriteLine(
            "Your full name is {0} {1}.", firstName, lastName);
    }
}
```

OUTPUT 1.5:

```
Hey you!
Enter your first name: Inigo
Enter your last name: Montoya
Your full name is Inigo Montoya.
```

Instead of writing out Your full name is followed by another Write statement for firstName, a third Write statement for the space, and finally a WriteLine statement for lastName, Listing 1.15 writes out the entire output using **composite formatting.** With composite formatting, the code first supplies a **format string** to define the output format. In this example, the format string is "Your full name is {0} {1}.". It identifies two indexed placeholders for data insertion in the string.

Note that the index value begins at zero. Each inserted parameter (known as a **format item**) appears after the format string in the order corresponding to the index value. In this example, since firstName is the first parameter to follow immediately after the format string, it corresponds to index value 0. Similarly, lastName corresponds to index value 1.

Note that the placeholders within the format string need not appear in order. For example, Listing 1.16 switches the order of the indexed placeholders and adds a comma, which changes the way the name is displayed (see Output 1.6).

LISTING 1.16: Swapping the Indexed Placeholders and Corresponding Variables

```
System.Console.WriteLine("Your full name is {1}, {0}",
    firstName, lastName);
```

OUTPUT 1.6:

```
Hey you!
Enter your first name: Inigo
Enter your last name: Montoya
Your full name is Montoya, Inigo
```

In addition to not having the placeholders appear consecutively within the format string, it is possible to use the same placeholder multiple times within a format string. Furthermore, it is possible to omit a placeholder. It is not possible, however, to have placeholders that do not have a corresponding parameter.

Comments

In this section, you will modify the program in Listing 1.15 by adding comments. In no way does this vary the execution of the program; rather, providing comments within the code makes it more understandable. Listing 1.17 shows the new code, and Output 1.7 shows the corresponding output.

LISTING 1.17: Commenting Your Code

```
class CommentSamples
{
  static void Main()
  {
                                    single-line comment
    string firstName; // Variable for storing the first name
    string lastName;  // Variable for storing the last name

    System.Console.WriteLine("Hey you!");

                     delimited comment inside statement
    System.Console.Write /* No new line */ (
        "Enter your first name: ");
    firstName = System.Console.ReadLine();

    System.Console.Write /* No new line */ (
        "Enter your last name: ");
    lastName = System.Console.ReadLine();

    /* Display a greeting to the console
       using composite formatting. */      } delimited comment
```

```
        System.Console.WriteLine("Your full name is {0} {1}.",
            firstName, lastName);
        // This is the end
        // of the program listing
    }
}
```

OUTPUT 1.7:

```
Hey you!
Enter your first name: Inigo
Enter your last name: Montoya
Your full name is Inigo Montoya.
```

In spite of the inserted comments, compiling and executing the new program produces the same output as before.

Programmers use comments to describe and explain the code they are writing, especially where the syntax itself is difficult to understand, or perhaps a particular algorithm implementation is surprising. Since comments are pertinent only to the programmer reviewing the code, the compiler ignores comments and generates an assembly that is devoid of any trace that comments were part of the original source code.

Table 1.2 shows four different C# comment types. The program in Listing 1.17 includes two of these.

TABLE 1.2: C# Comment Types

Comment Type	Description	Example
Delimited comments	A forward slash followed by an asterisk, /*, identifies the beginning of a delimited comment. To end the comment use an asterisk followed by a forward slash: */. Comments of this form may span multiple lines in the code file or appear embedded within a line of code. The asterisks that appear at the beginning of the lines but within the delimiters are simply for formatting.	/*comment*/

Continues

TABLE 1.2: C# Comment Types *(Continued)*

Comment Type	Description	Example
Single-line comments	Comments may also be declared with a delimiter comprising two consecutive forward slash characters: //. The compiler treats all text from the delimiter to the end of the line as a comment. Comments of this form comprise a single line. It is possible, however, to place sequential single-line comments one after another, as is the case with the last comment in Listing 1.17.	`//comment`
XML delimited comments	Comments that begin with /** and end with **/ are called XML delimited comments. They have the same characteristics as regular delimited comments, except that instead of ignoring XML comments entirely, the compiler can place them into a separate text file. XML delimited comments were only explicitly added in C# 2.0, but the syntax is compatible with C# 1.0.	`/**comment**/`
XML single-line comments	XML single-line comments begin with /// and continue to the end of the line. In addition, the compiler can save single-line comments into a separate file with the XML delimited comments.	`///comment`

A more comprehensive discussion of the XML comments appears in Chapter 9, where I discuss the various XML tags that are explicitly part of the XML standard.

▪ BEGINNER TOPIC

Extensible Markup Language (XML)

The Extensible Markup Language (XML) is a simple and flexible text format frequently used within web applications and for exchanging data between applications. XML is extensible because included within an XML document is information that describes the data, known as **metadata.** Here is a sample XML file.

```xml
<?xml version="1.0" encoding="utf-8" ?>
<body>
  <book title="Essential C# 4.0">
     <chapters>
          <chapter title="Introducing C#"/>
          <chapter title="Operators and Control Flow"/>
          ...
     </chapters>
  </book>
</body>
```

The file starts with a header indicating the version and character encoding of the XML file. After that appears one main "book" element. Elements begin with a word in angle brackets, such as <body>. To end an element, place the same word in angle brackets and add a forward slash to prefix the word, as in </body>. In addition to elements, XML supports attributes. title="Essential C# 4.0" is an example of an XML attribute. Note that the metadata (book title, chapter, and so on) describing the data ("Essential C# 4.0", "Operators and Control Flow") is included in the XML file. This can result in rather bloated files, but it offers the advantage that the data includes a description to aid in interpreting the data.

Managed Execution and the Common Language Infrastructure

The processor cannot directly interpret an assembly. Assemblies consist mainly of a second language known as the Common Intermediate Language (CIL), or IL for short.

■ NOTE

A third term for CIL is *Microsoft IL* (*MSIL*). This book uses the term *CIL* because it is the term adopted by the CLI standard. IL is prevalent in conversation among people writing C# code because they assume that IL refers to CIL rather than other types of intermediate languages.

The C# compiler transforms the C# source file into this intermediate language. An additional step, usually performed at execution time, is required to change the CIL code into **machine code** that the processor can understand. This involves an important element in the execution of a C# program: the **Virtual Execution System (VES).** The VES, also casually referred to as the **runtime,** compiles CIL code as needed (this process is known as **just-in-time** compilation or **jitting**). The code that executes under the context of an agent such as the runtime is **managed code,** and the process of executing under control of the runtime is **managed execution.** It is called managed code because the runtime controls significant portions of the program's behavior by managing aspects such as memory allocation, security, and just-in-time compilation. Code that does not require the runtime in order to execute is **unmanaged code.**

> **■ NOTE**
>
> The term *runtime* can refer to either execution time or the Virtual Execution System. To help clarify, this book uses the term *execution time* to indicate when the program is executing, and it uses the term *runtime* when discussing the agent responsible for managing the execution of a C# program while it executes.

The specification for a VES is included in a broader specification known as the **Common Language Infrastructure (CLI)** specification.[8] An international standard, the CLI includes specifications for

- The VES or runtime
- The CIL
- A type system that supports language interoperability, known as the **Common Type System (CTS)**
- Guidance on how to write libraries that are accessible from CLI-compatible languages (available in the **Common Language Specification [CLS]**)

---

8. Miller, J., and S. Ragsdale. 2004. *The Common Language Infrastructure Annotated Standard.* Boston: Addison-Wesley.

- Metadata that enables many of the services identified by the CLI (including specifications for the layout or file format of assemblies)
- A common programming framework, the Base Class Library (BCL), which developers in all languages can utilize

Running within the context of a CLI implementation enables support for a number of services and features that programmers do not need to code for directly, including the following.

- *Language interoperability:* interoperability between different source languages. This is possible because the language compilers translate each source language to the same intermediate language (CIL).
- *Type safety:* checks for conversion between types, ensuring that only conversions between compatible types will occur. This helps prevent the occurrence of buffer overruns, a leading cause of security vulnerabilities.
- *Code access security:* certification that the assembly developer's code has permission to execute on the computer.
- *Garbage collection:* memory management that automatically de-allocates space for data allocated by the runtime.
- *Platform portability:* support for potentially running the same assembly on a variety of operating systems. One obvious restriction is that no platform-dependent libraries are used; therefore, as with Java, there are inevitably some idiosyncrasies that need to be worked out.
- *BCL:* provides a large foundation of code that developers can depend on (in all CLI implementations) so that they do not have to develop the code themselves.

■ NOTE

This section gives a brief synopsis of the CLI to familiarize you with the context in which a C# program executes. It also provides a summary of some of the terms that appear throughout this book. Chapter 21 is devoted to the topic of the CLI and its relevance to C# developers. Although the chapter appears last in the book, it does not depend on any earlier chapters, so if you want to become more familiar with the CLI, you can jump to it at any time.

C# and .NET Versioning

Readers will notice that Output 1.1 refers to the ".NET Framework version 4.0." At the time of this writing, Microsoft had five major releases to the .NET Framework and only four major C# compiler releases. .NET Framework version 3.0 was an additional set of API libraries released in between C# compiler releases (and Visual Studio 2005 and 2008 versions). As a result, the .NET Framework version that corresponded with C# 3.0 was 3.5. With the release of C# 4.0 and the .NET Framework 4.0, the version numbers are synchronized. Table 1.3 is a brief overview of the C# and .NET releases.

TABLE 1.3: C# and .NET Versions

Comment Type	Description
C# 1.0 with .NET Framework 1.0/1.1 (Visual Studio 2002 and 2003)	The initial release of C#. A language built from the ground up to support .NET programming.
C# 2.0 with .NET Framework 2.0 (Visual Studio 2005)	Generics were added to the C# language and the .NET Framework 2.0 included libraries that supported generics.
.NET Framework 3.0	An additional set of APIs for distributed communications (Windows Communication Foundation—WCF), rich client presentation (Windows Presentation Foundation), workflow (Windows Workflow—WF), and web authentication (Cardspaces).
C# 3.0 with .NET Framework 3.5 (Visual Studio 2008)	Added support for LINQ, a significant improvement to the APIs used for programming collections. The .NET Framework 3.5 provided libraries that extended existing APIs to make LINQ possible.
C# 4.0 with .NET Framework 3.5 (Visual Studio 2010)	Added support for dynamic typing along with significant improvements in the API for writing multi-threaded programs that capitalized on multiple processors and cores within those processors.

The majority of all code within this text will work with platforms other than Microsoft's as long as the compiler version corresponds to the version of code required. Although I would very much have liked to provide full details on each C# platform so as not to detract from the focus of learning C#, I restrict information such as this to Microsoft's platform, .NET. This is simply because Microsoft has the predominant (by far) implementation. Furthermore, translation to another platform is fairly trivial.

Common Intermediate Language and ILDASM

As mentioned in the previous section, the C# compiler converts C# code to CIL code and not to machine code. The processor can directly understand machine code, but CIL code needs to be converted before the processor can execute it. Given an assembly (either a DLL or an executable), it is possible to view the CIL code using a CIL disassembler utility to deconstruct the assembly into its CIL representation. (The CIL disassembler is commonly referred to by its Microsoft-specific filename, ILDASM, which stands for IL Disassembler.) This program will disassemble a program or its class libraries, displaying the CIL generated by the C# compiler.

The exact command used for the CIL disassembler depends on which implementation of the CLI is used. You can execute the .NET CIL disassembler from the command line as shown in Output 1.8.

OUTPUT 1.8:

```
>ildasm /text HelloWorld.exe
```

The /text portion is used so that the output appears on the command console rather than in a new window. Similarly, the Mono disassembler implementation, which defaults to the command console, is shown in Output 1.9.

OUTPUT 1.9:

```
>monodis HelloWorld.exe
```

The stream of output that results by executing these commands is a dump of CIL code included in the HelloWorld.exe program. Note that CIL code is significantly easier to understand than machine code. For many developers, this may raise a concern because it is easier for programs to be decompiled and algorithms understood without explicitly redistributing the source code.

As with any program, CLI-based or not, the only foolproof way of preventing disassembly is to disallow access to the compiled program altogether (for example, only hosting a program on a web site instead of distributing it out to a user's machine). However, if decreased accessibility to the source code is all that is required, there are several obfuscators. These obfuscators open up the IL code and munge the code so that it does the same thing but in a way that is much more difficult to understand. This prevents the casual developer from accessing the code and instead creates assemblies that are much more difficult and tedious to decompile into comprehensible code. Unless a program requires a high degree of algorithm security, these obfuscators are generally sufficient.

■ ADVANCED TOPIC

CIL Output for `HelloWorld.exe`

Listing 1.18 shows the CIL code created by ILDASM.

LISTING 1.18: Sample CIL Output

```
//  Microsoft (R) .NET Framework IL Disassembler.
Version 4.0. 21006.1
//  Copyright (c) Microsoft Corporation.  All rights reserved.

// Metadata version: v4.0. 21006
.assembly extern mscorlib
{
  .publickeytoken = (B7 7A 5C 56 19 34 E0 89 )
// .z\V.4..
  .ver 4:0:0:0
}
.assembly HelloWorld
{
  .custom instance void
[mscorlib]System.Runtime.CompilerServices.CompilationRelaxationsAttribute::.
ctor(int32) = ( 01 00 08 00 00 00 00 00 )
  .custom instance void
[mscorlib]System.Runtime.CompilerServices.RuntimeCompatibilityAttribute::.
ctor() = ( 01 00 01 00 54 02 16 57 72 61 70 4E 6F 6E 45 78
// ....T..WrapNonEx
```

```
63 65 70 74 69 6F 6E 54 68 72 6F 77 73 01 )         // ceptionThrows.
  .hash algorithm 0x00008004
  .ver 0:0:0:0
}
.module HelloWorld.exe
// MVID: {1C3495D1-2133-41D6-A820-B4731061F3F8}
.imagebase 0x00400000
.file alignment 0x00000200
.stackreserve 0x00100000
.subsystem 0x0003       // WINDOWS_CUI
.corflags 0x00000001    //   ILONLY
// Image base: 0x00160000


// ============ CLASS MEMBERS DECLARATION ================

.class private auto ansi beforefieldinit HelloWorld
       extends [mscorlib]System.Object
{
  .method private hidebysig static void  Main() cil managed
  {
    .entrypoint
    // Code size       13 (0xd)
    .maxstack  8
    IL_0000:  nop
    IL_0001:  ldstr      "Hello. My name is Inigo Montoya."
    IL_0006:  call       void [mscorlib]System.Console::WriteLine(string)
    IL_000b:  nop
    IL_000c:  ret
  } // end of method HelloWorld::Main

  .method public hidebysig specialname rtspecialname
        instance void  .ctor() cil managed
  {
    // Code size       7 (0x7)
    .maxstack  8
    IL_0000:  ldarg.0
    IL_0001:  call       instance void [mscorlib]System.Object::.ctor()
    IL_0006:  ret
  } // end of method HelloWorld::.ctor

} // end of class HelloWorld


// =========================================================

// ********** DISASSEMBLY COMPLETE ***********************
```

The beginning of the listing is the manifest information. It includes not only the full name of the disassembled module (`HelloWorld.exe`), but also all the modules and assemblies it depends on, along with their version information.

Perhaps the most interesting thing that you can glean from such a listing is how relatively easy it is to follow what the program is doing compared to trying to read and understand machine code (assembler). In the listing, an explicit reference to `System.Console.WriteLine()` appears. There is a lot of peripheral information to the CIL code listing, but if a developer wanted to understand the inner workings of a C# module (or any CLI-based program) without having access to the original source code, it would be relatively easy unless an obfuscator is used. In fact, several free tools are available (such as Lutz Roeder/Red Gate's Reflector for .NET) that can decompile from CIL to C# automatically.

SUMMARY

This chapter served as a rudimentary introduction to C#. It provided a means of familiarizing you with basic C# syntax. Because of C#'s similarity to C++ style languages, much of what I presented here might not have been new material. However, C# and managed code do have some distinct characteristics, such as compilation down to CIL. Although it is not unique, another key characteristic is that C# includes full support for object-oriented programming. Even things such as reading and writing data to the console are object-oriented. Object orientation is foundational to C#, and you will see this throughout this book.

The next chapter examines the fundamental data types that are part of the C# language, and discusses how you can use these data types with operands to form expressions.

■2■
Data Types

F ROM CHAPTER 1'S HelloWorld program, you got a feel for the C# language, its structure, basic syntax characteristics, and how to write the simplest of programs. This chapter continues to discuss the C# basics by investigating the fundamental C# types.

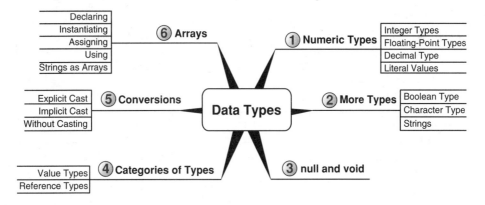

Until now, you have worked with only a few primitive data types, with little explanation. In C#, thousands of types exist, and you can combine types to create new types. A few types in C#, however, are relatively simple and are considered the building blocks of all other types. These types are **predefined types** or **primitives.** The C# language's primitive types include eight integer types, two binary floating-point types for scientific calculations and one decimal float for financial calculations, one Boolean type, and a character type. This chapter investigates these primitives, looks more closely at the string type, and introduces arrays.

Fundamental Numeric Types

The basic numeric types in C# have keywords associated with them. These types include integer types, floating-point types, and a special floating-point type called decimal to store large numbers with no representation error.

Integer Types

There are eight C# integer types. This variety allows you to select a data type large enough to hold its intended range of values without wasting resources. Table 2.1 lists each integer type.

TABLE 2.1: Integer Types

Type	Size	Range (Inclusive)	BCL Name	Signed
sbyte	8 bits	−128 to 127	System.SByte	Yes
byte	8 bits	0 to 255	System.Byte	No
short	16 bits	−32,768 to 32,767	System.Int16	Yes
ushort	16 bits	0 to 65,535	System.UInt16	No
int	32 bits	−2,147,483,648 to 2,147,483,647	System.Int32	Yes
uint	32 bits	0 to 4,294,967,295	System.UInt32	No
long	64 bits	−9,223,372,036,854,775,808 to 9,223,372,036,854,775,807	System.Int64	Yes
ulong	64 bits	0 to 18,446,744,073,709,551,615	System.UInt64	No

Included in Table 2.1 (and in Tables 2.2 and 2.3) is a column for the full name of each type. All the fundamental types in C# have a short name and a full name. The full name corresponds to the type as it is named in the Base Class Library (BCL). This name is the same across all languages and it uniquely identifies the type within an assembly. Because of the fundamental nature of primitive types, C# also supplies keywords as short names or abbreviations to the full names of fundamental types. From the compiler's perspective, both names are exactly the same, producing exactly the same code. In fact, an examination of the resultant CIL code would provide no indication of which name was used.

Language Contrast: C++—short Data Type

In C/C++, the short data type is an abbreviation for short int. In C#, short on its own is the actual data type.

Floating-Point Types (float, double)

Floating-point numbers have varying degrees of precision. If you were to read the value of a floating-point number to be 0.1, it could very easily be 0.099999999999999999 or 0.1000000000000000001 or some other number very close to 0.1. Alternatively, a large number such as Avogadro's number, 6.02E23, could be off by 9.9E9, which is something also exceptionally close to 6.02E23, considering its size. The accuracy of a floating-point number is in proportion to the magnitude of the number it represents. Accuracy, therefore, is determined by the number of significant digits, not by a fixed value such as ±0.01. In other words, absolute precision is a function of magnitude and significant digits; the number of significant digits tells you about the relative precision.

C# supports the two floating-point number types listed in Table 2.2.

TABLE 2.2: Floating-Point Types

Type	Size	Range (Inclusive)	BCL Name	Significant Digits
float	32 bits	$\pm 1.5 \times 10^{-45}$ to $\pm 3.4 \times 10^{38}$	System.Single	7
double	64 bits	$\pm 5.0 \times 10^{-324}$ to $\pm 1.7 \times 10^{308}$	System.Double	15–16

Binary numbers appear as base 10 (denary) numbers for human readability. The number of bits (binary digits) converts to 15 decimal digits, with a remainder that contributes to a sixteenth decimal digit as expressed in Table 2.2. Specifically, numbers between $1.7 * 10^{307}$ and less than $1 * 10^{308}$ have only 15 significant digits. However, numbers ranging from $1 * 10^{308}$ to $1.7 * 10^{308}$ will have 16 significant digits. A similar range of significant digits occurs with the decimal type as well.

Decimal Type

C# contains a numeric type with 128-bit precision (see Table 2.3). This is suitable for large and precise calculations, frequently financial calculations.

TABLE 2.3: *decimal* Type

Type	Size	Range (Inclusive)	BCL Name	Significant Digits
decimal	128 bits	1.0×10^{-28} to approximately 7.9×10^{28}	System.Decimal	28–29

Unlike floating-point numbers, the decimal type maintains exact accuracy for all denary numbers within its range. With the decimal type, therefore, a value of 0.1 is exactly 0.1. However, while the decimal type has greater precision than the floating-point types, it has a smaller range. Thus, conversions from floating-point types to the decimal type may result in overflow errors. Also, calculations with decimal are slightly slower.

■ ADVANCED TOPIC

Floating-Point Types and Decimals Dissected

Unless they are out of range, decimal numbers represent denary numbers exactly. In contrast, the floating-point representation of many denary numbers introduces a rounding error. This is analogous to how 1/3 is not exact in any finite number of decimal digits and 11/10 is not precise in any finite number of binary digits. In both cases, we end up with a rounding error of some kind. The difference between the decimal type and the C# floating-point types is that the base of a decimal type is a denary and the base of floating-point types is binary.

A decimal is represented by ±N * 10k where

- N, the mantissa, is a positive integer represented by 96 bits.
- k, the exponent, is given by -28 <= k <= 0.

In contrast, a float is any number ±N * 2k where

- N is a positive integer represented by a fixed number of bits (24 for float and 53 for double).
- k is any integer ranging from -149 to +104 for float and -1075 to +970 for double.

Literal Values

A **literal value** is a representation of a constant value within source code. For example, if you want to have System.Console.WriteLine() print out the integer value 42 and the double value 1.618034 (Phi), you could use the code shown in Listing 2.1.

LISTING 2.1: Specifying Literal Values

```
System.Console.WriteLine(42);
System.Console.WriteLine(1.618034);
```

Output 2.1 shows the results of Listing 2.1.

OUTPUT 2.1:

```
42
1.618034
```

▪ BEGINNER TOPIC

Use Caution When Hardcoding Values

The practice of placing a value directly into source code is called **hardcoding,** because changing the values means recompiling the code. Developers must carefully consider the choice between hardcoding values within their code and retrieving them from an external source, such as a configuration file, so that the values are modifiable without recompiling.

By default, when you specify a literal number with a decimal point, the compiler interprets it as a `double` type. Conversely, a literal value with no decimal point generally defaults to an `int`, assuming the value is not too large to be stored in an integer. If the value is too large, then the compiler will interpret it as a `long`. Furthermore, the C# compiler allows assignment to a numeric type other than an `int`, assuming the literal value is appropriate for the target data type. `short s = 42` and `byte b = 77` are allowed, for example. However, this is appropriate only for literal values; `b = s` is not appropriate without additional syntax, as discussed in the section Conversions between Data Types, later in this chapter.

As previously discussed in the section Fundamental Numeric Types, there are many different numeric types in C#. In Listing 2.2, a literal value is placed within C# code. Since numbers with a decimal point will default to the `double` data type, the output, shown in Output 2.2, is `1.61803398874989` (the last digit, 5, is missing), corresponding to the expected accuracy of a `double`.

LISTING 2.2: Specifying a Literal `double`

```
System.Console.WriteLine(1.618033988749895);
```

OUTPUT 2.2:

```
1.61803398874989
```

To view the intended number with its full accuracy, you must declare explicitly the literal value as a `decimal` type by appending an `m` (or `M`) (see Listing 2.3 and Output 2.3).

LISTING 2.3: Specifying a Literal `decimal`

```
System.Console.WriteLine(1.618033988749895m);
```

OUTPUT 2.3:

```
1.618033988749895
```

Now the output of Listing 2.3 is as expected: `1.618033988749895`. Note that `d` is for double. The `m` used to identify a `decimal` corresponds to its frequent use in monetary calculations.

You can also add a suffix to a value to explicitly declare a literal as `float` or `double` by using the `F` and `D` suffixes, respectively. For integer data types, the suffixes are `U`, `L`, `LU`, and `UL`. The type of an integer literal can be determined as follows.

- Numeric literals with no suffix resolve to the first data type that can store the value in this order: `int`, `uint`, `long`, and `ulong`.
- Numeric literals with the suffix `U` resolve to the first data type that can store the value in the order `uint` and then `ulong`.
- Numeric literals with the suffix `L` resolve to the first data type that can store the value in the order `long` and then `ulong`.
- If the numeric literal has the suffix `UL` or `LU`, it is of type `ulong`.

Note that suffixes for literals are case-insensitive. However, uppercase is generally preferred because of the similarity between the lowercase letter *l* and the digit 1.

In some situations, you may wish to use exponential notation instead of writing out several zeroes before or after the decimal point. To use exponential notation, supply the `e` or `E` infix, follow the infix character with a positive or negative integer number, and complete the literal with the appropriate data type suffix. For example, you could print out Avogadro's number as a `float`, as shown in Listing 2.4 and Output 2.4.

LISTING 2.4: **Exponential Notation**

```
System.Console.WriteLine(6.023E23f);
```

OUTPUT 2.4:

```
6.023E+23
```

▪▪ BEGINNER TOPIC

Hexadecimal Notation

Usually you work with numbers that are represented with a base of 10, meaning there are ten symbols (0–9) for each digit in the number. If a number is displayed with hexadecimal notation, then it is displayed with a base of 16 numbers, meaning 16 symbols are used: 0–9, A–F (lowercase can also be used). Therefore, 0x000A corresponds to the decimal value 10 and 0x002A corresponds to the decimal value 42. The actual number is the same. Switching from hexadecimal to decimal or vice versa does not change the number itself, just the representation of the number.

Each hex digit is four bits, so a byte can represent two hex digits.

In all discussions of literal numeric values so far, I have covered only base 10 type values. C# also supports the ability to specify hexadecimal values. To specify a hexadecimal value, prefix the value with 0x and then use any hexadecimal digit, as shown in Listing 2.5.

LISTING 2.5: Hexadecimal Literal Value

```
// Display the value 42 using a hexadecimal literal.
System.Console.WriteLine(0x002A);
```

Output 2.5 shows the results of Listing 2.5.

OUTPUT 2.5:

```
42
```

Note that this code still displays 42, not 0x002A.

▪▪ ADVANCED TOPIC

Formatting Numbers As Hexadecimal

To display a numeric value in its hexadecimal format, it is necessary to use the x or X numeric formatting specifier. The casing determines whether the hexadecimal letters appear in lower- or uppercase. Listing 2.6 shows an example of how to do this.

LISTING 2.6: Example of a Hexadecimal Format Specifier

```
// Displays "0x2A"
System.Console.WriteLine("0x{0:X}", 42);
```

Output 2.6 shows the results.

OUTPUT 2.6:

```
0x2A
```

Note that the numeric literal (42) can be in decimal or hexadecimal form. The result will be the same.

■ ADVANCED TOPIC

Round-Trip Formatting

By default, `System.Console.WriteLine(1.618033988749895);` displays `1.61803398874989`, with the last digit missing. To more accurately identify the string representation of the double value it is possible to convert it using a format string and the round-trip format specifier, R (or r). `string.Format("{0:R}", 1.618033988749895)`, for example, will return the result `1.6180339887498949`.

The round-trip format specifier returns a string that, if converted back into a numeric value, will always result in the original value. Listing 2.7, therefore, will show the numbers are not equal without the round trip format.

LISTING 2.7: Formatting Using the R Format Specifier

```
// ...
const double number = 1.618033988749895;
double result;
string text;

text = string.Format("{0}", number);
result = double.Parse(text);
System.Console.WriteLine("{0}: result != number",
  result != number);

text = string.Format("{0:R}", number);
```

```
result = double.Parse(text);
System.Console.WriteLine("{0}: result == number",
  result == number);
// ...
```

Output 2.7 shows the resultant output.

OUTPUT 2.7:

```
True: result != number
True: result == number
```

When assigning `text` the first time, there is no round-trip format specifier and, as a result, the value returned by `double.Parse(text)` is not the same as the original number value. In contrast, when the round-trip format specifier is used, `double.Parse(text)` returns the original value.

For those unfamiliar with the `==` syntax from C-based languages, `result == number` returns true if `result` is equal to `number`, while `result != number` does the opposite. Both assignment and equality operators are discussed in the next chapter.

More Fundamental Types

The fundamental types discussed so far are numeric types. C# includes some additional types as well: `bool`, `char`, and `string`.

Boolean Type (bool)

Another C# primitive is a Boolean or conditional type, `bool`, which represents true or false in conditional statements and expressions. Allowable values are the keywords `true` and `false`. The BCL name for `bool` is `System.Boolean`. For example, in order to compare two strings in a case-insensitive manner, you call the `string.Compare()` method and pass a `bool` literal of `true` (see Listing 2.8).

LISTING 2.8: A Case-Insensitive Comparison of Two Strings

```
string option;
...
int comparison = string.Compare(option, "/Help", true);
```

In this case, you make a case-insensitive comparison of the contents of the variable `option` with the literal text `/Help` and assign the result to `comparison`.

Although theoretically a single bit could hold the value of a Boolean, the size of `bool` is a byte.

Character Type (char)

A `char` type represents 16-bit characters whose set of possible values corresponds to the Unicode character set. Technically, a `char` is the same size as a 16-bit unsigned integer (`ushort`) with values between 0 and 65,535. However, `char` is a unique type in C# and code should treat it as such.

The BCL name for `char` is `System.Char`.

■ BEGINNER TOPIC

The Unicode Standard

Unicode is an international standard for representing characters found in the majority of human languages. It provides computer systems with functionality for building **localized** applications, applications that display the appropriate language and culture characteristics for different cultures.

■ ADVANCED TOPIC

16 Bits Is Too Small for All Unicode Characters

Unfortunately, not all Unicode characters are available within a 16-bit `char`. When Unicode was first started, its designers believed that 16 bits would be enough, but as more languages were supported, it was realized that this assumption was incorrect. The cumbersome result is that some Unicode characters are composed of surrogate `char` pairs totaling 32 bits.

To enter a literal character type, place the character within single quotes, as in `'A'`. Allowable characters comprise the full range of keyboard characters, including letters, numbers, and special symbols.

Some characters cannot be placed directly into the source code and instead require special handling. These characters are prefixed with a backslash (\) followed by a special character code. In combination, the backslash and special character code are an **escape sequence.** For example, '\n' represents a newline, and '\t' represents a tab. Since a backslash indicates the beginning of an escape sequence, it can no longer identify a simple backslash; instead, you need to use '\\' to represent a single backslash character.

Listing 2.9 writes out one single quote because the character represented by \' corresponds to a single quote.

LISTING 2.9: Displaying a Single Quote Using an Escape Sequence

```
class SingleQuote
{
  static void Main()
  {
      System.Console.WriteLine('\'');
  }
}
```

In addition to showing the escape sequence, Table 2.4 includes the Unicode representation of characters.

TABLE 2.4: Escape Characters

Escape Sequence	Character Name	Unicode Encoding
\'	Single quote	\u0027
\"	Double quote	\u0022
\\	Backslash	\u005C
\0	Null	\u0000
\a	Alert (system beep)	\u0007
\b	Backspace	\u0008
\f	Form feed	\u000C
\n	Line feed (sometimes referred to as a newline)	\u000A

TABLE 2.4: Escape Characters *(Continued)*

Escape Sequence	Character Name	Unicode Encoding
\r	Carriage return	\u000D
\t	Horizontal tab	\u0009
\v	Vertical tab	\u000B
\uxxxx	Unicode character in hex	\u0029
\x[n][n][n]n	Unicode character in hex (first three placeholders are options); variable length version of \uxxxx	\u3A
\Uxxxxxxxx	Unicode escape sequence for creating surrogate pairs	\UD840DC01 (㒡)

You can represent any character using Unicode encoding. To do so, prefix the Unicode value with \u. You represent Unicode characters in hexadecimal notation. The letter *A*, for example, is the hexadecimal value 0x41. Listing 2.10 uses Unicode characters to display a smiley face (:)), and Output 2.8 shows the results.

LISTING 2.10: Using Unicode Encoding to Display a Smiley Face

```
System.Console.Write('\u003A');
System.Console.WriteLine('\u0029');
```

OUTPUT 2.8:

```
:)
```

Strings

The fundamental string type in C# is the data type string, whose BCL name is System.String. The string includes some special characteristics that may be unexpected to developers familiar with other programming languages. The characteristics include a string verbatim prefix character, @, and the fact that a string is immutable.

Literals

You can enter a literal string into code by placing the text in double quotes ("), as you saw in the HelloWorld program. Strings are composed of characters, and because of this, escape sequences can be embedded within a string.

In Listing 2.11, for example, two lines of text are displayed. However, instead of using System.Console.WriteLine(), the code listing shows System.Console.Write() with the newline character, \n. Output 2.9 shows the results.

LISTING 2.11: Using the \n Character to Insert a Newline

```
class DuelOfWits
{
  static void Main()
  {
      System.Console.Write(
          "\"Truly, you have a dizzying intellect.\"");
      System.Console.Write("\n\"wait 'til I get going!\ "\n");
  }
}
```

OUTPUT 2.9:

```
"Truly, you have a dizzying intellect."
"Wait 'til I get going!"
```

The escape sequence for double quotes differentiates the printed double quotes from the double quotes that define the beginning and end of the string.

In C#, you can use the @ symbol in front of a string to signify that a backslash should not be interpreted as the beginning of an escape sequence. The resultant **verbatim string literal** does not reinterpret just the backslash character. Whitespace is also taken verbatim when using the @ string syntax. The triangle in Listing 2.12, for example, appears in the console exactly as typed, including the backslashes, newlines, and indentation. Output 2.10 shows the results.

Without the @ character, this code would not even compile. In fact, even if you changed the shape to a square, eliminating the backslashes, the code still would not compile because a newline cannot be placed directly within a string that is not prefaced with the @ symbol.

LISTING 2.12: Displaying a Triangle Using a Verbatim String Literal

```
class Triangle
{
  static void Main()
  {
        System.Console.Write(@"begin


            /\
           /  \
          /    \
         /      \
        /_____\
 end");
  }
}
```

OUTPUT 2.10:

```
begin
            /\
           /  \
        .  /    \
          /      \
         /_____\

 end
```

The only escape sequence the verbatim string does support is "", which signifies double quotes and does not terminate the string.

Language Contrast: C++—String Concatenation at Compile Time

Unlike C++, C# does not automatically concatenate literal strings. You cannot, for example, specify a string literal as follows:

```
"Major Strasser has been shot. " "Round up the usual suspects."
```

Rather, concatenation requires the use of the addition operator. (If the compiler can calculate the result at compile time, however, the resultant CIL code will be a single string.)

If the same literal string appears within an assembly multiple times, the compiler will define the string only once within the assembly and all variables will refer to the same string. That way, if the same string literal containing thousands of characters was placed multiple times into the code, the resultant assembly would reflect the size of only one of them.

String Methods

The string type, like the System.Console type, includes several methods. There are methods, for example, for formatting, concatenating, and comparing strings.

The Format() method in Table 2.5 behaves exactly like the Console.Write() and Console.WriteLine() methods, except that instead of displaying the result in the console window, string.Format() returns the result.

TABLE 2.5: **string Static Methods**

Statement	Example

static void
string.Format(
    string format,
    ...)
	string text, firstName, lastName;
	....
	text = string.Format("Your full name is {0} {1}.",
	    firstName, lastName);
	// Display
	// "Your full name is \<firstName\> \<LastName\>."
	System.Console.WriteLine(text);

static void
string.Concat(
    string str0,
    string str1)
	string text, firstName, lastName;
	...
	text = string.Concat(firstName, lastName);
	// Display "\<firstName\>\<LastName\>", notice
	// that there is no space between names.
	System.Console.WriteLine(text);

static int
string.Compare(
    string str0,
    string str1)
	string option;
	...
	// String comparison in which case matters.
	int result = string.Compare(option, "/help");
	
	// Display:
	// 0 if equal
	// negative if option \< /help
	// positive if option \> /help
	System.Console.WriteLine(result);

TABLE 2.5: **string** Static Methods *(Continued)*

Statement	Example

	``string option;
	...
	// Case-insensitive string comparison
	int result = string.Compare(
	    option, "/Help", true);
	
	// Display:
	// 0 if equal
	// < 0 if option < /help
	// > 0 if option > /help
	System.Console.WriteLine(result);```

All of the methods in Table 2.5 are **static.** This means that, to call the method, it is necessary to prefix the method name (for example, Concat) with the type that contains the method (for example, string). As illustrated below, however, some of the methods in the string class are **instance** methods. Instead of prefixing the method with the type, instance methods use the variable name (or some other reference to an instance). Table 2.6 shows a few of these methods, along with an example.

TABLE 2.6: **string** Methods

Statement	Example

bool StartsWith(
    string value)
bool EndsWith(
    string value)
	```string lastName```
	```...```
	```bool isPhd = lastName.EndsWith("Ph.D.");```
	```bool isDr = lastName.StartsWith("Dr.");```

string ToLower()
string ToUpper()
	```string severity = "warning";```
	```// Display the severity in uppercase```
	```System.Console.WriteLine(severity.ToUpper());```

string Trim() **string** Trim(...) **string** TrimEnd() **string** TrimStart()	```// Remove any whitespace at the start or end.``` ```username = username.Trim();```

string Replace(
    string oldValue,
    string newValue)
	```string filename;```
	```...```
	```// Remove ?'s altogether from the string```
	```filename = filename.Replace("?", "");;```

New Line

When writing out a new line, the exact characters for the new line will depend on the operating system on which you are executing. On Microsoft Windows platforms, the new line is the combination of both the '\r' and '\n' charters, while a single '\n' is used on Unix. One way to overcome the discrepancy between platforms is simply to use `System.Console.WriteLine()` in order to output a blank line. Another approach, virtually essential when you are not outputting to the console yet still require execution on multiple platforms, is to use `System.Environment.NewLine`. In other words, `System.Console.WriteLine("Hello World")` and `System.Console.Write("Hello World" + System.Environment.NewLine)` are equivalent.

■ ADVANCED TOPIC

C# Properties

Technically, the `Length` member referred to in the following section is not actually a method, as indicated by the fact that there are no parentheses following its call. `Length` is a property of `string`, and C# syntax allows access to a property as though it were a member variable (known in C# as a **field**). In other words, a property has the behavior of special methods called setters and getters, but the syntax for accessing that behavior is that of a field.

Examining the underlying CIL implementation of a property reveals that it compiles into two methods: `set_<PropertyName>` and `get_<PropertyName>`. Neither of these, however, is directly accessible from C# code, except through the C# property constructs. See Chapter 5 for more detail on properties.

String Length

To determine the length of a string you use a string member called `Length`. This particular member is called a **read-only property.** As such, it can't be set, nor does calling it require any parameters. Listing 2.13 demonstrates how to use the `Length` property, and Output 2.11 shows the results.

LISTING 2.13: Using **string's** Length Member

```
class PalindromeLength
{
  static void Main()
  {
      string palindrome;

      System.Console.Write("Enter a palindrome: ");
      palindrome = System.Console.ReadLine();

      System.Console.WriteLine(
          "The palindrome, \"{0}\" is {1} characters.",
          palindrome, palindrome.Length);
  }
}
```

OUTPUT 2.11:

```
Enter a palindrome: Never odd or even
The palindrome, "Never odd or even" is 17 characters.
```

The length for a string cannot be set directly; it is calculated from the number of characters in the string. Furthermore, the length of a string cannot change because a string is **immutable.**

Strings Are Immutable

The key characteristic of the `string` type is the fact that it is immutable. A string variable can be assigned an entirely new value, but for performance reasons, there is no facility for modifying the contents of a `string`. It is not possible, therefore, to convert a `string` to all uppercase letters. It is trivial to create a new string that is composed of an uppercase version of the old string, but the old string is not modified in the process. Consider Listing 2.14 as an example.

LISTING 2.14: Error; **string** Is Immutable

```
class Uppercase
{
  static void Main()
  {
      string text;

      System.Console.Write("Enter text: ");
      text = System.Console.ReadLine();
```

```
        // UNEXPECTED:   Does not convert text to uppercase
        text.ToUpper();

        System.Console.WriteLine(text);
    }
}
```

Output 2.12 shows the results of Listing 2.14.

OUTPUT 2.12:

```
Enter text: This is a test of the emergency broadcast system.
This is a test of the emergency broadcast system.
```

At a glance, it would appear that text.ToUpper() should convert the characters within text to uppercase. However, strings are immutable and, therefore, text.ToUpper() will make no such modification. Instead, text.ToUpper() returns a new string that needs to be saved into a variable or passed to System.Console.WriteLine() directly. The corrected code is shown in Listing 2.15, and its output is shown in Output 2.13.

LISTING 2.15: Working with Strings

```
class Uppercase
{
    static void Main()
    {
        string text, uppercase;

        System.Console.Write("Enter text: ");
        text = System.Console.ReadLine();

        // Return a new string in uppercase
        uppercase = text.ToUpper();

        System.Console.WriteLine(uppercase);
    }
}
```

OUTPUT 2.13:

```
Enter text: This is a test of the emergency broadcast system.
THIS IS A TEST OF THE EMERGENCY BROADCAST SYSTEM.
```

If the immutability of a string is ignored, mistakes similar to those shown in Listing 2.14 can occur with other string methods as well.

To actually change the value in text, assign the value from ToUpper() back into text, as in the following:

```
text = text.ToUpper();
```

System.Text.StringBuilder

If considerable string modification is needed, such as when constructing a long string in multiple steps, you should use the data type System.Text.StringBuilder rather than string. System.Text.StringBuilder includes methods such as Append(), AppendFormat(), Insert(), Remove(), and Replace(), some of which also appear on string. The key difference, however, is that on System.Text.StringBuilder these methods will modify the data in the StringBuilder itself, and will not simply return a new string.

null **and** void

Two additional keywords relating to types are null and void. null is a value which indicates that the variable does not refer to any valid object. void is used to indicate the absence of a type or the absence of any value altogether.

null

null can also be used as a type of string "literal." null indicates that a variable is set to nothing. Reference types, pointer types, and nullable value types can be assigned the value null. The only reference type covered so far in this book is string; Chapter 5 covers the topic of creating classes (which are reference types) in detail. For now, suffice it to say that a reference type contains a reference to a location in memory that is different from where the actual data resides. Code that sets a variable to null explicitly assigns the reference to point at nothing. In fact, it is even possible to check whether a reference type points to nothing. Listing 2.16 demonstrates assigning null to a string variable.

LISTING 2.16: Assigning null to a String

```
static void Main()
{
    string faxNumber;
```

```
// ...

// Clear the value of faxNumber.
faxNumber = null;

// ...
}
```

It is important to note that assigning the value `null` to a reference type is distinct from not assigning it at all. In other words, a variable that has been assigned `null` has still been set, and a variable with no assignment has not been set and therefore will often cause a compile error if used prior to assignment.

Assigning the value `null` to a `string` is distinctly different from assigning an empty string, `""`. `null` indicates that the variable has no value. `""` indicates that there is a value: an empty string. This type of distinction can be quite useful. For example, the programming logic could interpret a `faxNumber` of `null` to mean that the fax number is unknown, while a `faxNumber` value of `""` could indicate that there is no fax number.

The `void` Nontype

Sometimes the C# syntax requires a data type to be specified but no data is passed. For example, if no return from a method is needed C# allows the use of `void` to be specified as the data type instead. The declaration of `Main` within the `HelloWorld` program is an example. Under these circumstances, the data type to specify is `void`. The use of `void` as the return type indicates that the method is not returning any data and tells the compiler not to expect a value. `void` is not a data type per se, but rather an identification of the fact that there is no data type.

Language Contrast: C++—`void` Is a Data Type

In C++, void is a data type commonly used as void**. In C#, void is not considered a data type in the same way. Rather, it is used to identify that a method does not return a value.

Language Contrast: Visual Basic—Returning void **Is Like Defining a Subroutine**

The Visual Basic equivalent of returning a void in C# is to define a subroutine (Sub/End Sub) rather than a function that returns a value.

■ **ADVANCED TOPIC**

Implicitly Typed Local Variables

Additionally, C# 3.0 includes a contextual keyword, var, for declaring an **implicitly typed local variable.** As long as the code initializes a variable at declaration time with an unambiguous type, C# 3.0 allows for the variable data type to be implied. Instead of explicitly specifying the data type, an implicitly typed local variable is declared with the contextual keyword var, as shown in Listing 2.17.

LISTING 2.17: **Working with Strings**

```csharp
class Uppercase
{
  static void Main()
  {
      System.Console.Write("Enter text: ");
      var text = System.Console.ReadLine();

      // Return a new string in uppercase
      var uppercase = text.ToUpper();

      System.Console.WriteLine(uppercase);
  }
}
```

This listing is different from Listing 2.15 in two ways. First, rather than using the explicit data type string for the declaration, Listing 2.17 uses var. The resultant CIL code is identical to using string explicitly. However, var indicates to the compiler that it should determine the data type from the value (System.Console.ReadLine()) that is assigned within the declaration.

Second, the variables text and uppercase are not declared without assignment at declaration time. To do so would result in a compile error. As mentioned earlier, via assignment the compiler retrieves the data type of the right-hand side expression and declares the variable accordingly, just as it would if the programmer specified the type explicitly.

Although using var rather than the explicit data type is allowed, consider avoiding such use when the data type is known—for example, use string for the declaration of text and uppercase. Not only does this make the code more understandable, but it also verifies that the data type returned by the right-hand side expression is the type expected. When using a var declared variable, the right-hand side data type should be obvious; if it isn't, using the var declaration should be avoided.

var support was added to the language in C# 3.0 to support anonymous types. Anonymous types are data types that are declared on the fly within a method, rather than through explicit class definitions, as outlined in Chapter 14 (see Listing 2.18).

LISTING 2.18: Implicit Local Variables with Anonymous Types

```csharp
class Program
{
  static void Main()
  {
      var patent1 =
          new { Title = "Bifocals",
          YearOfPublication = "1784" };
      var patent2 =
          new { Title = "Phonograph",
          YearOfPublication = "1877" };

      System.Console.WriteLine("{0} ({1})",
          patent1.Title, patent1.YearOfPublication);
      System.Console.WriteLine("{0} ({1})",
          patent2.Title, patent1.YearOfPublication);
  }
}
```

The corresponding output is shown in Output 2.14.

OUTPUT 2.14:

```
Bifocals (1784)
Phonograph (1784)
```

Listing 2.18 demonstrates the anonymous type assignment to an implicitly typed (var) local variable. This type of operation provides critical functionality with C# 3.0 support for joining (associating) data types or reducing the size of a particular type down to fewer data elements.

Categories of Types

All types fall into two categories: **value types** and **reference types.** The differences between the types in each category stem from how they are copied: Value type data is always copied by value, while reference type data is always copied by reference.

Value Types

With the exception of string, all the predefined types in the book so far are value types. Value types contain the value directly. In other words, the variable refers to the same location in memory where the value is stored. Because of this, when a different variable is assigned the same value, a memory copy of the original variable's value is made to the location of the new variable. A second variable of the same value type cannot refer to the same location in memory as the first variable. So changing the value of the first variable will not affect the value in the second. Figure 2.1 demonstrates this. number1 refers to a particular location in memory that contains the value 42. After assigning number1 to number2, both variables will contain the value 42. However, modifying either variable's value will not affect the other.

Similarly, passing a value type to a method such as Console.Write-Line() will also result in a memory copy, and any changes to the parameter

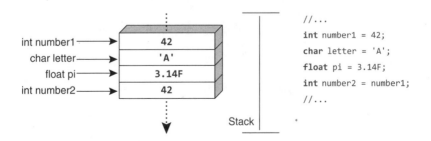

FIGURE 2.1: Value Types Contain the Data Directly

inside the method will not affect the original value within the calling function. Since value types require a memory copy, they generally should be defined to consume a small amount of memory (less than 16 bytes).

Reference Types

Reference types and the variables that refer to them point to the data storage location. Reference types store the reference where the data is located instead of storing the data directly. Therefore, to access the data the runtime will read the memory location out of the variable and then jump to the location in memory that contains the data. The memory area of the data a reference type points to is the **heap** (see Figure 2.2).

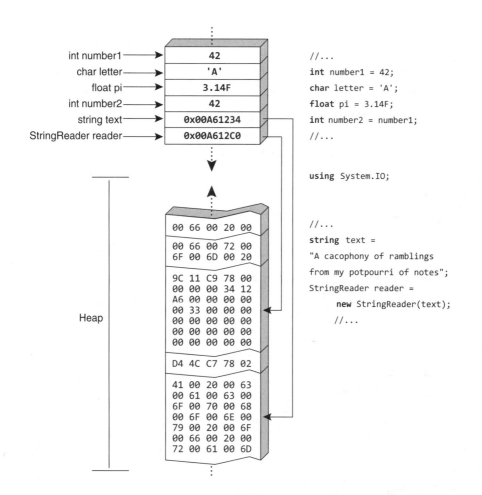

FIGURE 2.2: Reference Types Point to the Heap

A reference type does not require the same memory copy of the data that a value type does, resulting in circumstances when it is more efficient. When assigning one reference type variable to another reference type variable, only a memory copy of the address occurs, and as such, the memory copy required by a reference type is always the size of the address itself. (A 32-bit processor will copy 32 bits and a 64-bit processor will copy 64 bits, and so on.) Obviously, not copying the data would be faster than a value type's behavior if the latter's data size is large.

Since reference types copy only the address of the data, two different variables can point to the same data. Furthermore, changing the data through one variable will change the data for the other variable as well. This happens both for assignment and for method calls. Therefore, a method can affect the data of a reference type back at the caller. For this reason, a key determinant factor in the choice between defining a reference type or a value type is whether the object is logically like an immutable value of fixed size, and therefore a value type.

Besides `string` and any custom classes such as `Program`, all types discussed so far are value types. However, most types are reference types. Although it is possible to define custom value types, it is relatively rare to do so in comparison to the number of custom reference types.

Nullable Modifier

As I pointed out earlier, value types cannot be assigned `null` because, by definition, they can't contain references, including references to nothing. However, this presents a problem in the real world, where values are missing. When specifying a count, for example, what do you enter if the count is unknown? One possible solution is to designate a "magic" value, such as `0` or `int.MaxValue`, but these are valid integers. Rather, it is desirable to assign `null` to the value type because this is not a valid integer.

To declare variables that can store `null` you use the nullable modifier, ?. This feature, which started with C# 2.0, appears in Listing 2.19.

LISTING 2.19: Using the Nullable Modifier

```
static void Main()
{
  int? count = null;
```

```
do
  {
      // ...
  }
  while(count == null);
}
```

Assigning null to value types is especially attractive in database programming. Frequently, value type columns in database tables allow nulls. Retrieving such columns and assigning them to corresponding fields within C# code is problematic, unless the fields can contain null as well. Fortunately, the nullable modifier is designed to handle such a scenario specifically.

Conversions between Data Types

Given the thousands of types predefined in the various CLI implementations and the unlimited number of types that code can define, it is important that types support conversion from one to another where it makes sense. The most common operation that results in a conversion is **casting.**

Consider the conversion between two numerical types: converting from a variable of type long to a variable of type int. A long type can contain values as large as 9,223,372,036,854,775,808; however, the maximum size of an int is 2,147,483,647. As such, that conversion could result in a loss of data—for example, if the variable of type long contains a value greater than the maximum size of an int. Any conversion that could result in a loss of magnitude or an exception because the conversion failed requires an **explicit cast.** Conversely, a casting operation that will not lose magnitude and will not throw an exception regardless of the operand types is an **implicit conversion.**

Explicit Cast

In C#, you cast using the **cast operator.** By specifying the type you would like the variable converted to within parentheses, you acknowledge that if an explicit cast is occurring, there may be a loss of precision and data, or an exception may result. The code in Listing 2.20 converts a long to an int and explicitly tells the system to attempt the operation.

LISTING 2.20: Explicit Cast Example

```
long longNumber = 50918309109;
int intNumber = (int) longNumber;
                cast operator
```

With the cast operator, the programmer essentially says to the compiler, "Trust me, I know what I am doing. I know that the conversion could possibly not fit, but I am willing to take the chance." Making such a choice will cause the compiler to allow the conversion. However, with an explicit conversion, there is still a chance that an error, in the form of an exception, might occur while executing if the data does not convert successfully. It is, therefore, the programmer's responsibility to ensure the data will successfully convert, or else to provide the necessary error-handling code when it doesn't.

ADVANCED TOPIC

Checked and Unchecked Conversions

C# provides special keywords for marking a code block to indicate what should happen if the target data type is too small to contain the assigned data. By default, if the target data type cannot contain the assigned data, then the data will overflow truncate during assignment. For an example, see Listing 2.21.

LISTING 2.21: Overflowing an Integer Value

```
public class Program
{
  public static void Main()
  {
      // int.MaxValue equals 2147483647
      int n = int.MaxValue;
      n = n + 1 ;
      System.Console.WriteLine(n);
  }
}
```

Output 2.15 shows the results.

```
-2147483648
```

Listing 2.21 writes the value -2147483648 to the console. However, placing the code within a **checked block,** or using the checked option when running the compiler, will cause the runtime to throw an exception of type System.OverflowException. The syntax for a checked block uses the checked keyword, as shown in Listing 2.22.

LISTING 2.22: A Checked Block Example

```csharp
public class Program
{
  public static void Main()
  {
    checked
    {
      // int.MaxValue equals 2147483647
      int n = int.MaxValue;
      n = n + 1 ;
      System.Console.WriteLine(n);
    }
  }
}
```

Output 2.16 shows the results.

```
Unhandled Exception: System.OverflowException: Arithmetic operation
resulted in an overflow at Program.Main() in ...Program.cs:line 12
```

The result is that an exception is thrown if, within the checked block, an overflow assignment occurs at runtime.

The C# compiler provides a command-line option for changing the default checked behavior from unchecked to checked. C# also supports an unchecked block that overflows the data instead of throwing an exception for assignments within the block (see Listing 2.23).

LISTING 2.23: An Unchecked Block Example

```
using System;

public class Program
{
  public static void Main()
  {
      unchecked
      {
          // int.MaxValue equals 2147483647
          int n = int.MaxValue;
          n = n + 1 ;
          System.Console.WriteLine(n);
      }
  }
}
```

Output 2.17 shows the results.

OUTPUT 2.17:

```
-2147483648
```

Even if the checked option is on during compilation, the unchecked keyword in the preceding code will prevent the runtime from throwing an exception during execution.

You cannot convert any type to any other type simply because you designate the conversion explicitly using the cast operator. The compiler will still check that the operation is valid. For example, you cannot convert a long to a bool. No such cast operator is defined, and therefore, the compiler does not allow such a cast.

Language Contrast: Converting Numbers to Booleans

It may be surprising that there is no valid cast from a numeric type to a Boolean type, since this is common in many other languages. The reason no such conversion exists in C# is to avoid any ambiguity, such as whether −1 corresponds to true or false. More importantly, as you will see in the next chapter, this also reduces the chance of using the assignment operator in place of the equality operator (avoiding if(x=42){...} when if(x==42){...} was intended, for example).

Implicit Conversion

In other instances, such as going from an int type to a long type, there is no loss of precision and there will be no fundamental change in the value of the type. In these cases, code needs only to specify the assignment operator and the conversion is **implicit.** In other words, the compiler is able to determine that such a conversion will work correctly. The code in Listing 2.24 converts from an int to a long by simply using the assignment operator.

LISTING 2.24: Not Using the Cast Operator for an Implicit Cast

```
int intNumber = 31416;
long longNumber = intNumber;
```

Even when no explicit cast operator is required (because an implicit conversion is allowed), it is still possible to include the cast operator (see Listing 2.25).

LISTING 2.25: Using the Cast Operator for an Implicit Cast

```
int intNumber = 31416;
long longNumber = (long) intNumber;
```

Type Conversion without Casting

No conversion is defined from a string to a numeric type, so methods such as Parse() are required. Each numeric data type includes a Parse() function that enables conversion from a string to the corresponding numeric type. Listing 2.26 demonstrates this call.

LISTING 2.26: Using int.Parse() to Convert a string to a Numeric Data Type

```
string text = "9.11E-31";
float kgElectronMass = float.Parse(text);
```

Another special type is available for converting one type to the next. The type is System.Convert and an example of its use appears in Listing 2.27.

LISTING 2.27: Type Conversion Using System.Convert

```
string middleCText = "278.4375";
double middleC = System.Convert.ToDouble(middleCText);
bool boolean = System.Convert.ToBoolean(middleC);
```

`System.Convert` supports only a predefined number of types and it is not extensible. It allows conversion from any primitive type (`bool`, `char`, `sbyte`, `short`, `int`, `long`, `ushort`, `uint`, `ulong`, `float`, `double`, `decimal`, `DateTime`, and `string`) to any other primitive type.

Furthermore, all types support a `ToString()` method that can be used to provide a string representation of a type. Listing 2.28 demonstrates how to use this method. The resultant output is shown in Output 2.18.

LISTING 2.28: Using `ToString()` to Convert to a `string`

```
bool boolean = true;
string text = boolean.ToString();
// Display "True"
System.Console.WriteLine(text);
```

OUTPUT 2.18:

```
True
```

For the majority of types, the `ToString()` method will return the name of the data type rather than a string representation of the data. The string representation is returned only if the type has an explicit implementation of `ToString()`. One last point to make is that it is possible to code custom conversion methods, and many such methods are available for classes in the runtime.

■ ADVANCED TOPIC

TryParse()

Starting with C# 2.0 (.NET 2.0), all the numeric primitive types include a static `TryParse()` method. (In C# 1.0, only `double` includes such a method.) This method is very similar to the `Parse()` method, except that instead of throwing an exception if the conversion fails, the `TryParse()` method returns `false`, as demonstrated in Listing 2.29.

LISTING 2.29: Using `TryParse()` in Place of an Invalid Cast Exception

```
double number;
string input;
```

```
System.Console.Write("Enter a number: ");
input = System.Console.ReadLine();
if (double.TryParse(input, out number))
{
    // Converted correctly, now use number
    // ...
}
else
{
    System.Console.WriteLine(
        "The text entered was not a valid number.");
}
```

Output 2.19 shows the results of Listing 2.27.

OUTPUT 2.19:

```
Enter a number: forty-two
The text entered was not a valid number.
```

The resultant value the code parses from the input string is returned via an out parameter—in this case, number.

The key difference between Parse() and TryParse() is the fact that TryParse() won't throw an exception if it fails. Frequently, the conversion from a string to a numeric type depends on a user entering the text. It is expected, in such scenarios, that the user will enter invalid data that will not parse successfully. By using TryParse() rather than Parse(), you can avoid throwing exceptions in expected situations. (The expected situation in this case is that the user will enter invalid data.)

Arrays

One particular aspect of variable declaration that Chapter 1 didn't cover is array declaration. With array declaration, you can store multiple items of the same type using a single variable and still access them individually using the index when required. In C#, the array index starts at zero. Therefore, arrays in C# are **zero based**.

■ **BEGINNER TOPIC**

Arrays

Arrays provide a means of declaring a collection of data items that are of the same type using a single variable. Each item within the array is uniquely designated using an integer value called the **index.** The first item in a C# array is accessed using index 0. Programmers should be careful to specify an index value that is less than the array size. Since C# arrays are zero based, the index for the last element in an array is one less than the total number of items in the array.

For beginners, it is helpful sometimes to think of the index as an offset. The first item is zero away from the start of the array. The second item is one away from the start of the array—and so on.

Declaring an Array

In C#, you declare arrays using square brackets. First, you specify the element type of the array, followed by open and closed square brackets; then you enter the name of the variable. Listing 2.30 declares a variable called languages to be an array of strings.

LISTING 2.30: Declaring an Array

```
string[] languages;
```

Obviously, the first part of the array identifies the data type of the elements within the array. The square brackets that are part of the declaration identify the **rank,** or the number of dimensions, for the array; in this case it is an array of rank one. These two pieces form the data type for the variable languages.

Language Contrast: C++ and Java—Array Declaration

The square brackets for an array in C# appear immediately following the data type instead of after the variable declaration. This keeps all the type information together instead of splitting it up both before and after the identifier, as occurs in C++ and Java.

Listing 2.30 defines an array with a rank of one. Commas within the square brackets define additional dimensions. Listing 2.31, for example, defines a two-dimensional array of cells for a game of chess or tic-tac-toe.

LISTING 2.31: Declaring a Two-Dimensional Array

```
//    |   |
// ---+---+---
//    |   |
// ---+---+---
//    |   |
int[,] cells;
```

In Listing 2.29, the array has a rank of two. The first dimension could correspond to cells going across and the second dimension represents cells going down. Additional dimensions are added, with additional commas, and the total rank is one more than the number of commas. Note that the number of items that occur for a particular dimension is not part of the variable declaration. This is specified when creating (instantiating) the array and allocating space for each element.

Instantiating and Assigning Arrays

Once an array is declared, you can immediately fill its values using a comma-delimited list of items enclosed within a pair of curly braces. Listing 2.32 declares an array of strings and then assigns the names of nine languages within curly braces.

LISTING 2.32: Array Declaration with Assignment

```
string[] languages = { "C#", "COBOL", "Java",
    "C++", "Visual Basic", "Pascal",
    "Fortran", "Lisp", "J#"};
```

The first item in the comma-delimited list becomes the first item in the array; the second item in the list becomes the second item in the array, and so on. The curly brackets are the notation for defining an array literal.

The assignment syntax shown in Listing 2.32 is available only if you declare and assign the value within one statement. To assign the value after declaration requires the use of the keyword new as shown in Listing 2.33.

LISTING 2.33: Array Assignment Following Declaration

```
string[] languages;
languages = new string[]{"C#", "COBOL", "Java",
    "C++", "Visual Basic", "Pascal",
    "Fortran", "Lisp", "J#" };
```

Starting in C# 3.0, specifying the data type of the array (string) following new became optional as long as the data type of items within the array was compatible—the square brackets are still required.

C# also allows use of the new keyword as part of the declaration statement, so it allows the assignment and the declaration shown in Listing 2.34.

LISTING 2.34: Array Assignment with new during Declaration

```
string[] languages = new string[]{
    "C#", "COBOL", "Java",
    "C++", "Visual Basic", "Pascal",
    "Fortran", "Lisp", "J#"};
```

The use of the new keyword tells the runtime to allocate memory for the data type. It instructs the runtime to instantiate the data type—in this case, an array.

Whenever you use the new keyword as part of an array assignment, you may also specify the size of the array within the square brackets. Listing 2.35 demonstrates this syntax.

LISTING 2.35: Declaration and Assignment with the new Keyword

```
string[] languages = new string[9]{
    "C#", "COBOL", "Java",
    "C++", "Visual Basic", "Pascal",
    "Fortran", "Lisp", "J#"};
```

The array size in the initialization statement and the number of elements contained within the curly braces must match. Furthermore, it is possible to assign an array but not specify the initial values of the array, as demonstrated in Listing 2.36.

LISTING 2.36: Assigning without Literal Values

```
string[] languages = new string[9];
```

Assigning an array but not initializing the initial values will still initialize each element. The runtime initializes elements to their default values, as follows.

- Reference types (such as `string`) are initialized to `null`.
- Numeric types are initialized to zero.
- `bool` is initialized to `false`.
- `char` is initialized to `'\0'`.

Nonprimitive value types are recursively initialized by initializing each of their fields to their default values.

As a result, it is not necessary to individually assign each element of an array before using it.

In C# 2.0, it is possible to use the `default()` operator to determine the default value of a data type. `default()` takes a data type as a parameter. `default(int)`, for example, returns `0` and `default(char)` returns `\0`.

Because the array size is not included as part of the variable declaration, it is possible to specify the size at runtime. For example, Listing 2.37 creates an array based on the size specified in the `Console.ReadLine()` call.

LISTING 2.37: Defining the Array Size at Runtime

```
string[] groceryList;
System.Console.Write("How many items on the list? ");
int size = int.Parse(System.Console.ReadLine());
groceryList = new string[size];
// ...
```

C# initializes multidimensional arrays similarly. A comma separates the size of each rank. Listing 2.38 initializes a tic-tac-toe board with no moves.

LISTING 2.38: Declaring a Two-Dimensional Array

```
int[,] cells = int[3,3];
```

Initializing a tic-tac-toe board with a specific position instead could be done as shown in Listing 2.39.

LISTING 2.39: Initializing a Two-Dimensional Array of Integers

```
int[,] cells = {
        {1, 0, 2},
        {1, 2, 0},
        {1, 2, 1}
    };
```

The initialization follows the pattern in which there is an array of three elements of type int[], and each element has the same size; in this example, the size is 3. Note that the dimension of each int[] element must be identical. The declaration shown in Listing 2.40, therefore, is not valid.

LISTING 2.40: A Multidimensional Array with Inconsistent Size, Causing an Error

```
// ERROR:  Each dimension must be consistently sized.
int[,] cells = {
        {1, 0, 2, 0},
        {1, 2, 0},
        {1, 2}
        {1}
    };
```

Representing tic-tac-toe does not require an integer in each position. One alternative is a separate virtual board for each player, with each board containing a bool that indicates which positions the players selected. Listing 2.41 corresponds to a three-dimensional board.

LISTING 2.41: Initializing a Three-Dimensional Array

```
bool[,,] cells;
cells = new bool[2,3,3]
    {
        // Player 1 moves            // X |   |
        {   {true, false, false},    // ---+---+---
            {true, false, false},    // X |   |
            {true, false, true} },   // ---+---+---
                                     // X |   | X

        // Player 2 moves            //   |   | O
        {   {false, false, true},    // ---+---+---
            {false, true, false},    //   | O |
            {false, true, true} }    // ---+---+---
                                     //   | O |
    };
```

In this example, the board is initialized and the size of each rank is explicitly identified. In addition to identifying the size as part of the new expression, the literal values for the array are provided. The literal values of type bool[, ,] are broken into two arrays of type bool[,], size 3x3. Each two-dimensional array is composed of three bool arrays, size 3.

As already mentioned, each dimension in a multidimensional array must be consistently sized. However, it is also possible to define a **jagged array,** which is an array of arrays. Jagged array syntax is slightly different from that of a multidimensional array, and furthermore, jagged arrays do not need to be consistently sized. Therefore, it is possible to initialize a jagged array as shown in Listing 2.42.

LISTING 2.42: Initializing a Jagged Array

```
int[][]cells = {
    new int[]{1, 0, 2, 0},
    new int[]{1, 2, 0},
    new int[]{1, 2},
    new int[]{1}
};
```

A jagged array doesn't use a comma to identify a new dimension. Rather, a jagged array defines an array of arrays. In Listing 2.42, [] is placed after the data type int[], thereby declaring an array of type int[].

Notice that a jagged array requires an array instance (or null) for each internal array. In this example, you use new to instantiate the internal element of the jagged arrays. Leaving out the instantiation would cause a compile error.

Using an Array

You access a specific item in an array using the square bracket notation, known as the **array accessor.** To retrieve the first item from an array, you specify zero as the index. In Listing 2.43, the value of the fifth item (using the index 4 because the first item is index 0) in the languages variable is stored in the variable language.

LISTING 2.43: Declaring and Accessing an Array

```
string[] languages = new string[9]{
    "C#", "COBOL", "Java",
    "C++", "Visual Basic", "Pascal",
```

```
        "Fortran", "Lisp", "J#"};
// Retrieve 3rd item in languages array (Java)
string language = languages[4];
```

The square bracket notation is also used to store data into an array. Listing 2.44 switches the order of "C++" and "Java".

LISTING 2.44: Swapping Data between Positions in an Array

```
string[] languages = new string[9]{
    "C#", "COBOL", "Java",
    "C++", "Visual Basic", "Pascal",
    "Fortran", "Lisp", "J#"};
// Save "C++" to variable called language.
string language = languages[3];
// Assign "Java" to the C++ position.
languages[3] = languages[2];
// Assign language to location of "Java".
languages[2] = language;
```

For multidimensional arrays, an element is identified with an index for each dimension, as shown in Listing 2.45.

LISTING 2.45: Initializing a Two-Dimensional Array of Integers

```
int[,] cells = {
        {1, 0, 2},
        {0, 2, 0},
        {1, 2, 1}
    };
// Set the winning tic-tac-toe move to be player 1.
cells[1,0] = 1;
```

Jagged array element assignment is slightly different because it is consistent with the jagged array declaration. The first element is an array within the array of arrays. The second index specifies the item within the selected array element (see Listing 2.46).

LISTING 2.46: Declaring a Jagged Array

```
int[][] cells = {
    new int[]{1, 0, 2},
  new int[]{0, 2, 0},
  new int[]{1, 2, 1}
};

cells[1][0] = 1;
// ...
```

Length

You can obtain the length of an array, as shown in Listing 2.47.

LISTING 2.47: Retrieving the Length of an Array

```
Console.WriteLine("There are {0} languages in the array.",
languages.Length);
```

Arrays have a fixed length; they are bound such that the length cannot be changed without re-creating the array. Furthermore, overstepping the **bounds** (or length) of the array will cause the runtime to report an error. This can occur by accessing (either retrieving or assigning) the array with an index for which no element exists in the array. Such an error frequently occurs when you use the array length as an index into the array, as shown in Listing 2.48.

LISTING 2.48: Accessing Outside the Bounds of an Array, Throwing an Exception

```
string languages = new string[9];
...
// RUNTIME ERROR: index out of bounds - should
// be 8 for the last element
languages[4] = languages[9];
```

■ **NOTE**

The Length member returns the number of items in the array, not the highest index. The Length member for the languages variable is 9, but the highest index for the languages variable is 8, because that is how far it is from the start.

Language Contrast: C++—Buffer Overflow Bugs

Unmanaged C++ does not always check whether you overstep the bounds on an array. Not only can this be difficult to debug, but making this mistake can also result in a potential security error called a **buffer overrun**. In contrast, the Common Language Runtime protects all C# (and Managed C++) code from overstepping array bounds, virtually eliminating the possibility of a buffer overrun issue in managed code.

It is a good practice to use Length in place of the hardcoded array size. To use Length as an index, for example, it is necessary to subtract 1 to avoid an out-of-bounds error (see Listing 2.49).

LISTING 2.49: Using Length - 1 in the Array Index

```
string languages = new string[9];
...
languages[4] = languages[languages.Length - 1];
```

To avoid overstepping the bounds on an array use a length check to verify it has a length greater than 0 as well as using Length - 1 in place of a hardcoded value when accessing the last item in the array (see Listing 2.49).

Length returns the total number of elements in an array. Therefore, if you had a multidimensional array such as bool cells[,,] of size 2•3•3, Length would return the total number of elements, 18.

For a jagged array, Length returns the number of elements in the first array—a jagged array is an array of arrays, so Length evaluates only the outside, containing array and returns its element count, regardless of what is inside the internal arrays.

More Array Methods

Arrays include additional methods for manipulating the elements within the array. These include Sort(), BinarySearch(), Reverse(), and Clear() (see Listing 2.50).

LISTING 2.50: Additional Array Methods

```
class ProgrammingLanguages
{
  static void Main()
  {
      string[] languages = new string[]{
          "C#", "COBOL", "Java",
          "C++", "Visual Basic", "Pascal",
          "Fortran", "Lisp", "J#"};

      System.Array.Sort(languages);

      searchString = "COBOL";
```

```
        index = System.Array.BinarySearch(
            languages, searchString);
    System.Console.WriteLine(
        "The wave of the future, {0}, is at index {1}.",
        searchString, index);

    System.Console.WriteLine();
    System.Console.WriteLine("{0,-20}{1,-20}",
        "First Element", "Last Element");
    System.Console.WriteLine("{0,-20}{1,-20}",
        "-------------", "------------");
    System.Console.WriteLine("{0,-20}{1,-20}",
        languages[0], languages[languages.Length-1]);

    System.Array.Reverse(languages);
    System.Console.WriteLine("{0,-20}{1,-20}",
        languages[0], languages[languages.Length-1]);

    // Note this does not remove all items from the array.
    // Rather it sets each item to the type's default value.
    System.Array.Clear(languages, 0, languages.Length);
    System.Console.WriteLine("{0,-20}{1,-20}",
        languages[0], languages[languages.Length-1]);
    System.Console.WriteLine(
        "After clearing, the array size is: {0}",
        languages.Length);
    }
}
```

The results of Listing 2.50 are shown in Output 2.20.

OUTPUT 2.20:

```
The wave of the future, COBOL, is at index 1.

First Element       Last Element
-------------       ------------
C#                  Visual Basic
Visual Basic        C#

After clearing, the array size is: 9
```

Access to these methods is on the System.Array class. For the most part, using these methods is self-explanatory, except for two noteworthy items.

- Before using the `BinarySearch()` method, it is important to sort the array. If values are not sorted in increasing order, then the incorrect index may be returned. If the search element does not exist, then the value returned is negative. (Using the complement operator, `~index`, returns the first index, if any, that is larger than the searched value.)

- The `Clear()` method does not remove elements of the array and does not set the length to zero. The array size is fixed and cannot be modified. Therefore, the `Clear()` method sets each element in the array to its default value (`false`, `0`, or `null`). This explains why `Console.Write-Line()` creates a blank line when writing out the array after `Clear()` is called.

Language Contrast: Visual Basic—Redimensioning Arrays

Visual Basic includes a `Redim` statement for changing the number of items in an array. Although there is no equivalent C# specific keyword, there is a method available in .NET 2.0 that will re-create the array and then copy all the elements over to the new array. The method is called `System.Array.Resize`.

Array Instance Methods

Like strings, arrays have instance members that are accessed not from the data type, but directly from the variable. `Length` is an example of an instance member because access to `Length` is through the array variable, not the class. Other significant instance members are `GetLength()`, `Rank`, and `Clone()`.

Retrieving the length of a particular dimension does not require the `Length` property. To retrieve the size of a particular rank, an array includes a `GetLength()` instance method. When calling this method, it is necessary to specify the rank whose length will be returned (see Listing 2.51).

LISTING 2.51: **Retrieving a Particular Dimension's Size**

```
bool[,,] cells;
cells = new bool[2,3,3];
System.Console.WriteLine(cells.GetLength(0));    // Displays 2
```

The results of Listing 2.51 appear in Output 2.21.

OUTPUT 2.21:

```
2
```

Listing 2.51 displays 2 because this is the number of elements in the first dimension.

It is also possible to retrieve the entire array's rank by accessing the array's Rank member. cells.Rank, for example, will return 3.

By default, assigning one array variable to another copies only the array reference, not the individual elements of the array. To make an entirely new copy of the array, use the array's Clone() method. The Clone() method will return a copy of the array; changing any of the members of this new array will not affect the members of the original array.

Strings as Arrays

Variables of type string are accessible like an array of characters. For example, to retrieve the fourth character of a string called palindrome you can call palindrome[3]. Note, however, that because strings are immutable, it is not possible to assign particular characters within a string. C#, therefore, would not allow palindrome[3]='a', where palindrome is declared as a string. Listing 2.52 uses the array accessor to determine whether an argument on the command line is an option, where an option is identified by a dash as the first character.

LISTING 2.52: **Looking for Command-Line Options**

```
string[] args;
...
if(args[0][0]=='-')
{
    //This parameter is an option
}
```

This snippet uses the `if` statement, which is covered in Chapter 3. In addition, it presents an interesting example because you use the array accessor to retrieve the first element in the array of strings, `args`. Following the first array accessor is a second one, this time to retrieve the first character of the string. The code, therefore, is equivalent to that shown in Listing 2.53.

LISTING 2.53: Looking for Command-Line Options (Simplified)

```csharp
string[] args;
...
string arg = args[0];
if(arg[0] == '-')
{
    //This parameter is an option
}
```

Not only can string characters be accessed individually using the array accessor, but it is also possible to retrieve the entire string as an array of characters using the string's `ToCharArray()` method. Using this method, you could reverse the string using the `System.Array.Reverse()` method, as demonstrated in Listing 2.54, which determines whether a string is a palindrome.

LISTING 2.54: Reversing a String

```csharp
class Palindrome
{
  static void Main()
  {
      string reverse, palindrome;
      char[] temp;

      System.Console.Write("Enter a palindrome: ");
      palindrome = System.Console.ReadLine();

      // Remove spaces and convert to lowercase
      reverse = palindrome.Replace(" ", "");
      reverse = reverse.ToLower();

      // Convert to an array
      temp = reverse.ToCharArray();

      // Reverse the array
      System.Array.Reverse(temp);
```

```
        // Convert the array back to a string and
        // check if reverse string is the same.
        if(reverse == new string(temp))
        {
            System.Console.WriteLine("\"{0}\" is a palindrome.",
                palindrome);
        }
        else
        {
            System.Console.WriteLine(
                "\"{0}\" is NOT a palindrome.",
                palindrome);
        }
    }
}
```

The results of Listing 2.54 appear in Output 2.22.

OUTPUT 2.22:

```
Enter a palindrome: NeverOddOrEven
"NeverOddOrEven" is a palindrome.
```

This example uses the new keyword; this time, it creates a new string from the reversed array of characters.

Common Errors

This section introduced the three different types of arrays: single-dimension, multidimensional, and jagged arrays. Several rules and idiosyncrasies govern array declaration and use. Table 2.7 points out some of the most common errors and helps solidify the rules. Readers should consider reviewing the code in the Common Mistake column first (without looking at the Error Description and Corrected Code columns) as a way of verifying their understanding of arrays and their syntax.

TABLE 2.7: Common Array Coding Errors

Common Mistake	Error Description	Corrected Code
`int numbers[];`	The square braces for declaring an array appear after the data type, not after the variable identifier.	`int[] numbers;`

`int[] numbers;`
`numbers = {42, 84, 168 };`
	When assigning an array after declaration, it is necessary to use the new keyword and then specify the data type.	`int[] numbers;`
		`numbers = new int[]{`
		`42, 84, 168 }`

`int[3] numbers =` `{ 42, 84, 168 };`	It is not possible to specify the array size as part of the variable declaration.	`int[] numbers =` `{ 42, 84, 168 };`
`int[] numbers =` `new int[];`	The array size is required at initialization time unless an array literal is provided.	`int[] numbers =` `new int[3];`

`int[] numbers =`
`new int[3]{}`
	The array size is specified as 3, but there are no elements in the array literal. The array size must match the number of elements in the array literal.	`int[] numbers =`
		`new int[3]`
		`{ 42, 84, 168 };`

`int[] numbers =`
`new int[3];`
`Console.WriteLine(`
`numbers[3]);`
	Array indexes start at zero. Therefore, the last item is one less than the array size. (Note that this is a runtime error, not a compile-time error.)	`int[] numbers =`
		`new int[3];`
		`Console.WriteLine(`
		`numbers[2]);`

Continues

TABLE 2.7: Common Array Coding Errors *(Continued)*

Common Mistake	Error Description	Corrected Code
```int[] numbers = new int[3]; numbers[numbers.Length] = 42;```	Same as previous error: 1 needs to be subtracted from the Length to access the last element. (Note that this is a runtime error, not a compile-time error.)	```int[] numbers = new int[3]; numbers[numbers.Length-1] = 42;```
```int[] numbers; Console.WriteLine(numbers[0]);```	numbers has not yet been assigned an instantiated array, and therefore, it cannot be accessed.	```int[] numbers = {42, 84}; Console.WriteLine(numbers[0]);```
```int[,] numbers = { {42}, {84, 42} };```	Multidimensional arrays must be structured consistently.	```int[,] numbers = { {42, 168}, {84, 42} };```
```int[][] numbers = { {42, 84}, {84, 42} };```	Jagged arrays require instantiated arrays to be specified for the arrays within the array.	```int[][] numbers = { new int[]{42, 84}, new int[]{84, 42} };```

SUMMARY

Even for experienced programmers, C# introduces several new programming constructs. For example, as part of the section on data types, this chapter covered the type `decimal` that can be used accurately for financial calculations. In addition, the chapter introduced the fact that the Boolean type, `bool`, does not convert implicitly to an integer, thereby preventing the mistaken use of the assignment operator in a conditional expression. Other unique characteristics of C# from many of its predecessors are the @ verbatim string qualifier that forces a string to ignore the escape character and the fact that the `string` data type is immutable.

To convert data types between each other C# includes the cast operator in both an explicit and an implicit form. In the following chapters, you will learn how to define both cast operators on custom types.

This chapter closed with coverage of C# syntax for arrays, along with the various means of manipulating arrays. For many developers, the syntax can become rather daunting at first, so the section included a list of the common errors associated with coding arrays.

The next chapter looks at expressions and control flow statements. The `if` statement, which appeared a few times toward the end of this chapter, is discussed as well.

3
Operators and Control Flow

I N THIS CHAPTER, you will learn about operators and control flow statements. Operators provide syntax for performing different calculations or actions appropriate for the operands within the calculation. Control flow statements provide the means for conditional logic within a program or looping over a section of code multiple times. After introducing the if control flow statement, the chapter looks at the concept of Boolean expressions, which are embedded within many control flow statements. Included is mention of how integers will not cast (even explicitly) to bool and the

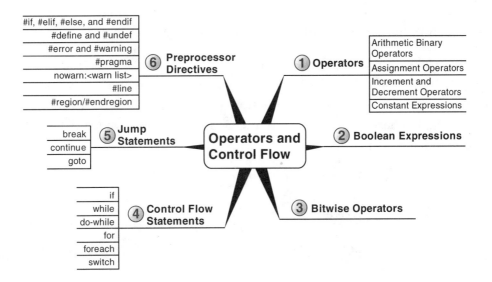

advantages of this restriction. The chapter ends with a discussion of the C#
"preprocessor" and its accompanying directives.

Operators

Now that you have been introduced to the predefined data types (refer to
Chapter 2), you can begin to learn more about how to use these data types
in combination with operators in order to perform calculations. For example, you can make calculations on variables that you have declared.

■ **BEGINNER TOPIC**

Operators

Operators specify operations within an expression, such as a mathematical
expression, to be performed on a set of values, called **operands,** to produce
a new value or result. For example, in Listing 3.1 there are two operands,
the numbers 4 and 2, that are combined using the subtraction operator, -.
You assign the result to the variable `difference`.

LISTING 3.1: A Simple Operator Example

```
difference = 4 - 2;
```

Operators are generally broken down into three categories: unary,
binary, and ternary, corresponding to the number of operands 1, 2, and 3,
respectively. This section covers some of the most basic unary and binary
operators. Introduction to the ternary operator appears later in the chapter.

Plus and Minus Unary Operators (+, -)

Sometimes you may want to change the sign of a numerical variable. In
these cases, the unary minus operator (-) comes in handy. For example,
Listing 3.2 changes the total current U.S. debt to a negative value to indicate that it is an amount owed.

LISTING 3.2: Specifying Negative Values[1]

```
//National Debt to the Penny
decimal debt = -11719258192538.99M;
```

Using the minus operator *is equivalent to subtracting the operand from zero.*

---

1. As of August 21, 2009, according to www.treasurydirect.gov.

The unary plus operator (+) has rarely[2] had any effect on a value. It is a superfluous addition to the C# language and was included for the sake of symmetry.

Arithmetic Binary Operators (+, -, *, /, %)

Binary operators require two operands in order to process an equation: a left-hand side operand and a right-hand side operand. Binary operators also require that the code assign the resultant value to avoid losing it.

Language Contrast: C++—Operator-Only Statements

Binary operators in C# require an assignment or call; they always return a new result. Neither operand in a binary operator expression can be modified. In contrast, C++ will allow a single statement, such as 4+5, to compile even without an assignment. In C#, call, increment, decrement, and new object expressions are allowed for operator-only statements.

The subtraction example in Listing 3.3 is an example of a binary operator—more specifically, an arithmetic binary operator. The operands appear on each side of the arithmetic operator and then the calculated value is assigned. The other arithmetic binary operators are addition (+), division (/), multiplication (*), and remainder (%; sometimes called the mod operator).

LISTING 3.3: Using Binary Operators

```
class Division
{
  static void Main()
  {
    int numerator;
    int denominator;
    int quotient;
    int remainder;

    System.Console.Write("Enter the numerator: ");
    numerator = int.Parse(System.Console.ReadLine());
```

---

2. The unary + operator is not defined on a short; it is defined on int, uint, long, ulong, float, double, and decimal. Therefore, using it on a short will convert it to one of these types as appropriate.

```
            System.Console.Write("Enter the denominator: ");
            denominator = int.Parse(System.Console.ReadLine());

            quotient = numerator / denominator;
            remainder = numerator % denominator;

            System.Console.WriteLine(
                "{0} / {1} = {2} with remainder {3}",
                numerator, denominator, quotient, remainder);
    }
}
```

Output 3.1 shows the results of Listing 3.3.

OUTPUT 3.1:

```
Enter the numerator: 23
Enter the denominator: 3
23 / 3 = 7 with remainder 2.
```

Note the order of associativity when using binary operators. The binary operator order is from left to right. In contrast, the assignment operator order is from right to left. On its own, however, associativity does not specify whether the division will occur before or after the assignment. The order of precedence defines this. The precedence for the operators used so far is as follows:

1. *, /, and %
2. + and -
3. =

Therefore, you can assume that the statement behaves as expected, with the division and remainder operators occurring before the assignment.

If you forget to assign the result of one of these binary operators, you will receive the compile error shown in Output 3.2.

OUTPUT 3.2:

```
... error CS0201: Only assignment, call, increment, decrement,
and new object expressions can be used as a statement
```

■ **BEGINNER TOPIC**

Associativity and Order of Precedence

As with mathematics, programming languages support the concept of **associativity**. Associativity refers to how operands are grouped and, therefore, the order in which operators are evaluated. Given a single operator that appears more than once in an expression, the operator associates the first duple and then the next operand until all operators are evaluated. For example, a-b-c associates as (a-b)-c, and not a-(b-c).

Associativity applies only when all the operators are the same. When different operators appear within a statement, the **order of precedence** for those operators dictates which operators are evaluated first. Order of precedence, for example, indicates that the multiplication operator be evaluated before the plus operator in the expression a+b*c.

Using the Plus Operator with Strings

Operators can also work with types that are not numeric. For example, it is possible to use the plus operator to concatenate two or more strings, as shown in Listing 3.4.

LISTING 3.4: Using Binary Operators with Non-Numeric Types

```
class FortyTwo
{
  static void Main()
  {
      short windSpeed = 42;
      System.Console.WriteLine(
          "The original Tacoma Bridge in Washington\nwas"
          + "brought down by a "
          + windSpeed + " mile/hour wind.");
  }
}
```

Output 3.3 shows the results of Listing 3.4.

OUTPUT 3.3:

```
The original Tacoma Bridge in Washington
was brought down by a 42 mile/hour wind.
```

Because sentence structure varies among languages in different cultures, developers should be careful not to use the plus operator with strings that require localization. Composite formatting is preferred (refer to Chapter 1).

Using Characters in Arithmetic Operations

When introducing the char type in the preceding chapter, I mentioned that even though it stores characters and not numbers, the char type is an **integral** type ("integral" means it is based on an integer). It can participate in arithmetic operations with other integer types. However, interpretation of the value of the char type is not based on the character stored within it, but rather on its underlying value. The digit 3, for example, contains a Unicode value of 0x33 (hexadecimal), which in base 10 is 51. The digit 4, on the other hand, contains a Unicode value of 0x34, or 52 in base 10. Adding 3 and 4 in Listing 3.5 results in a hexadecimal value of 0x167, or 103 in base 10, which is equivalent to the letter g.

LISTING 3.5: Using the Plus Operator with the char Data Type

```
int n = '3' + '4';
char c = (char)n;
System.Console.WriteLine(c);  // Writes out g.
```

Output 3.4 shows the results of Listing 3.5.

OUTPUT 3.4:

```
g
```

You can use this trait of character types to determine how far two characters are from one another. For example, the letter f is three characters away from the letter c. You can determine this value by subtracting the letter c from the letter f, as Listing 3.6 demonstrates.

LISTING 3.6: Determining the Character Difference between Two Characters

```
int distance = 'f' - 'c';
System.Console.WriteLine(distance);
```

Output 3.5 shows the results of Listing 3.6.

```
3
```

Special Floating-Point Characteristics

The floating-point types, float and double, have some special characteristics, such as the way they handle precision. This section looks at some specific examples, as well as some unique floating-point type characteristics.

A float, with seven digits of precision, can hold the value 1,234,567 and the value 0.1234567. However, if you add these two floats together, the result will be rounded to 1234567, because the decimal portion of the number is past the seven significant digits that a float can hold. This type of rounding can become significant, especially with repeated calculations or checks for equality (see the upcoming Advanced Topic, Unexpected Inequality with Floating-Point Types).

Note that inaccuracies can occur with a simple assignment, such as double number = 140.6F. Since the double can hold a more accurate value than the float can store, the C# compiler will actually evaluate this expression to double number = 140.600006103516;. 140.600006103516 is 140.6 as a float, but not quite 140.6 when represented as a double.

■ ADVANCED TOPIC

Unexpected Inequality with Floating-Point Types

The inaccuracies of floats can be very disconcerting when comparing values for equality, since they can unexpectedly be unequal. Consider Listing 3.7.

LISTING 3.7: Unexpected Inequality Due to Floating-Point Inaccuracies

```
decimal decimalNumber = 4.2M;
double doubleNumber1 = 0.1F * 42F;
double doubleNumber2 = 0.1D * 42D;
float floatNumber = 0.1F * 42F;

Trace.Assert(decimalNumber != (decimal)doubleNumber1);
// Displays: 4.2 != 4.20000006258488
System.Console.WriteLine(
    "{0} != {1}", decimalNumber, (decimal)doubleNumber1);
```

```
    Trace.Assert((double)decimalNumber != doubleNumber1);
    // Displays: 4.2 != 4.20000006258488
    System.Console.WriteLine(
        "{0} != {1}", (double)decimalNumber, doubleNumber1);

    Trace.Assert((float)decimalNumber != floatNumber);
    // Displays: (float)4.2M != 4.2F
    System.Console.WriteLine(
        "(float){0}M != {1}F",
        (float)decimalNumber, floatNumber);

    Trace.Assert(doubleNumber1 != (double)floatNumber);
    // Displays: 4.20000006258488 != 4.20000028610229
    System.Console.WriteLine(
        "{0} != {1}", doubleNumber1, (double)floatNumber);

    Trace.Assert(doubleNumber1 != doubleNumber2);
    // Displays: 4.20000006258488 != 4.2
    System.Console.WriteLine(
        "{0} != {1}", doubleNumber1, doubleNumber2);

    Trace.Assert(floatNumber != doubleNumber2);
    // Displays: 4.2F != 4.2D
    System.Console.WriteLine(
        "{0}F != {1}D", floatNumber, doubleNumber2);

    Trace.Assert((double)4.2F != 4.2D);
    // Display: 4.19999980926514 != 4.2
    System.Console.WriteLine(
        "{0} != {1}", (double)4.2F, 4.2D);

    Trace.Assert(4.2F != 4.2D);
    // Display: 4.2F != 4.2D
    System.Console.WriteLine(
        "{0}F != {1}D", 4.2F, 4.2D);
```

Output 3.6 shows the results of Listing 3.7.

OUTPUT 3.6:

```
4.2 != 4.20000006258488
4.2 != 4.20000006258488
(float)4.2M != 4.2F
4.20000006258488 != 4.20000028610229
4.20000006258488 != 4.2
4.2F != 4.2D
4.19999980926514 != 4.2
4.2F != 4.2D
```

The `Assert()` methods are designed to display a debug dialog whenever the parameter evaluates to `false`. However, all of the `Assert()` statements in this code listing will evaluate to `true`. Therefore, in spite of the apparent equality of the values in the code listing, they are in fact not equivalent due to the inaccuracies of a `float`. Furthermore, there is not some compounding rounding error. The C# compiler performs the calculations instead of the runtime. Even if you simply assign `4.2F` rather than a calculation, the comparisons will remain unequal.

To avoid unexpected results caused by the inaccuracies of floating-point types, developers should avoid using equality conditionals with these types. Rather, equality evaluations should include a tolerance. One easy way to achieve this is to subtract one value (operand) from the other and then evaluate whether the absolute value of the result is less than the maximum tolerance. Even better is to use the decimal type in place of the float type.

You should be aware of some additional unique floating-point characteristics as well. For instance, you would expect that dividing an integer by zero would result in an error, and it does with precision data types such as `int` and `decimal`. `float` and `double`, however, allow for certain special values. Consider Listing 3.8, and its resultant output, Output 3.7.

LISTING 3.8: Dividing a Float by Zero, Displaying NaN

```
float n=0f;
// Displays: NaN
System.Console.WriteLine(n / 0);
```

OUTPUT 3.7:

```
NaN
```

In mathematics, certain mathematical operations are undefined. In C#, the result of dividing 0F by the value 0 results in "Not a Number," and all attempts to print the output of such a number will result in `NaN`. Similarly, taking the square root of a negative number (`System.Math.Sqrt(-1)`) will result in `NaN`.

A floating-point number could overflow its bounds as well. For example, the upper bound of a float type is 3.4E38. Should the number overflow that bound, the result would be stored as "positive infinity" and the output of printing the number would be Infinity. Similarly, the lower bound of a float type is –3.4E38, and assigning a value below that bound would result in "negative infinity," which would be represented by the string -Infinity. Listing 3.9 produces negative and positive infinity, respectively, and Output 3.8 shows the results.

LISTING 3.9: Overflowing the Bounds of a float

```
// Displays: -Infinity
System.Console.WriteLine(-1f / 0);
// Displays: Infinity
System.Console.WriteLine(3.402823E+38f * 2f);
```

OUTPUT 3.8:

```
-Infinity
Infinity
```

Further examination of the floating-point number reveals that it can contain a value very close to zero, without actually containing zero. If the value exceeds the lower threshold for the float or double type, then the value of the number can be represented as "negative zero" or "positive zero," depending on whether the number is negative or positive, and is represented in output as -0 or 0.

Parenthesis Operator

Parentheses allow you to group operands and operators so that they are evaluated together. This is important because it provides a means of overriding the default order of precedence. For example, the following two expressions evaluate to something completely different:

```
(60 / 10) * 2
60 / (10 * 2)
```

The first expression is equal to 12; the second expression is equal to 3. In both cases, the parentheses affect the final value of the expression.

Sometimes the parenthesis operator does not actually change the result, because the order-of-precedence rules apply appropriately. However, it is often still a good practice to use parentheses to make the code more readable. This expression, for example:

```
fahrenheit = (celsius * 9.0 / 5.0) + 32.0;
```

is easier to interpret confidently at a glance than this one is:

```
fahrenheit = celsius * 9.0 / 5.0 + 32.0;
```

Developers should use parentheses to make code more readable, disambiguating expressions explicitly instead of relying on operator precedence.

Assignment Operators (+=, -=, *=, /=, %=)

Chapter 1 discussed the simple assignment operator, which places the value of the right-hand side of the operator into the variable on the left-hand side. Other assignment operators combine common binary operator calculations with the assignment operator. Take Listing 3.10, for example.

LISTING 3.10: Common Increment Calculation

```
int x;
x = x + 2;
```

In this assignment, first you calculate the value of x + 2 and then you assign the calculated value back to x. Since this type of operation is relatively frequent, an assignment operator exists to handle both the calculation and the assignment with one operator. The += operator increments the variable on the left-hand side of the operator with the value on the right-hand side of the operator, as shown in Listing 3.11.

LISTING 3.11: Using the += Operator

```
int x;
x += 2;
```

This code, therefore, is equivalent to Listing 3.10.

Numerous other combination assignment operators exist to provide similar functionality. You can use the assignment operator in conjunction with not only addition, but also subtraction, multiplication, division, and the remainder operators, as Listing 3.12 demonstrates.

LISTING 3.12: Other Assignment Operator Examples

```
x -= 2;
x /= 2;
x *= 2;
x %= 2;
```

Increment and Decrement Operators (++, --)

C# includes special operators for incrementing and decrementing coun-
ters. The **increment operator,** ++, increments a variable by one each time it
is used. In other words, all of the code lines shown in Listing 3.13 are
equivalent.

LISTING 3.13: Increment Operator

```
spaceCount = spaceCount + 1;
spaceCount += 1;
spaceCount++;
```

Similarly, you can also decrement a variable by one using the **decrement operator,** --. Therefore, all of the code lines shown in Listing 3.14 are
also equivalent.

LISTING 3.14: Decrement Operator

```
lines = lines - 1;
lines -= 1;
lines--;
```

■ BEGINNER TOPIC

A Decrement Example in a Loop

The increment and decrement operators are especially prevalent in loops,
such as the while loop described later in the chapter. For example, Listing
3.15 uses the decrement operator in order to iterate backward through
each letter in the alphabet.

LISTING 3.15: Displaying Each Character's ASCII Value in Descending Order

```
char current;
int asciiValue;

// Set the initial value of current.
```

```
current='z';

do
{
  // Retrieve the ASCII value of current.
  asciiValue = current;
  System.Console.Write("{0}={1}\t", current, asciiValue);

  // Proceed to the previous letter in the alphabet;
  current--;
}
while(current>='a');
```

Output 3.9 shows the results of Listing 3.15.

OUTPUT 3.9:

```
z=122   y=121   x=120   w=119   v=118   u=117   t=116   s=115   r=114
q=113   p=112   o=111   n=110   m=109   l=108   k=107   j=106   i=105
h=104   g=103   f=102   e=101   d=100   c=99    b=98    a=97
```

The increment and decrement operators are used to count how many times to perform a particular operation. Notice also that in this example, the increment operator is used on a character (char) data type. You can use increment and decrement operators on various data types as long as some meaning is assigned to the concept of "next" or "previous" for that data type.

Just as with the assignment operator, the increment operator also returns a value. In other words, it is possible to use the assignment operator simultaneously with the increment or decrement operator (see Listing 3.16 and Output 3.10).

LISTING 3.16: Using the Post-Increment Operator

```
int count;
int result;
count = 0;
result = count++;
System.Console.WriteLine("result = {0} and count = {1}",
    result, count);
```

OUTPUT 3.10:

```
result = 0 and count = 1
```

You might be surprised that `result` is assigned the value in `count` *before* count is incremented. In other words, `result` ends up with a value of 0 even though count ends up with a value of 1.

Where you place the increment or decrement operator determines whether the assigned value should be the value of the operand before or after the calculation, which affects how the code functions. If you want the value of `result` to include the increment (or decrement) calculation, you need to place the operator before the variable being incremented, as shown in Listing 3.17.

LISTING 3.17: Using the Pre-Increment Operator

```
int count;
int result;
count = 0;
result = ++count;
System.Console.WriteLine("result = {0} and count = {1}",
   result, count);
```

Output 3.11 shows the results of Listing 3.17.

OUTPUT 3.11:

```
result = 1 and count = 1
```

In this example, the increment operator appears before the operand so the value returned is the value assigned to the variable after the increment. If x is 1, then ++x will return 2. However, if a postfix operator is used, x++, the value returned by the expression will still be 1. Regardless of whether the operator is postfix or prefix, the resultant value of x will be incremented. The difference between prefix and postfix behavior appears in Listing 3.18. The resultant output is shown in Output 3.12.

LISTING 3.18: Comparing the Prefix and Postfix Increment Operators

```
class IncrementExample
{
  public static void Main()
  {
      int x;
```

```
        x = 1;
        // Display 1, 2.
        System.Console.WriteLine("{0}, {1}, {2}", x++, x++, x);
        // x now contains the value 3.

        // Display 4, 5.
        System.Console.WriteLine("{0}, {1}, {2}", ++x, ++x, x);
        // x now contains the value 5.
        // ...
    }
}
```

OUTPUT 3.12:

```
1, 2, 3
4, 5, 5
```

As Listing 3.18 demonstrates, where the increment and decrement operators appear relative to the operand can affect the result returned from the operator. Pre-increment/decrement operators return the result after incrementing/decrementing the operand. Post-increment/decrement operators return the result before changing the operand. Developers should use caution when embedding these operators in the middle of a statement. When in doubt as to what will happen, use these operators independently, placing them within their own statements. This way, the code is also more readable and there is no mistaking the intention.

■ ADVANCED TOPIC

Thread-Safe Incrementing and Decrementing

In spite of the brevity of the increment and decrement operators, these operators are not atomic. A thread context switch can occur during the execution of the operator and can cause a race condition. You could use a lock statement to prevent the race condition. However, for simple increments and decrements a less expensive alternative is to use the thread-safe Increment() and Decrement() methods from the System.Threading.Interlocked class. These methods rely on processor functions for performing fast thread-safe increments and decrements (see Chapter 19 for more detail).

Constant Expressions (const)

The preceding chapter discussed literal values, or values embedded directly into the code. It is possible to combine multiple literal values in a **constant expression** using operators. By definition, a constant expression is one that the C# compiler can evaluate at compile time (instead of calculating it when the program runs) because it is composed of constant operands. For example, the number of seconds in a day can be assigned as a constant expression whose result can then be used in other expressions.

The const keyword in Listing 3.19 locks the value at compile time. Any attempt to modify the value later in the code results in a compile error.

LISTING 3.19:

```
// ...
public long Main()
{                              Constant Expression
    const int secondsPerDay = 60 * 60 * 24;
    const int secondsPerWeek = secondsPerDay * 7;

                    Constant
    // ...
}
```

Note that even the value assigned to secondsPerWeek is a constant expression, because the operands in the expression are also constants, so the compiler can determine the result.

Introducing Flow Control

Later in this chapter is a code listing (Listing 3.43) that shows a simple way to view a number in its binary form. Even such a simple program, however, cannot be written without using control flow statements. Such statements control the execution path of the program. This section discusses how to change the order of statement execution based on conditional checks. Later on, you will learn how to execute statement groups repeatedly through loop constructs.

A summary of the control flow statements appears in Table 3.1. Note that the General Syntax Structure column indicates common statement use, not the complete lexical structure.

TABLE 3.1: Control Flow Statements

Statement	General Syntax Structure	Example
if statement	if(*boolean-expression*) *embedded-statement*	```if (input == "quit")
{
System.Console.WriteLine(
"Game end");
return;
}```

	if(*boolean-expression*)
	   embedded-statement
	else
	   embedded-statement
		``if (input == "quit")

{
System.Console.WriteLine(
"Game end");
return;
}
else
GetNextMove();```
while statement	while(*boolean-expression*) *embedded-statement*	```while(count < total)
{
System.Console.WriteLine(
"count = {0}", count);
count++;
}```

Continues

TABLE 3.1: Control Flow Statements *(Continued)*

Statement	General Syntax Structure	Example

do while statement	`do`
	    embedded-statement
	`while(boolean-expression);`
		```do { System.Console.WriteLine("Enter name:"); input = System.Console.ReadLine(); } while(input != "exit");```

for statement	`for(`*for-initializer;*
	    boolean-expression;
	    for-iterator)
	    embedded-statement
		```for (int count = 1; count <= 10; count++) { System.Console.WriteLine("count = {0}", count); }```

Foreach statement	`foreach(`*type identifier* `in`
	    expression)
	    embedded-statement
		```foreach (char letter in email) { if(!insideDomain) { if (letter == '@') { insideDomain = true; } continue; } System.Console.Write(letter); }```

continue statement	`continue;`	

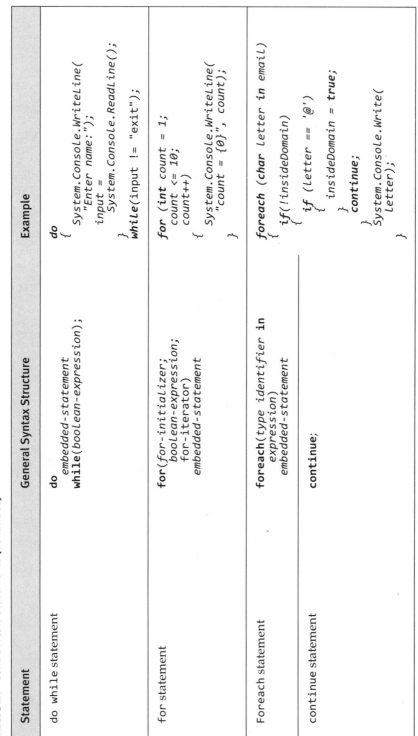

TABLE 3.1: Control Flow Statements *(Continued)*

Statement	General Syntax Structure	Example

switch statement	`switch(governing-type-expression)`
	`{`
	   `...`
	   `case const-expression:`
	      `statement-list`
	      `jump-statement`
	   `default:`
	      `statement-list`
	      `jump-statement`
	`}`
		`switch(input)`
		`{`
		  `case "exit":`
		  `case "quit":`
		    `System.Console.WriteLine(`
		    `"Exiting app....");`
		    `break;`
		  `case "restart":`
		    `Reset();`
		    `goto case "start";`
		  `case "start":`
		    `GetMove();`
		    `break;`

break statement	`break;`	`default:`
		    `System.Console.WriteLine(`
		    `input);`
		    `break;`
		`}`

goto statement	`goto identifier;`
	
	`goto case const-expression;`
	
	`goto default;`	

An embedded-statement in Table 3.1 corresponds to any statement, including a code block (but not a declaration statement or a label).

Each C# control flow statement in Table 3.1 appears in the tic-tac-toe[3] program found in Appendix B. The program displays the tic-tac-toe board, prompts each player, and updates with each move.

The remainder of this chapter looks at each statement in more detail. After covering the if statement, it introduces code blocks, scope, Boolean expressions, and bitwise operators before continuing with the remaining control flow statements. Readers who find the table familiar because of C#'s similarities to other languages can jump ahead to the section titled C# Preprocessor Directives or skip to the Summary section at the end of the chapter.

if Statement

The if statement is one of the most common statements in C#. It evaluates a **Boolean expression** (an expression that returns a Boolean), and if the result is true, the following statement (or block) is executed. The general form is as follows:

```
if(condition)
  consequence
[else
  alternative]
```

There is also an optional else clause for when the Boolean expression is false. Listing 3.20 shows an example.

LISTING 3.20: if/else Statement Example

```
class TicTacToe       // Declares the TicTacToe class.
{
  static void Main() // Declares the entry point of the program.
  {
    string input;

    // Prompt the user to select a 1- or 2- player game.
    System.Console.Write (
        "1 - Play against the computer\n" +
        "2 - Play against another player.\n" +
        "Choose:"
    );
    input = System.Console.ReadLine();
```

3.　Known as noughts and crosses to readers outside the United States.

```
        if(input=="1")
            // The user selected to play the computer.
            System.Console.WriteLine(
                "Play against computer selected.");
        else
            // Default to 2 players (even if user didn't enter 2).
            System.Console.WriteLine(
                "Play against another player.");
    }
}
```

In Listing 3.20, if the user enters 1, the program displays "Play against computer selected.". Otherwise, it displays "Play against another player.".

Nested if

Sometimes code requires multiple if statements. The code in Listing 3.21 first determines whether the user has chosen to exit by entering a number less than or equal to 0; if not, it checks whether the user knows the maximum number of turns in tic-tac-toe.

LISTING 3.21: Nested if Statements

```
1   class TicTacToeTrivia
2   {
3     static void Main()
4     {
5         int input;    // Declare a variable to store the input.
6
7         System.Console.Write(
8             "What is the maximum number " +
9             "of turns in tic-tac-toe?" +
10            "(Enter 0 to exit.): ");
11
12        // int.Parse() converts the ReadLine()
13        // return to an int data type.
14        input = int.Parse(System.Console.ReadLine());
15
16        if (input <= 0)
17                // Input is less than or equal to 0.
18                System.Console.WriteLine("Exiting...");
19        else
20            if (input < 9)
21                // Input is less than 9.
22                System.Console.WriteLine(
23                    "Tic-tac-toe has more than {0}" +
```

```
24                      "maximum turns.", input);
25          else
26              if(input>9)
27                  // Input is greater than 9.
28                  System.Console.WriteLine(
29                      "Tic-tac-toe has fewer than {0}" +
30                      "maximum turns.", input);
31              else
32                  // Input equals 9.
33                  System.Console.WriteLine(
34                      "Correct, " +
35                      "tic-tac-toe has a max. of 9 turns.");
36      }
37  }
```

Output 3.13 shows the results of Listing 3.21.

OUTPUT 3.13:

```
What's the maximum number of turns in tic-tac-toe? (Enter 0 to exit.): 9
Correct, tic-tac-toe has a max. of 9 turns.
```

Assume the user enters 9 when prompted at line 14. Here is the execution path:

1. *Line 16:* Check if input is less than 0. Since it is not, jump to line 20.
2. *Line 20:* Check if input is less than 9. Since it is not, jump to line 26.
3. *Line 26:* Check if input is greater than 9. Since it is not, jump to line 33.
4. *Line 33:* Display that the answer was correct.

Listing 3.21 contains nested if statements. To clarify the nesting, the lines are indented. However, as you learned in Chapter 1, whitespace does not affect the execution path. Without indenting and without newlines, the execution would be the same. The code that appears in the nested if statement in Listing 3.22 is equivalent to Listing 3.21.

LISTING 3.22: **if/else** Formatted Sequentially

```
if (input < 0)
  System.Console.WriteLine("Exiting...");
else if (input < 9)
  System.Console.WriteLine(
```

```
        "Tic-tac-toe has more than {0}" +
        " maximum turns.", input);
else if(input>9)
   System.Console.WriteLine(
        "Tic-tac-toe has less than {0}" +
        " maximum turns.", input);
else
   System.Console.WriteLine(
        "Correct, tic-tac-toe has a maximum of 9 turns.");
```

Although the latter format is more common, in each situation use the format that results in the clearest code.

Code Blocks ({})

In the previous if statement examples, only one statement follows if and else: a single System.Console.WriteLine(), similar to Listing 3.23.

LISTING 3.23: if Statement with No Code Block

```
if(input<9)
   System.Console.WriteLine("Exiting");
```

With curly braces, however, we can combine statements into a single unit called a **code block,** allowing the execution of multiple statements for a condition. Take, for example, the highlighted code block in the radius calculation in Listing 3.24.

LISTING 3.24: if Statement Followed by a Code Block

```
class CircleAreaCalculator
{
  static void Main()
  {
      double radius;  // Declare a variable to store the radius.
      double area;    // Declare a variable to store the area.

      System.Console.Write("Enter the radius of the circle: ");

      // double.Parse converts the ReadLine()
      // return to a double.
      radius = double.Parse(System.Console.ReadLine());

      if(radius>=0)
```

```
    {
        // Calculate the area of the circle.
        area = 3.14*radius*radius;
        System.Console.WriteLine(
            "The area of the circle is: {0}", area);
    }
    else
    {
        System.Console.WriteLine(
            "{0} is not a valid radius.", radius);
    }
  }
}
```

Output 3.14 shows the results of Listing 3.24.

OUTPUT 3.14:

```
Enter the radius of the circle: 3
The area of the circle is: 28.26
```

In this example, the if statement checks whether the radius is positive. If
so, the area of the circle is calculated and displayed; otherwise, an invalid
radius message is displayed.

Notice that in this example, two statements follow the first if. However, these two statements appear within curly braces. The curly braces
combine the statements into a code block.

If you omit the curly braces that create a code block in Listing 3.24, only
the statement immediately following the Boolean expression executes con-
ditionally. Subsequent statements will execute regardless of the if statement's Boolean expression. The invalid code is shown in Listing 3.25.

LISTING 3.25: Relying on Indentation, Resulting in Invalid Code

```
if(radius>=0)
  area = 3.14*radius*radius;
  System.Console.WriteLine( // Logic Error!! Needs code block.
      "The area of the circle is: {0}", area);
```

In C#, indentation is for code readability only. The compiler ignores it,
and therefore, the previous code is semantically equivalent to Listing 3.26.

LISTING 3.26: Semantically Equivalent to Listing 3.25

```
if(radius>=0)
{
  area = 3.14*radius*radius;
}
System.Console.WriteLine(    // Error!! Place within code block.
  "The area of the circle is: {0}", area);
```

Programmers should take great care to avoid subtle bugs such as this, perhaps even going so far as to always include a code block after a control flow statement, even if there is only one statement.

Although unusual, it is possible to have a code block that is not lexically a direct part of a control flow statement. In other words, placing curly braces on their own (without a conditional or loop, for example) is legal syntax.

■ **ADVANCED TOPIC**

Math Constants

In Listing 3.25 and Listing 3.26, the value of pi as 3.14 was hardcoded—a crude approximation at best. There are much more accurate definitions for pi and E in the System.Math class. Instead of hardcoding a value, code should use System.Math.PI and System.Math.E.

Scope and Declaration Space

Scope and **declaration space** are hierarchical contexts bound by a **code block.** Scope is the region of source code in which it is legal to refer to an item by its unqualified name because the name reference is unique and unambiguous.

The area in which declaring the name is unique is the declaration space. C# prevents two local variable declarations with the same name from appearing in the same declaration space. Similarly, it is not possible to declare two methods with the signature of Main() within the same class (declaration scope for the method name includes the full signature). The scope identifies what within a code block an unqualified name refers to; the declaration scope specifies the region in which declaring something with the same name will cause a conflict.

Scope restricts visibility. A local variable, for example, is not visible outside its defining method. Similarly, code that declares a variable in an if block makes the variable inaccessible outside the if block (even in the same method). In Listing 3.27, defining message inside the if statement restricts its scope to the statement only. To avoid the error, you must declare the string outside the if statement.

LISTING 3.27: Variables Inaccessible Outside Their Scope

```csharp
class Program
{
    static void Main(string[] args)
    {
        int playerCount;
        System.Console.Write(
            "Enter the number of players (1 or 2):");
        playerCount = int.Parse(System.Console.ReadLine());
        if (playerCount != 1 && playerCount != 2)
        {
            string message =
                "You entered an invalid number of players.";
        }
        else
        {
            // ...
        }
        // Error:  message is not in scope.
        System.Console.WriteLine(message);
    }
}
```

Output 3.15 shows the results of Listing 3.27.

OUTPUT 3.15:

```
...

...\Program.cs(18,26): error CS0103: The name 'message' does not exist
in the current context
```

Declaration space cascades down to child (or embedded) code blocks within a method. The C# compiler prevents the name of a local variable declared immediately within a method code block (or as a parameter) from being reused within a child code block. The declaration space is the parent code block of a variable, including any child blocks within the parent code block. From Listing 3.27, because `args` and `playerCount` are declared within the method code block, they cannot be used again within declarations anywhere within the method.

Scope is also bound by the parent code block. The name `message` applies only within the `if` block, not outside it. Similarly, `playerCount` refers to the same variable throughout the method following where the variable is declared—including within both the `if` and `else` child blocks.

Boolean Expressions

The portion of the `if` statement within parentheses is the **Boolean expression,** sometimes referred to as a **conditional.** In Listing 3.28, the Boolean expression is highlighted.

LISTING 3.28: Boolean Expression

```
if(input < 9)
{
    // Input is less than 9.
    System.Console.WriteLine(
        "Tic-tac-toe has more than {0}" +
        " maximum turns.", input);
}
// ...
```

Boolean expressions appear within many control flow statements. The key characteristic is that they always evaluate to `true` or `false`. For `input<9` to be allowed as a Boolean expression, it must return a `bool`. The compiler disallows x=42, for example, because it assigns x, returning the new value, instead of checking whether x's value is 42.

Language Contrast: C++—Mistakenly Using = in Place of ==

The significant feature of Boolean expressions in C# is the elimination of a common coding error that historically appeared in C/C++. In C++, Listing 3.29 is allowed.

Listing 3.29: C++, But Not C#, Allows Assignment as a Boolean Expression

```
if(input=9)    // COMPILE ERROR:  Allowed in C++, not in C#.
   System.Console.WriteLine(
       "Correct, tic-tac-toe has a maximum of 9 turns.");
```

Although this appears to check whether input equals 9, Chapter 1 showed that = represents the assignment operator, not a check for equality. The return from the assignment operator is the value assigned to the variable—in this case, 9. However, 9 is an int, and as such it does not qualify as a Boolean expression and is not allowed by the C# compiler.

Relational and Equality Operators

Included in the previous code examples was the use of relational operators. In those examples, relational operators were used to evaluate user input. Table 3.2 lists all the relational and equality operators.

Table 3.2: Relational and Equality Operators

Operator	Description	Example
<	Less than	input<9;
>	Greater than	input>9;
<=	Less than or equal to	input<=9;
>=	Greater than or equal to	input>=9;
==	Equality operator	input==9;
!=	Inequality operator	input!=9;

In addition to determining whether a value is greater than or less than another value, operators are also required to determine equivalency. You test for equivalence by using equality operators. In C#, the syntax follows the C/C++/Java pattern with ==. For example, to determine whether input equals 9 you use input==9. The equality operator uses two equal signs to distinguish it from the assignment operator, =.

The exclamation point signifies NOT in C#, so to test for inequality you use the inequality operator, !=.

The relational and equality operators are binary operators, meaning they compare two operands. More significantly, they always return a Boolean data type. Therefore, you can assign the result of a relational operator to a bool variable, as shown in Listing 3.30.

LISTING 3.30: Assigning the Result of a Relational Operator to a bool

```
bool result = 70 > 7;
```

In the tic-tac-toe program (see Appendix B), you use the equality operator to determine whether a user has quit. The Boolean expression of Listing 3.31 includes an OR (||) logical operator, which the next section discusses in detail.

LISTING 3.31: Using the Equality Operator in a Boolean Expression

```
if (input == "" || input == "quit")
{
   System.Console.WriteLine("Player {0} quit!!", currentPlayer);
   break;
}
```

Logical Boolean Operators

Logical operators have Boolean operands and return a Boolean result. Logical operators allow you to combine multiple Boolean expressions to form other Boolean expressions. The logical operators are ||, &&, and ^, corresponding to OR, AND, and exclusive OR, respectively.

OR Operator (||)

In Listing 3.31, if the user enters quit or presses the Enter key without typing in a value, it is assumed that she wants to exit the program. To enable two ways for the user to resign, you use the logical OR operator, ||.

The || operator evaluates Boolean expressions and returns a true value if *either* one of them is true (see Listing 3.32).

LISTING 3.32: Using the OR Operator

```
if((hourOfTheDay > 23) || (hourOfTheDay < 0))
  System.Console.WriteLine("The time you entered is invalid.");
```

Note that with the Boolean OR operator, it is not necessary to evaluate both sides of the expression. Like all operators in C#, the OR operators go from left to right, so if the left portion of the expression evaluates to true, then the right portion is ignored. Therefore, if hourOfTheDay has the value 33 then (hourOfTheDay > 23) will return true and the OR operator ignores the second half of the expression—**short-circuiting** it. Short-circuiting an expression also occurs with the Boolean AND operator.

AND Operator (&&)

The Boolean AND operator, &&, evaluates to true only if both operands evaluate to true. If either operand is false, the combined expression will return false.

Listing 3.33 displays that it is time for work as long as the current hour is both greater than 10 and less than 24.[4] As you saw with the OR operator, the AND operator will not always evaluate the right side of the expression. If the left operand returns false, then the overall result will be false regardless of the right operand, so the runtime ignores the right operand.

LISTING 3.33: Using the AND Operator

```
if ((10 < hourOfTheDay) && (hourOfTheDay < 24))
  System.Console.WriteLine(
  "Hi-Ho, Hi-Ho, it's off to work we go.");
```

Exclusive OR Operator (^)

The caret symbol, ^, is the "exclusive OR" (XOR) operator. When applied to two Boolean operands, the XOR operator returns true only if exactly one of the operands is true, as shown in Table 3.3.

Unlike the Boolean AND and Boolean OR operators, the Boolean XOR operator does not short-circuit: It always checks both operands, because the result cannot be determined unless the values of both operands are known.

---

4. The typical hours that programmers work.

TABLE 3.3: Conditional Values for the XOR Operator

Left Operand	Right Operand	Result
True	True	False
True	False	True
False	True	True
False	False	False

Logical Negation Operator (!)

Sometimes called the NOT operator, the **logical negation operator,** !, inverts a bool data type to its opposite. This operator is a unary operator, meaning it requires only one operand. Listing 3.34 demonstrates how it works, and Output 3.16 shows the results.

LISTING 3.34: Using the Logical Negation Operator

```
bool result;
bool valid = false;
result = !valid;
// Displays "result = True".
System.Console.WriteLine("result = {0}", result);
```

OUTPUT 3.16:

```
result = True
```

To begin, valid is set to false. You then use the negation operator on valid and assign a new value to result.

Conditional Operator (?)

In place of an if-else statement used to select one of two values, you can use the conditional operator. The conditional operator is a question mark (?), and the general format is as follows:

```
conditional? consequence: alternative;
```

The conditional operator is a ternary operator, because it has three operands: conditional, consequence, and alternative. If the conditional evaluates to true, then the conditional operator returns consequence. Alternatively, if the conditional evaluates to false, then it returns alternative.

Listing 3.35 is an example of how to use the conditional operator. The full listing of this program appears in Appendix B.

LISTING 3.35: Conditional Operator

```
public class TicTacToe
{
  public static string Main()
  {
      // Initially set the currentPlayer to Player 1;
      int currentPlayer = 1;

      // ...

      for (int turn = 1; turn <= 10; turn++)
      {
          // ...

          // Switch players
          currentPlayer = (currentPlayer == 2) ? 1 : 2;
      }
  }
}
```

The program swaps the current player. To do this, it checks whether the current value is 2. This is the conditional portion of the conditional statement. If the result is true, then the conditional operator returns the value 1. Otherwise, it returns 2. Unlike an if statement, the result of the conditional operator must be assigned (or passed as a parameter). It cannot appear as an entire statement on its own.

Use the conditional operator sparingly, because readability is often sacrificed and a simple if/else statement may be more appropriate.

Null Coalescing Operator (??)

Starting with C# 2.0, there is a shortcut to the conditional operator when checking for null. The shortcut is the **null coalescing operator,** and it evaluates an expression for null and returns a second expression if the value is null.

expression1?? expression2;

If the expression (expression1) is not null, then expression1 is returned. In other words, the null coalescing operator returns expression1 directly unless expression1 evaluates to null, in which case expression2 is returned. Unlike the conditional operator, the null coalescing operator is a binary operator.

Listing 3.36 is an example of how to use the null coalescing operator.

LISTING 3.36: Null Coalescing Operator

```
string fileName;
// ...
string fullName = fileName??"default.txt";
// ...
```

In this listing, we use the null coalescing operator to set fullName to "default.txt" if fileName is null. If fileName is not null, fullName is simply assigned the value of fileName.

Bitwise Operators (<<, >>, |, &, ^, ~)

An additional set of operators that is common to virtually all programming languages is the set of operators for manipulating values in their binary formats: the bit operators.

■ BEGINNER TOPIC

Bits and Bytes

All values within a computer are represented in a binary format of 1s and 0s, called **binary digits (bits).** Bits are grouped together in sets of eight, called **bytes.** In a byte, each successive bit corresponds to a value of 2 raised to a power, starting from 2^0 on the right, to 2^7 on the left, as shown in Figure 3.1.

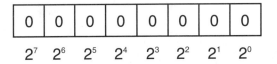

FIGURE 3.1: Corresponding Placeholder Values

In many instances, particularly when dealing with low-level or system services, information is retrieved as binary data. In order to manipulate these devices and services, you need to perform manipulations of binary data.

As shown in Figure 3.2, each box corresponds to a value of 2 raised to the power shown. The value of the byte (8-bit number) is the sum of the powers of 2 of all of the eight bits that are set to 1.

$$7 = 4 + 2 + 1$$

FIGURE 3.2: Calculating the Value of an Unsigned Byte

The binary translation just described is significantly different for signed numbers. Signed numbers (long, short, int) are represented using a 2s complement notation. This is so that addition continues to work when adding a negative number to a positive number as though both were positive operands. With this notation, negative numbers behave differently than positive numbers. Negative numbers are identified by a 1 in the leftmost location. If the leftmost location contains a 1, you add the locations with 0s rather than the locations with 1s. Each location corresponds to the negative power of 2 value. Furthermore, from the result, it is also necessary to subtract 1. This is demonstrated in Figure 3.3.

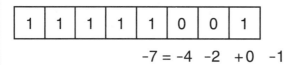

$$-7 = -4 \quad -2 \quad +0 \quad -1$$

FIGURE 3.3: Calculating the Value of a Signed Byte

Therefore, 1111 1111 1111 1111 corresponds to −1 and 1111 1111 1111 1001 holds the value −7. 1000 0000 0000 0000 corresponds to the lowest negative value that a 16-bit integer can hold.

Shift Operators (<<, >>, <<=, >>=)

Sometimes you want to shift the binary value of a number to the right or left. In executing a left shift, all bits in a number's binary representation are shifted to the left by the number of locations specified by the operand on the right of the shift operator. Zeroes are then used to backfill the locations on the right side of the binary number. A right-shift operator does almost the same thing in the opposite direction. However, if the number is negative, then the values used to backfill the left side of the binary number are ones and not zeroes. The shift operators are >> and <<, the right-shift and left-shift operators, respectively. In addition, there are combined shift and assignment operators, <<= and >>=.

Consider the following example. Suppose you had the int value -7, which would have a binary representation of 1111 1111 1111 1111 1111 1111 1111 1001. In Listing 3.37, you right-shift the binary representation of the number –7 by two locations.

LISTING 3.37: Using the Right-Shift Operator

```
int x;
x = (-7 >> 2); // 11111111111111111111111111111001 becomes
               // 11111111111111111111111111111110
// Write out "x is -2."
System.Console.WriteLine("x = {0}.", x);
```

Output 3.17 shows the results of Listing 3.37.

OUTPUT 3.17:

```
x = -2.
```

Because of the right shift, the value of the bit in the rightmost location has "dropped off" the edge and the negative bit indicator on the left shifts by two locations to be replaced with 1s. The result is -2.

Bitwise Operators (&, |, ^)

In some instances, you might need to perform logical operations, such as AND, OR, and XOR, on a bit-by-bit basis for two operands. You do this via the &, |, and ^ operators, respectively.

■ BEGINNER TOPIC

Logical Operators Explained

If you have two numbers, as shown in Figure 3.4, the bitwise operations will compare the values of the locations beginning at the leftmost significant value and continuing right until the end. The value of "1" in a location is treated as "true," and the value of "0" in a location is treated as "false."

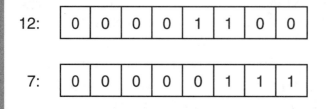

FIGURE 3.4: The Numbers 12 and 7 Represented in Binary

Therefore, the bitwise AND of the two values in Figure 3.4 would be the bit-by-bit comparison of bits in the first operand (12) with the bits in the second operand (7), resulting in the binary value 000000100, which is 4. Alternatively, a bitwise OR of the two values would produce 00001111, the binary equivalent of 15. The XOR result would be 00001011, or decimal 11.

Listing 3.38 demonstrates how to use these bitwise operators. The results of Listing 3.38 appear in Output 3.18.

LISTING 3.38: Using Bitwise Operators

```
byte and, or, xor;
and = 12 & 7;    // and = 4
or = 12 | 7;     // or = 15
xor = 12 ^ 7;    // xor = 11
System.Console.WriteLine(
    "and = {0} \nor = {1}\nxor = {2}"
    and, or, xor);
```

OUTPUT 3.18:

```
and = 4
or = 15
xor = 11
```

In Listing 3.38, the value 7 is the **mask;** it is used to expose or eliminate specific bits within the first operand using the particular operator expression.

In order to convert a number to its binary representation, you need to iterate across each bit in a number. Listing 3.39 is an example of a program that converts an integer to a string of its binary representation. The results of Listing 3.39 appear in Output 3.19.

LISTING 3.39: Getting a String Representation of a Binary Display

```csharp
public class BinaryConverter
{
  public static void Main()
  {
      const int size = 64;
      ulong value;
      char bit;

      System.Console.Write ("Enter an integer: ");
      // Use Long.Parse() so as to support negative numbers
      // Assumes unchecked assignment to ulong.
      value = (ulong)long.Parse(System.Console.ReadLine());

      // Set initial mask to 100....
      ulong mask = 1ul << size - 1;
      for (int count = 0; count < size; count++)
      {
          bit = ((mask & value) > 0) ? '1': '0';
          System.Console.Write(bit);
          // Shift mask one Location over to the right
          mask >>= 1;
      }
      System.Console.WriteLine();
  }
}
```

OUTPUT 3.19:

```
Enter an integer: 42
0000000000000000000000000000000000000000000000000000000000101010
```

Notice that within each iteration of the `for` loop (discussed shortly), you use the right-shift assignment operator to create a mask corresponding to each bit in `value`. By using the & bit operator to mask a particular bit, you can determine whether the bit is set. If the mask returns a positive result, you set the corresponding bit to 1; otherwise, it is set to 0. In this way, you create a string representing the binary value of an unsigned long.

Bitwise Assignment Operators (&=, |=, ^=)

Not surprisingly, you can combine these bitwise operators with assignment operators as follows: &=, |=, and ^=. As a result, you could take a variable, OR it with a number, and assign the result back to the original variable, which Listing 3.40 demonstrates.

LISTING 3.40: Using Logical Assignment Operators

```
byte and, or, xor;
and = 12;
and &= 7;    // and = 4
or = 12;
or |= 7;     // or = 15
xor = 12;
xor ^= 7;    // xor = 11
System.Console.WriteLine(
    "and = {0} \nor = {1} \nxor = {2}",
    and, or, xor);
```

The results of Listing 3.40 appear in Output 3.20.

OUTPUT 3.20:

```
and = 4
or = 15
xor = 11
```

Combining a bitmap with a mask using something like `fields &= mask` clears the bits in `fields` that are not set in the `mask`. The opposite, `fields &= ~mask`, clears out the bits in `fields` that are set in `mask`.

Bitwise Complement Operator (~)

The **bitwise complement operator** takes the complement of each bit in the operand, where the operand can be an `int`, `uint`, `long`, or `ulong`. ~1, therefore, returns 1111 1111 1111 1111 1111 1111 1111 1110 and ~(1<<31) returns 0111 1111 1111 1111 1111 1111 1111 1111.

Control Flow Statements, Continued

With the additional coverage of Boolean expressions, it's time to consider more of the control flow statements supported by C#. As indicated in the introduction to this chapter, many of these statements will be familiar to experienced programmers, so you can skim this section for information specific to C#. Note in particular the foreach loop, as this may be new to many programmers.

The while and do/while Loops

Until now, you have learned how to write programs that do something only once. However, one of the important capabilities of the computer is that it can perform the same operation multiple times. In order to do this, you need to create an instruction loop. The first instruction loop I will discuss is the while loop. The general form of the while statement is as follows:

```
while(boolean-expression )
  statement
```

The computer will repeatedly execute statement as long as boolean-expression evaluates to true. If the expression evaluates to false, then code execution continues at the instruction following statement. (Note that statement will continue to execute even if it causes boolean-expression to be false. It isn't until the boolean-expression is reevaluated within the while condition that the loop exits.) The Fibonacci calculator shown in Listing 3.41 demonstrates the while loop.

LISTING 3.41: while Loop Example

```
class FibonacciCalculator
{
  static void Main()
  {
      decimal current;
      decimal previous;
      decimal temp;
      decimal input;

      System.Console.Write("Enter a positive integer:");
```

```
    // decimal.Parse convert the ReadLine to a decimal.
    input = decimal.Parse(System.Console.ReadLine());

    // Initialize current and previous to 1, the first
    // two numbers in the Fibonacci series.
    current = previous = 1;

    // While the current Fibonacci number in the series is
    // less than the value input by the user.
    while(current <= input)
    {
        temp = current;
        current = previous + current;
        previous = temp;
    }

    System.Console.WriteLine(
        "The Fibonacci number following this is {0}",
        current);
    }
}
```

A **Fibonacci number** is a member of the **Fibonacci series,** which includes all numbers that are the sum of the previous two numbers in the series, beginning with 1 and 1. In Listing 3.41, you prompt the user for an integer. Then you use a `while` loop to find the Fibonacci number that is greater than the number the user entered.

■ BEGINNER TOPIC

When to Use a while Loop

The remainder of this chapter considers other types of statements that cause a block of code to execute repeatedly. The term *loop* refers to the block of code that is to be executed within the `while` statement, since the code is executed in a "loop" until the exit condition is achieved. It is important to understand which loop construct to select. You use a `while` construct to iterate while the condition evaluates to `true`. A `for` loop is used most appropriately whenever the number of repetitions is known, such as counting from 0 to *n*. A `do/while` is similar to a `while` loop, except that it will always loop at least once.

The do/while loop is very similar to the while loop except that a do/while loop is preferred when the number of repetitions is from 1 to *n* and *n* is indeterminate when iterating begins. This pattern occurs most commonly when repeatedly prompting a user for input. Listing 3.42 is taken from the tic-tac-toe program.

LISTING 3.42: do/while **Loop Example**

```
// Repeatedly request player to move until he
// enter a valid position on the board.
do
{
  valid = false;

  // Request a move from the current player.
  System.Console.Write(
    "\nplayer {0}: Enter move:", currentplayer);
  input = System.Console.ReadLine();

  // Check the current player's input.
  // ...

} while (!valid);
```

In Listing 3.42, you always initialize valid to false at the beginning of each **iteration,** or loop repetition. Next, you prompt and retrieve the number the user input. Although not shown here, you then check whether the input was correct, and if it was, you assign valid equal to true. Since the code uses a do/while statement rather than a while statement, the user will be prompted for input at least once.

The general form of the do/while loop is as follows:

```
do
    statement
while(boolean-expression );
```

As with all the control flow statements, the code blocks are not part of the general form. However, a code block is generally used in place of a single statement in order to allow multiple statements.

The for Loop

Increment and decrement operators are frequently used within a for loop. The for loop iterates a code block until a specified condition is reached in a way similar to the while loop. The difference is that the for loop has built-in syntax for initializing, incrementing, and testing the value of a counter.

Listing 3.43 shows the for loop used to display an integer in binary form. The results of this listing appear in Output 3.21.

LISTING 3.43: Using the for Loop

```
public class BinaryConverter
{
  public static void Main()
  {
      const int size = 64;
      ulong value;
      char bit;

      System.Console.Write ("Enter an integer: ");
      // Use Long.Parse() so as to support negative numbers
      // Assumes unchecked assignment to ulong.
      value = (ulong)long.Parse(System.Console.ReadLine());

      // Set initial mask to 100....
      ulong mask = 1ul << size - 1;
      for (int count = 0; count < size; count++)
      {
          bit = ((mask & value) > 0) ? '1': '0';
          System.Console.Write(bit);
          // Shift mask one location over to the right
          mask >>= 1;
      }
  }
}
```

OUTPUT 3.21:

```
Enter an integer: -42
1111111111111111111111111111111111111111111111111111111111010110
```

Listing 3.43 performs a bit mask 64 times, once for each bit in the number. The for loop declares and initializes the variable count, escapes once the count reaches 64, and increments the count during each iteration. Each expression within the `for` loop corresponds to a statement. (It is easy to remember that the separation character between expressions is a semicolon and not a comma, because each expression could be a statement.)

You write a `for` loop generically as follows:

```
for(initial; boolean-expression; loop)
    statement
```

Here is a breakdown of the `for` loop.

* The `initial` expression performs operations that precede the first iteration. In Listing 3.43, it declares and initializes the variable `count`. The `initial` expression does not have to be a declaration of a new variable. It is possible, for example, to declare the variable beforehand and simply initialize it in the `for` loop. Variables declared here, however, are bound within the scope of the `for` statement.
* The `boolean-expression` portion of the `for` loop specifies an end condition. The loop exits when this condition is false in a manner similar to the `while` loop's termination. The `for` loop will repeat only as long as `boolean-expression` evaluates to `true`. In the preceding example, the loop exits when `count` increments to 64.
* The `loop` expression executes after each iteration. In the preceding example, `count++` executes after the right shift of the mask (`mask >>= 1`), but before the Boolean expression is evaluated. During the sixty-fourth iteration, `count` increments to 64, causing `boolean-expression` to be `false` and, therefore, terminating the loop. Because each expression may be thought of as a separate statement, each expression in the `for` loop is separated by a semicolon.
* The `statement` portion of the `for` loop is the code that executes while the conditional expression remains true.

If you wrote out each `for` loop execution step in pseudocode without using a `for` loop expression, it would look like this:

1. Declare and initialize `count` to 0.
2. Verify that `count` is less than 64.

3. Calculate `bit` and display it.

4. Shift the mask.

5. Increment `count` by one.

6. If `count<64`, then jump back to line 3.

The `for` statement doesn't require any of the elements between parentheses. `for(;;){ ... }` is perfectly valid; although there still needs to be a means to escape from the loop to avoid executing infinitely. Similarly, the initial and loop expressions can be a complex expression involving multiple subexpressions, as shown in Listing 3.44.

LISTING 3.44: `for` Loop Using Multiple Expressions

```csharp
for(int x=0, y=5; ((x<=5) && (y>=0)); y--, x++)

{
  System.Console.Write("{0}{1}{2}\t",
     x, (x>y? '>' : '<'), y);
}
```

The results of Listing 3.44 appear in Output 3.22.

OUTPUT 3.22:

```
0<5     1<4     2<3     3>2     4>1     5>0
```

In this case, the comma behaves exactly as it does in a declaration statement, one that declares and initializes multiple variables. However, programmers should avoid complex expressions such as this one because they are difficult to read and understand.

Generically, you can write the `for` loop as a `while` loop, as shown here:

```csharp
initial;
while(boolean-expression)
{
  statement;
  loop;
}
```

■ BEGINNER TOPIC

Choosing between for and while Loops

Although you can use the two statements interchangeably, generally you would use the for loop whenever there is some type of counter, and the total number of iterations is known when the loop is initialized. In contrast, you would typically use the while loop when iterations are not based on a count or when the number of iterations is indeterminate when iterating commences.

The foreach Loop

The last loop statement within the C# language is foreach. foreach is designed to iterate through a collection of items, setting a variable to represent each item in turn. During the loop, operations may be performed on the item. One feature of the foreach loop is that it is not possible to accidentally miscount and iterate over the end of the collection.

The general form of the foreach statement is as follows:

```
foreach(type variable in collection)
    statement;
```

Here is a breakdown of the foreach statement.

- type is used to declare the data type of the variable for each item within the collection.
- variable is a read-only variable into which the foreach construct will automatically assign the next item within the collection. The scope of the variable is limited to the foreach loop.
- collection is an expression, such as an array, representing multiple items.
- statement is the code that executes for each iteration within the foreach loop.

Consider the foreach loop in the context of the simple example shown in Listing 3.45.

LISTING 3.45: Determining Remaining Moves Using the foreach Loop

```
class TicTacToe     // Declares the TicTacToe class.
{
  static void Main() // Declares the entry point of the program.
  {
      // Hardcode initial board as follows
      // ---+---+---
      //  1 | 2 | 3
      // ---+---+---
      //  4 | 5 | 6
      // ---+---+---
      //  7 | 8 | 9
      // ---+---+---
      char[] cells = {
          '1', '2', '3', '4', '5', '6', '7', '8', '9'
      };

      System.Console.Write(
          "The available moves are as follows: ");

      // Write out the initial available moves
      foreach (char cell in cells)
      {
          if (cell != 'O' && cell != 'X')
          {
              System.Console.Write("{0} ", cell);
          }
      }
  }
}
```

Output 3.23 shows the results of Listing 3.45.

```
The available moves are as follows: 1 2 3 4 5 6 7 8 9
```

When the execution engine reaches the foreach statement, it assigns to the variable cell the first item in the cells array—in this case, the value '1'. It then executes the code within the foreach statement block. The if statement determines whether the value of cell is 'O' or 'X'. If it is neither, then the value of cell is written out to the console. The next iteration then assigns the next array value to cell, and so on.

It is important to note that the compiler prevents modification of the variable (cell) during the execution of a foreach loop.

■ BEGINNER TOPIC

Where the switch Statement Is More Appropriate

Sometimes you might compare the same value in several continuous if statements, as shown with the input variable in Listing 3.46.

LISTING 3.46: Checking the Player's Input with an if Statement

```
// ...

bool valid = false;

// Check the current player's input.
if( (input == "1") ||
   (input == "2") ||
   (input == "3") ||
   (input == "4") ||
   (input == "5") ||
   (input == "6") ||
   (input == "7") ||
   (input == "8") ||
   (input == "9") )
{
    // Save/move as the player directed.
    // ...

    valid = true;
}
else if( (input == "") || (input == "quit") )
{
    valid = true;
}
else
{
    System.Console.WriteLine(
      "\nERROR:  Enter a Value from 1-9."
      + "Push ENTER to quit");
}

// ...
```

This code validates the text entered to ensure that it is a valid tic-tac-toe move. If the value of input were 9, for example, the program would have to perform nine different evaluations. It would be preferable to jump to the correct code after only one evaluation. To enable this, you use a switch statement.

The switch Statement

Given a variable to compare and a list of constant values to compare against, the switch statement is simpler to read and code than the if statement. The switch statement looks like this:

```
switch(test-expression)
{
  [case option-constant:
      statement
  [default:
      statement]
}
```

Here is a breakdown of the switch statement.

- test-expression returns a value that is compatible with the governing types. Allowable governing data types are sbyte, byte, short, ushort, int, uint, long, ulong, char, string, and an enum type (covered in Chapter 8).
- constant is any constant expression compatible with the data type of the governing type.
- statement is one or more statements to be executed when the governing type expression equals the constant value. The statement or statements must have no reachable endpoint. In other words, the statement, or last of the statements if there are more than one, must be a jump statement such as a break, return, or goto statement. If the switch statement appears within a loop, then continue is also allowed.

A switch statement should have at least one case statement or a default statement. In other words, switch(x){} will generate a warning.

Listing 3.47, with a switch statement, is semantically equivalent to the series of if statements in Listing 3.46.

LISTING 3.47: Replacing the **if** Statement with a **switch** Statement

```
static bool ValidateAndMove(
  int[] playerPositions, int currentPlayer, string input)
{
  bool valid = false;

  // Check the current player's input.
  switch (input)
  {
    case "1" :
    case "2" :
    case "3" :
    case "4" :
    case "5" :
    case "6" :
    case "7" :
    case "8" :
    case "9" :
      // Save/move as the player directed.
      ...
      valid = true;
      break;

    case "" :
    case "quit" :
      valid = true;
      break;
    default :
      // If none of the other case statements
      // is encountered then the text is invalid.
      System.Console.WriteLine(
        "\nERROR:  Enter a value from 1-9."
        + "Push ENTER to quit");
      break;
  }

  return valid;
}
```

In Listing 3.47, input is the governing type expression. Since input is a string, all of the constants are strings. If the value of input is 1, 2, ... 9, then the move is valid and you change the appropriate cell to match that of the current user's token (X or O). Once execution encounters a break statement, it immediately jumps to the instruction following the switch statement.

The next portion of the switch looks for "" or "quit", and sets valid to true if input equals one of these values. Ultimately, the default label is executed if no prior case constant was equivalent to the governing type.

There are several things to note about the switch statement.

- Placing nothing within the switch block will generate a compiler warning, but the statement will still compile.
- default does not have to appear last within the switch statement. case statements appearing after default are evaluated.
- When you use multiple constants for one case statement, they should appear consecutively, as shown in Listing 3.47.
- The compiler requires a jump statement (usually a break).

Language Contrast: C++—switch Statement Fall-through

Unlike C++, C# does not allow a switch statement to fall through from one case block to the next if the case includes a statement. A jump statement is always required following the statement within a case. The C# founders believed it was better to be explicit and require the jump statement in favor of code readability. If programmers want to use a fall-through semantic, they may do so explicitly with a goto statement, as demonstrated in the section The goto Statement, later in this chapter.

Jump Statements

It is possible to alter the execution path of a loop. In fact, with jump statements, it is possible to escape out of the loop or to skip the remaining portion of an iteration and begin with the next iteration, even when the conditional expression remains true. This section considers some of the ways to jump the execution path from one location to another.

The break Statement

To escape out of a loop or a switch statement, C# uses a break statement. Whenever the break statement is encountered, the execution path immediately jumps to the first instruction following the loop. Listing 3.48 examines the foreach loop from the tic-tac-toe program.

LISTING 3.48: Using break to Escape Once a Winner Is Found

```
class TicTacToe      // Declares the TicTacToe class.
{
  static void Main() // Declares the entry point of the program.
  {
      int winner=0;
      // Stores locations each player has moved.
      int[] playerPositions = {0,0};

      // Hardcoded board position
      // X | 2 | 0
      // ---+---+---
      // 0 | 0 | 6
      // ---+---+---
      // X | X | X
      playerPositions[0] = 449;
      playerPositions[1] = 28;

      // Determine if there is a winner
      int[] winningMasks = {
          7, 56, 448, 73, 146, 292, 84, 273 };

      // Iterate through each winning mask to determine
      // if there is a winner.
      foreach (int mask in winningMasks)
      {
          if ((mask & playerPositions[0]) == mask)
          {
              winner = 1;
              break;
          }
          else if ((mask & playerPositions[1]) == mask)
          {
              winner = 2;
              break;
          }
      }

      System.Console.WriteLine(
          "Player {0} was the winner", winner);
  }
}
```

Output 3.24 shows the results of Listing 3.48.

OUTPUT 3.24:

```
Player 1 was the winner
```

Listing 3.48 uses a break statement when a player holds a winning position. The break statement forces its enclosing loop (or a switch statement) to cease execution, and the program moves to the next line outside the loop. For this listing, if the bit comparison returns true (if the board holds a winning position), the break statement causes execution to jump and display the winner.

■ BEGINNER TOPIC

Bitwise Operators for Positions

The tic-tac-toe example uses the bitwise operators (Appendix B) to determine which player wins the game. First, the code saves the positions of each player into a bitmap called playerPositions. (It uses an array so that the positions for both players can be saved.)

To begin, both playerPositions are 0. As each player moves, the bit corresponding to the move is set. If, for example, the player selects cell 3, shifter is set to 3 – 1. The code subtracts 1 because C# is zero-based and you need to adjust for 0 as the first position instead of 1. Next, the code sets position, the bit corresponding to cell 3, using the shift operator 000000000000001 << shifter, where shifter now has a value of 2. Lastly, it sets playerPositions for the current player (subtracting 1 again to shift to zero-based) to 0000000000000100. Listing 3.49 uses |= so that previous moves are combined with the current move.

LISTING 3.49: Setting the Bit That Corresponds to Each Player's Move

```
int shifter;  // The number of places to shift
              // over in order to set a bit.
int position; // The bit which is to be set.

// int.Parse() converts "input" to an integer.
// "int.Parse(input) - 1" because arrays
// are zero-based.
shifter = int.Parse(input) - 1;

// Shift mask of 00000000000000000000000000000001
// over by cellLocations.
```

```
position = 1 << shifter;

// Take the current player cells and OR them to set the
// new position as well.
// Since currentPlayer is either 1 or 2,
// subtract one to use currentPlayer as an
// index in a 0-based array.
playerPositions[currentPlayer-1] |= position;
```

Later in the program, you can iterate over each mask corresponding to winning positions on the board to determine whether the current player has a winning position, as shown in Listing 3.48.

The continue Statement

In some instances, you may have a series of statements within a loop. If you determine that some conditions warrant executing only a portion of these statements for some iterations, you use the continue statement to jump to the end of the current iteration and begin the next iteration. The C# continue statement allows you to exit the current iteration (regardless of which additional statements remain) and jump to the loop conditional. At that point, if the loop conditional remains true, the loop will continue execution.

Listing 3.50 uses the continue statement so that only the letters of the domain portion of an email are displayed. Output 3.25 shows the results of Listing 3.50.

LISTING 3.50: Determining the Domain of an Email Address

```
class EmailDomain
{
  static void Main()
  {
    string email;
    bool insideDomain = false;
    System.Console.WriteLine("Enter an email address: ");

    email = System.Console.ReadLine();

    System.Console.Write("The email domain is: ");

    // Iterate through each letter in the email address.
    foreach (char letter in email)
    {
```

```
            if (!insideDomain)
            {
                if (letter == '@')
                {
                    insideDomain = true;
                }
                continue;
            }

            System.Console.Write(letter);
        }
    }
}
```

OUTPUT 3.25:

```
Enter an email address:
mark@dotnetprogramming.com
The email domain is: dotnetprogramming.com
```

In Listing 3.50, if you are not yet inside the domain portion of the email address, you need to use a continue statement to jump to the next character in the email address.

In general, you can use an if statement in place of a continue statement, and this is usually more readable. The problem with the continue statement is that it provides multiple exit points within the iteration, and this compromises readability. In Listing 3.51, the sample has been rewritten, replacing the continue statement with the if/else construct to demonstrate a more readable version that does not use the continue statement.

LISTING 3.51: Replacing a continue with an if Statement

```
foreach (char letter in email)
{
    if (insideDomain)
    {
        System.Console.Write(letter);
    }
    else
    {
        if (letter == '@')
        {
            insideDomain = true;
        }
    }
}
```

The goto **Statement**

With the advent of object-oriented programming and the prevalence of well-structured code, the existence of a goto statement within C# seems like an aberration to many experienced programmers. However, C# supports goto, and it is the only method for supporting fall-through within a switch statement. In Listing 3.52, if the /out option is set, code execution jumps to the default case using the goto statement; similarly for/f.

LISTING 3.52: Demonstrating a switch with goto Statements

```csharp
// ...
static void Main(string[] args)
{
  bool isOutputSet = false;
  bool isFiltered = false;

  foreach (string option in args)
  {
      switch (option)
      {
          case "/out":
              isOutputSet = true;
              isFiltered = false;
              goto default;
          case "/f":
              isFiltered = true;
              isRecursive = false;
              goto default;
          default:
              if (isRecursive)
              {
                  // Recurse down the hierarchy
                  // ...

              }
              else if (isFiltered)
              {
                  // Add option to list of filters.
                  // ...
              }
              break;
      }
  }

  // ...

}
```

Output 3.26 shows the results of Listing 3.52.

OUTPUT 3.26:

```
C:\SAMPLES>Generate /out fizbottle.bin /f "*.xml" "*.wsdl"
```

As demonstrated in Listing 3.52, goto statements are ugly. In this particular example, this is the only way to get the desired behavior of a `switch` statement. Although you can use `goto` statements outside `switch` statements, they generally cause poor program structure and you should deprecate them in favor of a more readable construct. Note also that you cannot use a `goto` statement to jump from outside a `switch` statement into a label within a `switch` statement. More generally, C# prevents using goto *into* something, and allows its use only *within* or *out of* something. By making this restriction, C# avoids most of the serious goto abuses available in other languages.

C# Preprocessor Directives

Control flow statements evaluate conditional expressions at runtime. In contrast, the C# preprocessor is invoked during compilation. The preprocessor commands are directives to the C# compiler, specifying the sections of code to compile or identifying how to handle specific errors and warnings within the code. C# preprocessor commands can also provide directives to C# editors regarding the organization of code.

Language Contrast: C++—Preprocessing

Languages such as C and C++ contain a **preprocessor**, a separate utility from the compiler that sweeps over code, performing actions based on special tokens. Preprocessor directives generally tell the compiler how to compile the code in a file and do not participate in the compilation process itself. In contrast, the C# compiler handles preprocessor directives as part of the regular lexical analysis of the source code. As a result, C# does not support preprocessor macros beyond defining a constant. In fact, the term *preprocessor* is generally a misnomer for C#.

Each preprocessor directive begins with a hash symbol (#), and all preprocessor directives must appear on one line. A newline rather than a semicolon indicates the end of the directive.

A list of each preprocessor directive appears in Table 3.4.

TABLE 3.4: Preprocessor Directives

Statement or Expression	General Syntax Structure	Example

#if directive	`#if` preprocessor-expression
	    code
	`#endif`
		`#if` CSHARP2
		    Console.Clear();
		`#endif`

#elif directive	`#if` preprocessor-expression1
	    code
	`#elif` preprocessor-expression2
	    code
	`#endif`
		`#if` LINUX
		...
		`#elif` WINDOWS
		...
		`#endif`

#else directive	`#if`
	    code
	`#else`
	    code
	`#endif`
		`#if` CSHARP1
		...
		`#else`
		...
		`#endif`

#define directive	`#define` conditional-symbol	`#define` CSHARP2
#undef directive	`#undef` conditional-symbol	`#undef` CSHARP2
#error directive	`#error` preproc-message	`#error` Buggy implementation
#warning directive	`#warning` preproc-message	`#warning` Needs code review
#pragma directive	`#pragma` warning	`#pragma` warning disable 1030
#line directive	`#line` org-line new-line `#line default`	`#line` 467 "TicTacToe.cs" ... `#line default`
#region directive	`#region` pre-proc-message code `#endregion`	`#region` Methods ... `#endregion`

Excluding and Including Code (#if, #elif, #else, #endif)

Perhaps the most common use of preprocessor directives is in controlling when and how code is included. For example, to write code that could be compiled by both C# 2.0 and later compilers and the prior version 1.2 compilers, you use a preprocessor directive to exclude C# 2.0-specific code when compiling with a 1.2 compiler. You can see this in the tic-tac-toe example and in Listing 3.53.

LISTING 3.53: Excluding C# 2.0 Code from a C# 1.x Compiler

```
#if CSHARP2
System.Console.Clear();
#endif
```

In this case, you call the `System.Console.Clear()` method, which is available only in the 2.0 CLI version and later. Using the `#if` and `#endif` preprocessor directives, this line of code will be compiled only if the preprocessor symbol `CSHARP2` is defined.

Another use of the preprocessor directive would be to handle differences among platforms, such as surrounding Windows- and Linux-specific APIs with `WINDOWS` and `LINUX` `#if` directives. Developers often use these directives in place of multiline comments (`/*...*/`) because they are easier to remove by defining the appropriate symbol or via a search and replace. A final common use of the directives is for debugging. If you surround code with an `#if DEBUG`, you will remove the code from a release build on most IDEs. The IDEs define the `DEBUG` symbol by default in a debug compile and `RELEASE` by default for release builds.

To handle an else-if condition, you can use the `#elif` directive within the `#if` directive, instead of creating two entirely separate `#if` blocks, as shown in Listing 3.54.

LISTING 3.54: Using #if, #elif, and #endif Directives

```
#if LINUX
...
#elif WINDOWS
...
#endif
```

Defining Preprocessor Symbols (#define, #undef)

You can define a preprocessor symbol in two ways. The first is with the #define directive, as shown in Listing 3.55.

LISTING 3.55: A #define Example

```
#define CSHARP2
```

The second method uses the define option when compiling for .NET, as shown in Output 3.27.

OUTPUT 3.27:

```
>csc.exe /define:CSHARP2 TicTacToe.cs
```

Output 3.28 shows the same functionality using the Mono compiler.

OUTPUT 3.28:

```
>mcs.exe -define:CSHARP2 TicTacToe.cs
```

To add multiple definitions, separate them with a semicolon. The advantage of the define complier option is that no source code changes are required, so you may use the same source files to produce two different binaries.

To undefine a symbol you use the #undef directive in the same way you use #define.

Emitting Errors and Warnings (#error, #warning)

Sometimes you may want to flag a potential problem with your code. You do this by inserting #error and #warning directives to emit an error or warning, respectively. Listing 3.56 uses the tic-tac-toe sample to warn that the code does not yet prevent players from entering the same move multiple times. The results of Listing 3.56 appear in Output 3.29.

LISTING 3.56: Defining a Warning with #warning

```
#warning     "Same move allowed multiple times."
```

OUTPUT 3.29:

```
Performing main compilation...
...\tictactoe.cs(471,16): warning CS1030: #warning: '"Same move allowed
multiple times."'

Build complete -- 0 errors, 1 warnings
```

By including the #warning directive, you ensure that the compiler will report a warning, as shown in Output 3.29. This particular warning is a way of flagging the fact that there is a potential enhancement or bug within the code. It could be a simple way of reminding the developer of a pending task.

Turning Off Warning Messages (#pragma)

Warnings are helpful because they point to code that could potentially be troublesome. However, sometimes it is preferred to turn off particular warnings explicitly because they can be ignored legitimately. C# 2.0 and later compilers provide the preprocessor #pragma directive for just this purpose (see Listing 3.57).

LISTING 3.57: Using the Preprocessor #pragma Directive to Disable the #warning Directive

```
#pragma warning disable  1030
```

Note that warning numbers are prefixed with the letters *CS* in the compiler output. However, this prefix is not used in the #pragma warning directive. The number corresponds to the warning error number emitted by the compiler when there is no preprocessor command.

To reenable the warning, #pragma supports the restore option following the warning, as shown in Listing 3.58.

LISTING 3.58: Using the Preprocessor #pragma Directive to Restore a Warning

```
#pragma warning restore  1030
```

In combination, these two directives can surround a particular block of code where the warning is explicitly determined to be irrelevant.

Perhaps one of the most common warnings to disable is CS1591, as this appears when you elect to generate XML documentation using the /doc compiler option, but you neglect to document all of the public items within your program.

nowarn:<warn list> Option

In addition to the #pragma directive, C# compilers generally support the nowarn:<warn list> option. This achieves the same result as #pragma, except that instead of adding it to the source code, you can insert the command as a compiler option. In addition, the nowarn option affects the entire compilation, and the #pragma option affects only the file in which it appears. Turning off the CS1591 warning, for example, would appear on the command line as shown in Output 3.30.

OUTPUT 3.30:

```
> csc /doc:generate.xml /nowarn:1591 /out:generate.exe Program.cs
```

Specifying Line Numbers (#line)

The #line directive controls on which line number the C# compiler reports an error or warning. It is used predominantly by utilities and designers that emit C# code. In Listing 3.59, the actual line numbers within the file appear on the left.

LISTING 3.59: The #line Preprocessor Directive

```
124        #line 113 "TicTacToe.cs"
125        #warning "Same move allowed multiple times."
126        #line default
```

Including the #line directive causes the compiler to report the warning found on line 125 as though it was on line 113, as shown in the compiler error message shown in Output 3.31.

OUTPUT 3.31:

```
Performing main compilation...
.../tictactoe.cs(113,18): warning CS1030: #warning: '"Same move allowed
multiple times."'

Build complete -- 0 errors, 1 warnings
```

Following the #line directive with default reverses the effect of all prior #line directives and instructs the compiler to report true line numbers rather than the ones designated by previous uses of the #line directive.

Hints for Visual Editors (#region, #endregion)

C# contains two preprocessor directives, #region and #endregion, that are useful only within the context of visual code editors. Code editors, such as the one in the Microsoft Visual Studio .NET IDE, can search through source code and find these directives to provide editor features when writing code. C# allows you to declare a region of code using the #region directive. You must pair the #region directive with a matching #endregion directive, both of which may optionally include a descriptive string following the directive. In addition, you may nest regions within one another.

Again, Listing 3.60 shows the tic-tac-toe program as an example.

LISTING 3.60: A #region and #endregion Preprocessor Directive

```
...
#region Display Tic-tac-toe Board

#if CSHARP2
  System.Console.Clear();
#endif

// Display the current board;
border = 0;   // set the first border (border[0] = "|")

// Display the top line of dashes.
// ("\n---+---+---\n")
System.Console.Write(borders[2]);
foreach (char cell in cells)
{
  // Write out a cell value and the border that comes after it.
  System.Console.Write(" {0} {1}", cell, borders[border]);

  // Increment to the next border;
```

```
    border++;

    // Reset border to 0 if it is 3.
    if (border == 3)
    {
        border = 0;
    }
}
#endregion Display Tic-tac-toe Board
...
```

One example of how these preprocessor directives are used is with Microsoft Visual Studio .NET. Visual Studio .NET examines the code and provides a tree control to open and collapse the code (on the left-hand side of the code editor window) that matches the region demarcated by the #region directives (see Figure 3.5).

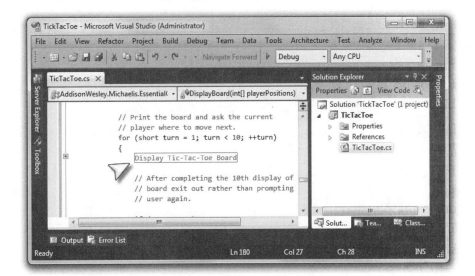

FIGURE 3.5: Collapsed Region in Microsoft Visual Studio .NET

SUMMARY

This chapter began with an introduction to the C# operators related to assignment and arithmetic. Next, you used the operators along with the const keyword to declare constant expressions. Coverage of all of the C#

operators was not sequential, however. Before discussing the relational and logical comparison operators, the chapter introduced the `if` statement and the important concepts of code blocks and scope. To close out the coverage of operators I discussed the bitwise operators, especially regarding masks.

Operator precedence was discussed earlier in the chapter, but Table 3.5 summarizes the order of precedence across all operators, including several that are not yet covered.

TABLE 3.5: Operator Order of Precedence*

Category	Operators

Primary	`x.y  f(x)  a[x]  x++  x--  new`
	`typeof(T)  checked(x)  unchecked(x) default(T)`
	`delegate{}  ()`

Unary	`+  -  !  ~  ++x  --x  (T)x`
Multiplicative	`*  /  %`
Additive	`+  -`
Shift	`<<  >>`
Relational and type testing	`<  >  <=  >=  is  as`
Equality	`==  !=`
Logical AND	`&`
Logical XOR	`^`
Logical OR	`|`
Conditional AND	`&&`
Conditional OR	`||`
Null coalescing	`??`
Conditional	`?:`
Assignment	`=  =>  *=  /=  %=  +=  -=  <<=  >>=  &=  ^=  |=`

* Rows appear in order of precedence from highest to lowest.

Given coverage of most of the operators, the next topic was control flow statements. The last sections of the chapter detailed the preprocessor directives and the bit operators, which included code blocks, scope, Boolean expressions, and bitwise operators.

Perhaps one of the best ways to review all of the content covered in Chapters 1–3 is to look at the tic-tac-toe program found in Appendix B. By reviewing the program, you can see one way in which you can combine all that you have learned into a complete program.

4

Methods and Parameters

F ROM WHAT YOU HAVE LEARNED about C# programming so far you should be able to write straightforward programs consisting of a list of statements, similar to the way programs were created in the 1970s. Programming has come a long way since the 1970s; as programs became more complex, new paradigms were needed to manage that complexity. "Procedural" or "structured" programming provides a construct into which statements are grouped together to form a unit. Furthermore, with structured programming, it is possible to pass data to a group of statements and then have data returned once the statements have executed.

This chapter covers how to group statements together into a method. In addition, it covers how to call a method, including how to pass data to a method and receive data from a method.

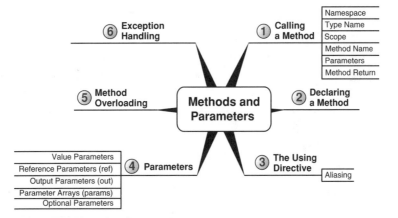

Besides the basics of calling and defining methods, this chapter also covers some slightly more advanced concepts—namely, recursion and method overloading, along with some new C# 4 features, namely optional and named parameters. All method calls discussed so far and through the end of this chapter are static (a concept which Chapter 5 explores in detail).

Even as early as the `HelloWorld` program in Chapter 1, you learned how to define a method. In that example, you defined the `Main()` method. In this chapter, you will learn about method creation in more detail, including the special C# syntax for parameters that pass data to and from a method (`ref`) using a single parameter, as well as parameters that only pass data out from a method (`out`). Lastly, I will touch on some rudimentary error handling.

Calling a Method

■ BEGINNER TOPIC

What Is a Method?

Up to this point, all of the statements in the programs you have written have appeared together in one grouping called a `Main()` method. As programs become even minimally larger, a single method implementation quickly becomes difficult to maintain and complex to read through and understand.

A **method** is a means of grouping together a sequence of statements to perform a particular action or compute a particular result. This provides greater structure and organization for the statements that comprise a program. Consider, for example, a `Main()` method that counts the lines of source code in a directory. Instead of having one large `Main()` method, you can provide a shorter version that allows you to hone in on the details of each method implementation as necessary. Listing 4.1 shows an example.

LISTING 4.1: Grouping Statements into Methods

```
class LineCount
{
  static void Main()
  {
      int lineCount;
      string files;
```

```
        DisplayHelpText();
        files = GetFiles();
        lineCount = CountLines(files);
        DisplayLineCount(lineCount);
    }
    // ...
}
```

Instead of placing all of the statements into Main(), the listing breaks them into groups called methods. Statements related to displaying the help text, a group of System.Console.WriteLine() statements, have been moved to the DisplayHelpText() method. All of the statements used to determine which files to count appear in the GetFiles() method. To actually count the files, the code calls the CountLines() method before displaying the results using the DisplayLineCount() method. With a quick glance, it is easy to review the code and gain an overview, because the method name describes the implementation.

A method is always associated with a **class,** and the class provides a means of grouping related methods together. Calling a method is conceptually the same as sending a message to a class.

Methods can receive data via **parameters.** Parameters are variables used for passing data from the **caller** (the method containing the method call) to the target method (Write(), WriteLine(), GetFiles(), CountLines(), and so on). In Listing 4.1, files and lineCount are examples of parameters passed to the CountLines() and DisplayLineCount() methods. Methods can also return data back to the caller via a **return value** (in Listing 4.1, the GetFiles() method call has a return value that is assigned to files).

To begin, you will reexamine System.Console.Write(), System.Console.WriteLine(), and System.Console.ReadLine() from Chapter 1. This time, look at them as examples of method calls in general, instead of looking at the specifics of printing and retrieving data from the console. Listing 4.2 shows each of the three methods in use.

LISTING 4.2: A Simple Method Call

```
class HeyYou
{
  static void Main()
  {
```

```
    string firstName;
    string lastName;

    System.Console.WriteLine("Hey you!");
```

```
    System.Console.Write("Enter your first name: ");
```

Namespace   Method Name   Parameters

Type Name

```
    firstName = System.Console.ReadLine();

    System.Console.Write("Enter your last name: ");
    lastName = System.Console.ReadLine();

    System.Console.WriteLine("Your full name is {0} {1}.",
        firstName, lastName);
  }
}
```

The parts of the method call include the namespace, type name, method name, parameters, and return data type. A period separates each part of a fully qualified method name.

Namespace

The first item in the method call is the **namespace.** The namespace is a categorization mechanism for grouping all types related to a particular functionality. Typically you want an outer namespace to be a company name, and then a product name, and then the functional area: Microsoft.Win32.Networking. The namespace helps to avoid type name collisions. For example, the compiler can distinguish between two types with the name "Program" as long as each type has a different namespace. The result is that the Main method in each class could be referred to using Awl.Windows.Program.Main() or Awl.Console.Program.Main().

System.Collections, System.Collections.Generics, System.IO, and System.Runtime.Serialization.Formatters are valid names for a namespace. Namespaces can include periods within their names. This enables the namespaces to give the appearance of being hierarchical. This improves human readability only, since the compiler treats all namespaces at a single level. For example, System.Collections.Generics appears within the System.Collections namespace hierarchy, but to the compiler these are simply two entirely different namespaces.

In Listing 4.2, the namespace for the `Console` type is `System`. The `System` namespace contains the types that enable the programmer to perform many fundamental programming activities. Virtually all C# programs use types within the `System` namespace. Table 4.1 provides a listing of other common namespaces.

TABLE 4.1: Common Namespaces

Namespace	Description
System	Contains the definition of fundamental types, conversion between types, mathematics, program invocation, and environment management.
System.Collections	Includes types for working with collections of objects. Collections can generally follow either list or dictionary type storage mechanisms.
System.Collections.Generics	This C# 2.0 added namespace works with strongly typed collections that depend on generics (type parameters).
System.Data	Contains types used for working with data that is stored within a database.
System.Drawing	Contains types for drawing to the display device and working with images.
System.IO	Contains types for working with files and directories and provides capabilities for manipulating, loading, and saving files.
System.Linq	Provides classes and interfaces for querying data in collections using a C# 3.0 added API, Language Integrated Query.
System.Text	Includes types for working with strings and various text encodings, and for converting between those encodings. This namespace includes a subnamespace called `System.Text.RegularExpressions`, which provides access to regular-expression-related APIs.
System.Threading	Handles thread manipulation and multithreaded programming.
System.Threading.Tasks	A family of classes for working with Threads that first appeared in .NET 4.

Continues

TABLE 4.1: Common Namespaces *(Continued)*

Namespace	Description
System.Web	A collection of types that enable browser-to-server communication, generally over HTTP. The functionality within this namespace is used to support a .NET technology called ASP.NET.
System.Web. Services	Contains types that send and retrieve data over HTTP using the Simple Object Access Protocol (SOAP).
System. Windows.Forms	Includes types for creating rich user interfaces and the components within them.
System.Xml	Contains standards-based support for XML processing.

It is not always necessary to provide the namespace when calling a method. For example, if you use a type in the same namespace as the target method, then the compiler can infer the namespace to be the same as the caller's namespace. Later in this chapter, you will see how the using directive avoids the need for a namespace qualifier as well.

Type Name

Calls to static methods (Chapter 5 covers static versus instance methods) require the type name qualifier as long as the target method is not within the same class[1] (such as a call from HelloWorld.Main() to Console.WriteLine()). However, just as with the namespace, C# allows the elimination of the type name from a method call whenever the method is available on the containing type. (Examples of method calls such as this appear in Listing 4.4.) The type name is unnecessary because the compiler infers the type from the calling method. If the compiler can make no such inference, the name must be provided as part of the method call.

At their core, types are a means of grouping together methods and their associated data. For example, Console is the type name that contains the Write(), WriteLine(), and ReadLine() methods (among others). All of these methods are in the same "group" because they belong to the Console type.

---

1. Or base class.

Scope

You already learned that the parent code block bounds declaration and visibility. Scope defines the inferred call context. A method call between two methods in the same type does not require the type qualifier because an item may be referred to by its unqualified name if it is in scope. Similarly, calls between two types in the same namespace do not require the namespace qualifier because the scope, in this case the namespace, is the same.

Method Name

After specifying which type contains the method you wish to call, it is time to identify the method itself. C# always uses a period between the type name and the method name, and a pair of parentheses following the method name. Between the parentheses must appear any parameters that the method requires.

Parameters

All methods can have any number of parameters, and each parameter in C# is of a specific data type. For example, the following method call, used in Listing 4.2, has three parameters:

```
System.Console.WriteLine(
    "Your full name is {1} {0}", lastName, firstName)
```

The first is a `string` and the second two are of type `object`. Although you pass parameter values of type `string` for the second two parameters as well, the compiler allows this because all types, including `string`, are compatible with the data type `object`.

Method Return

In contrast to `System.Console.WriteLine()`, `System.Console.ReadLine()` in Listing 4.2 does not have any parameters. However, this method happens to have a **method return.** The method return is a means of transferring results from a called method back to the caller. Because `System.Console.ReadLine()` has a return, it is possible to assign the return value to the variable `firstName`. In addition, it is possible to pass this method return as a parameter, as shown in Listing 4.3.

LISTING 4.3: Passing a Method Return as a Parameter to Another Method Call

```csharp
class Program
{
  static void Main()
  {
      System.Console.Write("Enter your first name: ");
      System.Console.WriteLine("Hello {0}!",
          System.Console.ReadLine());
  }
}
```

Instead of assigning a variable and then using it in the call to System.Console.WriteLine(), Listing 4.3 calls the System.Console.ReadLine() method within the call to System.Console.WriteLine(). At execution time, the System.Console.ReadLine() method executes first and its return is passed directly into the System.Console.WriteLine() method, rather than into a variable.

Not all methods return data. Both versions of System.Console.Write() and System.Console.WriteLine() are examples of such methods. As you will see shortly, these methods specify a return type of void just as the HelloWorld declaration of Main returned void.

Statement versus Method Call

Listing 4.3 provides a demonstration of the difference between a statement and a method call. Although System.Console.WriteLine("Hello {0}!", System.Console.ReadLine()); is a single statement, it contains two method calls. A statement generally contains one or more expressions, and in this example, each expression is a method call. Therefore, method calls form parts of statements.

Although coding multiple method calls in a single statement often reduces the amount of code, it does not necessarily increase the readability and seldom offers a significant performance advantage. Developers should favor readability over brevity.

> ▪ **NOTE**
>
> In general, developers should favor readability over brevity. Readability is critical to writing code that is self-documenting and, therefore, more maintainable over time.

Declaring a Method

This section expands on the explanation of declaring a method (such as `Main()`) to include any parameter or a return type. Listing 4.4 contains examples of these concepts, and Output 4.1 shows the results.

LISTING 4.4: Declaring a Method

```csharp
class IntroducingMethods
{
  static void Main()
  {
      string firstName;
      string lastName;
      string fullName;

      System.Console.WriteLine("Hey you!");

      firstName = GetUserInput("Enter your first name: ");
      lastName = GetUserInput("Enter your last name: ");

      fullName = GetFullName(firstName, lastName);

      DisplayGreeting(fullName);
  }

  static string GetUserInput(string prompt)
  {
      System.Console.Write(prompt);
      return System.Console.ReadLine();
  }

  static string GetFullName(string firstName, string lastName)
  {
      return firstName + " " + lastName;
  }

  static void DisplayGreeting(string name)
  {
      System.Console.WriteLine("Your full name is {0}.", name);
      return;
  }
}
```

OUTPUT 4.1:

```
Hey you!
Enter your first name: Inigo
Enter your last name: Montoya
Your full name is Inigo Montoya.
```

Four methods are declared in Listing 4.4. From `Main()` the code calls `GetUserInput()`, followed by a call to `GetFullName()`. Both of these methods return a value and take parameters. In addition, the listing calls `DisplayGreeting()`, which doesn't return any data. No method in C# can exist outside the confines of an enclosing class. Even the `Main` method examined in Chapter 1 must be within a class.

Language Contrast: C++/Visual Basic—Global Methods

C# provides no global method support; everything must appear within a class definition. This is why the `Main()` method was marked as `static`—the C# equivalent of a C++ global and Visual Basic module method.

■ **BEGINNER TOPIC**

Refactoring into Methods

Moving a set of statements into a method instead of leaving them inline within a larger method is a form of **refactoring.** Refactoring reduces code duplication, because you can call the method from multiple places instead of duplicating the code. Refactoring also increases code readability. As part of the coding process, it is a best practice to continually review your code and look for opportunities to refactor. This involves looking for blocks of code that are difficult to understand at a glance and moving them into a method with a name that clearly defines the code's behavior. This practice is often preferred over commenting a block of code, because the method name serves to describe what the implementation does.

For example, the `Main()` method that is shown in Listing 4.4 results in the same behavior as does the `Main()` method that is shown in Listing 1.15 in Chapter 1. Perhaps even more noteworthy is that although both listings are trivial to follow, Listing 4.4 is easier to grasp at a glance by just viewing the `Main()` method and not worrying about the details of each called method's implementation.

Parameter Declaration

Consider the declaration of the DisplayGreeting() and GetFullName() methods. The text that appears between the parentheses of a method declaration is the **parameter list.** Each parameter in the parameter list includes the type of the parameter along with the parameter name. A comma separates each parameter in the list.

Behaviorally, parameters are virtually identical to local variables, and the naming convention of parameters follows accordingly. Therefore, parameter names are camel case. Also, it is not possible to declare a local variable (a variable declared inside a method) with the same name as a parameter of the containing method, because this would create two "local variables" of the same name.

Method Return Declaration

In addition to GetUserInput() and GetFullName() requiring parameters to be specified, both of these methods also include a **method return.** You can tell there is a method return because a data type appears immediately before the method name of the method declaration. For both GetUser-Input() and GetFullName(), the data type is string. Unlike parameters, only one method return is allowable.

Once a method includes a return data type, and assuming no error occurs, it is necessary to specify a return statement for each **code path** (or set of statements that may execute consecutively) within the method declaration. A return statement begins with the return keyword followed by the value the method is returning. For example, the GetFullName() method's return statement is return firstName + " " + lastName. The C# compiler makes it imperative that the return type match the type of the data specified following the return keyword.

Return statements can appear in spots other than at the end of a method implementation, as long as all code paths include a return if the method has a return type. For example, an if or switch statement at the beginning of a method implementation could include a return statement within the conditional or case statement; see Listing 4.5 for an example.

LISTING 4.5: A return Statement before the End of a Method

```csharp
class Program
{
  static void Main()
```

```
    {
        string command;
        //...
        switch(command)
        {
            case "quit":
                return;
            // ...
        }
        // ...
    }
}
```

A `return` statement indicates a jump to the end of the method, so no break is required in a `switch` statement. Once the execution encounters a return, the method call will end.

If particular code paths include statements following the return, the compiler will issue a warning that indicates that the additional statements will never execute. In spite of the C# allowance for early returns, code is generally more readable and easier to maintain if there is a single exit location rather than multiple returns sprinkled through various code paths of the method.

Specifying `void` as a return type indicates that there is no return from the method. As a result, the method does not support assignment to a variable or use as a parameter type at the call site. Furthermore, the `return` statement becomes optional, and when it is specified, there is no value following the return keyword. For example, the return of `Main()` in Listing 4.4 is `void` and there is no `return` statement within the method. However, `DisplayGreeting()` includes a `return` statement that is not followed by any returned result.

Language Contrast: C++—Header Files

Unlike C++, C# classes never separate the implementation from the declaration. In C# there is no header (`.h`) file or implementation (`.cpp`) file. Instead, declaration and implementation appear together in the same file. Starting with C# 2.0, it is possible to spread a class across multiple files known as partial types. However, even then the declaration of a method and the implementation of that method must remain together. For C# to declare types and methods inline makes a cleaner and more maintainable language.

■ **BEGINNER TOPIC**

Namespaces

Namespaces are an organizational mechanism for all types. They provide a nested grouping mechanism so that types may be categorized. Developers will discover related types by examining other types within the same namespace as the initial type. Additionally, through namespaces, two or more types may have the same name as long as they are disambiguated by different namespaces.

The using **Directive**

It is possible to import types from one namespace into the parent namespace code block or the entire file if there is no parent code block. As a result, it would not be necessary for the programmer to fully qualify a type. To achieve this, the C# programmer includes a using directive, generally at the top of the file. For example, in Listing 4.6, Console is not prefixed with System. Instead, it includes the using directive, using System, at the top of the listing.

LISTING 4.6: using Directive Example

```csharp
// The using directive imports all types from the
// specified namespace into the entire file.
using System;

class HelloWorld
{
  static void Main()
  {
      // No need to qualify Console with System
      // because of the using directive above.
      Console.WriteLine("Hello, my name is Inigo Montoya");
  }
}
```

The results of Listing 4.6 appear in Output 4.2.

OUTPUT 4.2:

```
Hello, my name is Inigo Montoya
```

Namespaces are nested. That means that a using directive such as using System does not enable the omission of System from a method within a more specific namespace. If code accessed a type within the System.Text namespace, for example, you would have to either include an additional using directive for System.Text, or fully qualify the type. The using directive does not import any **nested namespaces.** Nested namespaces, identified by the period in the namespace, need to be imported explicitly.

Language Contrast: Java—Wildcards in import Directive

Java allows for importing namespaces using a wildcard such as:

```
import javax.swing.*;
```

In contrast, C# does not support a wildcard using directive, and instead requires each namespace to be imported explicitly.

Language Contrast: Visual Basic .NET—Project Scope Imports Directive

Unlike C#, Visual Basic .NET supports the ability to specify the using directive equivalent, Imports, for an entire project, rather than just for a specific file. In other words, Visual Basic .NET provides a command-line means of the using directive that will span an entire compilation.

Typically, prevalent use of types within a particular namespace results in a using directive for that namespace, instead of fully qualifying all types within the namespace. Following this tendency, virtually all files include the using System directive at the top. Throughout the remainder of this book, code listings will often omit the using System directive. Other namespace directives will be included explicitly, however.

One interesting effect of the using System directive is that the string data type can be identified with varying case: String or string. The former version relies on the using System directive and the latter uses the string keyword. Both are valid C# references to the System.String data type, and the resultant CIL code is unaffected by which version is chosen.[2]

■ ADVANCED TOPIC

Nested using Declaratives

Not only can you have using declaratives at the top of a file, but you also can include them at the top of a namespace declaration. For example, if a new namespace, Awl.Michaelis.EssentialCSharp, were declared, it would be possible to add a using declarative at the top of the namespace declaration (see Listing 4.7).

LISTING 4.7: Specifying the using Directive inside a Namespace Declaration

```csharp
namespace Awl.Michaelis.EssentialCSharp
{
    using System;

    class HelloWorld
    {
        static void Main()
        {
            // No need to qualify Console with System
            // because of the using directive above.
            Console.WriteLine("Hello, my name is Inigo Montoya");
        }
    }
}
```

The results of Listing 4.7 appear in Output 4.3.

OUTPUT 4.3:

```
Hello, my name is Inigo Montoya
```

The difference between placing the using declarative at the top of a file rather than at the top of a namespace declaration is that the declarative is

---

2. I prefer the string keyword, but whichever representation a programmer selects, ideally code within a project should be consistent.

active only within the namespace declaration. If the code includes a new namespace declaration above or below the `Awl.Michaelis.Essen-tialCSharp` declaration, then the `using System` directive within a different namespace would not be active. Code seldom is written this way, especially given the standard practice of a single type declaration per file.

Aliasing

The `using` directive also has a provision for **aliasing** a namespace or type. An alias is an alternative name that you can use within the text to which the `using` directive applies. The two most common reasons for aliasing are to disambiguate two types that have the same name and to abbreviate a long name. In Listing 4.8, for example, the `CountDownTimer` alias is declared as a means of referring to the type `System.Timers.Timer`. Simply adding a `using System.Timers` directive will not sufficiently enable the code to avoid fully qualifying the `Timer` type. The reason is that `System.Threading` also includes a type called `Timer`, and therefore, just using `Timer` within the code will be ambiguous.

LISTING 4.8: Declaring a Type Alias

```csharp
using System;
using System.Threading;
using CountDownTimer = System.Timers.Timer;

class HelloWorld
{
  static void Main()
  {
    CountDownTimer timer;

    // ...
  }
}
```

Listing 4.8 uses an entirely new name, `CountDownTimer`, as the alias. It is possible, however, to specify the alias as `Timer`, as shown in Listing 4.9.

LISTING 4.9: Declaring a Type Alias with the Same Name

```csharp
using System;
using System.Threading;

// Declare alias Timer to refer to System.Timers.Timer to
// avoid code ambiguity with System.Threading.Timer
```

```
using Timer = System.Timers.Timer;

class HelloWorld
{
  static void Main()
  {
      Timer timer;

      // ...
  }
}
```

Because of the alias directive, "Timer" is not an ambiguous reference. Furthermore, to refer to the System.Threading.Timer type, you will have to either qualify the type or define a different alias.

Returns and Parameters on Main()

So far, declaration of an executable's Main() method has been the simplest declaration possible. You have not included any parameters or return types in your Main() method declarations. However, C# supports the ability to retrieve the command-line arguments when executing a program, and it is possible to return a status indicator from the Main() method.

The runtime passes the command-line arguments to Main() using a single string array parameter. All you need to do to retrieve the parameters is to access the array, as demonstrated in Listing 4.10. The purpose of this program is to download a file whose location is given by a URL. The first command-line argument identifies the URL, and the optional second argument is the filename to which to save the file. The listing begins with a switch statement that evaluates the number of parameters (args.Length) as follows.

1. If there are zero parameters, display an error indicating that it is necessary to provide the URL.
2. If there is only one argument, calculate the second argument from the first argument.
3. The presence of two arguments indicates the user has provided both the URL of the resource and the download target filename.

LISTING 4.10: Passing Command-Line Arguments to Main

```csharp
using System;
using System.IO;
using System.Net;

class Program
{
    static int Main(string[] args)
    {
        int result;
        string targetFileName = ParseCommandLineArgs(args);

        switch (args.Length)
        {
            case 0:
                // No URL specified, so display error.
                Console.WriteLine(
                    "ERROR:  You must specify the "
                    + "URL to be downloaded");
                break;
            case 1:
                // No target filename was specified.
                targetFileName = Path.GetFileName(args[0]);
                break;
            case 2:
                targetFileName = args[1];
                break;
        }

        if (targetFileName != null)
        {
            WebClient webClient = new WebClient();
            webClient.DownloadFile(args[0], targetFileName);
            result = 0;
        }
        else
        {
            Console.WriteLine(
                "Downloader.exe <URL> <TargetFileName>");
            result = 1;
        }
        return result;
    }

    private static string ParseCommandLineArgs(string[] args)
    {
        string targetFileName = null;
        switch (args.Length)
        {
            case 0:
                // No URL specified, so display error.
                Console.WriteLine(
```

```
                "ERROR:  You must specify the "
                + "URL to be downloaded");
            break;
        case 1:
            // No target filename was specified.
            targetFileName = Path.GetFileName(args[0]);
            break;
        case 2:
            targetFileName = args[1];
            break;
    }
    return targetFileName;
}
}
```

The results of Listing 4.10 appear in Output 4.4.

OUTPUT 4.4:

```
>Downloader.exe
ERROR:  You must specify the URL to be downloaded
Downloader.exe <URL> <TargetFileName>
```

If you were successful in calculating the target filename, you would use it to save the downloaded file. Otherwise, you would display the help text. The Main() method also returns an int rather than a void. This is optional for a Main() declaration, but if it is used, the program can return a status code to a caller, such as a script or a batch file. By convention, a return other than zero indicates an error.

Although all command-line arguments can be passed to Main() via an array of strings, sometimes it is convenient to access the arguments from inside a method other than Main(). The System.Environment.GetCommand-LineArgs() method returns the command-line arguments array in the same form that Main(string[] args) passes the arguments into Main().

▪ ADVANCED TOPIC

Disambiguate Multiple Main() Methods

If a program includes two classes with Main() methods, it is possible to specify on the command line which class to use for the Main() declaration. csc.exe includes an /m option to specify the fully qualified class name of Main().

■ **BEGINNER TOPIC**

Call Stack and Call Site

As code executes, methods call more methods that in turn call additional methods, and so on. In the simple case of Listing 4.4, `Main()` calls `GetUser-Input()`, which in turn calls `System.Console.ReadLine()`, which in turn calls even more methods internally. The set of calls within calls within calls, and so on, is termed the **call stack.** As program complexity increases, the call stack generally gets larger and larger as each method calls another method. As calls complete, however, the call stack shrinks until another series of methods are invoked. The term for describing the process of removing calls from the call stack is **stack unwinding.** Stack unwinding always occurs in the reverse order of the method calls. The result of method completion is that execution will return to the **call site,** which is the location from which the method was invoked.

Parameters

So far, this chapter's examples have returned data via the method return. This section demonstrates the options of returning data via method parameters and via a variable number of parameters.

■ **BEGINNER TOPIC**

Matching Caller Variables with Parameter Names

In some of the previous listings, you matched the variable names in the caller with the parameter names in the callee (target method). This matching is simply for readability; whether names match is entirely irrelevant to the behavior of the method call.

Value Parameters

By default, parameters are **passed by value,** which means that the variable's stack data is copied into the target parameter. For example, in Listing 4.11, each variable that `Main()` uses when calling `Combine()` will be copied into the parameters of the `Combine()` method. Output 4.5 shows the results of this listing.

LISTING 4.11: Passing Variables by Value

```csharp
class Program
{
  static void Main()
  {
      // ...
      string fullName;
      string driveLetter = "C:";
      string folderPath  = "Data";
      string fileName     = "index.html";


      fullName = Combine(driveLetter, folderPath, fileName);


      Console.WriteLine(fullName);
      // ...
  }

  static string Combine(
      string driveLetter, string folderPath, string fileName)
  {
      string path;
      path = string.Format("{1}{0}{2}{0}{3}",
          System.IO.Path.DirectorySeparatorChar,
          driveLetter, folderPath, fileName);
      return path;
  }
}
```

OUTPUT 4.5:

```
C:\Data\index.html
```

Even if the Combine() method assigns null to driveLetter, folder-Path, and fileName before returning, the corresponding variables within Main() will maintain their original values because the variables are copied when calling a method. When the call stack unwinds at the end of a call, the copy is thrown away.

■ ADVANCED TOPIC

Reference Types versus Value Types
For the purposes of this section, it is inconsequential whether the parameter passed is a value type or a reference type. The issue is whether the

target method can assign the caller's original variable a new value. Since a copy is made, the caller's copy cannot be reassigned.

In more detail, a reference type variable contains an address of the memory location where the data is stored. If a reference type variable is passed by value, the address is copied from the caller to the method parameter. As a result, the target method cannot update the caller variable's address value but it may update the data within the reference type. Alternatively, if the method parameter is a value type, the value itself is copied into the parameter, and changing the parameter will not affect the original caller's variable.

Reference Parameters (ref)

Consider Listing 4.12, which calls a function to swap two values, and Output 4.6, which shows the results.

LISTING 4.12: Passing Variables by Reference

```
class Program
{
  static void Main()
  {
      // ...
      string first = "first";
      string second = "second";
      Swap(ref first, ref second);

      System.Console.WriteLine(
          @"first = ""{0}"", second = ""{1}""",
          first, second);
      // ...
  }

  static void Swap(ref string first, ref string second)
  {
      string temp = first;
      first = second;
      second = temp;
  }
}
```

OUTPUT 4.6:

```
first = "second", second = "first"
```

The values assigned to `first` and `second` are successfully switched, even though there is no return from the `Swap()` method. To do this, the variables are **passed by reference.** The obvious difference between the call to `Swap()` and Listing 4.11's call to `Combine()` is the use of the keyword `ref` in front of the parameter's data type. This keyword changes the call type to be by reference, so the called method can update the original caller's variable with a new value.

When the called method specifies a parameter as `ref`, the caller is required to place `ref` in front of the variables passed. In so doing, the caller explicitly recognizes that the target method could reassign any `ref` parameters it receives. Furthermore, it is necessary to initialize variables passed as `ref` because target methods could read data from `ref` parameters without first assigning them. In Listing 4.12, for example, `temp` is assigned the value of `first`, assuming that the variable passed in `first` was initialized by the caller. Effectively, a `ref` parameter is an alias for the variable passed. In other words, it is essentially giving a parameter name to an existing variable.

Output Parameters (`out`)

In addition to passing parameters into a method only (by value) and passing them in and back out (by reference), it is possible to pass data out only. To achieve this, code needs to decorate parameter types with the keyword `out`, as shown in the `GetPhoneButton()` method in Listing 4.13 that returns the phone button corresponding to a character.

LISTING 4.13: Passing Variables Out Only

```
class ConvertToPhoneNumber
{
  static int Main(string[] args)
  {
      char button;

      if(args.Length == 0)
      {
          Console.WriteLine(
              "ConvertToPhoneNumber.exe <phrase>");
          Console.WriteLine(
              "'_' indicates no standard phone button");
          return 1;
```

```csharp
        }
        foreach(string word in args)
        {
            foreach(char character in word)
            {
                if(GetPhoneButton(character, out button))
                {
                    Console.Write(button);
                }
                else
                {
                    Console.Write('_');
                }
            }
        }
        Console.WriteLine();
        return 0;
    }


    static bool GetPhoneButton(char character, out char button)
    {
        bool success = true;
        switch( char.ToLower(character) )
        {
            case '1':
                button = '1';
                break;
            case '2': case 'a': case 'b': case 'c':
                button = '2';
                break;

            // ...

            case '-':
                button = '-';
                break;
            default:
                // Set the button to indicate an invalid value
                button = '_';
                success = false;
                break;
        }
        return success;
    }
}
```

Output 4.7 shows the results of Listing 4.13.

OUTPUT 4.7:

```
>ConvertToPhoneNumber.exe CSharpIsGood
274277474663
```

In this example, the `GetPhoneButton()` method returns `true` if it can successfully determine the `character`'s corresponding phone button. The function also returns the corresponding button by using the `button` parameter which is decorated with `out`.

Whenever a parameter is marked with `out`, the compiler will check that the parameter is set for all code paths within the method that return normally (without an explicit error). If, for example, the code does not assign `button` a value, the compiler will issue an error indicating that the code didn't initialize `button`. Listing 4.13 assigns `button` to _ because even though it cannot determine the correct phone button, it is still necessary to assign a value.

Parameter Arrays (`params`)

In all the examples so far, the number of parameters is fixed by the target method declaration. However, sometimes the number of parameters may vary. Consider the `Combine()` method from Listing 4.11. In that method, you passed the drive letter, folder path, and filename. What if the number of folders in the path was more than one and the caller wanted the method to join additional folders to form the full path? Perhaps the best option would be to pass an array of strings for the folders. However, this would make the calling code a little more complex, because it would be necessary to construct an array to pass as a parameter.

For a simpler approach, C# provides a keyword that enables the number of parameters to vary in the calling code instead of being set by the target method. Before we discuss the method declaration, observe the calling code declared within `Main()`, as shown in Listing 4.14.

LISTING 4.14: Passing a Variable Parameter List

```csharp
using System.IO;

class PathEx
{
  static void Main()
  {
      string fullName;

      // ...

      // Call Combine() with four parameters
      fullName = Combine(
          Directory.GetCurrentDirectory(),
          "bin", "config", "index.html");
      Console.WriteLine(fullName);

      // ...

      // Call Combine() with only three parameters
      fullName = Combine(
          Environment.SystemDirectory,
          "Temp", "index.html");
      Console.WriteLine(fullName);

      // ...

      // Call Combine() with an array
      fullName = Combine(
          new string[] {
              "C:\", "Data",
              "HomeDir", "index.html"} );
      Console.WriteLine(fullName);
      // ...
  }

  static string Combine(params string[] paths)
  {
      string result = string.Empty;
      foreach (string path in paths)
      {
          result = System.IO.Path.Combine(result, path);
      }
      return result;
  }
}
```

Output 4.8 shows the results of Listing 4.14.

```
C:\Data\mark\bin\config\index.html
C:\WINDOWS\system32\Temp\index.html
C:\Data\HomeDir\index.html
```

In the first call to `Combine()`, four parameters are specified. The second call contains only three parameters. In the final call, parameters are passed using an array. In other words, the `Combine()` method takes a variable number of parameters, whether separated by a comma or as a single array.

To allow this, the `Combine()` method

1. Places `params` immediately before the last parameter in the method declaration
2. Declares the last parameter as an array

With a **parameter array** declaration, it is possible to access each parameter as a member of the `params` array. In the `Combine()` method implementation, you iterate over the elements of the `paths` array and call `System.IO.Path.Combine()`. This method automatically combines the parts of the path, appropriately using the platform-specific directory-separator-character. (`PathEx.Combine()` is identical to `Path.Combine()`, except that `PathEx.Combine()` handles a variable number of parameters rather than simply two.)

There are a few notable characteristics of the parameter array.

- The parameter array is not necessarily the only parameter on a method. However, the parameter array must be the last parameter in the method declaration. Since only the last parameter may be a parameter array, a method cannot have more than one parameter array.
- The caller can specify zero parameters for the parameter array, which will result in an array of zero items.

- Parameter arrays are type-safe—the type must match the type identified by the array.

- The caller can use an explicit array rather than a comma-separated list of parameters. The resultant CIL code is identical.

- If the target method implementation requires a minimum number of parameters, then those parameters should appear explicitly within the method declaration, forcing a compile error instead of relying on runtime error handling if required parameters are missing. For example, use int Max(int first, params int[] operands) rather than int Max(params int[] operands) so that at least one value is passed to Max().

Using a parameter array, you can pass a variable number of parameters of the same type into a method. The section Method Overloading, later in this chapter, discusses a means of supporting a variable number of parameters that are not necessarily of the same type.

Recursion

Calling a method **recursively** or implementing the method using **recursion** refers to the fact that the method calls itself. This is sometimes the simplest way to implement a method. Listing 4.15 counts the lines of all the C# source files (*.cs) in a directory and its subdirectory.

LISTING 4.15: Returning All the Filenames, Given a Directory

```csharp
using System.IO;

public static class LineCounter
{
  // Use the first argument as the directory
  // to search, or default to the current directory.
  public static void Main(string[] args)
  {
      int totalLineCount = 0;
      string directory;
      if (args.Length > 0)
      {
          directory = args[0];
      }
      else
```

```
    {
        directory = Directory.GetCurrentDirectory();
    }
    totalLineCount = DirectoryCountLines(directory);
    System.Console.WriteLine(totalLineCount);
}

static int DirectoryCountLines(string directory)
{
    int lineCount = 0;
    foreach (string file in
        Directory.GetFiles(directory, "*.cs"))
    {
        lineCount += CountLines(file);
    }

    foreach (string subdirectory in
        Directory.GetDirectories(directory))
    {
        lineCount += DirectoryCountLines(subdirectory);
    }

    return lineCount;
}

private static int CountLines(string file)
{
    string line;
    int lineCount = 0;
    FileStream stream =
        new FileStream(file, FileMode.Open);³
    StreamReader reader = new StreamReader(stream);
    line = reader.ReadLine();

    while(line != null)
    {
        if (line.Trim() != "")
        {
            lineCount++;
        }
        line = reader.ReadLine();
    }

    reader.Close();  // Automatically closes the stream
    return lineCount;
}
}
```

---

3. I could improve this code with a using statement, but I have avoided that construct because I have not yet introduced it.

Output 4.9 shows the results of Listing 4.15.

OUTPUT 4.9:

```
104
```

The program begins by passing the first command-line argument to
`DirectoryCountLines()`, or by using the current directory if no argument
was provided. This method first iterates through all the files in the current
directory and totals the source code lines for each file. After each file in the
directory, the code processes each subdirectory by passing the subdirectory back into the `DirectoryCountLines()` method, rerunning the method
using the subdirectory. The same process is repeated recursively through
each subdirectory until no more directories remain to process.

Readers unfamiliar with recursion may find it cumbersome at first.
Regardless, it is often the simplest pattern to code, especially with hierarchical type data such as the filesystem. However, although it may be the
most readable, it is generally not the fastest implementation. If performance becomes an issue, developers should seek an alternative solution in
place of a recursive implementation. The choice generally hinges on bal-
ancing readability with performance.

■ BEGINNER TOPIC

Infinite Recursion Error

A common programming error in recursive method implementations
appears in the form of a stack overflow during program execution. This
usually happens because of **infinite recursion,** in which the method continually calls back on itself, never reaching a point that indicates the end of
the recursion. It is a good practice for programmers to review any method
that uses recursion and verify that the recursion calls are finite.

A common pattern for recursion using pseudocode is as follows:

```
M(x)
{
  if x is trivial
```

```
      Return the result
   else
      a. Do some work to make the problem smaller
      b. Recursively call M to solve the smaller problem
      c. Compute the result based on a. and b.
      return the result
   }
```

Things go wrong when this pattern is not followed. For example, if you don't make the problem smaller or if you don't handle all possible "smallest" cases, the recursion never terminates.

Method Overloading

Listing 4.15 called `DirectoryCountLines()`, which counted the lines of `*.cs` files. However, if you want to count code in `*.h`/`*.cpp` files or in `*.vb` files, `DirectoryCountLines()` will not work. Instead, you need a method that takes the file extension, but still keeps the existing method definition so that it handles `*.cs` files by default.

All methods within a class must have a unique signature, and C# defines uniqueness by variation in the method name, parameter data types, or number of parameters. This does not include method return data types; defining two methods that have only a different return data type will cause a compile error. **Method overloading** occurs when a class has two or more methods with the same name and the parameter count and/or data types vary between the overloaded methods.

Method overloading is a type of **operational polymorphism.** Polymorphism occurs when the same logical operation takes on many ("poly") forms ("morphisms") because the data varies. Calling `WriteLine()` and passing a format string along with some parameters is implemented differently than calling `WriteLine()` and specifying an integer. However, logically, to the caller, the method takes care of writing the data and it is somewhat irrelevant how the internal implementation occurs. Listing 4.16 provides an example, and Output 4.10 shows the results.

LISTING 4.16: Returning All the Filenames, Given a Directory

```
using System.IO;

public static class LineCounter
```

```csharp
{
    public static void Main(string[] args)
    {
        int totalLineCount;

        if (args.Length > 1)
        {
            totalLineCount =
                DirectoryCountLines(args[0], args[1]);
        }
        if (args.Length > 0)
        {
            totalLineCount = DirectoryCountLines(args[0]);
        }
        else
        {
            totalLineCount = DirectoryCountLines();
        }

        System.Console.WriteLine(totalLineCount);
    }

    static int DirectoryCountLines()
    {
        return DirectoryCountLines(
            Directory.GetCurrentDirectory());
    }

    static int DirectoryCountLines(string directory)
    {
        return DirectoryCountLines(directory, "*.cs");
    }

    static int DirectoryCountLines(
        string directory, string extension)
    {
        int lineCount = 0;
        foreach (string file in
            Directory.GetFiles(directory, extension))
        {
            lineCount += CountLines(file);
        }

        foreach (string subdirectory in
            Directory.GetDirectories(directory))
        {
            lineCount += DirectoryCountLines(subdirectory);
        }

        return lineCount;
    }
```

```
private static int CountLines(string file)
{
    int lineCount = 0;
    string line;
    FileStream stream =
        new FileStream(file, FileMode.Open);⁴
    StreamReader reader = new StreamReader(stream);
    line = reader.ReadLine();
    while(line != null)
    {
        if (line.Trim() == "")
        {
            lineCount++;
        }
        line = reader.ReadLine();
    }

    reader.Close();  // Automatically closes the stream
    return lineCount;
}
}
```

OUTPUT 4.10:

```
>LineCounter.exe .\ *.cs
28
```

The effect of method overloading is to provide optional ways to call the method. As demonstrated inside Main(), you can call the DirectoryCount-Lines() method with or without passing the directory to search and the file extension.

Notice that the parameterless implementation of DirectoryCount-Lines() was changed to call the single-parameter version (int Directory-CountLines(string directory)). This is a common pattern when implementing overloaded methods. The idea is that developers implement only the core logic in one method and all the other overloaded methods will call that single method. If the core implementation changes, it needs to be modified in only one location rather than within each implementation. This pattern is especially prevalent when using method overloading to

---

4. This code could be improved with a using statement, a construct avoided because it has not yet been introduced.

enable optional parameters that do not have compile-time determined values and so they cannot be specified using optional parameters.

Optional Parameters

Starting with C# 4.0, the language designers added limited support for **optional parameters.** By allowing the assignment of a parameter to a constant value as part of the method declaration, it is possible to call a method without passing every parameter for the method (see Listing 4.17).

LISTING 4.17: Methods with Optional Parameters

```
using System.IO;

public static class LineCounter
{
  public static void Main(string[] args)
  {
    int totalLineCount;

    if (args.Length > 1)
    {
      totalLineCount =
        DirectoryCountLines(args[0], args[1]);
    }
    if (args.Length > 0)
    {
      totalLineCount = DirectoryCountLines(args[0]);
    }
    else
    {
      totalLineCount  = DirectoryCountLines();
    }

    System.Console.WriteLine(totalLineCount);
  }

  static int DirectoryCountLines()
  {
    // ...
  }

  /*
  static int DirectoryCountLines(string directory)
  { ... }
  */
```

```
static int DirectoryCountLines(
    string directory, string extension = "*.cs")
{
    int lineCount = 0;
    foreach (string file in
        Directory.GetFiles(directory, extension))
    {
        lineCount += CountLines(file);
    }

    foreach (string subdirectory in
        Directory.GetDirectories(directory))
    {
        lineCount += DirectoryCountLines(subdirectory);
    }

    return lineCount;
}

private static int CountLines(string file)
{
    // ...
}
}
```

In Listing 4.17, for example, the `DirectoryCountLines()` method declaration with a single parameter has been removed (commented out), but the call from `Main()` (specifying one parameter) remains. When no `extension` parameter is specified in the call, the value assigned to `extension` within the declaration (`*.cs` in this case) is used. This allows the calling code to not specify a value if desired, and eliminates the additional overload that would be required in C# 3.0 and earlier. Note that optional parameters must appear after all required parameters (those that don't have default values). Also, the fact that the default value needs to be a constant, compile-time-resolved value, is fairly restrictive. You can't, for example, declare a method using

```
DirectoryCountLines(
    string directory = Environment.CurrentDirectory,
    string extension = "*.cs")
```

since `Environment.CurrentDirectory` is not a literal. In contrast, since `default(string)` is compile-time-determined, C# 4.0 does allow it for the default value of an optional parameter.

A second method call feature made available in C# 4.0 was the use of **named parameters.** With named parameters it is possible for the caller to explicitly identify the name of the parameter to be assigned a value, rather than relying only on parameter order to correlate (see Listing 4.18).

LISTING 4.18: Specifying Parameters by Name

```csharp
class Program
{
  static void Main()
  {
      DisplayGreeting(
          firstName: "Inigo", lastName: "Montoya");
  }

  public void DisplayGreeting(
      string firstName,
      string middleName = default(string),
      string lastName = default(string))
  {

      // ...

  }
}
```

In Listing 4.18 the call to `DisplayGreeting()` from within `Main()` assigns a value to a parameter by name. Of the two optional parameters (`middleName` and `lastName`), only `lastName` is specified. For cases where a method has lots of parameters and many of them are optional (a common occurrence when accessing Microsoft COM libraries), using the named parameter syntax is certainly a convenience. However, notice that along with the convenience comes an impact on the flexibility of the method interface. In the past (at least from C#), parameter names could be changed without causing other calling code to no longer compile. With the addition of named parameters, the parameter name becomes part of the interface because changing the name would cause code that uses the named parameter to no longer compile.

For many experienced C# developers, this is a surprising restriction. However, the restriction has been imposed as part of the Common Language Specification ever since .NET 1.0. Therefore, library developers should already be following the practice of not changing parameter names to successfully interoperate with other .NET languages from version to version. C# 4.0 now imposes the same restriction on parameter name changes as many other .NET languages already require.

Given the combination of method overloading, optional parameters, and named parameters, resolving which method to call becomes less obvious. A call is **applicable** (compatible) with a method if all parameters have exactly one corresponding argument (either by name or by position) that is type-compatible unless the parameter is optional. Although this restricts the possible number of methods that will be called, it doesn't identify a unique method. To further distinguish which method specifically, the compiler uses only explicitly identified parameters in the caller, ignoring all optional parameters that were not specified at the caller. Therefore, if two methods are applicable because one of them has an optional parameter, the compiler will resolve to the method without the optional parameter.

■ ADVANCED TOPIC

Method Resolution

At a high level, selection by the compiler governing which method to call is determined to be whichever applicable method is most specific. There can be only one method that matches the caller parameters identically, so this will always take precedence. Assuming there are two applicable methods, each requiring an implicit conversion, the method that matches the most derived type will be used. (A method using `double` will be favored over a method using `object` if the caller passes an `int`. This is because `double` is more specific than `object`.) If more than one method is applicable and no unique best method can be determined, then the compiler will issue an error indicating that the call is ambiguous.

For example, given methods

```
Method( thing) // Fifth
Method( thing) // Fourth
Method( thing) // Third
Method( thing) // First
```

a Method(42) call will resolve in ascending order, starting with Method(int thing) and proceeding up to Method(long thing), and so on, if the former method does not exist.

The C# specification includes additional rules governing implicit conversion between byte, ushort, uint, ulong, and the other numeric types, but in general it is better to use a cast to make the intended target method more recognizable.

Basic Error Handling with Exceptions

An important aspect of calling methods relates to error handling; specifically, how to report an error back to the caller. This section examines how to handle error reporting via a mechanism known as **exception handling.**

With exception handling, a method is able to pass information about an error to a calling method without explicitly providing any parameters to do so. Listing 4.19 contains a slight modification to the HeyYou program from Chapter 1. Instead of requesting the last name of the user, it prompts for the user's age.

LISTING 4.19: Converting a string to an int

```
using System;

class ExceptionHandling
{
  static void Main()
  {
      string firstName;
      string ageText;
      int age;

      Console.WriteLine("Hey you!");

      Console.Write("Enter your first name: ");
      firstName = System.Console.ReadLine();

      Console.Write("Enter your age: ");
      ageText = Console.ReadLine();
      age = int.Parse(ageText);

      Console.WriteLine(
          "Hi {0}!  You are {1} months old.",
          firstName, age*12);
  }
}
```

Output 4.11 shows the results of Listing 4.19.

OUTPUT 4.11:

```
Hey you!
Enter your first name: Inigo
Enter your age: 42
Hi Inigo!  You are 504 months old.
```

The return value from `System.Console.ReadLine()` is stored in a variable called `ageText` and is then passed to a method on the `int` data type, called `Parse()`. This method is responsible for taking a string value that represents a number and converting it to an `int` type.

■ BEGINNER TOPIC

42 as a String versus 42 as an Integer

C# requires that every value has a well-defined type associated with it. Therefore, not only is the data value important, but the type associated with the data is important as well. A string value of 42, therefore, is distinctly different from an integer value of 42. The string is composed of the two characters 4 and 2, whereas the `int` is the number 42.

Given the converted string, the final `System.Console.WriteLine()` statement will print the age in months by multiplying the age value by 12.

However, what happens if the user does not enter a valid integer string? For example, what happens if the user enters "forty-two"? The `Parse()` method cannot handle such a conversion. It expects the user to enter a string that contains only digits. If the `Parse()` method is sent an invalid value, it needs some way to report this fact back to the caller.

Trapping Errors

To indicate to the calling method that the parameter is invalid, `int.Parse()` will **throw an exception.** Throwing an exception will halt further execution in the current program flow and instead will jump into the first code block within the call stack that handles the exception.

Since you have not yet provided any such handling, the program reports the exception to the user as an **unhandled exception.** Assuming there is no registered debugger on the system, the error will appear on the console with a message such as that shown in Output 4.12.

OUTPUT 4.12:

```
Hey you!
Enter your first name: Inigo
Enter your age: forty-two

Unhandled Exception: System.FormatException: Input string was
      not in a correct format.
   at System.Number.ParseInt32(String s, NumberStyles style,
      NumberFormatInfo info)
   at ExceptionHandling.Main()
```

Obviously, such an error is not particularly helpful. To fix this, it is necessary to provide a mechanism that handles the error, perhaps reporting a more meaningful error message back to the user.

This is known as **catching an exception.** The syntax is demonstrated in Listing 4.20, and the output appears in Output 4.13.

LISTING 4.20: Catching an Exception

```csharp
using System;

class ExceptionHandling
{
  static int Main()
  {
      string firstName;
      string ageText;
      int age;
      int result = 0;

      Console.Write("Enter your first name: ");
      firstName = Console.ReadLine();

      Console.Write("Enter your age: ");
      ageText = Console.ReadLine();

      try
      {
          age = int.Parse(ageText);
          Console.WriteLine(
              "Hi {0}!  You are {1} months old.",
```

```
            firstName, age*12);
    }
    catch (FormatException )
    {
        Console.WriteLine(
            "The age entered, {0}, is not valid.",
            ageText);
        result = 1;
    }
    catch(Exception exception)
    {
        Console.WriteLine(
            "Unexpected error:  {0}", exception.Message);
        result = 1;
    }
    finally
    {
        Console.WriteLine("Goodbye {0}",
            firstName);
    }

    return result;
  }
}
```

OUTPUT 4.13:

```
Enter your first name: Inigo
Enter your age: forty-two
The age entered, forty-two, is not valid.
Goodbye Inigo
```

To begin, surround the code that could potentially throw an exception (age = int.Parse()) with a **try block.** This block begins with the try keyword. It is an indication to the compiler that the developer is aware of the possibility that the code within the block could potentially throw an exception, and if it does, then one of the **catch blocks** will attempt to handle the exception.

One or more catch blocks (or the finally block) must appear immediately following a try block. The catch block header (see the Advanced Topic titled Generic catch, later in this chapter) optionally allows you to specify the data type of the exception, and as long as the data type matches the exception type, the catch block will execute. If, however, there is no appropriate catch block, the exception will fall through and go unhandled as though there were no exception handling.

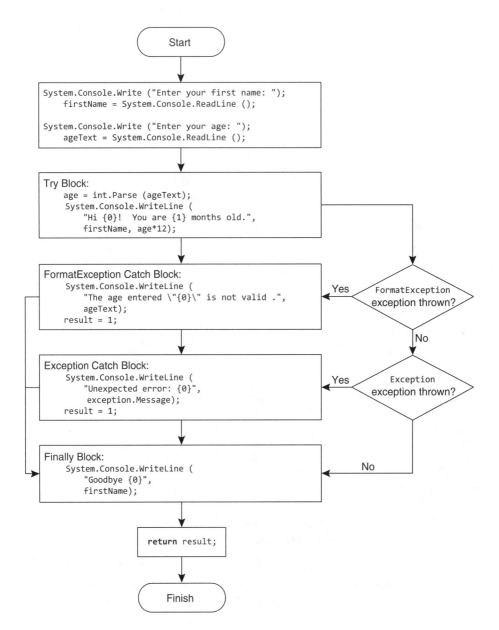

FIGURE 4.1: Exception-Handling Program Flow

The resultant program flow appears in Figure 4.1.

For example, assume the user enters "forty-two" for the age. In this case, `int.Parse()` will throw an exception of type `System.FormatException`, and control will jump to the set of catch blocks. (`System.FormatException` indicates that the string was not of the correct format to be parsed appropriately.) Since the first catch block matches the type of exception that `int.Parse()` threw, the code inside this block will execute. If a statement within the try block throws a different exception, then the second catch block would execute because (starting in C# 2.0) all exceptions are of type `System.Exception`.

If there were no `System.FormatException` catch block, then the `System.Exception` catch block would execute even though `int.Parse` throws a `System.FormatException`. This is because a `System.FormatException` is also of type `System.Exception`. (`System.FormatException` is a more specific implementation of the generic exception, `System.Exception`.)

Although the number of catch blocks varies, the order in which you handle exceptions is significant. Catch blocks must appear from most specific to least specific. The `System.Exception` data type is least specific and therefore it appears last. `System.FormatException` appears first because it is the most specific exception that Listing 4.20 handles.

Regardless of whether the code in the try block throws an exception, the **finally block** of code will execute. The purpose of the finally block is to provide a location to place code that will execute regardless of how the try/catch blocks exit—with or without an exception. Finally blocks are useful for cleaning up resources regardless of whether an exception is thrown. In fact, it is possible to have a try block with a finally block and no catch block. The finally block executes regardless of whether the try block throws an exception or whether a catch block is even written to handle the exception. Listing 4.21 demonstrates the try/finally block and Output 4.14 shows the results.

LISTING 4.21: Catching an Exception

```csharp
using System;

class ExceptionHandling
{
  static int Main()
  {
      string firstName;
      string ageText;
      int age;
      int result = 0;
```

```
        Console.Write("Enter your first name: ");
        firstName = Console.ReadLine();

        Console.Write("Enter your age: ");
        ageText = Console.ReadLine();

        try
        {
            age = int.Parse(ageText);
            Console.WriteLine(
                "Hi {0}!  You are {1} months old.",
                firstName, age*12);
        }
        finally
        {
            Console.WriteLine("Goodbye {0}",
                firstName);
        }

        return result;
    }
}
```

OUTPUT 4.14:

```
Enter your first name: Inigo
Enter your age: forty-two

Unhandled Exception: System.FormatException: Input string was not in a
correct format.
   at System.Number.StringToNumber(String str, NumberStyles options,
NumberBuffer& number, NumberFormatInfo info, Boolean parseDecimal)
   at System.Number.ParseInt32(String s, NumberStyles style,
NumberFormatInfo info)
   at ExceptionHandling.Main()
Goodbye Inigo
```

When this code executes, the finally block executes before printing an unhandled exception to the console (an unhandled exception dialog may also appear).

■ ADVANCED TOPIC

Exception Class Inheritance

Starting in C# 2.0, all exceptions derive from System.Exception. Therefore, they can be handled by the catch(System.Exception exception) block. It is preferable, however, to include a catch block that is specific to the most derived type (System.FormatException, for example), because then it is possible to get the most information about an exception and handle it less generically. In so doing, the catch statement that uses the most derived type is able to handle the exception type specifically, accessing data related to the exception thrown, and avoiding conditional logic to determine what type of exception occurred.

This is why C# enforces that catch blocks appear from most derived to least derived. For example, a catch statement that catches System.Exception cannot appear before a statement that catches System.Format Exception because System.FormatException derives from System.Exception.

A method could throw many exception types. Table 4.2 lists some of the more common ones within the framework.

TABLE 4.2: Common Exception Types

Exception Type	Description
System.Exception	A generic exception from which other exceptions derive.
System.ArgumentException	A means of indicating that one of the parameters passed into the method is invalid.
System.ArgumentNullException	Indicates that a particular parameter is null and that this is not valid for that parameter.
System.ApplicationException	To be avoided. Originally the idea that you might want to have one kind of handling for "system" exceptions and another for "application" exceptions, although plausible, doesn't actually work well in the real world.
System.FormatException	Indicates that the string format is not valid for conversion.
System.IndexOutOfRangeException	Indicates that an attempt was made to access an array element that does not exist.

Continues

TABLE 4.2: Common Exception Types *(Continued)*

Exception Type	Description
`System.InvalidCastException`	Indicates that an attempt to convert from one data type to another was not a valid conversion.
`System.NotImplementedException`	Indicates that although the method signature exists, it has not been fully implemented.
`System.NullReferenceException`	Throws when code tries to find the object referred to by a reference (such as a variable) which is null.
`System.ArithmeticException`	Indicates an invalid math operation, not including divide by zero.
`System.ArrayTypeMismatchException`	Occurs when attempting to store an element of the wrong type into an array.
`System.StackOverflowException`	Generally indicates that there is an infinite loop in which a method is calling back into itself (known as recursion).

▪ ADVANCED TOPIC

Generic `catch`

It is possible to specify a catch block that takes no parameters, as shown in Listing 4.22.

LISTING 4.22: General Catch Blocks

```
...
try
{
    age = int.Parse(ageText);
    System.Console.WriteLine(
        "Hi {0}!  You are {1} months old.",
        firstName, age*12);
}
catch (System.FormatException exception)
```

```
    {
        System.Console.WriteLine(
            "The age entered ,{0}, is not valid.",
            ageText);
        result = 1;
    }
    catch(System.Exception exception)
    {
        System.Console.WriteLine(
            "Unexpected error:  {0}", exception.Message);
        result = 1;
    }
    catch
    {
        System.Console.WriteLine(
            "Unexpected error!");
        result = 1;
    }
    finally
    {
        System.Console.WriteLine("Goodbye {0}",
            firstName);
    }
    ...
```

A catch block with no data type, called a **generic catch block,** is equivalent to specifying a catch block that takes an object data type: for instance, catch(object exception){...}. And since all classes ultimately derive from object, a catch block with no data type must appear last.

Generic catch blocks are rarely used because there is no way to capture any information about the exception. In addition, C# doesn't support the ability to throw an exception of type object. (Only libraries written in languages such as C++ allow exceptions of any type.)

The behavior starting in C# 2.0 varies slightly from the earlier C# behavior. In C# 2.0, if a language allows non-System.Exceptions, the object of the thrown exception will be wrapped in a System.Runtime. CompilerServices.RuntimeWrappedException which does derive from System.Exception. Therefore, all exceptions, whether deriving from System.Exception or not, will propagate into C# assemblies as derived from System.Exception.

The result is that System.Exception catch blocks will catch all exceptions not caught by earlier blocks, and a general catch block, following a

System.Exception catch block, will never be invoked. Because of this, following a System.Exception catch block with a general catch block in C# 2.0 or later will result in a compiler warning indicating that the general catch block will never execute.

Reporting Errors Using a throw Statement

Just as int.Parse() can throw an exception, C# allows developers to throw exceptions from their code, as demonstrated in Listing 4.23 and Output 4.15.

LISTING 4.23: Throwing an Exception

```csharp
using System;
class ThrowingExceptions
{
  static void Main()
  {
    try
    {
      Console.WriteLine("Begin executing");
      Console.WriteLine("Throw exception...");
      throw new Exception("Arbitrary exception");
      Console.WriteLine("End executing");
    }
    catch (FormatException exception)
    {
      Console.WriteLine(
        "A FormateException was thrown");
    }
    catch(Exception exception)
    {
      Console.WriteLine(
        "Unexpected error:  {0}", exception.Message);
    }
    catch
    {
      Console.WriteLine("Unexpected error!");
    }

    Console.WriteLine(
      "Shutting down...");
  }
}
```

OUTPUT 4.15:

```
Begin executing
Throw exception...
Unexpected error:   Arbitrary exception
Shutting down...
```

As the arrows in Listing 4.23 depict, throwing an exception jumps execution from where the exception is thrown into the first catch block within the stack that is compatible with the thrown exception type. In this case, the second catch block handles the exception and writes out an error message. In Listing 4.23, there is no final block, so execution falls through to the System.Console.WriteLine() statement following the try/catch block.

In order to throw an exception, it is necessary to have an instance of an exception. Listing 4.23 creates an instance using the keyword new followed by the data type of the exception. Most exception types allow a message as part of throwing the exception so that when the exception occurs, the message can be retrieved.

Sometimes a catch block will trap an exception but be unable to handle it appropriately or fully. In these circumstances, a catch block can rethrow the exception using the throw statement without specifying any exception, as shown in Listing 4.24.

LISTING 4.24: Rethrowing an Exception

```
    ...
        catch(Exception exception)
        {
            Console.WriteLine(
                "Rethrowing unexpected error:  {0}",
                exception.Message);
            throw;
        }
    ...
```

Avoid Using Exception Handling to Deal with Expected Situations

Developers should make an effort to avoid throwing exceptions for expected conditions or normal control flow. For example, developers should not expect users to enter valid text when specifying their age.[5] Therefore, instead of relying on an exception to validate data entered by the user, developers should provide a means of checking the data before attempting the conversion. (Better yet, you should prevent the user from entering invalid data in the first place.) Exceptions are designed specifically for tracking exceptional, unexpected, and potentially fatal situations. Using them for an unattended purpose such as expected situations will cause your code to be hard to read, understand, and maintain.

Additionally, (as with most languages) C# incurs a slight performance hit when throwing an exception—taking microseconds compared to the nanoseconds most operations take. This delay is generally not noticeable in human time—except when the exception goes unhandled. For example, when executing Listing 4.19 and entering an invalid age the exception is unhandled and there is a noticeable delay while the runtime searches the environment to see whether there is a debugger to load. Fortunately, slow performance when a program is shutting down isn't generally a factor to be concerned with.

■ ADVANCED TOPIC

Numeric Conversion with `TryParse()`

One of the problems with the `Parse()` method is that the only way to determine whether the conversion will be successful is to attempt the cast and then catch the exception if it doesn't work. Because throwing an exception is a relatively expensive operation, it is better to attempt the conversion without exception handling. In the first release of C#, the only data type that enabled this was a `double` method called `double.TryParse()`. However, the CLI added this method to all numeric primitive types in the CLI 2.0 version. It requires the use of the `out` keyword because the return from the `TryParse()` function is a `bool` rather than the converted value. Here is a code listing that demonstrates the conversion using `int.TryParse()`.

---

5. In general, developers should expect their users to perform unexpected actions, and therefore they should code defensively to handle "stupid user tricks."

```
...
if (int.TryParse(ageText, out age))
{
    System.Console.WriteLine(
        "Hi {0}!  You are {1} months old.", firstName,
        age * 12);
}
else
{
    System.Console.WriteLine(
        "The age entered ,{0}, is not valid.", ageText);
}
...
```

With the .NET Framework 4, a TryParse() method was also added to enum types.

With the TryParse() method, it is no longer necessary to include a try/catch block simply for the purpose of handling the string-to-numeric conversion.

SUMMARY

This chapter discussed the details of declaring and calling methods. In many ways, this construct is identical to its declaration in C-like languages. However, the addition of the keywords out and ref is more like COM in syntax (the predecessor to CLI technology) than C-like language's use of "&". In addition to method declaration, this chapter introduced exception handling.

Methods are a fundamental construct that is a key to writing readable code. Instead of writing large methods with lots of statements, you should use methods for "paragraphs" within your code, whose lengths target roughly ten lines or less. The process of breaking large functions into smaller pieces is one of the ways you can refactor your code to make it more readable and maintainable.

The next chapter considers the class construct and how it encapsulates methods (behavior) and fields (data) into a single unit.

◤5◼
Classes

Y OU BRIEFLY SAW IN CHAPTER 1 how to declare a new class called `HelloWorld`. In Chapter 2, you learned about the built-in primitive types included with C#. Since you have now also learned about control flow and how to declare methods, it is time to discuss defining your own

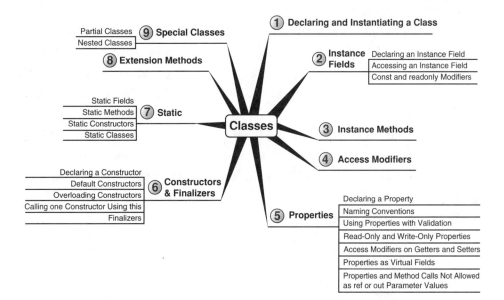

types. This is the core construct of any C# program, and the complete support for classes and the objects created from them is what defines C# as an object-oriented language.

This chapter introduces you to the basics of object-oriented programming using C#. A key focus is on how to define **classes,** which are the templates for objects themselves.

All of the constructs of structured programming from the previous chapters still apply within object-oriented programming. However, by wrapping those constructs within classes, you can create larger, more organized programs that are more maintainable. The transition from structured, control-flow-based programs to object-oriented programs somewhat revolutionized programming because it provided an extra level of organization. The result was that smaller programs were simplified somewhat; but more importantly, it was possible to create much larger programs because the code within those programs was better organized.

One of the key advantages of object-oriented programming is that instead of creating new programs entirely from scratch, you can assemble a collection of existing objects from prior work, extending the classes with new features, adding more classes, and then reassembling everything to provide new functionality.

Readers unfamiliar with object-oriented programming should read the Beginner Topic blocks for an introduction. The general text outside the Beginner Topics focuses on using C# for object-oriented programming with the assumption that readers are already familiar with object-oriented methodology.

This chapter delves into how C# supports encapsulation through its support of constructs such as classes, properties, and access modifiers (we covered methods in the preceding chapter). The next chapter builds on this foundation with the introduction of inheritance and the polymorphism that object-oriented programming enables.

■ BEGINNER TOPIC

Object-Oriented Programming

The key to programming successfully today is in the ability to provide organization and structure to the implementation of complex requirements fulfilled in larger and larger applications. Object-oriented programming provides one of the key methodologies in accomplishing this, to the point that it is difficult for object-oriented programmers to envision transitioning back to structured programming, except for the most trivial programs.

The most fundamental construct to object-oriented programming is the class or object itself. These form a programming abstraction, model, or template of what is often a real-world concept. The class `OpticalStorageMedia`, for example, may have an `Eject()` method on it that causes a CD/DVD to eject from the player. The `OpticalStorageMedia` class is the programming abstraction of the real-world object of a CD.

Classes are the foundation for three principal characteristics of object-oriented programming: encapsulation, inheritance, and polymorphism.

Encapsulation

Encapsulation allows you to hide detail. The detail can still be accessed when necessary, but by intelligently encapsulating the detail, large programs are easier to understand, data is protected from inadvertent modification, and code is easier to maintain because the effects of a code change are bound to the scope of the encapsulation. Methods are examples of encapsulation. Although it is possible to take the code from a method and embed it directly inline with the caller's code, refactoring of code into a method provides encapsulation benefits.

Inheritance

Consider the following example: A DVD is a type of optical media. It has a specific storage capacity along with the ability to hold a digital movie. A CD is also a type of optical media, but it has different characteristics. The copyright implementation on CDs is different from DVD copyright protection, and the storage capacity is different as well. Both CDs and DVDs are different from hard drives, USB drives, and floppy drives (remember those?). All fit into the category of storage media, but each has special characteristics, even for fundamental functions such as the supported filesystems and whether instances of the media are read-only or read-write.

Inheritance in object-oriented programming allows you to form "is a" relationships between these similar but different items. It is a reasonable assumption that a DVD "is a" type of storage media and that a CD "is a" type of storage media, and as such, that each has storage capacity.

Similarly, CDs and DVDs have "is a" relationships to the optical media type, which in turn has an "is a" relationship with the storage media type.

If you define classes corresponding to each type of storage media mentioned, you will have defined a **class hierarchy,** which is a series of "is a" relationships. The base type, from which all storage media derive, could be the class StorageMedia. As such, CDs, DVDs, hard drives, USB drives, and floppy drives are types of StorageMedia. However, CDs and DVDs don't need to derive from StorageMedia directly. Instead, they can derive from an intermediate type, OpticalStorageMedia. You can view the class hierarchy graphically using a Unified Modeling Language (UML)-like class diagram, as shown in Figure 5.1.

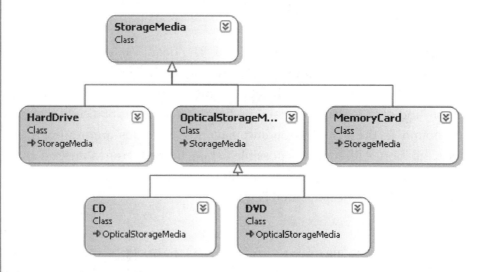

FIGURE 5.1: Class Hierarchy

The inheritance relationship involves a minimum of two classes such that one class is a more general version of the other; in Figure 5.1, StorageMedia is a more general version of HardDrive. Although the more specialized type, HardDrive, is a type of StorageMedia, the reverse is not true; a StorageMedia type is not necessarily a HardDrive. As Figure 5.1 shows, inheritance can involve more than two classes.

The more specialized type is the **derived** type or the **subtype.** The more generalized type is the **base** class or sometimes the **super** type. Other common terms for the classes in an inheritance relationship are *parent* and *child*; the former is the more generalized class.

To **derive** or **inherit** from another type is to **specialize** that type, which means to customize the base type so that it is geared for a specific purpose. Similarly, the base type is the generalized implementation of the derived types.

The key feature of inheritance is that all derived types inherit the members of the base type. Often, the implementation of the base members can be modified, but regardless, the derived type contains the base type's members in addition to any other members that the derived type contains explicitly.

Derived types allow you to organize your classes into a coherent hierarchy where the "child" types have greater specificity than their "parent" types.

Polymorphism

Polymorphism comprises a word meaning "many" and a word meaning "forms." In the context of objects, polymorphism means that a single method or type can have many forms of implementation. Suppose you have a media player. It follows that the media player could play both CD music discs and DVDs containing MP3s. However, the exact implementation of the `Play()` method will vary depending on the media type. Calling `Play()` on a music CD object or `Play()` on a music DVD will play music in both cases, because each type understands the intricacies of playing. All that the media player knows about is the common base type, `OpticalStorageMedia`, and the fact that it defines the `Play()` method signature. Polymorphism is the principle that a type can take care of the exact details of a method's implementation because the method appears on multiple derived types that each share a common base type (or interface) that also contains the same method signature.

Declaring and Instantiating a Class

Defining a class involves first specifying the keyword `class`, followed by an identifier, as shown in Listing 5.1.

LISTING 5.1: Defining a Class

```
class Employee
{
}
```

All code that belongs to the class will appear between the curly braces following the class declaration. Although not a requirement, generally you place each class into its own file. This makes it easier to find the code that defines a particular class, because the convention is to name the file using the class name.

Once you have defined a new class, you can use that class as though it were built into the framework. In other words, you can declare a variable of that type or define a method that takes a parameter of the new class type. Listing 5.2 demonstrates.

LISTING 5.2: Declaring Variables of the Class Type

```
class Program
{
  static void Main()
  {
      Employee employee1, employee2;
      // ...
  {


  static void IncreaseSalary (Employee  employee)
  {
      // ...
  }
}
```

■ BEGINNER TOPIC

Objects and Classes Defined

In casual conversation, the terms *class* and *object* appear interchangeably. However, object and class have distinct meanings. A **class** is a template for what an object will look like at instantiation time. An **object,** therefore, is an instance of a class. Classes are like the mold for what a widget will look like. Objects correspond to widgets created by the mold. The process of creating an object from a class is **instantiation** because an object is an instance of a class.

Now that you have defined a new class type, it is time to instantiate an object of that type. Mimicking its predecessors, C# uses the new keyword to instantiate an object (see Listing 5.3).

LISTING 5.3: Instantiating a Class

```csharp
class Program
{
  static void Main()
  {
      Employee employee1 = new Employee();
      Employee employee2;
      employee2 = new Employee();

      IncreaseSalary(employee1);
  }
}
```

Not surprisingly, the assignment can occur on the same line as the declaration, or on a separate line.

Unlike the primitive types you have worked with so far, there is no literal way to specify an Employee. Instead, the new operator provides an instruction to the runtime to allocate memory for an Employee object, instantiate the object, and return a reference to the instance.

In spite of the explicit operator for allocating memory, there is no such operator for restoring the memory. Instead, the runtime automatically reclaims the memory sometime after the object is last accessible but before the application closes down. The **garbage collector** is responsible for the automatic deallocation. It determines which objects are no longer referenced by other active objects and then de-allocates the memory for those objects. The result is that there is no compile-time-determined location where the memory will be restored to the system.

In this trivial example, no explicit data or methods are associated with an Employee and this renders the object essentially useless. The next section focuses on adding data to an object.

Language Contrast: C++—delete Operator

Programmers should view the new operator as a call to instantiate an object, not as a call to allocate memory. Both objects allocated on the heap and objects allocated on the stack support the new operator, emphasizing the point that new is not about memory allocation and whether de-allocation is necessary.

Therefore, and in contrast to C++, C# does avoid the need for the delete operator or an equivalent. Memory management is a detail that the runtime manages, allowing the developer to focus more on domain logic. However, although memory management is handled by the runtime, there is no implicit mechanism for resource management (database connections, network ports, and so on). In other words, there is no *implicit* way to program **deterministic destruction** (the occurrence of implicit object destruction at a compile-time-defined location in the code). Fortunately, C# does support explicit, deterministic resource management via a using statement or nondeterministic cleanup using finalizers.

■ BEGINNER TOPIC

Encapsulation Part 1: Objects Group Data with Methods

If you received a stack of index cards with employees' first names, a stack of index cards with their last names, and a stack of index cards with their salaries, the cards would be of little value unless you knew that the cards were in order in each stack. Even so, the data would be difficult to work with because determining a person's full name would require searching through two stacks. Worse, if you dropped one of the stacks, there would be no way to reassociate the first name with the last name and the salary. Instead, you would need one stack of employee cards in which all the data was grouped on one card. In this way, first names, last names, and salaries would be encapsulated together.

Outside the object-oriented programming context, to **encapsulate** a set of items is to enclose those items within a capsule. Similarly, object-oriented programming encapsulates methods and data together into an object. This provides a grouping of all of the class **members** (the data and methods within a class) so that they no longer need to be handled individually. Instead of passing first name, last name, and salary as three separate parameters to a method, objects enable a call to pass a reference to an employee object. Once the called method receives the object reference, it can send a message (it can call a method such as `AdjustSalary()`, for example) on the object to perform a particular operation.

Instance Fields

One of the key aspects of object-oriented design is the grouping of data to provide structure. This section discusses how to add data to the `Employee` class. The general object-oriented term for a variable that stores data within a class is **member variable.** This term is well understood in C#, but the more standard term and the one used in the specification is **field,** which is a named unit of storage associated with the containing type. **Instance fields** are variables declared at the class level to store data associated with an object. Hence, **association** is the relationship between the field data type and the containing field.

Declaring an Instance Field

In Listing 5.4, `Employee` has been modified to include three fields: `First-Name`, `LastName`, and `Salary`.

LISTING 5.4: Declaring Fields

```
class Employee
{
  public string FirstName;
  public string LastName;
  public string Salary;
}
```

With these fields added, it is possible to store some fundamental data with every `Employee` instance. In this case, you prefix the fields with an access modifier of `public`. `public` on a field indicates that the data within the field is accessible from classes other than `Employee` (see the section Access Modifiers, later in this chapter).

As with local variable declarations, a field declaration includes the data type to which the field refers. Furthermore, it is possible to assign fields an initial value at declaration time, as demonstrated with the `Salary` field in Listing 5.5.

LISTING 5.5: Setting Initial Values of Fields at Declaration Time

```
class Employee
{
  public string FirstName;
  public string LastName;
  public string Salary = "Not enough";
}
```

Accessing an Instance Field

You can set and retrieve the data within fields. However, the fact that the field does not include a `static` modifier indicates that it is an instance field. You can access an instance field only from an instance of the containing class (an object). You cannot access it from the class directly (without first creating an instance, in other words).

Listing 5.6 shows an updated look at the `Program` class and its utilization of the `Employee` class, and Output 5.1 shows the results.

LISTING 5.6: Accessing Fields

```
class Program
{
  static void Main()
  {
      Employee employee1 = new Employee();
      Employee employee2;
      employee2 = new Employee();

      employee1.FirstName = "Inigo";
      employee1.LastName = "Montoya";
      employee1.Salary = "Too Little";
      IncreaseSalary(employee1);
```

```
        Console.WriteLine(
            "{0} {1}: {2}",
            employee1.FirstName,
            employee1.LastName,
            employee1.Salary);
        // ...
    }

    static void IncreaseSalary(Employee employee)
    {
        employee.Salary = "Enough to survive on";
    }
}
```

OUTPUT 5.1:

```
Inigo Montoya: Enough to survive on
```

Listing 5.6 instantiates two Employee objects, as you saw before. Next, it sets each field, calls IncreaseSalary() to change the salary, and then displays each field associated with the object referenced by employee1.

Notice that you first have to specify which Employee instance you are working with. Therefore, the employee1 variable appears as a prefix to the field name when assigning and accessing the field.

Instance Methods

One alternative to formatting the names in the WriteLine() method call within Main() is to provide a method in the Employee class that takes care of the formatting. Changing the functionality to be within the Employee class rather than a member of Program is consistent with the encapsulation of a class. Why not group the methods relating to the employee's full name with the class that contains the data that forms the name?

Listing 5.7 demonstrates the creation of such a method.

LISTING 5.7: Accessing Fields from within the Containing Class

```
class Employee
{
  public string FirstName;
  public string LastName;
  public string Salary;
```

```
    public string GetName()
    {
        return FirstName + " " + LastName;
    }
}
```

There is nothing particularly special about this method compared to what you learned in Chapter 4, except that now the GetName() method accesses fields on the object instead of just local variables. In addition, the method declaration is not marked with static. As you will see later in this chapter, static methods cannot directly access instance fields within a class. Instead, it is necessary to obtain an instance of the class in order to call any instance member, whether a method or a field.

Given the addition of the GetName() method, you can update Program.Main() to use the new method, as shown in Listing 5.8 and Output 5.2.

LISTING 5.8: Accessing Fields from Outside the Containing Class

```
class Program
{
  static void Main()
  {
      Employee employee1 = new Employee();
      Employee employee2;
      employee2 = new Employee();

      employee1.FirstName = "Inigo";
      employee1.LastName = "Montoya";
      employee1.Salary = "Too Little";
      IncreaseSalary(employee1);
      Console.WriteLine(
          "{0}: {1}",
          employee1.GetName(),
          employee1.Salary);
      // ...
  }
  // ...
}
```

OUTPUT 5.2:

```
Inigo Montoya: Enough to survive on
```

Using the this Keyword

You can obtain the reference to a class from within instance members that belong to the class. To indicate explicitly that the field or method accessed is an instance member of the containing class in C#, you use the keyword this. this is conceptually an implicit parameter within every instance method that returns an instance of the object itself.

For example, consider the SetName() method shown in Listing 5.9.

LISTING 5.9: Using this to Identify the Field's Owner Explicitly

```csharp
class Employee
{
  public string FirstName;
  public string LastName;
  public string Salary;

  public string GetName()
  {
      return FirstName + " " + LastName;
  }

  public void SetName(string newFirstName, string newLastName)
  {
      this.FirstName = newFirstName;
      this.LastName = newLastName;
  }
}
```

This example uses the keyword this to indicate that the fields First-Name and LastName are instance members of the class.

▪ BEGINNER TOPIC

Relying on Coding Style to Avoid Ambiguity

In the SetName() method, you did not have to use the this keyword because FirstName is obviously different from newFirstName. Consider, however, if instead of calling the parameter "newFirstName" you called it "FirstName" (using Pascal case), as shown in Listing 5.10.

LISTING 5.10: **Using this to Avoid Ambiguity**

```csharp
class Employee
{
  public string FirstName;
  public string LastName;
  public string Salary;

  public string GetName()
  {
      return FirstName + " " + LastName;
  }

  // Caution:  Parameter names use Pascal case
  public void SetName(string FirstName, string LastName)
  {
      this.FirstName = FirstName;
      this.LastName = LastName;
  }
}
```

In this example, it is not possible to refer to the `FirstName` field without explicitly indicating that the `Employee` object owns the variable. `this` acts just like the `employee1` variable prefix used in the `Program.Main()` method (see Listing 5.8); it identifies the reference as the one on which `SetName()` was called.

Listing 5.10 does not follow the C# naming convention in which parameters are declared like local variables, using camel case. This can lead to subtle bugs because assigning `FirstName` (intending to refer to the field) to `FirstName` (the parameter) will still compile and even run. To avoid this problem it is a good practice to have a different naming convention for parameters and local variables than the naming convention for fields. I demonstrate one such convention later in this chapter.

Language Contrast: Visual Basic—Accessing a Class Instance with Me

The C# keyword `this` is identical to the Visual Basic keyword `Me`.

In Listing 5.9 and Listing 5.10, the this keyword is not used in the GetName() method—it is optional. However, if local variables or parameters exist with the same name as the field (see the SetName() method in Listing 5.10), then leaving off this would result in accessing the local variable/parameter rather than the field, so this would be required.

You also can use the keyword this to access a class's methods explicitly. this.GetName() is allowed within the SetName() method, for example, allowing you to print out the newly assigned name (see Listing 5.11 and Output 5.3).

LISTING 5.11: Using this with a Method

```csharp
class Employee
{
  // ...

  public string GetName()
  {
      return FirstName + " " + LastName;
  }

  public void SetName(string newFirstName, string newLastName)
  {
      this.FirstName = newFirstName;
      this.LastName = newLastName;
      Console.WriteLine("Name changed to '{0}'",
          this.GetName());
  }
}
```

```csharp
class Program
{
  static void Main()
  {
      Employee employee = new Employee();

      employee.SetName("Inigo", "Montoya");
      // ...
  }
  // ...
}
```

OUTPUT 5.3:

```
Name changed to 'Inigo Montoya'
```

Sometimes it may be necessary to use this in order to pass a reference to the currently executing object. Consider the Save() method in Listing 5.12.

LISTING 5.12: Passing this in a Method Call

```csharp
class Employee
{
  public string FirstName;
  public string LastName;
  public string Salary;

  public void Save()
  {
      DataStorage.Store(this);
  }
}
```

```csharp
class DataStorage
{
  // Save an employee object to a file
  // named with the Employee name.
  public static void Store(Employee employee)
  {
      // ...
  }
}
```

The Save() method calls a method on the DataStorage class, called Store(). The Store() method, however, needs to be passed the Employee object that needs to be persisted. This is done using the keyword this, which passes the instance of the Employee object on which Save() was called.

■ ADVANCED TOPIC

Storing and Loading with Files
The actual implementation of the Store() method inside DataStorage involves classes within the System.IO namespace, as shown in Listing 5.13. Inside Store(), you begin by instantiating a FileStream object that you

associate with a file corresponding to the employee's full name. The `File-Mode.Create` parameter indicates that you want a new file to be created if there isn't already one with the `<firstname><lastname>.dat` name; if the file exists already, it will be overwritten. Next, you create a `StreamWriter` class. The `StreamWriter` class is responsible for writing text into the `FileStream`. You write the data using `WriteLine()` methods, just as though writing to the console.

LISTING 5.13: Data Persistence to a File

```
using System;
// IO namespace
using System.IO;

class DataStorage
{
    // Save an employee object to a file
    // named with the Employee name.
    // Error handling not shown.
    public static void Store(Employee employee)
    {
        // Instantiate a FileStream using FirstNameLastName.dat
        // for the filename. FileMode.Create will force
        // a new file to be created or override an
        // existing file.
        FileStream stream = new FileStream(
            employee.FirstName + employee.LastName + ".dat",
            FileMode.Create);1

        // Create a StreamWriter object for writing text
        // into the FileStream
        StreamWriter writer = new StreamWriter(stream);

        // Write all the data associated with the employee.
        writer.WriteLine(employee.FirstName);
        writer.WriteLine(employee.LastName);
        writer.WriteLine(employee.Salary);

        // Close the StreamWriter and its Stream.
        writer.Close();  // Automatically closes the stream
    }
    // ...
}
```

---

1. This code could be improved with a `using` statement, a construct avoided because it has not yet been introduced.

Once the write operations are completed, both the `FileStream` and the `StreamWriter` need to be closed so that they are not left open indefinitely while waiting for the garbage collector to run. This listing does not include any error handling, so if an exception is thrown, neither `Close()` method will be called.

The load process is similar (see Listing 5.14).

LISTING 5.14: Data Retrieval from a File

```csharp
class Employee
{
  // ...
}
```

```csharp
// IO namespace
using System;
using System.IO;

class DataStorage
{
  // ...

  public static Employee Load(string firstName, string lastName)
  {
      Employee employee = new Employee();

      // Instantiate a FileStream using FirstNameLastName.dat
      // for the filename. FileMode.Open will open
      // an existing file or else report an error.
      FileStream stream = new FileStream(
          firstName + lastName + ".dat", FileMode.Open);²

      // Create a SteamReader for reading text from the file.
      StreamReader reader = new StreamReader(stream);

      // Read each line from the file and place it into
      // the associated property.
      employee.FirstName = reader.ReadLine();
      employee.LastName = reader.ReadLine();
      employee.Salary = reader.ReadLine();

      // Close the StreamReader and its Stream.
      reader.Close();  // Automatically closes the stream
```

---

2. This code could be improved with a `using` statement, a construct avoided because it has not yet been introduced.

```
        return employee;
    }
}
```

```
class Program
{
  static void Main()
  {
      Employee employee1;

      Employee employee2 = new Employee();
      employee2.SetName("Inigo", "Montoya");
      employee2.Save();

      // Modify employee2 after saving.
      IncreaseSalary(employee2);

      // Load employee1 from the saved version of employee2
      employee1 = DataStorage.Load("Inigo", "Montoya");

      Console.WriteLine(
          "{0}: {1}",
          employee1.GetName(),
          employee1.Salary);

      // ...
  }
  // ...
}
```

Output 5.4 shows the results.

OUTPUT 5.4:

```
Name changed to 'Inigo Montoya'
Inigo Montoya
```

The reverse of the save process appears in Listing 5.14, which uses a Stream-Reader rather than a StreamWriter. Again, Close() needs to be called on both FileStream and StreamReader once the data has been read.

Output 5.4 does not show any salary after "Inigo Montoya:" because Salary was not set to "Enough to survive on" by a call to IncreaseSalary() until after the call to Save().

Notice in `Main()` that we can call `Save()` from an instance of an employee, but to load a new employee we call `DataStorage.Load()`. To load an employee, we generally don't already have an employee instance to load into, so an instance method on `Employee` would be less than ideal. An alternative to calling `Load` on `DataStorage` would be to add a static `Load()` method (see the section Static, later in this chapter) to `Employee` so that it would be possible to call `Employee.Load()` (using the `Employee` class, not an instance of `Employee`).

Observe the inclusion of the `using System.IO` directive at the top of the listing. This makes each `IO` class accessible without prefixing it with the full namespace.

Access Modifiers

When declaring a field earlier in the chapter, you prefixed the field declaration with the keyword `public`. `public` is an **access modifier** that identifies the level of encapsulation associated with the member it decorates. Five access modifiers are available: `public`, `private`, `protected`, `internal`, and `protected internal`. This section considers the first two.

■ BEGINNER TOPIC

Encapsulation Part 2: Information Hiding

Besides wrapping data and methods together into a single unit, encapsulation is also about hiding the internal details of an object's data and behavior. To some degree, methods do this; from outside a method, all that is visible to a caller is the method declaration. None of the internal implementation is visible. Object-oriented programming enables this further, however, by providing facilities for controlling the extent to which members are visible from outside the class. Members that are not visible outside the class are **private members.**

In object-oriented programming, *encapsulation* is the term for not only grouping data and behavior, but also hiding data within a class (the capsule) so that minimum access about the inner workings of a class is exposed outside the class. This reduces the chances that callers will modify the data inappropriately.

The purpose of an access modifier is to provide encapsulation. By using public, you explicitly indicated that it is acceptable that the modified fields are accessible from outside the Employee class—in other words, that they are accessible from the Program class, for example.

Consider an Employee class that includes a Password field, however. It should be possible to call an Employee object and verify the password using a Logon() method. It should not be possible, however, to access the Password field on an Employee object from outside the class.

To define a Password field as hidden and inaccessible from outside the containing class, you use the keyword private for the access modifier, in place of public (see Listing 5.15). As a result, the Password field is not intended for access from inside the Program class, for example.

LISTING 5.15: Using the **private** Access Modifier

```
class Employee
{
  public string FirstName;
  public string LastName;
  public string Salary;
  private string Password;
  private bool IsAuthenticated;

  public bool Logon(string password)
  {
      if(Password == password)
      {
          IsAuthenticated = true;
      }
      return IsAuthenticated;
  }

  public bool GetIsAuthenticated()
  {
      return IsAuthenticated;
  }
  // ...
}
```

```
class Program
{
  static void Main()
  {
```

```
Employee employee = new Employee();

employee.FirstName = "Inigo";
employee.LastName = "Montoya";

// ...

// Password is private, so it cannot be
// accessed from outside the class.
// Console.WriteLine(
//     ("Password = {0}", employee.Password);
}
// ...
}
```

Although not shown in Listing 5.15, it is possible to decorate a method with an access modifier of `private` as well.

Note that if no access modifier is placed on a class member, the declaration will default to `private`. In other words, members are private by default and programmers need to specify explicitly that a member is to be public.

Properties

The preceding section, Access Modifiers, demonstrated how you can use the `private` keyword to encapsulate a password, preventing access from outside the class. This type of encapsulation is often too thorough, however. For example, sometimes you might need to define fields that external classes can only read but whose values you can change internally. Alternatively, perhaps you want to allow access to write some data in a class but you need to be able to validate changes made to the data. Still one more example is the need to construct the data on the fly.

Traditionally, languages enabled the features found in these examples by marking fields as private and then providing getter and setter methods for accessing and modifying the data. The code in Listing 5.16 changes both `FirstName` and `LastName` to private fields. Public getter and setter methods for each field allow their values to be accessed and changed.

LISTING 5.16: Declaring Getter and Setter Methods

```csharp
class Employee
{

  private string FirstName;
  // FirstName getter
  public string GetFirstName()
  {
      return FirstName;
  }
  // FirstName setter
  public void SetFirstName(string newFirstName)
  {
      if(newFirstName != null && newFirstName != "")
      {
          FirstName = newFirstName;
      }
  }

  private string LastName;
  // LastName getter
  public string GetLastName()
  {
      return LastName;
  }
  // LastName setter
  public void SetLastName(string newLastName)
  {
      if(newLastName != null && newLastName != "")
      {
          LastName = newLastName;
      }
  }
  // ...
}
```

Unfortunately, this change affects the programmability of the `Employee` class. No longer can you use the assignment operator to set data within the class, nor can you access data without calling a method.

Declaring a Property

Considering the frequency of this type of pattern, the C# designers decided to provide explicit syntax for it. This syntax is called a **property** (see Listing 5.17 and Output 5.5).

LISTING 5.17: Defining Properties

```csharp
class Profgram
{
  static void Main()
  {
    Employee employee = new Employee();

    // Call the FirstName property's setter.
    employee.FirstName = "Inigo";

    // Call the FirstName property's getter.
    System.Console.WriteLine(employee.FirstName);
  }
}
```

```csharp
class Employee
{
  // FirstName property
  public string FirstName
  {
    get
    {
      return _FirstName;
    }
    set
    {
      _FirstName = value;
    }
  }
  private string _FirstName;

  // LastName property
  public string LastName
  {
    get
    {
      return _LastName;
    }
    set
    {
      _LastName = value;
    }
  }
  private string _LastName;
  // ...
}
```

OUTPUT 5.5:

```
Inigo
```

The first thing to notice in Listing 5.17 is not the property code itself, but the code within the `Program` class. Although you no longer have the fields with the `FirstName` and `LastName` identifiers, you cannot see this by looking at the `Program` class. The API for accessing an employee's first and last names has not changed at all. It is still possible to assign the parts of the name using a simple assignment operator, for example (`employee.First Name = "Inigo"`).

The key feature is that properties provide an API that looks programmatically like a field. In actuality, however, no such fields exist. A property declaration looks exactly like a field declaration, but following it are curly braces in which to place the property implementation. Two optional parts make up the property implementation. The `get` part defines the getter portion of the property. It corresponds directly to the `GetFirstName()` and `GetLastName()` functions defined in Listing 5.16. To access the `First-Name` property you call `employee.FirstName`. Similarly, setters (the `set` portion of the implementation) enable the calling syntax of the field assignment:

```
employee.FirstName = "Inigo";
```

Property definition syntax uses three contextual keywords. You use the `get` and `set` keywords to identify either the retrieval or the assignment portion of the property, respectively. In addition, the setter uses the `value` keyword to refer to the right side of the assignment operation. When `Program.Main()` calls `employee.FirstName = "Inigo"`, therefore, `value` is set to "Inigo" inside the setter and can be used to assign `_FirstName`. Listing 5.17's property implementations are the most common. When the getter is called (such as in `Console.WriteLine(employee2.FirstName)`), the value from the field (`_FirstName`) is returned.

Automatically Implemented Properties

In C# 3.0, property syntax includes a shorthand version. Since a property with a single backing field that is assigned and retrieved by the get and set accessors is so trivial and common (see the implementations of `FirstName` and `LastName`), the C# 3.0 compiler allows the declaration of a property without any accessor implementation or backing field declaration. Listing 5.18 demonstrates the syntax, and Output 5.6 shows the results.

LISTING 5.18: Automatically Implemented Properties

```csharp
class Program
{
  static void Main()
  {
      Employee employee1 =
          new Employee();
      Employee employee2 =
          new Employee();

      // Call the FirstName property's setter.
      employee1.FirstName = "Inigo";

      // Call the FirstName property's getter.
      System.Console.WriteLine(employee1.FirstName);

      // Assign an auto-implemented property
      employee2.Title = "Computer Nerd";
      employee1.Manager = employee2;

      // Print employee1's manager's title.
    System.Console.WriteLine(employee1.Manager.Title);
  }
}
```

```csharp
class Employee
{
  // FirstName property
  public string FirstName
  {
      get
      {
          return _FirstName;
      }
      set
      {
          _FirstName = value;
      }
  }
  private string _FirstName;
```

```csharp
// LastName property
public string LastName
{
    get
    {
        return _LastName;
    }
    set
    {
        _LastName = value;
    }
}
private string _LastName;
// ...

// Title property
public string Title { get; set; }

// Manager property
public Employee Manager { get; set; }

}
```

OUTPUT 5.6:

```
Inigo
Computer Nerd
```

Auto-implemented properties provide for a simpler way of writing properties in addition to reading them. Furthermore, when it comes time to add something such as validation to the setter, any existing code that calls the property will not have to change even though the property declaration will have changed to include an implementation.

Throughout the remainder of the book, I will frequently use this C# 3.0 or later syntax without indicating that it is a C# 3.0 introduced feature.

Naming Conventions

Because the property name is FirstName, the field name changed from earlier listings to _FirstName. Other common naming conventions for the private field that backs a property are _firstName and m_FirstName (a holdover from C++ where the *m* stands for member variable), as well as the camel-case convention, just as with local variables.[3]

Regardless of which naming pattern you use for private fields, the coding standard for public fields and properties is Pascal case. Therefore, public properties should use the LastName and FirstName type patterns. Similarly, if no encapsulating property is created around a public field, Pascal case should be used for the field.

Using Properties with Validation

Notice in Listing 5.19 that the Initialize() method of Employee uses the property rather than the field for assignment as well. Although not required, the result is that any validation within the property setter will be invoked both inside and outside the class. Consider, for example, what would happen if you changed the LastName property so that it checked value for null or an empty string, before assigning it to _LastName.

LISTING 5.19: Providing Property Validation

```csharp
class Employee
{
  // ...
  public void Initialize(
      string newFirstName, string newLastName)
  {
      // Use property inside the Employee
      // class as well.
      FirstName = newFirstName;
      LastName = newLastName;
  }


  // LastName property
  public string LastName
  {
      get
      {
          return _LastName;
      }
      set
```

---

3. I prefer _FirstName because the *m* in front of the name is unnecessary when compared with simply _, and by using the same casing as the property, it is possible to have only one string within the Visual Studio code template expansion tools, instead of having one for both the property name and the field name.

```
        {
            // Validate LastName assignment
            if(value == null)
            {
                // Report error
                throw new ArgumentNullException ();
            }
            else
            {
                // Remove any whitespace around
                // the new last name.
                value = value.Trim();
                if(value == "")
                {
                    throw new ArgumentException (
                        "LastName cannot be blank.");4
                }
                else
                    _LastName = value;
            }
        }
    }
    private string _LastName;
    // ...
}
```

With this new implementation, the code throws an exception if Last-Name is assigned an invalid value, either from another member of the same class or via a direct assignment to LastName from inside Program.Main(). The ability to intercept an assignment and validate the parameters by providing a field-like API is one of the advantages of properties.

It is a good practice to only access a property-backing field from inside the property implementation. In other words, always use the property, rather than calling the field directly. In many cases, this is true even from code within the same class as the property. If following this practice, when code such as validation code is added, the entire class immediately takes advantage of it. (As described later in the chapter, one exception to this occurs when the field is marked as read-only because then the value cannot be set once class instantiation completes, even in a property setter.)

Although rare, it is possible to assign a value inside the setter, as Listing 5.19 does. In this case, the call to value.Trim() removes any whitespace surrounding the new last name value.

---

4. Apologies to Teller, Cher, Sting, Madonna, Bono, Prince, and Liberace, and so on.

Read-Only and Write-Only Properties

By removing either the getter or the setter portion of a property, you can change a property's accessibility. Properties with only a setter are write-only, which is a relatively rare occurrence. Similarly, providing only a getter will cause the property to be read-only; any attempts to assign a value will cause a compile error. To make Id read-only, for example, you would code it as shown in Listing 5.20.

LISTING 5.20: Defining a Read-Only Property

```csharp
class Program
{
  static void Main()
  {
      Employee employee1 = new Employee();
      employee1.Initialize(42);

      // ERROR:  Property or indexer 'Employee.Id'
      // cannot be assigned to -- it is read-only
      employee1.Id = "490";
  }
}

class Employee
{
  public void Initialize(int id)
  {
      // Use field because Id property has no setter,
      // it is read-only.
      _Id = id.ToString();
  }

  // ...
  // Id property declaration
  public string Id
  {
      get
      {
          return _Id;
      }
      // No setter provided.
  }
  private string _Id;

}
```

Listing 5.20 assigns the field from within the `Employee` constructor rather than the property (`_Id = id`). Assigning via the property causes a compile error, as it does in `Program.Main()`.

Access Modifiers on Getters and Setters

As previously mentioned, it is a good practice not to access fields from outside their properties because doing so circumvents any validation or additional logic that may be inserted. Unfortunately, C# 1.0 did not allow different levels of encapsulation between the getter and setter portions of a property. It was not possible, therefore, to create a public getter and a private setter so that external classes would have read-only access to the property while code within the class could write to the property.

In C# 2.0, support was added for placing an access modifier on either the get or the set portion of the property implementation (not on both), thereby overriding the access modifier specified on the property declaration. Listing 5.21 demonstrates how to do this.

LISTING 5.21: Placing Access Modifiers on the Setter

```
class Program
{
  static void Main()
  {
      Employee employee1 = new Employee();
      employee1.Initialize(42);
      // ERROR: The property or indexer 'Employee.Id'
      // cannot be used in this context because the set
      // accessor is inaccessible
      employee1.Id = "490";
  }
}


class Employee
{
  public void Initialize(int id)
  {
      // Set Id property
      Id = id.ToString();
  }

  // ...
```

```
// Id property declaration
public string Id
{
    get
    {
        return _Id;
    }
    // Providing an access modifier is in C# 2.0
    // and higher only
    private set
    {
        _Id = value;
    }
}
private string _Id;

}
```

By using `private` on the setter, the property appears as read-only to classes other than `Employee`. From within `Employee`, the property appears as read/write, so you can assign the property within the constructor. When specifying an access modifier on the getter or setter, take care that the access modifier is more restrictive than the access modifier on the property as a whole. It is a compile error, for example, to declare the property as `private` and the setter as `public`.

Properties as Virtual Fields

As you have seen, properties behave like virtual fields. In some instances, you do not need a backing field at all. Instead, the property getter returns a calculated value while the setter parses the value and persists it to some other member fields (if it even exists). Consider, for example, the `Name` property implementation shown in Listing 5.22. Output 5.7 shows the results.

LISTING 5.22: Defining Properties

```
class Program
{
    static void Main()
    {
        Employee employee1 = new Employee();

        employee1.Name = "Inigo Montoya";
        System.Console.WriteLine(employee1.Name);
```

```
            // ...
        }
    }
```

```
    class Employee
    {
      // ...

      // FirstName property
      public string FirstName
      {
          get
          {
              return _FirstName;
          }
          set
          {
              _FirstName = value;
          }
      }
      private string _FirstName;

      // LastName property
      public string LastName
      {
          get
          {
              return _LastName;
          }
          set
          {
              _LastName = value;
          }
      }
      private string _LastName;
      // ...

      // Name property
      public string Name
      {
          get
          {
              return FirstName + " " + LastName;
          }
          set
          {
              // Split the assigned value into
```

```
        // first and last names.
        string[] names;
        names = value.Split(new char[]{' '});
        if(names.Length == 2)
        {
            FirstName = names[0];
            LastName = names[1];
        }
        else
        {
            // Throw an exception if the full
            // name was not assigned.
            throw new System. ArgumentException (
                string.Format(
                "Assigned value '{0}' is invalid", value));
        }
    }
}

    // ...
}
```

OUTPUT 5.7:

```
Inigo Montoya
```

The getter for the Name property concatenates the values returned from the FirstName and LastName properties. In fact, the name value assigned is not actually stored. When the Name property is assigned, the value on the right side is parsed into its first and last name parts.

Properties and Method Calls Not Allowed as ref or out Parameter Values

C# allows properties to be used identically to fields, except when they are passed as ref or out parameter values. ref and out parameter values are internally implemented by passing the memory address to the target method. However, because properties can be virtual fields that have no backing field, or can be read/write-only, it is not possible to pass the address for the underlying storage. As a result, you cannot pass properties as ref or out parameter values. The same is true for method calls. Instead, when code needs to pass a property or method call as a ref or out parameter value, the code must first copy the value into a variable and then pass the variable. Once the method call has completed, the code must assign the variable back into the property.

■ ADVANCED TOPIC

Property Internals
Listing 5.23 shows that getters and setters are exposed as get_FirstName() and set_FirstName() in the CIL.

LISTING 5.23: CIL Code Resulting from Properties

```
.method public hidebysig specialname instance string
       get_FirstName() cil managed
{
  // Code size       12 (0xc)
  .maxstack  1
  .locals init ([0] string CS$1$0000)
  IL_0000:  nop
  IL_0001:  ldarg.0
  IL_0002:  ldfld       string Program::_FirstName
  IL_0007:  stloc.0
  IL_0008:  br.s        IL_000a
  IL_000a:  ldloc.0
  IL_000b:  ret
} // end of method Program::get_FirstName

.method public hidebysig specialname instance void
       set_FirstName(string 'value') cil managed
{
  // Code size       9 (0x9)
  .maxstack  8
  IL_0000:  nop
  IL_0001:  ldarg.0
  IL_0002:  ldarg.1
  IL_0003:  stfld       string Program::_FirstName
  IL_0008:  ret
} // end of method Program::set_FirstName
```

Just as important to their appearance as regular methods is the fact that properties are an explicit construct within the CIL, too. As Listing 5.24

shows, the getters and setters are called by CIL properties, which are an explicit construct within the CIL code. Because of this, languages and compilers are not restricted to always interpreting properties based on a naming convention. Instead, CIL properties provide a means for compilers and code editors to provide special syntax.

LISTING 5.24: Properties Are an Explicit Construct in CIL

```
.property instance string FirstName()
{
  .get instance string Program::get_FirstName()
  .set instance void Program::set_FirstName(string)
} // end of property Program::FirstName
```

Notice in Listing 5.23 that the getters and setters that are part of the property include the `specialname` metadata. This modifier is what IDEs, such as Visual Studio, use as a flag to hide the members from IntelliSense.

An automatically implemented property is virtually identical to one for which you define the backing field explicitly. In place of the manually defined backing field the C# compiler generates a field with the name `<PropertyName>k_BackingField` in IL. This generated field includes an attribute (see Chapter 17) called `System.Runtime.CompilerServices.CompilerGeneratedAttribute`. Both the getters and the setters are decorated with the same attribute because they too are generated—with the same implementation as in Listings 5.23 and 5.24.

Constructors

Now that you have added fields to a class and can store data, you need to consider the validity of that data. As you saw in Listing 5.3, it is possible to instantiate an object using the `new` operator. The result, however, is the ability to create an employee with invalid data. Immediately following the assignment of `employee`, you have an `Employee` object whose name and salary are not initialized. In this particular listing, you assigned the uninitialized fields immediately following the instantiation of an employee, but if you failed to do the initialization, you would not receive a warning from the compiler. As a result, you could end up with an `Employee` object with an invalid name.

Declaring a Constructor

To correct this, you need to provide a means of specifying the required data when the object is created. You do this using a constructor, demonstrated in Listing 5.25.

LISTING 5.25: Defining a Constructor

```csharp
class Employee
{
  // Employee constructor
  public Employee(string firstName, string lastName)
  {
    FirstName = firstName;
    LastName = lastName;
  }

  public string FirstName{ get; set; }
  public string LastName{ get; set; }
  public string Salary{ get; set; }

  // ...
}
```

To define a constructor you create a method with no return type, whose method name is identical to the class name.

The constructor is the method that the code calls to create an instance of the object. In this case, the constructor takes the first name and the last name as parameters, allowing the programmer to specify these names when instantiating the Employee object. Listing 5.26 is an example of how to call a constructor.

LISTING 5.26: Calling a Constructor

```csharp
class Program
{
  static void Main()
  {
    Employee employee;
    employee = new Employee("Inigo", "Montoya");
    employee.Salary = "Too Little";

    System.Console.WriteLine(
        "{0} {1}: {2}",
        employee.FirstName,
        employee.LastName,
```

```
              employee.Salary);
    }
    // ...
}
```

Notice that the new operator returns the type of the object being instantiated (even though no return type or return statement was specified explicitly in the constructor's declaration or implementation). In addition, you have removed the initialization code for the first and last names because that occurs within the constructor. In this example, you don't initialize Salary within the constructor, so the code assigning the salary still appears.

Developers should take care when using both assignment at declaration time and assignment within constructors. Assignments within the constructor will occur after any assignments are made when a field is declared (such as string Salary = "Not enough" in Listing 5.5). Therefore, assignment within a constructor will override any value assigned at declaration time. This subtlety can lead to a misinterpretation of the code by a casual reader whereby he assumes the value after instantiation is assigned at declaration time. Therefore, it is worth considering a coding style that does not mix both declaration assignment and constructor assignment within the same class.

■ ADVANCED TOPIC

Implementation Details of the new Operator

Internally, the interaction between the new operator and the constructor is as follows. The new operator retrieves memory from the memory manager and then calls the specified constructor, passing the initialized memory to the constructor. Next, the remainder of the constructor chain executes, passing around the initialized memory between constructors. None of the constructors have a return type (behaviorally they all return void). When execution completes on the constructor chain, the new operator returns the memory reference, now referring to the memory in its initialized form.

Default Constructors

It is important to note that by adding a constructor explicitly, you can no longer instantiate an `Employee` from within `Main()` without specifying the first and last names. The code shown in Listing 5.27, therefore, will not compile.

LISTING 5.27: Default Constructor No Longer Available

```csharp
class Program
{
  static void Main()
  {
      Employee employee;
      // ERROR:     No overload for method 'Employee'
      // takes '0' arguments.
      employee = new Employee();

      // ...
  }
}
```

If a class has no explicitly defined constructor, then the C# compiler adds one during compilation. This constructor takes no parameters and is, therefore, the **default constructor** by definition. As soon as you add an explicit constructor to a class, the C# compiler no longer provides a default constructor. Therefore, with `Employee(string firstName, string last-Name)` defined, the default constructor, `Employee()`, is not added by the compiler. You could manually add such a constructor, but then you would again be allowing construction of an `Employee` without specifying the employee name.

It is not necessary to rely on the default constructor defined by the compiler. It is also possible for programmers to define a default constructor explicitly, perhaps one that initializes some fields to particular values. Defining the default constructor simply involves declaring a constructor that takes no parameters.

Object Initializers

Starting with C# 3.0, the C# language team added functionality to initialize an object's accessible fields and properties using an **object initializer.** The object initializer consists of a set of member initializers enclosed in curly braces following the constructor call to create the object. Each member initializer is the assignment of an accessible field or property name with a value (see Listing 5.28).

LISTING 5.28: Calling an Object Initializer

```
class Program
{
  static void Main()
  {
      Employee employee1 = new Employee("Inigo", "Montoya")
          { Title = "Computer Nerd", Salary = "Not enough"};
      // ...
  }
}
```

Notice that the same constructor rules apply even when using an object initializer. In fact, the resultant CIL is exactly the same as it would be if the fields or properties were assigned within separate statements immediately following the constructor call. The order of member initializers in C# provides the sequence for property and field assignment in the statements following the constructor call within CIL.

■ ADVANCED TOPIC

Collection Initializers
Using a similar syntax to that of object initializers, collection initializers were added in C# 3.0. Collection initializers provide support for a similar feature set with collections. Specifically, a collection initializer allows the assignment of items within the collection at the time of the collection's instantiation. Borrowing on the same syntax used for arrays, the collection initializer initializes each item within the collection as part of collection creation. Initializing a list of Employees, for example, involves specifying each item within curly braces following the constructor call, as Listing 5.29 shows.

LISTING 5.29: Calling an Object Initializer

```
class Program
{
  static void Main()
  {
     List<Employee> employees = new List<Employee>()
       {
          new Employee("Inigo", "Montoya"),
          new Employee("Chuck", "McAtee")
       };
     // ...
  }
}
```

After the assignment of a new collection instance, the compiler-generated code instantiates each object in sequence and adds them to the collection via the Add() method.

■ ADVANCED TOPIC

Finalizers

Constructors define what happens during the instantiation process of a class. To define what happens when an object is destroyed, C# provides the finalizer construct. Unlike destructors in C++, finalizers do not run immediately after an object goes out of scope. Rather, the finalizer executes after an object is last active and before the program shuts down. Specifically, the garbage collector identifies objects with finalizers during a garbage collection cycle, and instead of immediately deallocating those objects, it adds them to a finalization queue. A separate thread runs through each object in the finalization queue and calls the object's finalizer before removing it from the queue and making it available for the garbage collector again. Chapter 9 discusses this process, along with resource cleanup, in depth.

Overloading Constructors

Constructors can be overloaded—you can have more than one constructor as long as the number or types of the parameters vary. For example, as

Listing 5.30 shows, you could provide a constructor that has an employee ID with first and last names, or even just the employee ID.

LISTING 5.30: Overloading a Constructor

```csharp
class Employee
{
  public Employee(string firstName, string lastName)
  {
      FirstName = firstName;
      LastName = lastName;
  }

    public Employee(
        int id, string firstName, string lastName )
    {
        Id = id;
        FirstName = firstName;
        LastName = lastName;
    }

    public Employee(int id)
    {
        Id = id;

        // Look up employee name...
        // ...
    }

    public int Id { get; set; }
    public string FirstName { get; set; }
    public string LastName { get; set; }
    public string Salary { get; set; }

    // ...
}
```

This enables Program.Main() to instantiate an employee from the first and last names either by passing in the employee ID only, or by passing both the names and the IDs. You would use the constructor with both the names and the IDs when creating a new employee in the system. You would use the constructor with only the ID to load up the employee from a file or a database.

Constructor Chaining: Calling another Constructor Using this

Notice in Listing 5.30 that the initialization code for the `Employee` object is now duplicated in multiple places and, therefore, has to be maintained in multiple places. The amount of code is small, but there are ways to eliminate the duplication by calling one constructor from another—**constructor chaining**—using **constructor initializers.** Constructor initializers determine which constructor to call before executing the implementation of the current constructor (see Listing 5.31).

LISTING 5.31: Calling One Constructor from Another

```csharp
class Employee
{
  public Employee(string firstName, string lastName)
  {
      FirstName = firstName;
      LastName = lastName;
  }

  public Employee(
      int id, string firstName, string lastName )
      : this(firstName, lastName)
  {
      Id = id;
  }

  public Employee(int id)
  {
      Id = id;

      // Look up employee name...
      // ...

      // NOTE:  Member constructors cannot be
      // called explicitly inline
      // this(id, firstName, LastName);
  }

  public int Id { get; set; }
  public string FirstName { get; set; }
  public string LastName { get; set; }
  public string Salary { get; set; }

  // ...
}
```

To call one constructor from another within the same class (for the same object instance) C# uses a colon followed by the this keyword followed by the parameter list on the callee constructor's declaration. In this case, the constructor that takes all three parameters calls the constructor that takes two. Often, the calling pattern is reversed; the constructor with the fewest parameters calls the constructor with the most parameters, passing defaults for the parameters that are not known.

■ BEGINNER TOPIC

Centralizing Initialization

Notice that in the Employee(int id) constructor implementation from Listing 5.31, you cannot call this(firstName, LastName) because no such parameters exist on this constructor. To enable such a pattern in which all initialization code happens through one method you must create a separate method, as shown in Listing 5.32.

LISTING 5.32: Providing an Initialization Method

```
class Employee
{
  public Employee(string firstName, string lastName)
  {
      int id;
      // Generate an employee ID...
      // ...
      Initialize(id, firstName, lastName);
  }

  public Employee(int id, string firstName, string lastName )
  {
      Initialize(id, firstName, lastName);
  }

  public Employee(int id)
  {
      string firstName;
      string lastName;
      Id = id;

      // Look up employee data
      // ...
```

```
            Initialize(id, firstName, lastName);
    }

    private void Initialize(
        int id, string firstName, string lastName)
    {

        Id = id;
        FirstName = firstName;
        LastName = lastName;
    }
    // ...
}
```

In this case, the method is called `Initialize()` and it takes both the names and the employee IDs. Note that you can continue to call one constructor from another, as shown in Listing 5.31.

■ ADVANCED TOPIC

Anonymous Types
C# 3.0 introduced support for anonymous types. These are data types that are generated by the compiler (on the fly) rather than through explicit class definitions. Listing 5.33 shows such a declaration.

LISTING 5.33: Implicit Local Variables with Anonymous Types

```
using System;

class Program
{
    static void Main()
    {
        var patent1 =
            new
            {
                Title = "Bifocals",
                YearOfPublication = "1784"
            };
        var patent2 =
            new
            {
                Title = "Phonograph",
                YearOfPublication = "1877"
            };
```

```
            var patent3 =
                new
                {
                    patent1.Title,
                    Year = patent1.YearOfPublication
                };

        System.Console.WriteLine("{0} ({1})",
            patent1.Title, patent1.YearOfPublication);
        System.Console.WriteLine("{0} ({1})",
            patent2.Title, patent1.YearOfPublication);

        Console.WriteLine();
        Console.WriteLine(patent1);
        Console.WriteLine(patent2);

        Console.WriteLine();
        Console.WriteLine(patent3);
    }
}
```

The corresponding output is shown in Output 5.8.

OUTPUT 5.8:

```
Bifocals (1784)
Phonograph (1877)

{ Title = Bifocals, YearOfPublication = 1784 }
{ Title = Phonograph, YearOfPublication = 1877 }

{ Title = Bifocals, Year = 1784 }
```

Listing 5.33 demonstrates the assignment of an anonymous type to an implicitly typed (var) local variable.

When the compiler encounters the anonymous type syntax, it generates a CIL class with properties corresponding to the named values and data types in the anonymous type declaration. Although there is no available name in C# for the generated type, it is still statically typed. For example, the properties of the type are fully accessible. In Listing 5.33, patent1. Title and patent2.YearOfPublication are called within the Console. WriteLine() statement. Any attempts to call nonexistent members will result in compile errors. Even IntelliSense in IDEs such as Visual Studio 2008 works with the anonymous type.

In Listing 5.33, member names on the anonymous types are explicitly identified using the assignment of the value to the name (see `Title` and `YearOfPublication` in `patent1` and `patent2` assignments). However, if the value assigned is a property or field, the name will default to the name of the field or property if not specified explicitly. `patent3`, for example, is defined using a property name "Title" rather than an assignment to an implicit name. As Output 5.8 shows, the resultant property name is determined by the compiler to match the property from where the value was retrieved.

Although the compiler allows anonymous type declarations such as the ones shown in Listing 5.33, you should generally avoid anonymous type declarations and even the associated implicit typing with `var` until you are working with lambda and query expressions that associate data from different types or you are horizontally projecting the data so that for a particular type, there is less data overall. Until frequent querying of data out of collections makes explicit type declaration burdensome, it is preferable to explicitly declare types as outlined in this chapter.

Static Members

The `HelloWorld` example in Chapter 1 first presented the keyword `static`; however, it did not define it fully. This section defines the `static` keyword fully.

To begin, consider an example. Assume that the employee `Id` value needs to be unique for each employee. One way to accomplish this is to store a counter to track each employee ID. If the value is stored as an instance field, however, every time you instantiate an object, a new `NextId` field will be created such that every instance of the `Employee` object would consume memory for that field. The biggest problem is that each time an `Employee` object instantiated, the `NextId` value on all of the previously instantiated `Employee` objects would need to be updated with the next ID value. What you need is a single field that all `Employee` object instances share.

Language Contrast: C++/Visual Basic—Global Variables and Functions

Unlike many of the languages that came before it, C# does not have global variables or global functions. All fields and methods in C# appear within the context of a class. The equivalent of a global field or function within the realm of C# is a static field or function. There is no functional difference between global variables/functions and C# static fields/methods, except that static fields/methods can include access modifiers, such as `private`, that can limit the access and provide better encapsulation.

Static Fields

To define data that is available across multiple instances, you use the static keyword, as demonstrated in Listing 5.34.

LISTING 5.34: Declaring a Static Field

```
class Employee
{
  public Employee(string firstName, string lastName)
  {
      FirstName = firstName;
      LastName = lastName;
      Id = NextId;
      NextId++;
  }

  // ...

  public static int NextId;
  public int Id { get; set; }
  public string FirstName { get; set; }
  public string LastName { get; set; }
  public string Salary { get; set; }

  // ...
}
```

In this example, the NextId field declaration includes the static modifier and therefore is called a **static field.** Unlike Id, a single storage location for NextId is shared across all instances of Employee. Inside the Employee constructor, you assign the new Employee object's Id the value of NextId immediately before incrementing it. When another `Employee` class is created, `NextId` will be incremented and the new `Employee` object's `Id` field will hold a different value.

Just as **instance fields** (nonstatic fields) can be initialized at declaration time, so can static fields, as demonstrated in Listing 5.35.

LISTING 5.35: Assigning a Static Field at Declaration

```
class Employee
{
  // ...
  public static int NextId = 42;
  // ...
}
```

Unlike with instance fields, if no initialization for a static field is provided, the static field will automatically be assigned its default value (0, `null`, `false`, and so on), and it will be possible to access the static field even if it has never been explicitly assigned.

Nonstatic fields, or instance fields, have a new value for each object to which they belong. In contrast, static fields don't belong to the instance, but rather to the class itself. As a result, you access a static field from outside a class via the class name. Consider the new `Program` class shown in Listing 5.36 (using the `Employee` class from Listing 5.34).

LISTING 5.36: Accessing a Static Field

```
using System;

class Program
{
  static void Main()
  {
    Employee.NextId = 1000000;

    Employee employee1 = new Employee(
        "Inigo", "Montoya");
    Employee employee2 = new Employee(
        "Princess", "Buttercup");

    Console.WriteLine(
        "{0} {1} ({2})",
        employee1.FirstName,
        employee1.LastName,
        employee1.Id);
```

```
        Console.WriteLine(
            "{0} {1} ({2})",
            employee2.FirstName,
            employee2.LastName,
            employee2.Id);

        Console.WriteLine("NextId = {0}", Employee.NextId);
    }

    // ...
}
```

Output 5.9 shows the results of Listing 5.36.

OUTPUT 5.9:

```
Inigo Montoya (1000000)
Princess Buttercup (1000001)
NextId = 1000002
```

To set and retrieve the initial value of the `NextId` static field, you use the class name, `Employee`, not a variable name. The only time you can eliminate the class name is from within code that appears within the class itself. In other words, the `Employee(...)` constructor did not need to use `Employee.NextId` because the code appeared within the context of the `Employee` class itself, and therefore, the context was already understood from the scope. In fact, the context is the scope.

Even though you refer to static fields slightly differently than instance fields, it is not possible to define a static and an instance field with the same name in the same class. The possibility of mistakenly referring to the wrong field is high, and therefore, the C# designers decided to prevent such code. Therefore, overlap in names will introduce conflict within the declaration space.

■ BEGINNER TOPIC

Data Can Be Associated with Both a Class and an Object

Both classes and objects can have associated data, just as can the molds and the widgets created from them.

For example, a mold could have data corresponding to the number of widgets it created, the serial number of the next widget, the current color of the plastic injected into the mold, and the number of widgets it produces per hour. Similarly, a widget has its own serial number, its own color, and perhaps the date and time when the widget was created. Although the color of the widget corresponds to the color of the plastic within the mold at the time the widget was created, it obviously does not contain data corresponding to the color of the plastic currently in the mold, or the serial number of the next widget to be produced.

In designing objects, programmers should take care to declare both fields and methods appropriately as static or instance-based. In general, you should declare methods that don't access any instance data as static methods, and methods that access instance data (where the instance is not passed in as a parameter) as instance methods. Static fields store data corresponding to the class, such as defaults for new instances or the number of instances that have been created. Instance fields store data associated with the object.

Static Methods

Just like static fields, you access static methods directly off the class name (`Console.ReadLine()`, for example). Furthermore, it is not necessary to have an instance in order to access the method.

Listing 5.37 provides another example of both declaring and calling a static method.

LISTING 5.37: Defining a Static Method on `DirectoryInfo`

```
public static class DirectoryInfoExtension
{
  public static void CopyTo(
      DirectoryInfo sourceDirectory, string target,
      SearchOption option, string searchPattern)
  {
      if (target[target.Length - 1] !=
          Path.DirectorySeparatorChar)
      {
          target += Path.DirectorySeparatorChar;
      }
      if (!Directory.Exists(target))
      {
```

```
            Directory.CreateDirectory(target);
    }

    for (int i = 0; i < searchPattern.Length; i++)
    {
        foreach (string file in
            Directory.GetFiles(
                sourceDirectory.FullName, searchPattern))
        {
            File.Copy(file,
                target + Path.GetFileName(file), true);
        }
    }

    //Copy SubDirectories (recursively)
    if (option == SearchOption.AllDirectories)
    {
        foreach(string element in
            Directory.GetDirectories(
                sourceDirectory.FullName))
        {
            Copy(element,
                target + Path.GetFileName(element),
                searchPattern);
        }
    }
  }
}
```

```
    // ...
    DirectoryInfo directory = new DirectoryInfo(".\\Source");
    directory.MoveTo(".\\Root");
    DirectoryInfoExtension.CopyTo(
        directory, ".\\Target",
        SearchOption.AllDirectories, "*");
    // ...
```

The `DirectoryInfoExtension.Copy()` method takes a `DirectoryInfo` object and copies the underlying directory structure to a new location.

Because static methods are not referenced through a particular instance, the `this` keyword is invalid inside a static method. In addition, it is not possible to access either an instance field or an instance method directly from within a static method without a reference to the particular instance to which the field or method belongs. (Note that `Main()` is another example of a static method.)

One might have expected this method on the `System.IO.Directory` class or as an instance method on `System.IO.DirectoryInfo`. Since neither exists, Listing 5.37 defines such a method on an entirely new class. In the section Extension Methods, later in this chapter, we show how to make it appear as an instance method on `DirectoryInfo`.

Static Constructors

In addition to static fields and methods, C# also supports **static constructors.** Static constructors are provided as a means to initialize a class (not the class instance). Static constructors are not called explicitly; instead, the runtime calls static constructors automatically upon first access to the class, whether via calling a regular constructor or accessing a static method or field on the class. You use static constructors to initialize the static data within the class to a particular value, mainly when the initial value involves more complexity than a simple assignment at declaration time. Consider Listing 5.38.

LISTING 5.38: Declaring a Static Constructor

```csharp
class Employee
{
  static Employee()
  {
      Random randomGenerator = new Random();
      NextId = randomGenerator.Next(101, 999);
  }

  // ...
  public static int NextId = 42;
  // ...
}
```

Listing 5.38 assigns the initial value of `NextId` to be a random integer between 100 and 1,000. Because the initial value involves a method call, the `NextId` initialization code appears within a static constructor and not as part of the declaration.

If assignment of `NextId` occurs within both the static constructor and the declaration, it is not obvious what the value will be when initialization concludes. The C# compiler generates CIL in which the declaration assignment is moved to be the first statement within the static constructor.

Therefore, `NextId` will contain the value returned by `randomGenera-tor.Next(101, 999)` instead of a value assigned during `NextId`'s declaration. Assignments within the static constructor, therefore, will take precedence over assignments that occur as part of the field declaration, as was the case with instance fields. Note that there is no support for defining a static finalizer.

▪ ADVANCED TOPIC

Favor Static Initialization during Declaration

Static constructors execute before the first access to any member of a class, whether it is a static field, another static member, or the constructor. In order to support this, the compiler injects a check into all type static members and constructors to ensure that the static constructor runs first.

Without the static constructor, the compiler instead initializes all static members to their default value and avoids adding the static constructor check. The result is for static assignment initialization to be called before accessing any static fields but not necessarily before all static methods or any instance constructor is invoked. This might provide a performance improvement if initialization of static members is expensive and not needed before accessing a static field.

Static Properties

You also can declare properties as static. For example, Listing 5.39 wraps the data for the next ID into a property.

LISTING 5.39: Declaring a Static Property

```csharp
class Employee
{
  // ...
  public static int NextId
  {
      get
      {
          return _NextId;
      }
      private set
      {
          _NextId = value;
```

```
        }
    }
    public static int _NextId = 42;
    // ...
}
```

It is almost always better to use a static property rather than a public static field because public static fields are callable from anywhere whereas a static property offers at least some level of encapsulation.

Static Classes

Some classes do not contain any instance fields. Consider, for example, a Math class that has functions corresponding to the mathematical operations Max() and Min(), as shown in Listing 5.40.

LISTING 5.40: Declaring a Static Class

```
// Static class introduced in C# 2.0
public static class SimpleMath
{
    // params allows the number of parameters to vary.
    static int Max(params int[] numbers)
    {
        // Check that there is a least one item in numbers.
        if(numbers.Length == 0)
        {
            throw new ArgumentException(
                "numbers cannot be empty");
        }

        int result;
        result = numbers[0];
        foreach (int number in numbers)
        {
            if(number > result)
            {
                result = number;
            }
        }
        return result;
    }

    // params allows the number of parameters to vary.
    static int Min(params int[] numbers)
    {
        // Check that there is a least one item in numbers.
        if(numbers.Length == 0)
```

```
    {
        throw new ArgumentException(
            "numbers cannot be empty");
    }

    int result;
    result = numbers[0];
    foreach (int number in numbers)
    {
        if(number < result)
        {
            result = number;
        }
    }
    return result;
}
}
```

This class does not have any instance fields (or methods), and therefore, creation of such a class would be pointless. Because of this, the class is decorated with the static keyword. The static keyword on a class provides two facilities. First, it prevents a programmer from writing code that instantiates the SimpleMath class. Second, it prevents the declaration of any instance fields or methods within the class. Since the class cannot be instantiated, instance members would be pointless.

One more distinguishing characteristic of the static class is that the C# compiler automatically marks it as abstract and sealed within the CIL. This designates the class as **inextensible;** in other words, no class can be derived from it or instantiate it.

Extension Methods

Consider the System.IO.DirectoryInfo class which is used to manipulate filesystem directories. The class supports functionality to list the files and subdirectories (DirectoryInfo.GetFiles()) as well as the capability to move the directory (DirectoryInfo.Move()). One feature it doesn't support directly is copy. If you needed such a method you would have to implement it, as shown earlier in Listing 5.37.

The DirectoryInfoExtension.Copy() method is a standard static method declaration. However, notice that calling this Copy() method is different from calling the DirectoryInfo.Move() method. This is unfortunate. Ideally, we want to add a method to DirectoryInfo so that, given an instance, we could call Copy() as an instance method—directory.Copy().

C# 3.0 simulates the creation of an instance method on a different class via **extension methods.** To do this we simply change the signature of our static method so that the first parameter, the data type we are extending, is prefixed with the this keyword (see Listing 5.41).

LISTING 5.41: Static Copy Method for DirectoryInfo

```csharp
public static class DirectoryInfoExtension
{
  public static void CopyTo(
      this DirectoryInfo sourceDirectory, string target,
    SearchOption option, string searchPattern)
  {
      // ...
  }
}
```

```csharp
// ...
    DirectoryInfo directory = new DirectoryInfo(".\\Source");
    directory.CopyTo(".\\Target",
        SearchOption.AllDirectories, "*");
    // ...
```

Via this simple addition to C# 3.0, it is now possible to add "instance methods" to any class, even classes that are not within the same assembly. The resultant CIL code, however, is identical to what the compiler creates when calling the extension method as a normal static method.

Extension method requirements are as follows.

- The first parameter corresponds to the type on which the method extends or operates.
- To designate the extension method, prefix the extended type with the this modifier.
- To access the method as an extension method, import the extending type's namespace via a using directive (or place the extending class in the same namespace as the calling code).

If the extension method signature matches a signature on the extended type already (that is, if CopyTo() already existed on DirectoryInfo), the extension method will never be called except as a normal static method.

Note that specializing a type via inheritance (which I will cover in Chapter 6) is preferable to using an extension method. Extension methods do not provide a clean versioning mechanism since the addition of a matching signature to the extended type will take precedence over the extension method without warning of the change. The subtlety of this is more pronounced for extended classes whose source code you don't control. Another minor point is that, although development IDEs support IntelliSense for extension methods, it is not obvious that a method is an extension method by simply reading through the calling code. In general, use extension methods sparingly.

Encapsulating the Data

In addition to properties and the access modifiers we looked at earlier in the chapter, there are several other specialized ways of encapsulating the data within a class. For instance, there are two more field modifiers. The first is the const modifier, which you already encountered when declaring local variables. The second is the capability of fields to be defined as read-only.

const

Just as with const values, a const field contains a compile-time-determined value that cannot be changed at runtime. Values such as pi make good candidates for constant field declarations. Listing 5.42 shows an example of declaring a const field.

LISTING 5.42: Declaring a Constant Field

```
class ConvertUnits
{
   public const float CentimetersPerInch = 2.54F;
   public const int CupsPerGallon = 16;
   // ...
}
```

Constant fields are static automatically, since no new field instance is required for each object instance. Declaring a constant field as static explicitly will cause a compile error.

It is important that the types of values used in public constant expressions are permanent in time. Values such as pi, Avogadro's number, and the circumference of the Earth are good examples. However, values that could potentially change over time are not. Build numbers, population counts, and exchange rates would be poor choices for constants.

■ ADVANCED TOPIC

Public Constants Should Be Permanent Values

public constants should be permanent because changing their value will not necessarily take effect in the assemblies that use it. If an assembly references constants from a different assembly, the value of the constant is compiled directly into the referencing assembly. Therefore, if the value in the referenced assembly is changed but the referencing assembly is not recompiled, then the referencing assembly will still use the original value, not the new value. Values that could potentially change in the future should be specified as readonly instead.

readonly

Unlike const, the readonly modifier is available only for fields (not for local variables) and it declares that the field value is modifiable only from inside the constructor or directly during declaration. Listing 5.43 demonstrates how to declare a readonly field.

LISTING 5.43: Declaring a Field As readonly

```csharp
class Employee
{
  public Employee(int id)
  {
      Id = id;
  }

  // ...
  public readonly int Id;
  public void SetId(int newId)
  {
      // ERROR:  read-only fields cannot be set
      //          outside the constructor.
      // Id = newId;
  }

  // ...
}
```

Unlike constant fields, readonly fields can vary from one instance to the next. In fact, a readonly field's value can change from its value during declaration to a new value within the constructor. Furthermore, readonly fields occur as either instance or static fields. Another key distinction is that you can assign the value of a readonly field at execution time rather than just at compile time.

Using readonly with an array does not freeze the contents of the array. It freezes the number of elements in the array because it is not possible to reassign the readonly field to a new instance. However, the elements of the array are still writeable.

Nested Classes

In addition to defining methods and fields within a class, it is also possible to define a class within a class. Such classes are **nested classes.** You use a nested class when the class makes little sense outside the context of its containing class.

Consider a class that handles the command-line options of a program. Such a class is generally unique to each program and there is no reason to make a CommandLine class accessible from outside the class that contains Main(). Listing 5.44 demonstrates such a nested class.

LISTING 5.44: Defining a Nested Class

```csharp
class Program
{
    // Define a nested class for processing the command line.
    private class CommandLine
    {
        public CommandLine(string[] arguments)
        {
            for(int argumentCounter=0;
                argumentCounter<arguments.Length;
                argumentCounter++)
            {
                switch (argumentCounter)
                {
                    case 0:
                        Action = arguments[0].ToLower();
                        break;
                    case 1:
                        Id = arguments[1];
                        break;
```

```
                    case 2:
                        FirstName = arguments[2];
                        break;
                    case 3:
                        LastName = arguments[3];
                        break;
                }
            }
        }
        public string Action;
        public string Id;
        public string FirstName;
        public string LastName;
    }

    static void Main(string[] args)
    {
        CommandLine commandLine = new CommandLine(args);

        switch (commandLine.Action)
        {
            case "new":
                // Create a new employee
                // ...
                break;
            case "update":
                // Update an existing employee's data
                // ...
                break;
            case "delete":
                // Remove an existing employee's file.
                // ...
                break;
            default:
                Console.WriteLine(
                    "Employee.exe " +
              "new|update|delete <id> [firstname] [lastname]");
                break;
        }
    }
}
```

The nested class in this example is Program.CommandLine. As with all class members, no containing class identifier is needed from inside the containing class, so you can simply refer to it as CommandLine.

One unique characteristic of nested classes is the ability to specify private as an access modifier for the class itself. Because the purpose of this class is to parse the command line and place each argument into a separate field, `Program.CommandLine` is relevant only to the `Program` class in this application. The use of the `private` access modifier defines the intended scope of the class and prevents access from outside the class. You can do this only if the class is nested.

The `this` member within a nested class refers to an instance of the nested class, not the containing class. One way for a nested class to access an instance of the containing class is if the containing class instance is explicitly passed, such as via a constructor or method parameter.

Another interesting characteristic of nested classes is that they can access any member on the containing class, including private members. The converse to accessing private members is not true, however. It is not possible for the containing class to access a private member on the nested class.

Nested classes are rare. Furthermore, treat `public` nested classes suspiciously; they indicate potentially poor code that is likely to be confusing and hard to discover.

Language Contrast: Java—Inner Classes

Java includes not only the concept of a nested class, but also the concept of an inner class. Inner classes correspond to objects that are associated with the containing class instance rather than just a syntactic relationship. In C#, you can achieve the same structure by including an instance field of a nested type within the outer class. A factory method or constructor can ensure a reference to the corresponding instance of the outer class is set within the inner class instance as well.

Partial Classes

Another language feature added in C# 2.0 is **partial classes.** Partial classes are portions of a class that the compiler can combine to form a complete class. Although you could define two or more partial classes within the same file, the general purpose of a partial class is to allow the splitting of a class definition across multiple files. Primarily this is useful for tools that are generating or modifying code. With partial classes, the tools can work on a file separate from the one the developer is manually coding.

Defining a Partial Class

C# 2.0 (and later) allows declaration of a partial class by prepending a contextual keyword, partial, immediately before class, as Listing 5.45 shows.

LISTING 5.45: Defining a Partial Class

```
// File: Program1.cs
partial class Program
{
}
```

```
// File: Program2.cs
partial class Program
{
}
```

In this case, each portion of Program is placed into a separate file, as identified by the comment. Besides their use with code generators, another common use of partial classes is to place any nested classes into their own files. This is in accordance with the coding convention that places each class definition within its own file. For example, Listing 5.46 places the Program.CommandLine class into a file separate from the core Program members.

LISTING 5.46: Defining a Nested Class in a Separate Partial Class

```
// File: Program.cs
partial class Program
{
  static void Main(string[] args)
  {
    CommandLine commandLine = new CommandLine(args);

    switch (commandLine.Action)
    {
      // ...
    }
  }
}
```

```
// File: Program+CommandLine.cs
partial class Program
```

```
{
  // Define a nested class for processing the command line.
  private class CommandLine
  {
    // ...
  }
}
```

Partial classes do not allow extending compiled classes, or classes in other assemblies. They are only a means of splitting a class implementation across multiple files within the same assembly.

Partial Methods

Beginning with C# 3.0, the language designers added the concept of partial methods, extending the partial class concept of C# 2.0. Partial methods are allowed only within partial classes, and like partial classes, the primary purpose is to accommodate code generation.

Consider a code generation tool that generates the `Person.Designer.cs` file for the `Person` class based on a `Person` table within a database. The tool will examine the table and create properties for each column in the table. The problem, however, is that frequently the tool cannot generate any validation logic that may be required because this logic is based on business rules that are not embedded into the database table definition. Instead, the developer of the `Person` class needs to add the validation logic. It is undesirable to modify `Person.Designer.cs` directly because if the file is regenerated (to accommodate an additional column in the database, for example), the changes would be lost. Instead, the structure of the code for `Person` needs to be separated out so that the generated code appears in one file and the custom code (with business rules) is placed into a separate file unaffected by any regeneration. As we saw in the preceding section, partial classes are well suited for the task of splitting a file across multiple files. However, they are not sufficient. Frequently, we also need **partial methods.**

Partial methods allow for a declaration of a method without requiring an implementation. However, when the optional implementation is included, it can be located in one of the sister partial class definitions, likely in a separate file. Listing 5.47 shows the partial method declaration and the implementation for the `Person` class.

LISTING 5.47: Defining a Nested Class in a Separate Partial Class

```csharp
// File: Person.Designer.cs
public partial class Person
{
    #region Extensibility Method Definitions
    partial void OnLastNameChanging(string value);
    partial void OnFirstNameChanging(string value);
    #endregion

    // ...
    public System.Guid PersonId
    {
        // ...
    }
    private System.Guid _PersonId;

    // ...
    public string LastName
    {
        get
        {
            return _LastName;
        }
        set
        {
            if ((_LastName != value))
            {
                OnLastNameChanging(value);
                _LastName = value;
            }
        }
    }
    private string _LastName;

    // ...
    public string FirstName
    {
        get
        {
            return _FirstName;
        }
        set
        {
            if ((_FirstName != value))
            {
                OnFirstNameChanging(value);
                _FirstName = value;
            }
        }
    }
```

```
        }
        private string _FirstName;


    }


    // File: Person.cs
    partial class Person
    {
        partial void OnLastNameChanging(string value)
        {
            if (value == null)
            {
                throw new ArgumentNullException("LastName");
            }
            if(value.Trim().Length == 0)
            {
                throw new ArgumentException(
                    "LastName cannot be empty.");
            }
        }
    }
```

In the listing of Person.Designer.cs are declarations for the OnLastName-Changing() and OnFirstNameChanging() methods. Furthermore, the properties for the last and first names make calls to their corresponding changing methods. Even though the declarations of the changing methods contain no implementation, this code will successfully compile. The key is that the method declarations are prefixed with the contextual keyword partial in addition to the class that contains such methods.

In Listing 5.47, only the OnLastNameChanging() method is implemented. In this case, the implementation checks the suggested new Last-Name value and throws an exception if it is not valid. Notice that the signatures for OnLastNameChanging() between the two locations match.

It is important to note that a partial method must return void. If the method didn't return void and the implementation was not provided, what would the expected return be from a call to a nonimplemented method? To avoid any invalid assumptions about the return, the C# designers decided not to prohibit methods with returns other than void. Similarly, out parameters are not allowed on partial methods. If a return value is required, ref parameters may be used.

In summary, partial methods allow generated code to call methods that have not necessarily been implemented. Furthermore, if there is no implementation provided for a partial method, no trace of the partial method appears in the CIL. This helps keep code size small while keeping flexibility high.

SUMMARY

This chapter explained C# constructs for classes and object orientation in C#. This included a discussion of fields, and a discussion of how to access them on a class instance.

This chapter also discussed the key concept of whether to store data on a per-instance basis or across all instances of a type. Static data is associated with the class and instance data is stored on each object.

In addition, the chapter explored encapsulation in the context of access modifiers for methods and data. The C# construct of properties was introduced, and you saw how to use it to encapsulate private fields.

The next chapter focuses on how to associate classes with each other via inheritance, and the benefits derived from this object-oriented construct.

6

Inheritance

THE PRECEDING CHAPTER DISCUSSED how one class can reference other classes via fields and properties. This chapter discusses how to use the inheritance relationship between classes to build class hierarchies.

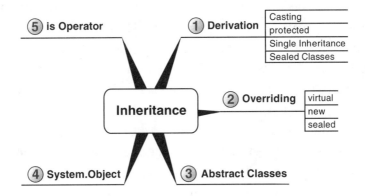

■ BEGINNER TOPIC

Inheritance Definitions

The preceding chapter provided an overview of inheritance. Here's a review of the defined terms.

- *Derive/inherit:* Specialize a base class to include additional members or customization of the base class members.

- *Derived/sub/child type:* The specialized type that inherits the members of the more general type.
- *Base/super/parent type:* The general type whose members a derived type inherits.

Inheritance forms an "is a" relationship. The derived type is always implicitly also of the base type. Just as a hard drive "is a" storage device, any other type derived from the storage device type "is a" type of storage device.

Derivation

It is common to want to extend a given type to add features, such as behavior and data. The purpose of inheritance is to do exactly that. Given a Person class, you create an Employee class that additionally contains EmployeeId and Department properties. The reverse approach may also occur. Given, for example, a Contact class within a Personal Digital Assistant (PDA), you decide you also can add calendaring support. Toward this effort, you create an Appointment class. However, instead of redefining the methods and properties that are common to both classes, you **refactor** the Contact class. Specifically, you move the common methods and properties on Contact into a base class called PdaItem from which both Contact and Appointment derive, as shown in Figure 6.1.

The common items in this case are Created, LastUpdated, Name, Object-Key, and the like. Through derivation, the methods defined on the base class, PdaItem, are accessible from all subclasses of PdaItem.

When defining a derived class, follow the class identifier with a colon and then the base class, as Listing 6.1 demonstrates.

LISTING 6.1: Deriving One Class from Another

```csharp
public class PdaItem
{
  public string Name { get; set; }

  public DateTime LastUpdated { get; set; }
}
```

```
// Define the Contact class as inheriting the PdaItem class
public class Contact : PdaItem
{
  public string Address { get; set; }
  public string Phone { get; set; }
}
```

Listing 6.2 shows how to access the properties defined in `Contact`.

LISTING 6.2: Using Inherited Methods

```
public class Program
{
  public static void Main()
  {
     Contact contact = new Contact();
     contact.Name = "Inigo Montoya";

     // ...
  }
}
```

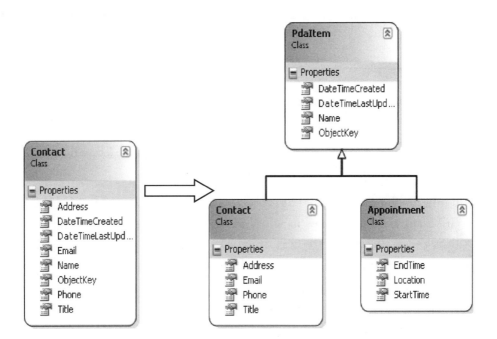

FIGURE 6.1: Refactoring into a Base Class

Even though `Contact` does not directly have a property called `Name`, all instances of `Contact` can still access the `Name` property from `PdaItem` and use it as though it was part of `Contact`. Furthermore, any additional classes that derive from `Contact` will also inherit the members of `PdaItem`, or any class from which `PdaItem` was derived. The inheritance chain has no practical limit and each derived class will have all the exposed members of its base class inheritance chain combined (see Listing 6.3).

LISTING 6.3: Classes Deriving from Each Other to Form an Inheritance Chain

```csharp
public class PdaItem : object
{
  // ...
}
```

```csharp
public class Appointment : PdaItem
{
  // ...
}
```

```csharp
public class Contact : PdaItem
{
  // ...
}
```

```csharp
public class Customer : Contact
{
  // ...
}
```

In other words, although `Customer` doesn't derive from `PdaItem` directly, it still inherits the members of `PdaItem`.

In Listing 6.3, `PdaItem` is shown explicitly to derive from `object`. Although C# allows such syntax, it is unnecessary because all classes that don't have some other derivation will derive from `object`, regardless of whether it is specified.

Casting between Base and Derived Types

As Listing 6.4 shows, because derivation forms an "is a" relationship, a derived type can always be directly assigned to a base type.

LISTING 6.4: Implicit Base Type Casting

```
public class Program
{
  pulic static void Main()
  {
      // Derived types can be implicitly converted to
      // base types
      Contact contact = new Contact();
      PdaItem item = contact;
      // ...

      // Base types must be cast explicitly to derived types
      contact = (Contact)item;
      // ...
  }
}
```

The derived type, Contact, is a PdaItem and can be assigned directly to a PdaItem. This is known as an **implicit conversion** because no specific operator is required and the conversion will, on principle, always succeed; it will not throw an exception.

The reverse, however, is not true. A PdaItem is not necessarily a Contact; it could be an Appointment or some other undefined, derived type. Therefore, casting from the base type to the derived type requires an explicit cast, which at runtime could fail. To perform an explicit cast, identify the target type within parentheses prior to the original reference, as Listing 6.4 demonstrates.

With the explicit cast, the programmer essentially communicates to the compiler to trust her, she knows what she is doing, and the C# compiler allows the conversion as long as the target type is derived from the originating type. Although the C# compiler allows an explicit conversion at compile time between potentially compatible types, the CLR will still verify the explicit cast at execution time, throwing an exception if in fact the object instance is not of the targeted type.

The C# compiler allows the cast operator even when the type hierarchy allows an implicit cast. For example, the assignment from contact to item could use a cast operator as follows:

```
item = (PdaItem)contact;
```

or even when no cast is necessary:

```
contact = (Contact)contact;
```

■ BEGINNER TOPIC

Casting within the Inheritance Chain

An implicit conversion to a base class does not instantiate a new instance. Instead, the same instance is simply referred to as the base type and the capabilities (the accessible members) are those of the base type. It is just like referring to a CD-ROM drive (CDROM) as a storage device. Since not all storage devices support an eject operation, a CDROM that is viewed as a storage device cannot be ejected either, and a call to storageDevice.Eject() would not compile even though the instantiated object may have been a CDROM object that supported the Eject() method.

Similarly, casting down from the base class to the derived class simply begins referring to the type more specifically, expanding the available operations. The restriction is that the actual instantiated type must be an instance of the targeted type (or something derived from it).

■ ADVANCED TOPIC

Defining Custom Conversions

Conversion between types is not limited to types within a single inheritance chain. It is possible to convert between entirely unrelated types as well. The key is the provision of a conversion operator between the two types. C# allows types to include either explicit or implicit conversion operators. Anytime the operation could possibly fail, such as in a cast from long to int, developers should choose to define an explicit conversion operator. This warns developers performing the conversion to do so only when they are certain the conversion will succeed, or else to be prepared to catch the exception if it doesn't. They should also use explicit conversions over an implicit conversion when the conversion is lossy. Converting from a float to an int, for example, truncates the decimal, which a return cast (from int back to float) would not recover.

Listing 6.5 shows implicit and explicit conversion operators for Address to string and vice versa.

LISTING 6.5: Defining Cast Operators

```
class GPSCoordinates
{
  // ...

  public static implicit operator UTMCoordinates(
      GPSCoordinates coordinates)
  {
      // ...
  }
}
```

In this case, you have an implicit conversion from GPSCoordinates to UTMCoordinates. A similar conversion could be written to reverse the process. Note that an explicit conversion could also be written by replacing implicit with explicit.

private **Access Modifier**

All public members of a base class are available to the derived class. However, private members are not. For example, in Listing 6.6, the private field, _Name, is not available on Contact.

LISTING 6.6: Private Members Are Not Inherited

```
public class PdaItem
{
  private string _Name;
  // ...
}
```

```
public class Contact : PdaItem
{
  // ...
}
```

```
public class Program
{
  public static void Main()
  {
      Contact contact = new Contact();

      // ERROR: 'PdaItem._Name' is inaccessible
      // due to its protection level
      contact._Name = "Inigo Montoya";
  }
}
```

As part of keeping with the principle of encapsulation, derived classes cannot access members declared as private.[1] This forces the base class developer to make an explicit choice as to whether a derived class gains access to a member. In this case, the base class is defining an API in which _Name can be changed only via the Name property. That way, if validation is added, the derived class will gain the validation benefit automatically because it was unable to access _Name directly from the start.

protected Access Modifier

Encapsulation is finer-grained than just public or private, however. It is possible to define members in base classes that only derived classes can access. Consider the ObjectKey property shown in Listing 6.7, for example.

LISTING 6.7: **protected** Members Are Accessible Only from Derived Classes

```csharp
public class Program
{
  public static void Main()
  {
     Contact contact = new Contact();
     contact.Name = "Inigo Montoya";

     // ERROR:  'PdaItem.ObjectKey' is inaccessible
     // due to its protection level
     contact.ObjectKey = Guid.NewGuid();
  }
}


public class PdaItem
{
  protected Guid ObjectKey
  {
     get { return _ObjectKey; }
     set { _ObjectKey = value; }
  }
  private Guid _ObjectKey;

  // ...
}
```

---

1. Except for the corner case when the derived class is also a nested class of the base class.

```csharp
public class Contact : PdaItem
{
  void Save()
  {
      // Instantiate a FileStream using <ObjectKey>.dat
      // for the filename.
      FileStream stream = System.IO.File.OpenWrite(
          ObjectKey + ".dat");

      void Load(PdaItem pdaItem)
      {
          // ERROR:  'pdaItem.ObjectKey' is inaccessible
          // due to its protection level
          pdaItem.ObjectKey = ...;

          Contact contact = pdaItem as Contact;
          if(contact != null)
          {
              contact.ObjectKey = ...;
          }
      }
      // ...
  }
}
```

ObjectKey is defined using the protected access modifier. The result is
that it is accessible outside of PdaItem only from classes that derive from
PdaItem. Contact derives from PdaItem and, therefore, all members of
Contact have access to ObjectKey. Since Program does not derive from
PdaItem, using the ObjectKey property within Program results in a compile
error.

A subtlety shown in the Contact.Load() method is worth noting.
Developers are often surprised that from code within Contact it is not possible to access the protected ObjectKey of an explicit PdaItem, even though
Contact derives from PdaItem. The reason is that a PdaItem could potentially be an Address, and Contact should not be able to access protected
members of Address. Therefore, encapsulation prevents Contact from
potentially modifying the ObjectKey of an Address. A successful cast to
Contact will bypass the restriction as shown. The governing rule is that
accessing a protected member from a derived class requires compile-time

determination that the protected member is an instance of the derived class (or one of its subclasses).

Extension Methods

One of the features included with extension methods is the fact that they too are inherited. If we extend a base class such as PdaItem, all the extension methods will also be available in the derived classes. However, as with all extension methods, priority is given to instance methods. If a compatible signature appears anywhere within the inheritance chain, this will take precedence over an extension method.

Requiring extension methods on base types is rare. As with extension methods in general, if the base type's code is available, it is preferable to modify the base type directly. Even in cases where the base type's code is unavailable, programmers should consider whether to add extension methods to an interface that the base type or individual derived types implement. I cover interfaces and using them with extension methods in the next chapter.

Single Inheritance

In theory, you can place an unlimited number of classes in an inheritance tree. For example, Customer derives from Contact, which derives from PdaItem, which derives from object. However, C# is a **single-inheritance** programming language (as is the CIL language to which C# compiles). This means that a class cannot derive from two classes directly. It is not possible, for example, to have Contact derive from both PdaItem and Person.

Language Contrast: C++—Multiple Inheritance

C#'s single inheritance is one of its major differences from C++. It makes for a significant migration path from programming libraries such as Active Template Library (ATL), whose entire approach relies on multiple inheritance.

For the rare cases that require a multiple-inheritance class structure, one solution is to use **aggregation;** instead of inheriting the second class, the class contains an instance of the class. Figure 6.2 shows an example of this class structure. Aggregation occurs when the association relationship defines a core part of the containing object. For multiple inheritance, this involves picking one class as the primary base class (PdaItem) and deriving a new class (Contact) from that. The second desired base class (Person) is added as a field in the derived class (Contact). Next, all the nonprivate members on the field (Person) are redefined on the derived class (Contact) which then delegates the calls out to the field (Person). Some code duplication occurs because methods are redeclared; however, this is minimal, since the real method body is implemented only within the aggregated class (Person).

In Figure 6.2, Contact contains a private property called InternalPerson that is drawn as an association to the Person class. Contact also contains the FirstName and LastName properties but with no corresponding fields. Instead, the FirstName and LastName properties simply delegate their calls out to InternalPerson.FirstName and InternalPerson.LastName, respectively. Listing 6.8 shows the resultant code.

LISTING 6.8: Working around Single Inheritance Using Aggregation

```
public class PdaItem
{
  // ...
}

public class Person
{
  // ...
}

public class Contact : PdaItem
{
   private Person InternalPerson { get; set; }

   public string FirstName
   {
       get { return InternalPerson.FirstName; }
       set { InternalPerson.FirstName = value; }
   }
```

```csharp
public string LastName
{
    get { return InternalPerson.LastName; }
    set { InternalPerson.LastName = value; }
}

// ...
}
```

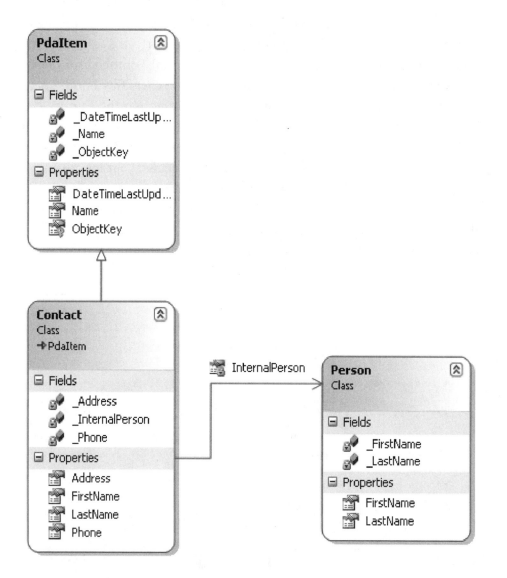

FIGURE 6.2: Working around Multiple Inheritance Using Aggregation

Besides the added complexity of delegation, another drawback is that any methods added to the field class (`Person`) will require manual addition to the derived class (`Contact`); otherwise, `Contact` will not expose the added functionality.

Sealed Classes

To design a class correctly that others can extend via derivation can be a tricky task which requires testing with examples to verify that the derivation will work successfully. To avoid unexpected derivation scenarios and problems you can mark classes as **sealed** (see Listing 6.9).

LISTING 6.9: Preventing Derivation with Sealed Classes

```
public sealed class CommandLineParser
{
  // ...
}
```

```
// ERROR:  Sealed classes cannot be derived from
public sealed class DerivedCommandLineParser :
  CommandLineParser
{
  // ...
}
```

Sealed classes include the `sealed` modifier, and the result is that they cannot be derived from. The `string` type is an example of a type that uses the `sealed` modifier to prevent derivation.

Overriding the Base Class

All `public` and `protected` members of a base class are inherited in the derived class. However, sometimes the base class does not have the optimal implementation of a particular member. Consider the `Name` property on `PdaItem`, for example. The implementation is probably acceptable when inherited by the `Appointment` class. For the `Contact` class, however, the `Name` property should return the `FirstName` and `LastName` properties combined. Similarly, when `Name` is assigned, it should be split across `FirstName` and `LastName`. In other words, the base class property declaration is appropriate for the derived class, but the implementation is not always valid. There needs to be a mechanism for **overriding** the base class implementation with a custom implementation in the derived class.

`virtual` Modifier

C# supports overriding on instance methods and properties but not on fields or any static members. It requires an explicit action within both the base class and the derived class. The base class must mark each member for which it allows overriding as `virtual`. If `public` or `protected` members do not include the `virtual` modifier, then subclasses will not be able to override those members.

Language Contrast: Java—Virtual Methods by Default

By default, methods in Java are virtual, and they must be explicitly sealed if nonvirtual behavior is preferred. In contrast, C# defaults to nonvirtual.

Listing 6.10 shows an example of property overriding.

LISTING 6.10: Overriding a Property

```csharp
public class PdaItem
{
    public virtual string Name { get; set; }
    // ...
}

public class Contact : PdaItem
{
    public override string Name
    {
        get
        {
            return FirstName + " " + LastName;
        }

        set
        {
            string[] names = value.Split(' ');
            // Error handling not shown.
            FirstName = names[0];
            LastName = names[1];
```

```
      }
  }

  public string FirstName { get; set; }
  public string LastName { get; set; }

  // ...
}
```

Not only does PdaItem include the virtual modifier on the Name property, but also, Contact's Name property is decorated with the keyword override. Eliminating virtual would result in an error and omitting override would cause a warning, as you will see shortly. C# requires the overriding methods to use the override keyword explicitly.

In other words, virtual identifies a method or property as available for replacement (overriding) in the derived type.

Language Contrast: Java and C++—Implicit Overriding

Unlike with Java and C++, the override keyword is required on the derived class. C# does not allow implicit overriding. In order to override a method, both the base class and the derived class members must match and have corresponding virtual and override keywords. Furthermore, if specifying the override keyword, the derived implementation is assumed to replace the base class implementation.

Overloading a member causes the runtime to call the most derived implementation (see Listing 6.11).

LISTING 6.11: Runtime Calling the Most Derived Implementation of a Virtual Method

```
public class Program
{
  public static void Main()
  {
      Contact contact;
      PdaItem item;

      contact = new Contact();
      item = contact;
```

```
    // Set the name via PdaItem variable
    item.Name = "Inigo Montoya";

    // Display that FirstName & LastName
    // properties were set.
    Console.WriteLine("{0} {1}",
        contact.FirstName, contact.LastName);
}
```

Output 6.1 shows the results of Listing 6.11.

OUTPUT 6.1:

```
Inigo Montoya
```

In Listing 6.11, item.Name is called, where item is declared as a PdaItem. However, the contact's FirstName and LastName are still set. The rule is that whenever the runtime encounters a virtual method, it calls the most derived and overriding implementation of the virtual member. In this case, the code instantiates a Contact and calls Contact.Name because Contact contains the most derived implementation of Name.

In creating a class, programmers should be careful when choosing to allow overriding a method, since they cannot control the derived implementation. Virtual methods should not include critical code because such methods may never be called if the derived class overrides them. Furthermore, converting a method from a virtual method to a nonvirtual method could break derived classes that override the method. This is a code-breaking change and you should avoid it, especially for assemblies intended for use by third parties.

Listing 6.12 includes a virtual Run() method. If the Controller programmer calls Run() with the expectation that the critical Start() and Stop() methods will be called, he will run into a problem.

LISTING 6.12: Carelessly Relying on a Virtual Method Implementation

```
public class Controller
{
  public void Start()
  {
      // Critical code
```

```
    }
    public virtual void Run()
    {
        Start();
        Stop();
    }
    public void Stop()
    {
        // Critical code
    }
}
```

In overriding Run(), a developer could perhaps not call the critical Start() and Stop() methods. To force the Start()/Stop() expectation, the Controller programmer should define the class, as shown in Listing 6.13.

LISTING 6.13: Forcing the Desirable Run() Semantics

```
public class Controller
{
    public void Start()
    {
        // Critical code
    }

    private void Run()
    {
        Start();
        InternalRun();
        Stop();
    }

    protected virtual void InternalRun()
    {
        // Default implementation
    }

    public void Stop()
    {
        // Critical code
    }
}
```

With this new listing, the Controller programmer prevents users from mistakenly calling InternalRun(), because it is protected. On the other hand, declaring Run() as public ensures that Start() and Stop() are invoked appropriately. It is still possible for users to modify the default implementation of how the Controller executes by overriding the protected InternalRun() member from within the derived class.

Virtual methods provide default implementations only, implementations that derived classes could override entirely. However, because of the complexities of inheritance design, it is important to consider (and preferably to implement) a specific scenario that requires the virtual method definition.

Language Contrast: C++ — Dispatch Method Calls during Construction

In C++, methods called during construction will not dispatch the virtual method. Instead, during construction, the type is associated with the base type rather than the derived type, and virtual methods call the base implementation. In contrast, C# dispatches virtual method calls to the most derived type. This is consistent with the principle of calling the most derived virtual member, even if the derived constructor has not completely executed. Regardless, in C# the situation should be avoided.

Finally, only instance members can be virtual. The CLR uses the concrete type, specified at instantiation time, to determine where to dispatch a virtual method call, so static virtual methods are meaningless and the compiler prohibits them.

new **Modifier**

When an overriding method does not use override, the compiler issues a warning similar to that shown in Output 6.2 or Output 6.3.

OUTPUT 6.2:

```
warning CS0114: '<derived method name>' hides inherited member
'<base method name>'. To make the current member override that
implementation, add the override keyword. Otherwise add the new
keyword.
```

OUTPUT 6.3:

```
warning CS0108: The keyword new is required on '<derived property name>'
because it hides inherited member '<base property name>'
```

The obvious solution is to add the override modifier (assuming the base member is virtual). However, as the warnings point out, the new modifier is also an option. Consider the scenario shown in Table 6.1—a specific example of the more general problem known as the **brittle base class** or **fragile base class** problem.

TABLE 6.1: Why the New Modifier?

Activity	Code

Programmer A defines class Person that includes properties FirstName and LastName.	`public class Person`
	`{`
	`    public string FirstName { get; set; }`
	`    public string LastName { get; set; }`
	`}`

Programmer B derives from Person and defines Contact with the additional property, Name. In addition, he defines the Program class whose Main() method instantiates Contact, assigns Name, and then prints out the name.	`public class Contact : Person`
	`{`
	`    public string Name`
	`    {`
	`        get`
	`        {`
	`            return FirstName + " " + LastName;`
	`        }`
	`        set`
	`        {`
	`            string[] names = value.Split(' ');`
	`            // Error handling not shown.`
	`            FirstName = names[0];`
	`            LastName = names[1];`
	`        }`
	`    }`
	`}`

Continues

TABLE 6.1: Why the New Modifier? *(Continued)*

Activity	Code
| Later, Programmer A adds the Name property, but instead of implementing the getter as FirstName + " " + LastName, she implements it as LastName + ", " + FirstName. Furthermore, she doesn't define the property as virtual, and she uses the property in a DisplayName() method. | ```csharp
public class Person
{
  public string Name
  {
    get
    {
        return LastName + ", " + FirstName;
    }

    set
    {
        string[] names = value.Split(', ');
        // Error handling not shown.
        LastName = names[0];
        FirstName = names[1];
    }
  }
  public static void Display(Person person)
  {
        // Display <LastName>, <FirstName>
        Console.WriteLine( person.Name );
  }
}
``` |

Because Person.Name is not virtual, Programmer A will expect Display() to use the Person implementation, even if a Person-derived data type, Contact, is passed in. However, Programmer B would expect Contact.Name to be used in all cases where the variable data type is a Contact. (Programmer B would have no code where Person.Name was used, since no Person.Name property existed initially.) To allow the addition of Person.Name without breaking either programmer's expected behavior, you cannot assume virtual was intended. Furthermore, since C# requires an override member to explicitly use the override modifier, some other semantic must be assumed, instead of allowing the addition of a member in the base class to cause the derived class to no longer compile.

The semantic is the new modifier, and it hides a redeclared member of the derived class from the base class. Instead of calling the most derived
```

member, a member of the base class calls the most derived member in the inheritance chain prior to the member with the new modifier. If the inheritance chain contains only two classes, then a member in the base class will behave as though no method was declared on the derived class (if the derived implementation overrides the base class member). Although the compiler will report the warning shown in either Output 6.2 or Output 6.3, if neither override nor new is specified, then new will be assumed, thereby maintaining the desired version safety.

Consider Listing 6.14, for example. Its output appears in Output 6.4.

LISTING 6.14: override versus new Modifier

```csharp
public class Program
{
  public class BaseClass
  {
     public void DisplayName()
     {
        Console.WriteLine("BaseClass");
     }
  }

    public class DerivedClass : BaseClass
    {
       // Compiler WARNING: DisplayName() hides inherited
       // member. Use the new keyword if hiding was intended.
       public virtual void DisplayName()
       {
          Console.WriteLine("DerivedClass");
       }
    }

  public class SubDerivedClass : DerivedClass
  {
     public override void DisplayName()
     {
        Console.WriteLine("SubDerivedClass");
     }
  }

  public class SuperSubDerivedClass : SubDerivedClass
  {
     public new void DisplayName()
     {
        Console.WriteLine("SuperSubDerivedClass");
     }
  }
}
```

```
public static void Main()
{
    SuperSubDerivedClass superSubDerivedClass
        = new SuperSubDerivedClass();

    SubDerivedClass subDerivedClass = superSubDerivedClass;
    DerivedClass derivedClass = superSubDerivedClass;
    BaseClass baseClass = superSubDerivedClass;

    superSubDerivedClass.DisplayName();
    subDerivedClass.DisplayName();
    derivedClass.DisplayName();
    baseClass.DisplayName();
    }
}
```

OUTPUT 6.4:

```
SuperSubDerivedClass
SubDerivedClass
SubDerivedClass
BaseClass
```

These results occur for the following reasons.

- SuperSubDerivedClass: SuperSubDerivedClass.DisplayName() displays SuperSubDerivedClass because there is no derived class and hence, no overload.

- SubDerivedClass: SubDerivedClass.DisplayName() is the most derived member to override a base class's virtual member. SuperSubDerivedClass.DisplayName() is hidden because of its new modifier.

- SubDerivedClass: DerivedClass.DisplayName() is virtual and SubDerivedClass.DisplayName() is the most derived member to override it. As before, SuperSubDerivedClass.DisplayName() is hidden because of the new modifier.

- BaseClass: BaseClass.DisplayName() does not redeclare any base class member and it is not virtual; therefore, it is called directly.

When it comes to the CIL, the new modifier has no effect on what statements the compiler generates. However, a "new" method results in the generation of the newslot metadata attribute on the method. From the C#

perspective, its only effect is to remove the compiler warning that would appear otherwise.

sealed **Modifier**

Just as you can prevent inheritance using the `sealed` modifier on a class, virtual members may be `sealed`, too (see Listing 6.15). This prevents a subclass from overriding a base class member that was originally declared as `virtual` higher in the inheritance chain. The situation arises when a subclass B overrides a base class A's member and then needs to prevent any further overriding below subclass B.

LISTING 6.15: Sealing Members

```csharp
class A
{
  public virtual void Method()
  {
  }
}
class B : A
{
   public override sealed void Method()
     {
  }
  }

class C : B
{
  // ERROR:  Cannot override sealed members
  // public override void Method()
  // {
  // }
}
```

In this example, the use of the sealed modifier on class B's `Method()` declaration prevents C's overriding of `Method()`.

base **Member**

In choosing to override a member, developers often want to invoke the member on the base class (see Listing 6.16).

LISTING 6.16: Accessing a Base Member

```csharp
public class Address
{
    public string StreetAddress;
```

```csharp
        public string City;
        public string State;
        public string Zip;

        public override string ToString()
        {
            return string.Format("{0}" + Environment.NewLine +
                "{1}, {2}  {3}",
                StreetAddress, City, State, Zip);
        }
    }

    public class InternationalAddress : Address
    {
        public string Country;

        public override string ToString()
        {
          return base.ToString() + Environment.NewLine +

                Country;
        }
    }
```

In Listing 6.16, `InternationalAddress` inherits from `Address` and implements `ToString()`. To call the parent class's implementation you use the `base` keyword. The syntax is virtually identical to `this`, including support for using `base` as part of the constructor (discussed shortly).

Parenthetically, in the `Address.ToString()` implementation, you are required to `override` as well because `ToString()` is also a member of `object`. Any members that are decorated with `override` are automatically designated as virtual, so additional child classes may further specialize the implementation.

Constructors

When instantiating a derived class, the runtime first invokes the base class's constructor so that the base class initialization is not circumvented. However, if there is no accessible (nonprivate) default constructor on the base class, then it is not clear how to construct the base class and the C# compiler reports an error.

To avoid the error caused by no accessible default constructor, programmers need to designate explicitly, in the derived class constructor header, which base constructor to run (see Listing 6.17).

LISTING 6.17: Specifying Which Base Constructor to Invoke

```csharp
public class PdaItem
{
  public PdaItem(string name)
  {
    Name = name;
  }

  // ...
}
```

```csharp
public class Contact : PdaItem
{
  public Contact(string name) :
      base(name)
  {
    Name = name;
  }

  public string Name { get; set; }
  // ...
}
```

By identifying the base constructor in the code, you let the runtime know which base constructor to invoke before invoking the derived class constructor.

Abstract Classes

Many of the inheritance examples so far have defined a class called PdaItem that defines the methods and properties common to Contact, Appointment, and so on, which are type objects that derive from PdaItem. PdaItem is not intended to be instantiated itself, however. A PdaItem instance has no meaning by itself; it has meaning only when it is used as a base class—to share default method implementations across the set of data types that derive from it. These characteristics are indicative of the need for PdaItem to be an **abstract** class rather than a **concrete** class. Abstract classes are designed for derivation only. It is not possible to instantiate an abstract class, except in the context of instantiating a class that derives from it. Classes that are not abstract and can instead be instantiated directly are concrete classes.

▪ BEGINNER TOPIC

Abstract Classes

Abstract classes represent abstract entities. Their **abstract members** define what an object derived from an abstract entity should contain, but they don't include the implementation. Often, much of the functionality within an abstract class is unimplemented, and before a class can successfully derive from an abstract class, it needs to provide the implementation for the abstract methods in its abstract base class.

To define an abstract class, C# requires the abstract modifier to the class definition, as shown in Listing 6.18.

LISTING 6.18: Defining an Abstract Class

```csharp
// Define an abstract class
public abstract class PdaItem
{
  public PdaItem(string name)
  {
    Name = name;
  }

  public virtual string Name { get; set; }
}
```

```csharp
public class Program
{
  public static void Main()
  {
    PdaItem item;
    // ERROR:  Cannot create an instance of the abstract class
    item = new PdaItem("Inigo Montoya");
  }
}
```

Although abstract classes cannot be instantiated, this restriction is a minor characteristic of an abstract class. Their primary significance is achieved when abstract classes include **abstract members.** An abstract member is a method or property that has no implementation. Its purpose is to force all derived classes to provide the implementation.

Consider Listing 6.19.

LISTING 6.19: Defining Abstract Members

```csharp
// Define an abstract class
public abstract class PdaItem
{
  public PdaItem(string name)
  {
     Name = name;
  }


  public virtual string Name { get; set; }
  public abstract string GetSummary();
}
```

```csharp
public class Contact : PdaItem
{
    public override string Name
    {
       get
       {
          return FirstName + " " + LastName;
       }

       set
       {
          string[] names = value.Split(' ');
          // Error handling not shown.
          FirstName = names[0];
          LastName = names[1];
       }
    }

    public string FirstName { get; set; }
    public string LastName { get; set; }
    public string Address { get; set; }

    public override string GetSummary()
    {
       return string.Format(
          "FirstName: {0}
          + "LastName: {1}
          + "Address: {2}", FirstName, LastName, Address);
    }

    // ...
}
```

```csharp
public class Appointment : PdaItem
{
  public Appointment(string name) :
    base(name)
  {
    Name = name;
  }

  public DateTime StartDateTime  { get; set; }
  public DateTime EndDateTime  { get; set; }
  public string Location  { get; set; }

  // ...

  public override string GetSummary()
  {
        return string.Format(
            "Subject: {0}" + Environment.NewLine
            + "Start: {1}" + Environment.NewLine
            + "End: {2}" + Environment.NewLine
            + "Location: {3}",
            Name, StartDateTime, EndDateTime, Location);
  }
}
```

Listing 6.19 defines the GetSummary() member as abstract, and therefore, it doesn't include any implementation. Then, the code overrides it within Contact and provides the implementation. Because abstract members are supposed to be overridden, such members are automatically virtual and cannot be declared so explicitly. In addition, abstract members cannot be private because derived classes would not be able to see them.

Language Contrast: C++ — Pure Virtual Functions

C++ allows for the definition of abstract functions using the cryptic notation =0. These functions are called pure virtual functions in C++. In contrast with C#, however, C++ does not require the class itself to have any special declaration. Unlike C#'s abstract class modifier, C++ has no class declaration change when the class includes pure virtual functions.

If you provide no GetSummary() implementation in Contact, the compiler will report an error.

> ### ■ NOTE
>
> By declaring an abstract member, the abstract class programmer states that in order to form an "is a" relationship between a concrete class and an abstract base class (that is, a `PdaItem`), it is necessary to implement the abstract members, the members for which the abstract class could not provide an appropriate default implementation.

■ BEGINNER TOPIC

Polymorphism

When the implementation for the same member signature varies between two or more classes, you have a key object-oriented principle: **polymorphism.** "Poly" meaning "many" and "morph" meaning "form," polymorphism refers to the fact that there are multiple implementations of the same signature. And since the same signature cannot be used multiple times within a single class, each implementation of the member signature occurs on a different class.

The idea behind polymorphism is that the object itself knows best how to perform a particular operation, and by enforcing common ways to invoke those operations, polymorphism is also a technique for encouraging code reuse when taking advantages of the commonalities. Given multiple types of documents, each document type class knows best how to perform a `Print()` method for its corresponding document type. Therefore, instead of defining a single print method that includes a `switch` statement with the special logic to print each document type, with polymorphism you call the `Print()` method corresponding to the specific type of document you wish to print. For example, calling `Print()` on a word processing document class behaves according to word processing specifics, and calling the same method on a graphics document class will result in print behavior specific to the graphic. Given the document types, however, all you have to do to print a document is to call `Print()`, regardless of the type.

Moving the custom print implementation out of a `switch` statement offers several maintenance advantages. First, the implementation appears in the context of each document type's class rather than in a location far removed; this is in keeping with encapsulation. Second, adding a new document type doesn't require a change to the switch statement. Instead, all that is necessary is for the new document type class to implement the Print() signature.

Abstract members are intended to be a way to enable polymorphism. The base class specifies the signature of the method and the derived class provides implementation (see Listing 6.20).

LISTING 6.20: Using Polymorphism to List the PdaItems

```
public class Program
{
  public static void Main()
  {
      PdaItem[] pda = new PdaItem[3];

      Contact contact = new Contact("Sherlock Holmes");
      contact.Address = "221B Baker Street, London, England";
      pda[0] = contact;

      Appointment appointment =
         new Appointment("Soccer tournament");
      appointment.StartDateTime = new DateTime(2008, 7, 18);
      appointment.EndDateTime = new DateTime(2008, 7, 19);
      appointment.Location = "Estádio da Machava";
      pda[1] = appointment;

      contact = new Contact("Anne Frank");
      contact.Address =
         "263 Prinsengracht, Amsterdam, Netherlands";
      pda[2] = contact;

      List(pda);
  }

  public static void List(PdaItem[] items)
  {
      // Implemented using polymorphism. The derived
      // type knows the specifics of implementing
      // GetSummary().
      foreach (PdaItem item in items)
      {
          Console.WriteLine("_____");
```

```
            Console.WriteLine(item.GetSummary());
        }
    }
}
```

The results of Listing 6.20 appear in Output 6.5.

OUTPUT 6.5:

```
FirstName: Sherlock
LastName: Holmes
Address: 221B Baker Street, London, England

Subject: Soccer tournament
Start: 7/18/2008 12:00:00 AM
End: 7/19/2008 12:00:00 AM
Location: Estádio da Machava

FirstName: Anne
LastName: Frank
Address: 263 Prinsengracht, Amsterdam, Netherlands
```

In this way, you can call the method on the base class but the implementation is specific to the derived class.

All Classes Derive from System.Object

Given any class, whether a custom class or one built into the system, the methods shown in Table 6.2 will be defined.

TABLE 6.2: Members of System.Object

Method Name	Description
public virtual bool Equals(object o)	Returns true if the object supplied as a parameter is equal in *value*, not necessarily in reference, to the instance.
public virtual int GetHashCode()	Returns an integer corresponding to an evenly spread hash code. This is useful for collections such as HashTable collections.

Continues

TABLE 6.2: Members of System.Object *(Continued)*

public Type GetType()	Returns an object of type System.Type corresponding to the type of the object instance.
public static bool ReferenceEquals(**object** a, **object** b)	Returns true if the two supplied parameters refer to the same object.
public virtual string ToString()	Returns a string representation of the object instance.
public virtual void Finalize()	An alias for the destructor; informs the object to prepare for termination. C# prevents calling this method directly.
protected object MemberwiseClone()	Clones the object in question by performing a shallow copy; references are copied, but not the data within a referenced type.

All of these methods appear on all objects through inheritance; all classes derive (either directly or via an inheritance chain) from object. Even literals include these methods, enabling somewhat peculiar-looking code such as this:

```
Console.WriteLine( 42.ToString() );
```

Even class definitions that don't have any explicit derivation from object derive from object anyway. The two declarations for PdaItem in Listing 6.21, therefore, result in identical CIL.

LISTING 6.21: System.Object Derivation Implied When No Derivation Is Specified Explicitly

```
public class PdaItem
{
  // ...
}
```

```
public class PdaItem : object
{
  // ...
}
```

When the object's default implementation isn't sufficient, programmers can override one or more of the three virtual methods. Chapter 9 describes the details for doing this.

Verifying the Underlying Type with the is Operator

Because C# allows casting down the inheritance chain, it is sometimes desirable to determine what the underlying type is before attempting a conversion. Also, checking the type may be necessary for type-specific actions where polymorphism was not implemented. To determine the underlying type, C# provides the is operator (see Listing 6.22).

LISTING 6.22: is Operator Determining the Underlying Type

```
public static void Save(object data)
{
    if (data is string)
    {
        data = Encrypt((string) data);
    }

    // ...
}
```

Listing 6.22 encrypts the data if the underlying type is a string. This is significantly different from encrypting, simply because it successfully casts to a string since many types support casting to a string, and yet their underlying type is not a string.

Although this capability is important, you should consider polymorphism prior to using the is operator. Polymorphism enables support for expanding a behavior to other data types without modifying the implementation that defines the behavior. For example, deriving from a common base type and then using that type as the parameter to the Save() method avoids having to check for string explicitly and enables other data types to support encryption during the save by deriving from the same base type.

Conversion Using the as Operator

The advantage of the is operator is that it enables verification that a data item is of a particular type. The as operator goes one step further. It attempts a conversion to a particular data type and assigns null if the source type is not inherently (within the inheritance chain) of the target type. This is significant because it avoids the exception that could result from casting. Listing 6.23 demonstrates using the as operator.

LISTING 6.23: Data Conversion Using the as Operator

```
object Print(IDocument document)
{
   if(thing != null)
   {
       // Print document...
   }
   else
   {
   }
}


static void Main()
{
   object data;

   // ...

   Print( data as Document );
}
```

By using the as operator, you are able to avoid additional try/catch handling code if the conversion is invalid, because the as operator provides a way to attempt a cast without throwing an exception if the cast fails.

One advantage of the is operator over the as operator is that the latter cannot successfully determine the underlying type. The latter potentially casts up or down an inheritance chain, as well as across to types supporting the cast operator. Therefore, unlike the as operator, the is operator can determine the underlying type.

SUMMARY

This chapter discussed how to specialize a class by deriving from it and adding additional methods and properties. This included a discussion of the `private` and `protected` access modifiers that control the level of encapsulation.

This chapter also investigated the details of overriding the base class implementation, and alternatively hiding it using the `new` modifier. To control overriding, C# provides the `virtual` modifier, which identifies to the deriving class developer which members she intends for derivation. For preventing any derivation altogether you learned about the `sealed` modifier on the class. Similarly, the `sealed` modifier on a member prevents further overriding from subclasses.

This chapter ended with a brief discussion of how all types derive from `object`. Chapter 9 discusses this derivation further, with a look at how `object` includes three virtual methods with specific rules and guidelines that govern overloading. Before you get there, however, you need to consider another programming paradigm that builds on object-oriented programming: interfaces. This is the subject of Chapter 7.

■7■
Interfaces

P OLYMORPHISM IS AVAILABLE not only via inheritance (as discussed in
the preceding chapter), but also via interfaces. Unlike abstract classes,
interfaces cannot include any implementation. Like abstract classes, however, interfaces define a set of members that callers can rely on to support a
particular feature.

By implementing an interface, a class defines its capabilities. The interface implementation relationship is a "can do" relationship: The class can
do what the interface requires. The interface defines the contract between
the classes that implement the interface and the classes that use the interface. Classes that implement interfaces define methods with the same signatures as the implemented interfaces. This chapter discusses defining,
implementing, and using interfaces.

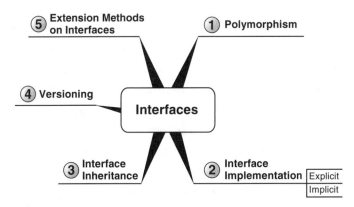

Introducing Interfaces

■ BEGINNER TOPIC

Why Interfaces?

Implemented interfaces are like appliances with wall plugs. The wall plug is the interface that appliances support in order to receive AC power. An appliance can use that power in countless ways, but in order to plug into a wall socket, an appliance must supply a compatible wall plug. What the appliance does with the power corresponds to how an interface implementation varies from class to class. The specification that defines a wall plug is the contract that must be supported in order for an appliance to plug into the wall plug. Similarly, an interface defines a contract that a class must support in order to gain the capability that the interface provides.

Consider the following example: An innumerable number of file compression formats are available (`.zip`, `.7-zip`, `.cab`, `.lha`, `.tar`, `.tar.gz`, `.tar.bz2`, `.bh`, `.rar`, `.arj`, `.arc`, `.ace`, `.zoo`, `.gz`, `.bzip2`, `.xxe`, `.mime`, `.uue`, and `.yenc`, just to name a few). If you created classes for each compression format, you could end up with different method signatures for each compression implementation and no ability for a standard calling convention across them. Although the method signature could be defined in an abstract member of a base class, deriving from a common base type uses up a class's one and only inheritance, with an unlikely chance of sharing code across the various compression implementations, thereby making the potential of a base class implementation useless. The key point, therefore, is that base classes let you share implementation along with the member signatures, whereas interfaces allow you to share the member signatures without the implementation.

Instead of sharing a common base class, each compression class needs to implement a common interface. Interfaces define the contract that a class supports in order to interact with the other classes that expect the interface. Although there are many potential compression algorithms, if all of them could implement the `IFileCompression` interface and its `Compress()` and `Uncompress()` methods, then the code for calling the algorithm on any particular compression class would simply involve a cast to the `IFileCompression` interface and a call into the members, regardless of which class implemented the methods. The result is polymorphism because each compression class has the same method signature but individual implementations of that signature.

The naming convention for interfaces is to use Pascal case, with an I prefix. The IFileCompression interface shown in Listing 7.1 is an example of such a name and interface definition.

LISTING 7.1: Defining an Interface

```
interface IFileCompression
{
  void Compress(string targetFileName, string[] fileList);
  void Uncompress(
      string compressedFileName, string expandDirectoryName);
}
```

IFileCompression defines the methods a class implements to work with other compression-related classes. The power of defining the interface concerns the ability to switch among implementations without modifying the calling code, as long as each compression class implements the IFileCompression interface.

One key characteristic of an interface is that it has no implementation and no data. Method declarations have a single semicolon in place of curly braces after the header. Fields (data) cannot appear on an interface. When an interface requires the derived class to have certain data, it uses a property rather than a field. Since the property does not contain any implementation as part of the interface declaration, it doesn't reference a backing field.

Given that the purpose of the interface is to define the contract among multiple classes, defining private or protected members would make them inaccessible to other classes, defeating the purpose of the interface. Therefore, C# does not allow access modifiers on interface members, and instead it automatically defines them as public.

Polymorphism through Interfaces

Consider another example (see Listing 7.2): IListable defines the members a class needs to support in order for the ConsoleListControl class to display it. As such, any class that implements IListable will have the capability of using the ConsoleListControl to display itself. The IListable interface requires a read-only property, ColumnValues.

LISTING 7.2: Implementing and Using Interfaces

```csharp
interface IListable
{
  // Return the value of each column in the row.
  string[] ColumnValues
  {
      get;
  }
}
```

```csharp
public abstract class PdaItem
{
  public PdaItem(string name)
  {
      Name = name;
  }

  public virtual string Name{get;set;}
}
```

```csharp
class Contact : PdaItem, IListable
{
    public Contact(string firstName, string lastName,
        string address, string phone) : base(null)
    {
        FirstName = firstName;
        LastName = lastName;
        Address = address;
        Phone = phone;
    }

    public string FirstName { get; set; }
    public string LastName { get; set; }
    public string Address { get; set; }
    public string Phone { get; set; }

    public string[] ColumnValues
    {
        get
        {
            return new string[]
            {
```

```
                        FirstName,
                        LastName,
                        Phone,
                        Address
                };
            }
        }

    public static string[] Headers
    {
        get
        {
            return new string[] {
                "First Name", "Last Name    ",
                "Phone         ",
                "Address                    " };
        }
    }

    // ...
}
```

```
class Publication : IListable
{
    public Publication(string title, string author, int year)
    {
        Title = title;
        Author = author;
        Year = year;
    }

    public string Title { get; set; }
    public string Author { get; set; }
    public int Year { get; set; }

    public string[] ColumnValues
    {
        get
        {
            return new string[]
            {
                Title,
                Author,
                Year.ToString()
            };
        }
    }

    public static string[] Headers
    {
```

```
        get
        {
            return new string[] {
                "Title                                  ",
                "Author                ",
                "Year" };
        }
    }

    // ...
}
```

```
class Program
{
    public static void Main()
    {
        Contact[] contacts = new Contact[6];
        contacts[0] = new Contact(
            "Dick", "Traci",
            "123 Main St., Spokane, WA   99037",
            "123-123-1234");
        contacts[1] = new Contact(
            "Andrew", "Littman",
            "1417 Palmary St., Dallas, TX 55555",
            "555-123-4567");
        contacts[2] = new Contact(
            "Mary", "Hartfelt",
            "1520 Thunder Way, Elizabethton, PA 44444",
            "444-123-4567");
        contacts[3] = new Contact(
            "John", "Lindherst",
            "1 Aerial Way Dr., Monteray, NH 88888",
            "222-987-6543");
        contacts[4] = new Contact(
            "Pat", "Wilson",
            "565 Irving Dr., Parksdale, FL 22222",
            "123-456-7890");
        contacts[5] = new Contact(
            "Jane", "Doe",
            "123 Main St., Aurora, IL 66666",
            "333-345-6789");

        // Classes are cast implicitly to
        // their supported interfaces
        ConsoleListControl.List(Contact.Headers, contacts);

        Console.WriteLine();

        Publication[] publications = new Publication[3] {
```

```
            new Publication("Celebration of Discipline",
                "Richard Foster", 1978),
            new Publication("Orthodoxy",
                "G.K. Chesterton", 1908),
            new Publication(
                "The Hitchhiker's Guide to the Galaxy",
                "Douglas Adams", 1979)
            };
        ConsoleListControl.List(
            Publication.Headers, publications);
    }
}
```

```
class ConsoleListControl
{
    public static void List(string[] headers, IListable[] items )
    {
        int[] columnWidths = DisplayHeaders(headers);

        for (int count = 0; count < items.Length; count++)
        {
            string[] values = items[count].ColumnValues;
            DisplayItemRow(columnWidths, values);
        }
    }

    /// <summary>Displays the column headers</summary>
    /// <returns>Returns an array of column widths</returns>
    private static int[] DisplayHeaders(string[] headers)
    {
        // ...
    }

    private static void DisplayItemRow(
        int[] columnWidths, string[] values)
    {
        // ...
    }
}
```

The results of Listing 7.2 appear in Output 7.1.

OUTPUT 7.1:

```
First Name  Last Name   Phone           Address
Dick        Traci       123-123-1234    123 Main St., Spokane, WA  99037
Andrew      Littman     555-123-4567    1417 Palmary St., Dallas, TX 55555
```

Continues

```
Mary        Hartfelt     444-123-4567   1520 Thunder Way, Elizabethton, ↵
PA 44444
John        Lindherst    222-987-6543   1 Aerial Way Dr., Monteray, ↵
NH 88888
Pat         Wilson       123-456-7890   565 Irving Dr., Parksdale, ↵
FL 22222
Jane        Doe          333-345-6789   123 Main St., Aurora, IL 66666

Title                                   Author            Year
Celebration of Discipline               Richard Foster    1978
Orthodoxy                               G.K. Chesterton   1908
The Hitchhiker's Guide to the Galaxy    Douglas Adam      1979
```

In Listing 7.2, the `ConsoleListControl` can display seemingly unrelated classes (`Contact` and `Publication`). A displayable class is defined simply by whether it implements the required interface. As a result, the `ConsoleListControl.List()` method relies on polymorphism to appropriately display whichever set of objects it is passed. Each class has its own implementation of `ColumnValues`, and converting a class to `IListable` still allows the particular class's implementation to be invoked.

Interface Implementation

Declaring a class to implement an interface is similar to deriving from a base class in that the implemented interfaces appear in a comma-separated list along with the base class (order is not significant between interfaces). The only difference is that classes can implement multiple interfaces. An example appears in Listing 7.3.

LISTING 7.3: Implementing an Interface

```csharp
public class Contact : PdaItem, IListable, IComparable
{
  // ...

  #region IComparable Members
  /// <summary>
  ///
  /// </summary>
  /// <param name="obj"></param>
  /// <returns>
  /// Less than zero:    This instance is less than obj.
  /// Zero               This instance is equal to obj.
  /// Greater than zero  This instance is greater than obj.
  /// </returns>
```

```csharp
    public int CompareTo (object obj)
    {
        int result;
        Contact contact = obj as Contact;

        if (obj == null)
        {
            // This instance is greater than obj.
            result = 1;
        }
        else if (obj != typeof(Contact))
        {
            throw new ArgumentException("obj is not a Contact");
        }
        else if( Contact.ReferenceEquals(this, obj) )
        {
            result = 0;
        }
        else
        {
            result = LastName.CompareTo(contact.LastName);
            if (result == 0)
            {
                result = FirstName.CompareTo(contact.FirstName);
            }
        }
        return result;
    }
    #endregion

    #region IListable Members
    string[] IListable.ColumnValues
    {
        get
        {
            return new string[]
            {
                FirstName,
                LastName,
                Phone,
                Address
            };
        }
    }
    #endregion
}
```

Once a class declares that it implements an interface, all members of the interface must be implemented. The member implementation may throw a

`NotImplementedException` type exception in the method body, but none-theless, the method has an implementation from the compiler's perspective.

One important characteristic of interfaces is that they can never be instantiated; you cannot use new to create an interface, and therefore, inter-faces cannot even have constructors or finalizers. Interface instances are available only from types that implement them. Furthermore, interfaces cannot include static members. One key interface purpose is polymor-phism, and polymorphism without an instance of the implementing type is of little value.

Each interface member behaves like an abstract method, forcing the derived class to implement the member. Therefore, it is not possible to use the abstract modifier on interface members explicitly. However, there are two variations on implementation: **explicit** and **implicit.**

Explicit Member Implementation

Explicitly implemented methods are available only by calling through the interface itself; this is typically achieved by casting an object to the inter-face. For example, to call `IListable.ColumnValues` in Listing 7.4, you must first cast the contact to `IListable` because of `ColumnValues'` explicit implementation.

LISTING 7.4: Calling Explicit Interface Member Implementations

```
string[] values;
Contact contact1, contact2;

// ...

// ERROR:  Unable to call ColumnValues() directly
//         on a contact.
// values = contact1.ColumnValues;

// First cast to IListable.
values = ((IListable)contact2).ColumnValues;
// ...
```

The cast and the call to `ColumnValues` occur within the same statement in this case. Alternatively, you could assign `contact2` to an `IListable` vari-able before calling `ColumnValues`.

To declare an explicit interface member implementation, prefix the member name with the interface name (see Listing 7.5).

LISTING 7.5: Explicit Interface Implementation

```csharp
public class Contact : PdaItem, IListable, IComparable
{
  // ...

  public int CompareTo(object obj)
  {
      // ...
  }

  #region IListable Members
  string[] IListable.ColumnValues
  {
      get
      {
          return new string[]
          {
              FirstName,
              LastName,
              Phone,
              Address
          };
      }
  }
  #endregion
}
```

Listing 7.5 implements `ColumnValues` explicitly, for example, because it prefixes the property with `IListable`. Furthermore, since explicit interface implementations are directly associated with the interface, there is no need to modify them with `virtual`, `override`, or `public`, and, in fact, these modifiers are not allowed. The C# compiler assumes these modifiers; otherwise, the implementation would be meaningless.

Implicit Member Implementation

Notice that `CompareTo()` in Listing 7.5 does not include the `IComparable` prefix; it is implemented implicitly. With implicit member implementation, it is only necessary for the class member's signature to match the interface member's signature. Interface member implementation does not require the override keyword or any indication that this member is tied to the interface. Furthermore, since the member is declared just as any other class member, code that calls implicitly implemented members can do so directly, just as it would any other class member:

```
result = contact1.CompareTo(contact2);
```

In other words, implicit member implementation does not require a cast because the member is not hidden from direct invocation on the implementing class.

Many of the modifiers disallowed on an explicit member implementation are required or are optional on an implicit implementation. For example, implicit member implementations must be public. Furthermore, virtual is optional depending on whether derived classes may override the implementation. Eliminating virtual will cause the member to behave as though it is sealed. Interestingly, override is not allowed because the interface declaration of the member does not include implementation, so override is not meaningful.

Explicit versus Implicit Interface Implementation

The key difference between implicit and explicit member interface implementation is obviously not in the method declaration, but in the visibility from outside the class. When building a class hierarchy, it's desirable to model real-world "is a" relationships—a giraffe is a mammal, for example. These are "semantic" relationships. Interfaces are often used to model "mechanism" relationships. A PdaItem "is not a" "comparable", but it might well be IComparable. This interface has nothing to do with the semantic model; it's a detail of the implementation mechanism. Explicit interface implementation is a technique for enabling the separation of mechanism concerns from model concerns. Forcing the caller to convert the object to an interface such as IComparable before treating the object as "comparable" explicitly separates out in the code when you are talking to the model and when you are dealing with its implementation mechanisms.

In general, it is preferable to limit the public surface area of a class to be "all model" with as little extraneous mechanism as possible. Unfortunately, some mechanisms are unavoidable in .NET. You cannot get a giraffe's hash code or convert a giraffe to a string. However, you can get a

Giraffe's hash code (GetHashCode()) and convert it to a string (ToString()). By using object as a common base class, .NET mixes model code with mechanism code even if only to a limited extent.

Here are several guidelines that will help you choose between an explicit and an implicit implementation.

- *Is the member a core part of the class functionality?*

  Consider the ColumnValues property implementation on the Contact class. This member is not an integral part of a Contact type but a peripheral member probably accessed only by the ConsoleListControl class. As such, it doesn't make sense for the member to be immediately visible on a Contact object, cluttering up what could potentially already be a large list of members.

  Alternatively, consider the IFileCompression.Compress() member. Including an implicit Compress() implementation on a ZipCompression class is a perfectly reasonable choice, since Compress() is a core part of the ZipCompression class's behavior, so it should be directly accessible from the ZipCompression class.

- *Is the interface member name appropriate as a class member?*

  Consider an ITrace interface with a member called Dump() that writes out a class's data to a trace log. Implementing Dump() implicitly on a Person or Truck class would result in confusion as to what operation the method performs. Instead, it is preferable to implement the member explicitly so that only from a data type of ITrace, where the meaning is clearer, can the Dump() method be called. Consider using an explicit implementation if a member's purpose is unclear on the implementing class.

- *Is there already a class member with the same name?*

  Explicit interface member implementation will uniquely distinguish a member. Therefore, if there is already a method implementation on a class, a second one can be provided with the same name as long as it is an explicit interface member.

Much of the decision regarding implicit versus explicit interface member implementation comes down to intuition. However, these questions provide suggestions about what to consider when making your choice.

Since changing an implementation from implicit to explicit results in a version-breaking change, it is better to err on the side of defining interfaces explicitly, allowing them to be changed to implicit later on. Furthermore, since the decision between implicit and explicit does not have to be consistent across all interface members, defining some methods as explicit and others as implicit is fully supported.

Converting between the Implementing Class and Its Interfaces

Just as with a derived class and a base type, a conversion from an object to its implemented interface is an implicit conversion. No cast operator is required because an instance of the implementing class will always contain all the members in the interface, and therefore, the object will always cast successfully to the interface type.

Although the conversion will always be successful from the implementing class to the implemented interface, many different classes could implement a particular interface, so you can never be certain that a downward cast from the interface to the implementing class will be successful. The result is that converting from an interface to its implementing class requires an explicit cast.

Interface Inheritance

Interfaces can derive from each other, resulting in an interface that inherits all the members in its base interfaces. As shown in Listing 7.6, the interfaces directly derived from `IReadableSettingsProvider` are the explicit base interfaces.

LISTING 7.6: Deriving One Interface from Another

```csharp
interface IReadableSettingsProvider
{
    string GetSetting(string name, string defaultValue);
}
```

```csharp
interface ISettingsProvider : IReadableSettingsProvider
{
    void SetSetting(string name, string value);
}
```

```
class FileSettingsProvider : ISettingsProvider
{
    #region ISettingsProvider Members
    public void SetSetting(string name, string value)
    {
        // ...
    }
    #endregion

    #region IReadableSettingsProvider Members
    public string GetSetting(string name, string defaultValue)
    {
        // ...
    }
    #endregion
}
```

In this case, ISettingsProvider derives from IReadableSettingsPro-vider and, therefore, inherits its members. If IReadableSettingsProvider also had an explicit base interface, ISettingsProvider would inherit those members too, and the full set of interfaces in the derivation hierarchy would simply be the accumulation of base interfaces.

It is interesting to note that if GetSetting() is implemented explicitly, it must be done using IReadableSettingsProvider. The declaration with ISettingsProvider in Listing 7.7 will not compile.

LISTING 7.7: **Explicit Member Declaration without the Containing Interface (Failure)**

```
// ERROR:  GetSetting() not available on ISettingsProvider
string ISettingsProvider.GetSetting(
  string name, string defaultValue)
{
  // ...
}
```

The results of Listing 7.7 appear in Output 7.2.

OUTPUT 7.2:

```
'ISettingsProvider.GetSetting' in explicit interface declaration
is not a member of interface.
```

This output appears in addition to an error indicating that IReadable-SettingsProvider.GetSetting() is not implemented. The fully qualified interface member name used for explicit interface member implementation must reference the interface name in which it was originally declared.

Even though a class implements an interface (`ISettingsProvider`) which is derived from a base interface (`IReadableSettingsProvider`), the class can still declare an implementation of both interfaces overtly, as Listing 7.8 demonstrates.

LISTING 7.8: Using a Base Interface in the Class Declaration

```
class FileSettingsProvider : ISettingsProvider,
    IReadableSettingsProvider
{
    #region ISettingsProvider Members
    public void SetSetting(string name, string value)
    {
        // ...
    }
    #endregion

    #region IReadableSettingsProvider Members
    public string GetSetting(string name, string defaultValue)
    {
        // ...
    }
    #endregion
}
```

In this listing, there is no change to the interface's implementations on the class, and although the additional interface implementation declaration on the class header is superfluous, it can provide better readability.

The decision to provide multiple interfaces rather than just one combined interface depends largely on what the interface designer wants to require of the implementing class. By providing an `IReadableSettings-Provider` interface, the designer communicates that implementers are required only to implement a settings provider that retrieves settings. They do not have to be able to write to those settings. This reduces the implementation burden by not imposing the complexities of writing settings as well.

In contrast, implementing `ISettingsProvider` assumes that there is never a reason to have a class that can write settings without reading them. The inheritance relationship between `ISettingsProvider` and

`IReadableSettingsProvider`, therefore, forces the combined total of both interfaces on the `ISettingsProvider` class.

One final but important note: Although *inheritance* is the correct term, conceptually it is more accurate to realize that an interface represents a contract; and one contract is allowed to specify that the provisions of another contract must also be followed. So, the code `ISettingsProvider : IReadableSettingsProvider` conceptually states that the `ISettingsProvider` contract requires also respecting the `IReadableSettingsProvider` contract rather than that the `ISettingsProvider` "is a kind of" `IReadableSettingsProvider`. That being said, the remainder of the chapter will continue using the inheritance relationship terminology in accordance with the standard C# terminology.

Multiple Interface Inheritance

Just as classes can implement multiple interfaces, interfaces can inherit from multiple interfaces, and the syntax is consistent with class derivation and implementation, as shown in Listing 7.9.

LISTING 7.9: Multiple Interface Inheritance

```
interface IReadableSettingsProvider
{
  string GetSetting(string name, string defaultValue);
}
```

```
interface IWriteableSettingsProvider
{
  void SetSetting(string name, string value);
}
```

```
interface ISettingsProvider : IReadableSettingsProvider,
    IWriteableSettingsProvider
{
}
```

It is unusual to have an interface with no members, but if implementing both interfaces together is predominant, it is a reasonable choice for this case. The difference between Listing 7.9 and Listing 7.6 is that it is now

possible to implement IWriteableSettingsProvider without supplying
any read capability. Listing 7.6's FileSettingsProvider is unaffected, but
if it used explicit member implementation, specifying which interface a
member belongs to changes slightly.

Extension Methods on Interfaces

Perhaps one of the most important features of extension methods is the
fact that they work with interfaces in addition to classes. The syntax is
identical to that of extension methods for classes. The extended type (the
first parameter and the parameter prefixed with this) is the interface that
we extend. Listing 7.10 shows an extension method for IListable(). It is
declared on Listable.

LISTING 7.10: Interface Extension Methods

```
class Program
{
  public static void Main()
  {
      Contact[] contacts = new Contact[6];
      contacts[0] = new Contact(
          "Dick", "Traci",
          "123 Main St., Spokane, WA  99037",
          "123-123-1234");
       // ...

          // Classes are implicitly converted to
          // their supported interfaces
          contacts.List(Contact.Headers);

      Console.WriteLine();

      Publication[] publications = new Publication[3] {
          new Publication("Celebration of Discipline",
              "Richard Foster", 1978),
          new Publication("Orthodoxy",
              "G.K. Chesterton", 1908),
          new Publication(
              "The Hitchhiker's Guide to the Galaxy",
              "Douglas Adams", 1979)
          };
      publications.List(Publication.Headers);
  }
}
```

```
static class Listable
{
    public static void List(
        this IListable[] items, string[] headers)
    {
        int[] columnWidths = DisplayHeaders(headers);

        for (int itemCount = 0; itemCount < items.Length; itemCount++)
        {
            string[] values = items[itemCount].ColumnValues;

            DisplayItemRow(columnWidths, values);
        }
    }
    // ...
            count < values.Length; count++)
        {
            Console.Write(
                "{0}{1,-" + columnWidths[count] + "}",
                tab, values[count]);
            {
                tab = "\t";
            }
        }
        Console.WriteLine();
}
```

Notice that in this example, the extension method is not on for an IListable parameter (although it could have been), but rather an IListable[] parameter. This demonstrates that C# allows extension methods not only on an instance of a particular object, but also on a collection of those objects. Support for extension methods is the foundation on which LINQ is implemented. IEnumerable is the fundamental interface which all collections implement. By defining extension methods for IEnumerable, LINQ support was added to all collections. This radically changed programming with collections of objects, a topic explored in detail in Chapter 14.

Implementing Multiple Inheritance via Interfaces

As Listing 7.3 demonstrated, a single class can implement any number of interfaces in addition to deriving from a single class. This feature provides a possible workaround for the lack of multiple inheritance support in C#

classes. The process uses aggregation as described in the preceding chapter, but you can vary the structure slightly by adding an interface to the mix, as shown in Listing 7.11.

LISTING 7.11: Working around Single Inheritance Using Aggregation with Interfaces

```csharp
public class PdaItem
{
  // ...
}
```

```csharp
interface IPerson
{
    string FirstName
    {
        get;
        set;
    }

    string LastName
    {
        get;
        set;
    }
}
```

```csharp
public class Person : IPerson
{
  // ...
}
```

```csharp
public class Contact : PdaItem, IPerson
{
  private Person Person
  {
      get { return _Person; }
      set { _Person = value; }
  }
  private Person _Person;


  public string FirstName
  {
      get { return _Person.FirstName; }
      set { _Person.FirstName = value; }
  }
```

```
public string LastName
{
    get { return _Person.LastName; }
    set { _Person.LastName = value; }
}

// ...
}
```

IPerson ensures that the signatures between the Person members and the same members duplicated onto Contact are consistent. The implementation is still not synonymous with multiple inheritance, however, because new members added to Person will not be added to Contact.

One possible improvement that works if the implemented members are methods (not properties) is to define interface extension methods for the additional functionality "derived" from the second base class. An extension method on IPerson could provide a method called VerifyCredentials(), for example, and all classes that implement IPerson, even an IPerson interface that had no members but just extension methods, would have a default implementation of VerifyCredentials(). What makes this a viable approach is that polymorphism is still available, as is overriding. Overriding is supported because any instance implementation of a method will take priority over an extension method with the equivalent static signature.

■ BEGINNER TOPIC

Interface Diagramming

Interfaces in a UML-like[1] figure take two possible forms. First, you can show the interface as though it is an inheritance relationship similar to a class inheritance, as demonstrated in Figure 7.1 between IPerson and IContact. Alternatively, you can show the interface using a small circle, often referred to as a lollipop, exemplified by IPerson and IContact in Figure 7.1.

---

1. Unified Modeling Language (UML), a standard specification for modeling object design using graphical notation.

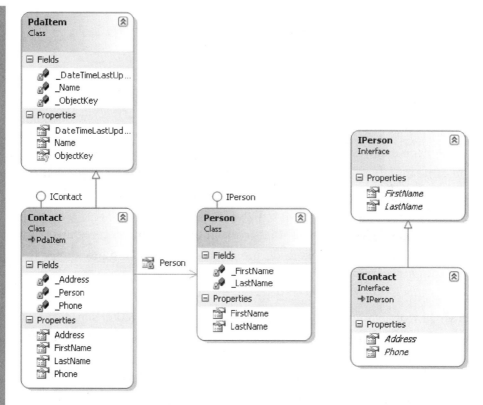

FIGURE 7.1: Working around Single Inheritances with Aggregation and Interfaces

In Figure 7.1, Contact derives from PdaItem and implements IContact. In addition, it aggregates the Person class, which implements IPerson. Although the Visual Studio 2005 Class Designer does not support this, interfaces are sometimes shown as using a derivation-type arrow to a class. For example, Person could have an arrow to IPerson instead of a lollipop.

Versioning

When creating a new version of a component or application that other developers have programmed against, you should not change interfaces. Because interfaces define a contract between the implementing class and the class using the interface, changing the interface is changing the contract, which will possibly break any code written against the interface.

Changing or removing a particular interface member signature is obviously a code-breaking change, as any call to that member will no longer compile without modification. The same is true when changing public or protected member signatures on a class. However, unlike with classes, adding members to an interface could also prevent code from compiling without additional changes. The problem is that any class implementing the interface must do so entirely, and implementations for all members must be provided. With new interface members, the compiler will require that developers add new interface members to the class implementing the interface.

The creation of `IDistributedSettingsProvider` in Listing 7.12 serves as a good example of extending an interface in a version-compatible way. Imagine that at first, only the `ISettingsProvider` interface is defined (as it was in Listing 7.6). In the next version, however, it is determined that per-machine settings are required. To enable this, the `IDistributedSettings-Provider` interface is created, and it derives from `ISettingsProvider`.

LISTING 7.12: Deriving One Interface from Another

```csharp
interface IDistributedSettingsProvider : ISettingsProvider
{
    /// <summary>
    /// Get the settings for a particular machine.
    /// </summary>
    /// <param name="machineName">
    /// The machine name the setting is related to</param>
    /// <param name="name">The name of the setting</param>
    /// <param name="defaultValue">
    /// The value returned if the setting is not found.</param>
    /// <returns>The specified setting</returns>
    string GetSetting(
        string machineName, string name, string defaultValue);

    /// <summary>
    /// Set the settings for a particular machine.
    /// </summary>
    /// <param name="machineName">
    /// The machine name the setting is related to.</param>
    /// <param name="name">The name of the setting.</param>
    /// <param name="value">The value to be persisted.</param>
    /// <returns>The specified setting</returns>
    void SetSetting(
        string machineName, string name, string value);
}
```

The important factor is that programmers with classes that implement ISettingsProvider can choose to upgrade the implementation to include IDistributedSettingsProvider, or they can ignore it.

If instead of creating a new interface, the machine-related methods are added to ISettingsProvider, then classes implementing this interface will no longer successfully compile with the new interface definition, and instead a version-breaking change will occur.

Changing interfaces during the development phase is obviously acceptable, although perhaps laborious if implemented extensively. However, once an interface is released, it should not be changed. Instead, a second interface should be created, possibly deriving from the original interface.

(Listing 7.12 includes XML comments describing the interface members, as discussed further in Chapter 9.)

Interfaces Compared with Classes

Interfaces introduce another category of data types. (They are one of the few categories of types that don't extend System.Object.[2]) Unlike classes, however, interfaces can never be instantiated. An interface instance is accessible only via a reference to an object that implements the interface. It is not possible to use the new operator with an interface; therefore, interfaces cannot contain any constructors or finalizers. Furthermore, static members are not allowed on interfaces.

Interfaces are closer to abstract classes, sharing such features as the lack of instantiation capability. Table 7.1 lists additional comparisons.

TABLE 7.1: Comparing Abstract Classes and Interfaces

Abstract Classes	Interfaces
Cannot be instantiated independently from their derived classes. Abstract class constructors are called only by their derived classes.	Cannot be instantiated.

---

2. The others being pointer types and type parameter types.

TABLE 7.1: Comparing Abstract Classes and Interfaces *(Continued)*

Abstract Classes	Interfaces
Define abstract member signatures that base classes must implement.	Implementation of all members of the interface occurs in the base class. It is not possible to implement only some members within the implementing class.
Are more extensible than interfaces, without breaking any version compatibility. With abstract classes, it is possible to add additional nonabstract members that all derived classes can inherit.	Extending interfaces with additional members breaks the version compatibility.
Can include data stored in fields.	Cannot store any data. Fields can be specified only on the deriving classes. The workaround for this is to define properties, but without implementation.
Allow for (virtual) members that have implementation and, therefore, provide a default implementation of a member to the deriving class.	All members are automatically virtual and cannot include any implementation.
Deriving from an abstract class uses up a subclass's one and only base class option.	Although no default implementation can appear, classes implementing interfaces can continue to derive from one another.

Given that abstract classes and interfaces have their own sets of advantages and disadvantages, you must make a cost-benefit decision based on the comparisons in Table 7.1 in order to make the right choice.

SUMMARY

Interfaces are a critical extension of object-oriented programming. They provide functionality similar to abstract classes but without using up the single-inheritance option, while constantly supporting derivation from multiple interfaces.

In C#, the implementation of interfaces can be either explicit or implicit, depending on whether the implementing class is to expose an interface member directly or only via a conversion to the interface. Furthermore, the granularity of whether the implementation is explicit or implicit is at the member level: One member may be implicit while another on the same interface is explicit.

The next chapter looks at value types and discusses the importance of defining custom value types; at the same time, the chapter points out the subtle foibles that they can introduce.

8
Value Types

YOU HAVE USED VALUE TYPES throughout this book. This chapter discusses not only using value types, but also defining custom value types. There are two categories of value types. The first category is structs. This chapter discusses how structs enable programmers to define new value types that behave very similarly to most of the predefined types discussed in Chapter 2. The key is that any newly defined value types have their own custom data and methods. The second category of value types is enums. This chapter discusses how to use enums to define sets of constant values.

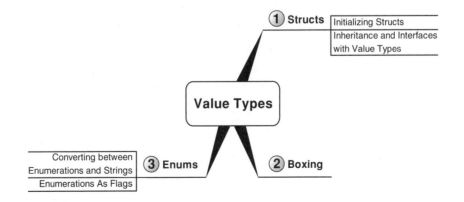

Structs

Categories of Types

All types discussed so far fall into two categories: reference types and value types. The differences between the types in each category stem from differences in copying strategies, which in turn results in each type being stored differently in memory. To review, this Beginner Topic reintroduces the value type/reference type discussion to familiarize those who are unfamiliar with it.

Value Types

Value types directly contain their values, as shown in Figure 8.1. The variable name equates to the location in memory where the value is stored. Because of this, when a different variable is assigned the original variable, a memory copy of the original variable's value is made to the location of the new variable. A second variable of the same value type cannot refer to the same location in memory as the first variable (again assuming no out or ref parameter). So, changing the value of the first variable will not affect the value in the second variable, since value types equate to a specific location in memory. Consequently, changing the value of one value type cannot affect the value of any other value type.

Similarly, passing a value type to a method such as Console.WriteLine() will also result in a memory copy, and any changes to the parameter value inside the method will not affect the original value within the calling function. Since value types require a memory copy, they generally should be defined to consume a small amount of memory (less than 16 bytes approximately).

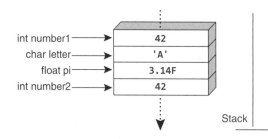

```
//...
int number1 = 42;
char letter = 'A';
float pi = 3.14F;
int number2 = number1;
//...
```

FIGURE 8.1: Value Types Contain the Data Directly

The amount of memory that is required for the value type is fixed at compile time and will not change at runtime. This fixed size allows value types to be stored in the area of memory known as the **stack.**

Reference Types

In contrast, **reference types** and the variables that refer to them point to the data storage location (see Figure 8.2). Reference types store the reference (memory address) where the data is located, instead of representing the data directly. Therefore, to access the data, the runtime will read the memory location out of the variable and then dereference it to reach the location in memory that contains the data. The memory area of the data a reference type points to is the **heap.**

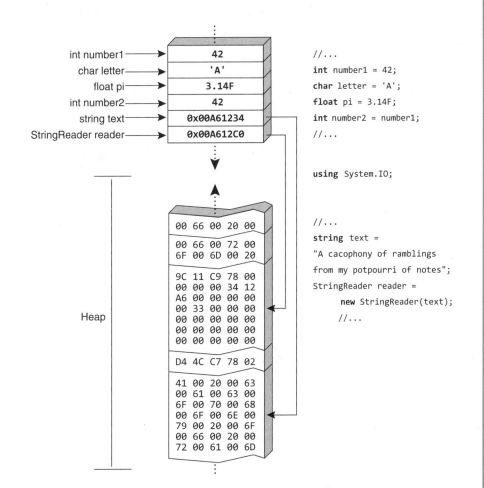

FIGURE 8.2: Reference Types Point to the Heap

Dereferencing a reference type to access its value involves an extra hop. However, a reference type does not require the same memory copy of the data that a value type does, resulting in circumstances when reference types are more efficient. When assigning one reference type variable to another reference type variable, only a memory copy of the address occurs, and as such, the memory copy required by a reference type is always the size of the address itself. (A 32-bit processor will copy 32 bits and a 64-bit processor will copy 64 bits, and so on.) Obviously, not copying the data would be faster than a value type's behavior if the data size is large.

Since reference types copy only the address of the data, two different variables can point to the same data, and changing the data through one variable will change the data for the other variable as well. This happens both for assignment and for method calls. Therefore, a method can affect the data of a reference type back at the caller.

Besides `string` and `object`, all the C# primitive types are value types. Furthermore, numerous additional value types are provided within the framework. It also is possible for developers to define their own value types that behave like user-defined primitives.

To define a custom value type, you use the same type of structure as you would to define classes and interfaces. The key difference in syntax is simply that value types use the keyword `struct`, as shown in Listing 8.1.

LISTING 8.1: Defining `struct`

```csharp
// Use keyword struct to declare a value type.
struct Angle
{
  public Angle(int hours, int minutes, int seconds)
  {
    _Hours = hours;
    _Minutes = minutes;
    _Seconds = seconds;
  }

  public int Hours
  {
    get { return _Hours; }
  }
```

```
    private int _Hours;

    public int Minutes
    {
        get { return _Minutes; }
    }
    private int _Minutes;

    public int Seconds
    {
        get { return _Seconds; }
    }
    private int _Seconds;

    public Angle Move(int hours, int minutes, int seconds)
    {
        return new Angle(
            Hours + hours,
            Minutes + minutes.
            Seconds + seconds)
    }

}

// Declaring a class - a reference type
// (declaring it as a struct would create a value type
// larger than 16 bytes.)
class Coordinate
{
  public Angle Longitude
  {
      get { return _Longitude; }
      set { _Longitude = value; }
  }
  private Angle _Longitude;

  public Angle Latitude
  {
      get { return _Latitude; }
      set { _Latitude = value; }
  }
  private Angle _Latitude;
}
```

This listing defines Angle as a value type that stores the hours, minutes, and seconds of an angle, either longitude or latitude. The resultant C# type is a **struct.**

> **"■ NOTE**
>
> Although nothing in the language requires it, a good guideline is for value types to be immutable: Once you have instantiated a value type, you should not be able to modify the same instance. In scenarios where modification is desirable, you should create a new instance. Listing 8.1 supplies a `Move()` method that doesn't modify the instance of `Angle`, but instead returns an entirely new instance.

Initializing structs

In addition to properties and fields, structs may contain methods and constructors. However, default (parameterless) constructors are not allowed. Sometimes (for instance, when instantiating an array) a value type's constructor will not be called because all array memory is initialized with zeroes instead. To avoid the inconsistency of default constructors being called only sometimes, C# prevents explicit definition of default constructors altogether. Because the compiler's implementation of an instance field assignment at declaration time is to place the assignment into the type's constructor, C# prevents instance field assignment at declaration time as well (see Listing 8.2).

LISTING 8.2: Initializing a struct Field within a Declaration, Resulting in an Error

```
struct Angle
{
  // ...
  // ERROR:  Fields cannot be initialized at declaration time
  // int _Hours = 42;
  // ...
}
```

This does not eliminate the need to initialize the field. In fact, just as with classes, the compiler will issue a warning on struct fields that remain uninitialized after instantiation if they also cannot be accessed from outside the assembly (because they are decorated with internal or private modifiers, for example).

Fortunately, C# supports constructors with parameters and they come with an interesting initialization requirement. They must initialize all fields within the struct. Failure to do so causes a compile error. The constructor in Listing 8.3 that initializes the property rather than the field, for example, produces a compile error.

LISTING 8.3: Accessing Properties before Initializing All Fields

```
// ERROR:  The 'this' object cannot be used before
//          all of its fields are assigned to
// public Angle(int hours, int minutes, int seconds)
// {
//     Hours = hours;      // Shorthand for this.Hours = hours;
//     Minutes = minutes   // Shorthand for this.Minutes = ...;
//     Seconds = seconds   // Shorthand for this.Seconds = ...;
// }
```

The error reports that methods and properties (Hours implies this.Hours) are accessed prior to the initialization of all fields. To resolve the issue, you need to initialize the fields directly, as demonstrated in Listing 8.1.

ADVANCED TOPIC

Using new with Value Types

Invoking the new operator on a reference type compiles to the CIL instruction newobj. new is available to value types as well, but in contrast, the underlying CIL instruction is initobj. This instruction initializes the memory with default values (the equivalent of assigning default(<type>) in C# 2.0).

Unlike classes, structs do not support finalizers. For local variable value types, memory is allocated on the stack, so there is no need for the garbage collector to handle the value type's cleanup and no finalizer is called before the stack is unwound. For value types that are part of a reference type, the data is stored on the heap and memory is cleaned up as part of the reference object's garbage collection.

Language Contrast: C++—struct Defines Type with Public Members

In C++, the difference between structs and classes is simply that by default, a struct's members are public. C# doesn't include this subtle distinction. The contrast is far greater in C#, where struct significantly changes the memory behavior from that of a class.

Using the `default` Operator

To provide a constructor that didn't require _Seconds would not avoid the requirement that _Seconds still required initialization. You can assign the default value of _Seconds using 0 explicitly or, in C# 2.0, using the `default` operator.

Listing 8.4 passes the default value into the `Angle` constructor that includes _Seconds. However, the default operator can be used outside the `this` constructor call (_Seconds = default(int), for example). It is a way to specify the value for the default of a particular type.

LISTING 8.4: Using the `default` Operator to Retrieve the Default Value of a Type

```
// Use keyword struct to declare a value type.
struct Angle
{
  public Angle(int hours, int minutes)
      : this( hours, minutes, default(int) )
  {
  }

  // ...
}
```

Inheritance and Interfaces with Value Types

All value types are sealed. In addition, all value types derive from `System.ValueType`. This means that the inheritance chain for structs is always from `object` to `ValueType` to the struct.

Value types can implement interfaces, too. Many of those built into the framework implement interfaces such as `IComparable` and `IFormattable`.

`ValueType` brings with it the behavior of value types, but it does not include any additional members (all of its members override `object`'s virtual members). However, as with classes, you can override the virtual members of `System.Object`. The rules for overriding are virtually the same as with reference types (see Chapter 9). However, one difference is that with value types, the default implementation for `GetHashCode()` is to forward the call to the first non-null field within the struct. Also, `Equals()`

makes significant use of reflection. This leads to the conclusion that if a value type is frequently used inside collections, especially dictionary-type collections that use hash codes, the value type should include overrides for both `Equals()` and `GetHashCode()` (see Chapter 9).

Boxing

Because local variable value types directly contain their data, and their interfaces and `System.Object` contain references to their data, an important question to consider is what happens when a value type is converted to one of its implemented interfaces or to its root base class, `object`. The conversion is known as **boxing** and it has special behavior. Converting from a value type that directly refers to its data to a reference type which points to a location on the heap involves several steps.

1. First, memory is allocated on the heap that will contain the value type's data and a little overhead (a `SyncBlockIndex` and method table pointer).
2. Next, a memory copy occurs from the value type's data on the stack, into the allocated location on the heap.
3. Finally, the object or interface reference is updated to point at the location on the heap.

The reverse operation is **unboxing.** By definition, the unbox CIL instruction simply references the data on the heap; it doesn't include the copy from the heap to the stack. In most cases with C#, however, a copy follows unboxing anyway.

Boxing and unboxing are important to consider because boxing has some performance and behavioral implications. Besides learning how to recognize them within C# code, a developer can count the box/unbox instructions in a particular snippet of code by looking through the CIL. Each operation has specific instructions, as shown in Table 8.1.

TABLE 8.1: Boxing Code in CIL

C# Code	CIL Code

static void Main()
 	
{
 	
    int number;
    object thing;
 	
    number = 42;
 	
    // Boxing
    thing = number;
 	
    // Unboxing
    number = (int)thing;
 	
    return;
}
	.method private hidebysig
	        static void Main() cil managed
	    {
	    .entrypoint
	    // Code size 21 (0x15)
	    .maxstack 1
	    .locals init ([0] int32 number,
	            [1] object thing)
	    IL_0000: nop
	    IL_0001: ldc.i4.s 42
	    IL_0003: stloc.0
	    IL_0004: ldloc.0
	    IL_0005: **box** [mscorlib]System.Int32
	    IL_000a: stloc.1
	    IL_000b: ldloc.1
	    IL_000c: **unbox.any** [mscorlib]System.Int32
	    IL_0011: stloc.0
	    IL_0012: br.s IL_0014
	    IL_0014: ret
	    } // end of method Program::Main

When boxing occurs in low volume, the performance concerns are irrelevant. However, boxing is sometimes subtle and frequent occurrences can make a difference with performance. Consider Listing 8.5 and Output 8.1.

LISTING 8.5: Subtle Box and Unbox Instructions

```csharp
class DisplayFibonacci
{
  static void Main()
  {

    int totalCount;
    System.Collections.ArrayList list =
        new System.Collections.ArrayList();

    Console.Write("Enter a number between 2 and 1000:");
    totalCount = int.Parse(Console.ReadLine());

    // Execution-time error:
    // list.Add(0);  // Cast to double or 'D' suffix required
                  // Whether cast or using 'D' suffix,
                  // CIL is identical.
    list.Add((double)0);
    list.Add((double)1);
```

```
        for (int count = 2; count < totalCount; count++)
        {
            list.Add(
                ((double)list[count - 1] +
                (double)list[count - 2]) );
        }

        foreach (double count in list)
        {
            Console.Write("{0}, ", count);
        }
    }
}
```

OUTPUT 8.1:

```
Enter a number between 2 and 1000:42
0, 1, 1, 2, 3, 5, 8, 13, 21, 34, 55, 89, 144, 233, 377, 610, 987, 1597,
2584, 4181, 6765, 10946, 17711, 28657, 46368, 75025, 121393, 196418,
317811, 514229, 832040, 1346269, 2178309, 3524578, 5702887, 9227465,
14930352, 24157817, 39088169, 63245986, 102334155, 165580141,
```

The code shown in Listing 8.5, when compiled, produces five box and three unbox instructions in the resultant CIL.

1. The first two box instructions occur in the initial calls to list.Add(). The signature for the ArrayList method is int Add(object value). As such, any value type passed to this method is boxed.

2. Next are two unbox instructions in the call to Add() within the for loop. The return from an ArrayList's index operator is always object because that is what ArrayList collects. In order to add the two values, however, you need to cast them back to doubles. This cast back from an object to a value type is an unbox call.

3. Now you take the result of the addition and place it into the ArrayList instance, which again results in a box operation. Note that the first two unbox instructions and this box instruction occur within a loop.

4. In the foreach loop, you iterate through each item in ArrayList and assign them to count. However, as you already saw, the items within ArrayList are objects, so assigning them to a double is unboxing each of them.

5. The signature for Console.WriteLine() that is called within the foreach loop is void Console.Write(string format, object arg). As a result, each call to it invokes a box operation back from double and into object.

Obviously, you can easily improve this code by eliminating many of the boxing operations. Using an object rather than double in the last foreach loop is one improvement you can make. Another would be to change the ArrayList data type to a generic collection (see Chapter 11). The point, however, is that boxing can be rather subtle, so developers need to pay special attention and notice situations where it could potentially occur repeatedly and affect performance.

There is another unfortunate runtime-boxing-related problem. If you wanted to change the initial two Add() calls so that they did not use a cast (or a double literal), you would have to insert integers into the array list. Since ints will implicitly cast to doubles, this would appear to be an innocuous modification. However, the casts to double from within the for loop, and again in the assignment to count in the foreach loops, would fail. The problem is that immediately following the unbox operation is an attempt to perform a memory copy of the int into a double. You cannot do this without first casting to an int, because the code will throw an InvalidCastException at execution time. Listing 8.6 shows a similar error commented out and followed by the correct cast.

LISTING 8.6: Unboxing Must Be to the Underlying Type

```
// ...
int number;
object thing;
double bigNumber;

number = 42;
thing = number;
// ERROR: InvalidCastException
// bigNumber = (double)thing;
bigNumber = (double)(int)thing;
// ...
```

■ ADVANCED TOPIC

Value Types in the `lock` Statement

C# supports a `lock` statement for synchronizing code. The statement compiles down to `System.Threading.Monitor`'s `Enter()` and `Exit()` methods. These two methods must be called in pairs. `Enter()` records the unique reference argument passed so that when `Exit()` is called with the same reference, the lock can be released. The trouble with using value types is the boxing. Therefore, each time `Enter()` or `Exit()` is called, a new value is created on the heap. Comparing the reference of one copy to the reference of a different copy will always return `false`, so you cannot hook up `Enter()` with the corresponding `Exit()`. Therefore, value types in the `lock()` statement are not allowed.

Listing 8.7 points out a few more runtime boxing idiosyncrasies and Output 8.2 shows the results.

LISTING 8.7: Subtle Boxing Idiosyncrasies

```csharp
interface IAngle
{
    void MoveTo(int hours, int minutes, int seconds);
}
```

```csharp
struct Angle : IAngle
{
    // ...

    // NOTE:  This makes Angle mutable, against the general
    //        guideline
    public void MoveTo(int hours, int minutes, int seconds)
    {
        _Hours = hours;
        _Minutes = minutes;
        _Seconds = seconds;
    }
}
```

```csharp
class Program
{
  static void Main()
```

```
    {
        // ...

        Angle angle = new Angle(25, 58, 23);
        object objectAngle = angle;  // Box
        Console.Write( ((Angle)objectAngle).Hours);

        // Unbox and discard
        ((Angle)objectAngle).MoveTo(26, 58, 23);
        Console.Write( ((Angle)objectAngle).Hours);

        // Box, modify, and discard
        ((IAngle)angle).MoveTo(26, 58, 23);
        Console.Write(", " + ((Angle)angle).Hours);

        // Modify heap directly
        ((IAngle)objectAngle).MoveTo(26, 58, 23);
        Console.WriteLine(", " + ((Angle)objectAngle).Hours);

        // ...
    }
}
```

OUTPUT 8.2:

```
25, 25, 25, 26
```

Listing 8.7 uses the Angle struct and IAngle interface from Listing 8.1. Note also that the IAngle.MoveTo() interface changes Angle to be mutable. This brings out some of the idiosyncrasies and, in so doing, demonstrates the importance of the guideline to make structs immutable.

In the first two lines, you initialize angle and then box it into a variable called objectAngle. Next, you call move in order to change Hours to 26. However, as the output demonstrates, no change actually occurs the first time. The problem is that in order to call MoveTo(), the compiler unboxes object-Angle and (by definition) makes a copy of the value. Although the stack value is successfully modified at execution time, this value is discarded and no change occurs on the heap location referenced by objectAngle.

In the next example, a similar problem occurs in reverse. Instead of calling MoveTo() directly, the value is cast to IAngle. The cast invokes a box instruction and the runtime copies the angle data to the heap. Next, the data on the heap is modified directly on the heap before the call returns.

The result is that no copy back from the heap to the stack occurs. Instead, the modified heap data is ready for garbage collection while the data in angle remains unmodified.

In the last case, the cast to IAngle occurs with the data on the heap already, so no copy occurs. MoveTo() updates the _Hours value and the code behaves as desired.

ADVANCED TOPIC

Unboxing Avoided

As discussed earlier, the unboxing instruction does not include the copy back to the stack. Although some languages support the ability to access value types on the heap directly, this is possible in C# only when the value type is accessed as a field on a reference type. Since interfaces are reference types, unboxing and copying can be avoided, when accessing the boxed value via its interface.

When you call an interface method on a value type, the instance must be a variable because the method might mutate the value. Since unboxing produces a managed address, the runtime has a storage location and hence a variable. As a result, the runtime simply passes that managed address on an interface and no unboxing operation is necessary.

Listing 8.7 added an interface implementation to the Angle struct. Listing 8.8 uses the interface to avoid unboxing.

LISTING 8.8: Avoiding Unboxing and Copying

```
int number;
object thing;
number = 42;
// Boxing
thing = number;
// No unbox instruction.
string text = ((IFormattable)thing).ToString(
    "X", null);
Console.WriteLine(text);
```

Interfaces are reference types anyway, so calling an interface member does not even require unboxing. Furthermore, calling a struct's ToString() method (that overrides object's ToString() method) does not require an unbox. When compiling, it is clear that a `struct`'s overriding `ToString()` method will always be called because all value types are sealed. The result is that the C# compiler can instruct a direct call to the method without unboxing.

Enums

Compare the two code snippets shown in Listing 8.9.

LISTING 8.9: Comparing an Integer Switch to an Enum Switch

```csharp
int connectionState;
// ...
switch (connectionState)
{
    case 0:
        // ...
        break;
    case 1:
        // ...
        break;
    case 2:
        // ...
        break;
    case 3:
        // ...
        break;
}
```

```csharp
ConnectionState connectionState;
// ...
switch (connectionState)
{
    case ConnectionState.Connected:
        // ...
        break;
    case ConnectionState.Connecting:
        // ...
        break;
    case ConnectionState.Disconnected:
        // ...
        break;
    case ConnectionState.Disconnecting:
        // ...
        break;
}
```

Obviously, the difference in terms of readability is tremendous because in the second snippet, the cases are self-documenting to some degree. However, the performance at runtime is identical. To achieve this, the second snippet uses **enum values** in each case statement.

An enum is a type that the developer can define. The key characteristic of an enum is that it identifies a compile-time-defined set of possible values, each value referred to by name, making the code easier to read. You define an enum using a style similar to that for a class, as Listing 8.10 shows.

LISTING 8.10: Defining an Enum

```
enum ConnectionState
{
  Disconnected,
  Connecting,
  Connected,
  Disconnecting
}
```

■ **NOTE**

An enum is helpful even for Boolean parameters. For example, a method call such as `SetState(true)` is less readable than `SetState(DeviceState.On)`.

You refer to an enum value by prefixing it with the enum name; to refer to the `Connected` value, for example, you use `ConnectionState.Connected`. You should not use the enum names within the enum value name, to avoid the redundancy of something such as `ConnectionState.ConnectionStateConnected`. By convention, the enum name itself should be singular, unless the enums are bit flags (discussed shortly).

By default, the first enum value is `0` (technically, it is `0` implicitly converted to the underlying enum type), and each subsequent entry increases by one. However, you can assign explicit values to enums, as shown in Listing 8.11.

LISTING 8.11: Defining an Enum Type

```
enum ConnectionState : short
{
  Disconnected,
  Connecting = 10,
  Connected,
  Joined = Connected,
  Disconnecting
}
```

Disconnected has a default value of 0, Connecting has been explicitly assigned 10, and consequently, Connected will be assigned 11. Joined is assigned 11, the value referred to by Connected. (In this case, you do not need to prefix Connected with the enum name, since it appears within its scope.) Disconnecting is 12.

An enum always has an underlying type, which may be int, uint, long, or ulong, but not char. In fact, the enum type's performance is equivalent to that of the underlying type. By default, the underlying value type is int, but you can specify a different type using inheritance type syntax. Instead of int, for example, Listing 8.11 uses a short. For consistency, the syntax emulates that of inheritance, but this doesn't actually make an inheritance relationship. The base class for all enums is System.Enum. Furthermore, these classes are sealed; you can't derive from an existing enum type to add additional members.

Successful conversion doesn't work just for valid enum values. It is possible to cast 42 into a ConnectionState, even though there is no corresponding ConnectionState enum value. If the value successfully converts to the underlying type, the conversion will be successful.

The advantage to allowing casting, even without a corresponding enum value, is that enums can have new values added in later API releases, without breaking earlier versions. Additionally, the enum values provide names for the known values while still allowing unknown values to be assigned at runtime. The burden is that developers must code defensively for the possibility of unnamed values. It would be unwise, for example, to replace case ConnectionState.Disconnecting with default and expect that the only possible value for the default case was ConnectionState.Disconnecting. Instead, you should handle the Disconnecting case explicitly and the Default case should report an error or behave innocuously. As indicated before, however, conversion between the enum and the underlying type, and vice versa, involves an explicit cast, not an implicit conversion. For example, code cannot call `ReportState(10)` where the signature is `void Report-State(ConnectionState state)`. (The only exception is passing `0` because there is an implicit conversion from `0` to any enum.) The compiler will perform a type check and require an explicit cast if the type is not identical.

Although you can add additional values to an enum in a later version of your code, you should do this with care. Inserting an enum value in the middle of an enum will bump the values of all later enums (adding `Flooded` or `Locked` before `Connected` will change the `Connected` value, for example). This will affect the versions of all code that is recompiled against the new version. However, any code compiled against the old version will continue to use the old values, making the intended values entirely different. Besides inserting an enum value at the end of the list, one way to avoid changing enum values is to assign values explicitly.

Enums are slightly different from other value types because enums derive from `System.Enum` before deriving from `System.ValueType`.

Type Compatibility between Enums

C# also does not support a direct cast between arrays of two different enums. However, there is a way to coerce the conversion by casting first to an array and then to the second enum. The requirement is that both enums share the same underlying type, and the trick is to cast first to `System.Array`, as shown at the end of Listing 8.12.

LISTING 8.12: Casting between Arrays of Enums

```
enum ConnectionState1
{
  Disconnected,
  Connecting,
  Connected,
  Disconnecting
}
```

```
enum ConnectionState2
{
  Disconnected,
  Connecting,
```

```
    Connected,
    Disconnecting
}
```

```
class Program
{
  static void Main()
  {
      ConnectionState1[] states =
          (ConnectionState1[])(Array)new ConnectionState2[42];
  }
}
```

This exploits the fact that the CLR's notion of assignment compatibility is more lenient than C#'s. (The same trick is possible for illegal conversions, such as int[] to uint[].) However, use this approach cautiously because there is no C# specification detailing that this should work across different CLR implementations.

Converting between Enums and Strings

One of the conveniences associated with enums is the fact that the ToString() method, which is called by methods such as System.Console.WriteLine(), writes out the enum value identifier:

```
System.Diagnostics.Trace.WriteLine(string.Format(
    "The Connection is currently {0}.",
    ConnectionState.Disconnecting));
```

The preceding code will write the text in Output 8.3 to the trace buffer.

OUTPUT 8.3:

```
The Connection is currently Disconnecting.
```

Conversion from a string to an enum is a little harder to find because it involves a static method on the System.Enum base class. Listing 8.13 provides an example of how to do it without generics (see Chapter 11), and Output 8.4 shows the results.

LISTING 8.13: Converting a String to an Enum Using Enum.Parse()

```
ThreadPriorityLevel priority = (ThreadPriorityLevel)Enum.Parse(
    typeof(ThreadPriorityLevel), "Idle");
Console.WriteLine(priority);
```

OUTPUT 8.4:

```
Idle
```

The first parameter to Enum.Parse() is the type, which you specify using the keyword typeof(). This is a compile-time way of identifying the type, like a literal for the type value (see Chapter 17).

Until .NET Framework 4, there was no TryParse() method, so code prior to then should include appropriate exception handling if there is a chance the string will not correspond to an enum value identifier. .NET Framework 4's TryParse<T>() method uses generics, but the type parameters can be implied, resulting in the to-enum conversion example shown in Listing 8.14.

LISTING 8.14: Converting a String to an Enum Using Enum.TryParse<T>()

```
System.Threading.ThreadPriorityLevel priority;
if(Enum.TryParse("Idle", out priority))
{
    Console.WriteLine(priority);
}
```

This conversion offers the advantage that there is no need to use exception handling if the string doesn't convert. Instead, code can check the Boolean result returned from the call to TryParse<T>().

Regardless of whether code uses the "Parse" or "TryParse" approach, the key caution about converting from a string to an enum is that such a cast is not localizable. Therefore, developers should use this type of cast only for messages that are not exposed to users (assuming localization is a requirement).

Enums as Flags

Many times, developers not only want enum values to be unique, but they also want to be able to combine them to represent a combinatorial value.

For example, consider System.IO.FileAttributes. This enum, shown in Listing 8.15, indicates various attributes on a file: read-only, hidden, archive, and so on. The difference is that unlike the ConnectionState attribute, where each enum value was mutually exclusive, the FileAttributes enum values can and are intended for combination: A file can be both read-only and hidden. To support this, each enum value is a unique bit (or a value that represents a particular combination).

LISTING 8.15: Using Enums As Flags

```
public enum FileAttributes
{
  ReadOnly =          1<<0,    // 000000000000001
  Hidden =            1<<1,    // 000000000000010
  System =            1<<2,    // 000000000000100
  Directory =         1<<4,    // 000000000010000
  Archive =           1<<5,    // 000000000100000
  Device =            1<<6,    // 000000001000000
  Normal =            1<<7,    // 000000010000000
  Temporary =         1<<8,    // 000000100000000
  SparseFile =        1<<9,    // 000001000000000
  ReparsePoint =      1<<10,   // 000010000000000
  Compressed =        1<<11,   // 000100000000000
  Offline =           1<<12,   // 001000000000000
  NotContentIndexed = 1<<13,   // 010000000000000
  Encrypted =         1<<14,   // 100000000000000
}
```

Because enums support combined values, the guideline for the enum name of bit flags is plural.

To join enum values you use a bitwise OR operator, as shown in Listing 8.16.

LISTING 8.16: Using Bitwise OR and AND with Flag Enums

```
using System;
using System.IO;

public class Program
{
 public static void Main()
 {
     // ...

     string fileName = @"enumtest.txt";
```

```
    System.IO.FileInfo file =
        new System.IO.FileInfo(fileName);

    file.Attributes = FileAttributes.Hidden |
        FileAttributes.ReadOnly;

    Console.WriteLine("{0} | {1} = {2}",
        FileAttributes.Hidden, FileAttributes.ReadOnly,
        (int)file.Attributes);

    if ( (file.Attributes & FileAttributes.Hidden) !=
        FileAttributes.Hidden)
    {
        throw new Exception("File is not hidden.");
    }

    if (( file.Attributes & FileAttributes.ReadOnly) !=
        FileAttributes.ReadOnly)
    {
        throw new Exception("File is not read-only.");
    }

    // ...
}
```

The results of Listing 8.16 appear in Output 8.5.

OUTPUT 8.5:

```
Hidden | ReadOnly = 3
```

Using the bitwise OR operator allows you to set the file to both read-only and hidden. In addition, you can check for specific settings using the bit-wise AND operator.

Each value within the enum does not need to correspond to only one flag. It is perfectly reasonable to define additional flags that correspond to frequent combinations of values. Listing 8.17 shows an example.

LISTING 8.17: Defining Enum Values for Frequent Combinations

```
enum DistributedChannel
{
  None = 0,
  Transacted = 1,
  Queued = 2,
```

```
    Encrypted = 4,
    Persisted = 16,
    FaultTolerant =
        Transacted | Queued | Persisted
}
```

Furthermore, flags such as None are appropriate if there is the possibility that none is a valid value. In contrast, avoid enum values corresponding to things such as Maximum as the last enum, because Maximum could be interpreted as a valid enum value. To check whether a value is included within an enum use the System.Enum.IsDefined() method.

ADVANCED TOPIC

FlagsAttribute

If you decide to use flag-type values, the enum should include FlagsAttribute. The attribute appears in square brackets (see Chapter 17), just prior to the enum declaration, as shown in Listing 8.18.

LISTING 8.18: Using FlagsAttribute

```csharp
// FileAttributes defined in System.IO.

[Flags] // Decorating an enum with FlagsAttribute.
public enum FileAttributes
{
    ReadOnly =        1<<0,     // 000000000000001
    Hidden =          1<<1,     // 000000000000010
    // ...
}
```

```csharp
using System;
using System.Diagnostics;
using System.IO;

class Program
{
    public static void Main()
    {
        string fileName = @"enumtest.txt";
        FileInfo file = new FileInfo(fileName);
        file.Open(FileMode.Create).Close();

        FileAttributes startingAttributes =
            file.Attributes;
```

```
        file.Attributes = FileAttributes.Hidden |
            FileAttributes.ReadOnly;

        Console.WriteLine("\"{0}\" outputs as \"{1}\"",
            file.Attributes.ToString().Replace(",", " |"),
            file.Attributes);

        FileAttributes attributes =
            (FileAttributes) Enum.Parse(typeof(FileAttributes),
            file.Attributes.ToString());

        Console.WriteLine(attributes);

        File.SetAttributes(fileName,
            startingAttributes);
        file.Delete();
    }
}
```

The results of Listing 8.18 appear in Output 8.6.

OUTPUT 8.6:

```
"ReadOnly | Hidden" outputs as "ReadOnly, Hidden"
ReadOnly, Hidden
```

The flag documents that the enum values can be combined. Furthermore, it changes the behavior of the `ToString()` and `Parse()` methods. For example, calling `ToString()` on an enum that is decorated with `FlagsAttribute` writes out the strings for each enum flag that is set. In Listing 8.18, `file.Attributes.ToString()` returns ReadOnly, Hidden rather than the 3 it would have returned without the `FileAttributes` flag. If two enum values are the same, the `ToString()` call would return the first value. As mentioned earlier, however, you should use this with caution because it is not localizable.

Parsing a value from a string to the enum also works. Each enum value identifier is separated by a comma.

It is important to note that `FlagsAttribute` does not automatically assign unique flag values or check that they have unique values. Doing this wouldn't make sense, since duplicates and combinations are often desirable. Instead, you must assign the values of each enum item explicitly.

SUMMARY

This chapter began with a discussion of how to define custom value types. One of the key guidelines that emerge is to create immutable value types. Boxing also was part of the value type discussion.

The idiosyncrasies introduced by boxing are subtle, and the vast majority of them lead to issues at execution time rather than at compile time. Although it is important to know about these in order to try to avoid them, in many ways, focused attention on the potential pitfalls overshadows the usefulness and performance advantages of value types. Programmers should not be overly concerned about using value types. Value types permeate virtually every chapter of this book, and yet the idiosyncrasies do not. I have staged the code surrounding each issue to demonstrate the concern, but in reality, these types of patterns rarely occur. The key to avoiding most of them is to follow the guideline of not creating mutable value types; this is why you don't encounter them within the primitive types.

Perhaps the only issue to occur with some frequency is repetitive boxing operations within loops. However, C# 2.0 greatly reduces the chance of this with the addition of generics, and even without that, performance is rarely affected enough to warrant avoidance until a particular algorithm with boxing is identified as a bottleneck.

Furthermore, custom structs (value types) are relatively rare. They obviously play an important role within C# development, but when compared to the number of classes, custom structs are rare—when custom structs are required, it is generally in frameworks targeted at interoperating with managed code or a particular problem space.

In addition to demonstrating structs, this chapter introduced enums. This is a standard construct available in most programming languages, and it deserves prominent consideration if you want to improve API usability and code readability.

The next chapter highlights more guidelines to creating well-formed types, both structs and otherwise. It begins by looking at overriding the virtual members of objects and defining operator-overloading methods. These two topics apply to both structs and classes, but they are somewhat more critical in completing a struct definition and making it well formed.

■9■
Well-Formed Types

T HE PREVIOUS CHAPTERS covered most of the constructs for defining classes and structs. However, several details remain concerning rounding out the type definition with fit-and-finish-type functionality. This chapter introduces how to put the final touches on a type declaration.

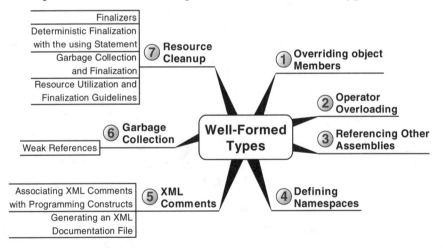

Overriding object Members

Chapter 6 discussed how all types derive from object. In addition, it reviewed each method available on object and discussed how some of them are virtual. This section discusses the details concerning overloading the virtual methods.

Overriding ToString()

By default, calling ToString() on any object will return the fully qualified name of the class. Calling ToString() on a System.IO.FileStream object will return the string System.IO.FileStream, for example. For some classes, however, ToString() can be more meaningful. On string, for example, ToString() returns the string value itself. Similarly, returning a Contact's name would make more sense. Listing 9.1 overrides ToString() to return a string representation of Coordinate.

LISTING 9.1: Overriding ToString()

```csharp
public struct Coordinate
{
  public Coordinate(Longitude longitude, Latitude latitude)
  {
      _Longitude = longitude;
      _Latitude = latitude;
  }

  public Longitude Longitude { get { return _Longitude; } }
  private readonly Longitude _Longitude;

  public Latitude Latitude { get { return _Latitude; } }
  private readonly Latitude _Latitude;

  public override string ToString()
  {
  return string.Format("{0} {1}", Longitude, Latitude);
  }
  // ...
}
```

Write methods such as Console.WriteLine() call an object's ToString() method, so overloading it often outputs more meaningful information than the default implementation.

Overriding GetHashCode()

Overriding GetHashCode() is more complex than overriding ToString(). Regardless, you should override GetHashCode() when you are overriding Equals(), and there is a compiler warning to indicate this. Overriding

GetHashCode() is also a good practice when you are using it as a key into a hash table collection (System.Collections.Hashtable and System.Collections.Generic.Dictionary, for example).

The purpose of the hash code is to *efficiently balance a hash table* by generating a number that corresponds to the value of an object. Here are some implementation principles for a good GetHashCode() implementation.

- *Required:* Equal objects must have equal hash codes (if a.Equals(b), then a.GetHashCode() == b.GetHashCode()).

- *Required:* GetHashCode()'s returns over the life of a particular object should be constant (the same value), even if the object's data changes. In many cases, you should cache the method return to enforce this.

- *Required:* GetHashCode() should not throw any exceptions; GetHashCode() must always successfully return a value.

- *Performance:* Hash codes should be unique whenever possible. However, since hash code returns only an int, there has to be an overlap in hash codes for objects that have potentially more values than an int can hold—virtually all types. (An obvious example is long, since there are more possible long values than an int could uniquely identify.)

- *Performance:* The possible hash code values should be distributed evenly over the range of an int. For example, creating a hash that doesn't consider the fact that distribution of a string in Latin-based languages primarily centers on the initial 128 ASCII characters would result in a very uneven distribution of string values and would not be a strong GetHashCode() algorithm.

- *Performance:* GetHashCode() should be optimized for performance. GetHashCode() is generally used in Equals() implementations to short-circuit a full equals comparison if the hash codes are different. As a result, it is frequently called when the type is used as a key type in dictionary collections.

- *Performance:* Small differences between two objects should result in large differences between hash code values—ideally, a 1-bit difference in the object results in around 16 bits of the hash code changing, on average. This helps ensure that the hash table remains balanced no matter how it is "bucketing" the hash values.

- *Security:* It should be difficult for an attacker to craft an object that has a particular hash code. The attack is to flood a hash table with large amounts of data that all hash to the same value. The hash table implementation then becomes O(n) instead of O(1), resulting in a possible denial-of-service attack.

Consider the GetHashCode() implementation for the Coordinate type shown in Listing 9.2.

LISTING 9.2: Implementing GetHashCode()

```csharp
public struct Coordinate
{
  public Coordinate(Longitude longitude, Latitude latitude)
  {
      _Longitude = longitude;
      _Latitude = latitude;
  }

  public Longitude Longitude { get { return _Longitude; } }
  private readonly Longitude _Longitude;

  public Latitude Latitude { get { return _Latitude; } }
  private readonly Latitude _Latitude;

  public override int GetHashCode()
  {
      int hashCode = Longitude.GetHashCode();
      // As long as the hash codes are not equal
      if(Longitude.GetHashCode() != Latitude.GetHashCode())
      {
          hashCode ^= Latitude.GetHashCode();  // eXclusive OR
      }
      return hashCode;
  }

  // ...
}
```

Generally, the key is to use the XOR operator over the hash codes from the relevant types, and to make sure the XOR operands are not likely to be close or equal—or else the result will be all zeroes. (In those cases where the operands are close or equal, consider using bitshifts and adds instead.) The alternative operands, AND and OR, have similar restrictions, but the restrictions occur more frequently. Applying AND multiple times tends toward all 0 bits, and applying OR tends toward all 1 bits.

For finer-grained control, split larger-than-int types using the shift operator. For example, GetHashCode() for a long called value is implemented as follows:

```
int GetHashCode() { return ((int)value ^ (int)(value >> 32)) };
```

Also, note that if the base class is not object, then base.GetHashCode() should be included in the XOR assignment.

Finally, Coordinate does not cache the value of the hash code. Since each field in the hash code calculation is readonly, the value can't change. However, implementations should cache the hash code if calculated values could change or if a cached value could offer a significant performance advantage.

Overriding Equals()

Overriding Equals() without overriding GetHashCode() results in a warning such as that shown in Output 9.1.

OUTPUT 9.1:

```
warning CS0659: '<Class Name>' overrides Object.Equals(object o) but
does not override Object.GetHashCode()
```

Generally, programmers expect overriding Equals() to be trivial, but it includes a surprising number of subtleties that require careful thought and testing.

Object Identity versus Equal Object Values

Two references are identical if both refer to the same instance. object, and therefore, all objects, include a static method called ReferenceEquals() that explicitly checks for this object identity (see Figure 9.1)

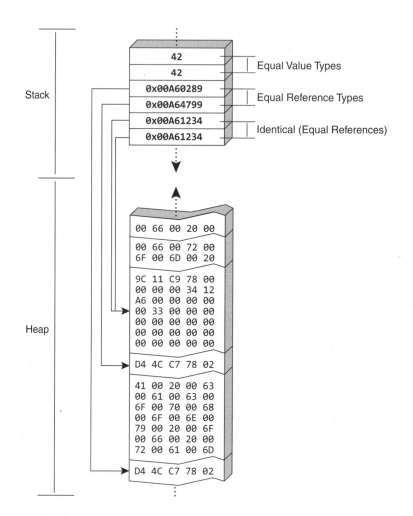

FIGURE 9.1: Identity

However, identical reference is not the only type of equality. Two object instances can also be equal if the values that identify them are equal. Consider the comparison of two ProductSerialNumbers shown in Listing 9.3.

LISTING 9.3: Equal

```
public sealed class ProductSerialNumber
{
    // See Appendix B
}
```

```
class Program
{
    static void Main()
    {
        ProductSerialNumber serialNumber1 =
            new ProductSerialNumber("PV", 1000, 09187234);
        ProductSerialNumber serialNumber2 = serialNumber1;
        ProductSerialNumber serialNumber3 =
            new ProductSerialNumber("PV", 1000, 09187234);

        // These serial numbers ARE the same object identity.
        if(!ProductSerialNumber.ReferenceEquals(serialNumber1,
            serialNumber2))
        {
            throw new Exception(
                "serialNumber1 does NOT " +
                "reference equal serialNumber2");
        }
        // and, therefore, they are equal
        else if(!serialNumber1.Equals(serialNumber2))
        {
            throw new Exception(
                "serialNumber1 does NOT equal serialNumber2");
        }
        else
        {
            Console.WriteLine(
                "serialNumber1 reference equals serialNumber2");
            Console.WriteLine(
                "serialNumber1 equals serialNumber2");
        }

        // These serial numbers are NOT the same object identity.
        if (ProductSerialNumber.ReferenceEquals(serialNumber1,
                serialNumber3))
        {
            throw new Exception(
                "serialNumber1 DOES reference " +
                "equal serialNumber3");
        }
        // but they are equal (assuming Equals is overloaded).
        else if(!serialNumber1.Equals(serialNumber3) ||
            serialNumber1 != serialNumber3)
        {
            throw new Exception(
                "serialNumber1 does NOT equal serialNumber3");
        }
```

```
            Console.WriteLine( "serialNumber1 equals serialNumber3" );
            Console.WriteLine( "serialNumber1 == serialNumber3" );
        }
    }
```

The results of Listing 9.3 appear in Output 9.2.

OUTPUT 9.2:

```
serialNumber1 reference equals serialNumber2
serialNumber1 equals serialNumber3
serialNumber1 == serialNumber3
```

As the last assertion demonstrates with `ReferenceEquals()`, serial-Number1 and `serialNumber3` are not the same reference. However, the code constructs them with the same values and both logically associate with the same physical product. If one instance was created from data in the database and another was created from manually entered data, you would expect the instances would be equal and, therefore, that the product would not be duplicated (reentered) in the database. Two identical references are obviously equal; however, two different objects could be equal but not reference equal. Such objects will not have identical object identities, but they may have key data that identifies them as being equal objects.

Only reference types can be reference equal, thereby supporting the concept of identity. Calling `ReferenceEquals()` on value types will always return `false` since, by definition, the value type directly contains its data, not a reference. Even when `ReferenceEquals()` passes the same variable in both (value type) parameters to `ReferenceEquals()`, the result will still be `false` because the very nature of value types is that they are copied into the parameters of the called method. Listing 9.4 demonstrates this behavior. In other words, `ReferenceEquals()` boxes the value types. Since each argument is put into a "different box" (location on the stack), they are never reference equal.

LISTING 9.4: Value Types Do Not Even Reference Equal Themselves

```
public struct Coordinate
{
    public Coordinate(Longitude longitude, Latitude latitude)
    {
```

```csharp
            _Longitude = longitude;
            _Latitude = latitude;
        }

        public Longitude Longitude { get { return _Longitude; } }
        private readonly Longitude _Longitude;

        public Latitude Latitude { get { return _Latitude; } }
        private readonly Latitude _Latitude;

        // ...
    }
```

```csharp
    class Program
    {
      public void Main()
      {
          //...

          Coordinate coordinate1 =
              new Coordinate( new Longitude(48, 52),
                              new Latitude(-2, -20));

          // Value types will never be reference equal.
          if ( Coordinate.ReferenceEquals(coordinate1,
              coordinate1) )
          {
              throw new Exception(
                  "coordinate1 reference equals coordinate1");
          }

          Console.WriteLine(
              "coordinate1 does NOT reference equal itself" );
      }
    }
```

In contrast to the definition of Coordinate as a reference type in Chapter 8, the definition going forward is that of a value type (struct) because the combination of Longitude and Latitude data is logically thought of as a value and the size is less than 16 bytes. (In Chapter 8, Coordinate aggregated Angle rather than Longitude and Latitude.) A contributing factor to declaring Coordinate as a value type is that it is a (complex) numeric value that has particular operations on it. In contrast, a reference type such as Employee is not a value that you manipulate numerically, but rather refers to an object in real life.

Implementing Equals()

To determine whether two objects are equal (they have same identifying data), you use an object's Equals() method. The implementation of this virtual method on object uses ReferenceEquals() to evaluate equality. Since this implementation is often inadequate, it is necessary to sometimes override Equals() with a more appropriate implementation.

For objects to *equal* each other, the expectation is that the identifying data within them is equal. For ProductSerialNumbers, for example, the ProductSeries, Model, and Id must be the same; however, for an Employee object, perhaps comparing EmployeeIds would be sufficient for equality. To correct object.Equals() implementation, it is necessary to override it. Value types, for example, override the Equals() implementation to instead use the fields that the type includes.

The steps for overriding Equals() are as follows.

1. Check for null.
2. Check for reference equality if the type is a reference type.
3. Check for equivalent types.
4. Invoke a typed helper method that can treat the operand as the compared type rather than an object (see the Equals(Coordinate obj) method in Listing 9.5).
5. Possibly check for equivalent hash codes to short-circuit an extensive, field-by-field comparison. (Two objects that are equal cannot have different hash codes.)
6. Check base.Equals() if the base class overrides Equals().
7. Compare each identifying field for equality.
8. Override GetHashCode().
9. Override the == and != operators (see the next section).

Listing 9.5 shows a sample Equals() implementation.

LISTING 9.5: Overriding Equals()

```csharp
public struct Longitude
{
    // ...
}
```

```csharp
public struct Latitude
{
  // ...
}
```

```csharp
public struct Coordinate
{
  public Coordinate(Longitude longitude, Latitude latitude)
  {
      _Longitude = longitude;
      _Latitude = latitude;
  }

  public Longitude Longitude { get { return _Longitude; } }
  private readonly Longitude _Longitude;

  public Latitude Latitude { get { return _Latitude; } }
  private readonly Latitude _Latitude;

  public override bool Equals(object obj)
  {
      // STEP 1: Check for null
      if (obj == null)
      {
          return false;
      }
      // STEP 3: equivalent data types
      if (this.GetType() != obj.GetType())
      {
          return false;
      }
      return Equals((Coordinate)obj);
  }
  public bool Equals(Coordinate obj)
  {
      // STEP 1: Check for null if a reference type
      // (e.g., a reference type)
      // if (obj == null)
      // {
      //     return false;
      // }

      // STEP 2: Check for ReferenceEquals if this
      // is a reference type
      // if ( ReferenceEquals(this, obj))
      // {
      //    return true;
      // }
```

```
        // STEP 4: Possibly check for equivalent hash codes
        // if (this.GetHashCode() != obj.GetHashCode())
        // {
        //     return false;
        // }

        // STEP 5: Check base.Equals if base overrides Equals()
        // System.Diagnostics.Debug.Assert(
        //     base.GetType() != typeof(object) );
        // if ( !base.Equals(obj) )
        // {
        //     return false;
        // }

        // STEP 6: Compare identifying fields for equality
        //           using an overload of Equals on Longitude.
        return ( (Longitude.Equals(obj.Longitude)) &&
            (Latitude.Equals(obj.Latitude)) );
    }

    // STEP 7: Override GetHashCode.
    public override int GetHashCode()
    {
        int hashCode = Longitude.GetHashCode();
        hashCode ^= Latitude.GetHashCode(); // Xor (eXclusive OR)
        return hashCode;
    }

}
```

In this implementation, the first two checks are relatively obvious. Checks 4–6 occur in an overload of Equals() that takes the Coordinate data type specifically. This way, a comparison of two Coordinates will avoid Equals(object obj) and its GetType() check altogether.

Since GetHashCode() is not cached and is no more efficient than step 5, the GetHashCode() comparison is commented out. Similarly, base.Equals() is not used since the base class is not overriding Equals(). (The assertion checks that base is not of type object, however it does not check that the base class overrides Equals(), which is required to appropriately call base.Equals().) Regardless, since GetHashCode() does not necessarily return a unique value (it only identifies when operands are different), on its own it does not conclusively identify equal objects.

Like GetHashCode(), Equals() should also never throw any exceptions. It is valid to compare any object with any other object, and doing so should never result in an exception.

Guidelines for Implementing Equality

While learning the details for overriding an object's virtual members, several guidelines emerge.

- Equals(), the == operator, and the != operator should be implemented together.
- A type should use the same algorithm within Equals(), ==, and != implementations.
- When implementing Equals(), ==, and !=, a type's GetHashCode() method should also be implemented.
- GetHashCode(), Equals(), ==, and != should never throw exceptions.
- When implementing IComparable, equality-related methods should also be implemented.

Operator Overloading

The preceding section looked at overriding Equals() and provided the guideline that the class should also implement == and !=. The term for implementing any operator is *operator overloading*, and this section describes how to do this, not only for == and !=, but also for other supported operators.

For example, string provides a + operator that concatenates two strings. This is perhaps not surprising, because string is a predefined type, so it could possibly have special compiler support. However, C# provides for adding + operator support to a class or struct. In fact, all operators are supported except x.y, f(x), new, typeof, default, checked, unchecked, delegate, is, as, =, and =>. One particular noteworthy operator that cannot be implemented is the assignment operator; there is no way to change the behavior of the = operator.

Comparison Operators (==, !=, <, >, <=, >=)

Once Equals() is overridden, there is a possible inconsistency. Two objects could return true for Equals() but false for the == operator because == performs a reference equality check by default as well. To correct this it is important to overload the equals (==) and not equals (!=) operators as well.

For the most part, the implementation for these operators can delegate the logic to Equals(), or vice versa. However, some initial null checks are required first (see Listing 9.6).

LISTING 9.6: Implementing the == and != Operators

```
public sealed class Coordinate
{

  // ...

  public static bool operator ==(
      Coordinate leftHandSide,
      Coordinate rightHandSide)
  {

      // Check if leftHandSide is null.
      // (operator== would be recursive)
      if (ReferenceEquals(leftHandSide, null))
      {
          // Return true if rightHandSide is also null
          // but false otherwise.
          return ReferenceEquals(rightHandSide, null);
      }

      return (leftHandSide.Equals(rightHandSide));
  }

  public static bool operator !=(
      Coordinate leftHandSide,
      Coordinate rightHandSide)
  {
      return !(leftHandSide == rightHandSide);
  }

}
```

Note that to perform the null checks, you cannot use an equality check for null (leftHandSide == null). Doing so would recursively call back into the method, resulting in a loop until overflowing the stack. To avoid this you call ReferenceEquals() to check for null.

Binary Operators (+, -, *, /, %, &, |, ^, <<, >>)

You can add an `Arc` to a `Coordinate`. However, the code so far provides no support for the addition operator. Instead, you need to define such a method, as Listing 9.7 shows.

LISTING 9.7: Adding an Operator

```
struct Arc
{
  public Arc(
      Longitude longitudeDifference,
      Latitude latitudeDifference)
  {
      _LongitudeDifference = longitudeDifference;
      _LatitudeDifference = latitudeDifference;
  }

  public Longitude LongitudeDifference
  {
      get
      {
          return _LongitudeDifference;
      }
  }
  private readonly Longitude _LongitudeDifference;

  public Latitude LatitudeDifference
  {
      get
      {
          return _LatitudeDifference;
      }
  }
  private readonly Latitude _LatitudeDifference;
}
```

```
struct Coordinate
{
  // ...
  public static Coordinate operator +(
      Coordinate source, Arc arc)
  {
      Coordinate result = new Coordinate(
          new Longitude(
              source.Longitude + arc.LongitudeDifference),
          new Latitude(
              source.Latitude + arc.LatitudeDifference));
      return result;
  }
}
```

The +, -, *, /, %, &, |, ^, <<, and >> operators are implemented as binary static methods where at least one parameter is of the containing type. The method name is the operator prefixed by the word *operator* as a keyword. As shown in Listing 9.8, given the definition of the - and + binary operators, you can add and subtract an Arc to and from the coordinate.

Note that Longitude and Latitude will also require implementations of the + operator because they are called by source.Longitude + arc.LongitudeDifference and source.Latitude + arc.LatitudeDifference.

LISTING 9.8: Calling the – and + Binary Operators

```
public class Program
{
  public static void Main()
  {
      Coordinate coordinate1,coordinate2;
      coordinate1 = new Coordinate(
          new Longitude(48, 52), new Latitude(-2, -20));
      Arc arc = new Arc(new Longitude(3), new Latitude(1));

      coordinate2 = coordinate1 + arc;
      Console.WriteLine(coordinate2);

      coordinate2 = coordinate2 - arc;
      Console.WriteLine(coordinate2);

      coordinate2 += arc;
      Console.WriteLine(coordinate2);
  }
}
```

The results of Listing 9.8 appear in Output 9.3.

OUTPUT 9.3:

```
51° 52' 0 E  -1° -20' 0 S
51° 52' 0 E  -1° -20' 0 S
54° 52' 0 E   0° -20' 0 S
```

For Coordinate, implement the – and + operators to return coordinate locations after subtracting Arc. This allows you to string multiple operators and operands together, as in result = coordinate1 + coordinate2 + coordinate3 – coordinate4;.

This works because the result of the first operand (`coordinate1 + coordinate2`) is another `Coordinate`, which you can then add to the next operand.

In contrast, consider if you provided a `-` operator that had two `Coordinate`s as parameters and returned a `double` corresponding to the distance between the two coordinates. Adding a `double` to a `Coordinate` is undefined and, therefore, you could not string operators and operands. Caution is in order when defining operators that behave this way, because doing so is counterintuitive.

Combining Assignment with Binary Operators (+=, -=, *=, /=, %=, &=...)

As previously mentioned, there is no support for overloading the assignment operator. However, assignment operators in combination with binary operators (+=, -=, *=, /=, %=, &=, |=, ^=, <<=, and >>=) are effectively overloaded when overloading the binary operator. Given the definition of a binary operator without the assignment, C# automatically allows for assignment in combination with the operator. Using the definition of `Coordinate` in Listing 9.7, therefore, you can have code such as:

```
coordinate += arc;
```

which is equivalent to the following:

```
coordinate = coordinate + arc;
```

Conditional Logical Operators (&&, ||)

Like assignment operators, conditional logical operators cannot be overloaded explicitly. However, since the logical operators & and | can be overloaded, and the conditional operators comprise the logical operators, effectively it is possible to overload conditional operators. `x && y` is processed as `x & y`, where `y` must evaluate to `true`. Similarly, `x || y` is processed as `x | y` only if `x` is `false`. To enable support for evaluating a type to `true` or `false`—in an `if` statement, for example—it is necessary to override the `true`/`false` unary operators.

Unary Operators (+, -, !, ~, ++, --, `true`, `false`)

Overloading unary operators is very similar to overloading binary operators, except that they take only one parameter, also of the containing type.

Listing 9.9 overloads the + and – operators for `Longitude` and `Latitude` and then uses these operators when overloading the same operators in `Arc`.

LISTING 9.9: Overloading the – and + Unary Operators

```csharp
public struct Latitude
{
  // ...
  public static Latitude operator -(Latitude latitude)
  {
      return new Latitude(-latitude.DecimalDegrees);
  }
  public static Latitude operator +(Latitude latitude)
  {
      return latitude;
  }
}


public struct Longitude
{
  // ...
  public static Longitude operator -(Longitude longitude)
  {
      return new Longitude(-longitude.DecimalDegrees);
  }
  public static Longitude operator +(Longitude longitude)
  {
      return longitude;
  }
}


public struct Arc
{
  // ...
  public static Arc operator -(Arc arc)
  {
      // Uses unary - operator defined on
      // Longitude and Latitude
      return new Arc(-arc.LongitudeDifference,
          -arc.LatitudeDifference);
  }
  public static Arc operator +(Arc arc)
  {
      return arc;
  }
}
```

Just as with numeric types, the + operator in this listing doesn't have any effect and is provided for symmetry.

Overloading `true` and `false` has the additional requirement that they both be overloaded. The signatures are the same as other operator overloads; however, the return must be a `bool`, as demonstrated in Listing 9.10.

LISTING 9.10: Overloading the `true` and `false` Operators

```
public static bool operator false(IsValid item)
{
    // ...
}
public static bool operator true(IsValid item)
{
    // ...
}
```

You can use types with overloaded `true` and `false` operators in `if`, `do`, `while`, and `for` controlling expressions.

Conversion Operators

Currently, there is no support in `Longitude`, `Latitude`, and `Coordinate` for casting to an alternate type. For example, there is no way to cast a `double` into a `Longitude` or `Latitude` instance. Similarly, there is no support for assigning a `Coordinate` using a `string`. Fortunately, C# provides for the definition of methods specifically to handle the converting of one type to another. Furthermore, the method declaration allows for specifying whether the conversion is implicit or explicit.

ADVANCED TOPIC

Cast Operator (())

Implementing the explicit and implicit conversion operators is not technically overloading the cast operator (()). However, this is effectively what takes place, so *defining a cast operator* is common terminology for implementing explicit or implicit conversion.

Defining a conversion operator is similar in style to defining any other operator, except that the "operator" is the resultant type of the conversion. Additionally, the `operator` keyword follows a keyword that indicates whether the conversion is implicit or explicit (see Listing 9.11).

LISTING 9.11: Providing an Implicit Conversion between Latitude and double

```csharp
public struct Latitude
{
  // ...

  public Latitude(double decimalDegrees)
  {
      _DecimalDegrees = Normalize(decimalDegrees);
  }

  public double DecimalDegrees
  {
      get { return _DecimalDegrees; }
  }
  private readonly double _DecimalDegrees;

  // ...

  public static implicit operator double(Latitude latitude)
  {
      return latitude.DecimalDegrees;
  }
  public static implicit operator Latitude(double degrees)
  {
      return new Latitude(degrees);
  }

  // ...
}
```

With these conversion operators, you now can convert doubles implicitly to and from Latitude objects. Assuming similar conversions exist for Longitude, you can simplify the creation of a Coordinate object by specifying the decimal degrees portion of each coordinate portion (for example, coordinate = new Coordinate(43, 172);).

> ■ **NOTE**
>
> When implementing a conversion operator, either the return or the parameter must be of the enclosing type—in support of encapsulation. C# does not allow you to specify conversions outside the scope of the converted type.

Guidelines for Conversion Operators

The difference between defining an implicit and an explicit conversion operator centers on preventing an unintentional implicit conversion that results in undesirable behavior. You should be aware of two possible consequences of using the explicit conversion operator. First, conversion operators that throw exceptions should always be explicit. For example, it is highly likely that a string will not conform to the appropriate format that a conversion from `string` to `Coordinate` requires. Given the chance of a failed conversion, you should define the particular conversion operator as explicit, thereby requiring that you be intentional about the conversion and that you ensure that the format is correct, or that you provide code to handle the possible exception. Frequently, the pattern for conversion is that one direction (`string` to `Coordinate`) is explicit and the reverse (`Coordinate` to `string`) is implicit.

A second consideration is the fact that some conversions will be lossy. Converting from a `float` (4.2) to an `int` is entirely valid, assuming an awareness of the fact that the decimal portion of the `float` will be lost. Any conversions that will lose data and not successfully convert back to the original type should be defined as explicit.

Referencing Other Assemblies

Instead of placing all code into one monolithic binary file, C# and the underlying CLI platform allow you to spread code across multiple assemblies. This enables you to reuse assemblies across multiple executables.

■ **BEGINNER TOPIC**

Class Libraries

The `HelloWorld.exe` program is one of the most trivial programs you can write. Real-world programs are more complex, and as complexity increases, it helps to organize the complexity by breaking programs into multiple parts. To do this, developers move portions of a program into separate compiled units called **class libraries** or, simply, **libraries.** Programs then reference and rely on class libraries to provide parts of their functionality. The power of this concept is that two programs can rely on the same class library, thereby sharing the functionality of that class library across the two programs and reducing the total amount of code needed.

In other words, it is possible to write features once, place them into a class library, and allow multiple programs to include those features by referencing the same class library. Later on, when developers fix a bug or add functionality to the class library, all the programs will have access to the increased functionality, just because they continue to reference the now improved class library.

To reuse the code within a different assembly, it is necessary to reference the assembly when running the C# compiler. Generally, the referenced assembly is a class library, and creating a class library requires a different assembly target from the default console executable targets you created thus far.

Changing the Assembly Target

The compiler allows you to create four different assembly types via the `/target` option.

- *Console executable:* This is the default type of assembly, and all compilation thus far has been to a console executable. (Leaving off the `/target` option or specifying `/target:exe` creates a console executable.)
- *Class library:* Classes that are shared across multiple executables are generally defined in a class library (`/target:library`).
- *Windows executable:* Windows executables are designed to run in the Microsoft Windows family of operating systems and outside the command console (`/target:winexe`).
- *Module:* In order to facilitate multiple languages within the same assembly, code can be compiled to a module and multiple modules can be combined to form an assembly (`/target:module`).

Assemblies to be shared across multiple applications are generally compiled as class libraries. Consider, for example, a library dedicated to functionality around longitude and latitude coordinates. To compile the

Coordinate, Longitude, and Latitude classes into their own library, you use the command line shown in Output 9.4.

OUTPUT 9.4:

```
>csc /target:library /out:Coordinates.dll Coordinate.cs IAngle.cs
Latitude.cs Longitude.cs Arc.cs
Microsoft (R) Visual C# 2010 Compiler version 4.0.20506.1
Copyright (C) Microsoft Corporation. All rights reserved.
```

Assuming you use .NET and the C# compiler is in the path, this builds an assembly library called Coordinates.dll.

Referencing an Assembly

To access code within a different assembly, the C# compiler allows the developer to reference the assembly on the command line. The option is /reference (/r is the abbreviation), followed by the list of references. The Program class listing from Listing 9.8 uses the Coordinate class, and if you place this into a separate executable, you reference Coordinates.dll using the .NET command line shown in Output 9.5.

OUTPUT 9.5:

```
csc.exe /R:Coordinates.dll Program.cs
```

The Mono command line appears in Output 9.6.

OUTPUT 9.6:

```
msc.exe /R:Coordinates.dll Program.cs
```

Encapsulation of Types

Just as classes serve as an encapsulation boundary for behavior and data, assemblies provide a similar boundary among groups of types. Developers can break a system into assemblies and then share those assemblies with multiple applications or integrate them with assemblies provided by third parties.

By default, a class without any access modifier is defined as internal.[1] The result is that the class is inaccessible from outside the assembly. Even

---

1. Excluding nested types which are private by default.

though another assembly references the assembly containing the class, all internal classes within the referenced assemblies will be inaccessible.

Just as `private` and `protected` provide levels of encapsulation to members within a class C# supports the use of access modifiers at the class level for control over the encapsulation of the classes within an assembly. The access modifiers available are `public` and `internal`, and in order to expose a class outside the assembly, the assembly must be marked as `public`. Therefore, before compiling the `Coordinates.dll` assembly, it is necessary to modify the type declarations as `public` (see Listing 9.12).

LISTING 9.12: Making Types Available Outside an Assembly

```
public struct Coordinate
{
  // ...
}
```

```
public struct Latitude
{
  // ...
}
```

```
public struct Longitude
{
  // ...
}
```

```
public struct Arc
{
  // ...
}
```

Similarly, declarations such as `class` and `enum` can also be either `public` or `internal`.

▪ ADVANCED TOPIC

Additional Class Access Modifiers

You can decorate nested classes with any access modifier available to other class members (`private`, for example). However, outside the class scope, the only available access modifiers are `public` and `internal`.

The internal access modifier is not limited to type declarations. It is also available on type members. Therefore, you can designate a type as `public` but mark specific methods within the type as `internal` so that the members are available only from within the assembly. It is not possible for the members to have a greater accessibility than the type. If the class is declared as `internal`, then public members on the type will be accessible only from within the assembly.

`protected internal` is another type member access modifier. Members with an accessibility modifier of `protected internal` will be accessible from all locations within the containing assembly *and* from classes that derive from the type, even if the derived class is not in the same assembly. The default state is `private`, so when you add an access modifier (other than `public`), the member becomes slightly more visible. Similarly, adding two modifiers compounds the effect.

■ BEGINNER TOPIC

Type Member Accessibility Modifiers

The full list of access modifiers appears in Table 9.1.

TABLE 9.1: Accessibility Modifiers

Modifier	Description
public	Declares that the member is accessible anywhere that the type is accessible. If the class is `internal`, the member will be internally visible. Public members will be accessible from outside the assembly if the containing type is public.
internal	The member is accessible from within the assembly only.
private	The member is accessible from within the containing type, but inaccessible otherwise.
protected	The member is accessible within the containing type and any subtypes derived from it, regardless of assembly.
protected internal	The member is accessible from anywhere within the containing assembly *and* from any types derived from the containing type, even if the derived types are within a different assembly.

Defining Namespaces

As mentioned in Chapter 2, all data types are identified by the combination of their namespace and their name. In fact, in the CLR there is no such thing as a "namespace." The type's name actually is the fully qualified type name. For the classes you defined earlier, there was no explicit namespace declaration. Classes such as these are automatically declared as members of the default global namespace. It is likely that such classes will experience a name collision, which occurs when you attempt to define two classes with the same name. Once you begin referencing other assemblies from third parties, the likelihood of a name collision increases even further.

To resolve this, you should place classes into namespaces. For example, classes outside the System namespace are generally placed into a namespace corresponding with the company, product name, or both. Classes from Addison-Wesley, for example, are placed into an Awl or AddisonWesley namespace, and classes from Microsoft (not System classes) are located in the Microsoft namespace. You should use the namespace keyword to create a namespace and to assign a class to it, as shown in Listing 9.13.

LISTING 9.13: Defining a Namespace

```
// Define the namespace AddisonWesley
namespace AddisonWesley
{
  class Program
  {
     // ...
  }
}
// End of AddisonWesley namespace declaration
```

All content between the namespace declaration's curly braces will then belong within the specified namespace. In Listing 9.13, Program is placed into the namespace AddisonWesley, making its full name AddisonWesley. Program.

Like classes, namespaces support nesting. This provides for a hierarchical organization of classes. All the System classes relating to network APIs are in the namespace System.Net, for example, and those relating to the Web are in System.Web.

There are two ways to nest namespaces. The first way is to nest them within each other (similar to classes), as demonstrated in Listing 9.14.

LISTING 9.14: Nesting Namespaces within Each Other

```csharp
// Define the namespace AddisonWesley
namespace AddisonWesley
{
  // Define the namespace AddisonWesley.Michaelis
  namespace Michaelis
  {
    // Define the namespace
    // AddisonWesley.Michaelis.EssentialCSharp
    namespace EssentialCSharp
    {
      // Declare the class
      // AddisonWesley.Michaelis.EssentialCSharp.Program
      class Program
      {
        // ...
      }
    }
  }
}
// End of AddisonWesley namespace declaration
```

Such a nesting will assign the Program class to the AddisonWesley.Michaelis. EssentialCSharp namespace.

The second way is to use the full namespace in a single namespace declaration in which a period separates each identifier, as shown in Listing 9.15.

LISTING 9.15: Nesting Namespaces Using a Period to Separate Each Identifier

```csharp
// Define the namespace AddisonWesley.Michaelis.EssentialCSharp
namespace AddisonWesley.Michaelis.EssentialCSharp
{
  class Program
  {
    // ...
  }
}
// End of AddisonWesley namespace declaration
```

Regardless of whether a namespace declaration follows Listing 9.14, Listing 9.15, or a combination of the two, the resultant CIL code will be identical. The same namespace may occur multiple times, in multiple files, and even across assemblies. For example, with the convention of one-to-one correlation between files and classes, you can define each class in its own file and surround it with the appropriate namespace declaration.

Namespace Alias Qualifier

Namespaces on their own deal with the vast majority of naming conflicts that might arise. However, sometimes (albeit rarely) conflict can arise because of an overlap in the namespace and class names. To account for this, the C# 2.0 compiler includes an option for providing an alias with the /reference option. For example, if the assemblies CoordinatesPlus.dll and Coordinates.dll have an overlapping type of Arc, you can reference both assemblies on the command line by assigning one or both references with a **namespace alias qualifier** that further distinguishes one class from the other. The results of such a reference appear in Output 9.7.

OUTPUT 9.7:

```
csc.exe /R:CoordPlus=CoordinatesPlus.dll /R:Coordinates.dll Program.cs
```

However, adding the alias during compilation is not sufficient on its own. In order to refer to classes in the aliased assembly, it is necessary to provide an extern directive that declares that the namespace alias qualifier is provided externally to the source code (see Listing 9.16).

LISTING 9.16: Using the extern Alias Directive

```
// extern must precede all other namespace elements
extern alias CoordPlus;

using System;
using CoordPlus::AddisonWesley.Michaelis.EssentialCSharp
// Equivalent also allowed
// using CoordPlus.AddisonWesley.Michaelis.EssentialCSharp

using global::AddisonWesley.Michaelis.EssentialCSharp
```

```
// Equivalent NOT allowed
// using global.AddisonWesley.Michaelis.EssentialCSharp

public class Program
{
  // ...
}
```

Once the `extern` alias for `CoordPlus` appears, you can reference the namespace using `CoordPlus`, followed by either two colons or a period.

To ensure that the lookup for the type occurs in the global namespace, C# 2.0 allows items to have the `global::` qualifier (but not `global.` because it could imaginably conflict with a real namespace of `global`).

XML Comments

Chapter 1 introduced comments. However, you can use XML comments for more than just notes to other programmers reviewing the source code. XML-based comments follow a practice popularized with Java. Although the C# compiler ignores all comments as far as the resultant executable goes, the developer can use command-line options to instruct the compiler[2] to extract the XML comments into a separate XML file. By taking advantage of the XML file generation, the developer can generate documentation of the API from the XML comments. In addition, C# editors can parse the XML comments in the code and display them to developers as distinct regions (for example, as a different color from the rest of the code), or parse the XML comment data elements and display them to the developer.

Figure 9.2 demonstrates how an IDE can take advantage of XML comments to assist the developer with a tip about the code he is trying to write.

---

2. The C# standard does not specify whether the C# compiler or a separate utility takes care of extracting the XML data. However, all mainstream C# compilers include the functionality via a compile switch instead of within an additional utility.

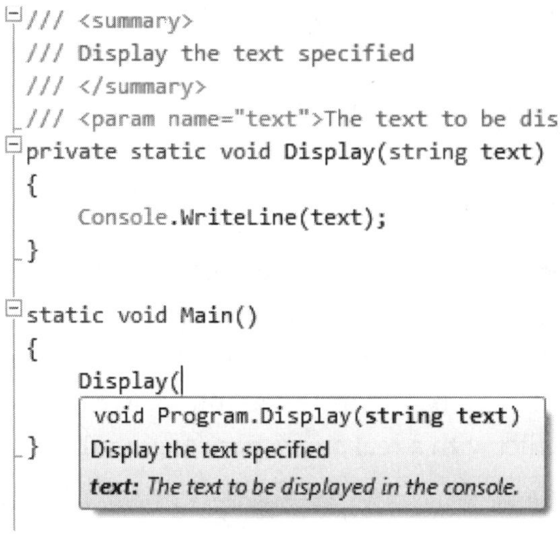

```
/// <summary>
/// Display the text specified
/// </summary>
/// <param name="text">The text to be displayed in the console.</param>
private static void Display(string text)
{
    Console.WriteLine(text);
}

static void Main()
{
    Display(|
        void Program.Display(string text)
        Display the text specified
        text: The text to be displayed in the console.
}
```

FIGURE 9.2: XML Comments as Tips in Visual Studio IDE

These coding tips offer significant assistance in large programs, especially when multiple developers share code. For this to work, however, the developer obviously must take the time to enter the XML comments within the code and then direct the compiler to create the XML file. The next section explains how to accomplish this.

Associating XML Comments with Programming Constructs

Consider the listing of the DataStorage class, as shown in Listing 9.17.

LISTING 9.17: Commenting Code with XML Comments

```
/// <summary>
/// DataStorage is used to persist and retrieve
/// employee data from the files.
/// </summary>
class DataStorage
{
    /// <summary>
    /// Save an employee object to a file
    /// named with the Employee name.
    /// </summary>
    /// <remarks>
    /// This method uses
    /// <seealso cref="System.IO.FileStream"/>
    /// in addition to
    /// <seealso cref="System.IO.StreamWriter"/>
```

⎫
⎬ Single-Line XML
⎭ Comment

```
/// </remarks>
/// <param name="employee">
/// The employee to persist to a file</param>
/// <date>January 1, 2000</date>
public static void Store(Employee employee)
{
    // ...
}

/**  <summary>
 *   Loads up an employee object
 *   </summary>
 *   <remarks>
 *   This method uses
 *   <seealso cref="System.IO.FileStream"/>
 *   in addition to
 *   <seealso cref="System.IO.StreamReader"/>
 *   </remarks>
 *   <param name="firstName">
 *   The first name of the employee</param>
 *   <param name="lastName">
 *   The last name of the employee</param>
 *   <returns>
 *   The employee object corresponding to the names
 *   </returns>
 *   <date>January 1, 2000</date>**/
public static Employee Load(
    string firstName, string lastName)
{
    // ...
}
}

class Program
{
    // ...
}
```

XML Delimited Comment (C# 2.0)

Listing 9.17 uses both XML delimited comments that span multiple lines, and single-line XML comments where each line requires a separate three-forward-slash delimiter (///).

Since XML comments are designed to document the API, they are intended for use only in association with C# declarations, such as the class or method shown in Listing 9.17. Any attempt to place an XML comment inline with the code, unassociated with a declaration, will result in a warning by the compiler. The compile makes the association simply because the XML comment appears immediately before the declaration.

Although C# allows any XML tag in comments, the C# standard explicitly defines a set of tags to be used. `<seealso cref="System.IO.Stream-Writer"/>` is an example of using the `seealso` tag. This tag creates a link between the text and the `System.IO.StreamWriter` class.

Generating an XML Documentation File

The compiler will check that the XML comments are well formed, and will issue a warning if they are not. To generate the XML file, you need to use the /doc option when compiling, as shown in Output 9.8.

OUTPUT 9.8:

```
>csc /doc:Comments.xml DataStorage.cs
```

The /doc option will create an XML file based on the name specified after the colon. Using the `CommentSamples` class listed earlier and the compiler options listed here, the resultant `CommentSamples.XML` file appears as shown in Listing 9.18.

LISTING 9.18: **Comments.xml**

```xml
<?xml version="1.0"?>
<doc>
    <assembly>
        <name>DataStorage</name>
    </assembly>
    <members>
        <member name="T:DataStorage">
            <summary>
            DataStorage is used to persist and retrieve
            employee data from the files.
            </summary>
        </member>
        <member name="M:DataStorage.Store(Employee)">
            <summary>
            Save an employee object to a file
```

```
                named with the Employee name.
                </summary>
                <remarks>
                This method uses
                <seealso cref="T:System.IO.FileStream"/>
                in addition to
                <seealso cref="T:System.IO.StreamWriter"/>
                </remarks>
                <param name="employee">
                The employee to persist to a file</param>
                <date>January 1, 2000</date>
            </member>
            <member name="M:DataStorage.Load(
                    System.String,System.String)">
                <summary>
                Loads up an employee object
                </summary>
                <remarks>
                This method uses
                <seealso cref="T:System.IO.FileStream"/>
                in addition to
                <seealso cref="T:System.IO.StreamReader"/>
                </remarks>
                <param name="firstName">
                The first name of the employee</param>
                <param name="lastName">
                The last name of the employee</param>
                <returns>
                The employee object corresponding to the names
                </returns>
                <date>January 1, 2000</date>*
            </member>
        </members>
    </doc>
```

The resultant file includes only the amount of metadata that is necessary to associate an element back to its corresponding C# declaration. This is important to note, because in general, it is necessary to use the XML output in combination with the generated assembly in order to produce any meaningful documentation. Fortunately, tools such as the free GhostDoc[3] and the open source project NDoc[4] can generate documentation.

---

3. See http://submain.com/ to learn more about GhostDoc.
4. See http://ndoc.sourceforge.net to learn more about NDoc.

Garbage Collection

Garbage collection is obviously a core function of the runtime. Its purpose is to restore memory consumed by objects that are no longer referenced. The emphasis in this statement lies with memory and references. The garbage collector is only responsible for restoring memory; it does not handle other resources such as database connections, handles (files, windows, and so on), network ports, and hardware devices such as serial ports. Also, the garbage collector determines what to clean up based on whether any references remain. Implicitly, this means that the garbage collector works with reference objects and restores memory on the heap only. Additionally, it means that maintaining a reference to an object will delay the garbage collector from reusing the memory consumed by the object.

■ **ADVANCED TOPIC**

Garbage Collection in .NET

Many details about the garbage collector pertain to the specific CLI implementation, and therefore, they could vary. This section discusses the .NET implementation, since it is the most prevalent.

In .NET, the garbage collector uses a mark-and-compact algorithm. At the beginning of an iteration, it identifies all **root references** to objects. Root references are any references from static variables, CPU registers, and local variables or parameter instances (and f-reachable objects). Given this list, the garbage collector is able to walk the tree identified by each root reference and determine recursively all the objects to which the root references point. In this manner, the garbage collector identifies a graph of all reachable objects.

Instead of enumerating all the inaccessible objects, the garbage collector performs garbage collection by compacting all reachable objects next to each other, thereby overwriting any memory consumed by objects that are inaccessible (and, therefore, are garbage).

Locating and moving all reachable objects requires that the system maintain a consistent state while the garbage collector runs. To achieve this, all managed threads within the process halt during garbage collection.

This obviously can result in brief pauses in an application, which is generally insignificant unless a particularly large garbage collection cycle is necessary. In order to reduce the likelihood of a garbage collection cycle at an inopportune time, however, the System.GC object includes a Collect() method, which can be called immediately before the critical performing code. This will not prevent the garbage collector from running, but it will reduce the likelihood that it will run, assuming no intense memory utilization occurs during the critical performance code.

One perhaps surprising aspect of .NET garbage collection behavior is that not all garbage is necessarily cleaned up during an iteration. Studies of object lifetimes reveal that recently created objects are more likely to need garbage collection than long-standing objects. Capitalizing on this behavior, the .NET garbage collector is generational, attempting to clean up short-lived objects more frequently than objects that have already survived a garbage collection iteration. Specifically, there are three generations of objects. Each time an object survives a garbage collection cycle, it is moved to the next generation, until it ends up in generation two (counting starts from zero). The garbage collector then runs more frequently for objects in generation zero than it does for objects in generation two.

Ultimately, in spite of the trepidation that .NET faced during its early beta releases when compared with unmanaged code time has shown that .NET's garbage collection is extremely efficient. More importantly, the gains created in development productivity have far outweighed the costs in development for the few cases where managed code is dropped to optimize particular algorithms.

Weak References

All references discussed so far are **strong references** because they maintain an object's accessibility and they prevent the garbage collector from cleaning up the memory consumed by the object. The framework also supports the concept of **weak references,** however. Weak references will not prevent garbage collection on an object, but they will maintain a reference so that if the garbage collector does not clean up the object, it can be reused.

Weak references are designed for objects that are expensive to create and are too expensive to keep around. Consider, for example, a large list of objects loaded from a database and displayed to the user. The loading of this list is potentially expensive, and once the user closes the list, it should be available for garbage collection. However, if the user requests the list multiple times, a second expensive load call will always be required. However, with weak references, it is possible to use code to check whether the list has not yet been cleaned up, and if not, to rereference the same list. In this way, weak references serve as a memory cache for objects. Objects within the cache are retrieved quickly, but if the garbage collector has recovered the memory of these objects, they will need to be re-created.

Once an object (or collection of objects) is recognized for potential weak reference consideration, it needs to be assigned to `System.WeakReference` (see Listing 9.19).

LISTING 9.19: Using a Weak Reference

```
// ...

    private WeakReference Data;

    public FileStream GetData()
    {
        FileStream data = (FileStream)Data.Target;
        if (data != null)
        {
            return data;
        }
        else
        {
            // Load data
            // ...

            // Create a weak reference
            // to data for use later.
            Data.Target = data;
        }
        return data;
    }

    // ...
```

Given the assignment of `WeakReference` (Data), you can check for garbage collection by seeing if the weak reference is set to `null`. The key in doing this, however, is to first assign the weak reference to a strong reference (`FileStream data = Data`) to avoid the possibility that between checking for null and accessing the data, the garbage collector runs and cleans up the weak reference. The strong reference obviously prevents the garbage collector from cleaning up the object, so it must be assigned first (instead of checking Target for null).

Resource Cleanup

Garbage collection is a key responsibility of the runtime. It is important to note, however, that the garbage collection relates to memory utilization. It is not about the cleaning up of file handles, database connection strings, ports, or other limited resources.

Finalizers

Finalizers allow programmers to write code that will clean up a class's resources. However, unlike constructors that are called explicitly using the new operator, finalizers cannot be called explicitly from within the code. There is no new equivalent such as a delete operator. Rather, the garbage collector is responsible for calling a finalizer on an object instance. Therefore, developers cannot determine at compile time exactly when the finalizer will execute. All they know is that the finalizer will run sometime between when an object was last used and before the application shuts down. (Finalizers will execute barring process termination prior to the natural closure of the process. For instance, events such as the computer being turned off or a forced termination of the process will prevent the finalizer from running.)

The finalizer declaration is identical to the destructor syntax of C#'s predecessor—namely, C++. As shown in Listing 9.20, the finalizer declaration is prefixed with a tilde before the name of the class.

LISTING 9.20: Defining a Finalizer

```
using System.IO;

class TemporaryFileStream
{
  public TemporaryFileStream()
  {
      _File = new FileInfo(Path.GetTempFileName());
      _Stream = new FileStream(
```

```
                 File.FullName, FileMode.OpenOrCreate,
                 FileAccess.ReadWrite);
    }

    // Finalizer
    ~TemporaryFileStream()
    {
        Close();
    }

    public FileStream Stream
    {
        get { return _Stream; }
    }
    readonly private FileStream _Stream;

    public FileInfo File
    {
        get { return _File; }
    }
    readonly private FileInfo _File =
        new FileInfo(Path.GetTempFileName());

    public void Close()
    {
        if(Stream != null)
        {
          Stream.Close();
        }
        if(File != null)
        {
          File.Delete();
        }
    }
}
```

Finalizers do not allow any parameters to be passed, and as a result, finalizers cannot be overloaded. Furthermore, finalizers cannot be called explicitly. Only the garbage collector can invoke a finalizer. Therefore, access modifiers on finalizers are meaningless, and as such, they are not supported. Finalizers in base classes will be invoked automatically as part of an object finalization call.

Because the garbage collector handles all memory management, finalizers are not responsible for de-allocating memory. Rather, they are responsible for freeing up resources such as database connections and file handles, resources that require an explicit activity that the garbage collector doesn't know about.

Note that finalizers will execute on their own thread, making their execution even less determinant. This indeterminacy makes an unhandled exception within a finalizer (outside of the debugger) difficult to diagnose because the circumstances that led to the exception are not clear. From the user's perspective, the unhandled exception will be thrown relatively randomly and with little regard for any action the user was performing. For this reason, take care to avoid exceptions within finalizers. Use defensive programming techniques such as checking for nulls (refer to Listing 9.20).

Deterministic Finalization with the `using` Statement

The problem with finalizers on their own is that they don't support **deterministic finalization** (the ability to know when a finalizer will run). Rather, finalizers serve the important role of a backup mechanism for cleaning up resources if a developer using a class neglects to call the requisite cleanup code explicitly.

For example, consider the `TemporaryFileStream` that not only includes a finalizer but also a `Close()` method. The class uses a file resource that could potentially consume a significant amount of disk space. The developer using `TemporaryFileStream` can explicitly call `Close()` in order to restore the disk space.

Providing a method for deterministic finalization is important because it eliminates a dependency on the indeterminate timing behavior of the finalizer. Even if the developer fails to call `Close()` explicitly, the finalizer will take care of the call. The finalizer will run later than if it was called explicitly, but it will be called.

Because of the importance of deterministic finalization, the Base Class Library includes a specific interface for the pattern and C# integrates the pattern into the language. The `IDisposable` interface defines the details of the pattern with a single method called `Dispose()`, which developers call on a resource class to "dispose" of the consumed resources. Listing 9.21 demonstrates the `IDisposable` interface and some code for calling it.

LISTING 9.21: Resource Cleanup with **IDisposable**

```csharp
using System;
using System.IO

class TemporaryFileStream : IDisposable
{
  public TemporaryFileStream()
  {
      _File = new FileInfo(Path.GetTempFileName());
      _Stream = new FileStream(
          File.FullName, FileMode.OpenOrCreate,
          FileAccess.ReadWrite);
  }

  ~TemporaryFileStream()
  {
      Close();
  }

  public FileStream Stream
  {
      get { return _Stream; }
  }
  readonly private FileStream _Stream;

  public FileInfo File
  {
      get { return _File; }
  }
  readonly private FileInfo _File;
  public void Close()
  {
      if(Stream != null)
      {
        Stream.Close();
      }
      if(File != null)
      {
        File.Delete();
      }
      // Turn off calling the finalizer
      System.GC.SuppressFinalize(this);
  }

  #region IDisposable Members
  public void Dispose()
  {
      Close();
  }
  #endregion
  }
```

```
class Program
{
  // ...
  static void Search()
  {
      TemporaryFileStream fileStream =
          new TemporaryFileStream();

      // Use temporary file stream;
      // ...

      fileStream.Dispose();

      // ...
  }
}
```

The steps for both implementing and calling the IDisposable interface are relatively simple. However, there are a couple of points you should not forget. First, there is a chance that an exception will occur between the time TemporaryFileStream is instantiated and Dispose() is called. If this happens, Dispose() will not be invoked and the resource cleanup will have to rely on the finalizer. To avoid this, callers need to implement a try/finally block. Instead of coding such a block explicitly, C# provides a using statement expressly for the purpose. The resultant code appears in Listing 9.22.

LISTING 9.22: Invoking the using Statement

```
class Program
{
  // ...

  static void Search()
  {
      using (TemporaryFileStream fileStream1 =
          new TemporaryFileStream(),
          fileStream2 = new TemporaryFileStream())
      {
          // Use temporary file stream;
      }
  }
}
```

The resultant CIL code is identical to the code that would be created if there was an explicit try/finally block, where fileStream.Dispose() is called in the finally block. The `using` statement, however, provides a syntax shortcut for the try/finally block.

Within a `using` statement, you can instantiate more than one variable by separating each variable with a comma. The key is that all variables are of the same type and that they implement `IDisposable`. To enforce the use of the same type, the data type is specified only once rather than before each variable declaration.

Garbage Collection and Finalization

The `IDisposable` pattern contains one additional important call. Back in Listing 9.21, the `Close()` method included a call to `System.GC.Suppress-Finalize()` (captured again in Listing 9.23). Its purpose was to remove the `TemporaryFileStream` class instance from the finalization (f-reachable) queue.

LISTING 9.23: Suppressing Finalization

```
// ...
public void Close()
{
    if(Stream != null)
    {
        Stream.Close();
    }
    if(File != null)
    {
        File.Delete();
    }
    // Turn off calling the finalizer
    System.GC.SuppressFinalize(this);
}
// ...
```

The **f-reachable queue** is a list of all the objects that are ready for garbage collection and that also have finalization implementations. The runtime cannot garbage-collect objects with finalizers until after their finalization methods have been called. However, garbage collection itself does not call the finalization method. Rather, references to finalization objects are added to the f-reachable queue, thereby ironically delaying garbage collection. This is because the f-reachable queue is a list of "references," and as such, the objects are not garbage until after their finalization methods are called and the object references are removed from the f-reachable queue.

Language Contrast: C++ — Deterministic Destruction

Although finalizers are similar to destructors in C++, the fact that their execution cannot be determined at compile time makes them distinctly different. The garbage collector calls C# finalizers sometime after they were last used, but before the program shuts down; C++ destructors are automatically called when the object (not a pointer) goes out of scope.

Although running the garbage collector can be a relatively expensive process, the fact that garbage collection is intelligent enough to delay running until process utilization is somewhat reduced offers an advantage over deterministic destructors, which will run at compile-time-defined locations, even when a processor is in high demand.

■ ADVANCED TOPIC

Resurrecting Objects

By the time an object's finalization method is called, all references to the object have disappeared and the only step before garbage collection is running the finalization code. However, it is possible to add a reference inadvertently for a finalization object back into the root reference's graph. In so doing, the rereferenced object is no longer inaccessible, and therefore, it is not ready for garbage collection. However, if the finalization method for the object has already run, it will not necessarily be run again unless it is explicitly marked for finalization (using the `GC.ReRegisterFinalize()` method).

Obviously, resurrecting objects like this is peculiar behavior and you should generally avoid it. Finalization code should be simple and should focus on cleaning up only the resources that it references.

Resource Utilization and Finalization Guidelines

When defining classes that manage resources, you should consider the following.

1. Implement `finalize` only on objects with resources that are scarce or expensive. Finalization delays garbage collection.

2. Objects with finalizers should implement `IDisposable` to support deterministic finalization.

3. Finalization methods generally invoke the same code called by `IDisposable`, perhaps simply calling the `Dispose()` method.

4. Finalizers should avoid causing any unhandled exceptions.

5. Deterministic finalization methods such as `Dispose()` and `Close()` should call `System.GC.SuppressFinalize()` so that garbage collection occurs sooner and resource cleanup is not repeated.

6. Code that handles resource cleanup may be invoked multiple times and should therefore be reentrant. (For example, it should be possible to call `Close()` multiple times.)

7. Resource cleanup methods should be simple and should focus on cleaning up resources referenced by the finalization instance only. They should not reference other objects.

8. If a base class implements `Dispose()`, then the derived implementation should call the base implementation.

9. Generally, objects should be coded as unusable after `Dispose()` is called. After an object has been disposed, methods other than `Dispose()` (which could potentially be called multiple times) should throw an `ObjectDisposedException()`.

Lazy Initialization

In this preceding section, we discussed how to deterministically dispose of an object with a `using` statement and how the finalization queue will dispose of resources in the event that no deterministic approach is used.

A related pattern is lazy initialization or lazy loading. Using lazy initialization, you can create (or obtain) objects when you need them rather than beforehand—especially when they were never used. Consider the `FileStream` property of Listing 9.24.

LISTING 9.24: Lazy Loading a Property

```csharp
using System.IO;

class DataCache
{
  // ...

  public TemporaryFileStream FileStream
  {
    get
    {
      if (_FileStream == null)
      {
        _FileStream = new TemporaryFileStream();
      }
      return _FileStream;
    }
  }
  private TemporaryFileStream _FileStream = null;

  // ...
}
```

In the `FileStream` property, we instantiate the `TemporaryFileStream` object only when the getter on the property is called. If the getter is never invoked, the `TemporaryFileStream` object would not get instantiated and we would save whatever execution time such an instantiation would cost. Obviously, if the instantiation is negligible or inevitable (and postponing the inevitable is less desirable), then simply assigning it during declaration or in the constructor makes sense. Deferring the initialization of an object until it is required is called **lazy initialization.**

■ **ADVANCED TOPIC**

Lazy Loading with Generics and Lambda Expressions

Starting with .NET Framework 4.0, a new class was added to the CLR to assist with lazy initialization: `System.Lazy<T>`. Listing 9.25 demonstrates how to use it.

LISTING 9.25: Lazy Loading a Property

```
using System.IO;

class DataCache
{
  // ...

  public string FileStreamName { get; set; }

  public DataCache()
  {
      _FileStream = new Lazy<TemporaryFileStream>(
          () => new TemporaryFileStream(FileStreamName));
  }

  public TemporaryFileStream FileStream
  {
      get
      {
          return _FileStream.Value;
      }
  }
  private Lazy<TemporaryFileStream> _FileStream;

  // ...
}
```

The System.Lazy<T> class takes a type parameter (T) that identifies what type the Value property on System.Lazy<T> will return. Instead of assigning a fully constructed TemporaryFileStream to the _FileStream field, an instance of Lazy<TemporaryFileStream> is assigned (a light-weight call), delaying the instantiation of the TemporaryFileStream itself, until the Value property (and therefore the FileStream property) is accessed.

If in addition to type parameters (generics) you use delegates, you can even provide a function for how to initialize an object when the Value property is accessed. Listing 9.25 demonstrates passing the delegate, a lambda expression in this case, into the constructor for System.Lazy<T>.

It is important to note that the lambda expression itself, () => new TemporaryFileStream(FileStreamName), does not execute until Value is called. Rather, the lambda expression provides a means of passing the instructions for what will happen, but not actually performing those instructions until explicitly requested.

SUMMARY

This chapter provided a whirlwind tour of many topics related to building solid class libraries. All the topics pertain to internal development as well, but they are much more critical to building robust classes. Ultimately, the topic is about forming more robust and programmable APIs. In the category of robustness fit namespaces and garbage collection. Both of these items fit in the programmability category, along with the other items covered: overriding `object`'s virtual members, operator overloading, and XML comments for documentation.

Exception handling uses inheritance heavily by defining an exception hierarchy and enforcing custom exceptions to fit within this hierarchy. Furthermore, the C# compiler uses inheritance to verify catch block order. In the next chapter, you will see why inheritance is such a core part of exception handling.

■ 10 ■
Exception Handling

C HAPTER 4 DISCUSSED using the try/catch/finally blocks for standard exception handling. In that chapter, the catch block always caught exceptions of type System.Exception. This chapter defines some additional details of exception handling—specifically, details surrounding additional exception types, defining custom exceptions, and multiple catch blocks for handling each type. This chapter also details exceptions because of their reliance on inheritance.

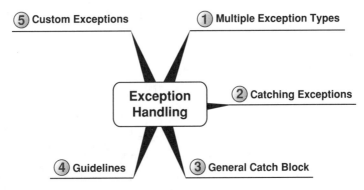

Multiple Exception Types

Listing 10.1 throws a System.ArgumentException, not the System.Exception type demonstrated in Chapter 4. C# allows code to throw any type that derives (perhaps indirectly) from System.Exception.

The code for throwing any exception is simply to prefix the exception instance with the keyword throw. The type of exception used is obviously the type that best describes the circumstances surrounding the error that caused the exception.

For example, consider the `TextNumberParser.Parse()` method in Listing 10.1.

LISTING 10.1: Throwing an Exception

```
public sealed class TextNumberParser
{
  public static int Parse(string textDigit)
  {
      string[] digitTexts =
          { "zero", "one", "two", "three", "four",
            "five", "six", "seven", "eight", "nine" };

      int result = Array.IndexOf(
          digitTexts, textDigit.ToLower());

      if (result < 0)
      {
          throw new ArgumentException(
              "The argument did not represent a digit",
              "textDigit");
      }

      return result;
  }
}
```

Instead of throwing `System.Exception`, it is more appropriate to throw `ArgumentException` because the type itself indicates what went wrong and includes special parameters for identifying which parameter was at fault.

Two similar exceptions are `ArgumentNullException` and `NullReferenceException`. `ArgumentNullException` should be thrown for the inappropriate passing of null arguments. This is a special case of an invalid parameter exception that would more generally (when it wasn't null) be thrown as an `ArgumentException` or an `ArgumentOutOfRangeException`. `NullReferenceException` is generally something that only the underlying runtime will throw with an attempt to dereference a null value—to call a member on an object whose value is null. Instead of causing a `NullReferenceException`, programmers should check parameters for null before accessing them and then throw an

`ArgumentNullException`, which can provide more contextual information such as the parameter name.

Catching Exceptions

Throwing a particular exception type enables the type itself to identify the problem. It is not necessary, in other words, to catch the exception and use a `switch` statement on the exception message to determine what action to take in light of the exception. Instead, C# allows for multiple catch blocks, each targeting a specific exception type, as Listing 10.2 shows.

LISTING 10.2: Catching Different Exception Types

```csharp
using System

public sealed class Program
{
  public static void Main(string[] args)
  {
    try
    {
        // ...
        throw new InvalidOperationException(
            "Arbitrary exception");
        // ...
    }
    catch (NullReferenceException exception)
    {
        // Handle NullReferenceException
    }
    catch (ArgumentException exception)
    {
        // Handle ArgumentException
    }
    catch (InvalidOperationException exception)
    {
        // Handle ApplicationException
    }
    catch (SystemException)
    {
        // Handle SystemException
    }
    catch (Exception exception)
    {
        // Handle Exception
    }
  }
}
```

Listing 10.2 has five catch blocks, each handling a different type of exception. When an exception occurs, the execution will jump to the catch block with the exception type that most closely matches. The closeness of a match is determined by the inheritance chain. For example, even though the exception thrown is of type `System.Exception`, this "is a" relationship occurs through inheritance because `System.ApplicationException` derives from `System.Exception`. Since `ApplicationException` most closely matches the exception thrown, `catch(ApplicationException ...)` will catch the exception instead of the `catch(Exception...)` block.

Catch blocks must appear in order, from most specific to most general, to avoid a compile error. For example, moving the `catch(Exception ...)` block before any of the other exceptions will result in a compile error, since all prior exceptions derive from `System.Exception` at some point in their inheritance chain.

As shown with the catch `(SystemException){  })` block, a named parameter for the catch block is not required. In fact, a final catch without even the type parameter is allowable, as you see in the next section.

Language Contrast: Java—Exception Specifiers

C# has no equivalent for Java's exception specifiers. With exception specifiers, the Java compiler is able to verify that all possible exceptions thrown within a function (or a function's call hierarchy) are either caught or declared as possibly rethrown. The C# team considered this option and concluded that the maintenance burden that it imposed was not worth the perceived benefit. Therefore, it is not necessary to maintain a list of all possible exceptions throughout a particular call stack, but neither is it feasible to easily determine the possible exceptions. (As it turns out, this wasn't possible for Java either. Calling virtual methods or using late binding, such as reflection, made it impossible to fully resolve at compile time what exceptions a method could possibly throw.)

General Catch Block

C# requires that any object that code throws must derive from System.Exception. However, this requirement is not universal to all languages. C/C++, for example, allows any object type to be thrown, including managed exceptions that don't derive from System.Exception. Starting with C# 2.0, all exceptions, whether deriving from System.Exception or not, will propagate into C# assemblies as derived from System.Exception. The result is that System.Exception catch blocks will catch all exceptions not caught by earlier blocks.

C# also supports a **general catch block** (catch{ }) that behaves identically to the catch(System.Exception exception) block except that there is no type or variable name. Also, the general catch block must appear last within the list of catch blocks. Since the general catch block is identical to the catch(System.Exception exception) block and the general catch block must appear last, the compiler issues a warning if both exist within the same try/catch statement because the general catch block will never be invoked (see the Advanced Topic, General Catch Blocks in C# 1.0, for more information on general catch blocks).

ADVANCED TOPIC

General Catch Blocks in C# 1.0

In C# 1.0, if a non-System.Exception-derived exception was thrown from a method call (residing in an assembly not written in C#), the exception would not be caught by a catch(System.Exception) block. If a different language throws a string, for example, the exception could go unhandled. To avoid this, C# includes a catch block that takes no parameters. The term for such a catch block is *general catch block,* and Listing 10.3 includes one.

LISTING 10.3: Catching Different Exception Types

```
using System

public sealed class Program
{
  public static void Main()
```

```
{
    try
    {
        // ...
        throw new InvalidOperationException (
            "Arbitrary exception");
        // ...
    }
    catch (NullReferenceException exception)
    {
        // Handle NullReferenceException
    }
    catch (ArgumentException exception)
    {
        // Handle ArgumentException
    }
    catch (InvalidOperationException exception)
    {
        // Handle ApplicationException
    }
    catch (SystemException exception)
    {
        // Handle SystemException
    }
    catch (Exception exception)
    {
        // Handle Exception
    }
    catch
    {
        // Any unhandled exception
    }
}
}
```

The general catch block will catch all exceptions, regardless of whether they derive from System.Exception, assuming an earlier catch block does not catch them. The disadvantage of such a block is simply that there is no exception instance to access and, therefore, no way to know the appropriate course of action. It wouldn't even be possible to recognize the unlikely case where such an exception is innocuous. The best course of action is to handle the exception with some cleanup code before shutting down the application. The catch block could save any volatile data, for example, before shutting down the application or rethrowing the exception.

Empty Catch Block Internals

The CIL code corresponding to an empty catch block is, in fact, a `catch(object)` block. This means that regardless of the type thrown, the empty catch block will catch it. Interestingly, it is not possible to explicitly declare a `catch(object)` exception block within C# code. Therefore, there is no means of catching a non-`System.Exception`-derived exception and having an exception instance to scrutinize.

Ironically, unmanaged exceptions from languages such as C++ generally result in `System.Runtime.InteropServices.SEHException` type exceptions, which derive from the `System.Exception` type. Therefore, not only can the unmanaged type exceptions be caught using a general catch block, but the non-`System.Exception`-managed types that are thrown can be caught as well—for instance, types such as `string`.

Guidelines for Exception Handling

Exception handling provides much-needed structure to the error-handling mechanisms that preceded it. However, it can still make for some unwieldy results if used haphazardly. The following guidelines offer some best practices for exception handling.

- Catch only the exceptions that you can handle.

  Generally it is possible to handle some types of exceptions but not others. For example, opening a file for exclusive read-write access may throw a `System.IO.IOException` because the file is already in use. In catching this type of exception, the code can report to the user that the file is in use and allow the user the option of canceling the operation or retrying it. Only exceptions for which there is a known action should be caught. Other exception types should be left for callers higher in the stack.

- Don't hide (bury) exceptions you don't fully handle.

  New programmers are often tempted to catch all exceptions and then continue executing instead of reporting an unhandled exception to the user. However, this may result in a critical system problem going undetected. Unless code takes explicit action to handle an exception or explicitly determines certain exceptions to be innocuous, catch blocks should rethrow exceptions instead of catching them and hiding them from the caller. Predominantly, catch(System.Exception) and general catch blocks should occur higher in the call stack, unless the block ends by rethrowing the exception.

- Use System.Exception and general catch blocks rarely.

  Virtually all exceptions derive from System.Exception. However, the best way to handle some System.Exceptions is to allow them to go unhandled or to gracefully shut down the application sooner rather than later. These exceptions include things such as System.OutOfMemoryException and System.StackOverflowException. In CLR 4, such exceptions were defaulted to nonrecoverable such that catching them without rethrowing them will cause the CLR to rethrow them anyway. These exceptions are runtime exceptions that the developer cannot write code to recover from. Therefore, the best course of action is to shut down the application—something the runtime will force in CLR 4. Code prior to CLR 4 should catch such exceptions only to run cleanup or emergency code (such as saving any volatile data) before shutting down the application or rethrowing the exception with throw;.

- Avoid exception reporting or logging lower in the call stack.

  Often, programmers are tempted to log exceptions or report exceptions to the user at the soonest possible location in the call stack. However, these locations are seldom able to handle the exception fully and they resort to rethrowing the exception. Such catch blocks should not log the exception or report it to a user while in the bowels of the call stack. If the exception is logged and rethrown, the callers higher in the call stack may do the same, resulting in duplicate log entries of the exception. Worse, displaying the exception to the user may not be appropriate for the type of application. (Using System.Console.WriteLine() in a Windows application will never be seen by the user, for example, and displaying a dialog in an unattended command-line process may go unnoticed and freeze the application.) Logging- and exception-related user interfaces should be reserved for high up in the call stack.

- Use `throw;` rather than `throw <exception object>` inside a catch block.

  It is possible to rethrow an exception inside a catch block. For example, the implementation of `catch(ArgumentNullException exception)` could include a call to `throw exception`. However, rethrowing the exception like this will reset the stack trace to the location of the rethrown call, instead of reusing the original throw point location. Therefore, unless you are rethrowing with a different exception type or intentionally hiding the original call stack, use `throw;` to allow the same exception to propagate up the call stack.

- Use caution when rethrowing different exceptions.

  From inside a catch block, rethrowing a different exception will not only reset the throw point, it will also hide the original exception. To preserve the original exception set the new exception's `InnerException` property, generally assignable via the constructor. Rethrowing a different exception should be reserved for the following situations.

  1. Changing the exception type clarifies the problem.

     For example, in a call to `Logon(User user)`, rethrowing a different exception type is perhaps more appropriate than propagating `System.IO.IOException` when the file with the user list is inaccessible.

  2. Private data is part of the original exception.

     In the preceding scenario, if the file path is included in the original `System.IO.IOException`, thereby exposing private security information about the system, the exception should be wrapped. This assumes, of course, that `InnerException` is not set with the original exception. (Funnily enough, a very early version of CLR v1 (pre-alpha even) had an exception that said something like "Security exception: You do not have permission to determine the path of `c:\temp\foo.txt`".)

  3. The exception type is too specific for the caller to handle appropriately.

     For example, instead of throwing an exception specific to a particular database system, a more generic exception is used so that database-specific code higher in the call stack can be avoided.

Defining Custom Exceptions

Once throwing an exception becomes the best course of action, it is preferable to use framework exceptions because they are well established and understood. Instead of throwing a custom invalid argument exception, for example, it is preferable to use the System.ArgumentException type. However, if the developers using a particular API will take special action—the exception-handling logic will vary to handle a custom exception type, for instance—it is appropriate to define a custom exception. For example, if a mapping API receives an address for which the ZIP Code is invalid, instead of throwing System.ArgumentException, it may be better to throw a custom InvalidAddressException. The key is whether the caller is likely to write a specific InvalidAddressException catch block with special handling rather than just a generic System.ArgumentException catch block.

Defining a custom exception simply involves deriving from System.Exception or some other exception type. Listing 10.4 provides an example.

LISTING 10.4: Creating a Custom Exception

```csharp
class DatabaseException : System.Exception
{
  public DatabaseException(
      System.Data.SqlClient.SQLException exception)
  {
      InnerException = exception;
      // ...
  }

  public DatabaseException(
      System.Data.OracleClient.OracleException exception)
  {
      InnerException = exception;
      // ...
  }

  public DatabaseException()
  {
      // ...
  }

  public DatabaseException(string message)
  {
      // ...
  }
```

```
public DatabaseException(
    string message, Exception innerException)
{
    InnerException = innerException;
    // ...
}
}
```

This custom exception might be created to wrap proprietary database exceptions. Since Oracle and SQL Server (for example) each throw different exceptions for similar errors, an application could define a custom exception that standardizes the database-specific exceptions into a common exception wrapper that the application can handle in a standard manner. That way, whether the application was using an Oracle or a SQL Server backend database, the same catch block could be used to handle the error higher up the stack.

The only requirement for a custom exception is that it derives from `System.Exception` or one of its descendents. However, there are several more good practices for custom exceptions.

- All exceptions should use the "Exception" suffix. This way, their purpose is easily established from the name.
- Generally, all exceptions should include constructors that take no parameters, a string parameter, and a parameter set of a string and an inner exception. Furthermore, since exceptions are usually constructed within the same statement in which they are thrown, any additional exception data should also be allowed as part of the constructor. (The obvious exception to creating all these constructors is if certain data is required and a constructor circumvents the requirements.)
- The inheritance chain should be kept relatively shallow (with fewer than approximately five levels).

The inner exception serves an important purpose when rethrowing an exception that is different from the one that was caught. For example, if a `System.Data.SqlClient.SqlException` is thrown by a database call but is caught within the data access layer to be rethrown as a `DatabaseException`, then the `DatabaseException` constructor that takes the `SqlException` (or inner exception) will save the original `SqlException` in the `Inner-Exception` property. That way, when requiring additional details about the original exception, developers can retrieve the exception from the `InnerException` property (for example, `exception.InnerException`).

■ ADVANCED TOPIC

Serializable Exceptions

Serializable objects are objects that the runtime can persist into a stream—a file stream, for example—and then reinstantiate out of the stream. In the case of exceptions, this may be necessary for certain distributed communication technologies. To support serialization, exception declarations should include the `System.SerializableAttribute` attribute or they should implement `ISerializable`. Furthermore, they must include a constructor that takes `System.Runtime.Serialization.Serialization-Info` and `System.Runtime.Serialization.StreamingContext`. Listing 10.5 shows an example of using `System.SerializableAttribute`.

LISTING 10.5: Defining a Serializable Exception

```
// Supporting serialization via an attribute
[Serializable]
class DatabaseException : System.ApplicationException
{
  // ...

  // Used for deserialization of exceptions
  public DatabaseException(
      SerializationInfo serializationInfo,
      StreamingContext context)
  {
      //...
  }

}
```

The preceding `DatabaseException` example demonstrates both the attribute and the constructor requirement for making an exception serializable.

Checked and Unchecked Conversions

As we first discussed in a Chapter 2 Advanced Topic, C# provides special keywords for marking a code block with instructions to the runtime of what should happen if the target data type is too small to contain the assigned data. By default, if the target data type cannot contain the assigned data, then the data will truncate during assignment. For an example, see Listing 10.6.

LISTING 10.6: Overflowing an Integer Value

```
using System;

public class Program
{
  public static void Main()
  {
      // int.MaxValue equals 2147483647
      int n = int.MaxValue;
      n = n + 1 ;
      System.Console.WriteLine(n);
  }
}
```

The results of Listing 10.6 appear in Output 10.1.

OUTPUT 10.1:

```
-2147483648
```

The code in Listing 10.6 writes the value -2147483648 to the console. However, placing the code within a checked block or using the checked option when running the compiler will cause the runtime to throw an exception of type System.OverflowException. The syntax for a checked block uses the checked keyword, as shown in Listing 10.7.

LISTING 10.7: A Checked Block Example

```
using System;

public class Program
{
```

```csharp
public static void Main()
{
    checked
    {
        // int.MaxValue equals 2147483647
        int n = int.MaxValue;
        n = n + 1 ;
        System.Console.WriteLine(n);
    }
}
}
```

If the calculation involves only constants, then the calculation will be checked by default. The results of Listing 10.7 appear in Output 10.2.

OUTPUT 10.2:

```
Unhandled Exception: System.OverflowException: Arithmetic operation
resulted in an overflow. at Program.Main() in ...Program.cs:line 12
```

In addition, depending on the version of Windows and whether a debugger is installed, a dialog may appear prompting the user to send an error message to Microsoft, check for a solution, or debug the application. Also, the location information (Program.cs:line X) will appear only in debug compilations—compilations using the /Debug option of the Microsoft csc.exe compiler.

The result is that an exception is thrown if, within the checked block, an overflow assignment occurs at runtime.

The C# compiler provides a command-line option for changing the default checked behavior from unchecked to checked. C# also supports an unchecked block that truncates the data instead of throwing an exception for assignments within the block (see Listing 10.8).

LISTING 10.8: An Unchecked Block Example

```csharp
using System;

public class Program
{
    public static void Main()
    {
        unchecked
        {
```

```
        // int.MaxValue equals 2147483647
        int n = int.MaxValue;
        n = n + 1 ;
        System.Console.WriteLine(n);
    }
  }
}
```

The results of Listing 10.8 appear in Output 10.3.

OUTPUT 10.3:

```
-2147483648
```

Even if the checked option is on during compilation, the unchecked keyword in the code in Listing 10.8 will prevent the runtime from throwing an exception during execution.

There are equivalent checked and unchecked expressions for cases where statements are not allowed, as is the case in a field initialize, for example:

```
int _Number = unchecked(int.MaxValue + 1);
```

SUMMARY

Throwing an exception causes a significant performance hit. A single exception causes lots of runtime stack information to be loaded and processed, data that would not otherwise be loaded, and it takes a considerable amount of time. As pointed out in Chapter 4, use exceptions only to handle exceptional circumstances; APIs should provide mechanisms to check whether an exception will be thrown instead of forcing a particular API to be called in order to determine whether an exception will be thrown.

The next chapter introduces generics, a C# 2.0 feature that significantly enhances the code written in C# 1.0. In fact, it essentially deprecates any use of the System.Collections namespace, which was formerly used in nearly every project.

11
Generics

A S YOUR PROJECTS BECOME more sophisticated, you will need a better way to reuse and customize existing software. To facilitate code reuse, especially the reuse of algorithms, C# includes a feature called **generics.** Just as methods are powerful because they can take parameters, classes that take type parameters have significantly more functionality as well, and this is what generics enable. Like their predecessor, templates, generics enable the definition of algorithms and pattern implementations once, rather than separately for each type. However, C# generics are a type-safe implementation of templates that differs slightly in syntax and greatly in implementation from its predecessors in C++ and Java. Note that generics were added to the runtime and C# with version 2.0.

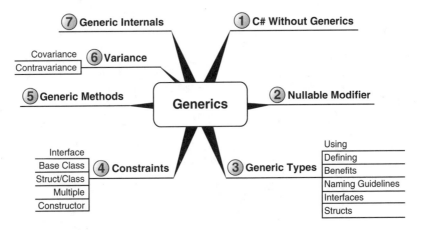

C# without Generics

I will begin the discussion of generics by examining a class that does not use generics. The class is System.Collections.Stack, and its purpose is to represent a collection of objects such that the last item to be added to the collection is the first item retrieved from the collection (called last in, first out, or LIFO). Push() and Pop(), the two main methods of the Stack class, add items to the stack and remove them from the stack, respectively. The declarations for the Pop() and Push() methods on the stack class appear in Listing 11.1.

LISTING 11.1: The Stack Definition Using a Data Type Object

```
public class Stack
{
    public virtual object Pop();
    public virtual void Push(object obj);
    // ...
}
```

Programs frequently use stack type collections to facilitate multiple undo operations. For example, Listing 11.2 uses the stack class for undo operations within a program which simulates the Etch A Sketch® game.

LISTING 11.2: Supporting Undo in a Program Similar to the Etch A Sketch Game

```
using System;
using System.Collections;

class Program
{
  // ...

  public void Sketch()
  {
      Stack path = new Stack();
      Cell currentPosition;
      ConsoleKeyInfo key;  // New with C# 2.0

      do
      {
          // Etch in the direction indicated by the
          // arrow keys that the user enters.
          key = Move();

          switch (key.Key)
          {
```

```
            case ConsoleKey.Z:
                // Undo the previous Move.
                if (path.Count >= 1)
                {
                    currentPosition = (Cell)path.Pop();
                    Console.SetCursorPosition(
                        currentPosition.X, currentPosition.Y);
                    Undo();
                }
                break;

            case ConsoleKey.DownArrow:
            case ConsoleKey.UpArrow:
            case ConsoleKey.LeftArrow:
            case ConsoleKey.RightArrow:
                // SaveState()
                currentPosition = new Cell(
                    Console.CursorLeft, Console.CursorTop);
                path.Push(currentPosition);
                break;

            default:
                Console.Beep();  // New with C#2.0
                break;
        }

    }
    while (key.Key != ConsoleKey.X);  // Use X to quit.

    }
}

public struct Cell
{
    readonly public int X;
    readonly public int Y;
    public Cell(int x, int y)
    {
        X = x;
        Y = y;
    }
}
```

The results of Listing 11.2 appear in Output 11.1.

Using the variable path, which is declared as a System.Collections.Stack, you save the previous move by passing a custom type, Cell, into the Stack.Push() method using path.Push(currentPosition). If the user enters a Z (or Ctrl+Z), then you undo the previous move by retrieving

OUTPUT 11.1:

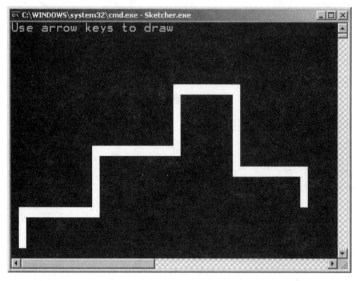

it from the stack using a Pop() method, setting the cursor position to be the previous position, and calling Undo(). (Note that this code uses some CLR 2.0-specific console functions as well.)

Although the code is functional, there is a fundamental drawback in the System.Collections.Stack class. As shown in Listing 11.1, the Stack class collects variables of type object. Because every object in the CLR derives from object, Stack provides no validation that the elements you place into it are homogenous or are of the intended type. For example, instead of passing currentPosition, you can pass a string in which X and Y are concatenated with a decimal point between them. However, the compiler must allow the inconsistent data types because in some scenarios, it is desirable.

Furthermore, when retrieving the data from the stack using the Pop() method, you must cast the return value to a Cell. But if the value returned from the Pop() method is not a Cell type object, an exception is thrown. You can test the data type, but splattering such checks builds complexity. The fundamental problem with creating classes that can work with multiple data types without generics is that they must use a common base type, generally object data.

Using value types, such as a struct or an integer, with classes that use object exacerbates the problem. If you pass a value type to the Stack.Push() method, for example, the runtime automatically boxes it.

Similarly, when you retrieve a value type, you need to explicitly unbox the data and cast the `object` reference you obtain from the `Pop()` method into a value type. Although the widening operation (cast to a base class) for a reference type has a negligible performance impact, the box operation for a value type introduces nontrivial overhead.

To change the `Stack` class to enforce storage on a particular data type using the preceding C# programming constructs, you must create a specialized stack class, as in Listing 11.3.

LISTING 11.3: Defining a Specialized Stack Class

```
public class CellStack
{
  public virtual Cell Pop();
  public virtual void Push(Cell cell);
  // ...
}
```

Because `CellStack` can store only objects of type `Cell`, this solution requires a custom implementation of the stack methods, which is less than ideal.

■ **BEGINNER TOPIC**

Another Example: Nullable Value Types

Chapter 2 introduced the capability of declaring variables that could contain null by using the nullable modifier, `?`, when declaring the value type variable. C# only began supporting this in version 2.0 because the right implementation required generics. Prior to the introduction of generics, programmers faced essentially two options.

The first option was to declare a nullable data type for each value type that needs to handle null values, as shown in Listing 11.4.

LISTING 11.4: Declaring Versions of Various Value Types That Store null

```
struct NullableInt
{
    /// <summary>
    /// Provides the value when HasValue returns true.
    /// </summary>
```

```
        public int Value{ get; set; }

        /// <summary>
        /// Indicates whether there is a value or whether
        /// the value is "null"
        /// </summary>
        public bool HasValue{ get; set; }

        // ...
    }

    struct NullableGuid
    {
        /// <summary>
        /// Provides the value when HasValue returns true.
        /// </summary>
        public Guid Value{ get; set; }

        /// <summary>
        /// Indicates whether there is a value or whether
        /// the value is "null"
        /// </summary>
        public bool HasValue{ get; set; }

        ...
    }
    ...
```

Listing 11.4 shows implementations for only `NullableInt` and `Nullable-Guid`. If a program required additional nullable value types, you would have to create a copy with the additional value type. If the nullable implementation changed (if it supported a cast from a null to the nullable type, for example), you would have to add the modification to all of the nullable type declarations.

The second option was to declare a nullable type that contains a `Value` property of type `object`, as shown in Listing 11.5.

LISTING 11.5: Declaring a Nullable Type That Contains a Value Property of Type object

```
    struct Nullable
    {
        /// <summary>
        /// Provides the value when HasValue returns true.
        /// </summary>
        public object Value{ get; set; }
```

```
        /// <summary>
        /// Indicates whether there is a value or whether
        /// the value is "null"
        /// </summary>
        public bool HasValue{ get; set; }


        ...

    }
```

Although this option requires only one implementation of a nullable type, the runtime always boxes value types when setting the `Value` property. Furthermore, calls to retrieve data from `Nullable.Value` will not be strongly typed, so retrieving the value type will require a cast operation, which is potentially invalid at runtime.

Neither option is particularly attractive. To deal with dilemmas such as this, C# 2.0 includes the concept of generics. In fact, the nullable modifier, ?, uses generics internally.

Introducing Generic Types

Generics provide a facility for creating data structures that are specialized to handle specific types when declaring a variable. Programmers define these **parameterized types** so that each variable of a particular generic type has the same internal algorithm but the types of data and method signatures can vary based on programmer preference.

To minimize the learning curve for developers, C# designers chose syntax that matched the similar templates concept of C++. In C#, therefore, the syntax for generic classes and structures uses the same angle bracket notation to identify the data types on which the generic declaration specializes.

Using a Generic Class

Listing 11.6 shows how you can specify the actual type used by the generic class. You instruct the `path` variable to use a `Cell` type by specifying `Cell` within angle bracket notation in both the instantiation and the declaration expressions. In other words, when declaring a variable (`path` in this case) using a generic data type, C# requires the developer to identify the actual type. An example showing the new `Stack` class appears in Listing 11.6.

LISTING 11.6: Implementing Undo with a Generic Stack Class

```csharp
using System;
using System.Collections.Generic;

class Program
{
  // ...

  public void Sketch()
  {
      Stack<Cell> path;         // Generic variable declaration
      path = new Stack<Cell>(); // Generic object instantiation
      Cell currentPosition;
      ConsoleKeyInfo key;         // New with C# 2.0

      do
      {
          // Etch in the direction indicated by the
          // arrow keys entered by the user.
          key = Move();

          switch (key.Key)
          {
              case ConsoleKey.Z:
                  // Undo the previous Move.
                  if (path.Count >= 1)
                  {
                      // No cast required.
                      currentPosition = path.Pop();
                      Console.SetCursorPosition(
                          currentPosition.X, currentPosition.Y);
                      Undo();
                  }
                  break;

              case ConsoleKey.DownArrow:
              case ConsoleKey.UpArrow:
              case ConsoleKey.LeftArrow:
              case ConsoleKey.RightArrow:
                  // SaveState()
                  currentPosition = new Cell(
                      Console.CursorLeft, Console.CursorTop);
                  // Only type Cell allowed in call to Push().
                  path.Push(currentPosition);
                  break;

              default:
                  Console.Beep();  // New with C#2.0
                  break;
          }
```

```
        } while (key.Key != ConsoleKey.X);  // Use X to quit.
    }
}
```

The results of Listing 11.6 appear in Output 11.2.

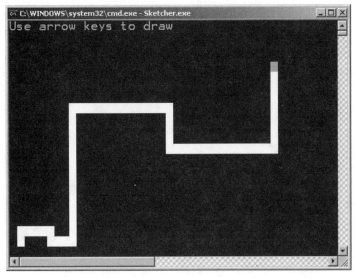

In the path declaration shown in Listing 11.6, you declare and create a new instance of a System.Collections.Generic.Stack<T> class and specify in angle brackets that the data type used for the path variable is Cell. As a result, every object added to and retrieved from path is of type Cell. In other words, you no longer need to cast the return of path.Pop() or ensure that only Cell type objects are added to path in the Push() method. Before we examine the generic advantages, the next section introduces the syntax for generic class definitions.

Defining a Simple Generic Class
Generics allow you to author algorithms and patterns, and reuse the code for different data types. Listing 11.7 creates a generic Stack<T> class similar to the System.Collections.Generic.Stack<T> class used in the code in Listing 11.6. You specify a **type parameter identifier** or **type parameter** (in this case, T) within angle brackets after the class declaration. Instances

of the generic Stack<T> then collect the type corresponding to the variable declaration without converting the collected item to type object. The type parameter T is a placeholder until variable declaration and instantiation, when the compiler requires the code to specify the type parameter. ¶In Listing 11.7, you can see that the type parameter will be used for the internal Items array, the type for the parameter to the Push() method, and the return type for the Pop() method.

LISTING 11.7: Declaring a Generic Class, Stack<T>

```csharp
public class Stack<T>
{
    private T[] _Items;

    public void Push(T data)
    {
        ...
    }

    public T Pop()
    {
        ...
    }
}
```

Benefits of Generics

There are several advantages to using a generic class (such as the System.Collections.Generic.Stack<T> class used earlier instead of the original System.Collections.Stack type).

1. Generics facilitate a strongly typed programming model, preventing data types other than those explicitly intended by the members within the parameterized class. In Listing 11.7, the parameterized stack class restricts you to the Cell data type for all instances of Stack<Cell>. (The statement path.Push("garbage") produces a compile-time error indicating that there is no overloaded method for System.Collections.Generic.Stack<T>.Push(T) that can work with the string garbage, because it cannot be converted to a Cell.)

2. Compile-time type checking reduces the likelihood of Invalid-CastException type errors at runtime.

3. Using value types with generic class members no longer causes a cast to `object`; they no longer require a boxing operation. (For example, `path.Pop()` and `path.Push()` do not require an item to be boxed when added or unboxed when removed.)

4. Generics in C# reduce code bloat. Generic types retain the benefits of specific class versions, without the overhead. (For example, it is no longer necessary to define a class such as `CellStack`.)

5. Performance increases because casting from an object is no longer required, thus eliminating a type check operation. Also, performance increases because boxing is no longer necessary for value types.

6. Generics reduce memory consumption by avoiding boxing and thus consuming less memory on the heap.

7. Code becomes more readable because of fewer casting checks and because of the need for fewer type-specific implementations.

8. Editors that assist coding via some type of IntelliSense® work directly with return parameters from generic classes. There is no need to cast the return data for IntelliSense to work.

At their core, generics offer the ability to code pattern implementations and then reuse those implementations wherever the patterns appear. Patterns describe problems that occur repeatedly within code, and templates provide a single implementation for these repeating patterns.

Type Parameter Naming Guidelines

Just as when you name a method parameter, you should be as descriptive as possible when naming a type parameter. Furthermore, to distinguish the parameter as being a type parameter, its name should include a *T* prefix. For example, in defining a class such as `EntityCollection<TEntity>` you use the type parameter name "TEntity."

The only time you would not use a descriptive type parameter name is when the description would not add any value. For example, using "T" in the `Stack<T>` class is appropriate, since the indication that "T" is a type parameter is sufficiently descriptive; the stack works for any type.

In the next section, you will learn about constraints. It is a good practice to use constraint-descriptive type names. For example, if a type parameter must implement `IComponent`, consider a type name of "TComponent."

Generic Interfaces and Structs

C# 2.0 supports the use of generics extensively within the C# language, including interfaces and structs. The syntax is identical to that used by classes. To define an interface with a type parameter, place the type parameter in angle brackets, as shown in the example of IPair<T> in Listing 11.8.

LISTING 11.8: Declaring a Generic Interface

```
interface IPair<T>
{
    T First { get; set; }
    T Second { get; set; }
}
```

This interface represents pairs of like objects, such as the coordinates of a point, a person's genetic parents, or nodes of a binary tree. The type contained in the pair is the same for both items.

To implement the interface, you use the same syntax as you would for a nongeneric class. However, implementing a generic interface without identifying the type parameter forces the class to be a generic class, as shown in Listing 11.9. In addition, this example uses a struct rather than a class, indicating that C# supports custom generic value types.

LISTING 11.9: Implementing a Generic Interface

```
public struct Pair<T>: IPair<T>
{
    public T First
    {
        get
        {
            return _First;
        }
        set
        {
            _First = value;
        }
    }
    private T _First;

    public T Second
    {
        get
        {
            return _Second;
```

```
        }
        set
        {
            _Second = value;
        }
    }
    private T _Second;
}
```

Support for generic interfaces is especially important for collection classes, where generics are most prevalent. Without generics, developers relied on a series of interfaces within the System.Collections namespace. Like their implementing classes, these interfaces worked only with type object, and as a result, the interface forced all access to and from these collection classes to require a cast. By using generic interfaces, you can avoid cast operations, because a stronger compile-time binding can be achieved with parameterized interfaces.

ADVANCED TOPIC

Implementing the Same Interface Multiple Times on a Single Class

One side effect of template interfaces is that you can implement the same interface many times using different type parameters. Consider the IContainer<T> example in Listing 11.10.

LISTING 11.10: Duplicating an Interface Implementation on a Single Class

```
public interface IContainer<T>
{
    ICollection<T> Items
    {
        get;
        set;
    }
}

public class Person: IContainer<Address>,
    IContainer<Phone>, IContainer<Email>
{
    ICollection<Address> IContainer<Address>.Items
    {
        get{...}
        set{...}
```

```
    }
    ICollection<Phone> IContainer<Phone>.Items
    {
        get{...}
        set{...}
    }
    ICollection<Email> IContainer<Email>.Items
    {
        get{...}
        set{...}
    }
}
```

In this example, the Items property appears multiple times using an explicit interface implementation with a varying type parameter. Without generics, this is not possible, and instead, the compiler would allow only one explicit IContainer.Items property.

One possible improvement on Person would be to also implement IContainer<object> and to have items return the combination of all three containers (Address, Phone, and Email).

Defining a Constructor and a Finalizer

Perhaps surprisingly, the constructor and destructor on a generic do not require type parameters in order to match the class declaration (in other words, not Pair<T>(){...}). In the pair example in Listing 11.11, the constructor is declared using public Pair(T first, T second).

LISTING 11.11: Declaring a Generic Type's Constructor

```
public struct Pair<T>: IPair<T>
{
    public Pair(T first, T second)
    {
        _Second = second;
        _Second = second;
    }

    public T First
    {
        get{ return _First; }
        set{ _First = value; }
    }
    private T _First;

    public T Second
```

```
    {
        get{ return _Second; }
        set{ _Second = value; }
    }
    private T _Second;
}
```

Specifying a Default Value

Listing 11.1 included a constructor that takes the initial values for both First and Second, and assigns them to _First and _Second. Since Pair<T> is a struct, any constructor you provide must initialize all fields. This presents a problem, however. Consider a constructor for Pair<T> that initializes only half of the pair at instantiation time.

Defining such a constructor, as shown in Listing 11.12, causes a compile error because the field _Second goes uninitialized at the end of the constructor. Providing initialization for _Second presents a problem since you don't know the data type of T. If it is a reference type, then null would work, but this would not suffice if T were a value type (unless it was nullable).

LISTING 11.12: Not Initializing All Fields, Causing a Compile Error

```
public struct Pair<T>: IPair<T>
{
    // ERROR:  Field 'Pair<T>._second' must be fully assigned
    //         before control leaves the constructor
    // public Pair(T first)
    // {
    //     _First = first;
    // }

    // ...
}
```

To deal with this scenario, C# 2.0 allows a dynamic way to code the default value of any data type using the default operator, first discussed in Chapter 8. In Chapter 8, I showed how the default value of int could be specified with default(int) while the default value of a string uses default(string) (which returns null, as it would for all reference types). In the case of T, which _Second requires, you use default(T) (see Listing 11.13).

LISTING 11.13: Initializing a Field with the `default` Operator

```
public struct Pair<T>: IPair<T>
{
  public Pair(T first)
  {
    _First = first;
    _Second = default(T);
  }

  // ...
}
```

The `default` operator is allowable outside the context of generics; any statement can use it.

Multiple Type Parameters

Generic types may employ any number of type parameters. The initial `Pair<T>` example contains only one type parameter. To enable support for storing a dichotomous pair of objects, such as a name/value pair, you need to extend `Pair<T>` to support two type parameters, as shown in Listing 11.14.

LISTING 11.14: Declaring a Generic with Multiple Type Parameters

```
interface IPair<TFirst, TSecond>
{
    TFirst First { get; set; }
    TSecond Second { get; set; }
}

public struct Pair<TFirst, TSecond>: IPair<TFirst, TSecond>
{
    public Pair(TFirst first, TSecond second)
    {
      _First = first;
      _Second = second;
    }

    public TFirst First
    {
        get{ return _First; }
        set{ _First = value; }
    }
    private TFirst _First;
```

```
    public TSecond Second
    {
        get{ return _Second; }
        set{ _Second = value; }
    }
    private TSecond _Second;
}
```

When you use the Pair<TFirst, TSecond> class, you supply multiple
type parameters within the angle brackets of the declaration and instantiation statements, and then you supply matching types to the parameters of
the methods when you call them, as shown in Listing 11.15.

LISTING 11.15: Using a Type with Multiple Type Parameters

```
Pair<int, string> historicalEvent =
    new Pair<int, string>(1914,
        "Shackleton leaves for South Pole on ship Endurance");
Console.WriteLine("{0}: {1}",
    historicalEvent.First, historicalEvent.Second);
```

The number of type parameters, the **arity,** uniquely distinguishes the
class. Therefore, it is possible to define both Pair<T> and Pair<TFirst,
TSecond> within the same namespace because of the arity variation.

Arity in Abundance

In C# 4.0 the CLR team defined nine new generic types all called Tuple. As
with Pair<...>, it was possible to reuse the same name because of the variation in arity (each class had a different number of type parameters) as
shown in Listing 11.16.

LISTING 11.16: Covariance Using the out Type Parameter Modifier

```
public class Tuple { ... }
public class Tuple<T1>:
    IStructuralEquatable, IStructuralComparable, IComparable {...}
public class Tuple<T1, T2>: ... {...}
public class Tuple<T1, T2, T3>: ... {...}
public class Tuple<T1, T2, T3, T4>: ... {...}
public class Tuple<T1, T2, T3, T4, T5>: ... {...}
public class Tuple<T1, T2, T3, T4, T5, T6>: ... {...}
public class Tuple<T1, T2, T3, T4, T5, T6, T7>: ... {...}
public class Tuple<T1, T2, T3, T4, T5, T6, T7, TRest>: ... {...}
```

The Tuple<...> set of classes was designed for the same purpose as the Pair<T> and Pair<TFirst, TSecond> classes, except together they can handle seven type parameters. In fact, using the last Tuple shown in Listing 11.16, TRest can be used to store another Tuple, making the potential limit to the size of the tuple practically unlimited.

Another interesting feature of the tuple set of classes is the Tuple (no type parameters). This class has eight static create methods for instantiating the various generic tuple types. Although each generic type could be instantiated directly using its constructor, the Tuple type's create methods allow for implied type parameters. Listing 11.17 shows the difference.

LISTING 11.17: Covariance Using the **out** Type Parameter Modifier

```
Tuple<string, Contact> keyValuePair;
keyValuePair =
   Tuple.Create(
      "555-55-5555", new Contact("Inigo Montoya"));
keyValuePair =
   new Tuple<string, Contact>(
      "555-55-5555", new Contact("Inigo Montoya"));
```

Obviously, when the Tuple gets large, the number of type parameters to specify could be cumbersome without the Create() methods.

Nested Generic Types

Type parameters on the containing type will cascade down to the nested type automatically. If the containing type includes a type parameter T, for example, then the type T will be available on the nested type as well. If the nested type includes its own type parameter named T, then this will hide the type parameter within the containing type and any reference to T in the nested type will refer to the nested T type parameter. Fortunately, reuse of the same type parameter name within the nested type will cause a compiler warning to prevent accidental overlap (see Listing 11.18).

LISTING 11.18: Nested Generic Types

```
class Container<T, U>
{
  // Nested classes inherit type parameters.
  // Reusing a type parameter name will cause
  // a warning.
```

```
    class Nested<U>
    {
        void Method(T param0, U param1)
        {
        }
    }
}
```

The behavior of making the container's type parameter available in the nested type is consistent with nested type behavior in the sense that private members of the containing type are also accessible from the nested type. The rule is simply that a type is available anywhere within the curly braces within which it appears.

Constraints

Generics support the ability to define constraints on type parameters. These constraints enforce the types to conform to various rules. Take, for example, the `BinaryTree<T>` class shown in Listing 11.19.

LISTING 11.19: Declaring a `BinaryTree<T>` Class with No Constraints

```
public class BinaryTree<T>
{
    public BinaryTree ( T item)
    {
        Item = item;
    }

    public T Item
    {
        get{ return _Item;    }
        set{ _Item = value; }
    }
    private T _Item;

    public Pair<BinaryTree<T>> SubItems
    {
        get{ return _SubItems; }
        set{ _SubItems = value; }
    }
    private Pair<BinaryTree<T>> _SubItems;
}
```

(An interesting side note is that BinaryTree<T> uses Pair<T> internally, which is possible because Pair<T> is simply another type.)

Suppose you want the tree to sort the values within the Pair<T> value as it is assigned to the SubItems property. In order to achieve the sorting, the SubItems set accessor uses the CompareTo() method of the supplied key, as shown in Listing 11.20.

LISTING 11.20: Needing the Type Parameter to Support an Interface

```csharp
public class BinaryTree<T>
{
    ...
    public Pair<BinaryTree<T>> SubItems
    {
        get{ return _SubItems; }
        set
        {
            IComparable<T> first;
            // ERROR: Cannot implicitly convert type...
            first = value.First.Item;  // Explicit cast required

            if (first.CompareTo(value.Second.Item) < 0)
            {
                // first is less than second.
                ...
            }
            else
            {
                // first and second are the same or
                // second is less than first.
                ...
            }
            _SubItems = value;
        }
    }
    private Pair<BinaryTree<T>> _SubItems;
}
```

At compile time, the type parameter T is generic. When the code is written as shown, the compiler assumes that the only members available on T are those inherited from the base type object, since every type has object as an ancestor. (Only methods such as ToString(), therefore, are available to the key instance of the type parameter T.) As a result, the compiler displays a compilation error because the CompareTo() method is not defined on type object.

You can cast the T parameter to the `IComparable<T>` interface in order to access the `CompareTo()` method, as shown in Listing 11.21.

LISTING 11.21: Needing the Type Parameter to Support an Interface or Exception Thrown

```csharp
public class BinaryTree<T>
{
    ...
    public Pair<BinaryTree<T>> SubItems
    {
        get{ return _SubItems; }
        set
        {
            IComparable<T> first;
            first = (IComparable<T>)value.First.Item;

            if (first.CompareTo(value.Second.Item) < 0)
            {
                // first is less than second.
                ...
            }
            else
            {
                // second is less than or equal to first.
                ...
            }
            _SubItems = value;
        }
    }
    private Pair<BinaryTree<T>> _SubItems;
}
```

Unfortunately, however, if you now declare a `BinaryTree` class variable and supply a type parameter that does not implement the `IComparable<T>` interface, you encounter an execution-time error—specifically, an `Invalid-CastException`. This defeats an advantage of generics.

To avoid this exception and instead provide a compile-time error, C# enables you to supply an optional list of **constraints** for each type parameter declared in the generic class. A constraint declares the type parameter characteristics that the generic requires. You declare a constraint using the where keyword, followed by a "parameter-requirements" pair, where the parameter must be one of those defined in the generic type and the requirements are to restrict the class or interface from which the type "derives," the presence of a default constructor, or a reference/value type restriction.

Language Contrast: C++—Templates

Generics in C# and the CLR differ from similar constructs in other languages. Although other languages provide similar functionality, C# is significantly more type-safe. Generics in C# are a language feature and a platform feature—the underlying 2.0 runtime contains deep support for generics in its engine.

C++ templates differ significantly from C# generics, because C# takes advantage of the CIL. C# generics are compiled into the CIL, causing specialization to occur at execution time for each value type only when it is used, and only once for reference types.

A distinct feature not supported by C++ templates is explicit constraints. C++ templates allow you to compile a method call that may or may not belong to the type parameter. As a result, if the member does not exist in the type parameter, an error occurs, likely with a cryptic error message and referring to an unexpected location in the source code. However, the advantage of the C++ implementation is that operators (+, -, and so on) may be called on the type. C# does not support the calling of operators on the type parameter because operators are static—they can't be identified by interfaces or base class constraints.

The problem with the error is that it occurs only when *using* the template, not when defining it. Because C# generics can declare constraints, the compiler can prevent such errors when defining the generic, thereby identifying invalid assumptions sooner. Furthermore, when declaring a variable of a generic type, the error will point to the declaration of the variable, not to the location in the generic implementation where the member is used.

It is interesting to note that Microsoft's CLI support in C++ includes both generics and C++ templates because of the distinct characteristics of each.

Interface Constraints

In order to satisfy the sort requirement, you need to use the CompareTo() method in the BinaryTree class. To do this most effectively, you impose a constraint on the T type parameter. You need the T type parameter to

implement the IComparable<T> interface. The syntax for this appears in
Listing 11.22.

LISTING 11.22: Declaring an Interface Constraint

```csharp
public class BinaryTree<T>
    where T: System.IComparable<T>
{
    ...
    public Pair<BinaryTree<T>> SubItems
    {
        get{ return _SubItems; }
        set
        {
            IComparable<T> first;
            // Notice that the cast can now be eliminated.
            first = value.First.Item;

            if (first.CompareTo(value.Second.Item) < 0)
            {
                // first is less than second
                ...
            }
            else
            {
                // second is less than or equal to first.
                ...
            }
            _SubItems = value;
        }
    }
    private Pair<BinaryTree<T>> _SubItems;
}
```

Given the interface constraint addition in Listing 11.22, the compiler
ensures that each time you use the BinaryTree class you specify a type
parameter that implements the IComparable<T> interface. Furthermore,
you no longer need to explicitly cast the variable to an IComparable<T>
interface before calling the CompareTo() method. Casting is not even
required to access members that use explicit interface implementation,
which in other contexts would hide the member without a cast. To resolve
what member to call, the compiler first checks class members directly, and
then looks at the explicit interface members. If no constraint resolves the
argument, only members of object are allowable.

If you tried to create a BinaryTree<T> variable using System. Text.StringBuilder as the type parameter, you would receive a compiler error because StringBuilder does not implement IComparable<T>. The error is similar to the one shown in Output 11.3.

OUTPUT 11.3:

```
error CS0309: The type 'System.Text.StringBuilder' must be convertible
to 'System.IComparable<T>' in order to use it as parameter 'T' in the
generic type or method 'BinaryTree<T>'
```

To specify an interface for the constraint you declare an **interface constraint.** This constraint even circumvents the need to cast in order to call an explicit interface member implementation.

Base Class Constraints

Sometimes you might want to limit the constructed type to a particular class derivation. You do this using a **base class constraint,** as shown in Listing 11.23.

LISTING 11.23: Declaring a Base Class Constraint

```
public class EntityDictionary<TKey, TValue>
    : System.Collections.Generic.Dictionary<TKey, TValue>
    where TValue : EntityBase
{
    ...
}
```

In contrast to System.Collections.Generic.Dictionary<TKey, TValue> on its own, EntityDictionary<TKey, TValue> requires that all TValue types derive from the EntityBase class. By requiring the derivation, it is possible to always perform a cast operation within the generic implementation, because the constraint will ensure that all type parameters derive from the base and, therefore, that all TValue type parameters used with EntityDictionary can be implicitly converted to the base.

The syntax for the base class constraint is the same as that for the interface constraint, except that base class constraints must appear first when multiple constraints are specified. However, unlike interface constraints, multiple base class constraints are not allowed since it is not possible to derive from multiple classes. Similarly, base class constraints cannot be specified for sealed classes or specific structs. For example, C# does not allow a constraint for a type parameter to be derived from `string` or `System.Nullable<T>`.

struct/class **Constraints**

Another valuable generic constraint is the ability to restrict type parameters to a value type or a reference type. The compiler does not allow specifying `System.ValueType` as the base class in a constraint. Instead, C# provides special syntax that works for reference types as well. Instead of specifying a class from which T must derive, you simply use the keyword `struct` or `class`, as shown in Listing 11.24.

LISTING 11.24: Specifying the Type Parameter As a Value Type

```
public struct Nullable<T> :
    IFormattable, IComparable,
    IComparable<Nullable<T>>, INullable
    where T : struct
{
    // ...
}
```

Because a base class constraint requires a particular base class, using `struct` or `class` with a base class constraint would be pointless, and in fact could allow for conflicting constraints. Therefore, you cannot use `struct` and `class` constraints with a base class constraint.

There is one special characteristic for the `struct` constraint. It limits possible type parameters as being only value types while at the same time preventing type parameters that are `System.Nullable<T>` type parameters. Why? Without this last restriction, it would be possible to define the nonsense type `Nullable<Nullable<T>>`, which is nonsense because `Nullable<T>` on its own allows a value type variable that supports nulls, so a nullable-nullable type becomes meaningless. Since the nullable operator (?) is a C# shortcut for declaring a nullable value type, the `Nullable<T>` restriction provided by the `struct` constraint also prevents code such as the following:

```
int?? number    // Equivalent to Nullable<Nullable<int> if allowed
```

Multiple Constraints

For any given type parameter, you may specify any number of interfaces as constraints, but no more than one class, just as a class may implement any number of interfaces but inherit from only one other class. Each new constraint is declared in a comma-delimited list following the generic type and a colon. If there is more than one type parameter, each must be preceded by the where keyword. In Listing 11.25, the EntityDictionary class contains two type parameters: TKey and TValue. The TKey type parameter has two interface constraints, and the TValue type parameter has one base class constraint.

LISTING 11.25: Specifying Multiple Constraints

```
public class EntityDictionary<TKey, TValue>
    : Dictionary<TKey, TValue>
    where TKey : IComparable<TKey>, IFormattable
    where TValue : EntityBase
{
    ...
}
```

In this case, there are multiple constraints on TKey itself and an additional constraint on TValue. When specifying multiple constraints on one type parameter, an AND relationship is assumed. TKey must implement IComparable<TKey> and IFormattable, for example.

Notice there is no comma between each where clause.

Constructor Constraints

In some cases, it is desirable to create an instance of a type parameter inside the generic class. In Listing 11.26, the New() method for the EntityDictionary<TKey, TValue> class must create an instance of the type parameter TValue.

LISTING 11.26: Requiring a Default Constructor Constraint

```
public class EntityBase<TKey>
{
    public TKey Key
    {
        get{ return _Key; }
        set{ _Key = value; }
    }
```

```
        private TKey _Key;
    }

    public class EntityDictionary<TKey, TValue> :
        Dictionary<TKey, TValue>
        where TKey: IComparable<TKey>, IFormattable
        where TValue : EntityBase<TKey>, new()
    {
        // ...

        public TValue New(TKey key)
        {
            TValue newEntity = new TValue();
            newEntity.Key = key;
            Add(newEntity.Key, newEntity);
            return newEntity;
        }

        // ...
    }
```

Because not all objects are guaranteed to have public default constructors, the compiler does not allow you to call the default constructor on the type parameter. To override this compiler restriction, you add the text new() after all other constraints are specified. This text is a **constructor constraint,** and it forces the type parameter decorated with the constructor constraint to have a default constructor. Only the default constructor constraint is available. You cannot specify a constraint for a constructor with parameters.

Constraint Inheritance

Constraints are inherited by a derived class, but they must be specified explicitly on the derived class. Consider Listing 11.27.

Listing 11.27: Inherited Constraints Specified Explicitly

```
    class EntityBase<T> where T : IComparable<T>
    {
        // ...
    }
```

```
    // ERROR:
    // The type 'T' must be convertible to 'System.IComparable<T>'
    // in order to use it as parameter 'T' in the generic type or
    // method.
```

```
// class Entity<T> : EntityBase<T>
// {
//     ...
// }
```

Because `EntityBase` requires that `T` implement `IComparable<T>`, the `Entity` class needs to explicitly include the same constraint. Failure to do so will result in a compile error. This increases a programmer's awareness of the constraint in the derived class, avoiding confusion when using the derived class and discovering the constraint but not understanding where it comes from.

In contrast, constraints on generic override (or explicit interface) methods are inherited implicitly and may not be restated (see Listing 11.28).

LISTING 11.28: Inherited Constraints Specified Explicitly

```
class EntityBase<T> where T : IComparable<T>
{
  public virtual void Method<T>(T t)
      where T : IComparable<T>
  {
      // ...
  }
}
```

```
class Entity<T> : EntityBase<T>
{
  public virtual void Method<T>(T t)
      // Error:  Constraints may not be
      // repeated on overriding members
      where T : IComparable<T>
  {
      // ...
  }
}
```

In the inheritance case the type parameter on the base class can be additionally constrained by adding not only the constraints on the base class (required), but also additional constraints as well. However, overriding members need to conform to the "interface" defined in the base class method. Additional constraints could break polymorphism, so they are not allowed and the type parameter constraints on the override method are implied.

Constraint Limitations

Constraints are appropriately limited to avoid nonsense code. For example, you cannot combine a base class constraint with a `struct` or `class` constraint, nor can you use `Nullable<T>` on struct constraint type parameters. Also, you cannot specify constraints to restrict inheritance to special types such as `object`, arrays, `System.ValueType`, `System.Enum` (enum), `System.Delegate`, and `System.MulticastDelegate`.

In some cases, constraint limitations are perhaps more desirable, but they still are not supported. The following subsections provide some additional examples of constraints that are not allowed.

Operator Constraints Are Not Allowed

Another restriction on constraints is that you cannot specify a constraint that a class supports on a particular method or operator, unless that method or operator is on an interface. Because of this, the generic `Add()` in Listing 11.29 does not work.

LISTING 11.29: Constraint Expressions Cannot Require Operators

```
public abstract class MathEx<T>
{
    public static T Add(T first, T second)
    {
        // Error: Operator '+' cannot be applied to
        // operands of type 'T' and 'T'.
        return first + second;
    }
}
```

In this case, the method assumes that the + operator is available on all types. However, because all types support only the methods of `object` (which does not include the + operator), an error occurs. Unfortunately, there is no way to specify the + operator within a constraint; therefore, creating an add method in this way is a lot more cumbersome. One reason for this limitation is that there is no way to constrain a type to have a static method. You cannot, for example, specify static methods on an interface.

OR Criteria Are Not Supported

If you supply multiple interfaces or class constraints for a type parameter, the compiler always assumes an AND relationship between constraints. For example, where T : IComparable<T>, IFormattable requires that both IComparable<T> and IFormattable are supported. There is no way to specify an OR relationship between constraints. Hence, an equivalent of Listing 11.30 is not supported.

LISTING 11.30: Combining Constraints Using an OR Relationship Is Not Allowed

```
public class BinaryTree<T>
    // Error:  OR is not supported.
    where T: System.IComparable<T> || System.IFormattable
{
    ...
}
```

Supporting this would prevent the compiler from resolving which method to call at compile time.

Constraints of Type Delegate and Enum Are Not Valid

Readers who are already familiar with C# 1.0 and are reading this chapter to learn newer features will be familiar with the concept of delegates, which are covered in Chapter 12. One additional constraint that is not allowed is the use of any delegate type as a class constraint. For example, the compiler will output an error for the class declaration in Listing 11.31.

LISTING 11.31: Inheritance Constraints Cannot Be of Type `System.Delegate`

```
// Error:  Constraint cannot be special class 'System.Delegate'
public class Publisher<T>
    where T : System.Delegate
{
    public event T Event;
    public void Publish()
    {
        if (Event != null)
        {
            Event(this, new EventArgs());
        }
    }
}
```

All delegate types are considered special classes that cannot be specified as type parameters. Doing so would prevent compile-time validation on the call to Event() because the signature of the event firing is unknown with the data types System.Delegate and System.MulticastDelegate. The same restriction occurs for any enum type.

Constructor Constraints Are Allowed Only for Default Constructors

Listing 11.26 includes a constructor constraint that forces TValue to support a default constructor. There is no constraint to force TValue to support a constructor other than the default. For example, it is not possible to make EntityBase.Key protected and only set it in a TValue constructor that takes a TKey parameter using constraints alone. Listing 11.32 demonstrates the invalid code.

LISTING 11.32: Constructor Constraints Can Be Specified Only for Default Constructors

```
public TValue New(TKey key)
{
    // Error: 'TValue': Cannot provide arguments
    // when creating an instance of a variable type.
    TValue newEntity = null;
    // newEntity = new TValue(key);
    Add(newEntity.Key, newEntity);
    return newEntity;
}
```

One way to circumvent this restriction is to supply a factory interface that includes a method for instantiating the type. The factory implementing the interface takes responsibility for instantiating the entity rather than the EntityDictionary itself (see Listing 11.33).

LISTING 11.33: Using a Factory Interface in Place of a Constructor Constraint

```
public class EntityBase<TKey>
{
    public EntityBase(TKey key)
    {
        Key = key;
    }
    public TKey Key
    {
        get { return _key; }
        set { _key = value; }
    }
    private TKey _key;
}

public class EntityDictionary<TKey, TValue, TFactory> :
        Dictionary<TKey, TValue>
    where TKey : IComparable<T>, IFormattable
```

```
   where TValue : EntityBase<TKey>
   where TFactory : IEntityFactory<TKey, TValue>, new()
{
  ...
  public TValue New(TKey key)
  {
     TValue newEntity = new TFactory().CreateNew(key);
     Add(newEntity.Key, newEntity);
     return newEntity;
  }
  ...
}


public interface IEntityFactory<TKey, TValue>
{
   TValue CreateNew(TKey key);
}
...
```

A declaration such as this allows you to pass the new key to a TValue constructor that takes parameters rather than the default constructor. It no longer uses the constructor constraint on TValue because TFactory is responsible for instantiating the order instead of EntityDictionary<...>. (One modification to the code in Listing 11.33 would be to save a copy of the factory. This would enable you to reuse the factory instead of reinstantiating it every time.)

A declaration for a variable of type EntityDictionary<TKey, TValue, TFactory> would result in an entity declaration similar to the Order entity in Listing 11.34.

LISTING 11.34: Declaring an Entity to Be Used in EntityDictionary<...>

```
public class Order : EntityBase<Guid>
{
  public Order(Guid key) :
     base(key)
  {
     // ...
  }
}


public class OrderFactory : IEntityFactory<Guid, Order>
{
  public Order CreateNew(Guid key)
  {
     return new Order(key);
  }
}
```

Generic Methods

You already learned that it is relatively simple to add a generic method to a class when the class is a generic. You did this in the generic class examples so far, and it also works for static methods. Furthermore, you can use generic classes within a generic class, as you did in earlier BinaryTree listings using the following line of code:

```
public Pair< BinaryTree<T> > SubItems;
```

Generic methods are methods that use generics even when the containing class is not a generic class or the method contains type parameters not included in the generic class type parameter list. To define generic methods, you add the type parameter syntax immediately following the method name, as shown in the MathEx.Max<T> and MathEx.Min<T> examples in Listing 11.35.

LISTING 11.35: Defining Generic Methods

```
public static class MathEx
{
  public static T Max<T>(T first, params T[] values)
      where T : IComparable<T>
  {
      T maximum = first;
      foreach (T item in values)
      {
          if (item.CompareTo(maximum) > 0)
          {
              maximum = item;
          }
      }
      return maximum;
  }

  public static T Min<T>(T first, params T[] values)
      where T : IComparable<T>
  {
      T minimum = first;

      foreach (T item in values)
      {
          if (item.CompareTo(minimum) < 0)
          {
              minimum = item;
          }
      }
  }
```

```
        return minimum;
    }
}
```

You use the same syntax on a generic class when the method requires an additional type parameter not included in the class type parameter list. In this example, the method is static but C# does not require this.

Note that generic methods, like classes, can include more than one type parameter. The arity (the number of type parameters) is an additional distinguishing characteristic of a method signature.

Type Inferencing

The code used to call the Min<T> and Max<T> methods looks like that shown in Listing 11.36.

LISTING 11.36: Specifying the Type Parameter Explicitly

```
Console.WriteLine(
    MathEx.Max<int>(7, 490));
Console.WriteLine(
    MathEx.Min<string>("R.O.U.S.", "Fireswamp"));
```

The output to Listing 11.36 appears in Output 11.4.

OUTPUT 11.4:

```
490
Fireswamp
```

Not surprisingly, the type parameters, int and string, correspond to the actual types used in the generic method calls. However, specifying the type is redundant because the compiler can infer the type from the parameters passed to the method. To avoid redundancy, you can exclude the type parameters from the call. This is known as **type inferencing,** and an example appears in Listing 11.37. The output appears in Output 11.5.

LISTING 11.37: Inferring the Type Parameter

```
Console.WriteLine(
    MathEx.Max(7, 490));
Console.WriteLine(
    MathEx.Min("R.O.U.S'", "Fireswamp"));
```

OUTPUT 11.5:

```
490
Fireswamp
```

For type inferencing to be successful, the types must match the method signature. However, starting with C# 3.0, the compiler added an enhancement to imply the type parameter as long as the types were implicitly compatible. For example, calling the Max<T> method using MathEx.Max(7.0, 490) will compile successfully. Even though the parameters are not both the same type (int and double), they will both implicitly convert to double, so the method call compiles. You can resolve the error by either casting explicitly or including the type argument. Also note that you cannot perform type inferencing purely on the return type. Parameters are required for type inferencing to be allowed.

Specifying Constraints

The generic method also allows constraints to be specified. For example, you can restrict a type parameter to implement IComparable<T>. The constraint is specified immediately following the method header, prior to the curly braces of the method block, as shown in Listing 11.38.

LISTING 11.38: Specifying Constraints on Generic Methods

```csharp
public class ConsoleTreeControl
{
    // Generic method Show<T>
    public static void Show<T>(BinaryTree<T> tree, int indent)
        where T : IComparable<T>
    {
        Console.WriteLine("\n{0}{1}",
            "+ --".PadLeft(5*indent, ' '),
            tree.Item.ToString());
        if (tree.SubItems.First != null)
            Show(tree.SubItems.First, indent+1);
        if (tree.SubItems.Second != null)
            Show(tree.SubItems.Second, indent+1);
    }
}
```

Notice that the Show<T> implementation itself does not use the IComparable<T> interface. Recall, however, that the BinaryTree<T> class did require this (see Listing 11.39).

LISTING 11.39: **BinaryTree<T>** Requiring **IComparable<T>** Type Parameters

```
public class BinaryTree<T>
    where T: System.IComparable<T>
{
    ...
}
```

Because the BinaryTree<T> class requires this constraint on T, and because Show<T> uses BinaryTree<T>, Show<T> also needs to supply the constraint.

■ ADVANCED TOPIC

Casting inside a Generic Method

Sometimes you should be wary of using generics—for instance, when using it specifically to bury a cast operation. Consider the following method, which converts a stream into an object:

```
public static T Deserialize<T>(
    Stream stream, IFormatter formatter)
{
    return (T)formatter.Deserialize(stream);
}
```

The formatter is responsible for removing data from the stream and converting it to an object. The Deserialize() call on the formatter returns data of type object. A call to use the generic version of Deserialize() looks something like this:

```
string greeting =
    Deserialization.Deserialize<string>(stream, formatter);
```

The problem with this code is that to the user of the method, Deserialize<T>() appears to be strongly typed. However, a cast operation is still performed implicitly rather than explicitly, as in the case of the nongeneric equivalent shown here:

```
string greeting =
    (string)Deserialization.Deserialize(stream, formatter);
```

A method using an explicit cast is more explicit about what is taking place than is a generic version with a hidden cast. Developers should use care when casting in generic methods if there are no constraints to verify cast validity.

Covariance and Contravariance

If you declare two variables with different type parameters using the same generic class, the variables are not type-compatible even if they are assigning from a more specific type to a more generic type—in other words, they are not **covariant**. For example, instances of a generic class, Pair<Contact> and Pair<PdaItem>, are not type-compatible even when the type parameters are compatible. In other words, the compiler prevents casting (implicitly or explicitly) Pair<Contact> to Pair<PdaItem>, even though Contact derives from PdaItem. Similarly, casting Pair<Contact> to IPair<PdaItem> will also fail (see Listing 11.40).

LISTING 11.40: Conversion between Generics with Different Type Parameters

```
// ...
// Error: Cannot convert type ...
Pair<PdaItem> pair = (Pair<PdaItem>) new Pair<Contact>();
IPair<PdaItem> duple = (IPair<PdaItem>) new Pair<Contact>();
```

To allow covariance such as this would allow the following (see Listing 11.41).

LISTING 11.41: Preventing Covariance Maintains Homogeneity

```
//...
Address address;
Contact contact1, contact2;
Pair<Contact> contacts
```

```
// Initialize variables...
```

```
// Error: Cannot convert type ...
IPair<PdaItem> pdaPair = (IPair<PdaItem>) contacts;
pair.First = address;
...
```

Thus, casting `Pair<Contact>` to `IPair<PdaItem>` would appear to allow `Pair<Contact>` to contain heterogeneous data rather than just with the `Contact` type as the type parameter specified. Although a failure would still occur at runtime, the compile time validation is preferable.

Similarly, the compiler prevents **contravariance,** or assigning of types from more generic to more specific. For example, the following will cause a compile error:

```
Pair<Contact> contacts = (IPair<PdaItem>) pdaPair;
```

Doing so would cause a similar problem to covariance. Items within pda-Pair could potentially be heterogeneous (addresses and contacts) and constraining to all contacts would be invalid.

Enabling Covariance with the out Type Parameter Modifier in C# 4.0

It is important to note that you can define an `IReadOnlyPair<T>` interface that doesn't encounter the covariance problem. The `IReadOnlyPair<T>` interfaces would only expose `T` out of the interface (return parameters or get property members) and never into it (input parameters or set property members). In so doing, the covariance problem just described would not occur (see Listing 11.42).

LISTING 11.42: Potentially Possible Covariance

```
interface IReadOnlyPair<T>
{
  T First { get; }
  T Second { get; }
}
```

```
interface IPair<T>
{
  T First { get; set; }
  T Second { get; set; }
}
```

```
public struct Pair<T> : IPair<T>, IReadOnlyPair<T>
{
  // ...
}
```

```
class Program
{
  static void Main()
  {
      // Error: Only theoretically possible without
      // the out type parameter modifier
      Pair<Contact> contacts =
          new Pair<Contact>(
              new Contact("Princess Buttercupt"),
              new Contact("Inigo Montoya") );
      IReadOnlyPair<PdaItem> pair = contacts;
      PdaItem pdaItem1 = pair.First;
      PdaItem pdaItem2 = pair.Second;
  }
}
```

By restricting the generic type declaration to only expose data out of the interface, there is no reason for the compiler to prevent covariance. All operations on an IReadOnlyPair<PdaItem> instance would convert Contacts (from the original Pair<Contact> object) up to the base class PdaItem—a perfectly valid conversion.

Support for valid covariance, in which the assigned type only exposed data out, was added to C# 4 with the out type parameter modifier (see Listing 11.43).

LISTING 11.43: Covariance Using the out Type Parameter Modifier

```
// ...
interface IReadOnlyPair<out T>
{
  T First { get; }
  T Second { get; }
}
```

```
interface IPair<T>
{
  T First { get; set; }
  T Second { get; set; }
}
```

```
public struct Pair<T> : IPair<T>, IReadOnlyPair<T>
{
  // ...
}
```

```
class Program
{
  static void Main()
  {
    // Allowed in C# 4.0
    Pair<Contact> contacts =
        new Pair<Contact>(
            new Contact("Princess Buttercup"),
            new Contact("Inigo Montoya") );
    IReadOnlyPair<PdaItem> pair = contacts;
    PdaItem pdaItem1 = pair.First;
    PdaItem pdaItem2 = pair.Second;
  }
}
```

Modifying the type parameter on the IReadOnlyPair<out T> interface with out will cause the compiler to verify that indeed, T is used only for member returns and property getters, never for input parameters or property setters. From then on, the compiler will allow any covariant assignments to the interface.

Enabling Contravariance with the in Type Parameter Modifier in C# 4.0

As I mentioned earlier, contravariance is also invalid. A Pair<PdaItem> could potentially be heterogeneous (containing both an Address and a Contact), and constraining it to only be Contacts when it contains Addresses would invalid. However, imagine an IWriteOnlyPair<T> (see Listing 11.44) such that through this interface only Contacts could be placed into First and Second. What was already stored within Pair<PdaItem> would be irrelevant (since IWriteOnlyPair<T> can't retrieve it), and assigning an Address directly via the Pair<PdaItem> would also not affect the validity of what the IWriteOnlyPair<T> allowed.

LISTING 11.44: Covariance Using the out Type Parameter Modifier

```
interface IReadOnlyPair<out T>
{
  //...
}
```

```csharp
interface IWriteOnlyPair<in T>
{
 T First { set; }
   T Second { set; }
 }
```

```csharp
interface IPair<T>
{
   T First { get; set; }
   T Second { get; set; }
 }
```

```csharp
public struct Pair<T>
   : IPair<T>, IReadOnlyPair<out T>, IWriteOnlyPair<in T>
{
 //...
 }
```

```csharp
class Program
{
  static void Main()
  {
      // Allowed in C# 4.0
      Pair<Contact> contacts = new Pair<PdaItem>(
          new Address("..."), new Contact("..."));;
      IWriteOnlyPair<Contact> pair = contacts;
      contacts.First = new Contact("Inigo Montoya");
      contacts.Second = new Contact("Princess Buttercup");
  }
 }
```

Since Pair<PdaItem> could safely contain any PdaItem, forcing only Contacts to be inserted would be valid. The invalid operation would occur only when retrieving items out of the pair, something that IWriteOnly-Pair<T> does not allow since it has only property setters.

Notice that similar to covariance support, contravariance uses a type parameter modifier: in, on the IWriteOnlyPair<T> interface. This instructs the compiler to check that T never appears on a property getter or as an out parameter on a method, thus enabling contravariance to the interface.

Not surprisingly, the covariance and contravariance type modifiers can be combined into the same interface. Imagine, for example, the IConvertible<in TSource, out TTarget> interface defined in Listing 11.45.

LISTING 11.45: Covariance Using the out Type Parameter Modifier

```
interface IConvertible<in TSource, out TTarget>
{
  TTarget Convert(TSource source);
}
```

Using this interface with the type parameter modifiers specified would enable a successful conversion from an IConvertible<PdaItem, Contact> to an IConvertible<Contact, PdaItem>.

Lastly, notice that the compiler will check validity of the covariance and contravariance type parameter modifiers throughout the source. Consider the PairInitializer<in T> interface in Listing 11.46.

LISTING 11.46: Covariance Using the out Type Parameter Modifier

```
// ERROR:  Invalid variance, the type parameter 'T' is not
//         invariantly valid
interface PairInitializer<in T>
{
  void Initialize(IPair<T> pair);
}
```

A casual observer may be tempted to think that since IPair<T> is only an input parameter, restricting T to in on PairInitializer is valid. However, inside the implementation of Initialize() we would expect to assign First and Second, thereby introducing the potential of assigning a value that does not convert to T.

Support for Parameter Covariance and Contravariance in Arrays

Unfortunately, ever since C# 1.0, arrays allowed for covariance and contravariance. For example, both PdaItem[] pdaItems = new Contact[] { } and Contact[] contacts = (Contact[])new PdaItem[] { } are valid assignments in spite of the negative implications discussed earlier. The result is that the covariant and contravariant restrictions imposed by the compiler in C# 2.0 and the loosening of those restrictions in C# 4.0 to enable valid scenarios do not apply to arrays. As regrettable as this is, the situation can be avoided. As Chapter 14 describes, a host of interfaces and collections are available that effectively supersede arrays and enable a super set of functionality. Support for generics in combination with C# 3.0

syntax for initializing arrays (see Collection Initializers in Chapter 14) eliminates any best practice use of arrays except when required by existing interfaces. Moving forward, arrays may be treated as deprecated.

Generic Internals

Given the discussions in earlier chapters about the prevalence of objects within the CLI type system, it is no surprise that generics are also objects. In fact, the type parameter on a generic class becomes metadata that the runtime uses to build appropriate classes when needed. Generics, therefore, support inheritance, polymorphism, and encapsulation. With generics, you can define methods, properties, fields, classes, interfaces, and delegates.

To achieve this, generics require support from the underlying runtime. So, the addition of generics to the C# language is a feature of both the compiler and the platform. To avoid boxing, for example, the implementation of generics is different for value-based type parameters than for generics with reference type parameters.

■ ADVANCED TOPIC

CIL Representation of Generics

When a generic class is compiled, it is no different from a regular class. The result of the compilation is nothing but metadata and CIL. The CIL is parameterized to accept a user-supplied type somewhere in code. Suppose you had a simple Stack class declared as shown in Listing 11.47.

LISTING 11.47: Stack<T> Declaration

```
public class Stack<T> where T : IComparable
{
    T[] items;
    // rest of the class here
}
```

When you compile the class, the generated CIL is parameterized and looks something like Listing 11.48.

LISTING 11.48: CIL Code for Stack<T>

```
.class private auto ansi beforefieldinit
    Stack'1<([mscorlib]System.IComparable)T>
    extends [mscorlib]System.Object
{
   ...
}
```

The first notable item is the '1 that appears following Stack on the second line. That number is the arity. It declares the number of parameter types that the generic class will include. A declaration such as EntityDictionary<TKey, TValue> would have an arity of 2.

In addition, the second line of the generated CIL shows the constraints imposed upon the class. The T type parameter is decorated with an interface declaration for the IComparable constraint.

If you continue looking through the CIL, you will find that the item's array declaration of type T is altered to contain a type parameter using "exclamation point notation," new to the generics-capable version of the CIL. The exclamation point denotes the presence of the first type parameter specified for the class, as shown in Listing 11.49.

LISTING 11.49: CIL with "Exclamation Point Notation" to Support Generics

```
.class public auto ansi beforefieldinit
    'Stack'1'<([mscorlib]System.IComparable) T>
    extends [mscorlib]System.Object
{
    .field private !0[ ] items
    ...
}
```

Beyond the inclusion of the arity and type parameter in the class header and the type parameter denoted with exclamation points in code, there is little difference between the CIL generated for a generic class and the CIL generated for a nongeneric class.

Instantiating Generics Based on Value Types

When a generic type is first constructed with a value type as a type parameter, the runtime creates a specialized generic type with the supplied type parameter(s) placed appropriately in the CIL. Therefore, the runtime creates new specialized generic types for each new parameter value type.

For example, suppose some code declared a `Stack` constructed of integers, as shown in Listing 11.50.

LISTING 11.50: `Stack<int>` Definition

```
Stack<int> stack;
```

When using this type, `Stack<int>`, for the first time, the runtime generates a specialized version of the `Stack` class with `int` substituted for its type parameter. From then on, whenever the code uses a `Stack<int>`, the runtime reuses the generated specialized `Stack<int>` class. In Listing 11.51, you declare two instances of a `Stack<int>`, both using the code already generated by the runtime for a `Stack<int>`.

LISTING 11.51: Declaring Variables of Type `Stack<T>`

```
Stack<int> stackOne = new Stack<int>();
Stack<int> stackTwo = new Stack<int>();
```

If later in the code, you create another `Stack` with a different value type as its type parameter (such as a `long` or a user-defined `struct`) the runtime generates another version of the generic type. The benefit of specialized value type classes is better performance. Furthermore, the code is able to avoid conversions and boxing because each specialized generic class "natively" contains the value type.

Instantiating Generics Based on Reference Types

Generics work slightly differently for reference types. The first time a generic type is constructed with a reference type, the runtime creates a specialized generic type with `object` references substituted for type parameters in the CIL, not a specialized generic type based on the type parameter. Each subsequent time a constructed type is instantiated with a reference type parameter, the runtime reuses the previously generated version of the generic type, even if the reference type is different from the first reference type.

For example, suppose you have two reference types, a `Customer` class and an `Order` class, and you create an `EntityDictionary` of `Customer` types, like so:

```
EntityDictionary<Guid, Customer> customers;
```

Prior to accessing this class, the runtime generates a specialized version of the `EntityDictionary` class that, instead of storing `Customer` as the specified data type, stores `object` references. Suppose the next line of code creates an `EntityDictionary` of another reference type, called `Order`:

```
EntityDictionary<Guid, Order> orders =
    new EntityDictionary<Guid, Order>();
```

Unlike value types, no new specialized version of the `EntityDictionary` class is created for the `EntityDictionary` that uses the `Order` type. Instead, an instance of the version of `EntityDictionary` that uses `object` references is instantiated and the `orders` variable is set to reference it.

To still gain the advantage of type safety, for each object reference substituted in place of the type parameter, an area of memory for an `Order` type is specifically allocated and the pointer is set to that memory reference.

Suppose you then encountered a line of code to instantiate an `EntityDictionary` of a `Customer` type as follows:

```
customers = new EntityDictionary<Guid, Customer>();
```

As with the previous use of the `EntityDictionary` class created with the `Order` type, another instance of the specialized `EntityDictionary` class (the one based on `object` references) is instantiated and the pointers contained therein are set to reference a `Customer` type specifically. This implementation of generics greatly reduces code bloat by reducing to one the number of specialized classes created by the compiler for generic classes of reference types.

Even though the runtime uses the same internal generic type definition when the type parameter on a generic reference type varies, this behavior is superseded if the type parameter is a value type. `Dictionary<int,`

`Customer>`, `Dictionary<Guid, Order>`, and `Dictionary<long, Order>` will require new internal type definitions, for example.

Language Contrast: Java—Generics

Sun's implementation of generics for Java occurs within the compiler entirely, not within the Java Virtual Machine. Sun did this to ensure that no updated Java Virtual Machine would need to be distributed because generics were used.

The Java implementation uses syntax similar to the templates in C++ and the generics in C#, including type parameters and constraints. But because it does not treat value types differently from reference types, the unmodified Java Virtual Machine cannot support generics for value types. As such, generics in Java do not gain the execution efficiency of C#. Indeed, whenever the Java compiler needs to return data, it injects automatic downcasts from the specified constraint, if one is declared, or the base `Object` type if it is not declared. Further, the Java compiler generates a single specialized type at compile time, which it then uses to instantiate any constructed type. Finally, because the Java Virtual Machine does not support generics natively, there is no way to ascertain the type parameter for an instance of a generic type at execution time, and other uses of reflection are severely limited.

SUMMARY

Generics transformed C# 1.0 coding style. In virtually all cases in which programmers used `object` within C# 1.0 code, generics became a better choice in C# 2.0 and later to the extent that using `object` in relation to collections, at a minimum, should act as a flag for a possible generics implementation. The increased type safety, cast avoidance, and reduction of code bloat offer significant improvements. Similarly, where code traditionally used the `System.Collections` namespace, `System.Collections.Generics` should be selected instead.

Chapter 16 looks at one of the most pervasive generic namespaces, `System.Collections.Generic`. This namespace is composed almost exclusively of generic types. It provides clear examples of how some types that originally used objects were then converted to use generics. However, before we tackle these topics, we will investigate expressions, which provide a significant C# 3.0 (and later) improvement for working with collections.

■ 12 ■
Delegates and Lambda Expressions

P REVIOUS CHAPTERS DISCUSSED extensively how to create classes using many of the built-in C# language facilities for object-oriented development. The objects instantiated from classes encapsulate data and operations on data. As you create more and more classes, you see common patterns in the relationships between these classes.

One such pattern is to pass an object that represents a method that the receiver can invoke. The use of methods as a data type and their support for publish-subscribe patterns is the focus of this chapter. Both C# 2.0 and C# 3.0 introduced additional syntax for programming in this area. Although C# 3.0 supports the previous syntax completely, in many cases C# 3.0 will deprecate the use of the older-style syntax. However, I have

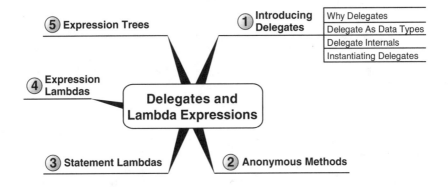

placed the earlier syntax into Advanced Topic blocks, which you can largely ignore unless you require support for an earlier compiler.

Introducing Delegates

Veteran C and C++ programmers have long used method pointers as a means to pass executable steps as parameters to another method. C# achieves the same functionality using a **delegate,** which encapsulates methods as objects, enabling an indirect method call bound at runtime. Consider an example of where this is useful.

Defining the Scenario

Although not necessarily efficient, perhaps one of the simplest sort routines is a bubble sort. Listing 12.1 shows the `BubbleSort()` method.

LISTING 12.1: BubbleSort() Method

```csharp
static class SimpleSort1
{
  public static void BubbleSort(int[] items)
  {
    int i;
    int j;
    int temp;

    if(items==null)
    {
      return;
    }

    for (i = items.Length - 1; i >= 0; i--)
    {
      for (j = 1; j <= i; j++)
      {
        if (items[j - 1] > items[j])
        {
          temp = items[j - 1];
          items[j - 1] = items[j];
          items[j] = temp;
        }
      }
    }
  }
  // ...
}
```

This method will sort an array of integers in ascending order.

However, if you wanted to support the option to sort the integers in descending order, you would have essentially two options. You could duplicate the code and replace the greater-than operator with a less-than operator. Alternatively, you could pass in an additional parameter indicating how to perform the sort, as shown in Listing 12.2.

LISTING 12.2: **BubbleSort( ) Method, Ascending or Descending**

```
class SimpleSort2
{
  public enum SortType
  {
      Ascending,
      Descending
  }

  public static void BubbleSort(int[] items, SortType sortOrder)
  {
      int i;
      int j;
      int temp;

      if(items==null)
      {
        return;
      }

      for (i = items.Length - 1; i >= 0; i--)
      {
          for (j = 1; j <= i; j++)
          {
              switch (sortOrder)
              {
                  case SortType.Ascending :
                      if (items[j - 1] > items[j])
                        {
                          temp = items[j - 1];
                          items[j - 1] = items[j];
                          items[j] = temp;
                        }

                      break;

                  case SortType.Descending :
                      if (items[j - 1] < items[j])
                        {
                          temp = items[j - 1];
                          items[j - 1] = items[j];
```

```
                              items[j] = temp;
                          }

                      break;
                  }
              }
          }
      }
      // ...
  }
```

However, this handles only two of the possible sort orders. If you wanted to sort them alphabetically, randomize the collection, or order them via some other criterion, it would not take long before the number of Bubble-Sort() methods and corresponding SortType values would become cumbersome.

Delegate Data Types

To increase the flexibility (and reduce code duplication), you can pass in the comparison method as a parameter to the BubbleSort() method. Moreover, in order to pass a method as a parameter, there needs to be a data type that can represent that method—in other words, a delegate. Listing 12.3 includes a modification to the BubbleSort() method that takes a delegate parameter. In this case, the delegate data type is ComparisonHandler.

LISTING 12.3: BubbleSort() Method with Delegate Parameter

```
class DelegateSample
{
  // ...

    public static void BubbleSort(
        int[] items, ComparisonHandler comparisonMethod)
    {
        int i;
        int j;
        int temp;

        if(items==null)
        {
          return;
        }
        if(comparisonMethod == null)
        {
```

```
            throw new ArgumentNullException("comparisonMethod");
        }

        for (i = items.Length - 1; i >= 0; i--)
        {
            for (j = 1; j <= i; j++)
            {
                if (comparisonMethod(items[j - 1], items[j]))
                {
                    temp = items[j - 1];
                    items[j - 1] = items[j];
                    items[j] = temp;
                }
            }
        }
    }
    // ...
}
```

ComparisonHandler is a data type that represents a method for comparing two integers. Within the BubbleSort() method you then use the instance of the ComparisonHandler, called comparisonMethod, inside the conditional expression. Since comparisonMethod represents a method, the syntax to invoke the method is identical to calling the method directly. In this case, comparisonMethod takes two integer parameters and returns a Boolean value that indicates whether the first integer is greater than the second one.

Perhaps more noteworthy than the particular algorithm, the ComparisonHandler delegate is strongly typed to return a bool and to accept only two integer parameters. Just as with any other method, the call to a delegate is strongly typed, and if the data types do not match up, then the C# compiler reports an error. Let us consider how the delegate works internally.

Delegate Internals

C# defines all delegates, including ComparisonHandler, as derived indirectly from System.Delegate, as shown in Figure 12.1.[1]

The first property is of type System.Reflection.MethodInfo, which I cover in Chapter 17. MethodInfo describes the signature of a particular method, including its name, parameters, and return type. In addition to

---

1. The C# standard doesn't specify the delegate implementation's class hierarchy. .NET's implementation, however, does derive indirectly from System.Delegate.

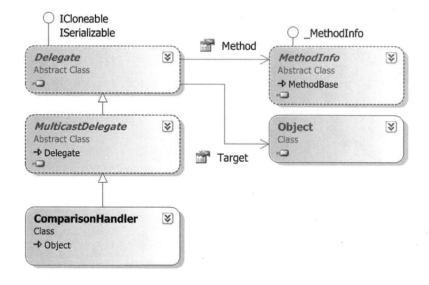

FIGURE 12.1: Delegate Types Object Model

MethodInfo, a delegate also needs the instance of the object containing the method to invoke. This is the purpose of the second property, Target. In the case of a static method, Target corresponds to the type itself. The purpose of the MulticastDelegate class is the topic of the next chapter.

It is interesting to note that all delegates are immutable. "Changing" a delegate involves instantiating a new delegate with the modification included.

Defining a Delegate Type

You saw how to define a method that uses a delegate, and you learned how to invoke a call to the delegate simply by treating the delegate variable as a method. However, you have yet to learn how to declare a delegate data type. For example, you have not learned how to define ComparisonHandler such that it requires two integer parameters and returns a bool.

Although all delegate data types derive indirectly from System.Delegate, the C# compiler does not allow you to define a class that derives directly or indirectly (via System.MulticastDelegate) from System.Delegate. Listing 12.4, therefore, is not valid.

LISTING 12.4: System.Delegate Cannot Explicitly Be a Base Class

```
// ERROR: 'ComparisonHandler' cannot
// inherit from special class 'System.Delegate'
public class ComparisonHandler: System.Delegate
{
  // ...
}
```

In its place, C# uses the `delegate` keyword. This keyword causes the compiler to generate a class similar to the one shown in Listing 12.4. Listing 12.5 shows the syntax for declaring a delegate data type.

LISTING 12.5: Declaring a Delegate Data Type

```
public delegate bool ComparisonHandler (
  int first, int second);
```

In other words, the `delegate` keyword is shorthand for declaring a reference type derived ultimately from `System.Delegate`. In fact, if the delegate declaration appeared within another class, then the delegate type, `ComparisonHandler`, would be a nested type (see Listing 12.6).

LISTING 12.6: Declaring a Nested Delegate Data Type

```
class DelegateSample
{
  public delegate bool ComparisonHandler (
    int first, int second);
}
```

In this case, the data type would be `DelegateSample.ComparisonHandler` because it is defined as a nested type within `DelegateSample`.

Instantiating a Delegate

In this final step of implementing the `BubbleSort()` method with a delegate, you will learn how to call the method and pass a delegate instance—specifically, an instance of type `ComparisonHandler`. To instantiate a delegate, you need a method that corresponds to the signature of the delegate type itself. In the case of `ComparisonHandler`, that method takes two integers and returns a `bool`. The name of the method is not significant. Listing 12.7 shows the code for a greater-than method.

LISTING 12.7: Declaring a `ComparisonHandler`-Compatible Method

```csharp
public delegate bool ComparisonHandler (
  int first, int second);
```

```csharp
class DelegateSample
{


  public static void BubbleSort(
    int[] items, ComparisonHandler comparisonMethod)
  {
     // ...
  }

  public static bool GreaterThan(int first, int second)
  {
    return first > second;
  }
  // ...
}
```

With this method defined, you can call `BubbleSort()` and pass the delegate instance that contains this method. Beginning with C# 2.0, you simply specify the name of the delegate method (see Listing 12.8).

LISTING 12.8: Passing a Delegate Instance As a Parameter in C# 2.0

```csharp
public delegate bool ComparisonHandler (
  int first, int second);
```

```csharp
class DelegateSample
{
  public static void BubbleSort(
      int[] items, ComparisonHandler comparisonMethod)
  {
     // ...
  }

  public static bool GreaterThan(int first, int second)
  {
      return first > second;
  }

  static void Main()
  {
     int[] items = new int[100];

     Random random = new Random();
```

```
    for (int i = 0; i < items.Length; i++)
    {
        items[i] = random.Next(int.MinValue, int.MaxValue);
    }


        BubbleSort(items, GreaterThan);

    for (int i = 0; i < items.Length; i++)
    {
        Console.WriteLine(items[i]);
    }
  }

 }
```

Note that the ComparisonHandler delegate is a reference type, but you do not necessarily use new to instantiate it. The facility to pass the name instead of using explicit instantiation is called **delegate inference,** a new syntax beginning with C# 2.0. With this syntax, the compiler uses the method name to look up the method signature and verify that it matches the method's parameter type.

▪ ADVANCED TOPIC

Delegate Instantiation in C# 1.0

Earlier versions of the compiler require instantiation of the delegate demonstrated in Listing 12.9.

LISTING 12.9: Passing a Delegate Instance As a Parameter Prior to C# 2.0

```
public delegate bool ComparisonHandler (
  int first, int second);
```

```
class DelegateSample
{
  public static void BubbleSort(
      int[] items, ComparisonHandler comparisonMethod)
  {
      // ...
  }

  public static bool GreaterThan(int first, int second)
  {
```

```
            return first > second;
        }

    static void Main(string[] args)
    {

        int i;
        int[] items = new int[5];

        for (i=0; i<items.Length; i++)
        {
            Console.Write("Enter an integer:");
            items[i] = int.Parse(Console.ReadLine());
        }

        BubbleSort(items,
            new ComparisonHandler(GreaterThan));

        for (i = 0; i < items.Length; i++)
        {
            Console.WriteLine(items[i]);
        }
    }

    // ...
}
```

Note that C# 2.0 and later support both syntaxes, but unless you are writing backward-compatible code, the 2.0 syntax is preferable. Therefore, throughout the remainder of the book, I will show only the C# 2.0 and later syntax. (This will cause some of the remaining code not to compile on version 1.0 compilers, unless you modify those compilers to use explicit delegate instantiation.)

The approach of passing the delegate to specify the sort order is significantly more flexible than the approach listed at the beginning of this chapter. With the delegate approach, you can change the sort order to be alphabetical simply by adding an alternative delegate to convert integers to strings as part of the comparison. Listing 12.10 shows a full listing that demonstrates alphabetical sorting, and Output 12.1 shows the results.

LISTING 12.10: Using a Different **ComparisonHandler**-Compatible Method

```
using System;
class DelegateSample
{
```

```csharp
public delegate bool ComparisonHandler(int first, int second);

public static void BubbleSort(
    int[] items, ComparisonHandler comparisonMethod)
{
    int i;
    int j;
    int temp;

    for (i = items.Length - 1; i >= 0; i--)
    {
        for (j = 1; j <= i; j++)
        {
            if (comparisonMethod(items[j - 1], items[j]))
            {
                temp = items[j - 1];
                items[j - 1] = items[j];
                items[j] = temp;
            }
        }
    }
}

public static bool GreaterThan(int first, int second)
{
    return first > second;
}

public static bool AlphabeticalGreaterThan(
    int first, int second)
{
    int comparison;
    comparison = (first.ToString().CompareTo(
        second.ToString()));

    return comparison > 0;
}

static void Main(string[] args)
{

    int i;
    int[] items = new int[5];

    for (i=0; i<items.Length; i++)
    {
        Console.Write("Enter an integer: ");
        items[i] = int.Parse(Console.ReadLine());
    }
```

```
        BubbleSort(items, AlphabeticalGreaterThan);

    for (i = 0; i < items.Length; i++)
    {
        Console.WriteLine(items[i]);
    }
  }
}
```

OUTPUT 12.1:

```
Enter an integer: 1
Enter an integer: 12
Enter an integer: 13
Enter an integer: 5
Enter an integer: 4
1
12
13
4
5
```

The alphabetic order is different from the numeric order. Note how simple it was to add this additional sort mechanism, however, compared to the process used at the beginning of the chapter.

The only changes to create the alphabetical sort order were the addition of the `AlphabeticalGreaterThan` method and then passing that method into the call to `BubbleSort()`.

Anonymous Methods

C# 2.0 and later include a feature known as **anonymous methods**. These are delegate instances with no actual method declaration. Instead, they are defined inline in the code, as shown in Listing 12.11.

LISTING 12.11: Passing an Anonymous Method

```
class DelegateSample
{
    // ...

    static void Main(string[] args)
    {
```

```
        int i;
        int[] items = new int[5];
        ComparisonHandler comparisonMethod;

        for (i=0; i<items.Length; i++)
        {
            Console.Write("Enter an integer:");
            items[i] = int.Parse(Console.ReadLine());
        }

        comparisonMethod =
            delegate(int first, int second)
            {
                return first < second;
            };

        BubbleSort(items, comparisonMethod);

        for (i = 0; i < items.Length; i++)
        {
            Console.WriteLine(items[i]);
        }
    }
}
```

In Listing 12.11, you change the call to `BubbleSort()` to use an anonymous method that sorts `items` in descending order. Notice that no `LessThan()` method is specified. Instead, the `delegate` keyword is placed directly inline with the code. In this context, the `delegate` keyword serves as a means of specifying a type of "delegate literal," similar to how quotes specify a string literal.

You can even call the `BubbleSort()` method directly, without declaring the `comparisonMethod` variable (see Listing 12.12).

LISTING 12.12: Using an Anonymous Method without Declaring a Variable

```
class DelegateSample
{

    // ...

    static void Main(string[] args)
    {

        int i;
        int[] items = new int[5];
```

```
    for (i=0; i<items.Length; i++)
    {
        Console.Write("Enter an integer:");
        items[i] = int.Parse(Console.ReadLine());
    }

    BubbleSort(items,
        delegate(int first, int second)
        {
            return first < second;
        }
    );

    for (i = 0; i < items.Length; i++)
    {
        Console.WriteLine(items[i]);
    }
  }
}
```

Note that in all cases, the parameter types and the return type must be compatible with the ComparisonHandler data type, the delegate type of the second parameter of BubbleSort().

In summary, C# 2.0 included a new feature, anonymous methods, that provided a means to declare a method with no name and convert it into a delegate.

■ ADVANCED TOPIC

Parameterless Anonymous Methods

Compatibility of the method signature with the delegate data type does not exclude the possibility of no parameter list. Unlike with lambda expressions, statement lambdas, and expression lambdas (see the next section), anonymous methods are allowed to omit the parameter list (delegate { return Console.ReadLine() != ""}, for example). This is atypical, but it does allow the same anonymous method to appear in multiple scenarios even though the delegate type may vary. Note, however, that although the parameter list may be omitted, the return type will still need to be compatible with that of the delegate (unless an exception is thrown).

System-**Defined Delegates:** Func<>

.NET 3.5 (C# 3.0) included a series of generic delegates with the names "Action" and "Func." System.Func represents delegates that had return types while System.Action corresponds when no return type occurs. The signatures for these delegates are shown in Listing 12.13 (although the in/out type modifiers were not added until C# 4.0, as discussed shortly).

LISTING 12.13: **Func and Action Delegate Declarations**

```
public delegate void Action ();
public delegate void Action<in T>(T arg)
public delegate void Action<in T1, in T2>(
    in T1 arg1, in T2 arg2)
public delegate void Action<in T1, in T2, in T3>(
    T1 arg1, T2 arg2, T3 arg3)
public delegate void Action<in T1, in T2, in T3, in T4(
    T1 arg1, T2 arg2, T3 arg3, T4 arg4)
...
public delegate void Action<
    in T1, in T2, in T3, in T4, in T5, in T6, in T7, in T8,
    in T9, in T10, in T11, in T12, in T13, in T14, in T16(
        T1 arg1, T2 arg2, T3 arg3, T4 arg4,
        T5 arg5, T6 arg6, T7 arg7, T8 arg8,
        T9 arg9, T10 arg10, T11 arg11, T12 arg12,
        T13 arg13, T14 arg14, T15 arg15, T16 arg16)

public delegate TResult Func<out TResult>();
public delegate TResult Func<in T, out TResult>(T arg)
public delegate TResult Func<in T1, in T2, out TResult>(
    in T1 arg1, in T2 arg2)
public delegate TResult Func<in T1, in T2, in T3, out TResult>(
    T1 arg1, T2 arg2, T3 arg3)
public delegate TResult Func<in T1, in T2, in T3, in T4,
    out TResult>(T1 arg1, T2 arg2, T3 arg3, T4 arg4)
...
public delegate TResult Func<
    in T1, in T2, in T3, in T4, in T5, in T6, in T7, in T8,
    in T9, in T10, in T11, in T12, in T13, in T14, in T16,
    out TResult>(
        T1 arg1, T2 arg2, T3 arg3, T4 arg4,
        T5 arg5, T6 arg6, T7 arg7, T8 arg8,
        T9 arg9, T10 arg10, T11 arg11, T12 arg12,
        T13 arg13, T14 arg14, T15 arg15, T16 arg16)
```

Since the delegate definitions in Listing 12.13 are generic, it is possible to use them instead of defining a custom delegate. For example, rather than declaring the ComparisonHandler delegate type, code could simply declare ComparisonHandler delegates using Func<int, int, bool>. The last type parameter of Func is always the return type of the delegate. The earlier type parameters correspond in sequence to the type of delegate parameters. In the case of ComparisonHandler, the return is bool (the last type parameter of the Func declaration) and the type arguments int and int correspond with the first and second parameters of ComparisonHandler. In many cases, the inclusion of Func delegates in the .NET 3.5 Framework eliminates the necessity to define delegates. You should use System.Action, or one of the generic versions, for delegates that have no return (TResult) and that take no parameters.

However, you should still declare delegate types when such a type would simplify coding with the delegate. For example, continuing to use the ComparisonHandler provides a more explicit indication of what the delegate is used for, whereas Func<int, int, bool> provides nothing more than an understanding of the method signature.

Evaluation about whether to declare a delegate is still meaningful and includes considerations such as whether the name of the delegate identifier is sufficient for indicating intent, whether the delegate type name would clarify its use, and whether the use of a .NET 3.5 type will limit the use of the assembly to .NET 3.5 clients unnecessarily.

Note that even though you can use a generic Func delegate in place of an explicitly defined delegate, the types are not compatible. You cannot assign one delegate type to a variable of another delegate type even if the type parameters match. For example, you cannot assign a ComparisonHandler variable to a Func<int, int, bool> variable or pass them interchangeably as parameters even though both represent signatures for a delegate that takes two int parameters and returns a bool.

However, notice the type parameter modifiers decorating the delegates in Listing 12.13. These do allow for some degree of casting between them, thanks to the variance support added in C# 4.0. Consider the following contravariant example: Because void Action<in T>(T arg) has the in type parameter decorator, it is possible to assign type Action<string> an object of type Action<object>. In other words, any methods with a void return and an object parameter will implicitly cast to the more restrictive delegate type that only allows parameters of type string. Similarly with covariance and a Func delegate—since TResult Func<out TResult>() includes the out type parameter modifier on TResult, it is possible to implicitly assign a Func<object> variable the value of a Func<string>. (See Listing 12.14.)

LISTING 12.14: Using Variance for Delegates

```
// Contravariance
Action<object> broadAction =
  delegate(object data)
  {
      Console.WriteLine(data);
  };
Action<string> narrowAction = broadAction;

// Contravariance
Func<string> narrowFunction =
  delegate()
  {
      return Console.ReadLine();
  };
Func<object> broadFunction = narrowFunction;

// Contravariance & Covariance Combined
Func<object, string> func1 =
  delegate(object data)
  {
      return data.ToString();
  };
Func<string, object> func2 = func1;
```

The last part of the listing combines both variance concepts into a single example, demonstrating how they can occur simultaneously if both in and out type parameters are involved.

The need for variance support within these generic delegates was a key contributing factor for why C# now includes the feature.[2]

---

2. The other was support for covariance to IEnumerable<out T>.

Lambda Expressions

Introduced in C# 3.0, **lambda expressions** are a more succinct syntax of **anonymous functions** than anonymous methods, where *anonymous functions* is a general term that includes both lambda expressions and anonymous methods. Lambda expressions are themselves broken into two types: statement lambdas and expression lambdas. Figure 12.2 shows the hierarchical relationship between the terms.

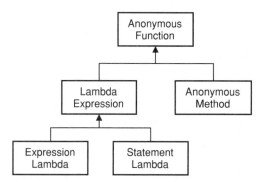

FIGURE 12.2: Anonymous Function Terminology

As mentioned earlier in the context of delegates, all anonymous functions are immutable.

Statement Lambdas

With statement lambdas, C# 3.0 provides a reduced syntax for anonymous methods, a syntax that does not include the `delegate` keyword and adds the **lambda operator, =>.** Listing 12.15 shows equivalent functionality to Listing 12.12, except that Listing 12.15 uses a statement lambda rather than an anonymous method.

LISTING 12.15: Passing a Delegate with a Statement Lambda

```
class DelegateSample
{

    // ...
```

```
static void Main(string[] args)
{

    int i;
    int[] items = new int[5];

    for (i=0; i<items.Length; i++)
    {
        Console.Write("Enter an integer:");
        items[i] = int.Parse(Console.ReadLine());
    }

    BubbleSort(items,
        (int first, int second) =>
        {
            return first < second;
        }
    );

    for (i = 0; i < items.Length; i++)
    {
        Console.WriteLine(items[i]);
    }
}
}
```

When reading code that includes a lambda operator, you would replace the lambda operator with the words *go/goes to*. For example, you would read n => { return n.ToString();} as "n goes to return n dot ToString." In Listing 12.15, you would read the second BubbleSort() parameter as "integers first and second go to returning the result of first less than second."

As readers will observe, the syntax in Listing 12.15 is virtually identical to that in Listing 12.12, apart from the changes already outlined. However, statement lambdas allow for an additional shortcut via type parameter inference. Rather than explicitly declaring the data type of the parameters, statement lambdas can omit parameter types as long as the compiler can infer the types. In Listing 12.16, the delegate data type is bool ComparisonHandler(int first, int second), so the compiler verifies that the return type is a bool and infers that the input parameters are both integers (int).

LISTING 12.16: Omitting Parameter Types from Statement Lambdas

```
// ...

        BubbleSort(items,
            (first, second) =>
            {
                return first < second;
            }
        );

// ...
```

In general, statement lambdas do not need parameter types as long as the compiler can infer the types or can implicitly convert them to the requisite expected types. If the types are specified, however, there must be an exact match for the delegate type. In cases where inference is not possible, the data type is required, although even when it is not required, you can specify the data type explicitly to increase readability; once the statement lambda includes one type, all types are required.

In general, C# requires a lambda expression to have parentheses around the parameter list regardless of whether the data type is specified. Even parameterless statement lambdas, representing delegates that have no input parameters, are coded using empty parentheses (see Listing 12.17).

LISTING 12.17: Parameterless Statement Lambdas

```
using System;
// ...
Func<string> getUserInput =
    () =>
    {
        string input;
        do
        {
            input = Console.ReadLine();
        }
        while(input.Trim().Length==0);
        return input;
    };
// ...
```

The exception to the parenthesis rule is that if the compiler can infer the data type and there is only a single input parameter, the statement lambda does not require parentheses (see Listing 12.18).

LISTING 12.18: **Statement Lambdas with a Single Input Parameter**

```
using System.Collections.Generic;
using System.Diagnostics;
using System.Linq;
 // ...
 IEnumerable<Process> processes = Process.GetProcesses().Where(
     process => { return process.WorkingSet64 > 2^30; });
 // ...
```

(In Listing 12.18, Where() returns a query for processes that have a physical memory utilization greater than 1GB.)

Note that back in Listing 12.17, the body of the statement lambda includes multiple statements inside the statement block (via curly braces). Although a statement lambda can have any number of statements, typically a statement lambda uses only two or three statements in its statement block.

Expression Lambdas

Unlike a statement lambda, which includes a statement block and, therefore, zero or more statements, an expression lambda has only an expression, with no statement block. Listing 12.19 is the same as Listing 12.15, except that it uses an expression lambda rather than a statement lambda.

LISTING 12.19: **Passing a Delegate with a Statement Lambda**

```
class DelegateSample
{

  // ...

  static void Main(string[] args)
  {

      int i;
      int[] items = new int[5];

      for (i=0; i<items.Length; i++)
      {
          Console.Write("Enter an integer:");
          items[i] = int.Parse(Console.ReadLine());
      }

      BubbleSort(items, (first, second) => first < second; );
```

```
    for (i = 0; i < items.Length; i++)
    {
        Console.WriteLine(items[i]);
    }
  }
}
```

The difference between a statement and an expression lambda is that the statement lambda has a statement block on the right side of the lambda operator, whereas the expression lambda has only an expression (no return statement or curly braces, for example).

Generally, you would read a lambda operator in an expression lambda in the same way you would a statement lambda: "go/goes to." In addition, "becomes" is sometimes clearer. In cases such as the BubbleSort() call, where the expression lambda specified is a **predicate** (returns a Boolean), it is frequently clearer to replace the lambda operator with "such that." This changes the pronunciation of the statement lambda in Listing 12.19 to read "first and second such that first is less than second." One of the most common places for a predicate to appear is in the call to System.Linq.Enumerable()'s Where() function. In cases such as this, neither "such that" nor "goes to" is needed. We would read names.Where(name => name.Contains(" ")) as "names where names dot Contains a space," for example. One pronunciation difference between the lambda operator in statement lambdas and in expression lambdas is that "such that" terminology applies more to expression lambdas than to statement lambdas since the latter tend to be more complex.

The anonymous function does not have any intrinsic type associated with it, although implicit conversion is possible for any delegate type as long as the parameters and return type are compatible. In other words, an anonymous method is no more a ComparisonHandler type than another delegate type such as LessThanHandler. As a result, you cannot use the typeof() operator (see Chapter 17) on an anonymous method, and calling GetType() is possible only after assigning or casting the anonymous method to a delegate variable.

Table 12.1 contains additional lambda expression characteristics.

TABLE 12.1: Lambda Expression Notes and Examples

Statement	Example
Lambda expressions themselves do not have type. In fact, there is no concept of a lambda expression in the CLR. Therefore, there are no members to call directly from a lambda expression. The . operator on a lambda expression will not compile, eliminating even the option of calls to object methods.	```// ERROR: Operator '.' cannot be applied to` `// operand of type 'Lambda expression'` `Type type = ((int x) => x).ToString();```
Given that a lambda expression does not have an intrinsic type, it cannot appear to the right of an is operator.	```// ERROR: The first operand of an 'is' or 'as'` `// operator may not be a Lambda expression or` `// anonymous method` `bool boolean = ((int x) => x) is Func<int, int>;```
Although there is no type on the lambda expression on its own, once assigned or cast, the lambda expression takes on a type. Therefore, it is common for developers to informally refer to the type of the lambda expression concerning type compatibility, for example.	```// ERROR: Lambda expression is not compatible with` `// Func<int, bool> type.` `Func<int, bool> expression = ((int x) => x);```
A lambda expression cannot be assigned to an implicitly typed local variable since the compiler does not know what type to make the variable given that lambda expressions do not have type.	```// ERROR: Cannot assign Lambda expression to an` `// implicitly typed local variable` `var thing = (x => x);```

Continues

TABLE 12.1: Lambda Expression Notes and Examples *(Continued)*

Statement	Example
| C# does not allow jump statements (break, goto, continue) inside anonymous functions if the target is outside the lambda expression. Similarly, you cannot target a jump statement from outside the lambda expression (or anonymous methods) into the lambda expression. | ```csharp
// ERROR: Control cannot leave the body of an
// anonymous method or lambda expression
string[] args;
Func<string> expression;
switch(args[0])
{

    case "/File":
    expression = () =>
        {

            if (!File.Exists(args[1]))
            {
                break;
            }
            // ...

            return args[1];

        };
    // ...

}
``` |
| Variables introduced within a lambda expression are visible only within the scope of the lambda expression body. | ```csharp
// ERROR:  The name 'first' does not
//            exist in the current context
Func<int, int, bool> expression =
        (first, second) => first > second;
first++;
``` |

TABLE 12.1: Lambda Expression Notes and Examples *(Continued)*

Statement	Example
| The compiler's flow analysis is unable to detect initialization of local variables in lambda expressions. | ```csharp
int number;
Func<string, bool> expression =
    text => int.TryParse(text, out number);
if (expression("1"))
{
    // ERROR: Use of unassigned local variable
    System.Console.Write(number);
}
``` |
| | ```csharp
int number;
Func<int, bool> isFortyTwo =
    x => 42 == (number = x);
if (isFortyTwo(42))
{
    // ERROR: Use of unassigned local variable
    System.Console.Write(number);
}
``` |

■**ADVANCED TOPIC**

Lambda Expression and Anonymous Method Internals

Lambda expressions (and anonymous methods) are not an intrinsic construct within the CLR. Rather, the C# compiler generates the implementation at compile time. Lambda expressions provide a language construct for an inline-declared delegate pattern. The C# compiler, therefore, generates the implementation code for this pattern so that the compiler automatically writes the code instead of the developer writing it manually. Given the earlier listings, therefore, the C# compiler generates CIL code that is similar to the C# code shown in Listing 12.20.

LISTING 12.20: C# Equivalent of CIL Generated by the Compiler for Lambda Expressions

```csharp
class DelegateSample
{

  // ...

  static void Main(string[] args)
  {

      int i;
      int[] items = new int[5];

      for (i=0; i<items.Length; i++)
      {
          Console.Write("Enter an integer:");
          items[i] = int.Parse(Console.ReadLine());
      }


      BubbleSort(items,
          DelegateSample.__AnonymousMethod_00000000);

      for (i = 0; i < items.Length; i++)
      {
          Console.WriteLine(items[i]);
      }

  }

  private static bool __AnonymousMethod_00000000(
      int first, int second)
  {
```

```
          return first < second;
    }

}
```

In this example, an anonymous method is converted into a separately declared static method that is then instantiated as a delegate and passed as a parameter.

Outer Variables

Local variables declared outside a lambda expression (including parameters), but **captured** (accessed) within the lambda expression, are **outer variables** of that lambda. this is also an outer variable. Outer variables captured by anonymous functions live on until after the anonymous function's delegate is destroyed. In Listing 12.21, it is relatively trivial to use an outer variable to count how many times BubbleSort() performs a comparison. Output 12.2 shows the results of this listing.

LISTING 12.21: Using an Outer Variable in a Lambda Expression

```
class DelegateSample
{

    // ...

    static void Main(string[] args)
    {

        int i;
        int[] items = new int[5];
        int comparisonCount=0;

        for (i=0; i<items.Length; i++)
        {
            Console.Write("Enter an integer:");
            items[i] = int.Parse(Console.ReadLine());
        }

        BubbleSort(items,
            (int first, int second) =>
            {
                comparisonCount++;
                return first < second;
```

```
            }
        );

        for (i = 0; i < items.Length; i++)
        {
            Console.WriteLine(items[i]);
        }

        Console.WriteLine("Items were compared {0} times.",
                            comparisonCount);

    }
}
```

OUTPUT 12.2:

```
Enter an integer:5
Enter an integer:1
Enter an integer:4
Enter an integer:2
Enter an integer:3
5
4
3
2
1
Items were compared 10 times.
```

comparisonCount appears outside the lambda expression and is incremented inside it. After calling the BubbleSort() method, comparisonCount is printed out to the console.

As this code demonstrates, the C# compiler takes care of generating CIL code that shares comparisonCount between the anonymous method and the call site, even though there is no parameter to pass comparisonCount within the anonymous delegate, nor within the BubbleSort() method. Given the sharing of the variable, it will not be garbage-collected until after the delegate that references it is garbage-collected. In other words, the lifetime of the captured variable is at least as long as that of the longest-lived delegate object capturing it.

ADVANCED TOPIC

Outer Variable CIL Implementation

The CIL code generated by the C# compiler for outer variables is more complex than the code for a simple anonymous method. Listing 12.22 shows the C# equivalent of the CIL code used to implement outer variables.

LISTING 12.22: C# Equivalent of CIL Code Generated by Compiler for Outer Variables

```csharp
class DelegateSample
{

  // ...

  private sealed class __LocalsDisplayClass_00000001
  {
      public int comparisonCount;
      public bool __AnonymousMethod_00000000(
          int first, int second)
      {
            comparisonCount++;
            return first < second;
      }
  }

  ...

  static void Main(string[] args)
  {

      int i;
      __LocalsDisplayClass_00000001 locals =
          new __LocalsDisplayClass_00000001();
      locals.comparisonCount=0;
      int[] items = new int[5];

      for (i=0; i<items.Length; i++)
      {
          Console.Write("Enter an integer:");
          items[i] = int.Parse(Console.ReadLine());
      }

      BubbleSort(items, locals.__AnonymousMethod_00000000);
      for (i = 0; i < items.Length; i++)
      {
          Console.WriteLine(items[i]);
      }

      Console.WriteLine("Items were compared {0} times.",
                    locals.comparisonCount);
  }
}
```

Notice that the captured local variable is never "passed" anywhere and is never "copied" anywhere. Rather, the captured local variable (comparisonCount) is a single variable whose lifetime we have extended by implementing it as an instance field rather than as a local variable. All references to the local variable are rewritten to be references to the field.

The generated class, `__LocalsDisplayClass`, is a **closure**—a data structure (class in C#) that contains an expression and the variables (public fields in C#) necessary to evaluate the expression. The variables (such as `comparisonCount`) enable the passing of data from one invocation of the expression to the next without changing the signature of the expression.

Expression Trees

Lambda expressions provide a succinct syntax for defining a method inline within your code. The compiler converts the code so that it is executable and callable later, potentially passing the delegate to another method. One feature for which it does not offer intrinsic support, however, is a representation of the expression as data—data that may be traversed and even serialized.

Using Lambda Expressions As Data

Consider the lambda expression in the following code:

```
persons.Where(
    person => person.Name.ToUpper() == "INIGO MONTOYA");
```

Assuming that `persons` is an array of `Persons`, the compiler compiles the lambda expression to a `Func<person, bool>` delegate type and then passes the delegate instance to the `Where()` method. Code and execution like this works very well. (The `Where()` method is an `IEnumerable` extension method from the class `System.Linq.Enumerable`, but this is irrelevant within this section.)

What if `persons` was not a `Person` array, but rather a collection of `Person` objects sitting on a remote computer, or perhaps in a database? Rather than returning all items in the `persons` collection, it would be preferable to send data describing the expression over the network and have the filtering occur remotely so that only the resultant selection returns over the network. In scenarios such as this, the data about the expression is needed, not the compiled CIL. The remote computer then compiles or interprets the expression data.

Interpreting is motivation for adding **expression trees** to the language. Lambda expressions that represent data about expressions rather than compiled code are expression trees. Since the expression tree represents data rather than compiled code, it is possible to convert the data to an alternative format—to convert it from the expression data to SQL code (SQL is the language generally used to query data from databases) that executes on a database, for example. The expression tree received by Where() may be converted into a SQL query that is passed to a database, for example (see Listing 12.23).

LISTING 12.23: Converting an Expression Tree to a SQL where Clause

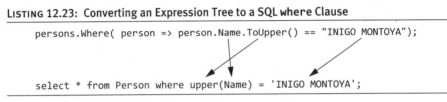

```
persons.Where( person => person.Name.ToUpper() == "INIGO MONTOYA");



select * from Person where upper(Name) = 'INIGO MONTOYA';
```

Recognizing the original Where() call parameter as data, you can see that it is made up of the following:

- The call to the Person property, Name
- A call to a string method called ToUpper()
- A constant value, "INIGO MONTOYA"
- An equality operator, ==

The Where() method takes this data and converts it to the SQL where clause by iterating over the data and building a SQL query string. However, SQL is just one example of what an expression tree may convert to.

Expression Trees Are Object Graphs

The data that an expression tree translates to is an object graph, an object graph that is represented by System.Linq.Expressions.Expression. Although an expression tree includes a method that will compile it into a delegate constructor call (executable CIL code), it is more likely that the expression tree (data) will be converted into a different format or set of instructions.

Any lambda expression, for example, is a type of expression that has a read-only collection of parameters, a return type, and a body—which is another expression (see Figure 12.3).

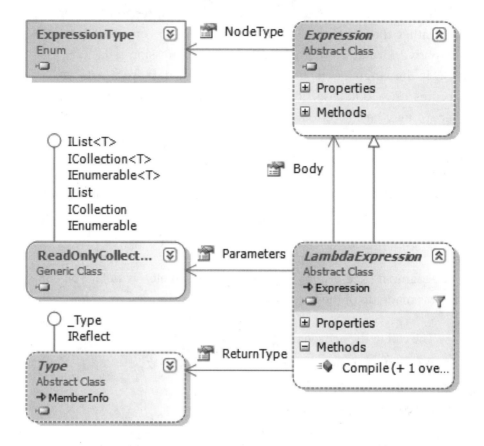

FIGURE 12.3: Object Graph of a Lambda Expression

This object graph is the data required to compile the LambdaExpression into CIL (or to convert some other representation). Similarly, we can create an object graph for a unary expression or binary expression (see Figure 12.4).

A unary expression (such as count++) is an expression composed of an Operand (of type Expression) and a Method—the operator. The BinaryExpression, which also derives from Expression, has two expression associations (Left and Right) in addition to the operator (Method). These object graphs sufficiently represent these types of expressions. However, there are another 30 or so expression types, such as NewExpression, ParameterExpression, MethodCallExpression, LoopExpression, and so forth.

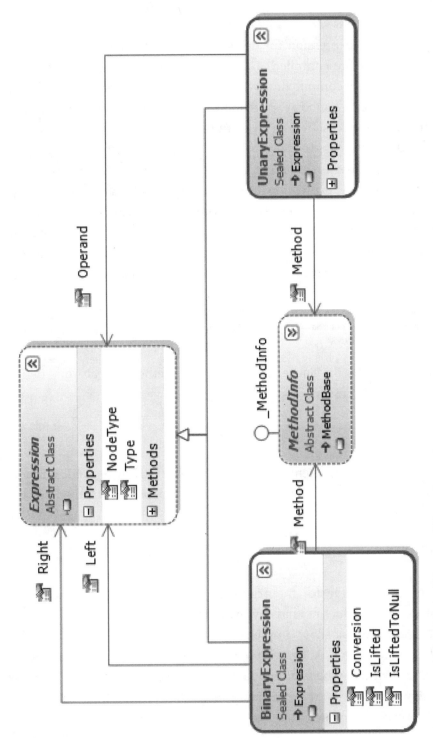

FIGURE 12.4: Object Graph of Unary and Binary Expressions

Lambda Expressions versus Expression Trees

Both a lambda expression for delegates and a lambda expression for an expression tree are compiled, and in both cases the syntax of the expression is verified at compile time with full semantic analysis. The difference, however, is that a lambda expression is compiled into a delegate in CIL. In contrast, an expression tree is compiled into a data structure of type `System.Linq.Expressions.Expression`.

Let us consider an example that highlights the difference between a delegate and an expression tree. `System.Linq.Enumerable` and `System.Linq.Queryable` are very similar. They each provide virtually identical extension methods to the collection interfaces they extend (`IEnumerable` and `IQueryable`, respectively). Consider, for example, the `Where()` method from Listing 12.23. Given a collection that supports `IEnumerable`, a call to `Where()` could be as follows:

```
persons.Where( person => person.Name.ToUpper() ==
    "INIGO MONTOYA");
```

Conceptually, the `Enumerable` extension method signature is defined on `IEnumerable<TSource>` as follows:

```
public IEnumerable<TSource> Where<TSource>(
    Func<TSource, bool> predicate);
```

However, the equivalent `Queryable` extension on the `IQueryable<TSource>` method call is identical, even though the conceptual `Where()` method signature (shown) is not:

```
public IQueryable<TSource> Where<TSource>(
    Expression<Func<TSource, bool>> predicate);
```

The calling code for the argument is identical because the lambda expression itself does not have type until it is assigned/cast.

`Enumerable`'s `Where()` implementation takes the lambda expression and converts it to a delegate that the `Where()` method's implementation calls. In contrast, when calling `Queryable`'s `Where()`, the lambda expression is converted to an expression tree so that the compiler converts the lambda expression into data. The object implementing `IQueryable` receives the expression data and manipulates it. As suggested before, the expression tree received by Where() may be converted into a SQL query that is passed to a database.

Examining an Expression Tree

Capitalizing on the fact that lambda expressions don't have intrinsic type, assigning a lambda expression to a System.Linq.Expressions.Expression<TDelegate> creates an expression tree rather than a delegate.

In Listing 12.24, we create an expression tree for the Func<int, int, bool>. (Recall that Func<int, int, bool> is functionally equivalent to the ComparisonHandler delegate.) Notice that just the simple act of writing an expression to the console, Console.WriteLine(expression) (where expression is of type Expression<TDelegate>), will result in a call to expression's ToString() method. However, this doesn't cause the expression to be evaluated or even to write out the fully qualified name of Func<int, int, bool> (as would happen if we used a delegate instance). Rather, displaying the expression writes out the data (in this case, the expression code) corresponding to the value of the expression tree.

LISTING 12.24: Examining an Expression Tree

```
using System;
using System.Linq.Expressions;

class Program
{
    static void Main()
    {
        Expression<Func<int, int, bool>> expression;
        expression = (x, y) => x > y;
        Console.WriteLine("-------------{0}-------------",
            expression);
        PrintNode(expression.Body, 0);
        Console.WriteLine();
        Console.WriteLine();
        expression = (x, y) => x * y > x + y;
        Console.WriteLine("-------------{0}-------------",
            expression);
        PrintNode(expression.Body, 0);
        Console.WriteLine();
        Console.WriteLine();
    }
```

```csharp
public static void PrintNode(Expression expression,
    int indent)
{
    if (expression is BinaryExpression)
        PrintNode(expression as BinaryExpression, indent);
    else
        PrintSingle(expression, indent);
}
private static void PrintNode(BinaryExpression expression,
  int indent)
{
    PrintNode(expression.Left, indent + 1);
    PrintSingle(expression, indent);
    PrintNode(expression.Right, indent + 1);
}
private static void PrintSingle(
    Expression expression, int indent)
{
    Console.WriteLine("{0," + indent * 5 + "}{1}",
      "", NodeToString(expression));
}
private static string NodeToString(Expression expression)
{
    switch (expression.NodeType)
    {
        case ExpressionType.Multiply:
            return "*";
        case ExpressionType.Add:
            return "+";
        case ExpressionType.Divide:
            return "/";
        case ExpressionType.Subtract:
            return "-";
        case ExpressionType.GreaterThan:
            return ">";
        case ExpressionType.LessThan:
            return "<";
        default:
            return expression.ToString() +
                " (" + expression.NodeType.ToString() + ")";
    }
}
}
}
```

In Output 12.3, we see that the Console.WriteLine() statements within Main() print out the body of the expression trees as text.

OUTPUT 12.3:

```
------------- (x, y) => x > y -------------
    x (Parameter)
>
    y (Parameter)


------------- (x, y) => (x * y) > (x + y) -------------
        x (Parameter)
    *
        y (Parameter)
>
        x (Parameter)
    +
        y (Parameter)
```

The output of the expression as text is due to conversion from the underlying data of an expression tree—conversion similar to the `Print-Node()` and `NodeTypeToString()` functions, only more comprehensive. The important point to note is that an expression tree is a collection of data, and by iterating over the data, it is possible to convert the data to another format. In the `PrintNode()` method, Listing 12.24 converts the data to a horizontal text interpretation of the data. However, the interpretation could be virtually anything.

Using recursion, the `PrintNode()` function demonstrates that an expression tree is a tree of zero or more expression trees. The contained expression trees are stored in an `Expression`'s `Body` property. In addition, the expression tree includes an `ExpressionType` property called `NodeType` where `ExpressionType` is an enum for each different type of expression. There are numerous types of expressions: `BinaryExpression`, `Condition-alExpression`, `LambdaExpression` (the root of an expression tree), `Method-CallExpression`, `ParameterExpression`, and `ConstantExpression` are examples. Each type derives from `System.Linq.Expressions.Expression`.

Generally, you can use statement lambdas interchangeably with expression lambdas. However, you cannot convert statement lambdas into expression trees. You can express expression trees only by using expression lambda syntax.

SUMMARY

This chapter began with a discussion of delegates and their use as references to methods or callbacks. It introduced a powerful concept for passing a set of instructions to call in a different location, rather than immediately, when the instructions are coded.

Following on the heels of a brief look at the C# 2.0 concept of anonymous methods, the chapter introduced the C# 3.0 concept of lambda expressions, a syntax which supersedes (although doesn't eliminate) the C# 2.0 anonymous method syntax. Regardless of the syntax, these constructs allow programmers to assign a set of instructions to a variable directly, without defining an explicit method that contains the instructions. This provides significant flexibility for programming instructions dynamically within the method—a powerful concept that greatly simplifies the programming of collections through an API known as LINQ, which stands for Language Integrated Query.

Finally, the chapter ended with the concept of expression trees, and how they compile into data that represents a lambda expression, rather than the delegate implementation itself. This is a key feature that enables such libraries as LINQ to SQL and LINQ to XML, libraries that interpret the expression tree and use it within contexts other than CIL.

The term *lambda expression* encompasses both *statement lambda* and *expression lambda*. In other words, both statement lambdas and expression lambdas are types of lambda expressions.

One thing that the chapter mentioned but did not elaborate on was multicast delegates. The next chapter investigates multicast delegates in detail and explains how they enable the publish-subscribe pattern with events.

13

Events

I N THE PRECEDING CHAPTER, you saw how to store a single method inside an instance of a delegate type and invoke that method via the delegate. Delegates comprise the building blocks of a larger pattern called publish-subscribe. The use of delegates and their support for publish-subscribe patterns is the focus of this chapter. Virtually everything described within this chapter is possible to do using delegates alone. However, the event constructs that this chapter focuses on providing additional encapsulation, making the publish-subscribe pattern easier to implement and less error-prone.

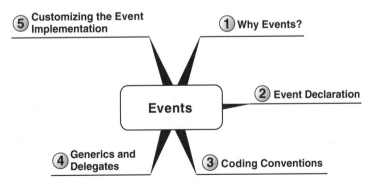

In the preceding chapter, all delegates were for a single callback (a multiplicity of one). However, a single delegate variable can reference a series of delegates in which each successive one points to a succeeding delegate in the form of a chain, sometimes known as a **multicast delegate.** With a multicast delegate, you can invoke a method chain via a single method object, create variables that refer to a method's chain, and pass the delegates as parameters to pass methods.

The C# implementation of multicast delegates is a common pattern that would otherwise require significant manual code. Known as the **observer** or **publish-subscribe pattern,** it represents scenarios where notifications of single events, such as a change in object state, are broadcast to multiple subscribers.

Coding the Observer Pattern with Multicast Delegates

Consider a temperature control example, where a heater and a cooler are hooked up to the same thermostat. In order for a unit to turn on and off appropriately, you notify the unit of changes in temperature. One thermostat publishes temperature changes to multiple subscribers—the heating and cooling units. The next section investigates the code.[1]

Defining Subscriber Methods

Begin by defining the Heater and Cooler objects (see Listing 13.1).

LISTING 13.1: **Heater and Cooler Event Subscriber Implementations**

```
class Cooler
{
    public Cooler(float temperature)
    {
        Temperature = temperature;
    }

    public float Temperature
    {
        get{return _Temperature;}
        set{_Temperature = value;}
    }
    private float _Temperature;
```

---

1. In this example, I use the term *thermostat* because people more commonly think of it in the context of heating and cooling systems. Technically, however, *thermometer* would be more appropriate.

```csharp
    public void OnTemperatureChanged(float newTemperature)
    {
        if (newTemperature > Temperature)
        {
            System.Console.WriteLine("Cooler: On");
        }
        else
        {
            System.Console.WriteLine("Cooler: Off");
        }
    }
}

class Heater
{
    public Heater(float temperature)
    {
        Temperature = temperature;
    }

    public float Temperature
    {
        get{return _Temperature;}
        set{_Temperature = value;}
    }
    private float _Temperature;

    public void OnTemperatureChanged(float newTemperature)
    {
        if (newTemperature < Temperature)
        {
            System.Console.WriteLine("Heater: On");
        }
        else
        {
            System.Console.WriteLine("Heater: Off");
        }
    }
}
```

The two classes are essentially identical, with the exception of the temperature comparison. (In fact, you could eliminate one of the classes if you used a delegate as a method pointer for comparison within the

OnTemperatureChanged method.) Each class stores the temperature for when to turn on the unit. In addition, both classes provide an OnTemperatureChanged() method. Calling the OnTemperatureChanged() method is the means to indicate to the Heater and Cooler classes that the temperature has changed. The method implementation uses newTemperature to compare against the stored trigger temperature to determine whether to turn on the device.

The OnTemperatureChanged() methods are the subscriber methods. It is important that they have the parameters and a return type that matches the delegate from the Thermostat class, which I will discuss next.

Defining the Publisher

The Thermostat class is responsible for reporting temperature changes to the heater and cooler object instances. The Thermostat class code appears in Listing 13.2.

LISTING 13.2: Defining the Event Publisher, Thermostat

```
public class Thermostat
{
  // Define the delegate data type
  public delegate void TemperatureChangeHandler(
      float newTemperature);

  // Define the event publisher
  public TemperatureChangeHandler OnTemperatureChange
  {
      get{ return _OnTemperatureChange;}
      set{ _OnTemperatureChange = value;}
  }
  private TemperatureChangeHandler _OnTemperatureChange;

  public float CurrentTemperature
  {
      get{return _CurrentTemperature;}
      set
      {
          if (value != CurrentTemperature)
          {
              _CurrentTemperature = value;
          }
      }
  }
  private float _CurrentTemperature;
}
```

The first member of the Thermostat class is the TemperatureChange-Handler delegate. Although not a requirement, Thermostat.TemperatureChangeHandler is a nested delegate because its definition is specific to the Thermostat class. The delegate defines the signature of the subscriber methods. Notice, therefore, that in both the Heater and the Cooler classes, the OnTemperatureChanged() methods match the signature of TemperatureChangeHandler.

In addition to defining the delegate type, Thermostat also includes a property called OnTemperatureChange that is of the OnTemperatureChange Handler delegate type. OnTemperatureChange stores a list of subscribers. Notice that only one delegate field is required to store all the subscribers. In other words, both the Cooler and the Heater classes will receive notifications of a change in the temperature from this single publisher.

The last member of Thermostat is the CurrentTemperature property. This sets and retrieves the value of the current temperature reported by the Thermostat class.

Hooking Up the Publisher and Subscribers

Finally, put all these pieces together in a Main() method. Listing 13.3 shows a sample of what Main() could look like.

LISTING 13.3: Connecting the Publisher and Subscribers

```csharp
class Program
{
  public static void Main()
  {
      Thermostat thermostat = new Thermostat();
      Heater heater = new Heater(60);
      Cooler cooler = new Cooler(80);
      string temperature;

      // Using C# 2.0 or later syntax.
      thermostat.OnTemperatureChange +=
          heater.OnTemperatureChanged;
      thermostat.OnTemperatureChange +=
          cooler.OnTemperatureChanged;

      Console.Write("Enter temperature: ");
      temperature = Console.ReadLine();
      thermostat.CurrentTemperature = int.Parse(temperature);
  }
}
```

The code in this listing has registered two subscribers (heater.OnTempera-tureChanged and cooler.OnTemperatureChanged) to the OnTempera-tureChange delegate by directly assigning them using the += operator. (As noted in the comment, you need to use the new operator with the Tempera-tureChangeHandler constructor if you are only using C# 1.0.)

By taking the temperature value the user has entered, you can set the CurrentTemperature of thermostat. However, you have not yet written any code to publish the change temperature event to subscribers.

Invoking a Delegate

Every time the CurrentTemperature property on the Thermostat class changes, you want to **invoke the delegate** to notify the subscribers (heater and cooler) of the change in temperature. To do this, modify the Current-Temperature property to save the new value and publish a notification to each subscriber. The code modification appears in Listing 13.4.

LISTING 13.4: Invoking a Delegate without Checking for null

```csharp
public class Thermostat
{
  ...
  public float CurrentTemperature
  {
      get{return _CurrentTemperature;}
      set
      {
          if (value != CurrentTemperature)
          {
              _CurrentTemperature = value;

              // INCOMPLETE:  Check for null needed
              // Call subscribers
              OnTemperatureChange(value);
          }
      }
  }
  private float _CurrentTemperature;
}
```

Now the assignment of CurrentTemperature includes some special logic to notify subscribers of changes in CurrentTemperature. The call to notify all subscribers is simply the single C# statement, OnTemperatureChange(value).

This single statement publishes the temperature change to the cooler and heater objects. Here, you see in practice that the ability to notify multiple subscribers using a single call is why delegates are more specifically known as multicast delegates.

Check for null

One important event of publishing code is missing from Listing 13.4. If no subscriber registered to receive the notification, then OnTemperatureChange would be null and executing the OnTemperatureChange(value) statement would throw a NullReferenceException. To avoid this, it is necessary to check for null before firing the event. Listing 13.5 demonstrates how to do this.

LISTING 13.5: Invoking a Delegate

```
public class Thermostat
{
    ...
    public float CurrentTemperature
    {
        get{return _CurrentTemperature;}
        set
        {
            if (value != CurrentTemperature)
            {
                _CurrentTemperature = value;
                // If there are any subscribers
                // then notify them of changes in
                // temperature
                TemperatureChangeHandler localOnChange =
                    OnTemperatureChange;
                if(localOnChange != null)
                {
                    // Call subscribers
                    localOnChange(value);
                }
            }
        }
    }
    private float _CurrentTemperature;
}
```

Instead of checking for null directly, first assign OnTemperatureChange to a second delegate variable, handlerCopy. This simple modification ensures that if all OnTemperatureChange subscribers are removed (by a different thread) between checking for `null` and sending the notification, you will not fire a `NullReferenceException`.

One more time: Remember to check the value of a delegate for `null` before invoking it.

ADVANCED TOPIC

-= Operator for a Delegate Returns a New Instance

Given that a delegate is a reference type, it is perhaps somewhat surprising that assigning a local variable and then using that local variable is sufficient for making the null check thread-safe. Since `localOnChange` points at the same location that `OnTemperatureChange` points, one would think that any changes in `OnTemperatureChange` would be reflected in `localOn-Change` as well.

This is not the case, because effectively, any calls to `OnTemperatureChange -= <listener>` will not simply remove a delegate from `OnTemperatureChange` so that it contains one less delegate than before. Rather, it will assign an entirely new multicast delegate without having any effect on the original multicast delegate to which `localOnChange` also points.

Delegate Operators

To combine the two subscribers in the `Thermostat` example, you used the `+=` operator. This takes the first delegate and adds the second delegate to the chain so that one delegate points to the next. Now, after the first delegate's method is invoked, it calls the second delegate. To remove delegates from a delegate chain, use the `-=` operator, as shown in Listing 13.6.

LISTING 13.6: Using the += and -= Delegate Operators

```
// ...
Thermostat thermostat = new Thermostat();
Heater heater = new Heater(60);
Cooler cooler = new Cooler(80);

Thermostat.TemperatureChangeHandler delegate1;
Thermostat.TemperatureChangeHandler delegate2;
Thermostat.TemperatureChangeHandler delegate3;

// use Constructor syntax for C# 1.0.
```

```
delegate1 = heater.OnTemperatureChanged;
delegate2 = cooler.OnTemperatureChanged;

Console.WriteLine("Invoke both delegates:");
delegate3 = delegate1;
delegate3 += delegate2;
delegate3(90);

Console.WriteLine("Invoke only delegate2");
delegate3 -= delegate1;
delegate3(30);
// ...
```

The results of Listing 13.6 appear in Output 13.1.

OUTPUT 13.1:

```
Invoke both delegates:
Heater: Off
Cooler: On
Invoke only delegate2
Cooler: Off
```

Furthermore, you can also use the + and – operators to combine delegates, as Listing 13.7 shows.

LISTING 13.7: Using the + and - Delegate Operators

```
// ...
Thermostat thermostat = new Thermostat();
Heater heater = new Heater(60);
Cooler cooler = new Cooler(80);

Thermostat.TemperatureChangeHandler delegate1;
Thermostat.TemperatureChangeHandler delegate2;
Thermostat.TemperatureChangeHandler delegate3;

// Note: Use new Thermostat.TemperatureChangeHandler(
//       cooler.OnTemperatureChanged) for C# 1.0 syntax.
delegate1 = heater.OnTemperatureChanged;
delegate2 = cooler.OnTemperatureChanged;

Console.WriteLine("Combine delegates using + operator:");
delegate3 = delegate1 + delegate2;
delegate3(60);

Console.WriteLine("Uncombine delegates using - operator:");
```

```
delegate3 = delegate3 - delegate2;
delegate3(60);
// ...
```

Use of the assignment operator clears out all previous subscribers and allows you to replace them with new subscribers. This is an unfortunate characteristic of a delegate. It is simply too easy to mistakenly code an assignment when, in fact, the += operator is intended. The solution, called events, appears in the Events section, later in this chapter.

It should be noted that both the + and – operators and their assignment equivalents, += and -=, are implemented internally using the static methods System.Delegate.Combine() and System.Delegate.Remove(). Both methods take two parameters of type delegate. The first method, Combine(), joins the two parameters so that the first parameter points to the second within the list of delegates. The second, Remove(), searches through the chain of delegates specified in the first parameter and then removes the delegate specified by the second parameter.

One interesting thing to note about the Combine() method is that either or both of the parameters can be null. If one of them is null, then Combine() returns the non-null parameter. If both are null, then Combine() returns null. This explains why you can call thermostat.OnTemperatureChange += heater.OnTemperatureChanged; and not throw an exception, even if the value of thermostat.OnTemperatureChange is not yet assigned.

Sequential Invocation

Figure 13.1 highlights the sequential notification of both heater and cooler.

Although you coded only a single call to OnTemperatureChange(), the call is broadcast to both subscribers so that from that one call, both cooler and heater are notified of the change in temperature. If you added more subscribers, they too would be notified by OnTemperatureChange().

Although a single call, OnTemperatureChange(), caused the notification of each subscriber, the subscribers are still called sequentially, not simultaneously, because a single delegate can point to another delegate that can, in turn, point to additional delegates.

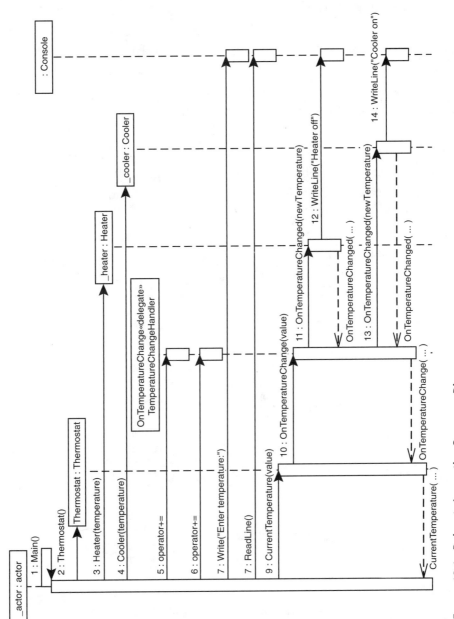

FIGURE 13.1: Delegate Invocation Sequence Diagram

517

■ ADVANCED TOPIC

Multicast Delegate Internals

To understand how events work, you need to revisit the first examination of the `System.Delegate` type internals. Recall that the `delegate` keyword is an alias for a type derived from `System.MulticastDelegate`. In turn, `System.MulticastDelegate` is derived from `System.Delegate`, which, for its part, comprises an object reference and a method pointer (of type `System.Reflection.MethodInfo`). When you create a delegate, the compiler automatically employs the `System.MulticastDelegate` type rather than the `System.Delegate` type. The `MulticastDelegate` class includes an object reference and method pointer, just like its `Delegate` base class, but it also contains a reference to another `System.MulticastDelegate` object.

When you add a method to a multicast delegate, the `MulticastDelegate` class creates a new instance of the delegate type, stores the object reference and the method pointer for the added method into the new instance, and adds the new delegate instance as the next item in a list of delegate instances. In effect, the `MulticastDelegate` class maintains a linked list of `Delegate` objects. Conceptually, you can represent the thermostat example as shown in Figure 13.2.

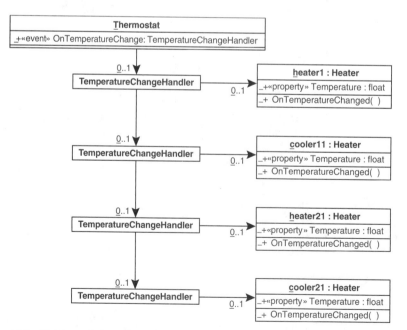

FIGURE 13.2: Multicast Delegates Chained Together

When invoking the multicast, each delegate instance in the linked list is called sequentially. Generally, delegates are called in the order they were added, but this behavior is not specified within the CLI specification, and furthermore, it can be overridden. Therefore, programmers should not depend on an invocation order.

Error Handling

Error handling makes awareness of the sequential notification critical. If one subscriber throws an exception, later subscribers in the chain do not receive the notification. Consider, for example, what would happen if you changed the Heater's OnTemperatureChanged() method so that it threw an exception, as shown in Listing 13.8.

LISTING 13.8: OnTemperatureChanged() Throwing an Exception

```
class Program
{
  public static void Main()
  {
      Thermostat thermostat = new Thermostat();
      Heater heater = new Heater(60);
      Cooler cooler = new Cooler(80);
      string temperature;

      // Using C# 2.0 or later syntax.
      thermostat.OnTemperatureChange +=
          heater.OnTemperatureChanged;
      // Using C# 3.0.  Change to anonymous method
      // if using C# 2.0
      thermostat.OnTemperatureChange +=
          (newTemperature) =>
            {
                throw new ApplicationException();
            };
      thermostat.OnTemperatureChange +=
          cooler.OnTemperatureChanged;

      Console.Write("Enter temperature: ");
      temperature = Console.ReadLine();
      thermostat.CurrentTemperature = int.Parse(temperature);
  }
}
```

Figure 13.3 shows an updated sequence diagram.

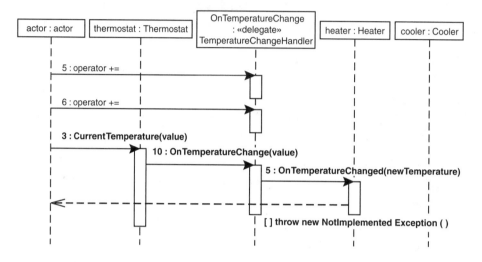

FIGURE 13.3: Delegate Invocation with Exception Sequence Diagram

Even though `cooler` and `heater` subscribed to receive messages, the lambda expression exception terminates the chain and prevents the `cooler` object from receiving notification.

To avoid this problem so that all subscribers receive notification, regardless of the behavior of earlier subscribers, you must manually enumerate through the list of subscribers and call them individually. Listing 13.9 shows the updates required in the `CurrentTemperature` property. The results appear in Output 13.2.

LISTING 13.9: Handling Exceptions from Subscribers

```
public class Thermostat
{
    // Define the delegate data type
    public delegate void TemperatureChangeHandler(
        float newTemperature);

    // Define the event publisher
    public event TemperatureChangeHandler OnTemperatureChange;
```

```csharp
public float CurrentTemperature
{
    get{return _CurrentTemperature;}
    set
    {
        if (value != CurrentTemperature)
        {
            _CurrentTemperature = value;
            if(OnTemperatureChange != null)
            {
                foreach(
                    TemperatureChangeHandler handler in
                    OnTemperatureChange.GetInvocationList() )
                {
                    try
                    {
                        handler(value);
                    }
                    catch(Exception exception)
                    {
                        Console.WriteLine(exception.Message);
                    }
                }
            }
        }
    }
    private float _CurrentTemperature;
}
```

OUTPUT 13.2:

```
Enter temperature: 45
Heater: On
Error in the application
Cooler: Off
```

This listing demonstrates that you can retrieve a list of subscribers from a delegate's GetInvocationList() method. Enumerating over each item in this list returns the individual subscribers. If you then place each invocation of a subscriber within a try/catch block, you can handle any error conditions before continuing with the enumeration loop. In this sample, even though the delegate listener throws an exception, cooler still receives notification of the temperature change.

Method Returns and Pass-by-Reference

There is another scenario where it is useful to iterate over the delegate invocation list instead of simply activating a notification directly. This scenario relates to delegates that either do not return void or have ref or out parameters. In the thermostat example so far, the OnTemperatureHandler delegate had a return type of void. Furthermore, it did not include any parameters that were ref or out type parameters, parameters that return data to the caller. This is important because an invocation of a delegate potentially triggers notification to multiple subscribers. If the subscribers return a value, it is ambiguous which subscriber's return value would be used.

If you changed OnTemperatureHandler to return an enumeration value, indicating whether the device was on because of the temperature change, the new delegate would look like Listing 13.10.

LISTING 13.10: Declaring a Delegate with a Method Return

```
public enum Status
{
    On,
    Off
}

// Define the delegate data type
public delegate Status TemperatureChangeHandler(
    float newTemperature);
```

All subscriber methods would have to use the same method signature as the delegate, and therefore, each would be required to return a status value. Assuming you invoke the delegate in a similar manner as before, what will the value of status be in Listing 13.11, for example?

LISTING 13.11: Invoking a Delegate Instance with a Return

```
Status status = OnTemperatureChange(value);
```

Since OnTemperatureChange potentially corresponds to a chain of delegates, status reflects only the value of the last delegate. All other values are lost entirely.

To overcome this issue, it is necessary to follow the same pattern that you used for error handling. In other words, you must iterate through each delegate invocation list, using the `GetInvocationList()` method, to retrieve each individual return value. Similarly, delegate types that use `ref` and out parameters need special consideration.

Events

There are two key problems with the delegates as you have used them so far in this chapter. To overcome these issues, C# uses the keyword `event`. In this section, you will see why you would use events, and how they work.

Why Events?

This chapter and the preceding one covered all you need to know about how delegates work. However, weaknesses in the delegate structure may inadvertently allow the programmer to introduce a bug. The issues relate to encapsulation that neither the subscription nor the publication of events can sufficiently control.

Encapsulating the Subscription

As demonstrated earlier, it is possible to assign one delegate to another using the assignment operator. Unfortunately, this capability introduces a common source for bugs. Consider Listing 13.12.

LISTING 13.12: Using the Assignment Operator = Rather Than +=

```csharp
class Program
{
  public static void Main()
  {
      Thermostat thermostat = new Thermostat();
      Heater heater = new Heater(60);
      Cooler cooler = new Cooler(80);
      string temperature;

      // Note: Use new Thermostat.TemperatureChangeHandler(
      //       cooler.OnTemperatureChanged) if C# 1.0
      thermostat.OnTemperatureChange =
          heater.OnTemperatureChanged;

      // Bug:  assignment operator overrides
      // previous assignment.
      thermostat.OnTemperatureChange =
          cooler.OnTemperatureChanged;
```

```
        Console.Write("Enter temperature: ");
        temperature = Console.ReadLine();
        thermostat.CurrentTemperature = int.Parse(temperature);
    }
}
```

Listing 13.12 is almost identical to Listing 13.6, except that instead of using the += operator, you use a simple assignment operator. As a result, when code assigns `cooler.OnTemperatureChanged` to `OnTemperatureChange`, `heater.OnTemperatureChanged` is cleared out because an entirely new chain is assigned to replace the previous one. The potential for mistakenly using an assignment operator, when in fact the += assignment was intended, is so high that it would be preferable if the assignment operator were not even supported for objects except within the containing class. It is the purpose of the event keyword to provide additional encapsulation such that you cannot inadvertently cancel other subscribers.

Encapsulating the Publication

The second important difference between delegates and events is that events ensure that only the containing class can trigger an event notification. Consider Listing 13.13.

LISTING 13.13: Firing the Event from Outside the Events Container

```
class Program
{
  public static void Main()
  {
      Thermostat thermostat = new Thermostat();
      Heater heater = new Heater(60);
      Cooler cooler = new Cooler(80);
      string temperature;

      // Note: Use new Thermostat.TemperatureChangeHandler(
      //       cooler.OnTemperatureChanged) if C# 1.0.
      thermostat.OnTemperatureChange +=
          heater.OnTemperatureChanged;

      thermostat.OnTemperatureChange +=
          cooler.OnTemperatureChanged;

      thermostat.OnTemperatureChange(42);
    }
}
```

In Listing 13.13, `Program` is able to invoke the `OnTemperatureChange` delegate even though the `CurrentTemperature` on thermostat did not change. `Program`, therefore, triggers a notification to all `thermostat` subscribers that the temperature changed, but in reality, there was no change in the thermostat temperature. As before, the problem with the delegate is that there is insufficient encapsulation. `Thermostat` should prevent any other class from being able to invoke the `OnTemperatureChange` delegate.

Declaring an Event

C# provides the `event` keyword to deal with both of these problems. Although seemingly like a field modifier, `event` defines a new type of member (see Listing 13.14).

LISTING 13.14: Using the event Keyword with the Event-Coding Pattern

```csharp
public class Thermostat
{
    public class TemperatureArgs: System.EventArgs
    {
        public TemperatureArgs( float newTemperature )
        {
            NewTemperature = newTemperature;
        }

        public float NewTemperature
        {
            get{return _newTemperature;}
            set{_newTemperature = value;}
        }
        private float _newTemperature;
    }

    // Define the delegate data type
    public delegate void TemperatureChangeHandler(
        object sender, TemperatureArgs newTemperature);

    // Define the event publisher
    public event TemperatureChangeHandler OnTemperatureChange =
        delegate { };

    public float CurrentTemperature
    {
        ...
    }
    private float _CurrentTemperature;
}
```

The new `Thermostat` class has four changes from the original class. First, the `OnTemperatureChange` property has been removed, and instead, `OnTemperatureChange` has been declared as a public field. This seems contrary to solving the earlier encapsulation problem. It would make more sense to increase the encapsulation, not decrease it by making a field public. However, the second change was to add the `event` keyword immediately before the field declaration. This simple change provides all the encapsulation needed. By adding the `event` keyword, you prevent use of the assignment operator on a public delegate field (for example, `thermostat.OnTemperatureChange = cooler.OnTemperatureChanged`). In addition, only the containing class is able to invoke the delegate that triggers the publication to all subscribers (for example, disallowing `thermostat.OnTemperatureChange(42)` from outside the class). In other words, the `event` keyword provides the needed encapsulation that prevents any external class from publishing an event or unsubscribing previous subscribers they did not add. This resolves the two issues with plain delegates and is one of the key reasons for the `event` keyword in C#.

Another potential pitfall with plain delegates was the fact that it was easy to forget to check for `null` before invoking the delegate. This resulted in an unexpected `NullReferenceException`. Fortunately, the encapsulation that the `event` keyword provides enables an alternative possibility during declaration (or within the constructor), as shown in Listing 13.14. Notice that when declaring the event we assign `delegate { }`—an empty delegate representing a collection of zero listeners. By assigning the empty delegate we can raise the event without checking whether there are any listeners. (The behavior is similar to assigning a variable with an array of zero items. Doing so allows the invocation of an array member without first checking whether the variable is `null`.) Of course, if there is any chance that the delegate could be reassigned with `null`, then a check will still be required. However, because the `event` keyword restricts assignment to occur only within the class, any reassignment of the delegate could occur only from within the class. Assuming `null` is never assigned, there will be no need to check for `null` whenever the code invokes the delegate.

Coding Conventions

All you need to do to gain the desired functionality is to change the original delegate variable declaration to a field, and add the `event` keyword.

With these two changes, you provide the necessary encapsulation and all other functionality remains the same. However, an additional change occurs in the delegate declaration in the code in Listing 13.14. To follow standard C# coding conventions, you changed `OnTemperatureChangeHandler` so that the single `temperature` parameter was replaced with two new parameters, `sender` and `temperatureArgs`. This change is not something that the C# compiler will enforce, but passing two parameters of these types is the norm for declaring a delegate intended for an event.

The first parameter, `sender`, should contain an instance of the class that invoked the delegate. This is especially helpful if the same subscriber method registers with multiple events—for example, if the `heater.OnTemperatureChanged` event subscribes to two different `Thermostat` instances. In such a scenario, either `Thermostat` instance can trigger a call to `heater.OnTemperatureChanged`. In order to determine which instance of `Thermostat` triggered the event, you use the `sender` parameter from inside `Heater.OnTemperatureChanged()`.

The second parameter, `temperatureArgs`, is of type `Thermostat.TemperatureArgs`. Using a nested class is appropriate because it conforms to the same scope as the `OnTemperatureChangeHandler` delegate itself. The important part about `TemperatureArgs`, at least as far as the coding convention goes, is that it derives from `System.EventArgs`. The only significant property on `System.EventArgs` is `Empty` and it is used to indicate that there is no event data. When you derive `TemperatureArgs` from `System.EventArgs`, however, you add an additional property, `NewTemperature`, as a means to pass the temperature from the thermostat to the subscribers.

To summarize the coding convention for events: The first argument, `sender`, is of type `object` and it contains a reference to the object that invoked the delegate. The second argument is of type `System.EventArgs` or something that derives from `System.EventArgs` but contains additional data about the event. You invoke the delegate exactly as before, except for the additional parameters. Listing 13.15 shows an example.

LISTING 13.15: Firing the Event Notification

```
public class Thermostat
{
    ...
```

```csharp
public float CurrentTemperature
{
    get{return _CurrentTemperature;}
    set
    {
        if (value != CurrentTemperature)
        {
            _CurrentTemperature = value;
            // If there are any subscribers
            // then notify them of changes in
            // temperature
            if(OnTemperatureChange != null)
            {
                // Call subscribers
                OnTemperatureChange(
                    this, new TemperatureArgs(value) );
            }
        }
    }
}
private float _CurrentTemperature;
}
```

You usually specify the sender using the container class (this) because that is the only class that can invoke the delegate for events.

In this example, the subscriber could cast the sender parameter to Thermostat and access the current temperature that way, as well as via the TemperatureArgs instance. However, the current temperature on the Thermostat instance may change via a different thread. In the case of events that occur due to state changes, passing the previous value along with the new value is a frequent pattern used to control what state transitions are allowable.

Generics and Delegates

The preceding section mentioned that the typical pattern for defining delegate data is to specify the first parameter, sender, of type object and the second parameter, eventArgs, to be a type deriving from System.EventArgs. One of the more cumbersome aspects of delegates in C# 1.0 was that you had to declare a new delegate type whenever the parameters on the handler change. Every creation of a new derivation from System.EventArgs (a relatively common occurrence) required the declaration of a new delegate data type that uses the new EventArgs derived type. For example, in order to use TemperatureArgs within the event notification code in Listing 13.15, it is necessary to declare the delegate type TemperatureChangeHandler that has TemperatureArgs as a parameter.

With generics, you can use the same delegate data type in many locations with a host of different parameter types, and remain strongly typed. Consider the delegate declaration example shown in Listing 13.16.

LISTING 13.16: Declaring a Generic Delegate Type

```
public delegate void EventHandler<T>(object sender, T e)
   where T : EventArgs;
```

When you use EventHandler<T>, each class that requires a particular sender-EventArgs pattern need not declare its own delegate definition. Instead, they can all share the same one, changing the thermostat example as shown in Listing 13.17.

LISTING 13.17: Using Generics with Delegates

```
public class Thermostat
{
  public class TemperatureArgs: System.EventArgs
  {
      public TemperatureArgs( float newTemperature )
      {
          NewTemperature = newTemperature;
      }

      public float NewTemperature
      {
          get{return _newTemperature;}
          set{_newTemperature = value;}
      }
      private float _newTemperature;
  }

    // TemperatureChangeHandler no longer needed
    // public delegate void TemperatureChangeHandler(
    //      object sender, TemperatureArgs newTemperature);

    // Define the event publisher without using
    //          TemperatureChangeHandler
    public event EventHandler<TemperatureArgs>
       OnTemperatureChange;
```

```
    public float CurrentTemperature
    {
        ...
    }
    private float _CurrentTemperature;
}
```

Listing 13.17 assumes, of course, that `EventHandler<T>` is defined some-where. In fact, `System.EventHandler<T>`, as just declared, is included in the version 2.0 Framework Class Library. Therefore, in the majority of cir-cumstances when using events in C# 2.0 or later, it is not necessary to declare a custom delegate data type.

Note that `System.EventHandler<T>` restricts T to derive from `EventArgs` using a constraint, exactly what was necessary to correspond with the gen-eral convention for the event declaration of C# 1.0.

■ ADVANCED TOPIC

Event Internals

Events restrict external classes from doing anything other than adding subscribing methods to the publisher via the += operator and then unsub-scribing using the -= operator. In addition, they restrict classes, other than the containing class, from invoking the event. To do this the C# compiler takes the public delegate variable with its event keyword modifier and declares the delegate as private. In addition, it adds a couple of methods and two special event blocks. Essentially, the event keyword is a C# shortcut for generating the appropriate encapsulation logic. Consider the example in the event declaration shown in Listing 13.18.

LISTING 13.18: Declaring the `OnTemperatureChange` Event

```
public class Thermostat
{
    // Define the delegate data type
    public delegate void TemperatureChangeHandler(
        object sender, TemperatureArgs newTemperature);

    public event TemperatureChangeHandler OnTemperatureChange

    ...
}
```

When the C# compiler encounters the event keyword, it generates CIL code equivalent to the C# code shown in Listing 13.19.

LISTING 13.19: C# Equivalent of the Event CIL Code Generated by the Compiler

```csharp
public class Thermostat
{
  // Define the delegate data type
  public delegate void TemperatureChangeHandler(
      object sender, TemperatureArgs newTemperature);

    // Declaring the delegate field to save the
  // list of subscribers.
  private TemperatureChangeHandler OnTemperatureChange;

  public void add_OnTemperatureChange(
      TemperatureChangeHandler handler)
  {
      System.Delegate.Combine(OnTemperatureChange, handler);
  }

  public void remove_OnTemperatureChange(
      TemperatureChangeHandler handler)
  {
      System.Delegate.Remove(OnTemperatureChange, handler);
  }

  public event TemperatureChangeHandler OnTemperatureChange
  {
      add
      {
          add_OnTemperatureChange(value)
      }
      remove
      {
          remove_OnTemperatureChange(value)
      }
  }
}
```

In other words, the code shown in Listing 13.18 is the C# shorthand that the compiler uses to trigger the code expansion shown in Listing 13.19.

The C# compiler first takes the original event definition and defines a private delegate variable in its place. As a result, the delegate becomes unavailable to any external class, even to classes derived from it.

Next, the C# compiler defines two methods, add_OnTemperatureChange() and remove_OnTemperatureChange(), where the OnTemperatureChange suffix is taken from the original name of the event. These methods are responsible for implementing the += and -= assignment operators, respectively. As Listing 13.19 shows, these methods are implemented using the static System.Delegate.Combine() and System.Delegate.Remove() methods, discussed earlier in the chapter. The first parameter passed to each of these methods is the private TemperatureChangeHandler delegate instance, OnTemperatureChange.

Perhaps the most curious part of the code generated from the event keyword is the last part. The syntax is very similar to that of a property's getter and setter methods except that the methods are add and remove. The add block takes care of handling the += operator on the event by passing the call to add_OnTemperatureChange(). In a similar manner, the remove block operator handles the -= operator by passing the call on to remove_OnTemperatureChange.

It is important to notice the similarities between this code and the code generated for a property. Readers will recall that the C# implementation of a property is to create get_<propertyname> and set_<propertyname>, and then to pass calls to the get and set blocks on to these methods. Clearly, the event syntax is very similar.

Another important characteristic to note about the generated CIL code is that the CIL equivalent of the event keyword remains in the CIL. In other words, an event is something that the CIL code recognizes explicitly; it is not just a C# construct. By keeping an equivalent event keyword in the CIL code, all languages and editors are able to provide special functionality because they can recognize the event as a special class member.

Customizing the Event Implementation

You can customize the code for += and -= that the compiler generates. Consider, for example, changing the scope of the OnTemperatureChange delegate so that it is protected rather than private. This, of course, would allow classes derived from Thermostat to access the delegate directly instead of being limited to the same restrictions as external classes. To enable this, C# allows the same property as the syntax shown in Listing 13.17. In other words, C# allows you to define custom add and remove blocks to provide implementation for each aspect of the event encapsulation. Listing 13.20 provides an example.

LISTING 13.20: Custom add and remove Handlers

```csharp
public class Thermostat
{
  public class TemperatureArgs: System.EventArgs
  {
      ...
  }

  // Define the delegate data type
  public delegate void TemperatureChangeHandler(
      object sender, TemperatureArgs newTemperature);

    // Define the event publisher
    public event TemperatureChangeHandler OnTemperatureChange
    {
        add
        {
            System.Delegate.Combine(value, _OnTemperatureChange);
        }
        remove
        {
            System.Delegate.Remove(_OnTemperatureChange, value);
        }
    }
    protected TemperatureChangeHandler _OnTemperatureChange;

  public float CurrentTemperature
  {
      ...
  }
  private float _CurrentTemperature;
}
```

In this case, the delegate that stores each subscriber, _OnTemperatureChange, was changed to protected. In addition, implementation of the add block switches around the delegate storage so that the last delegate added to the chain is the first delegate to receive a notification.

SUMMARY

Now that I have described events, it is worth mentioning that in general, method pointers are the only cases where it is advisable to work with a delegate variable outside the context of an event. In other words, given the additional encapsulation features of an event and the ability to customize the implementation when necessary, the best practice is always to use events for the observer pattern.

It may take a little practice to be able to code events from scratch without sample code. However, they are a critical foundation to the asynchronous, multithreaded coding of later chapters.

14

Collection Interfaces with Standard Query Operators

THE MOST SIGNIFICANT FEATURES added in C# 3.0 were in the area of collections. Extension methods and lambda expressions enabled a far superior API for working with collections. In fact, in earlier editions of this book, the chapter on collections came immediately after the chapter on generics and just before the one on delegates. However, lambda expressions make such a significant impact on collection APIs that it is no longer possible to cover collections without first covering delegates (the basis of lambda expressions). Now that you have a solid foundation on lambda expressions from the preceding chapter, we can delve into the details of collections, a topic that in this edition spans three chapters.

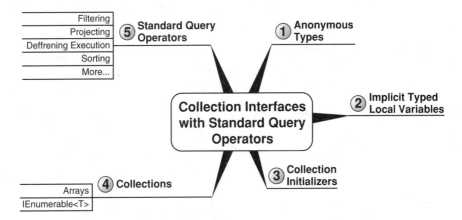

To begin, this chapter introduces anonymous types and collection initializers, topics which I covered only briefly in a few Advanced Topic sections in Chapter 5. Next, this chapter covers the various collection interfaces and how they relate to each other. This is the basis for understanding collections, so readers should cover the material with diligence. The section on collection interfaces includes coverage of the IEnumerable<T> extension methods that were added in C# 3.0, which provides the foundation on which standard query operators are implemented—another C# 3.0 feature discussed in the chapter.

There are two categories of collection-related classes and interfaces: those that support generics and those that don't. This chapter primarily discusses the generic collection interfaces. You should use collection classes that don't support generics only when you are writing components that need to interoperate with earlier versions of the runtime. This is because everything that was available in the nongeneric form has a generic replacement that is strongly typed. For *Essential C# 2.0,* I called out both the generic and the nongeneric versions of classes and interfaces. However, now that we are at C# 4.0, I leave out discussion of the nongeneric types, which were virtually deprecated in favor of their generic equivalents. Although the concepts still apply to both forms, I will not explicitly call out the names of the nongeneric versions.[1]

Anonymous Types and Implicitly Typed Local Variables

The changes in C# 3.0 provided a significant improvement for working with collections of items. What is amazing is that to support this advanced API, fewer than nine new language enhancements were made. However, these enhancements are critical to why C# 3.0 was such a marvelous improvement to the language. Two such enhancements were anonymous types and implicit local variables.

---

1. In fact, in Silverlight, the nongeneric collections have been removed.

Anonymous Types

Anonymous types are data types that are declared by the compiler, rather than through the explicit class definitions of Chapter 5. Like anonymous functions, when the compiler sees an anonymous type, it does the work to make that class for you and then lets you use it as though you had declared it explicitly. Listing 14.1 shows such a declaration.

LISTING 14.1: Implicit Local Variables with Anonymous Types

```csharp
using System;

class Program
{
  static void Main()
  {
    var patent1 =
      new
      {
          Title = "Bifocals",
          YearOfPublication = "1784"
      };
    var patent2 =
      new
      {
          Title = "Phonograph",
          YearOfPublication = "1877"
      };
    var patent3 =
      new
      {
          patent1.Title,
          // Renamed to show property naming.
          Year = patent1.YearOfPublication
      };

    Console.WriteLine("{0} ({1})",
        patent1.Title, patent1.YearOfPublication);
    Console.WriteLine("{0} ({1})",
        patent2.Title, patent2.YearOfPublication);

    Console.WriteLine();
    Console.WriteLine(patent1);
    Console.WriteLine(patent2);

    Console.WriteLine();
    Console.WriteLine(patent3);
  }
}
```

The corresponding output is shown in Output 14.1.

OUTPUT 14.1:

```
Bifocals (1784)
Phonograph (1784)

{ Title = Bifocals, YearOfPublication = 1784 }
{ Title = Phonograph, YearOfPublication = 1877 }

{ Title = Bifocals, Year = 1784 }
```

The construct of an anonymous type is implemented entirely by the C# compiler, with no explicit implementation awareness within the runtime. Rather, when the compiler encounters the anonymous type syntax, it generates a CIL class with properties corresponding to the named values and data types in the anonymous type declaration.

Implicitly Typed Local Variables (var)

Since an anonymous type by definition has no name, it is not possible to declare a local variable as explicitly being of an anonymous type. Rather, the local variable's type is replaced with var. However, by no means does this indicate that implicitly typed variables are untyped. On the contrary, they are fully typed to the data type of the value they are assigned. If an implicitly typed variable is assigned an anonymous type, the underlying CIL code for the local variable declaration will be of the type generated by the compiler. Similarly, if the implicitly typed variable is assigned a string, then its data type in the underlying CIL will be a string. In fact, there is no difference in the resultant CIL code for implicitly typed variables whose assignment is not an anonymous type (such as string) and those that are declared as type string. If the declaration statement is string text = "This is a test of the...", the resultant CIL code will be identical to an implicitly typed declaration, var text = "This is a test of the...". The compiler determines the data type of the implicitly typed variable from the data type assigned. In an explicitly typed local variable with an initializer (string s = "hello";), the compiler first determines the type of s from the declared type on the left-hand side, then analyzes the right-hand side and verifies that the expression on the right-hand side is assignable to that type. In an implicitly typed local variable, the process is in some sense reversed. First the right-hand side is analyzed to determine its type, and then the "var" is logically replaced with that type.

Although there is no available name in C# for the anonymous type, it is still strongly typed as well. For example, the properties of the type are fully accessible. In Listing 14.1, `patent1.Title` and `patent2.YearOfPublication` are called within the `Console.WriteLine` statement. Any attempts to call nonexistent members will result in compile errors. Even IntelliSense in IDEs such as Visual Studio 2008 works with the anonymous type.

You should use implicitly typed variable declarations sparingly. Obviously, for anonymous types, it is not possible to specify the data type, and the use of `var` is required. However, for cases where the data type is not an anonymous type, it is frequently preferable to use the explicit data type. As is the case generally, you should focus on making the semantics of the code more readable while at the same time using the compiler to verify that the resultant variable is of the type you expect. To accomplish this with implicitly typed local variables, use them only when the type assigned to the implicitly typed variable is entirely obvious. For example, in `var items = new Dictionary<string, List<Account>>();`, the resultant code is more succinct and readable. In contrast, when the type is not obvious, such as when a method return is assigned, developers should favor an explicit variable type declaration such as the following:

```
Dictionary<string, List<Account>> dictionary = GetAccounts();
```

■ **NOTE**

Implicitly typed variables should generally be reserved for anonymous type declaration rather than used indiscriminately when the data type is known at compile time, unless the type assigned to the variable is entirely obvious.

Language Contrast: C++/Visual Basic/JavaScript—void*, Variant, and var

It is important to understand that an implicitly typed variable is not the equivalent of void* in C++, a Variant in Visual Basic, or var in JavaScript. In each of these cases, the variable declaration is not very restrictive since the variable may be reassigned a different type, just as you could in C# with a variable declaration of type object. In contrast, var is definitively typed by the compiler, and once established at declaration, the type may not change, and type checks and member calls are verified at compile time.

More about Anonymous Types and Implicit Local Variables

In Listing 14.1, member names on the anonymous types are explicitly identified using the assignment of the value to the name for patent1 and patent2 (for example, Title = "Phonograph"). However, if the value assigned is a property or field call, the name may default to the name of the field or property rather than explicitly specifying the value. patent3, for example, is defined using a property named "Title" rather than an assignment to an explicit name. As Output 14.1 shows, the resultant property name is determined, by the compiler, to match the property from where the value was retrieved.

patent1 and patent2 both have the same property names with the same data types. Therefore, the C# compiler generates only one data type for these two anonymous declarations. patent3, however, forces the compiler to create a second anonymous type because the property name for the patent year is different from what it was in patent1 and patent2. Furthermore, if the order of the properties was switched between patent1 and patent2, then these two anonymous types would also not be type-compatible. In other words, the requirements for two anonymous types to be type-compatible within the same assembly are a match in property names, data types, and order of properties. If these criteria are met, the types are compatible even if they appear in different methods or classes. Listing 14.2 demonstrates the type incompatibilities.

LISTING 14.2: Type Safety and Immutability of Anonymous Types

```csharp
class Program
{
  static void Main()
  {
      var patent1 =
          new
          {
              Title = "Bifocals",
              YearOfPublication = "1784"
          };

      var patent2 =
          new
          {
              YearOfPublication = "1877",
              Title = "Phonograph"
          };

      var patent3 =
          new
          {
              patent1.Title,
              Year = patent1.YearOfPublication
          };

      // ERROR: Cannot implicitly convert type
      //        'AnonymousType#1' to 'AnonymousType#2'
      patent1 = patent2;
      // ERROR: Cannot implicitly convert type
      //        'AnonymousType#3' to 'AnonymousType#2'
      patent1 = patent3;

      // ERROR: Property or indexer 'AnonymousType#1.Title'
      //        cannot be assigned to -- it is read only'
      patent1.Title = "Swiss Cheese";
  }
}
```

The resultant two compile errors assert the fact that the types are not compatible, so they will not successfully convert from one to the other.

The third compile error is caused by the reassignment of the Title property. Anonymous types are immutable, so it is a compile error to change a property on an anonymous type once it has been instantiated.

Although not shown in Listing 14.2, it is not possible to declare a method with an implicit data type parameter (var). Therefore, instances of anonymous types can only be passed outside the method in which they are created in only two ways. First, if the method parameter is of type `object`, the anonymous type instance may pass outside the method because the anonymous type will convert implicitly. A second way is to use method type inference, whereby the anonymous type instance is passed as a method type parameter that the compiler can successfully infer. Calling `void Method<T>(T parameter)` using `Function(patent1)`, therefore, would succeed, although the available operations on `parameter` within `Function()` are limited to those supported by `object`.

In spite of the fact that C# allows anonymous types such as the ones shown in Listing 14.1, it is generally not recommended that you define them in this way. Anonymous types provide critical functionality with C# 3.0 support for projections, such as joining/associating collections, as we discuss later in the chapter. However, generally you should reserve anonymous type definitions for circumstances where they are required, such as aggregation of data from multiple types.

■ ADVANCED TOPIC

Anonymous Type Generation

Even though `Console.WriteLine()`'s implementation is to call `ToString()`, notice in Listing 14.1 that the output from `Console.WriteLine()` is not the default `ToString()`, which writes out the fully qualified data type name. Rather, the output is a list of `PropertyName = value` pairs, one for each property on the anonymous type. This occurs because the compiler overrides `ToString()` in the anonymous type code generation, and instead formats the `ToString()` output as shown. Similarly, the generated type includes overriding implementations for `Equals()` and `GetHashCode()`.

The implementation of `ToString()` on its own is an important reason that variance in the order of properties causes a new data type to be generated. If two separate anonymous types, possibly in entirely separate types and even namespaces, were unified and then the order of properties changed, changes in the order of properties on one implementation would have noticeable and possibly unacceptable effects on the others' `ToString()`

results. Furthermore, at execution time it is possible to reflect back on a type and examine the members on a type—even to call one of these members dynamically (determining at runtime which member to call). A variance in the order of members on two seemingly identical types could trigger unexpected results, and to avoid this, the C# designers decided to generate two different types.

Collection Initializers

Another feature added to C# in version 3.0 was **collection initializers.** A collection initializer allows programmers to construct a collection with an initial set of members at instantiation time in a manner similar to array declaration. Without collection initialization, elements had to be explicitly added to a collection after the collection was instantiated—using something like `System.Collections.Generic.ICollection<T>`'s `Add()` method. With collection initialization, the `Add()` calls are generated by the C# complier rather than explicitly coded by the developer. Listing 14.3 shows how to initialize the collection using a collection initializer instead.

LISTING 14.3: Filtering with `System.Linq.Enumerable.Where()`

```csharp
using System;
using System.Collections.Generic;

class Program
{
  static void Main()
  {
      List<string> sevenWorldBlunders;
      sevenWorldBlunders = new List<string>()
      {
          // Quotes from Ghandi
          "Wealth without work",
          "Pleasure without conscience",
          "Knowledge without character",
          "Commerce without morality",
          "Science without humanity",
          "Worship without sacrifice",
          "Politics without principle"
      };
```

```
        Print(sevenWorldBlunders);

    }

    private static void Print<T>(IEnumerable<T> items)
    {
        foreach (T item in items)
        {
            Console.WriteLine(item);
        }
    }
}
```

The syntax is similar not only to the array initialization, but also to an object initializer with the curly braces following the constructor. If no parameters are passed in the constructor, the parentheses following the data type are optional (as they are with object initializers).

A few basic requirements are needed in order for a collection initializer to compile successfully. Ideally, the collection type to which a collection initializer is applied would be of a type that implements `System.Collections.Generic.ICollection<T>`. This ensures that the collection includes an `Add()` that the compiler-generated code can invoke. However, a relaxed version of the requirement also exists and simply demands that one or more `Add()` methods exist on a type that implements `IEnumerable<T>`—even if the collection doesn't implement `ICollection<T>`. The `Add()` methods need to take parameters that are compatible with the values specified in the collection initializer.

Allowing initializers on collections that don't support `ICollection<T>` was important for two reasons. First, it turns out that the majority of collections (types that implement `IEnumerable<T>`) do not also implement `ICollection<T>`, thus significantly reducing the usefulness of collection initializers.

Second, matching on the method name and signature compatibility with the collection initialize items enables greater diversity in the items initialized into the collection. For example, the initializer now can support `new DataStore(){ a, {b, c}}` as long as there is one `Add()` method whose signature is compatible with `a` and a second `Add()` method compatible with `b, c`.

Note that you cannot have a collection initializer for an anonymous type since the collection initializer requires a constructor call, and it is impossible to name the constructor. The workaround is to define a method such as `static List<T> CreateList<T>(T t) { return new List<T>(); }`. Method type inference allows the type parameter to be implied rather than specified explicitly, and so this workaround successfully allows for the creation of a collection of anonymous types.

Another approach to initializing a collection of anonymous types is to use an array initializer. Since it is not possible to specify the data type in the constructor, array initialization syntax allows for anonymous array initializers using `new[]` (see Listing 14.4).

LISTING 14.4: **Initializing Anonymous Type Arrays**

```
using System;
using System.Collections.Generic;
using System.Linq;

class Program
{
  static void Main()
  {
    var worldCup2006Finalists = new[]
    {
      new
      {
          TeamName = "France",
          Players = new string[]
          {
              "Fabien Barthez", "Gregory Coupet",
              "Mickael Landreau", "Eric Abidal",
              // ...
          }
      },
      new
      {
          TeamName = "Italy",
          Players = new string[]
          {
              "Gianluigi Buffon", "Angelo Peruzzi",
              "Marco Amelia", "Cristian Zaccardo",
              // ...
          }
      }
    };
```

```
            Print(worldCup2006Finalists);
    }

    private static void Print<T>(IEnumerable<T> items)
    {
        foreach (T item in items)
        {
            Console.WriteLine(item);
        }
    }
}
```

The resultant variable is an array of the anonymous type items, which must be homogenous since it is an array.

What Makes a Class a Collection: IEnumerable<T>

By definition, a collection within .NET is a class that, at a minimum, implements IEnumerable<T> (technically, it would be the nongeneric type IEnumerable). This interface is a key because implementing the methods of IEnumerable<T> is the minimum implementation requirement needed to support iterating over the collection.

Chapter 3 showed how to use a foreach statement to iterate over an array of elements. The syntax is simple and avoids the complication of having to know how many elements there are. The runtime does not directly support the foreach statement, however. Instead, the C# compiler transforms the code as described in this section.

foreach with Arrays

Listing 14.5 demonstrates a simple foreach loop iterating over an array of integers and then printing out each integer to the console.

LISTING 14.5: foreach with Arrays

```
int[] array = new int[]{1, 2, 3, 4, 5, 6};

foreach (int item in array)
{
    Console.WriteLine(item);
}
```

From this code, the C# compiler creates a CIL equivalent of the for loop, as shown in Listing 14.6.

LISTING 14.6: Compiled Implementation of **foreach** with Arrays

```
int number;
int[] tempArray;
int[] array = new int[]{1, 2, 3, 4, 5, 6};

tempArray = array;
for (int counter = 0; (counter < tempArray.Length); counter++)
{
  int item = tempArray[counter];

  Console.WriteLine(item);
}
```

In this example, note that foreach relies on support for the Length property and the index operator ([ ]). With the Length property, the C# compiler can use the for statement to iterate through each element in the array.

foreach **with** IEnumerable<T>

Although the code shown in Listing 14.6 works well on arrays where the length is fixed and the index operator is always supported, not all types of collections have a known number of elements. Furthermore, many of the collection classes, including the Stack<T>, Queue<T>, and Dictionary<Tkey, Tvalue> classes, do not support retrieving elements by index. Therefore, a more general approach of iterating over collections of elements is needed. The iterator pattern provides this capability. Assuming you can determine the first, next, and last elements, knowing the count and supporting retrieval of elements by index is unnecessary.

The System.Collections.Generic.IEnumerator<T> and nongeneric System.Collections.IEnumerator interfaces (see Listing 14.8) are designed to enable the iterator pattern for iterating over collections of elements, rather than the length-index pattern shown in Listing 14.6. A class diagram of their relationships appears in Figure 14.1.

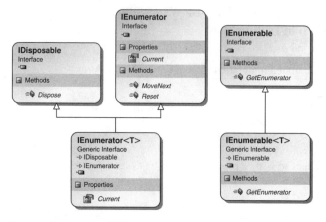

FIGURE 14.1: `IEnumerator<T>` and `IEnumerator` Interfaces

`IEnumerator`, which `IEnumerator<T>` derives from, includes three members. The first is `bool MoveNext()`. Using this method, you can move from one element within the collection to the next while at the same time detecting when you have enumerated through every item. The second member, a read-only property called `Current`, returns the element currently in process. `Current` is overloaded in `IEnumerator<T>`, providing a type-specific implementation of it. With these two members on the collection class, it is possible to iterate over the collection simply using a `while` loop, as demonstrated in Listing 14.7. (The `Reset()` method usually throws a `NotImplementedException` and, therefore, should never be called. If you need to restart an enumeration, just create a fresh enumerator.)

LISTING 14.7: Iterating over a Collection Using `while`

```
System.Collections.Generic.Stack<int> stack =
  new System.Collections.Generic.Stack<int>();
int number;
// ...

// This code is conceptual, not the actual code.
while (stack.MoveNext())
{
  number = stack.Current;
  Console.WriteLine(number);
}
```

In Listing 14.7, the MoveNext() method returns false when it moves past the end of the collection. This replaces the need to count elements while looping.

Listing 14.7 uses a System.Collections.Generic.Stack<T> as the collection type. Numerous other collection types exist; this is just one example. The key trait of Stack<T> is its design as a last in, first out (LIFO) collection. It is important to note that the type parameter T identifies the type of all items within the collection. Collecting one particular type of object within a collection is a key characteristic of a generic collection. It is important that the programmer understands the data type within the collection when adding, removing, or accessing items within the collection.

This preceding example shows the gist of the C# compiler output, but it doesn't actually compile that way because it omits two important details concerning the implementation: interleaving and error handling.

State Is Shared

The problem with an implementation such as Listing 14.7 is that if two such loops interleaved each other—one foreach inside another, both using the same collection—the collection must maintain a state indicator of the current element so that when MoveNext() is called, the next element can be determined. The problem is that one interleaving loop can affect the other. (The same is true of loops executed by multiple threads.)

To overcome this problem, the collection classes do not support IEnumerator<T> and IEnumerator interfaces directly. As shown in Figure 14.1, there is a second interface, called IEnumerable<T>, whose only method is GetEnumerator(). The purpose of this method is to return an object that supports IEnumerator<T>. Instead of the collection class maintaining the state, a different class, usually a nested class so that it has access to the internals of the collection, will support the IEnumerator<T> interface and will keep the state of the iteration loop. The enumerator is like a "cursor" or a "bookmark" in the sequence. You can have multiple bookmarks, and moving each of them enumerates over the collection independently of the other. Using this pattern, the C# equivalent of a foreach loop will look like the code shown in Listing 14.8.

LISTING 14.8: A Separate Enumerator Maintaining State during an Iteration

```
System.Collections.Generic.Stack<int> stack =
  new System.Collections.Generic.Stack<int>();
int number;
System.Collections.Generic.Stack<int>.Enumerator
  enumerator;

// ...

// If IEnumerable<T> is implemented explicitly,
// then a cast is required.
// ((IEnumerable<int>)stack).GetEnumerator();
enumerator = stack.GetEnumerator();
while (enumerator.MoveNext())
{
  number = enumerator.Current;
  Console.WriteLine(number);
}
```

Cleaning Up Following Iteration

Since the classes that implement the IEnumerator<T> interface maintain the state, sometimes you need to clean up the state after it exits the loop (because either all iterations have completed or an exception is thrown). To achieve this, the IEnumerator<T> interface derives from IDisposable. Enumerators that implement IEnumerator do not necessarily implement IDisposable, but if they do, Dispose() will be called as well. This enables the calling of Dispose() after the foreach loop exits. The C# equivalent of the final CIL code, therefore, looks like Listing 14.9.

LISTING 14.9: Compiled Result of foreach on Collections

```
System.Collections.Generic.Stack<int> stack =
  new System.Collections.Generic.Stack<int>();
System.Collections.Generic.Stack<int>.Enumerator
  enumerator;
IDisposable disposable;

enumerator = stack.GetEnumerator();
try
{
  int number;
  while (enumerator.MoveNext())
  {
      number = enumerator.Current;
      Console.WriteLine(number);
  }
}
```

```
finally
{
  // Explicit cast used for IEnumerator<T>.
  disposable = (IDisposable) enumerator;
  disposable.Dispose();

  // IEnumerator will use the as operator unless IDisposable
  // support is known at compile time.
  // disposable = (enumerator as IDisposable);
  // if (disposable != null)
  // {
  //     disposable.Dispose();
  // }
}
```

Notice that because the IDisposable interface is supported by IEnumerator<T>, the using statement can simplify the code in Listing 14.9 to that shown in Listing 14.10.

LISTING 14.10: Error Handling and Resource Cleanup with using

```
System.Collections.Generic.Stack<int> stack =
  new System.Collections.Generic.Stack<int>();
int number;

using(
  System.Collections.Generic.Stack<int>.Enumerator<int>
      enumerator = stack.GetEnumerator())
{
  while (enumerator.MoveNext())
  {
      number = enumerator.Current;
      Console.WriteLine(number);
  }
}
```

However, recall that the CIL also does not directly support the using keyword, so in reality, the code in Listing 14.9 is a more accurate C# representation of the foreach CIL code.

ADVANCED TOPIC

foreach **without** IEnumerable

Technically, the compiler doesn't require that IEnumerable/IEnumerable<T> be supported in order to iterate over a data type using foreach.

Rather, the compiler uses a concept known as "duck typing" such that if no `IEnumerable/IEnumerable<T>` method is found, it looks for the `GetEnumerator()` method to return a type with `Current()` and `MoveNext()` methods. Duck typing involves searching for a method by name rather than relying on an interface or explicit method call to the method.

Do Not Modify Collections during foreach Iteration

Chapter 3 showed that the compiler prevents assignment of the `foreach` variable (number). As is demonstrated in Listing 14.10, an assignment to number would not be a change to the collection element itself, so the C# compiler prevents such an assignment altogether.

In addition, neither the element count within a collection nor the items themselves can generally be modified during the execution of a `foreach` loop. If, for example, you called `stack.Push(42)` inside the `foreach` loop, it would be ambiguous whether the `iterator` should ignore or incorporate the change to `stack`—in other words, whether `iterator` should iterate over the newly added item or ignore it and assume the same state as when it was instantiated.

Because of this ambiguity, an exception of type `System.InvalidOperationException` is generally thrown upon accessing the enumerator if the collection is modified within a `foreach` loop, reporting that the collection was modified after the enumerator was instantiated.

Standard Query Operators

Besides the methods on `System.Object`, any type that implements `IEnumerable<T>` has only one method, `GetEnumerator()`. And yet, it makes more than 50 methods available to all types implementing `IEnumerable<T>`, not including any overloading—and this happens without needing to explicitly implement any method except the `GetEnumerator()` method. The additional functionality is provided using C# 3.0's extension methods and it all resides in the class `System.Linq.Enumerable`. Therefore, including the `using` declarative for `System.Linq` is all it takes to make these methods available.

Each method on `IEnumerable<T>` is a **standard query operator;** it provides querying capability over the collection on which it operates. In the following sections, we will examine some of the most prominent of these standard query operators.

Many of the examples will depend on an `Inventor` and/or `Patent` class, both of which are defined in Listing 14.11.

LISTING 14.11: Sample Classes for Use with Standard Query Operators

```csharp
using System;
using System.Collections.Generic;
using System.Linq;

public class Patent
{
  // Title of the published application
  public string Title { get; set; }

  // The date the application was officially published
  public string YearOfPublication { get; set; }

  // A unique number assigned to published applications
  public string ApplicationNumber { get; set; }

  public long[] InventorIds { get; set; }

  public override string ToString()
  {
      return string.Format("{0}({1})",
          Title, YearOfPublication);
  }
}

public class Inventor
{
  public long Id { get; set; }
  public string Name { get; set; }
  public string City { get; set; }
  public string State { get; set; }
  public string Country { get; set; }

  public override string ToString()
  {
      return string.Format("{0}({1}, {2})",
          Name, City, State);
  }
}

class Program
{
```

```csharp
static void Main()
{
  IEnumerable<Patent> patents = PatentData.Patents;
  Print(patents);

  Console.WriteLine();

  IEnumerable<Inventor> inventors = PatentData.Inventors;
  Print(inventors);
}

private static void Print<T>(IEnumerable<T> items)
{
    foreach (T item in items)
    {
        Console.WriteLine(item);
    }
}
}

public static class PatentData
{
  public static readonly Inventor[] Inventors = new Inventor[]
      {
          new Inventor(){
              Name="Benjamin Franklin", City="Philadelphia",
              State="PA", Country="USA", Id=1 },
          new Inventor(){
              Name="Orville Wright", City="Kitty Hawk",
              State="NC", Country="USA", Id=2},
          new Inventor(){
              Name="Wilbur Wright", City="Kitty Hawk",
              State="NC", Country="USA", Id=3},
          new Inventor(){
              Name="Samuel Morse", City="New York",
              State="NY", Country="USA", Id=4},
          new Inventor(){
              Name="George Stephenson", City="Wylam",
              State="Northumberland", Country="UK", Id=5},
          new Inventor(){
              Name="John Michaelis", City="Chicago",
              State="IL", Country="USA", Id=6},
          new Inventor(){
              Name="Mary Phelps Jacob", City="New York",
              State="NY", Country="USA", Id=7},
      };

  public static readonly Patent[] Patents = new Patent[]
      {
```

```
            new Patent(){
                Title="Bifocals", YearOfPublication="1784",
                InventorIds=new long[] {1}},
            new Patent(){
                Title="Phonograph", YearOfPublication="1877",
                InventorIds=new long[] {1}},
            new Patent(){
                Title="Kinetoscope", YearOfPublication="1888",
                InventorIds=new long[] {1}},
            new Patent(){
                Title="Electrical Telegraph",
                YearOfPublication="1837",
                InventorIds=new long[] {4}},
            new Patent(){
                Title="Flying machine", YearOfPublication="1903",
                InventorIds=new long[] {2,3}},
            new Patent(){
                Title="Steam Locomotive",
                YearOfPublication="1815",
                InventorIds=new long[] {5}},
            new Patent(){
                Title="Droplet deposition apparatus",
                YearOfPublication="1989",
                InventorIds=new long[] {6}},
            new Patent(){
                Title="Backless Brassiere",
                YearOfPublication="1914",
                InventorIds=new long[] {7}},
        };
    }
```

Listing 14.11 also provides a selection of sample data. Output 14.2 displays the results.

OUTPUT 14.2:

```
Bifocals(1784)
Phonograph(1877)
Kinetoscope(1888)
Electrical Telegraph(1837)
Flying machine(1903)
Steam Locomotive(1815)
Droplet deposition apparatus(1989)
Backless Brassiere(1914)

Benjamin Franklin(Philadelphia, PA)
Orville Wright(Kitty Hawk, NC)
Wilbur Wright(Kitty Hawk, NC)
Samuel Morse(New York, NY)
George Stephenson(Wylam, Northumberland)
John Michaelis(Chicago, IL)
Mary Phelps Jacob(New York, NY)
```

Filtering with Where()

In order to filter out data from a collection, we need to provide a filter method that returns true or false, indicating whether a particular element should be included or not. A delegate expression that takes an argument and returns a Boolean is called a **predicate,** and a collection's Where() method depends on predicates for identifying filter criteria, as shown in Listing 14.12. (Technically, the result of the Where() method is a **monad** which encapsulates the operation of filtering a given sequence with a given predicate.) The output appears in Output 14.3.

LISTING 14.12: Filtering with **System.Linq.Enumerable.Where()**

```csharp
using System;
using System.Collections.Generic;
using System.Linq;

class Program
{
  static void Main()
  {
    IEnumerable<Patent> patents = PatentData.Patents;
    patents = patents.Where(
        patent => patent.YearOfPublication.StartsWith("18"));
    Print(patents);
  }

  // ...
}
```

OUTPUT 14.3:

```
Phonograph(1877)
Kinetoscope(1888)
Electrical Telegraph(1837)
Steam Locomotive(1815)
```

Notice that the code assigns the output of the Where() call back to IEnumerable<T>. In other words, the output of IEnumerable<T>.Where() is a new IEnumerable<T> collection. In Listing 14.12, it is IEnumerable<Patent>.

Less obvious is that the `Where()` expression argument has not necessarily executed at assignment time. This is true for many of the standard query operators. In the case of `Where()`, for example, the expression is passed in to the collection and "saved" but not executed. Instead, execution of the expression occurs only when it is necessary to begin iterating over the items within the collection. A `foreach` loop, for example, such as the one in `Print()` (in Listing 14.11), will trigger the expression to be evaluated for each item within the collection. At least conceptually, the `Where()` method should be understood as a means of specifying the query regarding what appears in the collection, not the actual work involved with iterating over to produce a new collection with potentially fewer items.

Projecting with `Select()`

Since the output from the `IEnumerable<T>.Where()` method is a new `IEnumerable<T>` collection, it is possible to again call a standard query operator on the same collection. For example, rather than just filtering the data from the original collection, we could transform the data (see Listing 14.13).

LISTING 14.13: Projection with `System.Linq.Enumerable.Select()`

```
using System;
using System.Collections.Generic;
using System.Linq;

class Program
{
  static void Main()
  {
     IEnumerable<Patent> patents = PatentData.Patents;
     IEnumerable<Patent> patentsOf1800 = patents.Where(
         patent => patent.YearOfPublication.StartsWith("18"));
     IEnumerable<string> items = patentsOf1800.Select(
         patent => patent.ToString());

     Print(items);
  }

  // ...
}
```

In Listing 14.13, we create a new `IEnumerable<string>` collection. In this case, it just so happens that adding the `Select()` call doesn't change the output; but this is only because `Print()`'s `Console.WriteLine()` call used `ToString()` anyway. Obviously, a transform still occurred on each item from the `Patent` type of the original collection to the string type of the `items` collection.

Consider the example using `System.IO.FileInfo` in Listing 14.14.

LISTING 14.14: Projection with `System.Linq.Enumerable.Select()` and new

```
// ...
IEnumerable<string> fileList = Directory.GetFiles(
    rootDirectory, searchPattern);
IEnumerable<FileInfo> files = fileList.Select(
    file => new FileInfo(file));
// ...
```

`fileList` is of type `IEnumerable<string>`. However, using the projection offered by `Select`, we can transform each item in the collection to a `System.IO.FileInfo` object.

Lastly, capitalizing on anonymous types, we could create an `IEnumerable<T>` collection where `T` is an anonymous type (see Listing 14.15 and Output 14.4).

LISTING 14.15: Projection to an Anonymous Type

```
// ...
IEnumerable<string> fileList = Directory.GetFiles(
    rootDirectory, searchPattern);
var items = fileList.Select(
    file =>
    {
        FileInfo fileInfo = new FileInfo(file);
        return new
        {
            FileName = fileInfo.Name,
            Size = fileInfo.Length
        };
    });
// ...
```

OUTPUT 14.4:

```
{ FileName = AssemblyInfo.cs, Size = 1704 }
{ FileName = CodeAnalysisRules.xml, Size = 735 }
{ FileName = CustomDictionary.xml, Size = 199 }
{ FileName = EssentialCSharp.sln, Size = 40415 }
{ FileName = EssentialCSharp.suo, Size = 454656 }
{ FileName = EssentialCSharp.vsmdi, Size = 499 }
{ FileName = EssentialCSharp.vssscc, Size = 256 }
{ FileName = intelliTechture.ConsoleTester.dll, Size = 24576 }
{ FileName = intelliTechture.ConsoleTester.pdb, Size = 30208 }
{ FileName = LocalTestRun.testrunconfig, Size = 1388 }
```

The output of an anonymous type automatically shows the property names and their values as part of the generated `ToString()` method associated with the anonymous type.

Projection using the `Select()` method is very powerful. We already saw how to filter a collection vertically (reducing the number of items in the collection) using the `Where()` standard query operator. Now, via the `Select()` standard query operator, we can also reduce the collection horizontally (making fewer columns) or transform the data entirely. In combination, `Where()` and `Select()` provide a means for extracting only the pieces of the original collection that are desirable for the current algorithm. These two methods alone provide a powerful collection manipulation API that would otherwise result in significantly more code that is less readable.

■ ADVANCED TOPIC

Running LINQ Queries in Parallel

With the abundance of computers having multiple processors and multiple cores within those processors, the ability to easily take advantage of the additional processing power becomes far more important. To do this, programs need to be changed to support multiple threads so that work can happen simultaneously on different CPUs within the computer. Listing 14.16 demonstrates one way to do this using Parallel LINQ (PLINQ).

LISTING 14.16: Executing LINQ Queries in Parallel

```
// ...
IEnumerable<string> fileList = Directory.GetFiles(
    rootDirectory, searchPattern);
var items = fileList. AsParallel() .Select(
    file =>
    {
        FileInfo fileInfo = new FileInfo(file);
        return new
        {
            FileName = fileInfo.Name,
            Size = fileInfo.Length
        };
    });
// ...
```

As Listing 14.16 shows, the change in code to enable parallel support is minimal. All that it uses is a .NET Framework 4 introduced standard query operator, AsParallel(), on the static class System.Linq.ParallelEnumerable. Using this simple extension method, however, the runtime begins executing over the items within the fileList collection and returning the resultant objects in parallel. Each parallel operation in this case isn't particularly expensive (although it is relative to what other execution is taking place), but consider CPU-intensive operations such as encryption or compression. Paralyzing the execution across multiple CPUs can decrease execution time by a magnitude corresponding to the number of CPUs.

An important caveat to be aware of (and the reason why AsParallel() appears in an Advanced Block rather than the standard text) is that parallel execution can introduce race conditions such that an operation on one thread can be intermingled with an operation on a different thread, causing data corruption. To avoid this, synchronization mechanisms are required on data with shared access from multiple threads in order to force the operations to be atomic where necessary. Synchronization itself, however, can introduce deadlocks that freeze the execution, further complicating the effective parallel programming.

More details on this and additional multithreading topics are covered in Chapter 18 and Chapter 19.

Counting Elements with `Count()`

Another common query performed on a collection of items is to retrieve the count. To support this LINQ includes the `Count()` extension method.

Listing 14.17 demonstrates that `Count()` is overloaded to simply count all elements (no parameters) or to take a predicate that only counts items identified by the predicate expression.

LISTING 14.17: Counting Items with `Count()`

```
using System;
using System.Collections.Generic;
using System.Linq;

class Program
{
  static void Main()
  {
      IEnumerable<Patent> patents = PatentData.Patents;
      Console.WriteLine("Patent Count: {0}", patents.Count());
      Console.WriteLine("Patent Count in 1800s: {0}",
          patents.Count(patent =>
              patent.YearOfPublication.StartsWith("18")));
  }

  // ...
}
```

In spite of the simplicity of writing the `Count()` statement, `IEnumerable<T>` has not changed, so the executed code still involves iterating over all the items in the collection. Whenever a `Count` property is directly available on the collection, it is preferable to use that rather than LINQ's `Count()` method (a subtle difference). Fortunately, `ICollection<T>` includes the `Count` property, so code that calls the `Count()` method on a collection that supports `ICollection<T>` will cast the collection and call `Count` directly. However, if `ICollection<T>` is not supported, `Enumerable.Count()` will proceed to enumerate all the items in the collection rather than call the built-in `Count` mechanism. If the purpose of checking the count is only to see whether it is greater than zero (`if(patents.Count() > 0){...}`), a preferable approach would be to use the `Any()` operator (`if(patents.Any()){...}`). `Any()` attempts to iterate over only one of the items in the collection to return a true result, rather than the entire sequence.

Deferred Execution

One of the most important concepts to remember when using LINQ is deferred execution. Consider the code in Listing 14.18 and the corresponding output in Output 14.5.

Listing 14.18: Filtering with `System.Linq.Enumerable.Where()`

```csharp
using System;
using System.Collections.Generic;
using System.Linq;

// ...

        IEnumerable<Patent> patents = PatentData.Patents;
        bool result;
        patents = patents.Where(
            patent =>
            {
                if (result =
                    patent.YearOfPublication.StartsWith("18"))
                {
                    // Side effects like this in a predicate
                    // are used here to demonstrate a
                    // principle and should generally be
                    // avoided.
                    Console.WriteLine("\t" + patent);
                }
                return result;
            });

        Console.WriteLine("1. Patents prior to the 1900s are:");
        foreach (Patent patent in patents)
        {
        }

        Console.WriteLine();
        Console.WriteLine(
            "2. A second listing of patents prior to the 1900s:");
        Console.WriteLine(
            "   There are {0} patents prior to 1900.",
            patents.Count());

        Console.WriteLine();
        Console.WriteLine(
            "3. A third listing of patents prior to the 1900s:");
        patents = patents.ToArray();
```

```
Console.Write("   There are ");
Console.WriteLine("{0} patents prior to 1900.",
    patents.Count());
```

```
// ...
```

OUTPUT 14.5:

```
1. Patents prior to the 1900s are:
        Phonograph(1877)
        Kinetoscope(1888)
        Electrical Telegraph(1837)
        Steam Locomotive(1815)

2. A second listing of patents prior to the 1900s:
        Phonograph(1877)
        Kinetoscope(1888)
        Electrical Telegraph(1837)
        Steam Locomotive(1815)
    There are 4 patents prior to 1900.

3. A third listing of patents prior to the 1900s:
        Phonograph(1877)
        Kinetoscope(1888)
        Electrical Telegraph(1837)
        Steam Locomotive(1815)
    There are 4 patents prior to 1900.
```

Notice that `Console.WriteLine("1. Patents prior…`) executes before the lambda expression. This is a very important characteristic to pay attention to because it is not obvious to those who are unaware of its importance. In general, predicates should do exactly one thing—evaluate a condition—and they should not have any side effects (even printing to the console, as in this example).

To understand what is happening, recall that lambda expressions are delegates—references to methods—that can be passed around. In the context of LINQ and standard query operators, each lambda expression forms part of the overall query to be executed.

At the time of declaration, lambda expressions do not execute. It isn't until the lambda expressions are invoked that the code within them begins to execute. Figure 14.2 shows the sequence of operations.

As Figure 14.2 shows, three calls in Listing 14.16 trigger the lambda expression, and each time it is fairly implicit. If the lambda expression was

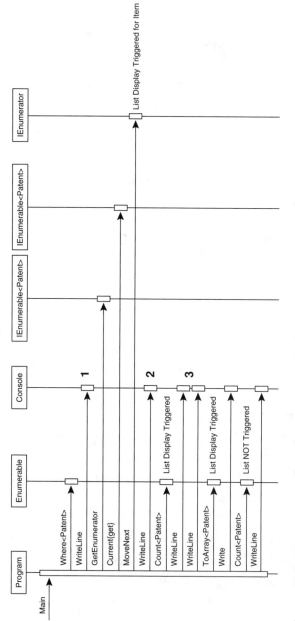

FIGURE 14.2: `IEnumerator<T>` and `IEnumerator` Interfaces

expensive (such as a call to a database) it would be important to minimize the lambda expression's execution.

First, the execution is triggered within the `foreach` loop. As I described earlier in the chapter, the `foreach` loop breaks down into a `MoveNext()` call and each call results in the lambda expression's execution for each item in the original collection. While iterating, the runtime invokes the lambda expression for each item to determine whether the item satisfies the predicate.

Second, a call to `Enumerable`'s `Count()` (the function) triggers the lambda expression for each item once more. Again, this is very subtle since `Count` (the property) is very common on collections that have not been queried with a standard query operator.

Third, the call to `ToArray()` (or `ToList()`, `ToDictionary()`, or `ToLook-up()`) triggers the lambda expression for each item. However, converting the collection with one of these "To" methods is extremely helpful. Doing so returns a collection on which the standard query operator has already executed. In Listing 14.16, the conversion to an array means that when `Length` is called in the final `Console.WriteLine()`, the underlying object pointed to by `patents` is in fact an array (which obviously implements `IEnumerable<T>`), and therefore, `System.Array`'s implementation of `Length` is called and not `System.Linq.Enumerable`'s implementation. Therefore, following a conversion to one of the collection types returned by a "To" method, it is generally safe to work with the collection (until another standard query operator is called). However, be aware that this will bring the entire result set into memory (it may have been backed by a database or file before this). Furthermore, the "To" method will snapshot the underlying data so that no fresh results will be returned upon requerying the "To" method result.

I strongly encourage readers to review the sequence diagram in Figure 14.2 along with the corresponding code and understand the fact that the deferred execution of standard query operators can result in extremely subtle triggering of the standard query operators; therefore, developers should use caution to avoid unexpected calls. The query object represents the query, not the results. When you ask the query for the results, the whole query executes (perhaps even again) because the query object doesn't know that the results will be the same as they were during a previous execution (if one existed).

> **■ NOTE**
>
> To avoid such repeated execution, it is necessary to cache the data that the executed query retrieves. To do this, you assign the data to a local collection using one of the "To" method's collection methods. During the assignment call of a "To" method, the query obviously executes. However, iterating over the assigned collection after that will not involve the query expression any further. In general, if you want the behavior of an in-memory collection snapshot, it is a best practice to assign a query expression to a cached collection to avoid unnecessary iterations.

Sorting with `OrderBy()` and `ThenBy()`

Another common operation on a collection is to sort it. This involves a call to `System.Linq.Enumerable`'s `OrderBy()`, as shown in Listing 14.19 and Output 14.6.

LISTING 14.19: Ordering with `System.Linq.Enumerable.OrderBy()/ThenBy()`

```
using System;
using System.Collections.Generic;
using System.Linq;

// ...

        IEnumerable<Patent> items;
        Patent[] patents = PatentData.Patents;
        items = patents.OrderBy(
            patent => patent.YearOfPublication).ThenBy(
            patent => patent.Title);
        Print(items);
        Console.WriteLine();

        items = patents.OrderByDescending(
            patent => patent.YearOfPublication).ThenByDescending(
            patent => patent.Title);
        Print(items);

    // ...
```

OUTPUT 14.6:

```
Bifocals  (1784)
Steam Locomotive(1815)
Electrical Telegraph(1837)
Phonograph(1877)
Kinetoscope(1888)
Flying machine  (1903)
Backless Brassiere(1914)
Droplet deposition apparatus(1989)

Droplet deposition apparatus(1989)
Backless Brassiere(1914)
Flying machine  (1903)
Kinetoscope(1888)
Phonograph(1877)
Electrical Telegraph(1837)
Steam Locomotive(1815)
Bifocals  (1784)
```

The OrderBy() call takes a lambda expression that identifies the key on which to sort. In Listing 14.19, the initial sort uses the year that the patent was published.

However, notice that the OrderBy() call takes only a single parameter, which uses the name keySelector, to sort on. To sort on a second column, it is necessary to use a different method: ThenBy(). Similarly, code would use ThenBy() for any additional sorting.

OrderBy() returns an IOrderedEnumerable<T> interface, not an IEnumerable<T>. Furthermore, IOrderedEnumerable<T> derives from IEnumerable<T>, so all the standard query operators (including OrderBy()) are available on the OrderBy() return. However, repeated calls to OrderBy() would undo the work of the previous call such that the end result would sort by only the keySelector in the final OrderBy() call. As a result, be careful not to call OrderBy() on a previous OrderBy() call.

Instead, you should specify additional sorting criteria using ThenBy(). Although ThenBy() is an extension method, it is not an extension of IEnumerable<T>, but rather IOrderedEnumerable<T>. The method, also defined on System.Linq.Extensions.Enumerable, is declared as follows:

```
public static IOrderedEnumerable<TSource>
   ThenBy<TSource, TKey>(
      this IOrderedEnumerable<TSource> source,
      Func<TSource, TKey> keySelector)
```

In summary, use `OrderBy()` first, followed by zero or more calls to `ThenBy()` to provide additional sorting "columns." The methods `OrderBy-Descending()` and `ThenByDescending()` provide the same functionality except with descending order. Mixing and matching ascending and descending methods is not a problem, but if sorting further, use a `ThenBy()` call (either ascending or descending).

Two more important notes about sorting: First, the actual sort doesn't occur until you begin to access the members in the collection, at which point the entire query is processed. This occurs because you can't sort unless you have all the items to sort; otherwise, you can't determine whether you have the first item. The fact that sorting is delayed until you begin to access the members is due to deferred execution, as I describe earlier in this chapter. Second, each subsequent call to sort the data (`Orderby()` followed by `ThenBy()` followed by `ThenByDescending()`, for example) does involve additional calls to the `keySelector` lambda expression of the earlier sorting calls. In other words, a call to `OrderBy()` will call its corresponding `keySelector` lambda expression once you iterate over the collection. Furthermore, a subsequent call to `ThenBy()` will again make calls to `OrderBy()`'s `keySelector`.

■ BEGINNER TOPIC

Join Operations

Consider two collections of objects as shown in the Venn diagram in Figure 14.3.

The left circle in the diagram includes all inventors, and the right circle contains all patents. Within the intersection, we have both inventors and patents and a line is formed for each case where there is a match of inventors to patents. As the diagram shows, each inventor may have multiple patents and each patent can have one or more inventors. Each patent has an inventor, but in some cases inventors do not yet have patents.

Matching up inventors within the intersection to patents is an **inner join.** The result is a collection of inventor-patent pairs in which both patents and inventions exist for a pair. A **left outer join** includes all the items within the left circle regardless of whether they have a corresponding patent. In this

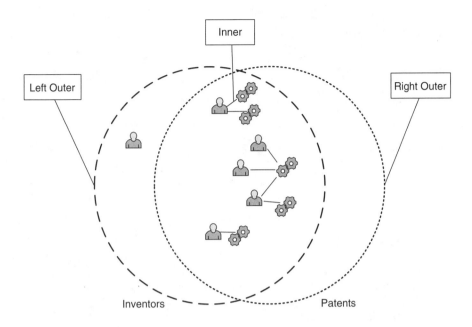

FIGURE 14.3: Venn Diagram of Inventor and Patent Collections

particular example, a **right outer join** would be the same as an inner join since there are no patents without inventors. Furthermore, the designation of left versus right is arbitrary, so there is really no distinction between left and outer joins. A **full outer join,** however, would include records from both outer sides; it is relatively rare to perform a full outer join.

Another important characteristic in the relationship between inventors and patents is that it is a **many-to-many** relationship. Each individual patent can have one or more inventors (the flying machine's invention by both Orville and Wilbur Wright, for example). Furthermore, each inventor can have one or more patents (Benjamin Franklin's invention of both bifocals and the phonograph, for example).

Another common relationship is a **one-to-many** relationship. For example, a company department may have many employees. However, each employee can belong to only one department at a time. (However, as is common with one-to-many relationships, adding the factor of time can transform them into many-to-many relationships. A particular employee may move from one department to another so that over time, she could potentially be associated with multiple departments, making another many-to-many relationship.)

Listing 14.20 provides a sample listing of Employee and Department data, and Output 14.7 shows the results.

LISTING 14.20: Sample Employee and Department Data

```csharp
public class Department
{
    public long Id { get; set; }
    public string Name { get; set; }
    public override string ToString()
    {
        return string.Format("{0}", Name);
    }
}
```

```csharp
public class Employee
{
    public int Id { get; set; }
    public string Name { get; set; }
    public string Title { get; set; }
    public int DepartmentId { get; set; }
    public override string ToString()
    {
        return string.Format("{0} ({1})", Name, Title);
    }
}
```

```csharp
public static class CorporateData
{
    public static readonly Department[] Departments =
        new Department[]
      {
          new Department(){
              Name="Corporate", Id=0},
          new Department(){
              Name="Finance", Id=1},
          new Department(){
              Name="Engineering", Id=2},
          new Department(){
              Name="Information Technology",
              Id=3},
          new Department(){
              Name="Research",
              Id=4},
          new Department(){
              Name="Marketing",
              Id=5},
      };
```

```csharp
    public static readonly Employee[] Employees = new Employee[]
    {
        new Employee(){
            Name="Mark Michaelis",
            Title="Chief Computer Nerd",
            DepartmentId = 0},
        new Employee(){
            Name="Michael Stokesbary",
            Title="Senior Computer Wizard",
            DepartmentId=2},
        new Employee(){
            Name="Brian Jones",
            Title="Enterprise Integration Guru",
            DepartmentId=2},
        new Employee(){
            Name="Jewel Floch",
            Title="Bookkeeper Extraordinaire",
            DepartmentId=1},
        new Employee(){
            Name="Robert Stokesbary",
            Title="Expert Mainframe Engineer",
            DepartmentId = 3},
        new Employee(){
            Name="Paul R. Bramsman",
            Title="Programmer Extraordinaire",
            DepartmentId = 2},
        new Employee(){
            Name="Thomas Heavey",
            Title="Software Architect",
            DepartmentId = 2},
        new Employee(){
            Name="John Michaelis",
            Title="Inventor",
            DepartmentId = 4}
    };
}
```

```csharp
class Program
{
    static void Main()
    {
        IEnumerable<Department> departments =
            CorporateData.Departments;
        Print(departments);

        Console.WriteLine();

        IEnumerable<Employee> employees =
            CorporateData.Employees;
```

```
        Print(employees);
    }

    private static void Print<T>(IEnumerable<T> items)
    {
        foreach (T item in items)
        {
            Console.WriteLine(item);
        }
    }
}
```

OUTPUT 14.7:

```
Corporate
Finance
Engineering
Information Technology
Research
Marketing

Mark Michaelis (Chief Computer Nerd)
Michael Stokesbary (Senior Computer Wizard)
Brian Jones (Enterprise Integration Guru)
Jewel Floch (Bookkeeper Extraordinaire)
Robert Stokesbary (Expert Mainframe Engineer)
Paul R. Bramsman (Programmer Extraordinaire)
Thomas Heavey (Software Architect)
John Michaelis (Inventor)
```

We will use the same data within the following section on joining data.

Performing an Inner Join with `Join()`

In the world of objects on the client side, relationships between objects are generally already set up. For example, the relationship between files and the directories in which they lie are preestablished with the `Directory-Info.GetFiles()` method and the `FileInfo.Directory` method. Frequently, however, this is not the case with data being loaded from nonobject stores. Instead, the data needs to be joined together so that you can navigate from one type of object to the next in a way that makes sense for the data.

Consider the example of employees and company departments. In Listing 14.21, we join each employee to his or her department and then list each employee with his or her corresponding department. Since each employee belongs to only one (and exactly one) department, the total number of items in the list is equal to the total number of employees—each employee appears only once (each employee is said to be **normalized**). Output 14.8 follows.

LISTING 14.21: An Inner Join Using `System.Linq.Enumerable.Join()`

```csharp
using System;
using System.Linq;

// ...

    Department[] departments = CorporateData.Departments;
    Employee[] employees = CorporateData.Employees;

    var items = employees.Join(
        departments,
        employee => employee.DepartmentId,
        department => department.Id,
        (employee, department) => new
        {
            employee.Id,
            employee.Name,
            employee.Title,
            Department = department
        });

    foreach (var item in items)
    {
        Console.WriteLine("{0} ({1})",
            item.Name, item.Title);
        Console.WriteLine("\t" + item.Department);
    }

// ...
```

OUTPUT 14.8:

```
Mark Michaelis (Chief Computer Nerd)
        Corporate
Michael Stokesbary (Senior Computer Wizard)
        Engineering
Brian Jones (Enterprise Integration Guru)
        Engineering
Jewel Floch (Bookkeeper Extraordinaire)
        Finance
Robert Stokesbary (Expert Mainframe Engineer)
        Information Technology
Paul R. Bramsman (Programmer Extraordinaire)
        Engineering
Thomas Heavey (Software Architect)
        Engineering
John Michaelis (Inventor)
        Research
```

The first parameter for `Join()` has the name `inner`. It specifies the collection, `departments`, that `employees` joins to. The next two parameters are lambda expressions that specify how the two collections will connect. `employee => employee.DepartmentId` (with a parameter name of `outerKeySelector`) identifies that on each employee the key will be `DepartmentId`. The next lambda expression, (`department => department.Id`) specifies the `Department`'s `Id` property as the key. In other words, for each employee, join a department where `employee.DepartmentId` equals `department.Id`. The last parameter, the anonymous type, is the resultant item that is selected. In this case, it is a class with `Employee`'s `Id`, `Name`, and `Title` as well as a `Department` property with the joined `department` object.

Notice in the output that *Engineering* appears multiple times—once for each employee in `CorporateData`. In this case, the `Join()` call produces a **Cartesian product** between all the departments and all the employees such that a new record is created for every case where a record exists in both collections and the specified department IDs are the same. This type of join is an **inner join.**

The data could also be joined in reverse such that `department` joins to each employee so as to list each department-to-employee match. Notice that the output includes more records than there are departments because there are multiple employees for each department and the output is a record for each match. As we saw before, the Engineering department appears multiple times, once for each employee.

The code in Listing 14.22 and Output 14.9 is similar to that in Listing 14.21, except that the objects, `Departments` and `Employees`, are reversed. The first parameter to `Join()` is `employees`, indicating what `departments` joins to. The next two parameters are lambda expressions that specify how the two collections will connect: `department => department.Id` for departments and `employee => employee.DepartmentId` for employees. Just like before, a join occurs whenever `department.Id` equals `employee.EmployeeId`. The final anonymous type parameter specifies a class with `int Id`, `string Name`, and `Employee Employee` properties.

LISTING 14.22: Another Inner Join with **System.Linq.Enumerable.Join()**

```
using System;
using System.Linq;
```

```
// ...

    Department[] departments = CorporateData.Departments;
    Employee[] employees = CorporateData.Employees;

    var items = departments.Join(
        employees,
        department => department.Id,
        employee => employee.DepartmentId,
        (department, employee) => new
        {
            department.Id,
            department.Name,
            Employee = employee
        });

    foreach (var item in items)
    {
        Console.WriteLine("{0}",
            item.Name);
        Console.WriteLine("\t" + item.Employee);
    }

// ...
```

OUTPUT 14.9:

```
Corporate
        Mark Michaelis (Chief Computer Nerd)
Finance
        Jewel Floch (Bookkeeper Extraordinaire)
Engineering
        Michael Stokesbary (Senior Computer Wizard)
Engineering
        Brian Jones (Enterprise Integration Guru)
Engineering
        Paul R. Bramsman (Programmer Extraordinaire)
Engineering
        Thomas Heavey (Software Architect)
Information Technology
        Robert Stokesbary (Expert Mainframe Engineer)
Research
        John Michaelis (Inventor)
```

Grouping Results with GroupBy()

In addition to ordering and joining a collection of objects, frequently you might want to group objects with like characteristics together. For the employee data, you might want to group employees by department, region, job title, and so forth. Listing 14.23 shows an example of how to do this using the GroupBy() standard query operator (see Output 14.10 to view the output).

LISTING 14.23: Grouping Items Together Using System.Linq.Enumerable.GroupBy()

```csharp
using System;
using System.Linq;

// ...

    IEnumerable<Employee> employees = CorporateData.Employees;

    IEnumerable<IGrouping<int, Employee>> groupedEmployees =
      employees.GroupBy((employee) => employee.DepartmentId);

    foreach(IGrouping<int, Employee> employeeGroup in
        groupedEmployees)
    {
        Console.WriteLine();
        foreach(Employee employee in employeeGroup)
        {
            Console.WriteLine("\t" + employee);
        }
        Console.WriteLine(
          "\tCount: " + employeeGroup.Count());
    }
// ...
```

OUTPUT 14.10:

```
Mark Michaelis (Chief Computer Nerd)
    Count: 1

Michael Stokesbary (Senior Computer Wizard)
Brian Jones (Enterprise Integration Guru)
Paul R. Bramsman (Programmer Extraordinaire)
Thomas Heavey (Software Architect)
    Count: 4

Jewel Floch (Bookkeeper Extraordinaire)
    Count: 1

Robert Stokesbary (Expert Mainframe Engineer)
    Count: 1

John Michaelis (Inventor)
    Count: 1
```

Note that the items output from a `GroupBy()` call are of type `IGrouping<TKey, TElement>` which has a property for the key that the query is grouping on (`employee.DepartmentId`). However, it does not have a property for the items within the group. Rather, `IGrouping<TKey, TElement>` derives from `IEnumerable<T>`, allowing for enumeration of the items within the group using a `foreach` statement or for aggregating the data into something such as a count of items (`employeeGroup.Count()`).

Implementing a One-to-Many Relationship with `GroupJoin()`

Listing 14.21 and Listing 14.22 are virtually identical. Either `Join()` call could have produced the same output just by changing the anonymous type definition. When trying to create a list of employees, Listing 14.21 provides the correct result. `department` ends up as a property of each anonymous type representing the joined employee. However, Listing 14.22 is not optimal. Given support for collections, a preferable representation of a department would have a collection of employees rather than a single anonymous type record for each department-employee relationship. Listing 14.24 demonstrates; Output 14.11 shows the preferred output.

LISTING 14.24: Creating a Child Collection with `System.Linq.Enumerable.GroupJoin()`

```csharp
using System;
using System.Linq;

// ...

        Department[] departments = CorporateData.Departments;
        Employee[] employees = CorporateData.Employees;

        var items = departments.GroupJoin(
            employees,
            department => department.Id,
            employee => employee.DepartmentId,
            (department, departmentEmployees) => new
            {
                department.Id,
                department.Name,
```

```
                    Employees = departmentEmployees
            });

        foreach (var item in items)
        {
            Console.WriteLine("{0}",
                item.Name);
            foreach (Employee employee in item.Employees)
            {
                Console.WriteLine("\t" + employee);
            }
        }

// ...
```

OUTPUT 14.11:

```
Corporate
        Mark Michaelis (Chief Computer Nerd)
Finance
        Jewel Floch (Bookkeeper Extraordinaire)
Engineering
        Michael Stokesbary (Senior Computer Wizard)
        Brian Jones (Enterprise Integration Guru)
        Paul R. Bramsman (Programmer Extraordinaire)
        Thomas Heavey (Software Architect)
Information Technology
        Robert Stokesbary (Expert Mainframe Engineer)
Research
        John Michaelis (Inventor)
```

To achieve the preferred result we use System.Linq.Enumerable's GroupJoin() method. The parameters are the same as those in Listing 14.21, except for the final anonymous type selected. In Listing 14.21, the lambda expression is of type Func<Department, IEnumerable<Employee>, TResult> where TResult is the selected anonymous type. Notice that we use the second type argument (IEnumerable<Employee>) to project the collection of employees for each department onto the resultant department anonymous type.

(Readers familiar with SQL will notice that, unlike Join(), GroupJoin() doesn't have a SQL equivalent since data returned by SQL is record-based, and not hierarchical.)

Implementing an Outer Join with GroupJoin()

The earlier inner joins are *equi-joins* because they are based on an equivalent evaluation of the keys. Records appear in the resultant collection only if there are objects in both collections. On occasion, however, it is desirable to create a record even if the corresponding object doesn't exist. For example, rather than leave the Marketing department out from the final department list simply because it doesn't have any employees, it would be preferable if we included it with an empty employee list. To accomplish this we perform a left outer join using a combination of both GroupJoin() and SelectMany() along with DefaultIfEmpty(). This is demonstrated in Listing 14.25 and Output 14.12.

LISTING 14.25: Implementing an Outer Join Using GroupJoin() with SelectMany()

```csharp
using System;
using System.Linq;

// ...

        Department[] departments = CorporateData.Departments;
        Employee[] employees = CorporateData.Employees;

    var items = departments.GroupJoin(
        employees,
        department => department.Id,
        employee => employee.DepartmentId,
        (department, departmentEmployees) => new
        {
            department.Id,
            department.Name,
            Employees = departmentEmployees
        }).SelectMany(
            departmentRecord =>
                departmentRecord.Employees.DefaultIfEmpty(),
            (departmentRecord, employee) => new
                {
                    departmentRecord.Id,
                    departmentRecord.Name,
                    Employees =
                        departmentRecord.Employees
                }).Distinct();
```

```
        foreach (var item in items)
        {
            Console.WriteLine("{0}",
                item.Name);
            foreach (Employee employee in item.Employees)
            {
                Console.WriteLine("\t" + employee);
            }
        }

// ...
```

OUTPUT 14.12:

```
Corporate
        Mark Michaelis (Chief Computer Nerd)
Finance
        Jewel Floch (Bookkeeper Extraordinaire)
Engineering
        Michael Stokesbary (Senior Computer Wizard)
        Brian Jones (Enterprise Integration Guru)
        Paul R. Bramsman (Programmer Extraordinaire)
        Thomas Heavey (Software Architect)
Information Technology
        Robert Stokesbary (Expert Mainframe Engineer)
Research
        John Michaelis (Inventor)
Marketing
```

Calling SelectMany()

On occasion, you may have collections of collections. Listing 14.26 provides an example of such a scenario. The teams array contains two teams, each with a string array of players.

LISTING 14.26: Calling SelectMany()

```
using System;
using System.Collections.Generic;
using System.Linq;

// ...

        var worldCup2006Finalists = new[]
        {
            new
            {
                TeamName = "France",
                Players = new string[]
```

```
                          {
                              "Fabien Barthez", "Gregory Coupet",
                              "Mickael Landreau", "Eric Abidal",
                              "Jean-Alain Boumsong", "Pascal Chimbonda",
                              "William Gallas", "Gael Givet",
                              "Willy Sagnol", "Mikael Silvestre",
                              "Lilian Thuram", "Vikash Dhorasoo",
                              "Alou Diarra", "Claude Makelele",
                              "Florent Malouda", "Patrick Vieira",
                              "Zinedine Zidane", "Djibril Cisse",
                              "Thierry Henry", "Franck Ribery",
                              "Louis Saha", "David Trezeguet",
                              "Sylvain Wiltord",
                          }
                      },
                      new
                      {
                          TeamName = "Italy",
                          Players = new string[]
                          {
                              "Gianluigi Buffon", "Angelo Peruzzi",
                              "Marco Amelia", "Cristian Zaccardo",
                              "Alessandro Nesta", "Gianluca Zambrotta",
                              "Fabio Cannavaro", "Marco Materazzi",
                              "Fabio Grosso", "Massimo Oddo",
                              "Andrea Barzagli", "Andrea Pirlo",
                              "Gennaro Gattuso", "Daniele De Rossi",
                              "Mauro Camoranesi", "Simone Perrotta",
                              "Simone Barone", "Luca Toni",
                              "Alessandro Del Piero", "Francesco Totti",
                              "Alberto Gilardino", "Filippo Inzaghi",
                              "Vincenzo Iaquinta",
                          }
                      }
                  };

          IEnumerable<string> players =
              worldCup2006Finalists.SelectMany(
                  team => team.Players);

          Print(players);

// ...
```

The output from this listing has each player's name displayed on its own line in the order in which it appears in the code. The difference between Select() and SelectMany() is the fact that Select() would return two items, one corresponding to each item in the original collection.

Select() may project out a transform from the original type, but the number of items would not change. For example, teams.Select(team => team.Players) will return an IEnumerable<string[]>.

In contrast, SelectMany() iterates across each item identified by the lambda expression (the array selected by Select() earlier) and hoists out each item into a new collection that includes a union of all items within the child collection. Instead of two arrays of players, SelectMany() combines each array selected and produces a single collection of all items.

More Standard Query Operators

Listing 14.27 shows code that uses some of the simpler APIs enabled by Enumerable; Output 14.13 shows the results.

LISTING 14.27: More System.Linq.Enumerable Method Calls

```csharp
using System;
using System.Collections.Generic;
using System.Linq;
using System.Text;

class Program
{
  static void Main()
  {
      IEnumerable<object> stuff =
        new object[] { new object(), 1, 3, 5, 7, 9,
             "\"thing\"", Guid.NewGuid() };
      Print("Stuff: {0}", stuff);
      IEnumerable<int> even = new int[] { 0, 2, 4, 6, 8 };
      Print("Even integers: {0}", even);

      IEnumerable<int> odd = stuff. OfType<int>();
      Print("Odd integers: {0}", odd);

      IEnumerable<int> numbers = even. Union(odd);
      Print("Union of odd and even: {0}", numbers);

      Print("Union with even: {0}", numbers.Union(even));
      Print("Concat with odd: {0}", numbers.Concat(odd));
      Print("Intersection with even: {0}",
          numbers. Intersect(even));
      Print("Distinct: {0}", numbers.Concat(odd).Distinct());
      if (!numbers. SequenceEqual(
          numbers.Concat(odd).Distinct()))
      {
          throw new Exception("Unexpectedly unequal");
```

```
            }
            else
            {
                Console.WriteLine(
                    @"Collection ""SequenceEquals""" +
                    " collection.Concat(odd).Distinct())");
                Print("Reverse: {0}", numbers.Reverse());

                Print("Average: {0}", numbers.Average());
                Print("Sum: {0}", numbers.Sum());
                Print("Max: {0}", numbers.Max());
                Print("Min: {0}", numbers.Min());
            }
    }

    private static void Print<T>(
        string format, IEnumerable<T> items)
    {
        StringBuilder text = new StringBuilder();
        foreach (T item in items.Take(items.  Count() -1))
        {
            text.Append(item + ", ");
        }
        text.Append(items.Last());

        Console.WriteLine(format, text);
    }

    private static void Print<T>(string format, T item)
    {
        Console.WriteLine(format, item);
    }
}
```

OUTPUT 14.13:

```
Stuff: System.Object, 1, 3, 5, 7, 9, "thing", 24c24a41-ee05-41b9-958e-
50dd12e3981e
Even integers: 0, 2, 4, 6, 8
Odd integers: 1, 3, 5, 7, 9
Union of odd and even: 0, 2, 4, 6, 8, 1, 3, 5, 7, 9
Union with even: 0, 2, 4, 6, 8, 1, 3, 5, 7, 9
Concat with odd: 0, 2, 4, 6, 8, 1, 3, 5, 7, 9, 1, 3, 5, 7, 9
Intersection with even: 0, 2, 4, 6, 8
Distinct: 0, 2, 4, 6, 8, 1, 3, 5, 7, 9
Collection "SequenceEquals"collection.Concat(odd).Distinct()
Reverse: 9, 7, 5, 3, 1, 8, 6, 4, 2, 0
Average: 4.5
Sum: 45
Max: 9
Min: 0
```

None of the API calls in Listing 14.20 require a lambda expression. Table 14.1 and Table 14.2 describe each method and provide an example.

TABLE 14.1: Simpler Standard Query Operators

Comment Type	Description
OfType<T>()	Forms a query over a collection that returns only the items of a particular type, where the type is identified in the type parameter of the OfType<T>() method call.
Union()	Combines two collections to form a superset of all the items in both collections. The final collection does not include duplicate items even if the same item existed in both collections to start.
Concat()	Combines two collections together to form a superset of both collections. Duplicate items are not removed from the resultant collection. Concat() will preserve the ordering. That is, concatting {A, B} with {C, D} will produce {A, B, C, D}.
Intersect()	Extracts the collection of items that exist in both original collections.
Distinct()	Filters out duplicate items from a collection so that each item within the resultant collection is unique.
SequenceEquals()	Compares two collections and returns a Boolean indicating whether the collections are identical, including the order of items within the collection. (This is a very helpful message when testing expected results.)
Reverse()	Reverses the items within a collection so that they occur in reverse order when iterating over the collection.

Included on System.Linq.Enumerable is a collection of aggregate functions that enumerate the collection and calculate a result. Count is one example of an aggregate function already shown within the chapter.

TABLE 14.2: Aggregate Functions on `System.Linq.Enumerable`

Comment Type	Description
`Count()`	Provides a total count of the number of items within the collection
`Average()`	Calculates the average value for a numeric key selector
`Sum()`	Computes the sum values within a numeric collection
`Max()`	Determines the maximum value among a collection of numeric values
`Min()`	Determines the minimum value among a collection of numeric values

Note that each method listed in Tables 14.1 and 14.2 will trigger deferred execution.

■ ADVANCED TOPIC

Queryable **Extensions for** IQueryable<T>

One virtually identical interface to `IEnumerable<T>` is `IQueryable<T>`. Because `IQueryable<T>` derives from `IEnumerable<T>`, it has all the members of `IEnumerable<T>` but only those declared directly (`GetEnumerator()`, for example). Extension methods are not inherited, so `IQueryable<T>` doesn't have any of the `Enumerable` extension methods. However, it has a similar extending class called `System.Linq.Queryable` that adds to `IQueryable<T>` virtually all of the same methods that `Enumerable` added to `IEnumerable<T>`. Therefore, it provides a very similar programming interface.

What makes `IQueryable<T>` unique is the fact that it enables custom LINQ providers. A LINQ provider subdivides expressions into their constituent parts. Once divided, the expression can be translated into another language, serialized for remote execution, injected with an asynchronous execution pattern, and much more. Essentially, LINQ providers allow for an interception mechanism into a standard collection API, and via this seemingly limitless functionality, behavior relating to the queries and collection can be injected.

For example, LINQ providers allow for the translation of a query expression from C# into SQL that is then executed on a remote database. In so doing, the C# programmer can remain in her primary object-oriented language and leave the translation to SQL to the underlying LINQ provider. Through this type of expression, programming languages are able to span the impedance mismatch between the object-oriented world and the relational database.

In the case of `IQueryable<T>`, vigilance regarding deferred execution is even more critical. Imagine, for example, a LINQ provider that returns data from a database. Rather than retrieve the data from a database regardless of the selection criteria, the lambda expression would provide an implementation of `IQueryable<T>` that possibly includes context information such as the connection string, but not the data itself. The data retrieval wouldn't occur until the call to `GetEnumerator()` or even `MoveNext()`. However, the `GetEnumerator()` call is generally implicit, such as when iterating over the collection with `foreach` or calling an `Enumerable` method such as `Count<T>()` or `Cast<T>()`. Obviously, cases such as this require developers to be wary of the subtle and repeated calls to any expensive operation that deferred execution might involve. For example, if calling `GetEnumerator()` involves a distributed call over the network to a database, avoid unintentional duplicate calls to iterations with `Count()` or `foreach`.

SUMMARY

After introducing anonymous types, implicit variables, and collection initializers, this chapter described the internals of how the `foreach` loop works and what interfaces are required for its execution. In addition, developers frequently filter a collection so that there are fewer items and project the collection so that the items take a different form. Toward that end, this chapter discussed the details of how to use the standard query operators, common collection APIs on the `System.Linq.Enumerable` class, to perform collection manipulation.

In the introduction to standard query operators, we spent a few pages detailing deferred execution and how developers should take care to avoid unintentionally reexecuting an expression via a subtle call that enumerates over the collection contents. The deferred execution and resultant implicit execution of standard query operators is a significant quality, especially when the query execution is expensive. Programmers should treat the query object as the query object, not the results, and expect the query to execute fully even if it executed already. The query object doesn't know that the results will be the same as they were during a previous execution.

Listing 14.25 appeared within an Advanced Topic section because of the complexity of calling multiple standard query operators one after the other. Although requirements for similar execution may be common, it is not necessary to rely on standard query operators directly. C# 3.0 includes query expressions, a SQL-like syntax for manipulating collections in a way that is frequently easier to code and read, as I'll show in the next chapter.

▪15▪
LINQ with Query Expressions

T HE END OF CHAPTER 14 showed a query using standard query operators for GroupJoin(), SelectMany(), and Distinct(), in addition to
the creation of two anonymous types. The result was a statement that
spanned multiple lines and was fairly complex to comprehend, certainly a
lot more complex than statements typically written in C# 2.0, even though
it appears fully compatible with C# 2.0 syntax. The introduction of standard query operators facilitated scenarios where such complex statements
were desirable even though the resultant code may be complex and hard
to read. In addition, the queries which standard query operators implemented were functionally very similar to queries generally implemented
in SQL.

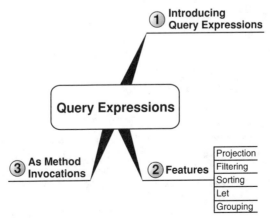

The culmination of these two factors resulted in the C# language designers adding a new syntax to C# 3.0: query expressions. With query expressions, many standard query operator statements are transformed into more readable code, code that looks very much like SQL.

In this chapter, I introduce the new syntax of query expressions and use this syntax to explain how to express many of the queries from the preceding chapter.

Introducing Query Expressions

Besides iterating over all the items within a collection, one of the most frequent operations developers perform is filtering the collection so that there are fewer items to iterate over or projecting the collection so that the items take a different form. For example, given a collection of files, we could filter it vertically to create a new collection of only the files with a ".cs" extension, or only the ten largest files. Alternatively, we could project across the file collection to create a new collection of paths to the directories the files are located in and the corresponding directory size. There are many ways to perform this type of operation, but one of the easiest was introduced in C# 3.0: query expressions.

Query expressions always begin with a "from clause" and end with a "select clause" or a "groupby clause". Each clause is identified by the `from`, `select`, or group contextual keywords, respectively. Listing 15.1 shows a query expression example and Output 15.1 shows the results.

LISTING 15.1: Simple Query Expression

```
using System;
using System.Collections.Generic;
using System.Linq;

// ...

    static string[] Keywords = {
        "abstract", "add*", "alias*", "as", "ascending*", "base",
        "bool", "break", "by*", "byte", "case", "catch", "char",
        "checked", "class", "const", "continue", "decimal",
        "default", "delegate", "descending*", "do", "double",
        "dynamic*", "else", "enum", "event", "equals*",
        "explicit", "extern", "false", "finally", "fixed",
        "from*", "float", "for", "foreach", "get*", "global*",
```

```
"group*", "goto", "if", "implicit", "in", "int",
"into*", "interface", "internal", "is", "lock", "long",
"join*", "let*", "namespace", "new", "null", "object",
"on*", "operator", "orderby*", "out", "override",
"params", "partial*", "private", "protected", "public",
"readonly", "ref", "remove*", "return", "sbyte", "sealed",
"select*", "set*", "short", "sizeof", "stackalloc",
"static", "string", "struct", "switch", "this", "throw",
"true", "try", "typeof", "uint", "ulong", "unchecked",
"unsafe", "ushort", "using", "value*", "var*", "virtual",
"void", "volatile", "where*", "while", "yield*"};
```

```csharp
private static void ShowContextualKeywords1()
{
    IEnumerable<string> selection = from word in Keywords
                                    where !word.Contains('*')
                                    select word;

    foreach (string keyword in selection)
    {
        Console.Write(" " + keyword);
    }
}

// ...
```

OUTPUT 15.1:

```
 abstract as base bool break byte case catch char checked class const
continue decimal default delegate do double else enum event explicit
extern false finally fixed float for foreach goto if implicit in int
interface internal is lock long namespace new null object operator out
override params private protected public readonly ref return sbyte
sealed short sizeof stackalloc static string struct switch this throw
true try typeof uint ulong unchecked unsafe ushort using virtual void
volatile while
```

In this query expression, `selection` is assigned the collection of C# keywords but not contextual keywords. The query expression in this example includes a `where` clause that filters out the noncontextual keywords.

Developers familiar with SQL will notice that query expressions have a syntax that is similar to that of SQL so as to be familiar to the thousands of programmers who know SQL. In spite of the similarities, however, there are some obvious inconsistencies. The most notable of these is the fact that rather than starting an expression with `select`, as SQL so often does, C# query expressions begin with the contextual keyword `from`.

The reason for this is to enable IntelliSense, or the ability to predict the members on the objects being selected. For example, because from appears first and identifies the string array Keywords as the data source, the code editor knows that word is of type string. This enables IntelliSense—member access (a dot operation) on word will display only the members of string. If the from clause appeared after the select, then any dot operations prior to the from clause would not know what the data type of word was and, therefore, would not be able to display a list of word's members. In Listing 15.1, for example, it wouldn't be possible to predict that Contains() was a possible member of word. word is referred to as a **range variable;** it represents each item in the collection.

Projection

The output of a query expression is an IEnumerable<T> or IQueryable<T> collection.[1] The data type of T is inferred from the select or groupby clause. In Listing 15.1, for example, the data type of string is inferred from select word because word is a string. word's data type is the type argument of the IEnumerable<T> collection in the from clause. Since Keywords is a string array, it implements IEnumerable<string>, and therefore, word is a string.

The type resulting from an expression which queries a collection of a certain type is by no means limited to be a sequence of that original type. Rather, the select clause allows for projection of data into an entirely different type. Consider the query expression in Listing 15.2, and its corresponding output in Output 15.2.

LISTING 15.2: Projection Using Query Expressions

```
using System;
using System.Collections.Generic;
using System.Linq;
using System.IO;

// ...
```

---

1. Query expression output is practically always IEnumerable<T>, but theoretically, not necessarily. Nothing is stopping anyone from coming up with an implementation of the query operators that returns something else. To do so would be somewhat perverse, but there is no *requirement* in the language that query operators return IEnumerable<T>.

```
    static void List1(string rootDirectory, string searchPattern)
    {
        IEnumerable<FileInfo> files =
            from fileName in Directory.GetFiles(
                rootDirectory, searchPattern)
            select new FileInfo(fileName);

        foreach (FileInfo file in files)
        {
            Console.WriteLine(".{0}({1})",
                file.Name, file.LastWriteTime);
        }
    }

// ...
```

OUTPUT 15.2:

```
Account.cs(11/22/2007 11:56:11 AM)
Bill.cs(8/10/2007 9:33:55 PM)
Contact.cs(8/19/2007 11:40:30 PM)
Customer.cs(11/17/2007 2:02:52 AM)
Employee.cs(8/17/2007 1:33:22 AM)
Person.cs(10/22/2007 10:00:03 PM)
```

Notice that this query expression returns an IEnumerable<FileInfo> rather than the IEnumerable<string> data type returned by System.IO.Directory.GetFiles(). The select clause of the query expression can potentially project out a data type that is different from what was collected by the from clause expression (Directory.GetFiles()).

In fact, projection such as this is the key driving factor for why C# 3.0 includes anonymous types within the language. Via anonymous types, it becomes possible to select out the exact data you seek without having to define an explicit type. For example, Listing 15.3 provides output similar to that in Listing 15.2, but via anonymous types rather than FileInfo.

LISTING 15.3: Anonymous Types within Query Expressions

```
    using System;
    using System.Collections.Generic;
    using System.Linq;
    using System.IO;

// ...

    static void List2(string rootDirectory, string searchPattern)
    {
```

```
        var files =
            from fileName in Directory.GetFiles(
                rootDirectory, searchPattern)
            select new
            {
                Name = fileName,
                LastWriteTime = File.GetLastWriteTime(fileName)
            };

        foreach (var file in files)
        {
            Console.WriteLine("{0}({1})",
                file.Name, file.LastWriteTime);
        }
    }

// ...
```

In this example, the query projects out only the filename and its last file write time. A projection such as the one in Listing 15.3 makes little difference when working with something small such as FileInfo. However, horizontal projection that filters down the amount of data associated with each item in the collection is extremely powerful when the amount of data is significant and retrieving it (perhaps from a different computer over the Internet) is expensive. Rather than retrieving all the data when a query executes, the use of anonymous types enables the capability of storing and retrieving only the required data into the collection. Imagine, for example, a large database that has tables with 30 or more columns. If there were no anonymous types, developers would be required to either use objects containing unnecessary information or define small, specialized classes useful only for storing the specific data required. Instead, anonymous types enable support for types to be defined by the compiler—types that contain only the data needed for their immediate scenario. Other scenarios can have a different projection of only the properties needed for that scenario.

■ BEGINNER TOPIC

Deferred Execution with Query Expressions

The topic of deferred execution appeared in the preceding chapter as well. The same principles also apply to query expressions. Consider again the assignment of selection in Listing 15.1. The assignment itself does not execute the query expression. In other words, during the assignment of selection, word.Contains("*") is not called. Rather, the query expression saves off the selection criteria to be used when iterating over the collection identified by the selection variable.

To demonstrate this point, consider Listing 15.4 and the corresponding output (Output 15.3).

LISTING 15.4: Deferred Execution and Query Expressions (Example 1)

```
using System;
using System.Collections.Generic;
using System.Linq;

// ...

    private static void ShowContextualKeywords2()
    {
        IEnumerable<string> selection = from word in Keywords
                                        where IsKeyword(word)
                                        select word;

        foreach (string keyword in selection)
        {
            Console.Write(keyword);
        }
    }

    // Side effect (console output) included in predicate to show
    // deferred execution not as a best practice.
    private static bool IsKeyword(string word)
    {
        if (word.Contains('*'))
        {
            Console.Write(" ");
            return true;
        }
        else
        {
            return false;
        }
    }
// ...
```

OUTPUT 15.3:

```
add* alias* ascending* by* descending* dynamic* equals* from* get*
global* group* into* join* let* on* orderby* partial* remove* select*
set* value* var* where* yield*
```

Notice that in Listing 15.4, no space is output within the foreach loop. The space between the contextual keywords is output in the IsKeyword() function, demonstrating that the IsKeyword() function isn't called until the code iterates over selection rather than when selection is assigned.

The point is that although selection is a collection (it is of type IEnumerable<T> after all), at the time of assignment everything following the from clause comprises the selection criteria. Not until we begin to iterate over selection are the criteria applied.

Consider a second example (see Listing 15.5 and Output 15.4).

LISTING 15.5: Deferred Execution and Query Expressions (Example 2)

```csharp
using System;
using System.Collections.Generic;
using System.Linq;

// ...

  private static void CountContextualKeywords()
  {
      int delegateInvocations = 0;
      Func<string, string> func =
          text=>
          {
              delegateInvocations++;
              return text;
          };

      IEnumerable<string> selection =
          from keyword in Keywords
          where keyword.Contains('*')
          select func(keyword);


      Console.WriteLine(
          "1. delegateInvocations={0}", delegateInvocations);

      // Executing count should invoke func once for
      // each item selected.
      Console.WriteLine(
          "2. Contextual keyword count={0}", selection.Count());

      Console.WriteLine(
          "3. delegateInvocations={0}", delegateInvocations);

      // Executing count should invoke func once for
```

```
        // each item selected.
        Console.WriteLine(
            "4. Contextual keyword count={0}", selection.Count());

        Console.WriteLine(
            "5. delegateInvocations={0}", delegateInvocations);

        // Cache the value so future counts will not trigger
        // another invocation of the query.
        List<string> selectionCache = selection.ToList();

        Console.WriteLine(
            "6. delegateInvocations={0}", delegateInvocations);

        // Retrieve the count from the cached collection.
        Console.WriteLine(
            "7. selectionCache count={0}",selectionCache.Count());

        Console.WriteLine(
            "8. delegateInvocations={0}", delegateInvocations);

    }

// ...
```

OUTPUT 15.4:

```
1. delegateInvocations=0
2. Contextual keyword count=15
3. delegateInvocations=15
4. Contextual keyword count=15
5. delegateInvocations=30
6. delegateInvocations=45
7. selectionCache count=15
8. delegateInvocations=45
```

Rather than defining a separate method, Listing 15.5 uses an anonymous method that counts the number of times the method is called.

Three things in the output are remarkable. First, notice that after selection is assigned, DelegateInvocations remains at zero. At the time of assignment to selection, no iteration over Keywords is performed. If Keywords were a property, the property call would run—in other words, the from clause executes at the time of assignment. However, neither the projection, the filtering, nor anything after the from clause will execute until the code iterates over the values within selection. It is as though at the time of assignment, selection would more appropriately be called "query."

However, once we call Count(), a term such as *selection* or *items* that indicates a container or collection is appropriate because we begin to count the items within the collection. In other words, the variable selection serves a dual purpose of saving the query information as well as acting like a container from which the data is retrieved.

A second important characteristic to notice is that calling Count() twice causes func to again be invoked once on each item selected. Since selection behaves both as a query and as a collection, requesting the count requires that the query be executed again by iterating over the IEnumerable<string> collection selection refers to and counting the items—returning the most up-to-date results. Similarly, a foreach loop over selection would trigger func to be called again for each item. The same is true of all the other extension methods provided via System.Linq.Enumerable.

Filtering

In Listing 15.1, we include a where clause that filters out pure keywords but not contextual keywords. The where clause filters the collection vertically so that there are fewer items within the collection. The filter criteria are expressed with a *predicate*—a lambda expression that returns a bool such as word.Contains() (as in Listing 15.1) or File.GetLastWrite-Time(file) < DateTime.Now.AddMonths(-1) (as in Listing 15.6, the output of which appears in Output 15.5).

LISTING 15.6: Anonymous Types within Query Expressions

```
using System;
using System.Collections.Generic;
using System.Linq;
using System.IO;

// ...

   static void FindMonthOldFiles(
       string rootDirectory, string searchPattern)
   {
       IEnumerable<FileInfo> files =
           from fileName in Directory.GetFiles(
               rootDirectory, searchPattern)
```

```
            where File.GetLastWriteTime(fileName) <
                DateTime.Now.AddMonths(-1)
            select new FileInfo(fileName);

    foreach (FileInfo file in files)
    {
        // As simplification, current directory is
        // assumed to be a subdirectory of
        // rootDirectory
        string relativePath = file.FullName.Substring(
                Environment.CurrentDirectory.Length);
        Console.WriteLine(".{0}({1})",
            relativePath, file.LastWriteTime);
    }
  }
}

// ...
```

OUTPUT 15.5:

```
.\TestData\Bill.cs(8/10/2007 9:33:55 PM)
.\TestData\Contact.cs(8/19/2007 11:40:30 PM)
.\TestData\Employee.cs(8/17/2007 1:33:22 AM)
.\TestData\Person.cs(10/22/2007 10:00:03 PM)
```

Sorting

To order the items using a query expression we rely on the orderby clause (see Listing 15.7).

LISTING 15.7: Sorting Using a Query Expression with an **orderby** Clause

```
using System;
using System.Collections.Generic;
using System.Linq;
using System.IO;

// ...
  static void ListByFileSize1(
      string rootDirectory, string searchPattern)
  {
      IEnumerable<string> fileNames =
          from fileName in Directory.GetFiles(
              rootDirectory, searchPattern)
          orderby (new FileInfo(fileName)).Length descending,
              fileName
          select fileName;
```

```
        foreach (string fileName in fileNames)
        {
            Console.WriteLine("{0}", fileName);
        }
    }
// ...
```

Listing 15.7 uses the `orderby` clause to sort the files returned by `Directory.GetFiles()` first by file size in descending order and then by filename in ascending order. Multiple sort criteria are separated by a comma such that first the items are ordered by size, and if the size is the same they are ordered by filename. `ascending` and `descending` are contextual keywords indicating the sort order direction. Specifying the order as ascending or descending is optional (`filename` order is absent); if the direction is omitted, the default is `ascending`.

The Let Clause

In Listing 15.8, we have a query that is very similar to that in Listing 15.7, except that the type argument of `IEnumerable<T>` is `FileInfo`. One of the problems with the `groupby` clause in Listing 15.8 is that in order to evaluate the size of the file, an instance of `FileInfo` needs to be available in both the `orderby` clause and the `select` clause.

LISTING 15.8: Projecting a `FileInfo` Collection and Sorting by File Size

```
using System;
using System.Collections.Generic;
using System.Linq;
using System.IO;

// ...
    static void ListByFileSize2(
        string rootDirectory, string searchPattern)
    {
        IEnumerable<FileInfo> files =
            from fileName in Directory.GetFiles(
                rootDirectory, searchPattern)
            orderby new FileInfo(fileName).Length, fileName
            select new FileInfo(fileName);

        foreach (FileInfo file in files)
        {
            // As simplification, current directory is
            // assumed to be a subdirectory of
```

```
        // rootDirectory
        string relativePath = file.FullName.Substring(
            Environment.CurrentDirectory.Length);
        Console.WriteLine(".{0}({1})",
            relativePath, file.Length);
    }
  }
// ...
```

Unfortunately, although the end result is correct, Listing 15.8 ends up instantiating a `FileInfo` object twice for each item in the source collection. `FileInfo` is instantiated not only in the `select` clause, but also when the `orderby` clause is evaluated. To avoid unnecessary overhead like this—overhead that could potentially be expensive—the query expression syntax includes a `let` expression, as demonstrated in Listing 15.9.

LISTING 15.9: Ordering the Results in a Query Expression

```
using System;
using System.Collections.Generic;
using System.Linq;
using System.IO;

// ...
  static void ListByFileSize3(
      string rootDirectory, string searchPattern)
  {
      IEnumerable<FileInfo> files =
          from fileName in Directory.GetFiles(
              rootDirectory, searchPattern)
          let file = new FileInfo(fileName)
          orderby file.Length, fileName
          select file;

      foreach (FileInfo file in files)
      {
          // As simplification, current directory is
          // assumed to be a subdirectory of
          // rootDirectory
          string relativePath = file.FullName.Substring(
              Environment.CurrentDirectory.Length);
          Console.WriteLine(".{0}({1})",
              relativePath, file.Length);
      }
  }
// ...
```

The `let` clause provides a location to place an expression that is used throughout the query expression. To place a second `let` expression, simply add it as an additional clause to the query after the first `from` clause but before the final `select`/`group by` clause. No operator is needed to separate out the expressions.

Grouping

Another common collection scenario is the grouping of items. In SQL, this generally involves aggregating the items into a summary header or total—an aggregate value. However, C# is more expressive than this. In addition to providing aggregate information about each grouping, query expressions allow for the individual items in the group to form a series of subcollections to each item in the overall parent list. For example, it is possible to group the contextual keywords separately from the regular keywords and automatically associate the individual words within the keyword type grouping to each other. Listing 15.10 and Output 15.6 demonstrate the query expression.

LISTING 15.10: Grouping Together Query Results

```csharp
using System;
using System.Collections.Generic;
using System.Linq;

// ...

  private static void GroupKeywords1()
  {
      IEnumerable<IGrouping<bool, string>> selection =
          from word in Keywords
          group word by word.Contains('*');

      foreach (IGrouping<bool, string> wordGroup
          in selection)
      {
          Console.WriteLine(Environment.NewLine + "{0}:",
              wordGroup.Key ?
                  "Contextual Keywords" : "Keywords");
          foreach (string keyword in wordGroup)
          {
              Console.Write(" " +
                  (wordGroup.Key ?
                      keyword.Replace("*", null) : keyword));
          }
      }
```

```
        }
    }

    // ...
```

OUTPUT 15.6:

```
Keywords:
 abstract as base bool break byte case catch char checked class const
continue decimal default delegate do double else enum event explicit
extern false finally fixed float for foreach goto if implicit in int
interface internal is lock long namespace new null object operator out
override params private protected public readonly ref return sbyte
sealed short sizeof stackalloc static string struct switch this throw
true try typeof uint ulong unchecked unsafe ushort using virtual void
volatile while
Contextual Keywords:
 add alias ascending by descending dynamic equals from get
global group into join let on orderby partial remove select
set value var where yield
```

There are several things to note in this listing. First, each item in the list is of type IGrouping<bool, string>. The type parameters of IGrouping<TKey, TElement> are determined by the data type following group and by—that is, TElement is a string because word is a string. Type parameter TKey is determined by the data type following by. In this case, word.Contains() returns a Boolean, so TKey is a bool.

A second characteristic of a query expression's groupby clause is the fact that it enables a nested foreach loop via which the code can iterate over the subcollection mentioned earlier in this section. In Listing 15.10, we first iterate over the groupings and print out the type of keyword as a header. Nested within the first iteration is a second foreach loop that prints each keyword as an item below the header.

Third, we can append a select clause to the end of a groupby clause, allowing support for projection (see Listing 15.11 and Output 15.7). More generally, the addition of the select clause is enabled via query continuation—any query body that handles the elements of the first query can be appended to the first query body.

LISTING 15.11: Selecting an Anonymous Type Following the groupby Clause

```
using System;
using System.Collections.Generic;
```

```csharp
using System.Linq;

// ...

    private static void GroupKeywords1()
    {
        IEnumerable<IGrouping<bool, string>> keywordGroups =
            from word in Keywords
            group word by word.Contains('*');

        var selection = from groups in keywordGroups
            select new
            {
                IsContextualKeyword = groups.Key,
                Items = groups
            };

        foreach (var wordGroup in selection)
        {
            Console.WriteLine(Environment.NewLine + "{0}:",
                wordGroup.IsContextualKeyword ?
                    "Contextual Keywords" : "Keywords");
            foreach (var keyword in wordGroup.Items)
            {
                Console.Write(" " +
                    keyword.Replace("*", null));
            }
        }
    }

// ...
```

OUTPUT 15.7:

```
Keywords:
 abstract as base bool break byte case catch char checked class const
continue decimal default delegate do double else enum event explicit
extern false finally fixed float for foreach goto if implicit in int
interface internal is lock long namespace new null object operator out
override params private protected public readonly ref return sbyte
sealed short sizeof stackalloc static string struct switch this throw
true try typeof uint ulong unchecked unsafe ushort using virtual void
volatile while
Contextual Keywords:
 add alias ascending by descending dynamic equals from get
global group into join let on orderby partial remove select
set value var where yield
```

The groupby clause returns a collection of `IGrouping<TKey, TElement>` objects—just as the `GroupBy()` standard query operator did (see Chapter 14).

The `select` clause defines an anonymous type, renaming `IGrouping<TKey, TElement>.Key` to be `IsContextualKeyword` and naming the subcollection property `Items`. With this change, the nested `foreach` uses `wordGroup.Items` rather than `wordGroup` directly, as shown in Listing 15.10. Another potential property to add to the anonymous type would be the count of items within the subcollection. However, this is available on `wordGroup.Items.Count()`, so the benefit of adding it to the anonymous type directly is questionable.

Query Continuation with `into`

Following the groupby query is a second query that projects out an anonymous type from the grouping. Rather than write an additional query, you can extend the query with a query continuation clause using the contextual keyword `into` that allows you to name each item returned by the groupby clause with a range variable (groups in Listing 15.11). The `into` clause serves as a generator for additional query commands—specifically, a `select` clause, as shown in Listing 15.12.

LISTING 15.12: **Selecting without the Query Continuation**

```csharp
using System;
using System.Collections.Generic;
using System.Linq;

// ...

    private static void GroupKeywords1()
    {
        var selection =
            from word in Keywords
            group word by word.Contains('*')
            into groups
                select new
                {
                    IsContextualKeyword = groups.Key,
                    Items = groups
                };

        // ...

    }

// ...
```

The ability to run additional queries on the results of an existing query using into is not specific to groupby clauses, but rather is a feature of all query expressions. Query continuation provides a form of shorthand in place of writing multiple individual query expressions. The query in Listing 15.12 is identical to the one in Listing 15.11, but without using into. In other words, into shortcuts the need to write a second query using the results of the first query; it serves as a pipeline operator, combining the results of the first query with those of the second query.

■ BEGINNER TOPIC

Distinct Members

Often, it is desirable to return only distinct items from within a collection—all duplicates are combined into a single item. Query expressions don't have explicit syntax for distinct members, but the functionality is available via the query operator Distinct(), as introduced in the preceding chapter. Listing 15.13 demonstrates calling it directly from the query expression, and Output 15.8 shows the results.

LISTING 15.13: Obtaining Distinct Members from a Query Expression

```csharp
using System;
using System.Collections.Generic;
using System.Linq;

// ...

        public static void ListMemberNames()
        {
            IEnumerable<string> enumerableMethodNames = (
                from method in typeof(Enumerable).GetMembers(
                    System.Reflection.BindingFlags.Static |
                    System.Reflection.BindingFlags.Public)
                select method.Name).Distinct();
            foreach(string method in enumerableMethodNames)
            {
                Console.Write(" {0},", method);
            }
        }

// ...
```

```
, FirstOrDefault, Last, LastOrDefault,
entAt, ElementAtOrDefault, Repeat, Empty,
ontains, Aggregate, Sum, Min, Max, Aver-
y, Take, TakeWhile, Skip, SkipWhile, Join,
scending, ThenBy, ThenByDescending,
ion, Intersect, Except, Reverse, Sequence-
    ToList, ToDictionary, ToLookup,
    Range
```

umerable).GetMembers() returns a list of all
rties, and so on) on System.Linq.Enumerable.
nbers are overloaded, sometimes more than
e same member multiple times, Distinct() is
on. This eliminates the duplicate names from
peof() and GetMembers() in Chapter 17.)

ession is a series of method calls to the under-
not have any concept of query expressions. In
es with expression trees, there was no change
to support query expressions. Rather, query
a changes to the C# compiler only.
compiler translates the query expression to
e query expression from Listing 15.1 trans-
numerable's Where() extension method and
ring>(). The criteria identified by the where
clause are just like they were in the Where() (or FindAll()) method
described in the preceding chapter.

■ ADVANCED TOPIC

Implementing Implicit Execution

The capability of saving the selection criteria into selection (see Listing 15.1)
rather than executing the query at the time of assignment is implemented
through delegates. The compiler translates the query expression to methods

on the target (that is, Keywords) that take delegates as parameters. Delegates are objects that save information about what code to execute when the delegate is called, and since delegates contain only the data regarding what to execute, they can be stored until a later time when they are executed.

In the case of collections that implement IQueryable<T> (LINQ providers), the lambda expressions are translated into expression trees. An expression tree is a hierarchical data structure broken down recursively into subexpressions. Each subexpression represents a portion of the lambda expression that is further broken down until each part is the most fundamental unit that can no longer be broken down. Frequently, expression trees are then enumerated and reconstructed as the original expression tree is translated into another language, such as SQL.

Query Expressions as Method Invocations

In spite of the power and relative simplicity associated with query expressions, the CLR and IL do not require any query expression implementation. Rather, the C# compiler translates query expressions into method calls. Consider, for example, the query expression from Listing 15.1, a portion of which appears in Listing 15.14.

LISTING 15.14: Simple Query Expression

```
private static void ShowContextualKeywords1()
{
    IEnumerable<string> selection = from word in Keywords
                                    where word.Contains('*')
                                    select word;
    // ...
}

// ...
```

After compilation, the expression from Listing 15.14 is converted to an IEnumerable<T> extension method call from System.Linq.Enumerable, as shown in Listing 15.15.

LISTING 15.15: Query Expression Translated to Standard Query Operator Syntax

```
private static void ShowContextualKeywords3()
{
```

```
    IEnumerable<string> selection =
        Keywords.Where(word => word.Contains('*'));

  // ...
}

// ...
```

Furthermore, as discussed in Chapter 14, the lambda expression is translated to IL corresponding to a delegate invocation.

Moreover, the combination of extension methods and lambda expressions provides a superset of the functionality available through query expressions. For example, there is no query expression equivalent for the extension method `TakeWhile<T>(Func<T, bool> predicate)`, which repeatedly returns items from the collection as long as the predicate returns `true`. Not all method invocations can be translated to query expressions, but the reverse, translating from query expressions to method expressions, is always possible. Regardless, where translation is possible in either direction, it is not consistently more understandable. Some queries are better suited for query expressions whereas others are more readable as method invocations. I find the general rule is to use query expressions where possible, but to rely on method invocations otherwise. Regardless, it is frequently helpful to refactor a complex query into multiple statements or even methods.

SUMMARY

This chapter introduced a new syntax, that of query expressions. Readers familiar with SQL will immediately see the similarities between query expressions and SQL. However, query expressions also introduce additional functionality, such as grouping into a hierarchical set of new objects, which was unavailable with SQL. All of the functionality of query expressions was already available via standard query operators, but query expressions frequently provide a simpler syntax for expressing such a query. Whether through standard query operators or query expression syntax, however, the end result is a significant improvement in the way developers are able to code against collection APIs, an improvement that ultimately provides a paradigm shift in the way object-oriented languages are able to interface with relational databases.

In the next chapter, we continue our discussion of collections: investigating some of the .NET Framework collection types as well as how to define custom collections.

■ 16 ■

Building Custom Collections

C HAPTER 14 COVERED standard query operators, a set of extension
methods on IEnumerable<T> that added a common set of methods to
all collections. However, this did not make all collections the same. There
is still a strong need for different collection types. Some collections are
better suited to searching by key, whereas others are better suited to index

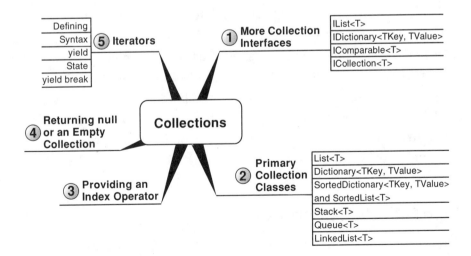

retrieval. Similarly, some collections follow a queue behavior of first in, first out, whereas others are more like a stack, as in last in, last out. The .NET Framework contains a plethora of different collections suited for the vast array of scenarios in which collections are needed. This chapter provides an introduction to many of these collections, along with more collection interfaces. Furthermore, the chapter introduces how to define a custom collection that supports standard collection functionality, such as indexing and `foreach` iteration via iterators. Iterators not only encapsulate the internal data structure of the collection classes, but they also improve control over end-user access and the use of data within a collection.

Perhaps the most prevalent use of generics in any language is in the area of collections. Collections deal with sets of like objects and with managing those objects as a group. This chapter looks at the collection classes provided with the runtime and how you use them within your applications. It also covers the various collection interfaces and how they relate to each other, and it includes a discussion of how to create custom collections using iterators. This C# 2.0 feature simplifies implementation of how the `foreach` statement iterates over the elements in a collection.

There are two types of collection-related classes: those that support generics and those that don't. This chapter primarily discusses the generic collection classes. Generally, you should use collection classes that don't support generics only when writing components that need to interoperate with earlier versions of the runtime. This is because everything that was available in the nongeneric form has a generic replacement that is strongly typed. In this edition, I focus on the generic collections and do not discuss nongeneric collection types.

More Collection Interfaces

This section delves into the collection-related interfaces to help you understand the common capabilities of all collection classes and where the commonalities possibly diverge.

Figure 16.1 shows the hierarchy of interfaces that make up the collection classes.

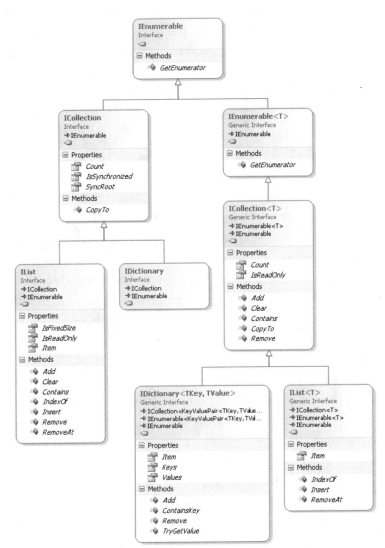

FIGURE 16.1: Generic Collection Interface Hierarchy

You use these interfaces to establish capabilities such as iterating over a collection using a `foreach` loop, indexing into a collection, and determining the total number of elements in a collection. This section examines these interfaces, starting at the bottom of Figure 16.1 and moving up.

IList<T> **versus** IDictionary<TKey, TValue>

In a sense, lists are just the special case of dictionaries where the "key" is always an integer, and the key set is always a contiguous set of non-negative integers starting with zero. But that is a strong enough difference that it is worth having an entirely different class to represent it. When selecting a collection class, the first two interfaces to look for are IList<T> and IDictionary<TKey, TValue>. These interfaces determine whether the collection type is focused on retrieval via index or retrieval via key. If the type of collection you are using should be key-centric, use a collection class that implements the IDictionary<TKey, TValue> interface. Alternatively, the IList<T> interface provides support for element retrieval via index. In other words, although both of these interfaces require that the indexer be implemented, the implementations are fundamentally different. In the case of IList<T>, the parameter passed to the array operator corresponds to the index of the element being retrieved, the *nth* element in the list. In the case of the IDictionary<TKey, TValue> interface, the parameter corresponds to the key of a previously inserted element. When you assign using the key, a new item will be inserted if one doesn't already exist for the specified key.

IComparable<T>

Before I discuss the next interface in Figure 16.1, I need to discuss an interface that does not appear in the diagram but is nonetheless important to both IList<T> and IDictionary<TKey, TValue>. The IComparable<T> interface is crucial for any sorting operation by classes implementing these interfaces. For example, if the List<T>.Sort() method is called, you need a means to compare objects to determine their order. One way to do this is via the IComparable<T> interface. This interface has one method, CompareTo(). It returns an integer indicating whether the element passed is greater than, less than, or equal to the current element. For this to work the key data type needs to implement IComparable<T>.

■ ADVANCED TOPIC

Using IComparer<T> for Sorting

Another way to handle custom sorting is to pass an element that implements IComparer<T> into the sort method. This interface performs a function similar to IComparable<T>, but is not generally supported directly by the element being collected. For example, consider providing an IComparable<T>.CompareTo() method for Contact. What sort order would be used: age; last name; country of residence? At issue is the fact that the sort order varies, and therefore, providing one comparison method directly on the Contact class would be an arbitrary choice.

A more appropriate solution is to provide a special sort class for each comparison implementation. Instead of the comparison method performing a comparison between the sort class instance and a single Contact instance, it would accept two Contact arguments and it would perform the comparison between these two instances. Listing 16.1 shows a sample implementation of a LastName, FirstName comparison.

LISTING 16.1: Implementing IComparer<T>

```
class Contact;
{
  public string FirstName { get; set; }
  }

  public string LastName { get; set; }
}
```

```
using System;
using System.Collections.Generic;

class NameComparison : IComparer<Contact>
{
  public int Compare(Contact x, Contact y)
  {
    int result;

    if (Contact.ReferenceEquals(x, y))
    {
      result = 0;
    }
    else
    {
      if (x == null)
      {
        result = 1;
      }
      else if (y == null)
      {
        result = -1;
      }
```

```
        else
        {
            result = StringCompare(x.LastName, y.LastName);
            if (result == 0)
            {
                result =
                    StringCompare(x.FirstName, y.FirstName);
            }
        }
    }
    return result;
}

private static int StringCompare(string x, string y)
{
    int result;
    if (x == null)
    {
      if (y == null)
      {
          result = 0;
      }
      else
      {
          result = 1;
      }
    }
    else
    {
      result = x.CompareTo(y);
    }
    return result;
  }
}
```

To use the new Compare() function you pass it to a sort method such as List<Contact>.Sort(IComparer<Contact> comparer).

ICollection<T>

Both IList<T> and IDictionary<TKey, TValue> implement ICollection<T>. A collection that does not implement either IList<T> or IDictionary<TKey, TValue> is more than likely going to implement ICollection<T> (although not necessarily, since collections could implement the lesser requirement of IEnumerable or IEnumerable<T>).

`ICollection<T>` is derived from `IEnumerable<T>` and includes two members: `Count` and `CopyTo()`.

- The `Count` property returns the total number of elements in the collection. Initially, it may appear that this would be sufficient to iterate through each element in the collection using a `for` loop, but in order for this to be possible the collection would also need to support retrieval by index, which the `ICollection<T>` interface does not include (although `IList<T>` does include it).
- The `CopyTo()` method provides the ability to convert the collection into an array. The method includes an `index` parameter so that you can specify where to insert elements in the target array. Note that to use the method you must initialize the array target with sufficient capacity, starting at the `index`, to contain all the elements in `ICollection<T>`.

Primary Collection Classes

There are five key categories of collection classes, and they differ from each other in terms of how data is inserted, stored, and retrieved. Each generic class is located in the `System.Collections.Generic` namespace, and their nongeneric equivalents are in the `System.Collections` namespace.

List Collections: `List<T>`

The `List<T>` class has properties similar to an array. The key difference is that these classes automatically expand as the number of elements increases. (In contrast, an array size is constant.) Furthermore, lists can shrink via explicit calls to `TrimToSize()` or `Capacity` (see Figure 16.2).

These classes are categorized as **list collections** whose distinguishing functionality is that each element can be individually accessed by index, just like an array. Therefore, you can set and access elements in the list collection classes using the index operator, where the index parameter value corresponds to the position of an element in the collection. Listing 16.2 shows an example, and Output 16.1 shows the results.

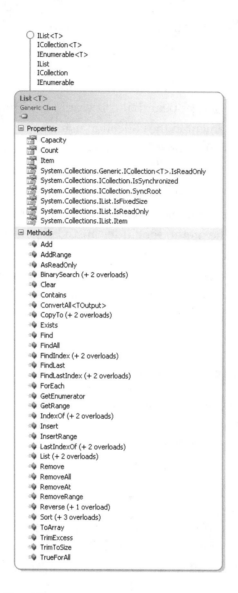

FIGURE 16.2: List<> Class Diagrams

LISTING 16.2: Using List<T>

```csharp
using System;
using System.Collections.Generic;

class Program
{
  static void Main()
  {
      List<string> list = new List<string>();
```

```
        // Lists automatically expand as elements
        // are added.
        list.Add("Sneezy");
        list.Add("Happy");
        list.Add("Dopey");
        list.Add("Doc");
        list.Add("Sleepy");
        list.Add("Bashful");
        list.Add("Grumpy");

        list.Sort();

        Console.WriteLine(
            "In alphabetical order {0} is the "
            + "first dwarf while {1} is the last.",
            list[0], list[6]);

        list.Remove("Grumpy");
    }
}
```

OUTPUT 16.1:

```
In alphabetical order Bashful is the first dwarf while Sneezy is the
last.
```

C# is zero-index-based; therefore, index zero in Listing 16.2 corresponds to the first element and index 6 indicates the seventh element. Retrieving elements by index does not involve a search. It involves a quick and simple "jump" operation to a location in memory.

When you use the Add() method, elements maintain the order in which you added them. Therefore, prior to the call to Sort() in Listing 16.2, "Sneezy" is first and "Grumpy" is last. Although List<T> supports a Sort() method, nothing states that all list collections require such a method.

There is no support for automatic sorting of elements as they are added. In other words, an explicit call to Sort() is required for the elements to be sorted (items must implement IComparable). To remove an element, you use the Remove() method.

To search List<T> for a particular element, you use the Contains(), IndexOf(), LastIndexOf(), and BinarySearch() methods. The first three methods search through the array, starting at the first element (the last element for LastIndexOf()), and examine each element until the equivalent one is found. The execution time for these algorithms is proportional to the number of elements searched before a hit occurs. Be aware that the collection classes do not require that all the elements within the collection are unique. If two or more elements in the collection are the same, then IndexOf() returns the first index and LastIndexOf() returns the last index.

BinarySearch() uses a binary search algorithm and requires that the elements be sorted. A useful feature of the BinarySearch() method is that if the element is not found, a negative integer is returned. The bitwise complement (~) of this value is the index of the next element larger than the element being sought, or the total element count if there is no greater value. This provides a convenient means to insert new values into the list at the specific location so as to maintain sorting (see Listing 16.3).

LISTING 16.3: Using the Bit Complement of the BinarySearch() Result

```csharp
using System;
using System.Collections.Generic;

class Program
{
  static void Main()
  {
      List<string> list = new List<string>();
      int search;

      list.Add("public");
      list.Add("protected");
      list.Add("private");

      list.Sort();

      search = list.BinarySearch("protected internal");
      if (search < 0)
      {
        list.Insert(~search, "protected internal");
      }

      foreach (string accessModifier in list)
      {
          Console.WriteLine(accessModifier);
      }
  }
}
```

Beware that if the list is not first sorted, an element will not necessarily be found, even if it is in the list. The results of Listing 16.3 appear in Output 16.2.

OUTPUT 16.2:

```
private
protected
protected internal
public
```

▪ ADVANCED TOPIC

Finding Multiple Items with FindAll()

Sometimes you must find multiple items within a list and your search criteria are more complex than looking for specific values. To support this, System.Collections.Generic.List<T> includes a FindAll() method. FindAll() takes a parameter of type Predicate<T>, which is a reference to a method called a delegate. Listing 16.4 demonstrates how to use the FindAll() method.

LISTING 16.4: Demonstrating FindAll() and Its Predicate Parameter

```
using System;
using System.Collections.Generic;

class Program
{
  static void Main()
  {
      List<int> list = new List<int>();
      list.Add(1);
      list.Add(2);
      list.Add(3);
      list.Add(2);

      List<int> results = list.FindAll(Even);

      foreach(int number in results)
      {
          Console.WriteLine(number);
      }
  }

  public static bool Even(int value)
  {
      return (value % 2) == 0;
  }
}
```

In Listing 16.4's call to FindAll(), you pass a delegate instance, Even(). This method returns true when the integer argument value is even.

`FindAll()` takes the delegate instance and calls into `Even()` for each item within the list (this listing uses C# 2.0's delegate type inferencing). Each time the return is `true`, it adds it to a new `List<T>` instance and then returns this instance once it has checked each item within `list`. A complete discussion of delegates occurs in Chapter 12.

Dictionary Collections: `Dictionary<TKey, TValue>`

Another category of collection classes is the dictionary classes—specifically, `Dictionary<Tkey, Tvalue>` (see Figure 16.3). Unlike the list collections, dictionary classes store name/value pairs. The name functions as a unique key that can be used to look up the corresponding element in a manner similar to that of using a primary key to access a record in a database. This adds some complexity to the access of dictionary elements, but because lookups by key are efficient operations, this is a useful collection. Note that the key may be any data type, not just a string or a numeric value.

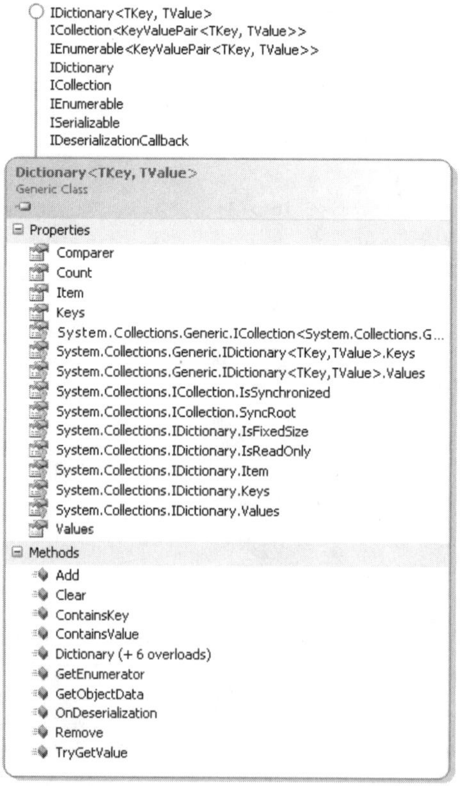

```
○ IDictionary<TKey, TValue>
  ICollection<KeyValuePair<TKey, TValue>>
  IEnumerable<KeyValuePair<TKey, TValue>>
  IDictionary
  ICollection
  IEnumerable
  ISerializable
  IDeserializationCallback

Dictionary<TKey, TValue>
Generic Class

□ Properties
   Comparer
   Count
   Item
   Keys
   System.Collections.Generic.ICollection<System.Collections.G...
   System.Collections.Generic.IDictionary<TKey,TValue>.Keys
   System.Collections.Generic.IDictionary<TKey,TValue>.Values
   System.Collections.ICollection.IsSynchronized
   System.Collections.ICollection.SyncRoot
   System.Collections.IDictionary.IsFixedSize
   System.Collections.IDictionary.IsReadOnly
   System.Collections.IDictionary.Item
   System.Collections.IDictionary.Keys
   System.Collections.IDictionary.Values
   Values
□ Methods
   Add
   Clear
   ContainsKey
   ContainsValue
   Dictionary (+ 6 overloads)
   GetEnumerator
   GetObjectData
   OnDeserialization
   Remove
   TryGetValue
```

FIGURE 16.3: Dictionary Class Diagrams

One option for inserting elements into a dictionary is to use the `Add()` method, passing both the key and the value, as shown in Listing 16.5.

LISTING 16.5: Adding Items to a `Dictionary<TKey, TValue>`

```
using System;
using System.Collections.Generic;

class Program
{
  static void Main()
  {
      Dictionary<Guid,string> dictionary =
          new Dictionary<Guid, string>();
      Guid key = Guid.NewGuid();

      dictionary.Add(key, "object");
  }
}
```

Listing 16.5 inserts the string `"object"` using a `Guid` as its key. If an element with the same key has already been added, an exception is thrown.

An alternative is to use the indexer, as shown in Listing 16.6.

LISTING 16.6: Inserting Items in a `Dictionary<TKey, TValue>` Using the Index Operator

```
using System;
using System.Collections.Generic;

class Program
{
  static void Main()
  {
      Dictionary<Guid, string> dictionary =
          new Dictionary<Guid, string>();
      Guid key = Guid.NewGuid();

      dictionary[key] = "object";
      dictionary[key] = "byte";
  }
}
```

The first thing to observe in Listing 16.6 is that the index operator does not require an integer. Instead, the index data type is specified by the first type parameter, `TKey`, when declaring a `Dictionary<TKey, TValue>`

variable. In this example, the key data type used is `Guid`, and the value data type is `string`.

The second thing to notice in Listing 16.6 is the reuse of the same index. In the first assignment, no dictionary element corresponds to key. Instead of throwing an out-of-bounds exception, as an array would, dictionary collection classes insert a new object. During the second assignment, an element with the specified key already exists, so instead of inserting an additional element, the existing element corresponding to key is updated from "object" to "byte".

Accessing a value from a dictionary using the index operator (`[]`) with a nonexistent key throws an exception of type `System.Collections.Generic.` `KeyNotFoundException`. The `ContainsKey()` method, however, allows you to check whether a particular key is used before accessing its value, thereby avoiding the exception. Also, since the keys are stored in a hash table, the search is relatively efficient.

By contrast, checking whether there is a particular value in the dictionary collections is a time-consuming operation with linear performance characteristics. To do this you use the `ContainsValue()` method, which searches sequentially through each element in the collection.

You remove a dictionary element using the `Remove()` method, passing the key, not the element value.

There is no particular order for the dictionary classes. Elements are arranged into a hash table using hash codes for rapid retrieval (acquired by calling `GetHashCode()` on the key). Iterating through a dictionary class using the `foreach` loop, therefore, accesses values in no particular order. Because both the key and the element value are required to add an element to the dictionary, the data type returned from the `foreach` loop is `KeyValuePair<TKey, TValue>` for `Dictionary<TKey, TValue>`. Listing 16.7 shows a snippet of code demonstrating the `foreach` loop with the `Dictionary<TKey, TValue>` collection class. The output appears in Output 16.3.

LISTING 16.7: Iterating over `Dictionary<TKey, TValue>` with `foreach`

```
using System;
using System.Collections.Generic;

class Program
{
  static void Main()
```

```
    {
        Dictionary<string,string> dictionary = new
            Dictionary<string,string>();

        int index =0;

        dictionary.Add(index++.ToString(), "object");
        dictionary.Add(index++.ToString(), "byte");
        dictionary.Add(index++.ToString(), "uint");
        dictionary.Add(index++.ToString(), "ulong");
        dictionary.Add(index++.ToString(), "float");
        dictionary.Add(index++.ToString(), "char");
        dictionary.Add(index++.ToString(), "bool");
        dictionary.Add(index++.ToString(), "ushort");
        dictionary.Add(index++.ToString(), "decimal");
        dictionary.Add(index++.ToString(), "int");
        dictionary.Add(index++.ToString(), "sbyte");
        dictionary.Add(index++.ToString(), "short");
        dictionary.Add(index++.ToString(), "long");
        dictionary.Add(index++.ToString(), "void");
        dictionary.Add(index++.ToString(), "double");
        dictionary.Add(index++.ToString(), "string");

        Console.WriteLine("Key   Value    Hashcode");
        Console.WriteLine("---   -------  --------");
        foreach (KeyValuePair<string, string> i in dictionary)
        {
            Console.WriteLine("{0,-5}{1,-9}{2}",
                i.Key, i.Value, i.Key.GetHashCode());
        }
    }
}
}
```

OUTPUT 16.3:

```
Key   Value    Hashcode
---   -------  ----------
0     object   -842352752
1     byte     -842352753
2     uint     -842352754
3     ulong    -842352755
4     float    -842352756
5     char     -842352757
6     bool     -842352758
7     ushort   -842352759
8     decimal  -842352744
9     int      -842352745
10    sbyte    -843401329
11    short    -843466865
12    long     -843532401
13    void     -843597937
14    double   -843663473
15    string   -843729009
```

If you want to deal only with keys or only with elements within a dictionary class, they are available via the Keys and Values properties. The data type returned from these properties is of type ICollection<T>. The data returned by these properties is a reference to the data within the original dictionary collection, so changes within the dictionary are automatically reflected in the ICollection type returned by the Keys and Values properties.

Sorted Collections: SortedDictionary<TKey, TValue> and SortedList<T>

The sorted collection classes (see Figure 16.4) differ from unsorted implementation collections in that the elements are sorted by key for SortedDictionary<TKey, TValue> and by value for SortedList<T>. (There is also a nongeneric SortedList implementation.) A foreach iteration of sorted collections returns the elements sorted in key order (see Listing 16.8).

LISTING 16.8: Using SortedDictionary<TKey, TValue>

```
using System;
using System.Collections.Generic;

class Program
{
  static void Main()
  {
      SortedDictionary<string,string> sortedDictionary =
          new SortedDictionary<string,string>();

      int index =0;

      sortedDictionary.Add(index++.ToString(), "object");
      // ...
      sortedDictionary.Add(index++.ToString(), "string");

      Console.WriteLine("Key  Value    Hashcode");
      Console.WriteLine--- ------- ----------");
      foreach (
          KeyValuePair<string, string> i in sortedDictionary)
      {
          Console.WriteLine("{0,-5}{1,-9}{2}",
              i.Key, i.Value, i.Key.GetHashCode());
      }
  }
}
```

The results of Listing 16.8 appear in Output 16.4.

OUTPUT 16.4:

```
Key   Value     Hashcode
---   -----     --------
0     object    -842352752
1     byte      -842352753
10    sbyte     -843401329
11    short     -843466865
12    long      -843532401
13    void      -843597937
14    double    -843663473
15    string    -843729009
2     uint      -842352754
3     ulong     -842352755
4     float     -842352756
5     char      -842352757
6     bool      -842352758
7     ushort    -842352759
8     decimal   -842352744
9     int       -842352745
```

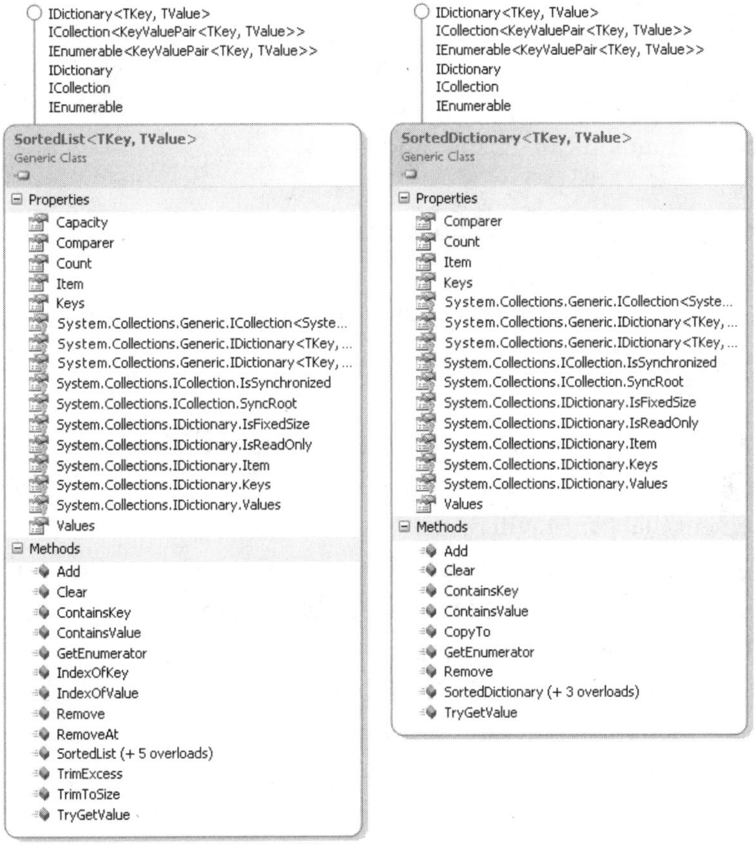

IDictionary<TKey, TValue>
ICollection<KeyValuePair<TKey, TValue>>
IEnumerable<KeyValuePair<TKey, TValue>>
IDictionary
ICollection
IEnumerable

SortedList<TKey, TValue>
Generic Class

Properties
- Capacity
- Comparer
- Count
- Item
- Keys
- System.Collections.Generic.ICollection<Syste...
- System.Collections.Generic.IDictionary<TKey, ...
- System.Collections.Generic.IDictionary<TKey, ...
- System.Collections.ICollection.IsSynchronized
- System.Collections.ICollection.SyncRoot
- System.Collections.IDictionary.IsFixedSize
- System.Collections.IDictionary.IsReadOnly
- System.Collections.IDictionary.Item
- System.Collections.IDictionary.Keys
- System.Collections.IDictionary.Values
- Values

Methods
- Add
- Clear
- ContainsKey
- ContainsValue
- GetEnumerator
- IndexOfKey
- IndexOfValue
- Remove
- RemoveAt
- SortedList (+ 5 overloads)
- TrimExcess
- TrimToSize
- TryGetValue

IDictionary<TKey, TValue>
ICollection<KeyValuePair<TKey, TValue>>
IEnumerable<KeyValuePair<TKey, TValue>>
IDictionary
ICollection
IEnumerable

SortedDictionary<TKey, TValue>
Generic Class

Properties
- Comparer
- Count
- Item
- Keys
- System.Collections.Generic.ICollection<Syste...
- System.Collections.Generic.IDictionary<TKey, ...
- System.Collections.Generic.IDictionary<TKey, ...
- System.Collections.ICollection.IsSynchronized
- System.Collections.ICollection.SyncRoot
- System.Collections.IDictionary.IsFixedSize
- System.Collections.IDictionary.IsReadOnly
- System.Collections.IDictionary.Item
- System.Collections.IDictionary.Keys
- System.Collections.IDictionary.Values
- Values

Methods
- Add
- Clear
- ContainsKey
- ContainsValue
- CopyTo
- GetEnumerator
- Remove
- SortedDictionary (+ 3 overloads)
- TryGetValue

FIGURE 16.4: SortedList<> and SortedDictionary<> Class Diagrams

Note that the elements in the key (not the value) are in alphabetical rather than numerical order, because the data type of the key is a string, not an integer.

When inserting or removing elements from a sorted dictionary collection, maintenance of order within the collection slightly increases execution time when compared to the straight dictionary classes described earlier. Behaviorally, there are two internal arrays, one for key retrieval and one for index retrieval. On a `System.Collections.Sorted` sorted list, indexing is supported via the `GetByIndex()` and `SetByIndex()` methods. With `System.Collections.Generic.SortedList<TKey, TValue>`, the `Keys` and `Values` properties return `IList<TKey>` and `IList<TValue>` instances, respectively. These methods enable the sorted list to behave both as a dictionary and as a list type collection.

Stack Collections: `Stack<T>`

Chapter 11 discussed the stack collection classes (see Figure 16.5). The stack collection classes are designed as last in, first out (LIFO) collections. The two key methods are `Push()` and `Pop()`.

- `Push()` places elements into the collection. The elements do not have to be unique.
- `Pop()` retrieves and removes elements in the reverse order of how they were added.

To access the elements on the stack without modifying the stack, you use the `Peek()` and `Contains()` methods. The `Peek()` method returns the next element that `Pop()` will retrieve.

As with most collection classes, you use the `Contains()` method to determine whether an element exists anywhere in the stack. As with all collections, it is also possible to use a `foreach` loop to iterate over the elements in a stack. This allows you to access values from anywhere in the stack. Note, however, that accessing a value via the `foreach` loop does not remove it from the stack. Only `Pop()` provides this functionality.

Queue Collections: Queue<T>

Queue collection classes, shown in Figure 16.6, are identical to stack collection classes, except they follow the ordering pattern of first in, first out (FIFO). In place of the Pop() and Push() methods are the Enqueue() and Dequeue() methods. The queue collection behaves like a circular array or pipe. You place objects into the queue at one end using the Enqueue() method, and you remove them from the other end using the Dequeue() method. As with stack collection classes, the objects do not have to be unique, and queue collection classes automatically increase in size as required. When data is no longer needed, you recover the capacity using the TrimToSize() method.

Linked Lists: LinkedList<T>

In addition, System.Collections.Generic supports a linked list collection that enables both forward and reverse traversal. Figure 16.7 shows the class diagram. Notice there is no corresponding nongeneric type.

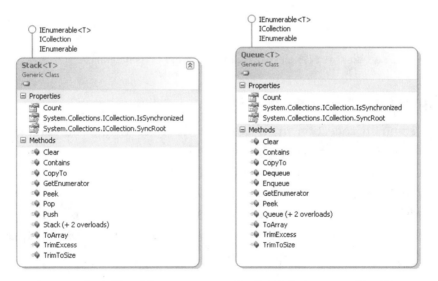

FIGURE 16.5: Stack<T> Class Diagram

FIGURE 16.6: Queue<T> Class Diagram

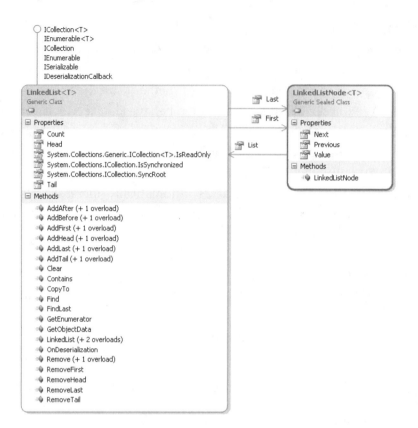

FIGURE 16.7: `LinkedList<T>` and `LinkedListNode<T>` Class Diagrams

Providing an Index Operator

The common collection interfaces provide much of the foundation for what members are needed when implementing custom collections. However, there is one more member: the **index operator.**

The index operator is a pair of square brackets that are generally used to index into a collection. Not only is this available on each collection type, but it is also a member that programmers can add to their custom classes. Listing 16.9 shows an example using `Pair<T>`.

LISTING 16.9: Defining an Index Operator

```
interface IPair<T>
{
  T First
  {
      get;
  }
```

```
   T Second
   {
      get;
   }

   T this[PairItem index]
   {
      get;
   }
}
```

```
public enum PairItem
{
   First,
   Second
}
```

```
public struct Pair<T> : IPair<T>
{
   public Pair(T first, T second)
   {
      _first = first;
      _second = second;
   }
   public T First
   {
      get{ return _first; }
      private set{ _first = value; }
   }
   private T _first;
   public T Second
   {
      get{ return _second; }
      private set{ _second = value; }
   }
   private T _second;

   public T this[PairItem index]
   {
      get
      {
         switch (index)
         {
            case PairItem.First:
               return First;
            case PairItem.Second:
               return Second;
            default :
               throw new NotImplementedException(
                  string.Format(
```

```
                              "The enum {0} has not been implemented",
                              index.ToString()));
                    }
            }
        set
        {
            switch (index)
            {
                case PairItem.First:
                    First = value;
                    break;
                case PairItem.Second:
                    Second = value;
                    break;
                default:
                    throw new NotImplementedException(
                        string.Format(
                        "The enum {0} has not been implemented",
                        index.ToString()));
            }
        }
    }
}
```

To define an index operator, you must name the member this and follow it with square brackets that identify the parameters. The implementation is like a property with get and set blocks. As Listing 16.9 shows, the parameter does not have to be an int, and in fact, the index can take multiple parameters and can even be overloaded. This example uses an enum to reduce the likelihood that callers will supply an index for a nonexistent item.

The resultant CIL code the C# compiler creates from an index operator is a special property called Item that takes an argument. Properties that accept arguments cannot be created explicitly in C#, so the Item property is unique in this aspect. This is because any additional member with the identifier Item, even if it has an entirely different signature, will conflict with the compiler-created member, and will therefore not be allowed.

■ ADVANCED TOPIC

Assigning the Indexer Property Name Using IndexerName
As indicated earlier, the CIL property name for an indexer defaults to Item. Using the IndexerNameAttribute you can specify a different name, however. Listing 16.10, for example, changes the name to "Entry".

LISTING 16.10: Changing the Indexer's Default Name

```
[System.Runtime.CompilerServices.IndexerName("Entry")]
public T this[params PairItem[] branches]
{
    // ...
}
```

This makes no difference to C# callers of the index, but it specifies the name for languages that do not support indexers directly.

Compilers consume this attribute and modify the generated CIL code. The attribute itself does not appear in the CIL output, and therefore, it is not available via reflection.

ADVANCED TOPIC

Defining an Index Operator with Variable Parameters

An index operator can also take a variable parameter list. For example, Listing 16.11 defines an index operator for BinaryTree<T> discussed in Chapter 11 (and again in the next section).

LISTING 16.11: Defining an Index Operator with Variable Parameters

```
using System;
using System.Collections.Generic;

public class BinaryTree<T>:
    IEnumerable<T>
{

    // ...

    public T this[params PairItem[] branches]
    {
        get
        {
            BinaryTree<T> currentNode = this;
            int totalLevels =
                (branches == null) ? 0 : branches.Length;
            int currentLevel = 0;

            while (currentLevel < totalLevels)
            {
                currentNode = currentNode.SubItems[
                    branches[currentLevel]];
                if (currentNode == null)
```

```
        {
            // The binary tree at this location is null.
            throw new IndexOutOfRangeException();
        }
        currentLevel++;
    }

    return currentNode.Value;
}
set
{
    // ...
}
    }
}
```

Each item within branches is a PairItem and indicates which branch to navigate down in the binary tree.

Returning Null or an Empty Collection

When returning an array or collection, you must indicate that there are zero items by returning either null or a collection instance with no items. The better choice in general is to return a collection instance with no items. In so doing, you avoid forcing the caller to check for null before iterating over the items in the collection. For example, given a zero-size IEnumerable<T> collection, the caller can immediately and safely use a foreach loop over the collection without concern that the generated call to GetEnumerator() will throw a NullReferenceException.

One of the few times to deviate from this guideline is when null is intentionally indicating something different from zero items. A null value for a phone number on a string, for example, may indicate that the phone number is not set, and an empty string could indicate explicitly that there is no phone number.

Iterators

Earlier, this chapter went into detail on the internals of the foreach loop. This section discusses how to use **iterators** to create your own implementation of the IEnumerator<T> and nongeneric IEnumerator interfaces for custom collections. Iterators provide clean syntax for specifying how to iterate on data in collection classes, especially using the foreach loop. The iterator allows end-users of a collection to navigate its internal structure without knowledge of that structure.

ADVANCED TOPIC

Origin of Iterators
In 1972, Barbara Liskov and a team of scientists at MIT began researching programming methodologies, focusing on user-defined data abstractions. To prove much of their work, they created a language called CLU that had a concept called "clusters" (CLU being the first three letters), a predecessor to the primary data abstraction programmers use today, objects. As part of their research, the team realized that although they were able to use the CLU language to abstract some data representation away from end-users of their types, they consistently found themselves having to reveal the inner structure of their data in order to allow others to intelligently consume it. Through their consternation came the creation of a language construct called an iterator. (The CLU language offered many insights into what would eventually be popularized as object-oriented programming.)

If classes want to support iteration using the foreach loop construct, they must implement the enumerator pattern. As you saw in the earlier section, in C# the foreach loop construct is expanded by the compiler into the while loop construct based on the IEnumerator<T> interface that is retrieved from the IEnumerable<T> interface.

The problem with the enumeration pattern is that it can be cumbersome to implement manually, because it maintains an internal state machine. This internal state machine may be simple for a list collection type class, but for data structures that require recursive traversal, such as binary trees, the state machine can be quite complicated. To overcome the challenges and effort associated with implementing this pattern, C# 2.0 included a construct that makes it easier for a class to dictate how the foreach loop iterates over its contents.

Defining an Iterator

Iterators are a means to implement methods of a class, and they are syntactic shortcuts for the more complex enumerator pattern. When the C# compiler encounters an iterator, it expands its contents into CIL code that implements the enumerator pattern. As such, there are no runtime dependencies for implementing iterators. Because the C# compiler handles implementation through CIL code generation, there is no real runtime performance benefit to using iterators. However, there is a substantial programmer productivity gain in choosing iterators over manual implementation of the enumerator pattern. To begin, the next section examines how an iterator is defined in code.

Iterator Syntax

An iterator provides shorthand implementation of iterator interfaces, the combination of the IEnumerable<T> and IEnumerator<T> interfaces. Listing 16.12 declares an iterator for the generic BinaryTree<T> type by creating a GetEnumerator() method. Next, you will add support for the iterator interfaces.

LISTING 16.12: Iterator Interfaces Pattern

```
using System;
using System.Collections.Generic;

public class BinaryTree<T>:
    IEnumerable<T>
{
    public BinaryTree ( T value)
    {
        Value = value;
    }

    #region IEnumerable<T>
    public IEnumerator<T> GetEnumerator()
    {
        ...
    }
    #endregion IEnumerable<T>

    public T Value
    {
        get{ return _value;    }
        set{ _value = value;     }
```

```
        }
        private T _value;

        public Pair<BinaryTree<T>> SubItems
        {
            get{ return _subItems; }
            set{ _subItems = value;      }
        }
        private Pair<BinaryTree<T>> _subItems;
    }

    public struct Pair<T>
    {
        public Pair(T first, T second)
        {
            _first = first;
            _second = second;
        }
        public T First
        {
            get{ return _first; }
            private set{ _first = value; }
        }
        private T _first;
        public T Second
        {
            get{ return _second; }
            private set{ _second = value; }
        }
        private T _second;
    }
```

To begin, add the declaration for the IEnumerator<T> IEnumerable<T>
.GetEnumerator() method.

Yielding Values from an Iterator

Iterators are like functions, but instead of returning values, they *yield* them.
In the case of BinaryTree<T>, the yield type of the iterator corresponds to the
type parameter, T. If the nongeneric version of IEnumerator is used, then the
return type will instead be object. To correctly implement the iterator pattern, you need to maintain an internal state machine in order to keep track of
where you are while enumerating the collection. In the BinaryTree<T> case,
you track which elements within the tree have already been enumerated and
which are still to come.

Iterators have built-in state machines to keep track of the current and next elements. The `yield return` statement returns values each time an iterator encounters it. Then, when the next iteration starts, the code begins to execute immediately following the last `yield return` statement. In Listing 16.13, you return the C# primitive data type keywords sequentially.

LISTING 16.13: Yielding the C# Keywords Sequentially

```csharp
using System;
using System.Collections.Generic;

public class CSharpPrimitiveTypes; IEnumerable<string>
{
  public IEnumerator<string> GetEnumerator()
  {
      yield return "object";
      yield return "byte";
      yield return "uint";
      yield return "ulong";
      yield return "float";
      yield return "char";
      yield return "bool";
      yield return "ushort";
      yield return "decimal";
      yield return "int";
      yield return "sbyte";
      yield return "short";
      yield return "long";
      yield return "void";
      yield return "double";
      yield return "string";
  }

      // IEnumerator also required because IEnumerator<T>
      // derives from it.
    System.Collections.IEnumerator
      System.Collections.IEnumerable.GetEnumerator()
  {
      // Invoke IEnumerator<string> GetEnumerator() above
      return GetEnumerator();
  }
}

public class Program
{
  static void Main()
  {
```

```
        CSharpPrimitiveTypes primitives =
            new CSharpPrimitiveTypes();

        foreach (string primitive in primitives)
        {
            Console.WriteLine(primitive);
        }
    }
}
```

The results of Listing 16.13 appear in Output 16.5.

OUTPUT 16.5:

```
object
byte
uint
ulong
float
char
bool
ushort
decimal
int
sbyte
short
long
void
double
string
```

The output from this listing is a listing of the C# primitive types.[1]

Iterators and State

When an iterator is first called in a foreach statement (such as foreach (string primitive in primitives) in Listing 16.13), its state is initialized within the enumerator. The iterator maintains its state as long as the foreach statement at the call site continues to execute. When you yield a value, process it, and resume the foreach statement at the call site, the iterator continues where it left off the previous time around the loop and

---

1. In alpha versions of the C# 2.0 compiler, yield was a keyword rather than a contextual keyword. However, such a change could result in an incompatibility between C# 1.0 and C# 2.0. Instead, yield became a contextual keyword that must appear before return. As a result, no code-breaking change occurred because C# 1.0 did not allow any text (besides comments) prior to the return keyword.

continues processing. When the `foreach` statement at the call site terminates, the iterator's state is no longer saved. It is always safe to call the iterator again since the generated code never resets the state of the iterator but instead creates a new one when needed.

Figure 16.8 shows a high-level sequence diagram of what takes place. Remember that the `MoveNext()` method appears on the `IEnumerator<T>` interface.

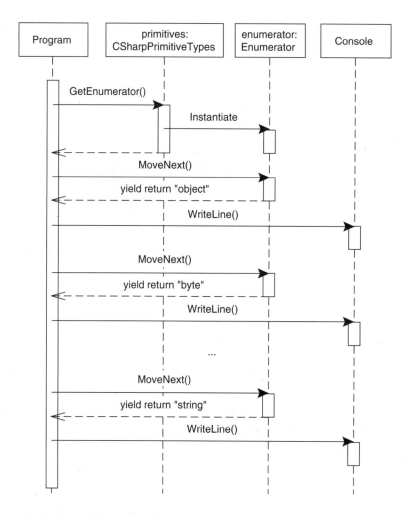

FIGURE 16.8: Sequence Diagram with `yield return`

In Listing 16.13, the `foreach` statement at the call site initiates a call to `GetEnumerator()` on the `CSharpPrimitiveTypes` instance called primitives. Given the iterator instance (referenced by `iterator`), `foreach` begins each iteration with a call to `MoveNext()`. Within the iterator, you yield a value back to the `foreach` statement at the call site. After the `yield return` statement, the `GetEnumerator()` method seemingly pauses until the next `MoveNext()` request. Back at the call site, the `foreach` statement displays the yielded value on the screen. It then loops back around and calls `MoveNext()` on the iterator again. Notice that the second time, processing picks up at the second `yield return` statement. Once again, the `foreach` displays on the screen what `CSharpPrimitiveTypes` yielded and starts the loop again. This process continues until there are no more `yield return` statements within the iterator. At that point, the `foreach` loop at the call site terminates.

More Iterator Examples

Before you modify `BinaryTree<T>`, you must modify `Pair<T>` to support the `IEnumerable<T>` interface using an iterator. Listing 16.14 is an example that yields each element in `Pair<T>`.

LISTING 16.14: Using `yield` to Implement `BinaryTree<T>`

```csharp
public struct Pair<T>: IPair<T>,
    IEnumerable<T>
{
    public Pair(T first, T second)
    {
        _first = first;
        _second = second;
    }
    public T First
    {
        get{ return _first; }
        private set{ _first = value; }
    }
    private T _first;
    public T Second
    {
        get{ return _second; }
        private set{ _second = value; }
    }
```

```csharp
    private T _second;

    #region IEnumerable<T>
    public IEnumerator<T> GetEnumerator()
    {
        yield return First;
        yield return Second;
    }
    #endregion IEnumerable<T>

    #region IEnumerable Members
    System.Collections.IEnumerator
        System.Collections.IEnumerable.GetEnumerator
    {
        return GetEnumerator();
    }
    #endregion
}
```

In Listing 16.14, the iteration over the Pair<T> data type loops twice: first through yield return First, and then through yield return Second. Each time the yield return statement within GetEnumerator() is encountered, the state is saved and execution appears to "jump" out of the GetEnumerator() method context and into the context of the call site. When the second iteration starts, GetEnumerator() begins to execute again with the yield return Second statement.

System.Collections.Generic.IEnumerable<T> inherits from System.Collections.IEnumerable. Therefore, when implementing IEnumerable<T>, it is also necessary to implement IEnumerable. In Listing 16.14, you do so explicitly, and the implementation simply involves a call to IEnumerable<T>'s GetEnumerator() implementation. This call from IEnumerable.GetEnumerator() to IEnumerable<T>.GetEnumerator() will always work because of the type compatibility (via inheritance) between IEnumerable<T> and IEnumerable. Since the signatures for both GetEnumerator()s are identical (the return type does not distinguish a signature), one or both implementations must be explicit. Given the additional type safety offered by IEnumerable<T>'s version, you implement IEnumerable's implementation explicitly.

Listing 16.15 uses the Pair<T>.GetEnumerator() method and displays "Inigo" and "Montoya" on two consecutive lines.

```csharp
Pair<string> fullname = new Pair<string>("Inigo", "Montoya");
foreach (string name in fullname)
{
    Console.WriteLine(name);
}
```

Notice that the call to `GetEnumerator()` is implicit within the `foreach` loop.

Placing a `yield return` within a Loop

It is not necessary to hardcode each `yield return` statement, as you did in both `CSharpPrimitiveTypes` and `Pair<T>`. Using the `yield return` statement, you can return values from inside a loop construct. Listing 16.16 uses a `foreach` loop. Each time the `foreach` within `GetEnumerator()` executes, it returns the next value.

```csharp
public class BinaryTree<T>: IEnumerable<T>
{
  // ...

  #region IEnumerable<T>
  public IEnumerator<T> GetEnumerator()
  {
      // Return the item at this node.
      yield return Value;

      // Iterate through each of the elements in the pair.
      foreach (BinaryTree<T> tree in SubItems)
      {
          if (tree != null)
          {
              // Since each element in the pair is a tree,
              // traverse the tree and yield each
              // element.
              foreach (T item in tree)
              {
                  yield return item;
              }
          }
      }
  }
  #endregion IEnumerable<T>
```

```
#region IEnumerable Members
System.Collections.IEnumerator
    System.Collections.IEnumerable.GetEnumerator()
{
    return GetEnumerator();
}
#endregion
}
```

In Listing 16.16, the first iteration returns the root element within the binary tree. During the second iteration you traverse the pair of subelements. If the subelement pair contains a non-null value, then you traverse into that child node and yield its elements. Note that `foreach(T item in tree)` is a recursive call to a child node.

As observed with `CSharpPrimitiveTypes` and `Pair<T>`, you can now iterate over `BinaryTree<T>` using a `foreach` loop. Listing 16.17 demonstrates this, and Output 16.6 shows the results.

LISTING 16.17: Using foreach with BinaryTree\<string>

```
// JFK
jfkFamilyTree = new BinaryTree<string>(
    "John Fitzgerald Kennedy");

jfkFamilyTree.SubItems = new Pair<BinaryTree<string>>(
    new BinaryTree<string>("Joseph Patrick Kennedy"),
    new BinaryTree<string>("Rose Elizabeth Fitzgerald"));

// Grandparents (Father's side)
jfkFamilyTree.SubItems.First.SubItems =
    new Pair<BinaryTree<string>>(
    new BinaryTree<string>("Patrick Joseph Kennedy"),
    new     BinaryTree<string>("Mary Augusta Hickey"));

// Grandparents (Mother's side)
jfkFamilyTree.SubItems.Second.SubItems =
    new Pair<BinaryTree<string>>(
    new BinaryTree<string>("John Francis Fitzgerald"),
    new BinaryTree<string>("Mary Josephine Hannon"));
foreach (string name in jfkFamilyTree)
{
    Console.WriteLine(name);
}
```

OUTPUT 16.6:

```
John Fitzgerald Kennedy
Joseph Patrick Kennedy
Patrick Joseph Kennedy
Mary Augusta Hickey
Rose Elizabeth Fitzgerald
John Francis Fitzgerald
Mary Josephine Hannon
```

■ BEGINNER TOPIC

struct **versus** class

An interesting side effect of defining Pair<T> as a struct rather than a class is that SubItems.First and SubItems.Second cannot be assigned directly. The following will produce a compile error indicating that Sub-Items cannot be modified, "because it is not a variable":

```
jfkFamilyTree.SubItems.First =
    new BinaryTree<string>("Joseph Patrick Kennedy");
```

The issue is that SubItems is a property of type Pair<T>, a struct. Therefore, when the property returns the value, a copy of _SubItems is made, and assigning First on a copy that is promptly lost at the end of the statement would be misleading. Fortunately, the C# compiler prevents this.

To overcome the issue, don't assign it (see the approach in Listing 16.17), use class rather than struct for Pair<T>, don't create a SubItems property and instead use a field, or provide properties in BinaryTree<T> that give direct access to _SubItems members.

Canceling Further Iteration: yield break

Sometimes you might want to cancel further iteration. You can do this by including an if statement so that no further statements within the code are executed. However, you can also jump back to the call site, causing MoveNext() to return false. Listing 16.18 shows an example of such a method.

LISTING 16.18: Escaping Iteration via `yield break`

```
public System.Collections.Generic.IEnumerable<T>
    GetNotNullEnumerator()
{
    if((First == null) || (Second == null))
    {
        yield break;
    }
    yield return Second;
    yield return First;
}
```

This method cancels the iteration if either of the elements in the `Pair<T>` class is `null`.

A `yield break` statement is similar to placing a `return` statement at the top of a function when it is determined that there is no work to do. It is a way to exit from further iterations without surrounding all remaining code with an `if` block. As such, it allows multiple exits, and therefore, you should use it with caution because casual reading of the code may miss the early exit.

■ ADVANCED TOPIC

How Iterators Work

When the C# compiler encounters an iterator, it expands the code into the appropriate CIL for the corresponding enumerator design pattern. In the generated code, the C# compiler first creates a nested private class to implement the `IEnumerator<T>` interface, along with its `Current` property and a `MoveNext()` method. The `Current` property returns a type corresponding to the return type of the iterator. Listing 16.14 of `Pair<T>` contains an iterator that returns a `T` type. The C# compiler examines the code contained within the iterator and creates the necessary code within the `MoveNext` method and the `Current` property to mimic its behavior. For the `Pair<T>` iterator, the C# compiler generates roughly equivalent code (see Listing 16.19).

LISTING 16.19: C# Equivalent of Compiler-Generated C# Code for Iterators

```
using System;
using System.Collections.Generic;
```

```csharp
public class Pair<T> : IPair<T>, IEnumerable<T>
{
  // ...

  // The iterator is expanded into the following
  // code by the compiler
  public virtual IEnumerator<T> GetEnumerator()
  {
      __ListEnumerator result = new __ListEnumerator(0);
      result._Pair = this;
      return result;
  }
  public virtual System.Collections.IEnumerator
      System.Collections.IEnumerable.GetEnumerator()
  {
      return new GetEnumerator();
  }

  private sealed class __ListEnumerator<T> : IEnumerator<T>
  {
      public __ListEnumerator(int itemCount)
      {
          _ItemCount = itemCount;
      }

      Pair<T> _Pair;
      T _Current;
      int _ItemCount;

      public object Current
      {
          get
          {
              return _Current;
          }
      }

      public bool MoveNext()
      {
          switch (_ItemCount)
          {
              case 0:
                  _Current = _Pair.First;
                  _ItemCount++;
                  return true;
              case 1:
                  _Current = _Pair.Second;
                  _ItemCount++;
```

```
                        return true;
                default:
                        return false;
            }
        }
    }
}
```

Because the compiler takes the `yield return` statement and generates classes that correspond to what you probably would have written manually, iterators in C# exhibit the same performance characteristics as classes that implement the enumerator design pattern manually. Although there is no performance improvement, the programmer productivity gained is significant.

Creating Multiple Iterators in a Single Class

Previous iterator examples implemented `IEnumerable<T>.GetEnumerator()`. This is the method that `foreach` seeks implicitly. Sometimes you might want different iteration sequences, such as iterating in reverse, filtering the results, or iterating over an object projection other than the default. You can declare additional iterators in the class by encapsulating them within properties or methods that return `IEnumerable<T>` or `IEnumerable`. If you want to iterate over the elements of `Pair<T>` in reverse, for example, you provide a `GetReverseEnumerator()` method, as shown in Listing 16.20.

LISTING 16.20: Using `yield return` in a Method That Returns `IEnumerable<T>`

```
public struct Pair<T>: IEnumerable<T>
{
    ...

    public IEnumerable<T> GetReverseEnumerator()
    {
        yield return Second;
        yield return First;
    }
    ...
}

public void Main()
{
    Pair<string> game = new Pair<string>("Redskins", "Eagles");
```

```
    foreach (string name in game.GetReverseEnumerator())
    {
        Console.WriteLine(name);
    }
}
```

Note that you return IEnumerable<T>, not IEnumerator<T>. This is different from IEnumerable<T>.GetEnumerator(), which returns IEnumerator<T>. The code in Main() demonstrates how to call GetReverseEnumerator() using a foreach loop.

yield **Statement Characteristics**

You can declare the yield return statement only in members that return an IEnumerator<T> or IEnumerable<T> type, or their nongeneric equivalents. More specifically, you can use yield only in GetEnumerator() methods that return IEnumerator<T>, or in methods that return IEnumerable<T> but are not called GetEnumerator().

Methods that include a yield return statement may not have a simple return. If the method uses the yield return statement, then the C# compiler generates the necessary code to maintain the state machine for the iterator. In contrast, if the method uses the return statement instead of yield return, the programmer is responsible for maintaining his own state machine and returning an instance of one of the iterator interfaces. Further, just as all code paths in a method with a return type must contain a return statement accompanied by a value (assuming they don't throw an exception), all code paths in an iterator must contain a yield return statement if they are to return any data.

Additional restrictions on the yield statement that result in compiler errors are as follows.

- The yield statement may not appear outside a method, operator, or property accessor.
- The yield statement may not appear in an anonymous method (see Chapter 12).
- The yield statement may not appear inside the catch and finally clauses of the try statement. Furthermore, a yield statement may appear in a try block only if there is no catch block.

SUMMARY

The generic collection classes and interfaces made available in C# 2.0 are universally superior to their nongeneric counterparts; by avoiding boxing penalties and enforcing type rules at compile time, they are faster and safer. Unless you are limited to C# 1.0, you should consider the entire namespace of `System.Collections` as obsolete (in fact, it has been excluded from the Silverlight CLR entirely). In other words, don't go back and necessarily remove all code that already uses this namespace. Instead, use `System.Collections.Generics` for any new code and, over time, consider migrating existing code to use the corresponding generic collections which contain both the interfaces and the classes for working with collections of objects.

Providing the `System.Collections.Generic` namespace is not the only change that C# 2.0 brought to collections. Another significant addition is the iterator. Iterators involve a new contextual keyword, `yield`, that C# uses to generate underlying CIL code that implements the iterator pattern used by the `foreach` loop.

■ 17 ■
Reflection, Attributes, and Dynamic Programming

TTRIBUTES ARE A MEANS of inserting additional metadata into an assembly and associating the metadata with a programming construct such as a class, method, or property. This chapter investigates the details surrounding attributes that are built into the framework, as well as how to define custom attributes. In order to take advantage of custom attributes, it is necessary to identify them. This is handled through reflection. This chapter begins with a look at reflection, including how you can use it to dynamically bind at runtime and call a member using its name at compile time. This is frequently performed within tools such as a code generator. In addition, reflection is used at execution time when the call target is unknown.

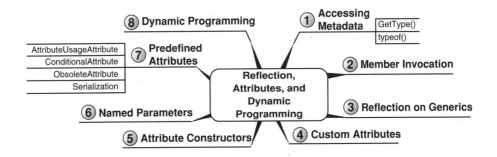

The chapter ends with a discussion of dynamic programming, a feature added in C# 4.0 that greatly simplifies working with data that is dynamic and requires execution-time rather than compile-time binding.

Reflection

Using reflection, it is possible to do the following:

- Access the metadata for types within an assembly. This includes constructs such as the full type name, member names, and any attributes decorating the construct.
- Dynamically invoke a type's member at runtime using the metadata, rather than a compile-time-defined binding.

Reflection is the process of examining the metadata within an assembly. Traditionally, when code compiles down to a machine language, all the metadata (such as type and method names) about the code is discarded. In contrast, when C# compiles into the CIL, it maintains most of the metadata about the code. Furthermore, using reflection, it is possible to enumerate through all the types within an assembly and search for those that match certain criteria. You access a type's metadata through instances of System.Type, and this object includes methods for enumerating the type instance's members. Furthermore, it is possible to invoke those members on particular objects that are of the examined type.

The facility for reflection enables a host of new paradigms that otherwise are unavailable. For example, reflection enables you to enumerate over all the types within an assembly, along with their members, and in the process create stubs for documentation of the assembly API. You can then combine the metadata retrieved from reflection with the XML document created from XML comments (using the /doc switch) to create the API documentation. Similarly, programmers use reflection metadata to generate code for persisting (serializing) business objects into a database. It could also be used in a list control that displays a collection of objects. Given the collection, a list control could use reflection to iterate over all the properties of an object in the collection, defining a column within the list for each property. Furthermore, by invoking each property on each object, the list control could populate each row and column with the data contained in the object, even though the data type of the object is unknown at compile time.

XmlSerializer, ValueType, and DataBinder are a few of the classes in the framework that use reflection for portions of their implementation as well.

Accessing Metadata Using System.Type

The key to reading a type's metadata is to obtain an instance of System.Type that represents the target type instance. System.Type provides all the methods for retrieving the information about a type. You can use it to answer questions such as the following.

- What is the type's name (Type.Name)?
- Is the type public (Type.IsPublic)?
- What is the type's base type (Type.BaseType)?
- Does the type support any interfaces (Type.GetInterfaces())?
- Which assembly is the type defined in (Type.Assembly)?
- What are a type's properties, methods, fields, and so on (Type.Get-Properties(), Type.GetMethods(), Type.GetFields(), and so on)?
- What attributes decorate a type (Type.GetCustomAttributes())?

There are more such members, but in summary, they all provide information about a particular type. The key is to obtain a reference to a type's Type object, and the two primary ways to do this are through object.GetType() and typeof().

Note that the GetMethods() call does not return extension methods. They are available only as static members on the implementing type.

GetType()

object includes a GetType() member, and therefore, all types include this function. You call GetType() to retrieve an instance of System.Type corresponding to the original object. Listing 17.1 demonstrates this, using a Type instance from DateTime. Output 17.1 shows the results.

LISTING 17.1: Using Type.GetProperties() to Obtain an Object's Public Properties

```
DateTime dateTime = new DateTime();

Type type = dateTime.GetType();
foreach (
    System.Reflection.PropertyInfo property in
        type.GetProperties())
{
    Console.WriteLine(property.Name);
}
```

OUTPUT 17.1:

```
Date
Day
DayOfWeek
DayOfYear
Hour
Kind
Millisecond
Minute
Month
Now
UtcNow
Second
Ticks
TimeOfDay
Today
Year
```

After calling GetType(), you iterate over each System.Reflection.PropertyInfo instance returned from Type.GetProperties() and display the property names. The key to calling GetType() is that you must have an object instance. However, sometimes no such instance is available. Static classes, for example, cannot be instantiated, so there is no way to call GetType().

typeof()

Another way to retrieve a Type object is with the typeof expression. typeof binds at compile time to a particular Type instance, and it takes a type directly as a parameter. Listing 17.2 demonstrates the use of typeof with Enum.Parse().

LISTING 17.2: Using **typeof()** to Create a **System.Type** Instance

```
using System.Diagnostics;
// ...
    ThreadPriorityLevel priority;
    priority = (ThreadPriorityLevel)Enum.Parse(
        typeof(ThreadPriorityLevel), "Idle");
// ...
```

Enum.Parse() takes a Type object identifying an enum and then converts a string to the specific enum value. In this case, it converts "Idle" to System.Diagnostics.ThreadPriorityLevel.Idle.

Member Invocation

The possibilities with reflection don't stop with retrieving the metadata. The next step is to take the metadata and dynamically invoke the members it references. Consider the possibility of defining a class to represent an application's command line. The difficulty with a CommandLineInfo class such as this has to do with populating the class with the actual command-line data that started the application. However, using reflection, you can map the command-line options to property names and then dynamically set the properties at runtime. Listing 17.3 demonstrates this example.

LISTING 17.3: Dynamically Invoking a Member

```
using System;
using System.Diagnostics;

public partial class Program
{
  public static void Main(string[] args)
  {
      string errorMessage;
      CommandLineInfo commandLine = new CommandLineInfo();
      if (!CommandLineHandler.TryParse(
          args, commandLine, out errorMessage))
      {
          Console.WriteLine(errorMessage);
          DisplayHelp();
      }

      if (commandLine.Help)
      {
```

```
                DisplayHelp();
        }
        else
        {
            if (commandLine.Priority !=
                ProcessPriorityClass.Normal)
            {
                // Change thread priority
            }

        }
        // ...

    }

    private static void DisplayHelp()
    {
        // Display the command-line help.
    }
}
```

```
using System;
using System.Diagnostics;

public partial class Program
{
  private class CommandLineInfo
  {
      public bool Help { get; set; }

      public string Out { get; set; }

      public ProcessPriorityClass Priority
      {
          get { return _Priority; }
          set { _Priority = value; }
      }
      private ProcessPriorityClass _Priority =
          ProcessPriorityClass.Normal;
  }

}
```

```
using System;
using System.Diagnostics;
using System.Reflection;

public class CommandLineHandler
{
```

```csharp
public static void Parse(string[] args, object commandLine)
{
    string errorMessage;
    if (!TryParse(args, commandLine, out errorMessage))
    {
        throw new ApplicationException(errorMessage);
    }
}

public static bool TryParse(string[] args, object commandLine,
    out string errorMessage)
{
    bool success = false;
    errorMessage = null;
    foreach (string arg in args)
    {
        string option;
        if (arg[0] == '/' || arg[0] == '-')
        {
            string[] optionParts = arg.Split(
                new char[] { ':' }, 2);

            // Remove the slash|dash
            option = optionParts[0].Remove(0, 1);
            PropertyInfo property =
                commandLine.GetType().GetProperty(option,
                    BindingFlags.IgnoreCase |
                    BindingFlags.Instance |
                    BindingFlags.Public);
            if (property != null)
            {
                if (property.PropertyType == typeof(bool))
                {
                    // Last parameters for handling indexers
                    property.SetValue(
                        commandLine, true, null);
                    success = true;
                }
                else if (
                    property.PropertyType == typeof(string))
                {
                    property.SetValue(
                        commandLine, optionParts[1], null);
                    success = true;
                }
                else if (property.PropertyType.IsEnum)
                {
                    try
                    {
                        property.SetValue(commandLine,
                            Enum.Parse(
```

```
                            typeof(ProcessPriorityClass),
                            optionParts[1], true),
                        null);
                    success = true;
                }
                catch (ArgumentException )
                {
                    success = false;
                    errorMessage =
                        string.Format(
                            "The option '{0}' is " +
                            "invalid for '{1}'",
                            optionParts[1], option);
                }
            }
            else
            {
                success = false;
                errorMessage = string.Format(
                    "Data type '{0}' on {1} is not"
                    + " supported.",
                    property.PropertyType.ToString(),
                    commandLine.GetType().ToString());
            }
        }
        else
        {
            success = false;
            errorMessage = string.Format(
                "Option '{0}' is not supported.",
                option);
        }
    }
}
return success;
    }
}
```

Although Listing 17.3 is long, the code is relatively simple. Main()
begins by instantiating a CommandLineInfo class. This type is defined specifically to contain the command-line data for this program. Each property
corresponds to a command-line option for the program where the command line is as shown in Output 17.2.

OUTPUT 17.2:

```
Compress.exe /Out:<file name> /Help
    /Priority:RealTime|High|AboveNormal|Normal|BelowNormal|Idle
```

The `CommandLineInfo` object is passed to the `CommandLineHandler`'s `TryParse()` method. This method begins by enumerating through each option and separating out the option name (`Help` or `Out`, for example). Once the name is determined, the code reflects on the `CommandLineInfo` object, looking for an instance property with the same name. If the property is found, it assigns the property using a call to `SetValue()` and specifies the data corresponding to the property type. (For arguments, this call accepts the object on which to set the value, the new value, and an additional `index` parameter that is `null` unless the property is an indexer.) This listing handles three property types: Boolean, string, and enum. In the case of enums, you parse the option value and assign the property the text's enum equivalent. Assuming the `TryParse()` call was successful, the method exits and the `CommandLineInfo` object is initialized with the data from the command line.

Interestingly, in spite of the fact that `CommandLineInfo` is a private class nested within `Program`, `CommandLineHandler` has no trouble reflecting over it and even invoking its members. In other words, reflection is able to circumvent accessibility rules as long as appropriate code access security (CAS; see chapter 21) permissions are established. If, for example, `Out` was private, it would still be possible for the `TryParse()` method to assign it a value. Because of this, it would be possible to move `CommandLineHandler` into a separate assembly and share it across multiple programs, each with their own `CommandLineInfo` class.

In this particular example, you invoke a member on `CommandLineInfo` using `PropertyInfo.SetValue()`. Not surprisingly, `PropertyInfo` also includes a `GetValue()` method for retrieving data from the property. For a method, however, there is a `MethodInfo` class with an `Invoke()` member. Both `MethodInfo` and `PropertyInfo` derive from `MemberInfo` (although indirectly), as shown in Figure 17.1.

The CAS permissions are set up to allow private member invocation in this case because the program runs from the local computer, and by default, locally installed programs are part of the trusted zone and have appropriate permissions granted. Programs run from a remote location will need to be explicitly granted such a right.

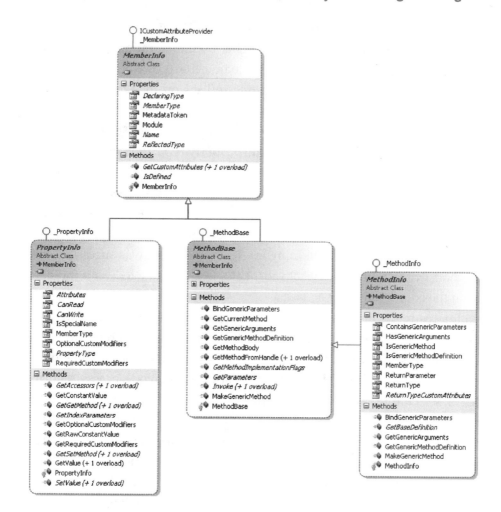

FIGURE 17.1: MemberInfo Derived Classes

Reflection on Generic Types

Just as you can use reflection on nongeneric types, the 2.0 framework included provisions for reflecting on generic types. Runtime reflection on generics determines whether a class or method contains a generic type, and any type parameters or arguments it may include.

Determining the Type of Type Parameters

In the same way that you can use a typeof operator with nongeneric types to retrieve an instance of System.Type, you can use the typeof operator on type parameters in a generic type or generic method. Listing 17.4 applies the typeof operator to the type parameter in the Add method of a Stack class.

LISTING 17.4: Declaring the Stack<T> Class

```
public class Stack<T>
{
    ...
    public void Add(T i)
    {
        ...
        Type t = typeof(T);
        ...
    }
    ...
}
```

Once you have an instance of the Type object for the type parameter, you may then use reflection on the type parameter itself to determine its behavior and tailor the Add method to the specific type more effectively.

Determining Whether a Class or Method Supports Generics

In the System.Type class for CLI 2.0, a handful of methods were added to determine whether a given type supports generic parameters and arguments. A generic argument is a type parameter supplied when a generic class is instantiated. You can determine whether a class or method contains generic parameters that have not yet been set by querying the Type.ContainsGenericParameters Boolean property, as demonstrated in Listing 17.5.

LISTING 17.5: Reflection with Generics

```
using System;

public class Program
{
    static void Main()
    {
        Type type;
        type = typeof(System.Nullable<>);
        Console.WriteLine(type.ContainsGenericParameters);
        Console.WriteLine(type.IsGenericType);

        type = typeof(System.Nullable<DateTime>);
        Console.WriteLine(!type.ContainsGenericParameters);
        Console.WriteLine(type.IsGenericType);
    }
}
```

Output 17.3 shows the results of Listing 17.5.

```
True
True
True
True
```

Type.IsGenericType is a Boolean property that evaluates whether a type is generic.

Obtaining Type Parameters for a Generic Class or Method

You can obtain a list of generic arguments, or type parameters, from a generic class by calling the GetGenericArguments() method. The result is an array of System.Type instances that corresponds to the order in which they are declared as type parameters of the generic class. Listing 17.6 reflects into a generic type and obtains each type parameter. Output 17.4 shows the results.

LISTING 17.6: Using Reflection with Generic Types

```
using System;
using System.Collections.Generic;

public partial class Program
{
  public static void Main()
  {

      Stack<int> s = new Stack<int>();

      Type t = s.GetType();

      foreach(Type type in t.GetGenericArguments())
      {
          System.Console.WriteLine(
              "Type parameter: " + type.FullName);
      }
      // ...
  }
}
```

OUTPUT 17.4:

```
Type parameter: System.Int32
```

Attributes

Before delving into details on how to program attributes, you should consider a use case that demonstrates their utility. In the CommandLine-Handler example in Listing 17.3, you dynamically set a class's properties based on the command-line option matching the property name. This approach is insufficient, however, when the command-line option is an invalid property name. /?, for example, cannot be supported. Furthermore, this mechanism doesn't provide any way of identifying which options are required versus which are optional.

Instead of relying on an exact match between the option name and the property name, attributes provide a way of identifying additional metadata about the decorated construct—in this case, the option that the attribute decorates. With attributes, you can decorate a property as Required and provide a /? option alias. In other words, attributes are a means of associating additional data with a property (and other constructs).

Attributes appear within square brackets preceding the construct they decorate. For example, you can modify the CommandLineInfo class to include attributes, as shown in Listing 17.7.

LISTING 17.7: Decorating a Property with an Attribute

```csharp
class CommandLineInfo
{
  [CommandLineSwitchAlias("?")]
  public bool Help
  {
      get { return _Help; }
      set { _Help = value; }
  }
  private bool _Help;

  [CommandLineSwitchRequired]
  public string Out
  {
      get { return _Out; }
      set { _Out = value; }
  }
  private string _Out;

  public System.Diagnostics.ProcessPriorityClass Priority
  {
      get { return _Priority; }
```

```
        set { _Priority = value; }
    }
    private System.Diagnostics.ProcessPriorityClass _Priority =
        System.Diagnostics.ProcessPriorityClass.Normal;
}
```

In Listing 17.7, the Help and Out properties are decorated with attributes. The purpose of these attributes is to allow an alias of/? for/Help, and to indicate that /Out is a required parameter. The idea is that from within the CommandLineHandler.TryParse() method, you enable support for option aliases and, assuming the parsing was successful, you can check that all the required switches were specified.

There are two ways to combine attributes on the same construct. You can either separate the attributes with commas within the same square brackets, or place each attribute within its own square brackets, as shown in Listing 17.8.

LISTING 17.8: Decorating a Property with Multiple Attributes

```
[CommandLineSwitchRequired]
[CommandLineSwitchAlias("FileName")]
public string Out
{
    get { return _Out; }
    set { _Out = value; }
}
```

```
[CommandLineSwitchRequired,
CommandLineSwitchAlias("FileName")]
public string Out
{
    get { return _Out; }
    set { _Out = value; }
}
```

In addition to decorating properties, developers can use attributes to decorate classes, interfaces, structs, enums, delegates, events, methods, constructors, fields, parameters, return values, assemblies, type parameters, and modules. For the majority of these, applying an attribute involves the same square bracket syntax shown in Listing 17.8. However, this syntax doesn't work for return values, assemblies, and modules.

Assembly attributes are used to add additional metadata about the assembly. Visual Studio's Project Wizard, for example, generates an AssemblyInfo.cs file that includes numerous attributes about the assembly. Listing 17.9 is an example of such a file.

LISTING 17.9: Assembly Attributes within `AssemblyInfo.cs`

```csharp
using System.Reflection;
using System.Runtime.CompilerServices;
using System.Runtime.InteropServices;

// General information about an assembly is controlled
// through the following set of attributes. Change these
// attribute values to modify the information
// associated with an assembly.
[assembly: AssemblyTitle("CompressionLibrary")]
[assembly: AssemblyDescription("")]
[assembly: AssemblyConfiguration("")]
[assembly: AssemblyCompany("Michaelis.net")]
[assembly: AssemblyProduct("CompressionLibrary")]
[assembly: AssemblyCopyright("Copyright © Michaelis.net 2006")]
[assembly: AssemblyTrademark("")]
[assembly: AssemblyCulture("")]

// Setting ComVisible to false makes the types in this
// assembly not visible to COM components. If you need to
// access a type in this assembly from COM, set the ComVisible
// attribute to true on that type.
[assembly: ComVisible(false)]

// The following GUID is for the ID of the typelib if this project is
// exposed to COM
[assembly: Guid("417a9609-24ae-4323-b1d6-cef0f87a42c3")]

// Version information for an assembly consists
// of the following four values:
//
//      Major Version
//      Minor Version
//      Build Number
//      Revision
//
// You can specify all the values or you can
// default the Revision and Build Numbers
// by using the '*' as shown below:
// [assembly: AssemblyVersion("1.0.*")]
[assembly: AssemblyVersion("1.0.0.0")]
[assembly: AssemblyFileVersion("1.0.0.0")]
```

The `assembly` attributes define things such as company, product, and assembly version number. Similar to `assembly`, identifying an attribute usage as `module` requires prefixing it with `module:`. The restriction on `assembly` and `module` attributes is that they appear after the `using` directive but before any namespace or class declarations.

Return attributes, such as the one shown in Listing 17.10, appear before a method declaration but use the same type of syntax structure.

LISTING 17.10: Specifying a Return Attribute

```
[return: Description(
    "Returns true if the object is in a valid state.")]
public bool IsValid()
{
  // ...
  return true;
}
```

In addition to `assembly:` and `return:`, C# allows for explicit target identifications of `module:`, `class:`, and `method:`, corresponding to attributes that decorate the module, class, and method. `class:` and `method:`, however, are optional, as demonstrated earlier.

One of the conveniences of using attributes is that the language takes into consideration the attribute naming convention, which is to place `Attribute` at the end of the name. However, in all the attribute *uses* in the preceding listings, no such suffix appears, despite the fact that each attribute used follows the naming convention. This is because although the full name (`DescriptionAttribute`, `AssemblyVersionAttribute`, and so on) is allowed when applying an attribute, C# makes the suffix optional. Generally, no such suffix appears when *applying* an attribute; it appears only when defining one or using the attribute inline (such as `typeof(DescriptionAttribute)`).

Custom Attributes

Defining a custom attribute is relatively trivial. Attributes are objects; therefore, to define an attribute, you need to define a class. The characteristic that turns a general class into an attribute is that it derives from `System.Attribute`. Therefore, you can create a `CommandLineSwitchRequiredAttribute` class, as shown in Listing 17.11.

LISTING 17.11: Defining a Custom Attribute

```
public class CommandLineSwitchRequiredAttribute : Attribute
{
}
```

With that simple definition, you now can use the attribute as demonstrated in Listing 17.7. So far, no code responds to the attribute; therefore, the Out property that includes the attribute will have no effect on command-line parsing.

Looking for Attributes

In addition to providing properties for reflecting on a type's members, Type includes methods to retrieve the Attributes decorating that type. Similarly, all the reflection types (PropertyInfo and MethodInfo, for example) include members for retrieving a list of attributes that decorate a type. Listing 17.12 defines a method to return a list of required switches that are missing from the command line.

LISTING 17.12: Retrieving a Custom Attribute

```
using System;
using System.Collections.Specialized;
using System.Reflection;

public class CommandLineSwitchRequiredAttribute : Attribute
{
  public static string[] GetMissingRequiredOptions(
      object commandLine)
  {
      StringCollection missingOptions = new StringCollection();
      PropertyInfo[] properties =
          commandLine.GetType().GetProperties();

      foreach (PropertyInfo property in properties)
      {
          Attribute[] attributes =
              (Attribute[])property.GetCustomAttributes(
                  typeof(CommandLineSwitchRequiredAttribute),
                  false);
          if ((attributes.Length > 0) &&
              (property.GetValue(commandLine, null) == null))
          {
              if (property.GetValue(commandLine, null) == null)
              {
```

```
                    missingOptions.Add(property.Name);
            }
        }
    return missingOptions.Add(property.Name);
    }
}
```

The code that checks for an attribute is relatively simple. Given a `Prop-`
`ertyInfo` object (obtained via reflection), you call `GetCustomAttributes()`
and specify the attribute sought, followed by whether to check any overloaded methods. (Alternatively, you can call the `GetCustomAttributes()`
method without the attribute type to return all of the attributes.)

Although it is possible to place code for finding the `CommandLine-`
`SwitchRequiredAttribute` attribute within the `CommandLineHandler`'s
code directly, it makes for better object encapsulation to place the code
within the `CommandLineSwitchRequiredAttribute` class itself. This is frequently the pattern for custom attributes. What better location to place
code for finding an attribute than in a static method on the attribute
class?

Initializing an Attribute through a Constructor

The call to `GetCustomAttributes()` returns an array of objects that will
successfully cast to an `Attribute` array. However, since the attribute in
this example didn't have any instance members, the only metadata information that it provided in the returned attribute was whether it
appeared. Attributes can also encapsulate data, however. Listing 17.13
defines a `CommandLineAliasAttribute` attribute. This is another custom
attribute, and it provides alias command-line options. For example, you
can provide command-line support for /Help or /? as an abbreviation.
Similarly, /S could provide an alias to /Subfolders that indicates that the
command should traverse all the subdirectories.

To support this, you need to provide a constructor on the attribute. Specifically, for the alias you need a constructor that takes a string argument.
(Similarly, if you want to allow multiple aliases, you need to define an
attribute that has a `params string` array for a parameter.)

LISTING 17.13: Providing an Attribute Constructor

```csharp
public class CommandLineSwitchAliasAttribute : Attribute
{
    public CommandLineSwitchAliasAttribute(string alias)
    {
        Alias = alias;
    }

    public string Alias
    {
        get { return _Alias; }
        set { _Alias = value; }
    }
    private string _Alias;
}
```

```csharp
class CommandLineInfo
{
    [CommandLineSwitchAlias("?")]
    public bool Help
    {
        get { return _Help; }
        set { _Help = value; }
    }
    private bool _Help;

    // ...
}
```

The only restriction on the constructor is that when applying an attribute to a construct, only literal values and types (such as `typeof(int)`) are allowed as arguments. This is to enable their serialization into the resultant CIL. Therefore, it is not possible to call a static method when applying an attribute. In addition, providing a constructor that takes arguments of type `System.DateTime` would be of little value, since there is no `System.DateTime` literal.

Given the constructor call, the objects returned from `PropertyInfo.GetCustomAttributes()` will be initialized with the specified constructor arguments, as demonstrated in Listing 17.14.

LISTING 17.14: Retrieving a Specific Attribute and Checking Its Initialization

```csharp
PropertyInfo property =
    typeof(CommandLineInfo).GetProperty("Help");
```

```
CommandLineSwitchAliasAttribute attribute =
    (CommandLineSwitchAliasAttribute)
        property.GetCustomAttributes(
        typeof(CommandLineSwitchAliasAttribute), false)[0];
if(attribute.Alias == "?")
{
  Console.WriteLine("Help(?)");
};
```

Furthermore, as Listing 17.15 and Listing 17.16 demonstrate, you can use similar code in a `GetSwitches()` method on `CommandLineAliasAttribute` that returns a dictionary collection of all the switches, including those from the property names, and associate each name with the corresponding attribute on the command-line object.

LISTING 17.15: **Retrieving Custom Attribute Instances**

```
using System;
using System.Reflection;
using System.Collections.Generic;

public class CommandLineSwitchAliasAttribute : Attribute
{
  public CommandLineSwitchAliasAttribute(string alias)
  {
      Alias = alias;
  }

  public string Alias
  {
      get { return _Alias; }
      set { _Alias = value; }
  }
  private string _Alias;

  public static Dictionary<string, PropertyInfo> GetSwitches(
      object commandLine)
  {
      PropertyInfo[] properties = null;
      Dictionary<string, PropertyInfo> options =
          new Dictionary<string, PropertyInfo>();

      properties = commandLine.GetType().GetProperties(
          BindingFlags.Public | BindingFlags.NonPublic |
          BindingFlags.Instance);
      foreach (PropertyInfo property in properties)
      {
          options.Add(property.Name.ToLower(), property);
```

```
        foreach (CommandLineSwitchAliasAttribute attribute in
            property.GetCustomAttributes(
            typeof(CommandLineSwitchAliasAttribute), false))
        {
            options.Add(attribute.Alias.ToLower(), property);
        }
    }
    return options;
  }
}
```

LISTING 17.16: Updating **CommandLineHandler.TryParse()** to Handle Aliases

```
using System;
using System.Reflection;
using System.Collections.Generic;

public class CommandLineHandler
{
  // ...

  public static bool TryParse(
      string[] args, object commandLine,
      out string errorMessage)
  {
      bool success = false;
      errorMessage = null;

      Dictionary<string, PropertyInfo> options =
          CommandLineSwitchAliasAttribute.GetSwitches(
              commandLine);

      foreach (string arg in args)
      {
          PropertyInfo property;
          string option;
          if (arg[0] == '/' || arg[0] == '-')
          {
              string[] optionParts = arg.Split(
                  new char[] { ':' }, 2);
              option = optionParts[0].Remove(0, 1).ToLower();

              if (options.TryGetValue(option, out property))
              {
                  success = SetOption(
                      commandLine, property,
                      optionParts, ref errorMessage);
              }
              else
              {
```

```csharp
                success = false;
                errorMessage = string.Format(
                    "Option '{0}' is not supported.",
                    option);
            }
        }
    }

    return success;
}

private static bool SetOption(
    object commandLine, PropertyInfo property,
    string[] optionParts, ref string errorMessage)
{
    bool success;

    if (property.PropertyType == typeof(bool))
    {
        // Last parameters for handling indexers
        property.SetValue(
            commandLine, true, null);
        success = true;
    }
    else
    {

        if ((optionParts.Length < 2)
            || optionParts[1] == ""
            || optionParts[1] == ":")
        {
            // No setting was provided for the switch.
            success = false;
            errorMessage = string.Format(
                "You must specify the value for the {0} option.",
                property.Name);
        }
        else if (
            property.PropertyType == typeof(string))
        {
            property.SetValue(
                commandLine, optionParts[1], null);
            success = true;
        }
        else if (property.PropertyType.IsEnum)
        {
            success = TryParseEnumSwitch(
                commandLine, optionParts,
                property, ref errorMessage);
        }
```

```
        else
        {
            success = false;
            errorMessage = string.Format(
                "Data type '{0}' on {1} is not supported.",
                property.PropertyType.ToString(),
                commandLine.GetType().ToString());
        }
    }
    return success;
}
}
```

System.AttributeUsageAttribute

Most attributes are intended to decorate only particular constructs. For example, it makes no sense to allow CommandLineOptionAttribute to decorate a class or an assembly. Those contexts would be meaningless. To avoid inappropriate use of an attribute, custom attributes can be decorated with System.AttributeUsageAttribute. Listing 17.17 (for CommandLine-OptionAttribute) demonstrates how to do this.

LISTING 17.17: **Restricting the Constructs an Attribute Can Decorate**

```
[AttributeUsage(AttributeTargets.Property)]
public class CommandLineSwitchAliasAttribute : Attribute
{
  // ...
}
```

If the attribute is used inappropriately, as it is in Listing 17.18, it will cause a compile-time error, as Output 17.5 demonstrates.

LISTING 17.18: **AttributeUsageAttribute Restricting Where to Apply an Attribute**

```
// ERROR: The attribute usage is restricted to properties
[CommandLineSwitchAlias("?")]
class CommandLineInfo
{
}
```

OUTPUT 17.5:

```
...Program+CommandLineInfo.cs(24,17): error CS0592: Attribute
'CommandLineSwitchAlias' is not valid on this declaration type. It is
valid on 'property, indexer' declarations only.
```

AttributeUsageAttribute's constructor takes an AttributesTargets flag. This enum provides a list of all the possible targets that the runtime allows an attribute to decorate. For example, if you also allowed Command-LineSwitchAliasAttribute on a field, you would update the Attribute-UsageAttribute class as shown in Listing 17.19.

LISTING 17.19: Limiting an Attribute's Usage with AttributeUsageAttribute

```csharp
// Restrict the attribute to properties and methods
[AttributeUsage(
  AttributeTargets.Field | AttributeTargets.Property)]
public class CommandLineSwitchAliasAttribute : Attribute
{
  // ...
}
```

Named Parameters

In addition to restricting what an attribute can decorate, AttributeUsage-Attribute provides a mechanism for allowing duplicates of the same attribute on a single construct. The syntax appears in Listing 17.20.

LISTING 17.20: Using a Named Parameter

```csharp
[AttributeUsage(AttributeTargets.Property, AllowMultiple=true)]
public class CommandLineSwitchAliasAttribute : Attribute
{
  // ...
}
```

The syntax is different from the constructor initialization syntax discussed earlier. The AllowMultiple parameter is a **named parameter,** similar to the name parameter syntax used for optional method parameters (added in C# 4.0). Named parameters provide a mechanism for setting specific public properties and fields within the attribute constructor call, even though the constructor includes no corresponding parameters. The named attributes are optional designations, but they provide a means of setting additional instance data on the attribute without providing a constructor parameter for the purpose. In this case, AttributeUsageAttribute includes a public member called AllowMultiple. Therefore, you can set this member using a named parameter assignment when you use the attribute. Assigning named parameters must occur as the last portion of a constructor, following any explicitly declared constructor parameters.

Named parameters allow for assigning attribute data without providing constructors for every conceivable combination of which attribute properties are specified and which are not. Since many of an attribute's properties may be optional, this is a useful construct in many cases.

BEGINNER TOPIC

FlagsAttribute
Chapter 8 introduced enums and included an Advanced Topic in regard to `FlagsAttribute`. This is a framework-defined attribute that targets enums which represent flag type values. Here is similar text as a Beginner Topic, starting with the sample code shown in Listing 17.21.

LISTING 17.21: Using **FlagsAttribute**

```
// FileAttributes defined in System.IO.

[Flags]  // Decorating an enum with FlagsAttribute.
public enum FileAttributes
{
  ReadOnly =        1<<0,    // 000000000000001
  Hidden =          1<<1,    // 000000000000010
  // ...
}
```

```
using System;
using System.Diagnostics;
using System.IO;

class Program
{
  public static void Main()
  {
    // ...

      string fileName = @"enumtest.txt";
      FileInfo file = new FileInfo(fileName);

      file.Attributes = FileAttributes.Hidden |
        FileAttributes.ReadOnly;

      Console.WriteLine("\"{0}\" outputs as \"{1}\"",
        file.Attributes.ToString().Replace(",", " |"),
```

```
            file.Attributes);

        FileAttributes attributes =
            (FileAttributes)Enum.Parse(typeof(FileAttributes),
            file.Attributes.ToString());

        Console.WriteLine(attributes);

        // ...
    }
}
```

Output 17.6 shows the results of Listing 17.21.

OUTPUT 17.6:

```
"ReadOnly | Hidden" outputs as "ReadOnly, Hidden"
```

The flag documents that the enumeration values can be combined. Furthermore, it changes the behavior of the ToString() and Parse() methods. For example, calling ToString() on an enumeration that is decorated with FlagsAttribute writes out the strings for each enumeration flag that is set. In Listing 17.21, file.Attributes.ToString() returns "ReadOnly, Hidden" rather than the 3 it would have returned without the FlagsAttribute flag. If two enumeration values are the same, the ToString() call would return the first one. As mentioned earlier, however, you should use this with caution because it is not localizable.

Parsing a value from a string to the enumeration also works, provided each enumeration value identifier is separated by a comma.

It is important to note that FlagsAttribute does not automatically assign the unique flag values or check that they have unique values. The values of each enumeration item still must be assigned explicitly.

Predefined Attributes

The AttributeUsageAttribute attribute has a special characteristic that you didn't see in the custom attributes you have created thus far in this book. This attribute affects the behavior of the compiler, causing the compiler to sometimes report an error. Unlike the reflection code you wrote earlier for retrieving `CommandLineRequiredAttribute` and `CommandLine-SwitchAliasAttribute`, `AttributeUsageAttribute` has no runtime code; instead, it has built-in compiler support.

`AttributeUsageAttribute` is a predefined attribute. Not only do such attributes provide additional metadata about the constructs they decorate, but also the runtime and compiler behave differently in order to facilitate these attributes' functionality. Attributes such as `AttributeUsageAttribute`, `FlagsAttribute`, `ObsoleteAttribute`, and `ConditionalAttribute` are examples of predefined attributes. They include special behavior that only the CLI provider or compiler can offer because there are no extension points for additional noncustom attributes. In contrast, custom attributes are entirely passive. Listing 17.21 includes a couple of predefined attributes; Chapter 18 includes a few more.

System.ConditionalAttribute

Within a single assembly, the `System.Diagnostics.ConditionalAttribute` attribute behaves a little like the `#if`/`#endif` preprocessor identifier. However, instead of eliminating the CIL code from the assembly, `System.Diagnostics.ConditionalAttribute` will optionally cause the call to behave like a **no-op,** an instruction that does nothing. Listing 17.22 demonstrates the concept, and Output 17.7 shows the results.

LISTING 17.22: Using Reflection with Generic Types

```
#define CONDITION_A

using System;
using System.Diagnostics;

public class Program
{
  public static void Main()
  {
      Console.WriteLine("Begin...");
      MethodA();
      MethodB();
      Console.WriteLine("End...");
  }

  [Conditional("CONDITION_A")]
  static void MethodA()
  {
```

```
        Console.WriteLine("MethodA() executing...");
    }

    [Conditional("CONDITION_B")]
    static void MethodB()
    {
        Console.WriteLine("MethodB() executing...");
    }
}
```

OUTPUT 17.7:

```
Begin...
MethodA() executing...
End...
```

This example defined CONDITION_A, so MethodA() executed normally. CONDITION_B, however, was not defined either through #define or by using the csc.exe /Define option. As a result, all calls to Program.MethodB() from within this assembly will do nothing and don't even appear in the code.

Functionally, ConditionalAttribute is similar to placing an #if/#endif around the method invocation. The syntax is cleaner, however, because developers create the effect by adding the ConditionalAttribute attribute to the target method without making any changes to the caller itself.

Note that the C# compiler notices the attribute on a called method during compilation, and assuming the preprocessor identifier exists, it eliminates any calls to the method. Note also that ConditionalAttribute does not affect the compiled CIL code on the target method itself (besides the addition of the attribute metadata). Instead, it affects the call site during compilation by removing the calls. This further distinguishes ConditionalAttribute from #if/#endif when calling across assemblies. Because the decorated method is still compiled and included in the target assembly, the determination of whether to call a method is based not on the preprocessor identifier in the callee's assembly, but rather on the caller's assembly. In other words, if you create a second assembly that defines CONDITION_B, any calls to Program.MethodB() from the second assembly will execute. This is a useful characteristic in many tracing and testing scenarios. In fact, calls to `System.Diagnostics.Trace` and `System.Diagnostics.Debug` use this trait with `ConditionalAttributes` on `TRACE` and `DEBUG` preprocessor identifiers.

Because methods don't execute whenever the preprocessor identifier is not defined, `ConditionalAttribute` may not be used on methods that include an out parameter or specify a return other than `void`. Doing so causes a compile-time error. This makes sense because possibly none of the code within the decorated method will execute, so it is unknown what to return to the caller. Similarly, properties cannot be decorated with `ConditionalAttribute`. The `AttributeUsage` (see the section titled `System .AttributeUsageAttribute`, earlier in this chapter) for `ConditionalAttri-bute` is `AttributeTargets.Class` (starting in .NET 2.0) and `Attribute-Targets.Method`. This allows the attribute to be used on either a method or a class. However, the class usage is special because `ConditionalAttribute` is allowed only on `System.Attribute`-derived classes.

When `ConditionalAttribute` decorates a custom attribute, a feature started in .NET 2.0, the latter can be retrieved via reflection only if the conditional string is defined in the calling assembly. Without such a conditional string, reflection that looks for the custom attribute will fail to find it.

System.ObsoleteAttribute

As mentioned earlier, predefined attributes affect the compiler's and/or the runtime's behavior. `ObsoleteAttribute` provides another example of attributes affecting the compiler's behavior. The purpose of `ObsoleteAt-tribute` is to help with the versioning of code, providing a means of indicating to callers that a particular member or type is no longer current. Listing 17.23 is an example of `ObsoleteAttribute` usage. As Output 17.8 shows, any callers that compile code that invokes a member marked with `ObsoleteAttribute` will cause a compile-time warning, optionally an error.

LISTING 17.23: Using `ObsoleteAttribute`

```csharp
class Program
{
  public static void Main()
  {
      ObsoleteMethod();
```

```
    }

    [Obsolete]
    public static void ObsoleteMethod()
    {
    }
}
```

OUTPUT 17.8:

```
c:\SampleCode\ObsoleteAttributeTest.cs(24,17): warning CS0612:
Program.ObsoleteMethod()' is obsolete
```

In this case, `ObsoleteAttribute` simply displays a warning. However, there are two additional constructors on the attribute. One of them, `ObsoleteAttribute(string message)`, appends the additional message argument to the compiler's obsolete message. The best practice for this message is to provide direction on what replaces the obsolete code. The second, however, is a `bool error` parameter that forces the warning to be recorded as an error instead.

`ObsoleteAttribute` allows third parties to notify developers of deprecated APIs. The warning (not an error) allows the original API to work until the developer is able to update the calling code.

Serialization-Related Attributes

Using predefined attributes, the framework supports the capacity to serialize objects onto a stream so that they can be deserialized back into objects at a later time. This provides a means of easily saving a document type object to disk before shutting down an application. Later on, the document may be deserialized so that the user can continue to work on it.

In spite of the fact that an object can be relatively complex and can include links to many other types of objects that also need to be serialized, the serialization framework is easy to use. In order for an object to be serializable, the only requirement is that it includes a `System.SerializableAttribute`. Given the attribute, a formatter class reflects over the serializable object and copies it into a stream (see Listing 17.24).

LISTING 17.24: Saving a Document Using System.SerializableAttribute

```csharp
using System;
using System.IO;
using System.Runtime.Serialization.Formatters.Binary;

class Program
{
  public static void Main()
  {
      Stream stream;
      Document documentBefore = new Document();
      documentBefore.Title =
          "A cacophony of ramblings from my potpourri of notes";
      Document documentAfter;

      using (stream = File.Open(
          documentBefore.Title + ".bin", FileMode.Create))
      {
          BinaryFormatter formatter =
              new BinaryFormatter();
          formatter.Serialize(stream, documentBefore);
      }

      using (stream = File.Open(
          documentBefore.Title + ".bin", FileMode.Open))
      {
          BinaryFormatter formatter =
              new BinaryFormatter();
          documentAfter = (Document)formatter.Deserialize(
              stream);
      }

      Console.WriteLine(documentAfter.Title);
  }
}
```

```csharp
// Serializable classes use SerializableAttribute.
[Serializable]
class Document
{

  public string Title = null;
  public string Data = null;

  [NonSerialized]
  public long _WindowHandle = 0;
```

```
class Image
{
}
[NonSerialized]
private Image Picture = new Image();
}
```

Output 17.9 shows the results of Listing 17.24.

```
A cacophony of ramblings from my potpourri of notes
```

Listing 17.24 serializes and deserializes a Document object. Serialization involves instantiating a formatter (this example uses System.Runtime. Serialization.Formatters.Binary.BinaryFormatter) and calling Serialization() with the appropriate stream object. Deserializing the object simply involves a call to the formatter's Deserialize() method, specifying the stream that contains the serialized object as an argument. However, since the return from Deserialize() is of type object, you also need to cast it specifically to the type that was serialized.

Notice that serialization occurs for the entire object graph (all the items associated with the serialized object [Document] via a field). Therefore, all fields in the object graph also must be serializable.

System.NonSerializable. Fields that are not serializable should be decorated with the System.NonSerializable attribute. This tells the serialization framework to ignore them. The same attribute should appear on fields that should not be persisted for use case reasons. Passwords and Windows handles are good examples of fields that should not be serialized: Windows handles because they change each time a window is re-created, and passwords because data serialized into a stream is not encrypted and can easily be accessed. Consider the Notepad view of the serialized document in Figure 17.2.

Listing 17.24 set the Title field and the resultant *.BIN file includes the text in plain view.

FIGURE 17.2: BinaryFormatter Does Not Encrypt Data

Providing Custom Serialization.   One way to add encryption is to provide custom serialization. Ignoring the complexities of encrypting and decrypting, this requires implementing the ISerializable interface in addition to using SerializableAttribute. The interface requires only the GetObject-Data() method to be implemented. However, this is sufficient only for serialization. In order to also support deserialization, it is necessary to provide a constructor that takes parameters of type System.Runtime.Serialization.SerializationInfo and System.Runtime.Serialization.Streaming-Context (see Listing 17.25).

LISTING 17.25: Implementing System.Runtime.Serialization.ISerializable

```csharp
using System;
using System.Runtime.Serialization;

[Serializable]
class EncryptableDocument :
    ISerializable
{
  public EncryptableDocument(){ }

  enum Field
  {
      Title,
      Data
  }
  public string Title;
  public string Data;

  public static string Encrypt(string data)
  {
      string encryptedData = data;
      // Key-based encryption . . .
```

```
            return encryptedData;
    }

    public static string Decrypt(string encryptedData)
    {
        string data = encryptedData;
      // Key-based decryption. . .
        return data;
    }

#region ISerializable Members
        public void GetObjectData(
        SerializationInfo info, StreamingContext context)
    {
        info.AddValue(
            Field.Title.ToString(), Title);
        info.AddValue(
            Field.Data.ToString(), Encrypt(Data));
    }

    public EncryptableDocument(
        SerializationInfo info, StreamingContext context)
    {
        Title = info.GetString(
            Field.Title.ToString());
        Data = Decrypt(info.GetString(
            Field.Data.ToString()));
    }
#endregion
    }
```

Essentially, the `System.Runtime.Serialization.SerializationInfo` object is a collection of name/value pairs. When serializing, the `GetObject()` implementation calls `AddValue()`. To reverse the process, you call one of the `Get*()` members. In this case, you encrypt and decrypt prior to serialization and deserialization, respectively.

Versioning the Serialization. One more serialization point deserves mentioning: versioning. Objects such as documents may be serialized using one version of an assembly and deserialized using a newer version, sometimes the reverse. Without paying attention, however, version incompatibilities can easily be introduced, sometimes unexpectedly. Consider the scenario shown in Table 17.1.

Surprisingly, even though all you did was to add a new field, deserializing the original file throws a `System.Runtime.Serialization.Serialization`

TABLE 17.1: Deserialization of a New Version Throws an Exception

Step	Description	Code
1	Define a class decorated with System.Serializ-ableAttribute.	```[Serializable] class Document { public string Title; public string Data; }```
2	Add a field or two (public or private) of any serializable type.	
3	Serialize the object to a file called *.v1.bin.	```Stream stream; Document documentBefore = new Document(); documentBefore.Title = "A cacophony of ramblings from my potpourri of notes"; Document documentAfter; using (stream = File.Open(documentBefore.Title + ".bin", FileMode.Create)) { BinaryFormatter formatter = new BinaryFormatter(); formatter.Serialize(stream, documentBefore); }```
4	Add an additional field to the serializable class.	```[Serializable] class Document { public string Title; public string Author; public string Data; }```
5	Deserialize the *v1.bin file into the new object (Document) version.	```using (stream = File.Open(documentBefore.Title + ".bin", FileMode.Open)) { BinaryFormatter formatter = new BinaryFormatter(); documentAfter = (Document)formatter.Deserialize(stream); }```

Exception. This is because the formatter looks for data corresponding to the new field within the stream. Failure to locate such data throws an exception.

To avoid this, the 2.0 framework and later includes a `System.Runtime.Serialization.OptionalFieldAttribute`. When you require backward compatibility, you must decorate serialized fields—even private ones—with `OptionalFieldAttribute` (unless, of course, a latter version begins to require it).

Unfortunately, `System.Runtime.Serialization.OptionalFieldAttribute` is not supported in the earlier framework version. Instead, it is necessary to implement `ISerializable`, just as you did for encryption, saving and retrieving only the fields that are available. Assuming the addition of the `Author` field, for example, the implementation shown in Listing 17.26 is required for backward-compatibility support prior to the 2.0 framework.

LISTING 17.26: Backward Compatibility Prior to the 2.0 Framework

```
[Serializable]
public class VersionableDocument : ISerializable
{
  enum Field
  {
      Title,
      Author,
      Data,
  }

  public VersionableDocument()
  {
  }

  public string Title;
  public string Author;
  public string Data;

  #region ISerializable Members
  public void GetObjectData(
      SerializationInfo info, StreamingContext context)
  {
      info.AddValue(Field.Title.ToString(), Title);
      info.AddValue(Field.Author.ToString(), Author);
      info.AddValue(Field.Data.ToString(), Data);
  }
  public VersionableDocument(
```

```
        SerializationInfo info, StreamingContext context)
    {
        foreach(SerializationEntry entry in info)
        {
            switch ((Field)Enum.Parse(typeof(Field), entry.Name))
            {
                case Field.Title:
                    Title = info.GetString(
                        Field.Title.ToString());
                    break;
                case Field.Author:
                    Author = info.GetString(
                        Field.Author.ToString());
                    break;
                case Field.Data:
                    Data = info.GetString(
                        Field.Data.ToString());
                    break;
            }
        }
    }
    #endregion
}
```

Serializing in GetObjectData() simply involves serializing all fields (assume here that version 1 does not need to open documents from version 2). On deserialization, however, you can't simply call Get-String("Author") because if no such entry exists, it will throw an exception. Instead, iterate through all the entries that are in info and retrieve them individually.

▪ ADVANCED TOPIC

System.SerializableAttribute **and the CIL**

In many ways, the serialize attributes behave just like custom attributes. At runtime, the formatter class searches for these attributes, and if the attributes exist, the classes are formatted appropriately. One of the characteristics that make System.SerializableAttribute not just a custom attribute, however, is the fact that the CIL has a special header notation for serializable classes. Listing 17.27 shows the class header for the Person class in the CIL.

LISTING 17.27: The CIL for `SerializableAttribute`

```
class auto ansi serializable nested private
  beforefieldinit Person
  extends [mscorlib]System.Object
{
} // end of class Person
```

In contrast, attributes (including most predefined attributes) generally appear within a class definition (see Listing 17.28).

LISTING 17.28: The CIL for Attributes in General

```
.class private auto ansi beforefieldinit Person
      extends [mscorlib]System.Object
{
   .custom instance void CustomAttribute::.ctor() =
      ( 01 00 00 00 )
} // end of class Person
```

In Listing 17.28, `CustomAttribute` is the full name of the decorating attribute.

`SerializableAttribute` translates to a set bit within the metadata tables. This makes `SerializableAttribute` a **pseudoattribute,** an attribute that sets bits or fields in the metadata tables.

Programming with Dynamic Objects

The introduction of dynamic objects in C# 4.0 simplifies a host of programming scenarios and enables several new ones previously not available. At its core, programming with dynamic objects enables developers to code operations using a dynamic dispatch mechanism that the runtime will resolve at execution time, rather than the compiler verifying and binding to it at compile time.

Why? At a high level, there are many times when objects are inherently not statically typed. Examples include loading data from an XML/CSV file, a database table, the Internet Explorer DOM, or COM's `IDispatch` interface, or calling code in a dynamic language such as an IronPython object. C# 4.0's Dynamic object support provides a common solution for talking to runtime environments that don't necessarily have a compile-time-defined structure. In the initial implementation of dynamic objects in C# 4.0, four binding methods are available:

1. Using reflection against an underlying CLR type
2. Invoking a custom `IDynamicMetaObjectProvider` which makes available a `DynamicMetaObject`
3. Calling through the `IUnknown` and `IDispatch` interfaces of COM
4. Calling type defined by dynamic languages such as IronPython

Of these, we are going to delve into the first two. The principles found there translate seamlessly to the remaining cases—COM interoperability and dynamic language interoperability.

Invoking Reflection Using `dynamic`

One of the key features of reflection is the ability to dynamically find and invoke a member on a particular type based on an execution time identification of the member name or some other quality, such as an attribute (see Listing 17.3). However, C# 4.0's addition of dynamic objects provides a simpler way of invoking a member by reflection, assuming compile-time knowledge of the member signature. Again: The restriction is that at compile time we need to know the member name along with the signature (number of parameters and whether the specified parameters will be type-compatible with the signature). Listing 17.29 (with Output 17.10) provides an example.

LISTING 17.29: Dynamic Programming Using "Reflection"

```
using System;

// ...
dynamic data =
  "Hello!  My name is Inigo Montoya";
Console.WriteLine(data);
data = (double)data.Length;
data = data*3.5 + 28.6;
if(data == 2.4 + 112 + 26.2)
{
  Console.WriteLine(
      "{0} makes for a long triathlon.", data);
}
```

```
  else
  {
    data.NonExistentMethodCallStillCompiles()
  }
  // ...
```

OUTPUT 17.10:

```
Hello!  My name is Inigo Montoya
140.6 makes for a long triathlon.
```

In this example, there is no explicit code for determining the object type, finding a particular MemberInfo instance, and then invoking it. Instead, data is declared as type dynamic and methods are called against it directly. At compile time, there is no check as to whether the members specified are available, or even a check regarding what type underlies the dynamic object. Hence, it is possible at compile time to make any call so long as the syntax is valid. At compile time, it is irrelevant whether there is a corresponding member or not.

However, type safety is not abandoned altogether. For standard CLR types (such as those used in Listing 17.29), the same type checker normally used at compile time for non-dynamic types is instead invoked at execution time for the dynamic type. Therefore, at execution time, if in fact no such member is available, then the call will result in a Microsoft.CSharp.RuntimeBinder.RuntimeBinderException.

Note again that this is not nearly as flexible as the reflection earlier in the chapter, although the API is undoubtedly simpler. The key difference when using a dynamic object is that it is necessary to identify the signature at compile time, rather than determine things such as the member name at runtime (like we did when parsing the command-line arguments).

dynamic Principles and Behaviors

Listing 17.29 and the accompanying text reveal several characteristics of the dynamic data type.

- dynamic is a directive to the compiler to generate code.

  dynamic involves an interception mechanism so that when a dynamic call is encountered by the runtime, it can compile the request to CIL and then invoke the newly compiled call (see the Advanced Block titled `dynamic` Uncovered, later in this chapter).

The principle at work when a type is assigned to `dynamic` is to conceptually "wrap" the original type so that no compile-time validation occurs. Additionally, when a member is invoked at run-time, the "wrapper" intercepts the call and dispatches it appropriately (or rejects it). Calling `GetType()` on the `dynamic` object reveals the type underlying the dynamic instance—it does not return `dynamic` as a type.

- Any type will convert to `dynamic`.

In Listing 17.29, we successfully cast both a value type (`double`) and a reference type (`string`) to `dynamic`. In fact, all types can successfully be converted into a `dynamic` object. There is an implicit conversion from any reference type to `dynamic`. Similarly, there is an implicit conversion (a boxing conversion) from a value type to `dynamic`. In addition, there is an implicit conversion from `dynamic` to `dynamic`. This is perhaps obvious, but with `dynamic` this is more complicated than simply copying the "pointer" (address) from one location to the next.

- Successful conversion from `dynamic` to an alternate type depends on support in the underlying type.

Conversion from a `dynamic` object to a standard CLR type is an explicit cast (for example, `(double)data.Length`). Not surprisingly, if the target type is a value type, then an unboxing conversion is required. If the underlying type supports the conversion to the target type, the conversion from `dynamic` will also succeed.

- The type underlying the dynamic type can change from one assignment to the next.

Unlike the implicitly typed variable (`var`) which cannot be reassigned to a different type, `dynamic` involves an interception mechanism for compilation before the underlying type's code is executed. Therefore, it is possible to successfully swap out the underlying type instance to an entirely different type. This will result in another interception call site that will need to be compiled before invocation.

- Verification that the specified signature exists on the underlying type doesn't occur until runtime—but it does occur.

  As the method call to `person.NonExistentMethodCallStillCompiles()` demonstrates, the compiler makes no verification of operations on a `dynamic` type. This is left entirely to the work of the runtime when the code executes. And if the code never executes, even though surrounding code does (as in the case with `person.NonExistentMethodCallStillCompiles()`), no verification and binding to the member will ever occur.

- The return from any `dynamic` member invocation is a `dynamic` object (`data = data*3.5 + 28.6`).

  A call to any member on a `dynamic` object will return a dynamic object. Therefore, calls such as `data.ToString()` will return a `dynamic` object rather than the underlying `string` type. However, at execution time, when `GetType()` is called on the `dynamic` object, the code will have been compiled, so the compiled type is returned.

- If the member specified does not exist at runtime, the runtime will throw a `Microsoft.CSharp.RuntimeBinder.RuntimeBinderException` exception.

  If an attempt to invoke a member at execution time does occur, the runtime will verify that in fact the member call is valid (that the signatures are type-compatible in the case of reflection, for example). If the method signatures are not compatible, the runtime will throw a `Microsoft.CSharp.RuntimeBinder.RuntimeBinderException`.

- `dynamic` with reflection does not support extension methods.

  Just like with reflection using `System.Type`, reflection using `dynamic` does not support extension methods. Invocation of extension methods is still available on the implementing type (`System.Linq.Enumerable`, for example), just not on the extended type directly.

- At its core, `dynamic` is a `System.Object`.

  Given that any object will successfully convert to `dynamic` and `dynamic` may be explicitly converted to a different object type, `dynamic` behaves like `System.Object`. Like `System.Object`, it even returns `null` for its default value (`default(dynamic)`), indicating it is a reference type. The special dynamic behavior of dynamic that distinguishes it from a System.Object appears only at invocation time.

■ ADVANCED TOPIC

dynamic **Uncovered**

ILDASM reveals that within the CIL, the dynamic type is actually a System.Object. In fact, without any invocations, declaration of the dynamic type is indistinguishable from System.Object. However, the difference is apparent when invoking a member. In order to invoke the member, the compiler declares a variable of type System.Runtime.CompilerServices.CallSite<T>. T varies based on the member signature, but something simple such as the invocation of ToString() would require instantiation of the following type: CallSite<Func<CallSite, object, string>>, and a method call with parameters of CallSite site, object dynamicTarget, and string result. site is the call site itself, dynamicTarget is the object on which the method call is invoked, and result is the underlying return value from the ToString() method call. Rather than instantiate CallSite<Func<CallSite _site, object dynamicTarget, string result>> directly, there is a Create() factory method for instantiating it. (Create() takes a parameter of type Microsoft.CSharp.Runtime-Binder.CSharpConvertBinder.) Given an instance of the CallSite<T>, the final step involves a call to CallSite<T>.Target() to invoke the actual member.

Under the covers at execution time, the framework uses "reflection" to look up members and to verify that the signatures match. Next, the runtime builds an expression tree that represents the dynamic expression as defined by the call site. Once the tree expression is compiled we have a CIL result that is similar to what the compiler would have generated. This CIL code is then injected into the call site and the invocation occurs using a delegate invoke. Since the CIL is now injected at the call site, the next invocation doesn't require all the reflection and compilation overhead again.

Why Dynamic Binding?

In addition to reflection, we can define custom types to invoke dynamically. Consider using dynamic invocation to retrieve the values of an XML element, for example. Rather than using the strongly typed syntax of Listing 17.30, using dynamic invocation we could call person.FirstName and person.LastName.

LISTING 17.30: The CIL for Attributes in General

```
using System;
using System.Xml.Linq;

// ...
XElement person = XElement.Parse(
   @"<Person>
      <FirstName>Inigo</FirstName>
      <LastName>Montoya</LastName>
</Person>");

Console.WriteLine("{0} {1}",
  person.Descendants("FirstName").FirstOrDefault().Value,
  person.Descendants("LastName").FirstOrDefault().Value);
// ...
```

Although the code in Listing 17.30 is not overly complex, compare it to Listing 17.31—an alternative approach that uses a dynamically typed object.

LISTING 17.31: The CIL for Attributes in General

```
using System;

// ...
dynamic person = DynamicXml.Parse(
  @"<Person>
      <FirstName>Inigo</FirstName>
      <LastName>Montoya</LastName>
  </Person>");

Console.WriteLine("{0} {1}",
    person.FirstName, person.LastName);
// ...
```

The advantages are clear, but does that mean dynamic programming is preferable to static compilation?

Static Compilation versus Dynamic Programming

In Listing 17.31, we have the same functionality as in Listing 17.30, but there is one very important difference. Listing 17.30 is entirely statically typed. This means that at compile time, all types and their member signatures are verified. Method names are required to match, and all parameters are checked for type compatibility. This is a key feature of C# and something I have highlighted throughout the book.

In contrast, Listing 17.31 has virtually no statically typed code; the variable person is instead dynamic. As a result, there is no compile-time verification that person has a FirstName or LastName property, or any other members, for that matter. Furthermore, when coding within an IDE, there is no IntelliSense identifying any members on person.

The loss of typing would seem to result in a significant decrease in functionality. Why is such a possibility even available in C#—a functionality that was added in C# 4.0, in fact? Let's examine Listing 17.31 again. Notice the call to retrieve the "FirstName" element: Element.Descendants("Last-Name").FirstOrDefault().Value. The listing uses a string ("LastName") to identify the element name. However, there is no compile-time verification that the string is correct. If the casing was inconsistent with the element name or if there was a space, the compile would still succeed, even though a NullReferenceException would occur with the call to the Value property. Furthermore, the compiler makes no verification that the "FirstName" element even exists, and if it doesn't, we would also get the NullReferenceException. In other words, in spite of all the type-safety advantages, type safety doesn't offer much advantage to accessing the dynamic data stored within the XML element.

Listing 17.31 is no better than Listing 17.30 when it comes to compile-time verification of the element retrieval. If there is a case mismatch or if the FirstName element didn't exist, there would still be an exception.[1] However, compare the call to access the first name in Listing 17.31 (person.FirstName) with the call in Listing 17.30. The call is undoubtedly significantly simpler. In summary, there are situations where type safety

---

1. You cannot use a space in the FirstName property call, but if XML supported spaces in element names, this would be a potential disadvantage, so let's ignore this fact.

doesn't—and likely can't—make certain checks. And in such cases, being able to make a dynamic call that is only runtime-verified rather than also compile-time verified is significantly more readable and succinct. Obviously, if compile-time verification is possible, statically typed programming is preferred because readable and succinct APIs could accompany it. However, in the cases where it isn't effective, C# 4.0 enables simpler code rather than the purity of type safety.

Implementing a Custom Dynamic Object

Listing 17.31 included a method call to `DynamicXml.Parse(...)` that was essentially a factory method call for `DynamicXml`—a custom type rather than one built into the CLR Framework. However, `DynamicXml` doesn't implement a `FirstName` or `LastName` property. To do so would break the dynamic support for retrieving data from the XML file at execution time, rather than compile-time-based implementation of the XML elements. In other words, `DynamicXml` does not use reflection for accessing its members, but rather it dynamically binds to the values based on the XML content.

The key to defining a custom dynamic type is implementation of the `System.Dynamic.IDynamicMetaObjectProvider` interface. Rather than implementing the interface from scratch, however, the preferred approach is to derive the custom dynamic type from `System.Dynamic.DynamicObject`. This provides default implementation for a host of members and allows you to override the ones that don't fit. Listing 17.32 shows the full implementation.

LISTING 17.32: Implementing a Custom Dynamic Object

```csharp
using System;
using System.Dynamic;
using System.Xml.Linq;

public class DynamicXml : DynamicObject
{
  private XElement Element { get; set; }

  public DynamicXml(System.Xml.Linq.XElement element)
  {
      Element = element;
  }

  public static DynamicXml Parse(string text)
  {
      return new DynamicXml(XElement.Parse(text));
```

```
    }

    public override bool TryGetMember(
        GetMemberBinder binder, out object result)
    {
        bool success = false;
        result = null;
        XElement firstDescendant =
            Element.Descendants(binder.Name).FirstOrDefault();
        if (firstDescendant != null)
        {
            if (firstDescendant.Descendants().Count() > 0)
            {
                result = new DynamicXml(firstDescendant);
            }
            else
            {
                result = firstDescendant.Value;
            }
            success = true;
        }
        return success;
    }

    public override bool TrySetMember(
        SetMemberBinder binder, object value)
    {
        bool success = false;
        XElement firstDescendant =
            Element.Descendants(binder.Name).FirstOrDefault();
        if (firstDescendant != null)
        {
            if (value.GetType() == typeof(XElement))
            {
                firstDescendant.ReplaceWith(value);
            }
            else
            {
                firstDescendant.Value = value.ToString();
            }
            success = true;
        }
        return success;
    }
}
```

The key dynamic implementation methods for this use case are TryGet-
Member() and the TrySetMember() (assuming you also want to assign the
elements as well). Only these two method implementations are necessary

to support the invocation of the dynamic getter and setter properties. Furthermore, the implementations are straightforward. First, they examine the contained XElement, looking for an element with the same name as the binder.Name—the name of the member invoked. If a corresponding XML element exists, then the value is retrieved (or set). The return value is set to true if the element exists and false if it doesn't. Automatically, a return value of false will cause the runtime to throw a Microsoft.CSharp.RuntimeBinder.RuntimeBinderException at the call site of the dynamic member invocation.

System.Dynamic.DynamicObject supports additional virtual methods if additional dynamic invocations are required. Listing 17.33 shows the list of all the overridable members.

LISTING 17.33: Overridable Members on System.Dynamic.DynamicObject

```csharp
using System.Dynamic;

public class DynamicObject : IDynamicMetaObjectProvider
{
  protected DynamicObject();

  public virtual IEnumerable<string> GetDynamicMemberNames();
  public virtual DynamicMetaObject GetMetaObject(
      Expression parameter);
  public virtual bool TryBinaryOperation(
      BinaryOperationBinder binder, object arg,
          out object result);
  public virtual bool TryConvert(
      ConvertBinder binder, out object result);
  public virtual bool TryCreateInstance(
      CreateInstanceBinder binder, object[] args,
          out object result);
  public virtual bool TryDeleteIndex(
      DeleteIndexBinder binder, object[] indexes);
  public virtual bool TryDeleteMember(
      DeleteMemberBinder binder);
  public virtual bool TryGetIndex(
      GetIndexBinder binder, object[] indexes,
          out object result);
  public virtual bool TryGetMember(
      GetMemberBinder binder, out object result);
  public virtual bool TryInvoke(
      InvokeBinder binder, object[] args, out object result);
  public virtual bool TryInvokeMember(
```

```
        InvokeMemberBinder binder, object[] args,
            out object result);
    public virtual bool TrySetIndex(
        SetIndexBinder binder, object[] indexes, object value);
    public virtual bool TrySetMember(
        SetMemberBinder binder, object value);
    public virtual bool TryUnaryOperation(
        UnaryOperationBinder binder, out object result);
}
```

As Listing 17.33 shows there are member implementations for everything—from casts and various operations, through to index invocations. In addition, there is a method for retrieving all the possible member names: GetDynamicMemberNames().

SUMMARY

This chapter discussed how to use reflection to read the metadata that is compiled into the CIL. Using reflection, you saw how to provide a late binding in which the code to call is defined at execution time rather than at compile time. Although reflection is entirely feasible for deploying a dynamic system, it is considerably slower than statically linked (compile-time), defined code. This tends to make it more prevalent and useful in development tools.

Reflection also enables the retrieval of additional metadata decorating various constructs in the form of attributes. Typically, custom attributes are sought using reflection. It is possible to define your own custom attributes that insert additional metadata of your own choosing into the CIL. At runtime, it is then possible to retrieve this metadata and use it within the programming logic.

Many view attributes as a precursor to a concept known as aspect-oriented programming, in which you add functionality through constructs such as attributes instead of manually implementing the functionality wherever it is needed. It will take some time before you see true aspects within C# (if ever); however, attributes provide a clear steppingstone in that direction, without forcing a significant risk to the stability of the language.

Finally, the chapter included a C# 4.0 introduced feature—dynamic programming using the new type `dynamic`. This section included a discussion of why static binding, although preferred when the API is strongly typed, has limitations when working with dynamic data.

The next chapter looks at multithreading, where attributes are used for synchronization.

18

Multithreading

PRIOR TO 2004, increasing computer power primarily involved increasing the power of a single processor. Limits imposed by the physics of today's silicon microchip technology have forestalled further increases in the power of single processors. Figure 18.1 shows the plateau and even a small drop back, as the threshold of computing power versus heat dissipation stabilized to more maintainable levels.

In spite of the plateau, computer power continues to grow and Moore's Law remains on track as multiple cores (within a single processor) and multiple processors (the microchips that plug into the motherboard) became standard on mainline servers, workstations, and now laptops. Microsoft Windows reflects this available power by showing eight processors on the Windows Task Manager for a four-core machine with Hyper-Threading.

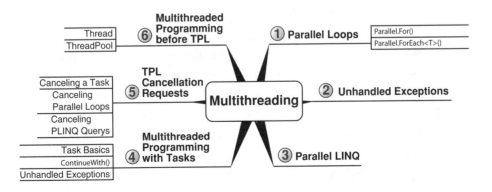

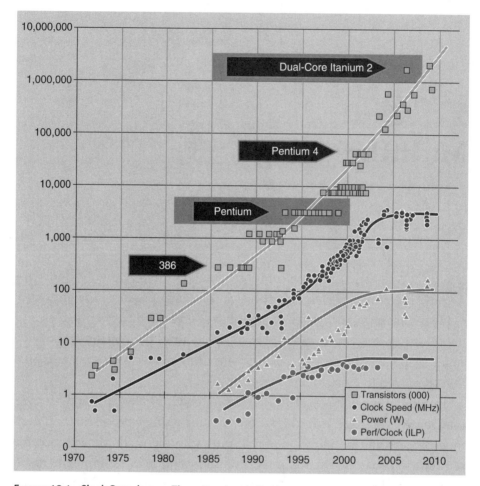

FIGURE 18.1: Clock Speeds over Time. (Graph compiled by Herb Sutter. Used with permission. Original at www.gotw.ca.)

Although the average computer now comes with multiple processing units or CPUs, the programs discussed so far use only one of those CPUs at a time because each program is single-threaded. This chapter and the next discuss how to write code to take advantage of the processing potential of multiple processing units in a single computer.

We achieve the additional throughput that multiple processing units enable by writing multithreaded code, and this involves delving into the System.Threading and System.Threading.Tasks namespaces. These namespaces contain the API for manipulating threads.

.NET 4 introduced two new sets of APIs for multithreaded programming: the Task Parallel Library (TPL) and Parallel LINQ (PLINQ). Although the threading API from earlier versions of the framework still exists and is fully supported, future enhancements will center on the new APIs and so this chapter focuses on these. However, since prior APIs are still relevant to those targeting earlier frameworks, one section in this chapter covers multithreading prior to .NET Framework 4. In addition, the multithreading chapters from the preceding edition of this book (*Essential C# 3.5*) are available for download at http://intelliTechture.com/EssentialCSharp, since much of the material that appeared in earlier editions is just as relevant and important today as it was then if you do not have the luxury of targeting only the .NET Framework 4.

Furthermore (albeit unsupported), Microsoft released the Reactive Extensions to .NET (Rx), a separate download that adds support for TPL and PLINQ within the .NET 3.5 Framework. Therefore, any references to .NET Framework 4-introduced capabilities within this chapter and the next imply similar capabilities within .NET 3.5 given references to the System.Threading.dll assembly from the Rx library.

■ BEGINNER TOPIC

Thread Basics

A **thread** is a sequence of instructions that may run concurrently with other instruction sequences. A program that enables more than one sequence to execute concurrently is **multithreaded.** For example, in order to import a large file while simultaneously allowing a user to click Cancel, a developer creates an additional thread to perform the import. By performing the import on a different thread, the user can request cancellation instead of freezing the user interface until the import completes.

An operating system simulates multiple threads running concurrently via a mechanism known as **time slicing.** Even with multiple processors, there is generally a demand for more threads than there are processors, and as a result, time slicing occurs. Time slicing is a mechanism whereby the operating system switches execution from one thread (sequence of instructions) to the next so quickly that it appears the threads are executing simultaneously. The period of time that the processor executes a particular thread before switching to another is the **time slice** or **quantum.**

The effect is similar to that of a fiber optic telephone line in which the fiber optic line represents the processor and each conversation represents a thread. A (single-mode) fiber optic telephone line can send only one signal at a time, but many people can hold simultaneous conversations over the line. The fiber optic channel is fast enough to switch between conversations so quickly that each conversation appears uninterrupted. Similarly, each thread of a multithreaded process appears to run continuously with other threads.

Since a thread is often waiting for various events, such as an I/O operation, switching to a different thread results in more efficient execution, because the processor is not idly waiting for the operation to complete. However, switching from one thread to the next does create some overhead. If there are too many threads, the switching overhead begins to noticeably affect performance, and adding additional threads will likely decrease performance further; the processor spends time switching from one thread to another instead of accomplishing the work of each thread.

Even readers new to programming will have heard the term *multithreading,* most likely in a conversation about its complexity. In designing both the C# language and the framework, considerable time was spent on simplifying the programming API that surrounds multithreaded programming. However, considerable complexity remains, not so much in writing a program that has multiple threads, but in doing so in a manner that maintains atomicity, avoids deadlocks, and does not introduce execution uncertainty such as race conditions.

Atomicity

Consider code that transfers money from a bank account. First, the code verifies whether there are sufficient funds; if there are, the transfer occurs. If after checking the funds, a different thread removes the funds, an invalid transfer may occur when execution returns to the initial thread. Controlling account access so that only one thread can access the account at a time fixes the problem and makes the transfer **atomic.** A set of operations is atomic if one of the following two conditions is met:

- The entire set of operations must complete before any operation appears to have executed.
- The apparent state of the system must return to the state prior to any operation executing—as though no steps executed.

Returning to the bank transfer example, although composed of multiple steps, the entire set must be one atomic operation. In the process of performing each step, no interruptions (such as a debit) should occur until the complete set finishes. And if the complete set does not finish, it should appear that none did (you can't debit the money from one account and not credit it to a second, for example). Identifying and implementing atomicity is one of the primary complexities of multithreaded programming.

Unfortunately, the complexity increases because the majority of C# statements are not atomic. Count++, for example, is a simple statement in C#, but it translates to multiple instructions for the processor.

1. The processor reads the data in Count.
2. The processor calculates the new value.
3. Count is assigned a new value (even this may not be atomic).

After the data is accessed, but before the new value is assigned, a different thread may modify the original value (perhaps also checking the value prior to modifying it), creating a **race condition** because the value in Count has, for at least one thread's perspective, changed unexpectedly.

Deadlock

To avoid such race conditions, languages support the ability to restrict blocks of code to a specified number of threads, generally one. However, if the order of lock acquisition between threads varies, a **deadlock** could occur such that threads freeze, each waiting for the other to release its lock. For example:

	THREAD A	THREAD B
	Acquires a lock on a	Acquires a lock on b
Time	Requests a lock on b	Requests a lock on a
	Deadlocks, waiting for b	Deadlocks, waiting for a

At this point, each thread is waiting on the other thread before proceeding, so each thread is blocked, leading to an overall deadlock in the execution of that code.

Uncertainty

The problem with code that is not atomic or causes deadlocks is that it depends on the order in which processor instructions across multiple threads occur. This dependency introduces uncertainty concerning program execution. The order in which one instruction will execute relative to an instruction in a different thread is unknown. Many times, the code will appear to behave uniformly, but occasionally it will not, and this is the crux of multithreaded programming. Because such race conditions are difficult to replicate in the laboratory, much of the quality assurance of multithreaded code depends on long-running stress tests, specially designed code analysis tools, and a significant investment in code analysis/reviews.

Running and Controlling a Separate Thread

The operating system implements threads and provides various unmanaged APIs to create and manage those threads. The CLR wraps these unmanaged threads and exposes them in managed code via the `System.Threading.Tasks.Task` class, which represents an asynchronous operation. However, a `Task` does not map directly to an unmanaged thread. Rather, the `Task` provides a degree of abstraction to the underlying unmanaged thread construct.

Creating a thread is a relatively expensive operation. Therefore, whenever you can reuse a thread between two or more sets of instructions (rather than re-creating the thread for each set) the overall execution is potentially more efficient. In .NET Framework 4, instead of creating an operating system thread each time a `Task` is created, the `Task` requests a thread from the **thread pool.** The thread pool evaluates whether to create an entirely new thread or to allocate an existing thread (such as one that previously finished executing) to the `Task` request.

By abstracting the concept of a thread into `Task`, the .NET multi-threading API reduces the complexities of efficiently managing the thread—that is, when to create a new operating system thread and when to reuse an existing one. Similarly, the internal behavior of the `Task` (via `System.Threading.ThreadPool`) manages when to return a thread to the thread pool for later reuse and when to deallocate the thread and release any resources it may be consuming.

The work of programming the `Task` involves assigning the set of instructions the `Task` will execute and then starting the `Task`. Not surprisingly, assigning the instructions is heavily dependent on delegates. Listing 18.1 provides a simple example, and Output 18.1 shows a partial listing of the results.

LISTING 18.1: Starting a Method in a Separate Thread

```
using System;
using System.Threading.Tasks;

public class Program
{
  public static void Main()
  {
      const int repetitions = 10000;
      Task task = new Task(() =>
          {
              for (int count = 0; count < repetitions; count++)
              {
                  Console.Write('-');
              }
          });

      task.Start();
      for (int count = 0; count < repetitions; count++)
      {
          Console.Write('.');
      }

      // Wait until the Task completes
      task.Wait();
  }
}
```

OUTPUT 18.1:

```
.............................--------------------------------------
--------------------------------------------------------------------
--------------------------------------------------------------------
--------------------------------------------------------------------
--------------------------------------------------------------------
-----------------------------------------------------------------.....
............................................................--......
............................................................-.......
............................................................-.......
............................................................-.......
...........................................................-........
............................................................-.......
............................-.......................................
--------------------------------------------------------------------
--------------------------------------------------------------------
--------------------------------------------------------------------
.............................................................-......
.............................................................-......
............................................................-.......
.............................................................-......
.............................................................-......
.............................................................-......
.............................................................-......
--------------------------------------------------------------------
-----------------------------------........................-........
......................-------------------------............-........
.............................................................-......
.................................................................
```

The code that is to run in a new thread is defined in the delegate (of type Action in this case) passed to the Task() constructor. This delegate (in the form of a lambda expression) prints out . to the console repeatedly during each iteration within a loop. The for loop following the Task declaration is virtually identical, except that it displays -. The resultant output from the program is a series of dashes until the thread context switches, at which time the program displays periods until the next thread switch, and so on. (On Windows, it is possible to increase the chances of a thread context switch by using Start /low /b <program.exe> to execute the program. This will assign the entire process a lower priority, causing its threads to be interrupted more frequently, and thus causing more frequent thread switches.) The fact that the output has periods and dashes interleaving indicates that both for loops were running simultaneously—in parallel.

Notice that following the Task declaration there is a call to Start(). Until this call is executed, the Action specified to Task doesn't start executing. Additionally, the call to task.Wait() forces the main thread (the one executing the second for loop) to stop and "Wait" until all the work assigned to task has completed executing.

Similarly, if the work executed in the task returns a result, then any request for the result will automatically block until the task completes. Listing 18.2 demonstrates Task<TResult>, which returns a value by executing a Func<TResult> rather than simply an Action.

LISTING 18.2: Returning a Result from a Task<TResult>

```csharp
using System;
using System.Threading.Tasks;

public class Program
{
  public static void Main()
  {
      Task<string> task = Task.Factory.StartNew<string>(
          () => PiCalculator.Calculate(100));

      foreach (char busySymbol in Utility.BusySymbols())
      {
          if (task.IsCompleted)
          {
              Console.Write('\b');
              break;
          }
          Console.Write(busySymbol);
      }

      Console.WriteLine();
      // Blocks until task completes.
      Console.WriteLine(task.Result);
      System.Diagnostics.Trace.Assert(
          task.IsCompleted);
  }
}


public class Utility
{
  public static IEnumerable<char> BusySymbols()
  {
      string busySymbols = @"-\|/-\|/";
      int next = 0;
      while (true)
      {
          yield return busySymbols[next];
          next = (++next) % busySymbols.Length;
```

```
            yield return '\b';
        }
    }
}
```

This listing shows that the data type of the task is Task<TResult> (specifically a string in this case). The generic version of a task includes a Result property from which to retrieve the value returned by the Func<TResult> that the Task<TResult> executes.

A second noteworthy characteristic of Listing 18.2 is the fact that there is no call to task.Start(). Instead, it uses the StartNew() method of the static Factory property on Task. The result is similar to instantiating the Task except that the return from Task.Factory.StartNew<TResult>() is already started. It is rare that using StartNew() won't suffice unless there is the need to separate instantiating a Task from scheduling it.

In addition to the IsCompleted property on Task, there are several others worth noting:

Status

Status returns a System.Threading.Tasks.TaskStatus enum indicating the status of the task. Values include Created, WaitingForActivation, WaitingToRun, Running, WaitingForChildrenToComplete, RanToCompletion, Canceled, and Faulted.

IsCompleted

IsCompleted is set to true when a task completes whether it faulted or not. IsCompleted is true whenever the Status is RanToCompletion, Canceled, or Faulted.

Id

Id is a unique identifier of the task. This is especially useful in debugging when trying to work through multithreading problems such as race and deadlocks.

AsyncState

The Id property is useful for identifying the task—naming it, for example. Furthermore, AsyncState can track additional data. For example, imagine a List<T> of values that various tasks are calculating. One way to place the result into the correct location of the list is to store the list index targeted to contain the result into the AsyncState property. This way, when the task completes, the code can index into the list using the AsyncState (first casting it to an int). (Note that calling List<T>.Add() is not a safe operation across multiple threads, and calling it will result in a race condition that is likely to result in data loss.)

Task.CurrentId

Task.CurrentId is a static property on the Task that returns an identifier for the currently executing Task (the one executing the Task.CurrentId call). Since the property is static, it is available anywhere and is mostly useful for debugging and diagnostic-type activities.

As discussed within the context of Task cancellation later in the chapter, additional properties on Task are also available.

ContinueWith()

A Task includes a ContinueWith() method for chaining tasks together such that as soon as the first one in the chain completes it triggers the ones that have registered to begin executing after it. Since the Continue-With() methods return another Task, the chain of work can continue to be added to.

It is interesting to note that it is possible to add multiple tasks using ContinueWith() and that such "continue-with" tasks are free to commence immediately upon completion of the **antecedent task**—the Task instance against which the ContinueWith() method was called. Furthermore, when ContinueWith() is called multiple times on the same antecedent task instance, all tasks that are added will commence running in parallel when the antecedent task completes.

The full list of available flags with descriptions from the MSDN Task-ContinuationOptions documentation appears in Table 18.1. The values are flags, so they can be combined using the logical OR operator (|).

The items decorated with a star (*) are particularly useful for "registering" for "notifications" of the antecedent task's behavior. Listing 18.3 demonstrates this.

TABLE 18.1:   List of Available `TaskContinuationOptions` Enums[1]

Enum	Description
None	The default continuation option which indicates continue asynchronously with no special task options. It specifies that the continue-with-task should execute "when the antecedent task completes, regardless of the task's final `System.Threading.Tasks.TaskStatus`."
PreferFairness	"A hint to a `System.Threading.Tasks.TaskScheduler` to schedule a task in as fair a manner as possible, meaning that tasks scheduled sooner will be more likely to be run sooner, and tasks scheduled later will be more likely to be run later."
LongRunning	"Specifies that a task will be a long-running, course-grained operation. It provides a hint to the `System.Threading.Tasks.Task-Scheduler` that oversubscription may be warranted."
AttachedToParent	Specifies that a task is attached to a parent in the task hierarchy.
NotOnRanToCompletion*	Specifies that the continuation task should not be scheduled if its antecedent ran to completion. This option is not valid for multitask continuations.
NotOnFaulted*	Specifies that the continuation task should not be scheduled if its antecedent threw an unhandled exception. This option is not valid for multitask continuations.
OnlyOnCanceled*	Specifies that the continuation task should be scheduled only if its antecedent was canceled. This option is not valid for multitask continuations.
NotOnCanceled*	Specifies that the continuation task should not be scheduled if its antecedent was canceled. This option is not valid for multitask continuations.

---

1. MSDN .NET Framework Developer Center, http://msdn.microsoft.com/en-us/library/ system.threading.tasks.taskcontinuationoptions(VS.100).aspx.

TABLE 18.1: List of Available `TaskContinuationOptions` Enums[1] *(Continued)*

Enum	Description
`OnlyOnFaulted*`	Specifies that the continuation task should be scheduled only if its antecedent threw an unhandled exception. This option is not valid for multitask continuations.
`OnlyOnRanToCompletion*`	Specifies that the continuation task should be scheduled only if its antecedent ran to completion. This option is not valid for multitask continuations.
`ExecuteSynchronously`	Specifies that the continuation task should be executed synchronously. With this option specified, the continuation will be run on the same thread that causes the antecedent task to transition into its final state. If the antecedent is already complete when the continuation is created, the continuation will run on the thread creating the continuation.

* Indicates when to run the task.

LISTING 18.3: Registering for "Notifications" with `ContinueWith()`

```csharp
using System;
using System.Threading.Tasks;

public class Program
{
  public static void Main()
  {
      Task<string> task = Task.Factory.StartNew<string>(
          () => PiCalculator.Calculate(10));

      Task faultedTask = task.ContinueWith(
          (antecedentTask) =>
          {
              Trace.Assert(task.IsFaulted);
              Console.WriteLine("Task State: Faulted");
          },
          TaskContinuationOptions.OnlyOnFaulted);
      Task canceledTask = task.ContinueWith(
          (antecedentTask) =>
          {
              //Trace.Assert(task.IsCanceled);
              Console.WriteLine("Task State: Canceled");
          },
```

```
        TaskContinuationOptions.OnlyOnCanceled);
    Task completedTask = task.ContinueWith(
        (antecedentTask) =>
        {
            Trace.Assert(task.IsCompleted);
            Console.WriteLine("Task State: Completed");
        },
    TaskContinuationOptions.OnlyOnRanToCompletion);

    completedTask.Wait();
  }
}
```

In this listing, we effectively register for "events" on the antecedent's task so that if the event occurs, the particular "listening" task will begin executing. This is a powerful capability, especially when using a fire-and-forget behavior on the task—no Wait()-type behavior is invoked on the task. Instead, we can just call Start() or Factory.StartNew(), register for the "notifications," and then discard the reference to the task. The task will begin executing asynchronously without any need for follow-up code that "checks" the status. In this case, we leave the completedTask.Wait() call so that the program does not exit before the completed output appears (see Output 18.2).

OUTPUT 18.2:

```
Task State: Completed.
```

Even if the task hasn't finished executing, the program will still exit if no explicit wait is specified.

The Wait() method is a means of joining tasks back to the calling thread so that the thread calling Wait() will continue only when the other task (the instance on which Wait() is called) has completed. Typically, this is necessary because one task is relying on the effects or results of the other task.

Note that we can't successfully call Wait() on canceledTask or faultedTask; since the task didn't and won't complete the work there is nothing to wait for. The continuation options in Listing 18.3 happen to be mutually exclusive, so when the antecedent task runs to completion and completedTask executes, the runtime cancels the canceledTask and faultedTask since they will never run. Therefore, calling Wait() or any of the other task completion methods (Result or Task.WaitAll()) on either of these tasks will throw an exception indicating that they are no longer executable.

Next we take a look at the faulted case.

Unhandled Exception Handling on Task

Unlike exception handling on a single thread, we cannot simply wrap Task.Start() in order to catch an exception within the delegate passed to the Task because any exception will obviously occur after the task starts. Exceptions caught and handled within the task execution are also not a problem since try/catch blocks will work just as they would anywhere. What does require care is handling unhandled exceptions thrown from a different thread.

Starting with the CLR 2.0, unhandled exceptions on the finalizer thread, thread pool threads, and user-created threads will generally bubble up, triggering the Windows Error Reporting dialog and an application exit as a way of explicitly identifying that there is likely a problem that needs to be addressed. All exceptions for which there is a known handling mechanism, therefore, require an explicit catch block or else they will cause the program to close.

Although bubbling up all unhandled exceptions is an improvement over the alternative of ignoring them, it still is not ideal. If an exception occurs for which there is no appropriate handling mechanism within the Task's execution, but there is appropriate handling logic outside the task, it needs to be possible to catch the exception within higher-level handlers rather than crashing the application. Fortunately, Task supports this.

The unhandled exception during the Task's execution will be suppressed until a call to one of the task completion members: Wait(), Result, Task.WaitAll(), or Task.WaitAny(). Each of these members will throw any unhandled exceptions that occurred within the task's execution. Listing 18.4 demonstrates the behavior, the output of which is the message, "ERROR: Error in the application." demonstrating that indeed an exception is thrown (see Output 18.3). By placing the task completion member within a try/catch block, the unhandled exception can be trapped and addressed if desired.

LISTING 18.4: Handling a Task's Unhandled Exception

```csharp
using System;
using System.Threading.Tasks;

public class Program
{
  public static void Main()
  {
      Task task = Task.Factory.StartNew(() =>
      {
          throw new ApplicationException();
      });

      try
      {
          task.Wait();
      }
      catch (AggregateException exception)
      {
          foreach (Exception item in
              exception.InnerExceptions)
          {
              Console.WriteLine(
                  "ERROR: {0}", item.Message);
          }
      }
  }
}
```

OUTPUT 18.3:

```
ERROR: Error in the application.
```

Listing 18.4 demonstrates how the unhandled framework passes the task's unhandled exception back to the main thread. Notice that the data type of the exception is System.AggregateException—a collection of exceptions that may throw in connection with the (potential) hierarchy of tasks associated with the root task. (We discuss System.AggregateException further in the next major section, Executing Iterations in Parallel.)

Task-Related Finalization Exceptions Suppressed during Application Shutdown

Earlier in this section, I stated that, "unhandled exceptions on the finalizer thread… will *generally* bubble up…., triggering the Windows Error Reporting dialog and an application exit as a way of explicitly identifying that there is likely a problem that needs to be addressed." Although relatively rare, one of the exceptions for the general rule happens to be on `Task`. It is possible that a `Task` that completes during the execution of the program will still have items in the finalization queue when the application shuts down. Any `Task`-based exceptions thrown from the finalization queue during application exit will go suppressed. The behavior is set this way because frequently the effort to handle such an exception is too complex to offset the likely benign nature of the exception occurring at application exit.

Another approach for unhandled exceptions that doesn't require try/catch is to use a `ContinueWith()` task. The `task` parameter on the `ContinueWith()` delegate allows for an evaluation of the antecedent task's `Exception` property to check for the exception (see Listing 18.5 and Output 18.4).

LISTING 18.5: Unhandled Exceptions Using `ContinueWith()`

```csharp
using System;
using System.Diagnostics;
using System.Threading.Tasks;

public class Program
{
  public static void Main()
  {
      bool parentTaskFaulted = false;
      Task task = new Task(() =>
          {
              throw new ApplicationException();
          });
      Task faultedTask = task.ContinueWith(
          (parentTask) =>
          {
              parentTaskFaulted = parentTask.IsFaulted;
          }, TaskContinuationOptions.OnlyOnFaulted);
```

```
        task.Start();
        faultedTask.Wait();
        Trace.Assert(parentTaskFaulted);
        if (!task.IsFaulted)
        {
            task.Wait();
        }
        else
        {
            Console.WriteLine(
                "ERROR: {0}", task.Exception.Message);
        }
    }
}
```

OUTPUT 18.4:

```
ERROR: in the application.
```

Rather than calling task.Wait() and throwing an exception, Listing 18.5 uses a ContinueWith() task and calls continueWithTask.Wait() on this task to determine that the original task completed. In addition, the call to task.ContinueWith() passes a TaskContinuationOptions.OnlyOnFaulted parameter causing this continuation task to execute only if the antecedent task throws an exception. Without the additional parameter, the code execution would have been the same as Listing 18.5 because it would have executed regardless. By specifying the TaskContinuationOptions.Only-OnFaulted flag, we are able to "register" for the fault "notification."

Notice that to retrieve the unhandled exception on the original task we use the Exception property. The result is an output identical to Output 18.3.

Canceling a Task

One particular functional difference between the .NET 3.5 and earlier APIs versus the .NET Framework 4 APIs is support for cancellation requests on threads. The threading API in .NET 3.5 and earlier has little support for cancellation requests and instead relies on a "rude" interruption approach. In this approach, the cancellation of a thread is forced and the target thread has little or no choice about the matter. Calling thread-abort, unloading the AppDomain, or killing the process are all examples of "rude" interruption. Such unexpected interruptions as aborting a thread can potentially occur during execution of a vital code block, threatening data integrity caused by partial data updates or inadequate resource de-allocation. Aborting a thread causes a `ThreadAbortException` exception to occur anywhere within the target thread's execution. This introduces uncertainty into the thread's behavior. (To complicate matters, the target thread's abort call could be rejected by handling the `ThreadAbortException` exception and issuing a reset abort method call inside the abort-targeted thread—rendering uncertainty in the abort-issuing thread.) Similarly, if the abort-targeted thread is running unmanaged code, the `ThreadAbortException` exception will not throw until the code returns to managed execution. As a result, except in rare circumstances, developers should consider the rude interruption approach a last resort at best.

Of course, the earlier APIs are still fully available in the .NET Framework 4, but the additional PLINQ- and TPL-based APIs support only a cancellation request approach in which the target `Task` opts in to the cancellation request—a process known as **cooperative cancellation.** Instead of one "thread" aborting another, the cancellation API "requests" a `Task` to cancel. By checking the cancellation flag—a `System.Threading.CancellationToken`—the task targeted for cancellation can respond appropriately to the cancellation request.

Listing 18.6 demonstrates both the request and the response to the request. Note that this sample uses a `PiCalculator.Calculate()` method that we will delve into further in the Executing Iterations in Parallel section.

LISTING 18.6: Canceling a Task Using `CancellationToken`

```csharp
using System;
using System.Diagnostics;
using System.Threading;
using System.Threading.Tasks;

public class Program
{
  public static void Main()
  {
      string stars = "*".PadRight(Console.WindowWidth-1, '*');
```

```
        Console.WriteLine("Push ENTER to exit.");

      CancellationTokenSource cancellationTokenSource =
          new CancellationTokenSource();
      Task task = Task.Factory.StartNew(
          () =>
  WritePi(cancellationTokenSource.Token),
          cancellationTokenSource.Token);

      // Wait for the user's input
      Console.ReadLine();

      cancellationTokenSource.Cancel();
      Console.WriteLine(stars);
      task.Wait();
      Console.WriteLine();
  }

  private static void WritePi(
      CancellationToken cancellationToken)
  {
      const int batchSize = 1;
      string piSection = string.Empty;
      int i = 0;

      while
  (!cancellationToken.IsCancellationRequested
          || i == int.MaxValue)
      {
          piSection = PiCalculator.Calculate(
              batchSize, (i++) * batchSize);
          Console.Write(piSection);
      }
  }
}
```

After starting the Task, a Console.Read() blocks the main thread. At the same time, the task continues to execute, calculating the next digit of pi and printing it out. Once the user presses Enter, the execution encounters a call to CancellationTokenSource.Cancel(). In Listing 18.6, we split the call to task.Cancel() from the call to task.Wait() and print out * in between. The purpose of this is to show that quite possibly an additional iteration will occur before the cancellation token is observed—hence the additional 2 in Output 18.5 following the stars. The 2 appears because the CancellationTokenSource.Cancel() doesn't rudely stop the Task from executing.

OUTPUT 18.5:

```
Push ENTER to exit.
3.1415926535897932384626433832795028841971693993751058209749445923078164
0628620899862803482534211706798214808651328230664709384460955058223172535
9408128481117450
**********************************************************************
2
```

Rather, the `Cancel()` call sets the `IsCancellationRequested` property on all cancellation tokens copied from `CancellationTokenSource.Token`. There are a couple things to note from the previous sentence.

- *Cancellation token:* A `CancellationToken`, not a `CancellationToken-Source`, is evaluated in the asynchronous task. A `CancellationToken` is seemingly similar to the `CancellationTokenSource` except that the `CancellationToken` is for monitoring and responding to a cancellation request while the `CancellationTokenSource` is for canceling the task itself (see Figure 18.2).

- *Copied:* A `CancellationToken` is a struct, so calling `Cancellation-TokenSource.Token` will create a copy of the token. As a result, all instances of the cancellation token will be thread-safe.

FIGURE 18.2: **CancellationTokenSource** and **CancellationToken** Class Diagrams

To monitor the `IsCancellationRequested` property an instance of the `CancellationToken` (retrieved from `CancellationTokenSource.Token`) is passed to the parallel task. In Listing 18.6, we then check the `IsCancellationRequested` property on the `CancellationToken` parameter after each digit calculation. If `IsCancellationRequested` returns `true`, the `while` loop exits.

One other point to note about the `CancellationToken` is the overloaded `Register()` method. Via this method, you can register an action that will be invoked whenever the token is canceled. In other words, calling the `Register()` method subscribes to a listener delegate on the corresponding `CancellationTokenSource`'s `Cancel()` (see Listing 18.7 later in the chapter).

Since canceling before completing is expected behavior in this program, Listing 18.6 does not throw a `System.Threading.Tasks.TaskCanceledException`. Because of this, `task.Status` will return `TaskStatus.RanToCompletion`—providing no indication that the work of the task was in fact cancelled. In this example, there is no need for such an indication; however, TPL does include the capability to do this. If the cancel call were disruptive in some way—preventing a valid result from returning, for example—throwing a `TaskCanceledException` (which derives from `System.OperationCanceledException`) would be the TPL pattern for reporting it. Instead of throwing the exception explicitly, `CancellationToken` includes a `ThrowIfCancellationRequested()` method to report the exception more easily, assuming an instance of `CancellationToken` is available.

Throwing the `TaskCanceledException` on the executing `Task` results in an `AggregateException` throw on `Task` completion members: `task.Wait()` `Task.WaitAny()`, or `task.Result`.

This example demonstrates how a long-running operation (calculating pi almost indefinitely) can monitor for a cancellation request and respond if one occurs. There are some cases, however, when cancellation can occur without explicitly coding for it within the target task. (For example, the `Parallel` class discussed later in the chapter offers such a behavior by default.)

Long-Running Tasks

As noted earlier in the chapter, `Tasks` provide an abstraction over the operating system threads so that the thread pool can efficiently manage allocation and de-allocation of the threads. The result is that Tasks use underlying threads that are a shared resource and it is expected that the tasks will be cooperative and return the thread in a timely manner so that other requests can be fulfilled using the same shared resource.

However, if the developer knows that a Task is going to be long-running and holding on to an underlying thread resource for a long time, the developer needs to notify the thread pool that it is unlikely to return the shared thread anytime soon. This allows the thread pool to increase the likelihood of creating a dedicated thread for the task, rather than pulling one of the shared threads. To accomplish this, use the TaskCreationOptions.LongRunning option when calling StartNew() as shown in Listing 18.7.

LISTING 18.7: Cooperatively Executing Long-Running Tasks

```
using System.Threading.Tasks;

// ...

    Task task = Task.Factory.StartNew(
        () =>
WritePi(cancellationTokenSource.Token),
            TaskCreationOptions.LongRunning);
// ...
```

Technically, TaskCreationOptions.LongRunning is actually something that the scheduler needs to take into consideration. However, since the default scheduler is the ThreadPoolTaskScheduler by default, it is the thread pool that takes the long-running parameter into consideration.

Disposing a Task

In the listings that depended on Task so far we generally call the task's Wait() method to ensure that the program doesn't exit before the task has completed executing. This falls in accordance with the cooperative canceling approach built into TPL since we don't close the program before the task finishes executing. However, what happens if the program does exit before a task completes?

If the Task is still running when the application begins to exit, the underlying thread on which the Task relies will be aborted by the CLR. Therefore, whatever undesirable effects the abort would cause could potentially occur on application exit. The preferable approach would be cooperative cancellation in which the Task supports cancellation and the application invokes the cancellation and waits for the task to complete.

Note that Task also supports IDisposable. This is necessary to support the Wait() functionality. Wait() relies on WaitHandle, and since WaitHandle supports IDisposable, Task also supports IDisposable in accordance with best practices. However, readers will note that the preceding code samples do not include a Dispose() call nor do they rely on such a call implicitly via the using statement. Technically, invoking Dispose() would be better code, however, so reasonable attempts should generally be made to do this.

Although instantiations of a task should generally include a corresponding Dispose() call and without it, any call to Wait() could result in a WaitHandle instance without a Dispose() call, missing this call is not critical. For example, listings in this chapter don't include Task.Dispose() calls, relying instead on an automatic WaitHandle finalizer invocation when the program exits. In these examples, any call to Dispose() would be inconsequential, so it was left off in favor of elucidation. However, technically, it should be there and developers should generally include it unless the code becomes ugly such that relying on the finalization queue is an acceptable trade-off. Although calling Dispose() does reduce pressure on the finalization queue later on, unless there is an exorbitant number of Tasks and corresponding WaitHandles, there is not a significant resource consumed by not calling Dispose() as soon as possible. Therefore, allowing finalize to be responsible for the resource cleanup is not unreasonable—in cases when a fire-and-forget invocation pattern is desirable, for example.

Executing Iterations in Parallel

Consider the for loop statement and the following code that uses such a loop (see Listing 18.8 and the corresponding Output 18.6). The listing calls a method for calculating a section of pi where the first parameter is the number of digits (BatchSize) and the digit to start with (i * BatchSize). The actual calculation is not germane to the discussion, so a full listing appears in the appendix. However, one characteristic that makes this great for multithreading is the fact that the calculation can be split into pieces.

LISTING 18.8: For Loop Synchronously Calculating Pi in Sections

```csharp
using System;

const int TotalDigits = 100;
const int BatchSize = 10;

class Program
{
  void Main()
  {
      string pi = null;
      int iterations = TotalDigits / BatchSize;
      for (int i = 0; i < iterations; i++)
      {
          pi += PiCalculator.Calculate(
              BatchSize, i * BatchSize);
      }

      Console.WriteLine(pi);
  }
}
```

```csharp
using System;

class PiCalculator
{
  public static string Calculate(int digits, int startingAt)
  {
    // ...
  }

  // ...
}
```

OUTPUT 18.6:

```
>3.141592653589793238462643383279502884197169399375105820974944592307816
406286208998628034825342117067982148086513282306647093844609550582231725
359408128481117450284102701938521105559644622948954930381964428810975665
933446128475648233786783165271201909145648566923460348610454326648213393
607260249141273724587006606315588174881520920962829254091715364367892590
360011330530548820466521384146951941511609433057270365759595919530921861117
381932611793105118548074462379962749567351885752724891227938183011949129
```

The for loop executes each iteration synchronously and sequentially. However, since the pi calculation algorithm splits the pi calculation into independent pieces, it is not necessary to complete the pieces sequentially as long as they are still all appended sequentially. Therefore, imagine if you could have iterations run simultaneously, overlapping each other because each processor could take an iteration and execute it in parallel with other processors executing other iterations. Given the simultaneous execution of iterations, we could decrease the execution time more and more based on the number of processors.

```
Parallel.For()
```

.NET 4 includes such a parallel for capability through an API on System. Threading.Tasks.Parallel, as shown in Listing 18.9.

LISTING 18.9: For Loop Calculating Pi in Sections in Parallel

```csharp
using System;
using System.Threading;

// ...

class Program
{
  void Main()
  {
      string pi = null;
      int iterations = TotalDigits / BatchSize;
      string[] sections = new string[iterations];
      Parallel.For(0, iterations, (i) =>
      {
          sections[i] += PiCalculator.Calculate(
              BatchSize, i * BatchSize);
      });
      pi = string.Join("", sections);
      Console.WriteLine(pi);
  }
}
```

The output for Listing 18.9 is identical to Output 18.6; however, the execution time is significantly faster (assuming multiple CPUs). The Parallel.For() API is designed to look similar to a standard for loop. The first parameter is the fromInclusive value, the second is the toExclusive value, and the last is the Action<int> to perform. When using an expression statement (with curly brackets) for the action, the code looks similar to a for loop statement except now each iteration may execute in parallel.

As with the for loop, the call to `Parallel.For()` will not complete until all iterations are complete. In other words, by the time execution reaches the `string.Join()` statement, all sections of pi will have been calculated.

It is important to note that the code for combining the various sections of pi no longer occurs inside the iteration (`action`). Since sections of the pi calculation will very likely not complete sequentially, appending a section whenever an iteration completes will likely append them out of order. Even if sequence was not a problem, there is still a potential race condition because the += operator is not atomic. To address both of these problems, each section of pi is stored into an array and no two or more iterations will access a single element within the array simultaneously. Only once all sections of pi are calculated does `string.Join()` combine them. In other words, we postpone concatenating the sections until after the `Parallel.For()` loop has completed. This avoids any race condition caused by sections not yet calculated or sections concatenating out of order.

```
Parallel.ForEach()
```

Parallel execution of a loop is not limited to the construct of for. `Parallel.ForEach()` provides similar capabilities for the foreach loop, as shown in Listing 18.10.

LISTING 18.10: Parallel Execution of a foreach Loop

```csharp
using System;
using System.Collections.Generic;
using System.IO;
using System.Threading.Tasks;

class Program
{
    // ...
    static void EncryptFiles(
        string directoryPath, string searchPattern)
    {

        IEnumerable<string> files = Directory.GetFiles(
            directoryPath, searchPattern,
            SearchOption.AllDirectories);

        Parallel.ForEach(files, (fileName) =>
        {
            Encrypt(fileName);
        });
```

```
    }
    // ...
}
```

In this example, we call a method that encrypts each file within the `files` collection and it does so in parallel, executing as many threads as the API determines is efficient. Efficiency is determined by a "hill climbing" algorithm in which additional threads are created until the overhead of additional threads begins to decrease overall performance—at which point the most efficient number of threads is determined (dynamically). The **degree of parallelism** corresponds to the number of threads that run simultaneously at any particular time.

Parallel Exception Handling with `System.AggregateException`

While executing the query in parallel, there is the potential for multiple exceptions—one for each started iteration. Notice, therefore, that if an exception throws while the loop is executing, the exception type is a `System.AggregateException`—an exception that contains multiple inner exceptions. In this way, all exceptions within the loop are handled with a single try/catch block. The `System.Threading.Task` namespace uses the `System.AggregateException` consistently for grouping together unhandled exceptions because, with parallel operations, there is frequently the potential for multiple exceptions. Consider the example in Listing 18.11 and its output in Output 18.7.

LISTING 18.11: Unhandled Exception Handling for Parallel Iterations

```
using System;
using System.Collections.Generic;
using System.IO;
using System.Threading;

class Program
{
  // ...
  static void EncryptFiles(
      string directoryPath, string searchPattern)
  {
      IEnumerable<string> files = Directory.GetFiles(
          directoryPath, searchPattern,
          SearchOption.AllDirectories);
      try
```

```
    {
        Parallel.ForEach(files, (fileName) =>
        {
            Encrypt(fileName);
        });
    }
    catch (AggregateException exception)
    {
        Console.WriteLine(
            "ERROR: {0}:",
            exception.GetType().Name);
        foreach (Exception item in
            exception.InnerExceptions)
        {
            Console.WriteLine("   {0} - {1}",
                item.GetType().Name, item.Message);
        }
    }
}
// ...
}
```

OUTPUT 18.7:

```
ERROR: AggregateException:
  UnauthorizedAccessException - Attempted to perform an unauthorized
operation.
  UnauthorizedAccessException - Attempted to perform an unauthorized
operation.
  UnauthorizedAccessException - Attempted to perform an unauthorized
operation.
```

Output 18.7 shows that three exceptions occurred while executing the Parallel.ForEach<T>(...) loop. However, in the code, there is only one catch of type System.AggregationException. The UnauthorizedAccessExceptions were retrieved from the InnerExceptions property on the AggregationException. With a Parallel.ForEach<T>() loop, each iteration could potentially throw an exception and so the System.AggregationException thrown by the method call will contain each of those exceptions within its InnerExceptions property.

Canceling a Parallel Loop

Unlike a task which requires an explicit call in order to block until it completes, a parallel loop executes iterations in parallel but still blocks until the entire Parallel.For() or Parallel.ForEach<T>() loop completes. Canceling a parallel loop, therefore, generally involves invocation of the cancellation request from a thread other than the one executing the parallel loop. In Listing 18.12, we invoke Parallel.ForEach<T>() using Task.Factory.StartNew(). In this manner, not only does the query execute in parallel, but it also executes asynchronously, allowing the code to prompt the user to "Push ENTER to exit."

LISTING 18.12: Canceling a Parallel Loop

```csharp
using System;
using System.Diagnostics;
using System.Threading;
using System.Threading.Tasks;

public class Program
{
    // ...

  static void EncryptFiles(
      string directoryPath, string searchPattern)
  {

      IEnumerable<string> files = Directory.GetFiles(
          directoryPath, searchPattern,
          SearchOption.AllDirectories);

      CancellationTokenSource cts =
          new CancellationTokenSource();
      ParallelOptions parallelOptions =
          new ParallelOptions
              { CancellationToken = cts.Token };
      cts.Token.Register(
          () => Console.WriteLine("Cancelling..."));

      Console.WriteLine("Push ENTER to exit.");

      Task task = Task.Factory.StartNew(() =>
          {
              try
              {
                  Parallel.ForEach(
                      files, parallelOptions,
                      (fileName, loopState) =>
                      {
                          Encrypt(fileName);
                      });
```

```
        }
        catch(OperationCanceledException){}
    });

    // Wait for the user's input
    Console.Read();

    // Cancel the query
    cts.Cancel();
    Console.Write(stars);
    task.Wait();
  }
}
```

The parallel loops use the same cancellation token pattern that Tasks use. The CancellationTokenSource.Token property is associated with the parallel loop via overloads on the parallel loops—overloads that take a System.Threading.ParallelOptions object. This object includes a Token property of type CancellationTokenSource.

Note that internally the parallel loop case prevents new iterations that haven't started yet from commencing via the IsCancellationRequested property. Existing executing iterations will run to their respective termination points. Furthermore, calling Cancel() even after all iterations have completed will still cause the registered cancel event (via cts.Token.Register()) to execute.

Also, the only means by which Parallel is able to acknowledge that the cancellation request has been processed (versus completed successfully) is via the OperationCanceledException. Given that cancellation in this example is an option for the user, the exception is caught and ignored, allowing the application to display "Canceling . . ." followed by a line of stars before exiting.

■ ADVANCED TOPIC

Parallel Results and Options

Although uncommon, it is possible to control the maximum degree of parallelism via the ParallelOptions parameter on overloads of both the Parallel.For() and Parallel.ForEach<T>() loops. Although Microsoft has invested significantly across a wide range of processor counts, to determine optimal numbers for the degree of parallelism—at least in the general case—there are specific cases where the developer knows more about the specific algorithm or circumstance such that changing the maximum degree of parallelism makes sense. Circumstances include:

- Setting the value to 1. This can be a means of turning off parallelism in order to simplify debugging.
- Knowing that the algorithm doesn't scale beyond a certain upper bound—for example, if the algorithm is limited by additional hardware constraints such as the number of USB ports that are available.
- If the body of the iteration is blocked for long periods, and creating additional parallel iterations (possibly also with extended blocking) will not increase the throughput and instead will cause unnecessary context switching with little to no progress.

To control the maximum degree of parallel, use the `ParallelOptions.Max-DegreeOfParallelism` property.

Additional settings available on an instance of `ParallelOptions` include a specific task scheduler (`ParallelOptions.TaskScheduler`) and the cancellation token (`ParallelOptions.CancellationToken`). The task scheduler has complete control over a `Task`'s execution, including when, in what sequence, and on what thread a task executes. For example, if a user repeatedly clicks Next to proceed to the next screen—and all of the screens are loaded asynchronously—you may want to execute iterations that load the data in last in, first out (LIFO) order because the user perhaps only wants to see the last screen he requested. Alternatively, if the save operation occurs multiple times, again asynchronously, you probably want to enter the save requests in first in, first out (FIFO) order to avoid any overwriting of later changes. The task scheduler provides a means of specifying how the tasks will execute in relation to each other.

The `CancellationToken` provides a mechanism to communicate to the loop that no further iterations should start. Additionally, the body of an iteration can watch the cancellation token to determine if an early exit from the iteration is in order. Like a standard `for` loop, `Parallel`'s loops also support the concept of breaking to exit the loop and canceling any further iterations. In the context of parallel for execution, however, break identifies that no *new* iterations following the breaking iteration should start. All currently executing iterations will run to completion.

For example, given the following circumstances:

- A total of ten iterations numbered sequentially from 1 to 10
- Iteration 1 has run to completion
- Iterations 3, 5, 7, and 9 are currently executing (remember, the order of execution is determined by the task scheduler and is not necessarily sequential)
- A break (`ParallelLoopState.Break()`) executes on iterations 5 and 7 at the conclusion of the parallel loop, iterations 1 through 5, 7, and 9 will complete. Iterations 6 and 8 will not complete (they never even started before 5 was canceled).

To determine the lowest iteration to execute a break and identify whether the break prevented one or more iterations from starting, the parallel `For()`/`Foreach()` method returns a `System.Threading.Parallel-LoopResult` object. This result object has the following properties:

- `IsCompleted`: returns a Boolean indicating whether all iterations started.
- `LowestBreakIteration`: identifies the lowest iteration that executed a break. The value is of type `long?`, where a value of null indicates no break statement was encountered.

Returning to the ten-iteration example, the `IsCompleted` property will return `false` and the `LowestBreakIteration` will return a value of 5. The C# break statement equivalent is possible using the `ParallelLoop-State.Break()` method where the `ParallelLoopState` is a type parameter on the `Action<int, ParallelLoopState>` specified in some of the parallel `For()`/`Foreach()`loop overloads.

In addition to `ParallelLoopState.Break()` there is also a `Parallel-LoopState.Stop()`. The behavior is similar to break except that iterations that have not yet started, even those prior to the iteration executing the

ParallelLoopState.Stop(), will not be allowed to start. Returning to the ten-iteration example but replacing the break with a stop (ParallelLoop-State.Stop()) will vary the results slightly. Instead of iterations 1 through 7 executing through completion, only the odd iterations will run to completion.

Further overloads on both parallel functions include Func<TLocal> and Action<TLocal> parameters for handling initialization and final execution expressions, respectively, for each *task* used in the parallel loop. Overloads are available for passing state regarding early exit to be passed between iterations.

Running LINQ Queries in Parallel

With Listing 18.10, we enumerate over the collection using Parallel.ForEach<T>(). It is also possible to execute LINQ queries in parallel using the Parallel LINQ API, PLINQ. Consider Listing 18.13.

LISTING 18.13: LINQ Select()

```csharp
using System.Linq;

class Cryptographer
{
  // ...
  public List<string> SynchronousEncrypt(List<string> data)
  {
      return data.Select(
          (item) => Encrypt(item)).ToList();
  }
  // ...
}
```

In Listing 18.13, we have a LINQ query using the Select() standard query operator to encrypt each string within the collection.

Consider the same code in Listing 18.14, except that in this listing, the code encrypts the strings in parallel.

LISTING 18.14: Parallel LINQ Select()

```csharp
using System.Linq;

class Cryptographer
```

```
{
  // ...
  public List<string> ParallelEncrypt(List<string> data)
  {
      return data.AsParallel().Select(
          (item) => Encrypt(item)).ToList();
  }
  // ...
}
```

As Listing 18.14 shows, the change to enable parallel support is minimal. All that it uses is a .NET Framework 4-introduced standard query operator, AsParallel(), on the static class System.Linq.ParallelEnumerable. Using this simple extension method, the runtime begins executing over the items within the data collection and encrypting them in parallel. The result is a completion time that gets noticeably shorter than the synchronous alternative over a significantly sized set when there are multiple processors.

System.Linq.ParallelEnumerable includes a superset of the query operators available on System.Linq.Enumerable, resulting in possible performance improvements for all of the predominant query operators including those used for filtering (Where()), projecting (Select()), joining, grouping, and aggregating.

LISTING 18.15: Parallel LINQ with Standard Query Operators

```
// ...
      ParallelQuery<IGrouping<char, string>>
parallelGroups;
      parallelGroups = data.AsParallel().
          OrderBy(item => item).

      // Show the total count of items still
      // matches the original count
      System.Diagnostics.Trace.Assert(
          data.Count == parallelGroups.Sum(
              item => item.Count()));
// ...
```

As Listing 18.15 shows, invoking the parallel version simply involves a call to the IEnumerable<T>.AsParallel() extension method. Furthermore, the result of calling a parallel standard query operator is a parallel enumerator, usually `ParallelQuery<T>`, which means that further operations on the result of a PLINQ query will be performed in parallel.

To use PLINQ with query expressions, the process is very similar (see Listing 18.16).

LISTING 18.16: Parallel LINQ with Query Expressions

```
// ...
        ParallelQuery<IGrouping<char, string>> parallelGroups;
        parallelGroups =
            from text in data.AsParallel()
              orderby text
              group text by text[0];

        // Show the total count of items still
        // matches the original count
        System.Diagnostics.Trace.Assert(
            data.Count == parallelGroups.Sum(
            item => item.Count()));
// ...
```

As you saw in the previous examples, converting a query to execute in parallel is simple. There is one significant caveat, however. As we will discuss in depth in the next chapter, you must take care not to allow multiple threads to inappropriately access and modify the same memory simultaneously. Doing so will cause a race condition.

Just as with parallel `for` and `foreach`, PLINQ operations also have the potential of returning multiple exceptions for the exact same reason (simultaneous execution of iterations). Fortunately, the mechanism for catching the exceptions is the same as well; PLINQ exceptions are accessible via the `InnerExceptions` property of the `AggregateException`. Therefore, wrapping a PLINQ query in a try/catch block with the exception type of `System.AggregateException` will successfully handle any exceptions within each iteration that were unhandled.

Canceling a PLINQ Query

Not surprisingly, the cancellation request pattern is also available on PLINQ queries. Listing 18.16 (with Output 18.8) provides an example. Like the parallel loops, canceled PLINQ queries will throw a `System.Opera-tionCanceledException`. Also, PLINQ queries block the calling thread until they complete. Therefore, Listing 18.17 also wraps the query in a task.

LISTING 18.17: Canceling a Parallel Loop

```
using System;
using System.Collections.Generic;
using System.Linq;
using System.Threading;
using System.Threading.Tasks;

public class Program
{

  public static List<string> ParallelEncrypt(
      List<string> data,
      CancellationToken cancellationToken)
  {
      return data.AsParallel().WithCancellation(
          cancellationToken).Select(
              (item) => Encrypt(item)).ToList();
  }

  public static void Main()
  {
      List<string> data = Utility.GetData(1000000).ToList();

      CancellationTokenSource cts =
          new CancellationTokenSource();

      Console.WriteLine("Push ENTER to exit.");

      Task task = Task.Factory.StartNew(() =>
          {
              data = ParallelEncrypt(data, cts.Token);
          } , cts.Token);

      // Wait for the user's input
      Console.Read();

      cts.Cancel();
      Console.Write(stars);
      try{task.Wait();}
      catch (AggregateException){}  }

  // ...
  }
```

OUTPUT 18.8:

```
ERROR: The operation was canceled.
```

As with a parallel loop, canceling a PLINQ query requires a `Cancella-tionToken`, which is available on a `CancellationTokenSource.Token` property. However, rather than overloading every PLINQ query to support the cancellation token, the `ParallelQuery<T>` object returned by `IEnumerable`'s `AsParallel()` method includes a `WithCancellation()` extension method that simply takes a `CancellationToken`. As a result, calling `Cancel()` on the `CancellationTokenSource` object will request the parallel query to cancel—because it checks the `IsCancellationRequested` property on the `CancellationToken`.

As mentioned, canceling a PLINQ query will throw an exception in place of returning the complete result. Therefore, all canceled PLINQ queries will need to be wrapped by `try{…}/catch(OperationCanceledException){…}` blocks to avoid an unhandled exception. Alternatively, as shown in Listing 18.17, pass the `CancellationToken` to both `ParallelEncrypt()` and as a second parameter on `StartNew()`. This will cause `task.Wait()` to throw an `AggregateException` whose `InnerException` property will be set to a `TaskCanceledException`.

Multithreading before .NET Framework 4

TPL is a fantastic library covering a multitude of multithreading patterns with extensibility points to handle even more. However, there is one significant drawback to TPL: It is available only for the .NET Framework 4 or for use with the Rx library in .NET 3.5. In this section, we cover multithreading technology before TPL.

Asynchronous Operations with System.Threading.Thread

Listing 18.18 (with Output 18.9) provides an example. Like TPL, there is a fundamental type, `System.Threading.Thread`, which is used to control an asynchronous operation. Like `System.Threading.Tasks.Task` in TPL, `Thread` includes a `Start` method and a wait equivalent, `Join()`.

LISTING 18.18: Starting a Method Using System.Threading.Thread

```
using System;
using System.Threading;

public class RunningASeparateThread
```

```
{
  public const int Repetitions = 1000;

  public static void Main()
  {
      ThreadStart threadStart = DoWork;
      Thread thread = new Thread(threadStart);
      thread.Start();
      for (int count = 0; count < Repetitions; count++)
      {
          Console.Write('-');
      }
      thread.Join();
  }

  public static void DoWork()
  {
      for (int count = 0; count < Repetitions; count++)
      {
          Console.Write('.');
      }
  }
}
```

OUTPUT 18.9:

```
................................------------------------------------------------
--------------------------------------------------------------------------------
--------------------------------------------------------------------------------
--------------------------------------------------------------------------------
--------------------------------------------------------------------------------
--------------------------------------------------------------------------------
................................................................................
................................................................................
................................................................................
................................................................................
................................................................................
.....................................-------------------------------------------
--------------------------------------------------------------------------------
--------------------------------------------------------------------------------
--------------------------------------------------------------------------------
--------------------------------------------------------------------------------
................................................................................
................................................................................
................................................................................
................................................................................
................................................................................
.........-----------------------------------------------------------------------
--------------------------------------------------------------------------------
--------------------------------------------------------------------------------
................................................................................
................................................................................
```

Like the output of Listing 18.9, which used TPL, Listing 18.18's code (see Output 18.9) intersperses . and – in the output. The code that is to execute in a new thread appears in the `DoWork()` method. The `DoWork()` method outputs a . during each iteration within a loop. Besides the fact that it contains code for starting another thread, the `Main()` method is virtually identical in structure to `DoWork()`, except that it displays -. The resultant output is due to a series of dashes until the thread context switches, at which time the program displays periods until the next thread switch, and so on.[2]

In order for code to run under the context of a different thread, you need a delegate of type `System.Threading.ThreadStart` or `System.Threading.ParameterizedThreadStart` (the latter allows for a single parameter of type `object`), identifying the code to execute. Given a `Thread` instance created using the thread-start delegate constructor, you can start the thread executing with a call to `thread.Start()`. (Listing 18.18 shows the `ThreadStart` explicitly to identify the delegate type. In general, `DoWork` could be passed directly to the thread constructor using C# 2.0's delegate inference.) Starting the thread simply involves a call to `Thread.Start()`. As soon as the `DoWork()` method begins execution, the call to `Thread.Start()` returns and executes the `for` loop in the `Main()` method. The threads are now independent and neither waits for the other. The output from Listing 18.18 and Listing 18.19 will intermingle the output of each thread, instead of creating a series of . followed by -.

Thread Management

Threads include a number of methods and properties for managing their execution.

- `Join()`: Once threads are started, you can cause a "wait for completion" with a call to `thread.Join()`. The calling thread will wait until the `thread` instance terminates. The `Join()` method is overloaded to take either an `int` or a `TimeSpan` to support a maximum time to wait for thread completion before continuing execution.

---

2. As mentioned earlier, it is possible to increase the chances of a thread context switch by using `Start /low /b <program.exe>` to execute the program.

- IsBackground: Another thread configuration option is the thread.IsBackGround property. By default, a thread is a foreground thread, meaning the process will not terminate until the thread completes. In contrast, setting the IsBackground property to true will allow process execution to terminate prior to a thread's completion.

- Priority: When using the Join() method, you can increase or decrease the thread's priority by setting the Priority to a new ThreadPriority enum value (Lowest, BelowNormal, Normal, Above-Normal, or Highest).

- ThreadState: A thread's state is accessible through the ThreadState property, a more precise reflection of the Boolean IsAlive property. The ThreadState enum flag values are Aborted, AbortRequested, Background, Running, Stopped, StopRequested, Suspended, Suspend-Requested, Unstarted, and WaitSleepJoin. The flag names indicate activities that may occur on a thread. Two noteworthy methods are Thread.Sleep() and Abort().

- Thread.Sleep(): Thread.Sleep() is a static method that pauses the current thread for a period. A single parameter (in milliseconds, or a TimeSpan) specifies how long the active thread waits before continuing execution. This enables switching to a different thread for a specific period.

  This method is not for accurate timing. Returns can occur hundreds of milliseconds *before* or *after* the specified time.

- Abort(): A thread's Abort() method causes a ThreadAbortException to be thrown within the target thread at whatever location the thread is executing when Abort() is invoked. As already detailed, aborting a thread introduces uncertainty into the thread's behavior and could cause data integrity and resource cleanup problems. Developers should consider the Abort() method to be a last resort. Instead, they should rely on threads running to completion and/or signaling them to escape out of whatever code is running via some with shared state.

From this list of Thread members, only Join() and ThreadState have Task equivalents. For the most part, this is because there are generally preferable equivalents or the behavior of the member is undesirable as a best practice. For example, aborting a thread may threaten data integrity or inadequate resource de-allocation, as mentioned earlier in the chapter. Therefore, given the .NET Framework 4, developers should generally avoid these members in favor of their task equivalents or alternative patterns entirely.

In summary, the general priority for selecting from the asynchronous class options is Task, ThreadPool, and Thread. In other words, use TPL, but if that doesn't fit, use ThreadPool; if that still doesn't suffice, use Thread.

One particular Thread member that is likely to crop up more frequently because there is no Task or ThreadPool equivalent is Thread.Sleep(). Although, if it doesn't introduce too much unnecessary complexity, consider using a timer in place of Sleep().

Thread Pooling

Regardless of the number of processors, an excess of threads negatively affects performance. To efficiently manage thread creation, TPL makes extensive use of CLR's thread pool, System.Threading.ThreadPool. Most importantly, the thread pool dynamically determines when to use existing threads rather than creating new ones. Fortunately, the .NET 3.5 Framework includes a version of the System.Threading.ThreadPool, so it is available even without TPL.

Accessing threads in ThreadPool is similar to explicit use of the Thread class except that the invocation is via a static method, QueueUser-WorkItem() (see Listing 18.19).

LISTING 18.19: Using ThreadPool Instead of Instantiating Threads Explicitly

```csharp
using System;
using System.Threading;

public class Program
{
  public const int Repetitions = 1000;
  public static void Main()
  {
      ThreadPool.QueueUserWorkItem(DoWork, '.');

      for (int count = 0; count < Repetitions; count++)
      {
```

```
            Console.Write('-');
        }

        // Pause until the thread completes
        Thread.Sleep(1000);
    }
    public static void DoWork(object state)
    {
        for (int count = 0; count < Repetitions; count++)
        {
            Console.Write(state);
        }
    }
}
```

The output is similar to Output 18.9, an intermingling of . and -. This provides more-efficient execution on single- and multiprocessor computers. The efficiency is achieved by reusing threads over and over, rather than reconstructing them for every asynchronous call.

Unfortunately, thread pool use is not without its pitfalls. Activities such as I/O operations and other framework methods that internally use the thread pool can consume threads as well. Consuming all threads within the pool can delay execution and, in extreme cases, cause a deadlock. Similarly, if the asynchronous code will take a long time to execute, then it is inappropriate to consume a shared thread from the thread pool and instead favor explicit Thread instantiation (use TaskCreationOptions.LongRunning given TPL as mentioned earlier).

Unfortunately, another disadvantage with the thread pool is that, unlike either Thread or Task, the ThreadPool API does not return a handle to the thread or task itself. This prevents the calling thread from controlling it with the thread management functions described earlier in the chapter. Just monitoring state is not available without explicitly adding a custom implementation. Assuming these deficiencies are not critical, developers should consider using the thread pool over explicit thread creation because of it increased efficiency—at least prior to .NET Framework 4 and TPL; the fact that TPL uses the thread pool internally indicates the significance of using it for the majority of multithreading scenarios.

Unhandled Exceptions on the AppDomain

To catch all exceptions from a thread (for which appropriate handling is known), you surround the root code block with a try/catch/finally block, just as you would for all code within Main(). However, what happens if a third-party component creates an alternate thread and throws an unhandled exception from that thread? Similarly, what if queued work on the thread pool throws an exception? A try/catch block in Main() will not catch an exception on an alternate thread. Furthermore, without access to any "handle" that invoked the thread (such as a Task) there is no way to catch any exceptions that it might throw. Even if there was, the code could never appropriately recover from all possible exceptions and continue executing (in fact, this is why in .NET 4.0 exceptions such as System.StackOverflowException, for example, will not be caught and instead will tear down the application). The general unhandled-exceptions guideline is for the program to shut down and restart in a clean state instead of behaving erratically or hanging because of an invalid state.

However, instead of crashing suddenly or ignoring an unhandled exception entirely if it occurs on an alternate thread, it is often desirable to save any working data and/or log the exception for error reporting and future debugging. This requires a mechanism to register for notifications of unhandled exceptions.

Registering for unhandled exceptions on the main application domain occurs via an application domain's UnhandledException event. Listing 18.20 demonstrates that process, and Output 18.10 shows the results.

LISTING 18.20: Registering for Unhandled Exceptions

```
using System;
using System.Threading;

public class Program
{
  public static void Main()
  {
      try
      {
          // Register a callback to
          // receive notifications
          // of any unhandled exception.
          AppDomain.CurrentDomain.UnhandledException
              += OnUnhandledException;
```

```
            ThreadPool.QueueUserWorkItem(
                state =>
                {
                    throw new Exception(
                        "Arbitrary Exception");
                });

            // ...

            // Wait for the unhandled exception to fire
            // ADVANCED: Use ManualResetEvent to avoid
            // timing dependent code.
            Thread.Sleep(10000);

            Console.WriteLine("Still running...");
        }
        finally
        {
            Console.WriteLine("Exiting...");
        }
    }

    static void OnUnhandledException(
        object sender,
        UnhandledExceptionEventArgs eventArgs)
    {
        Exception exception =
            (Exception)eventArgs.ExceptionObject;
        Console.WriteLine("ERROR ({0}):{1} ---> {2}",
            exception.GetType().Name,
            exception.Message,
            exception.InnerException.Message);
    }

    public static void ThrowException()
    {
        throw new ApplicationException(
            "Arbitrary exception");
    }
}
```

OUTPUT 18.10:

```
Still running...
Exiting...
ERROR (AggregateException):One or more errors occurred. ---> Arbitrary
Exception
```

The `UnhandledException` callback will fire for all unhandled exceptions on threads within the application domain, including the main thread. This is a notification mechanism, not a mechanism to catch and process exceptions so that the application can continue. After the event, the application will exit. In fact, the unhandled exception will cause the Windows Error dialog to display (Dr. Watson). And for console applications, the exception will appear on the console.

Astute readers will note that in Listing 18.20 we use `ThreadPool` rather than `Task`. This is because of the likelihood that the garbage collector will not have executed on `Task` before the application begins to shut down and any exceptions within the finalization will be suppressed rather than going unhandled. The likelihood of this case in most programs is generally low, but the best practice to avoid significant unhandled exceptions during application exit is to support task cancellation to cancel the task and wait for it to exit before shutting down the application.

SUMMARY

This chapter delved into the details surrounding the creation and manipulation of threads using the .NET Framework 4-introduced Task Parallel Library or TPL. This library includes new APIs for executing `for` and `foreach` loops such that iterations can potentially run in parallel. Underlying TPL is a new fundamental threading class, `System.Threading.Tasks.Task`, the basic threading unit on which all of TPL is based. It provides the standard multithreaded programming and monitoring activities and keeps them relatively simple. Given that `Task` forms the basis for parallel loops (`Parallel.For()` and `Parallel.ForEach()`), PLINQ, and more, it is clear that `Task` and its peer classes also enable a multitude of more complex threading scenarios—including unhandled exception handling and `Task` chaining/notifications—via `Task.ContinueWith<T>`.

In addition, the chapter demonstrated Parallel LINQ (PLINQ) in which a single extension method, `AsParallel()`, transforms all further LINQ queries to run in parallel. The elegance and simplicity with which this fits into the framework is superb.

The chapter closes with a section on multithreaded programming prior to TPL. The foundational class for this is `System.Threading.Thread`, and when appropriate, static methods on `ThreadPool` provide efficient means for reusing `Thread`s rather than creating new ones—a relatively inefficient operation. The priority order for choosing an asynchronous class is `Task`, `ThreadPool`, and `Thread`, resorting to a `Thread.Sleep()`, for example, because neither `Task` nor `ThreadPool` offers an equivalent. In making this evaluation, don't forget to consider using the Rx library in order to gain access to TPL and PLINQ within .NET 3.5.

There is one glaring omission from the chapter: synchronization. The introduction mentioned multithreading problems such as deadlocks and race conditions, but the chapter never discussed how to avoid them. This is the topic of the next chapter.

19

Synchronization and More Multithreading Patterns

IN THE PRECEDING CHAPTER, we discussed the details of multithreaded programming using the Task Parallel Library (TPL) and Parallel LINQ (PLINQ). One topic specifically avoided, however, was thread synchronization that prevents race conditions while avoiding deadlocks. Thread synchronization is the topic of this chapter.

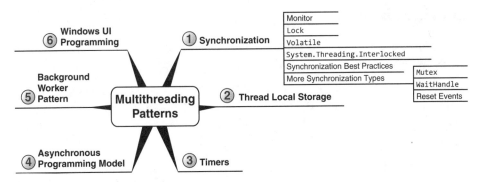

We begin with a multithreaded example with no thread synchronization around shared data—resulting in a race condition in which data integrity is lost. This serves as the introduction for why we need thread synchronization followed by myriad mechanisms and best practices for doing it.

The second half of the chapter looks at some additional multithreading patterns. This is really a continuation of the patterns first introduced in

Chapter 18 except that they depend on several of the synchronization tools introduced in this chapter. In addition, the chapter includes a discussion of three timers and Windows-based user interface programming.

This entire chapter uses TPL, so the samples cannot be compiled on frameworks prior to .NET Framework 4. However, unless specifically identified as a .NET Framework 4 API, the only reason for the .NET Framework 4 restriction is the use of the `System.Threading.Tasks.Task` class to execute the asynchronous operation. Modifying the code to instantiate a `System.Threading.Thread` and use a `Thread.Join()` to wait for the thread to execute will allow the vast majority of samples to compile on earlier frameworks.

Furthermore (as mentioned in the preceding chapter), Microsoft released the Reactive Extensions to .NET (Rx), a separate download that adds support for TPL and PLINQ within the .NET 3.5 framework. This framework also includes the concurrent and synchronization types introduced in this chapter. For this reason, code listings that depend on `Task` or that introduce C# 4.0 synchronization classes are, in fact, available from .NET 3.5 using the functionality backported to the .NET 3.5 Framework via Rx and reference to the `System.Threading.dll` assembly.

Synchronization

Running a new thread is a relatively simple programming task. What makes multithreaded programming difficult, however, is identifying which data multiple threads could access simultaneously. The program must synchronize such data to prevent simultaneous access. Consider Listing 19.1.

LISTING 19.1: Unsynchronized State

```csharp
using System;
using System.Threading.Tasks;

class Program
{
    const int _Total = int.MaxValue;
    static long _Count = 0;

    public static void Main()
    {
        Task task = Task.Factory.StartNew(Decrement);
```

```
    // Increment
    for (int i = 0; i < _Total; i++)
    {
        _Count++;
    }

    task.Wait();
    Console.WriteLine("Count = {0}", _Count);
}

static void Decrement()
{
    // Decrement
    for (int i = 0; i < _Total; i++)
    {
        _Count--;
    }
}
}
```

One possible result of Listing 19.1 appears in Output 19.1.

OUTPUT 19.1:

```
Count = 113449949
```

The important thing to note about Listing 19.1 is that the output is not 0. It would have been if Decrement() was called directly (sequentially). However, when calling Decrement() asynchronously, a race condition occurs because the individual steps within _Count++ and _Count-- statements intermingle. (As discussed in the Thread Basics Beginner Topic early in Chapter 18, a single statement in C# will likely involve multiple steps.) Consider the sample execution in Table 19.1.

Table 19.1 shows a parallel execution (or a thread context switch) by the transition of instructions appearing from one column to the other. The value of _Count after a particular line has completed appears in the last column. In this sample execution, _Count++ executes twice and _Count-- occurs once. However, the resultant _Count value is 0, not 1. Copying a result back to _Count essentially wipes out any _Count value changes that occurred since the read of _Count on the same thread.

TABLE 19.1: Sample Pseudocode Execution

Main Thread	Decrement Thread	Count
. . .	. . .	. . .
Copy the value 0 out of _Count.		0
Increment the copied value (0), resulting in 1.		0
Copy the resultant value (1) into _Count.		1
Copy the value 1 out of _Count.		1
	Copy the value 1 out of _Count.	1
Increment the copied value (1), resulting in 2.		1
Copy the resultant value (2) into _Count.		2
	Decrement the copied value (1), resulting in 0.	2
	Copy the resultant value (0) into _Count.	0
. . .	. . .	. . .

The problem in Listing 19.1 is a race condition, where multiple threads have simultaneous access to the same data elements. As this sample execution demonstrates, allowing multiple threads to access the same data elements likely undermines data integrity, even on a single-processor computer. To remedy this, the code needs synchronization around the data. Code or data synchronized for simultaneous access by multiple threads is **thread-safe.**

There is one important point to note about atomicity of reading and writing to variables. The runtime guarantees that a type whose size is no bigger than a native (pointer-size) integer will not be read or written partially. Assuming a 64-bit operating system, therefore, reads and writes to a `long` (64 bits) will be atomic. However, reads and writes to a 128-bit variable such as `decimal` may not be atomic. Therefore, write operations to change a `decimal` variable may be interrupted after copying only 32 bits, resulting in the reading of an incorrect value, known as a **torn read**.

■ **BEGINNER TOPIC**

Multiple Threads and Local Variables

Note that it is not necessary to synchronize local variables. Local variables are loaded onto the stack and each thread has its own logical stack. Therefore, each local variable has its own instance for each method call. By default, local variables are not shared across method calls; therefore, they are also not shared among multiple threads.

However, this does not mean local variables are entirely without concurrency issues since code could easily expose the local variable to multiple threads. A parallel `for` loop that shares a local variable between iterations, for example, will expose the variable to concurrent access and a race condition (see Listing 19.2).

LISTING 19.2: Unsynchronized Local Variables

```csharp
using System;
using System.Threading.Tasks;

class Program
{
  public static void Main()
  {
      int x = 0;
      Parallel.For(0, int.MaxValue, i =>
      {
          x++;
          x--;
      });
      Console.WriteLine("Count = {0}", x);
  }
}
```

In this example, x (a local variable) is accessed within a parallel for loop and so multiple threads will modify it simultaneously, creating a race condition very similar to Listing 19.1. The output is unlikely to yield the value 0 even though x is incremented and decremented the same number of times.

Synchronization Using Monitor

To synchronize multiple threads so that they cannot execute particular sections of code simultaneously, use a **monitor** to block the second thread from entering a protected code section before the first thread has exited that section. The monitor functionality is part of a class called System.Threading.Monitor, and the beginning and end of protected code sections are marked with calls to the static methods Monitor.Enter() and Monitor.Exit(), respectively.

Listing 19.3 demonstrates synchronization using the Monitor class explicitly. As this listing shows, it is important that all code between calls to Monitor.Enter() and Monitor.Exit() be surrounded with a try/finally block. Without this, an exception could occur within the protected section and Monitor.Exit() may never be called, thereby blocking other threads indefinitely.

LISTING 19.3: Synchronizing with a Monitor Explicitly

```csharp
using System;
using System.Threading;
using System.Threading.Tasks;

class Program
{
    readonly static object _Sync = new object();
    const int _Total = int.MaxValue;
    static long _Count = 0;

    public static void Main()
    {
        Task task = Task.Factory.StartNew(Decrement);

        // Increment
        for (int i = 0; i < _Total; i++)
```

```
        {
            bool lockTaken = false;
            Monitor.Enter(_Sync, ref lockTaken);
            try
            {
                _Count++;
            }
            finally
            {
                if (lockTaken)
                {
                    Monitor.Exit(_Sync);
                }              }
        }

    task.Wait();
    Console.WriteLine("Count = {0}", _Count);
}

static void Decrement()
{
    for (int i = 0; i < _Total; i++)
    {
        bool lockTaken = false;
        Monitor.Enter(_Sync, ref lockTaken);
        try
        {
            _Count--;
        }
        finally
        {
            if (lockTaken)
            {
                Monitor.Exit(_Sync);
            }
        }
    }
}
}
```

The results of Listing 19.3 appear in Output 19.2.

OUTPUT 19.2:

```
Count = 0
```

Note that calls to `Monitor.Enter()` and `Monitor.Exit()` are associated with each other by sharing the same object reference passed as the parameter (in this case `_Sync`).

The `Monitor.Enter()` overload method that takes the `lockTaken` parameter was only added to the framework in .NET 4.0. Before that, no such `lockTaken` parameter was available and there was no way to reliably catch an exception that occurred between the `Monitor.Enter()` and try block. Placing the try block immediately following the `Monitor.Enter()` call was reliable in release code because the JIT prevented any such asynchronous exception from sneaking in. However, anything other than a try block immediately following the `Monitor.Enter()`, including any instructions that the compiler may have injected within debug code, could prevent the JIT from reliably returning execution within the try block. Therefore, if an exception did occur, it would leak the lock (the lock remains acquired) rather than executing the final block and releasing it—likely causing a deadlock when another thread tries to acquire the lock.

`Monitor` also supports a `Pulse()` method for allowing a thread to enter the "ready queue," indicating it is up next for execution. This is a common means of synchronizing producer-consumer patterns so that no "consume" occurs until there has been a "produce." The producer thread that owns the monitor (by calling `Monitor.Enter()`) calls `Monitor.Pulse()` to signal the consumer thread (which may already have called `Monitor.Enter()`) that an item is available for consumption, so "get ready." For a single `Pulse()` call, only one thread (consumer in this case) can enter the ready queue. When the producer thread calls `Monitor.Exit()`, the consumer thread takes the lock (`Monitor.Enter()` completes) and enters the critical section to begin "consuming" the item. Once the consumer processes the waiting item, it calls `Exit()`, thus allowing the producer (currently blocked with `Monitor.Enter()`) to produce again. In this example, only one thread can enter the ready queue at a time, ensuring that there is no "consumption" without "production" and vice versa.

Using the `lock` Keyword

Because of the frequent need for synchronization using `Monitor` in multi-threaded code, and the fact that the try/finally block could easily be forgotten, C# provides a special keyword to handle this locking synchronization pattern. Listing 19.4 demonstrates the use of the `lock` keyword, and Output 19.3 shows the results.

LISTING 19.4: Synchronization Using the `lock` Keyword

```csharp
using System;
using System.Threading;
using System.Threading.Tasks;

class Program
{
    readonly static object _Sync = new object();
    const int _Total = int.MaxValue;
    static long _Count = 0;

    public static void Main()
    {
        Task task = Task.Factory.StartNew(Decrement);

        // Increment
        for (int i = 0; i < _Total; i++)
        {
            lock (_Sync)
            {
                _Count++;
            }
        }

        task.Wait();
        Console.WriteLine("Count = {0}", _Count);
    }

    static void Decrement()
    {
        for (int i = 0; i < _Total; i++)
        {
            lock (_Sync)
            {
                _Count--;
            }
```

```
            }
        }
    }
```

OUTPUT 19.3:

```
Count = 0
```

By locking the section of code accessing _Count (using either lock or Monitor), you make the Main() and Decrement() methods thread-safe, meaning they can be safely called from multiple threads simultaneously. (Prior to C# 4.0 the concept was the same except the compiler-emitted code depended on the Monitor.Enter() method without the lockTaken parameter and the Monitor.Enter() called was emitted before the try block.)

Synchronization comes at a cost to performance. Listing 19.4, for example, takes an order of magnitude longer to execute than Listing 19.1 does, which demonstrates lock's relatively slow execution compared to the execution of incrementing and decrementing the count.

Even when lock is insignificant in comparison with the work it synchronizes, programmers should avoid indiscriminate synchronization in order to avoid the possibility of deadlocks and unnecessary synchronization on multiprocessor computers that could instead be executing code in parallel. The general best practice for object design is to synchronize mutable static state (there is no need to synchronize something that never changes) and not any instance data. Programmers who allow multiple threads to access a particular object must provide synchronization for the object. Any class that explicitly deals with threads is likely to want to make instances thread-safe to some extent.

Choosing a lock Object

Whether or not the lock keyword or the Monitor class is explicitly used, it is crucial that programmers carefully select the lock object.

In the previous examples, the synchronization variable, _Sync, is declared as both private and read-only. It is declared read-only to ensure that the value is not changed between calls to Monitor.Enter() and Monitor.Exit(). This allows correlation between entering and exiting the synchronized block.

Similarly, the code declares _Sync as private so that no synchronization block outside the class can synchronize the same object instance, causing the code to block.

If the data is public, then the synchronization object may be public so that other classes can synchronize using the same object instance. This makes it harder to avoid deadlock. Fortunately, the need for this pattern is rare. For public data, it is preferable to leave synchronization entirely outside the class, allowing the calling code to take locks with its own synchronization object.

It's important that the synchronization object not be a value type. If the lock keyword is used on a value type, then the compiler will report an error. (In the case of accessing the System.Threading.Monitor class explicitly [not via lock], no such error will occur at compile time. Instead, the code will throw an exception with the call to Monitor.Exit(), indicating there was no corresponding Monitor.Enter() call.) The issue is that when using a value type, the runtime makes a copy of the value, places it in the heap (boxing occurs), and passes the boxed value to Monitor.Enter(). Similarly, Monitor.Exit() receives a boxed copy of the original variable. The result is that Monitor.Enter() and Monitor.Exit() receive different synchronization object instances so that no correlation between the two calls occurs.

Why to Avoid Locking on this, typeof(type), and string

One common pattern is to lock on the this keyword for instance data in a class, and on the type instance obtained from typeof(type) (for example, typeof(MyType)) for static data. Such a pattern provides a synchronization target for all states associated with a particular object instance when this is used, and all static data for a type when typeof(type) is used. The problem is that the synchronization target that this (or typeof(type)) points to could participate in the synchronization target for an entirely different synchronization block created in an unrelated block of code. In other words, although only the code within the instance itself can block using the this keyword, the caller that created the instance can pass that instance to a synchronization lock.

The result is that two different synchronization blocks that synchronize two entirely different sets of data could block each other. Although perhaps unlikely, sharing the same synchronization target could have an unintended performance impact and, in extreme cases, even cause a deadlock. Instead of locking on `this` or even `typeof(type)`, it is better to define a private, read-only field on which no one will block except for the class that has access to it.

Another lock type to avoid is `string` due to string interning. If the same `string` constant appears within multiple locations it is likely that all locations will refer to the same instance, making the scope of the lock a lot greater than expected.

In summary, use a per-synchronization context instance of type `object` for the lock target.

■ ADVANCED TOPIC

Avoid Synchronizing with `MethodImplAttribute`

One synchronization mechanism that was introduced in .NET 1.0 was the `MethodImplAttribute`. Used in conjunction with the `MethodImplOptions.Synchronized` method, this attribute marks a method as synchronized so that only one thread can execute the method at a time. To achieve this, the just-in-time compiler essentially treats the method as though it was surrounded by `lock(this)` or locking on the type in the case of a static method. Such an implementation means that, in fact, the method and all other methods on the same class, decorated with the same attribute and enum parameter, are synchronized, not just each method relative to itself. In other words, given two or more methods on the same class decorated with the attribute, only one of them will be able to execute at a time and the one executing will block all calls by other threads to itself or to any other method in the class with the same decoration. Furthermore, since the synchronization is on `this` (or even worse, on the type), it suffers the same detriments as `lock(this)` (or worse, for the static) discussed in the previous section. As a result, it is a best practice to avoid the attribute altogether.

Declaring Fields as `volatile`

On occasion, the compiler and/or CPU may optimize code in such a way that the instructions do not occur in the exact order they are coded, or some instructions are optimized out. Such optimizations are innocuous when code executes on one thread. However, with multiple threads, such optimizations may have unintended consequences because the optimizations may change the order of execution of a field's read or write operations relative to an alternate thread's access to the same field.

One way to stabilize this is to declare fields using the volatile keyword. This keyword forces all reads and writes to the volatile field to occur at the exact location the code identifies instead of at some other location that the optimization produces. The volatile modifier identifies that the field is susceptible to modification by the hardware, operating system, or another thread. As such, the data is "volatile," and the keyword instructs the compilers and runtime to handle it more exactly.

Using the System.Threading.Interlocked Class

The mutual exclusion pattern described so far provides the minimum of tools for handling synchronization within a process (application domain). However, synchronization with System.Threading.Monitor is a relatively expensive operation, and an alternative solution that the processor supports directly targets specific synchronization patterns.

Listing 19.5 sets _Data to a new value as long as the preceding value was null. As indicated by the method name, this pattern is the compare/exchange pattern. Instead of manually placing a lock around behaviorally equivalent compare and exchange code, the Interlocked.CompareExchange() method provides a built-in method for a synchronous operation that does the same check for a value (null) and swaps the first two parameters if the value is equal. Table 19.2 shows other synchronization methods supported by Interlocked.

LISTING 19.5: Synchronization Using System.Threading.Interlocked

```
class SynchronizationUsingInterlocked
{
    private static object _Data;

    // Initialize data if not yet assigned.
    static void Initialize(object newValue)
    {
        // If _Data is null then set it to newValue.
        Interlocked.CompareExchange(
            ref _Data, newValue, null);
    }

    // ...
}
```

TABLE 19.2: Interlock's Synchronization-Related Methods

Method Signature	Description

```public static T CompareExchange<T>(```
  ```T location,```
  ```T value,```
  ```T comparand```
```);```
	Checks location for the value in comparand. If the values are equal, it sets location to value and returns the original data stored in location.

```public static T Exchange<T>(```
  ```T location,```
  ```T value```
```);```
	Assigns location with value and returns the previous value.

```public static int Decrement(```
  ```ref int location```
```);```
	Decrements location by one. It is equivalent to the -- operator, except Decrement() is thread-safe.

```public static int Increment(```
  ```ref int location```
```);```
	Increments location by one. It is equivalent to the ++ operator, except Increment() is thread-safe.

```public static int Add(```
  ```ref int location,```
  ```int value```
```);```
	Adds value to location and assigns location the result. It is equivalent to the += operator.

```public static long Read(```
  ```ref long location```
```);```
	Returns a 64-bit value in a single atomic operation.

Most of these methods are overloaded with additional data type signatures, such as support for long. Table 19.2 provides the general signatures and descriptions. For example, the System.Threading namespace does not include generic method signatures until C# 2.0, although earlier versions do include nongeneric equivalents.

Note that you can use Increment() and Decrement() in place of the synchronized ++ and -- operators from Listing 19.5, and doing so will yield better performance. Also note that if a different thread accessed `location` using a noninterlocked method, then the two accesses would not be synchronized correctly.

Event Notification with Multiple Threads

One area where developers often overlook synchronization is when firing events. The unsafe thread code for publishing an event is similar to Listing 19.6.

LISTING 19.6: Firing an Event Notification

```
// Not thread-safe
if(OnTemperatureChanged != null)
{
  // Call subscribers
  OnTemperatureChanged(
      this, new TemperatureEventArgs(value) );
}
```

This code is valid as long as there is no race condition between this method and modifying the event. However, the code is not atomic, so multiple threads could introduce a race condition. It is possible that between the time when `OnTemperatureChange` is checked for `null` and the event is actually fired, `OnTemperatureChange` could be set to `null`, thereby throwing a `NullReferenceException`. In other words, if multiple threads could possibly access a delegate simultaneously, it is necessary to synchronize the assignment and firing of the delegate.

Fortunately, the operators for adding and removing listeners are thread-safe and static (operator overloading is done with static methods). To correct Listing 19.6 and make it thread-safe, assign a copy, check the copy for `null`, and fire the copy (see Listing 19.7).

LISTING 19.7: Thread-Safe Event Notification

```
// ...
TemperatureChangedHandler localOnChange =
    OnTemperatureChanged;
if(localOnChanged != null)
{
    // Call subscribers
    localOnChanged(
      this, new TemperatureEventArgs(value) );
}
// ...
```

Given that a delegate is a reference type, it is perhaps surprising that assigning a local variable and then firing with the local variable is sufficient for making the null check thread-safe. Since localOnChange points to the same location that OnTemperatureChange points to, one would think that any changes in OnTemperatureChange would be reflected in localOnChange as well.

However, this is not the case because any calls to OnTemperatureChange += <listener> will not add a new delegate to OnTemperatureChange, but rather will assign it an entirely new multicast delegate without having any effect on the original multicast delegate to which localOnChange also points. This makes the code thread-safe because only one thread will access the localOnChange instance, and OnTemperatureChange will be an entirely new instance if listeners are added or removed.

Synchronization Design Best Practices

Along with the complexities of multithreaded programming come several best practices for handling the complexities.

Avoiding Deadlock

With the introduction of synchronization comes the potential for deadlock. Deadlock occurs when two or more threads wait for each other to release a synchronization lock. For example, Thread 1 requests a lock on _Sync1, and then later requests a lock on _Sync2 before releasing the lock on _Sync1. At the same time, Thread 2 requests a lock on _Sync2, followed by a lock on _Sync1, before releasing the lock on _Sync2. This sets the stage for the deadlock. The deadlock actually occurs if both Thread 1 and Thread 2 successfully acquire their initial locks (_Sync1 and _Sync2, respectively) before obtaining their second locks.

For a deadlock to occur, four fundamental conditions must be met:

1. *Mutual exclusion:* One thread (ThreadA) exclusively owns a resource such that no other thread (ThreadB) can acquire the same resource.
2. *Hold and wait:* One thread (ThreadA) with a mutual exclusion is waiting to acquire a resource held by another thread (ThreadB).
3. *No preemption:* The resource held by a thread (ThreadA) cannot be forcibly removed (ThreadA needs to release its own locked resource).

4. *Circular wait condition:* Two or more threads form a circular chain such that they lock on the same two or more resources and each waits on the resource held by the next thread in the chain.

Removing any one of these conditions will prevent the deadlock.

A scenario likely to cause a deadlock is when two or more threads request exclusive ownership on the same two or more synchronization targets (resources) and the locks are requested in different orders. This is avoided when developers are careful to ensure that multiple lock acquisitions are always in the same order. Another cause of a deadlock is locks that are not **reentrant.** When a lock from one thread can block the same thread—that is, it is re-requesting the same lock—the lock is not reentrant. For example, if ThreadA acquires a lock and then re-requests the same lock but is blocked because the lock is already owned, the lock is not reentrant and the additional request will deadlock. Therefore, locks that are not reentrant can occur only with a single thread.

The code generated by the lock keyword (with the underlying Monitor class) is reentrant. However, as we shall see in the More Synchronization Types section, there are lock types that are not re-entrant.

When to Provide Synchronization

As already discussed, all static data should be thread-safe. Therefore, synchronization needs to surround static data that is mutable. Generally, this means that programmers should declare private static variables and then provide public methods for modifying the data. Such methods should internally handle the synchronization.

In contrast, instance state is not expected to include synchronization. Synchronization may significantly decrease performance and increase the chance of a lock contention or deadlock. With the exception of classes that are explicitly designed for multithreaded access, programmers sharing objects across multiple threads are expected to handle their own synchronization of the data being shared.

Avoiding Unnecessary Locking

Without compromising data integrity, programmers should avoid unnecessary synchronization where possible. For example, use immutable types between threads so that no synchronization is necessary (this approach has proven invaluable in functional programming languages such as F#). Similarly, avoid locking on operations on thread-safe operations such as simple reads and writes of an int.

More Synchronization Types

In addition to System.Threading.Monitor and System.Threading.Interlocked, several more synchronization techniques are available.

System.Threading.Mutex

System.Threading.Mutex is similar in concept to the System.Threading.Monitor class (without the Pulse() method support), except that the lock keyword does not use it and Mutexes can be named so that they support synchronization across multiple processes. Using the Mutex class, you can synchronize access to a file or some other cross-process resource. Since Mutex is a cross-process resource, .NET 2.0 added support to allow for setting the access control via a System.Security.AccessControl.MutexSecurity object. One use for the Mutex class is to limit an application so that it cannot run multiple times simultaneously, as Listing 19.8 demonstrates.

LISTING 19.8: Creating a Single Instance Application

```csharp
using System;
using System.Threading;
using System.Reflection;

class Program
{
    public static void Main()
    {
        // Indicates whether this is the first
        // application instance
        bool firstApplicationInstance;

        // Obtain the mutex name from the full
        // assembly name.
        string mutexName =
            Assembly.GetEntryAssembly().FullName;

        using( Mutex mutex = new Mutex(false, mutexName,
            out firstApplicationInstance) )
        {
```

```
            if(!firstApplicationInstance)
            {
                Console.WriteLine(
                    "This application is already running.");
            }
            else
            {
                Console.WriteLine("ENTER to shutdown");
                Console.ReadLine();
            }
        }
    }
}
```

The results from running the first instance of the application appear in Output 19.4.

OUTPUT 19.4:

```
ENTER to shutdown
```

The results of the second instance of the application while the first instance is still running appear in Output 19.5.

OUTPUT 19.5:

```
This application is already running.
```

In this case, the application can run only once on the machine, even if it is launched by different users. To restrict the instances to one per user, prefix `Assembly.GetEntryAssembly().FullName` with `System.Windows.Forms.Application.UserAppDataPath.Replace( "\\", "+" )` instead. This requires a reference to the `System.Windows.Forms` assembly.

`Mutex` derives from `System.Threading.WaitHandle` and, therefore, includes `WaitAll()`, `WaitAny()`, and `SignalAndWait()` methods, allowing it to acquire multiple locks automatically (something `Monitor` does not support).

WaitHandle
The base class for `Mutex` is a `System.Threading.WaitHandle`. This is a fundamental synchronization class used by the `Mutex`, `EventWaitHandle`, and

Semaphore synchronization classes. The key methods on a `WaitHandle` are the `WaitOne()` methods. These methods block execution until the `WaitHandle` instance is signaled or set. The `WaitOne()` methods include several overloads allowing for an indefinite wait: `void WaitOne()`, a millisecond timed wait; `bool WaitOne(int milliseconds)`; and `bool WaitOne(TimeSpan timeout)`, a `TimeSpan` wait. The versions that return a Boolean will return a value of `true` whenever the `WaitHandle` is signaled before the timeout.

In addition to the `WaitHandle` instance methods, there are two key static members: `WaitAll()` and `WaitAny()`. Like their instance cousins, the static members also support timeouts. In addition, they take a collection of `WaitHandles`, in the form of an array, so that they can respond to signals coming from any within the collection.

One last point to note about `WaitHandle` is that it contains a handle (of type `SafeWaitHandle`) that implements `IDisposable`. As such, care is needed to ensure that `WaitHandles` are disposed when they are no longer needed.

Reset Events: *ManualResetEvent* and *ManualResetEventSlim*

One way to control uncertainty about when particular instructions in a thread will execute relative to instructions in another thread is with reset events. In spite of the term *events,* reset events have nothing to do with C# delegates and events. Instead, reset events are a way to force code to wait for the execution of another thread until the other thread signals. These are especially useful for testing multithreaded code because it is possible to wait for a particular state before verifying the results.

The reset event types are `System.Threading.ManualResetEvent` and the .NET Framework 4–added lightweight, version `System.Threading.Manual ResetEventSlim`. (As discussed in the Advanced Topic on page 772, there is a third type, `System.Threading.AutoResetEvent`, but programmers should avoid it in favor of one of the first two.) The key methods on the reset events are `Set()` and `Wait()` (called `WaitOne()` on `ManualResetEvent`). Calling the `Wait()` method will cause a thread to block until a different thread calls

Set(), or until the wait period times out. Listing 19.9 demonstrates how this works, and Output 19.6 shows the results.

LISTING 19.9: Waiting for `ManualResetEventSlim`

```csharp
using System;
using System.Threading;
using System.Threading.Tasks;

public class Program
{
  static ManualResetEventSlim MainSignaledResetEvent;
  static ManualResetEventSlim DoWorkSignaledResetEvent;

  public static void DoWork()
  {
      Console.WriteLine("DoWork() started....");
      DoWorkSignaledResetEvent.Set();
      MainSignaledResetEvent.Wait();
      Console.WriteLine("DoWork() ending....");
  }

  public static void Main()
  {
      using(MainSignaledResetEvent =
          new ManualResetEventSlim())
      using (DoWorkSignaledResetEvent =
          new ManualResetEventSlim())
      {
          Console.WriteLine(
              "Application started....");
          Console.WriteLine("Starting task....");

          Task task = Task.Factory.StartNew(DoWork);

          // Block until DoWork() has started.
          DoWorkSignaledResetEvent.Wait();
          Console.WriteLine("Thread executing...");
          MainSignaledResetEvent.Set();
          task.Wait();
          Console.WriteLine("Thread completed");
          Console.WriteLine(
              "Application shutting down....");
      }
  }
}
```

OUTPUT 19.6:

```
Application started....
Starting thread....
DoWork() started....
Waiting while thread executes...
DoWork() ending....
Thread completed
Application shutting down....
```

Listing 19.9 begins by instantiating and starting a new Task. Table 19.3 shows the execution path in which each column represents a thread. In cases where code appears on the same row, it is indeterminate which side executes first.

TABLE 19.3: Execution Path with ManualResetEvent Synchronization

Main()	DoWork()
...	
Console.WriteLine("Application started....");	
Task task = new Task(DoWork);	
Console.WriteLine("Starting thread....");	
task.Start();	
DoWorkSignaledResetEvent.Wait();	Console.WriteLine("DoWork() started....");
	DoWorkSignaledResetEvent.Set();
Console.WriteLine("Thread executing...");	MainSignaledResetEvent.Wait();
MainSignaledResetEvent.Set();	
task.Wait();	Console.WriteLine("DoWork() ending....");

TABLE 19.3: Execution Path with **ManualResetEvent** Synchronization *(Continued)*

Main()	DoWork()
`Console.WriteLine(` `    "Thread completed");`	
`Console.WriteLine(` `    "Application exiting....");`	

Calling a reset event's `Wait()` method (for a `ManualResetEvent` it is called `WaitOne()`) blocks the calling thread until another thread signals and allows the blocked thread to continue. Instead of blocking indefinitely, `Wait()`/`WaitOne()` overrides include a parameter, either in milliseconds or as a `TimeSpan` object, for the maximum amount of time to block. When specifying a timeout period, the return from `WaitOne()` will be `false` if the timeout occurs before the reset event is signaled. `ManualResetEvent.Wait()` also includes a version that takes a cancellation token, allowing cancellation requests as discussed in the preceding chapter.

The difference between `ManualResetEventSlim` and `ManualReset Event` is the fact that the latter uses kernel synchronization by default whereas the former is optimized to avoid trips to the kernel except as a last resort. Thus, `ManualResetEventSlim` is more performant even though it could possibly use more CPU cycles. Therefore, use `ManualResetEventSlim` in general unless waiting on multiple events or across processes is required.

Notice that reset events implement `IDisposable`, so they should be disposed when they are no longer needed. In Listing 19.9, we do this via a using statement. (`CancellationTokenSource` contains a `ManualResetEvent`, which is why it too implements `IDisposable`.)

Although not exactly the same, `System.Threading.Monitor`'s `Wait()` and `Pulse()` methods provide similar functionality to reset events in some circumstances.

■ ADVANCED TOPIC

Favor ManualResetEvent and Semaphores over AutoResetEvent

There is a third reset event, System.Threading.AutoResetEvent, that, like ManualResetEvent, allows one thread to signal (with a call to Set()) another thread that this first thread has reached a certain location in the code. The difference is that the AutoResetEvent unblocks only one thread's Wait() call because after the first thread passes through the auto-reset gate, it goes back to locked. With the auto-reset event, however, it is too easy to mistakenly code the producer thread with more iterations than the consumer thread. Therefore, it is generally preferred to favor using Monitor's Wait()/Pulse() pattern or to use a semaphore (if fewer than n threads can participate in a particular block).

In contrast to an AutoResetEvent, the ManualResetEvent won't return to the unsignaled state until Reset() is called explicitly.

Semaphore/SemaphoreSlim and CountdownEvent

Semaphore and SemaphoreSlim have the same performance differences as ManualResetEvent and ManualResetEventSlim. Unlike ManualResetEvent/ ManualResetEventSlim, which provide a lock (like a gate) that is either open or closed, semaphores restrict only calls to pass within a critical section simultaneously. The semaphore essentially keeps a count on a pool of resources. When the count reaches zero, it blocks any further access to the pool until one of the resources is returned, making it available for the next blocked request that is queued.

CountdownEvent is much like the semaphore except it achieves the opposite synchronization. Rather than protecting further access to a pool of resources that are all used up, the CountdownEvent allows access only once the count reaches zero. Consider, for example, a parallel operation that downloads a multitude of stock quotes. Only when all of the quotes are downloaded can a particular search algorithm execute. The CountdownEvent may be used for synchronizing the search algorithm, decrementing as each stock is downloading and then releasing the search to start once the count reaches zero.

Notice that SemaphoreSlim and CountdownEvent were introduced with the .NET Framework 4.

Concurrent Collection Classes

Another series of classes introduced with the .NET Framework 4 is the concurrent collection classes. These classes are especially designed to include built-in synchronization code so that they can support simultaneous access by multiple threads without concern for race conditions. A list of the concurrent collection classes appears in Table 19.4.

TABLE 19.4: Concurrent Collection Classes

Collection Class	Description
`BlockingCollection<T>`	Provides a blocking collection that enables producer/consumer scenarios in which producers write data into the collection while consumers read the data. This class provides a generic collection type that synchronizes add and remove operations without concern for the backend storage (whether a queue, stack, list, etc.). `BlockingCollection<T>` provides blocking and bounding support for collections that implement the `IProducerConsumerCollection<T>` interface.
`*ConcurrentBag<T>`	A thread-safe unordered collection of T type objects.
`ConcurrentDictionary<TKey, TValue>`	A thread-safe dictionary; a collection of keys and values.
`*ConcurrentQueue<T>`	A thread-safe queue supporting first in, first out (FIFO) semantics on objects of type T.
`*ConcurrentStack<T>`	A thread-safe stack supporting first in, last out (FILO) semantics on objects of type T.

* Collection classes that implement `IProducerConsumerCollection<T>`.

A common pattern enabled by concurrent collections is support for thread-safe access by producers and consumers. Classes that implement `IProducerConsumerCollection<T>` (identified by * in Table 19.4) are specifically designed to support this. This enables one or more classes to be pumping data into the collection while a different set reads it out, removing it. The order in which data is added and removed is determined by the individual collection classes that implement the IProducerConsumerCollection<T> interface.

Thread Local Storage

In some cases, using synchronization locks can lead to unacceptable performance and scalability restrictions. In other instances, providing synchronization around a particular data element may be too complex, especially when it is added after the original coding.

One alternative solution to synchronization is isolation and one method for implementing isolation is **thread local storage.** With thread local storage, each thread has its own dedicated instance of a variable. As a result, there is no need for synchronization, as there is no point in synchronizing data that occurs within only a single thread's context. Two examples of thread local storage implementations are ThreadLocal<T> and ThreadStaticAttribute.

ThreadLocal<T>

To use thread local storage with the .NET Framework 4 involves declaring a field (or variable in the case of closure by the complier) of type ThreadLocal<T>. The result is a different instance of the field for each thread as demonstrated in Listing 19.10 and Output 19.7. Note that a different instance exists even if the field is static.

LISTING 19.10: Using ThreadLocal<T> for Thread Local Storage

```csharp
using System;
using System.Threading;

class Program
{
  static ThreadLocal<double> _Count =
      new ThreadLocal<double>(() => 0.01134);
  public static double Count
  {
      get { return _Count.Value; }
      set { _Count.Value = value; }
  }

  public static void Main()
  {
      Thread thread = new Thread(Decrement);
```

```
        thread.Start();

        // Increment
        for (double i = 0; i < short.MaxValue; i++)
        {
            Count++;
        }

        thread.Join();
        Console.WriteLine("Main Count = {0}", Count);
    }

    static void Decrement()
    {
        Count = -Count;
        for (double i = 0; i < short.MaxValue; i++)
        {
            Count--;
        }
        Console.WriteLine(
            "Decrement Count = {0}", Count);
    }
}
```

OUTPUT 19.7:

```
Decrement Count = -32767.01134
Main Count = 32767.01134
```

As Output 19.7 demonstrates, the value of Count for the thread executing Main() is never decremented by the thread executing Decrement(). For Main()'s thread the initial value is 0.01134 and the final value is 32767.01134. Decrement() has similar values except they are negative. Since Count is based on the static field of type ThreadLocal<T>, the thread running Main() and the thread running Decrement() have independent values stored in _Count.Value.

ThreadStaticAttribute

Decorating a static field with a ThreadStaticAttribute, as in Listing 19.11, is a second way to designate a static variable as an instance per thread. This technique has a caveat over ThreadLocal<T> but it also has the advantage that it is available prior to .NET Framework 4. (Also, since Thread-Local<T> is based on the ThreadStaticAttribute, it would consume less memory and give a slight performance advantage given frequently enough repeated small iterations.)

LISTING 19.11: Using **ThreadStaticAttribute** for Thread Local Storage

```csharp
using System;
using System.Threading;

class Program
{
    [ThreadStatic]
    static double _Count = 0.01134;
    public static double Count
    {
        get { return Program._Count; }
        set { Program._Count = value; }
    }

    public static void Main()
    {
        Thread thread = new Thread(Decrement);
        thread.Start();

        // Increment
        for (int i = 0; i < short.MaxValue; i++)
        {
            Count++;
        }

        thread.Join();
        Console.WriteLine("Main Count = {0}", Count);
    }

    static void Decrement()
    {
        for (int i = 0; i < short.MaxValue; i++)
        {
            Count--;
        }
        Console.WriteLine("Decrement Count = {0}", Count);
    }
}
```

The results of Listing 19.11 appear in Output 19.8.

OUTPUT 19.8:

```
Decrement Count = -32767
Main Count = 32767.01134
```

As in the preceding listing, the value of Count for the thread executing Main() is never decremented by the thread executing Decrement(). For Main()'s thread the initial value is a negative _Total and the final value is 0. In other words, with ThreadStaticAttribute the value of Count for each thread is specific to the thread and not accessible across threads.

Notice that unlike Listing 19.10, the value displayed for the "Decrement Count" does not have any decimal digits indicating it was never initialized to 0.01134. Although the value of _Count is assigned during declaration—private double _Count = 0.01134 in this example—only the thread static instance associated with the thread running the static constructor will be initialized. In Listing 19.11, only the thread executing Main() will have a thread local storage variable initialized to 0.01134. The value of _Count that Decrement() decrements will always be initialized to 0 (default(double) since _Count is an int). Similarly, if a constructor initializes a thread local storage field, only the constructor calling that thread will initialize the thread local storage instance. For this reason, it is a good practice to initialize a thread local storage field within the method that each thread initially calls.

The decision to use thread local storage requires some degree of cost-benefit analysis. For example, consider using thread local storage for a database connection. Depending on the database management system, database connections are relatively expensive, so creating a connection for every thread could be costly. Similarly, locking a connection so that all database calls are synchronized places a significantly lower ceiling on scalability. Each pattern has its costs and benefits, and the correct choice depends largely on the individual implementation.

Another reason to use thread local storage is to make commonly needed context information available to other methods without explicitly passing the data via parameters. For example, if multiple methods in the call stack require user security information you can pass the data using thread local storage fields instead of as parameters. This keeps APIs cleaner while still making the information available to methods in a thread-safe manner. This requires that you ensure that the thread local data is always set, and it is especially important on Tasks or other thread pool threads because the underlying threads are reused.

Timers

One area where threading issues relating to the user interface may arise unexpectedly is when using one of the timer classes. The problem is that when timer notification callbacks fire, the thread may not be the user interface thread, and therefore, it cannot safely access user interface controls and forms.

Several timer classes are available, including `System.Windows.Forms.Timer`, `System.Timers.Timer`, and `System.Threading.Timer`. In creating `System.Windows.Forms.Timer`, the development team designed it specifically for use within a rich client user interface. Programmers can drag it onto a form as a nonvisual control and control the behavior from within the Properties window. Most importantly, it will always safely fire an event from a thread that can interact with the user interface.

The other two timers are very similar. `System.Timers.Timer` is a wrapper for `System.Threading.Timer`, abstracting and layering on functionality. Specifically, `System.Threading.Timer` does not derive from `System.ComponentModel.Component`, and therefore, you cannot use it as a component within a component container, something that implements `System.ComponentModel.IContainer`. Another difference is that `System.Threading.Timer` enables the passing of state, an object parameter, from the call to start the timer and then into the call that fires the timer notification. The remaining differences are simply in the API usability with `System.Timers.Timer` supporting a synchronization object and having calls that are slightly more intuitive. Both `System.Timers.Timer` and `System.Threading.Timer` are designed for use in server-type processes, but `System.Timers.Timer` includes a synchronization object to allow it to interact with the UI. Furthermore, both timers use the system thread pool. Table 19.5 provides an overall comparison of the various timers.

Using `System.Windows.Forms.Timer` is a relatively obvious choice for user interface programming. The only caution is that a long-running operation on the user interface thread may delay the arrival of a timer's expiration. Choosing between the other two options is less obvious, and generally, the difference between the two is insignificant. If hosting within an `IContainer` is necessary, then `System.Timers.Timer` is the right choice. However, if no specific `System.Timers.Timer` feature is required, then

TABLE 19.5: Overview of the Various Timer Characteristics

Feature Description	System.Timers.Timer	System.Threading.Timer	System.Windows.Forms.Timer
Support for adding and removing listeners after the timer is instantiated	Yes	No	Yes
Supports callbacks on the user interface thread	Yes	No	Yes
Calls back from threads obtained from the thread pool	Yes	Yes	No
Supports drag-and-drop in the Windows Forms Designer	Yes	No	Yes
Suitable for running in a multithreaded server environment	Yes	Yes	No
Includes support for passing arbitrary state from the timer initialization to the callback	No	Yes	No
Implements `IDisposable`	Yes	Yes	Yes
Supports on-off callbacks as well as periodic repeating callbacks	Yes	Yes	Yes
Accessible across application domain boundaries	Yes	Yes	Yes
Supports `IComponent`; hostable in an `IContainer`	Yes	No	Yes

choose `System.Threading.Timer` by default, simply because it is a slightly lighter-weight implementation.

Listing 19.12 and Listing 19.13 provide sample code for using `System.Timers.Timer` and `System.Threading.Timer`, respectively. Their code is

very similar, including the fact that both support instantiation within a
using statement because both support IDispose. The output for both listings is identical, and it appears in Output 19.9.

LISTING 19.12: Using System.Timers.Timer

```csharp
using System;
using System.Timers;
using System.Threading;
// Because Timer exists in both the System.Timers and
// System.Threading namespaces, you disambiguate "Timer"
// using an alias directive.
using Timer = System.Timers.Timer;

class UsingSystemTimersTimer
{
    private static int _Count=0;
    private static readonly ManualResetEvent _ResetEvent =
        new ManualResetEvent(false);
    private static int _AlarmThreadId;

    public static void Main()
    {
        using( Timer timer = new Timer() )
        {
            // Initialize Timer
            timer.AutoReset = true;
            timer.Interval = 1000;
            timer.Elapsed +=
                new ElapsedEventHandler(Alarm);

            timer.Start();

            // Wait for Alarm to fire for the 10th time.
            _ResetEvent.WaitOne();
        }

        // Verify that the thread executing the alarm
        // Is different from the thread executing Main
        if(_AlarmThreadId ==
            Thread.CurrentThread.ManagedThreadId)
        {
            throw new ApplicationException(
                "Thread Ids are the same.");
        }
        if(_Count < 9)
        {
            throw new ApplicationException(
                " _Count < 9");
```

```
        };

        Console.WriteLine(
            "(Alarm Thread Id) {0} != {1} (Main Thread Id)",
            _AlarmThreadId,
            Thread.CurrentThread.ManagedThreadId);
        Console.WriteLine(
            "Final Count = {0}", _Count);
    }

    static void Alarm(
        object sender, ElapsedEventArgs eventArgs)
    {
        _Count++;

        Console.WriteLine("{0}:- {1}",
            eventArgs.SignalTime.ToString("T"),
            _Count);

        if (_Count >= 9)
        {
            _AlarmThreadId =
                Thread.CurrentThread.ManagedThreadId;
            _ResetEvent.Set();
        }
    }
}
```

In Listing 19.12, you have using directives for both System.Threading and System.Timers. This makes the Timer type ambiguous. Therefore, use an alias to explicitly associate Timer with System.Timers.Timer.

One noteworthy characteristic of System.Threading.Timer is that it takes the callback delegate and interval within the constructor.

LISTING 19.13: Using System.Threading.Timer

```
using System;
using System.Threading;

class UsingSystemThreadingTimer
{
    private static int _Count=0;
    private static readonly AutoResetEvent _ResetEvent =
        new AutoResetEvent(false);
    private static int _AlarmThreadId;

    public static void Main()
    {
```

```csharp
        // Timer(callback, state, dueTime, period)
        using( Timer timer =
            new Timer(Alarm, null, 0, 1000) )
    {
    // Wait for Alarm to fire for the 10th time.
    _ResetEvent.WaitOne();
    }


    // Verify that the thread executing the alarm
    // Is different from the thread executing Main
    if(_AlarmThreadId ==
        Thread.CurrentThread.ManagedThreadId)
    {
        throw new ApplicationException(
            "Thread Ids are the same.");
    }
    if(_Count < 9)
    {
        throw new ApplicationException(
            " _Count < 9");
    };

    Console.WriteLine(
        "(Alarm Thread Id) {0} != {1} (Main Thread Id)",
        _AlarmThreadId,
        Thread.CurrentThread.ManagedThreadId);
    Console.WriteLine(
        "Final Count = {0}", _Count);
}

static void Alarm(object state)
{
    _Count++;

    Console.WriteLine("{0}:- {1}",
        DateTime.Now.ToString("T"),
        _Count);

    if (_Count >= 9)
    {
        _AlarmThreadId =
            Thread.CurrentThread.ManagedThreadId;
        _ResetEvent.Set();
    }
}
}
```

OUTPUT 19.9:

```
12:19:36 AM:- 1
12:19:37 AM:- 2
12:19:38 AM:- 3
12:19:39 AM:- 4
12:19:40 AM:- 5
12:19:41 AM:- 6
12:19:42 AM:- 7
12:19:43 AM:- 8
12:19:44 AM:- 9
(Alarm Thread Id) 4 != 1 (Main Thread Id)
Final Count = 9
```

You can change the interval or time due after instantiation on `System.Threading.Timer` via the `Change()` method. However, you cannot change the callback listeners after instantiation. Instead, you must create a new instance.

Asynchronous Programming Model

Multithreaded programming includes the following complexities:

1. *Monitoring an asynchronous operation state for completion:* This includes determining when an asynchronous operation has completed, preferably not by polling the thread's state or by blocking and waiting.

2. *Thread pooling:* This avoids the significant cost of starting and tearing down threads. In addition, thread pooling avoids the creation of too many threads, such that the system spends more time switching threads than running them.

3. *Avoiding deadlocks:* This involves preventing the occurrence of deadlocks while attempting to protect the data from simultaneous access by two different threads.

4. *Providing atomicity across operations and synchronizing data access:* Adding synchronization around groups of operations ensures that operations execute as a single unit and that they are appropriately interrupted by another thread. Locking is provided so that two different threads do not access the data simultaneously.

Furthermore, anytime a method is long-running, it is probable that multithreaded programming is going to be required—invoking the long-running method asynchronously. As developers write more multi-threaded code, a common set of scenarios and programming patterns for handling those scenarios emerges. The key scenarios relate to notifications of when a thread performing a long-running action completes.

One particularly prominent pattern established is the Asynchronous Programming Model (APM) pattern. Given a long-running synchronous method X(), APM uses a `BeginX()` method to start X() equivalent work asynchronously and an `EndX()` method to conclude it. (Henceforth we will name these methods X, BeginX, and EndX.)

Calling the APM

Listing 19.14 demonstrates the pattern using the `System.Net.WebRequest` class to download a Web page. Fulfilling Web requests is a relatively long-running task since they involve network I/O and they are very likely to go across the Internet. `WebRequest` supports the APM pattern with the methods `BeginGetResponse()` (BeginX) and `EndGetResponse()` (EndX)—asynchronous versions of the synchronous `GetResponse()` (X) method.

LISTING 19.14: Calling the APM on `WebRequest`

```
using System;
using System.IO;
using System.Net;
using System.Linq;

public class Program
{
  public static void Main(string[] args)
  {
      string url = "http://www.intelliTechture.com";
      if (args.Length > 0)
      {
          url = args[0];
      }

      Console.Write(url);
      WebRequest webRequest = WebRequest.Create(url);

      IAsyncResult asyncResult =
          webRequest.BeginGetResponse(null, null);
```

```
        // Indicate busy using dots
        while (
            !asyncResult.AsyncWaitHandle.WaitOne(100))
        {
            Console.Write('.');
        }

        // Retrieve the results when finished
        // downloading
        WebResponse response =
            webRequest.EndGetResponse(asyncResult);
        using (StreamReader reader =
            new StreamReader(response.GetResponseStream()))
        {
            int length = reader.ReadToEnd().Length;
            Console.WriteLine(FormatBytes(length));
        }
    }

    static public string FormatBytes(long bytes)
    {
        string[] magnitudes =
            new string[] { "GB", "MB", "KB", "Bytes" };
        long max =
            (long)Math.Pow(1024, magnitudes.Length);

        return string.Format("{1:##.##} {0}",
            magnitudes.FirstOrDefault(
                magnitude =>
                    bytes > (max /= 1024) )?? "0 Bytes",
                (decimal)bytes / (decimal)max).Trim();
    }
}
```

The results of Listing 19.14 appear in Output 19.10.

OUTPUT 19.10:

```
http://www.intelliTechture.com..........29.36 KB
```

As mentioned, the key aspect of the APM is the pair of BeginX and EndX methods with well-established signatures. The BeginX returns a System. IAsyncResult object providing access to the state of the asynchronous call in order to wait or poll for completion. The EndX method then takes this return as an input parameter. This pairs up the two methods so that it is clear which BeginX method call pairs with which EndX method call. The nature of the APM requires that for all BeginX invocations there must be exactly one EndX invocation, so no two calls to EndX for the same IAsyncResult instance should occur.

In Listing 19.14, we also use the IAsyncResult's WaitHandle to determine when the asynchronous method completes. As we iteratively poll the WaitHandle we print out periods to the console indicating that the download is running. Following that, we call EndGetResponse().

The EndX method serves four purposes. First, calling EndX will block further execution until the work requested completes successfully (or errors out with an exception). Second, if method X returns data, this data is accessible from the EndX method call. Third, if an exception occurs while performing the requested work, the exception will be rethrown on the call to EndX, ensuring that the exception is visible to the calling code as though it had occurred on a synchronous invocation. Finally, if any resource needs cleanup due to X's invocation, EndX will be responsible for cleaning up these resources.

APM Signatures

Together, the combination of the BeginX and EndX APM methods should match the synchronous version of the signature. Therefore, the return parameter on EndX should match the return parameters on the X method (Get-Reponse() in this case). Furthermore, the input parameters on the BeginX method also need to match. In the case of WebRequest.GetResponse() there are no parameters, but let's consider a fictitious synchronous method, bool TryDoSomething(string url, ref string data, out string[] links). The parameters map from the synchronous method to the APM methods as shown in Figure 19.1.

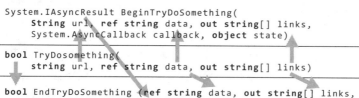

```
System.IAsyncResult BeginTryDoSomething(
    String url, ref string data, out string[] links,
    System.AsyncCallback callback, object state)

bool TryDoSomething(
    string url, ref string data, out string[] links)

bool EndTryDoSomething (ref string data, out string[] links,
    System.IAyncResult result);
```

FIGURE 19.1: APM Parameter Distribution

All input parameters map to the `BeginX` method. Similarly, the return parameter maps to the `EndX` return parameter. Also, notice that since `ref` and out parameters return results, these are included in the `EndX` method signature. In contrast, since `url` is only an input parameter, it is not included in the `EndX` method.

Continuation Passing Style (CPS) with `AsyncCallback`

There are two additional parameters on the `BeginX` method that were not included in the synchronous method. These are the callback parameter, a `System.AsyncCallback` delegate to be called when the method completes, and a `state` parameter of type `object`. Listing 19.15 demonstrates how they are used. (The output is the same as Output 19.10).

LISTING 19.15: Invoking the APM with Callback and State

```
using System;
using System.IO;
using System.Net;
using System.Linq;
using System.Threading;

public class Program
{
    public static void Main(string[] args)
    {
        string url = "http://www.intelliTechture.com";
        if (args.Length > 0)
        {
            url = args[0];
        }

        Console.Write(url);
        WebRequest webRequest = WebRequest.Create(url);
        State state = new State(webRequest);
        IAsyncResult asyncResult =
            webRequest.BeginGetResponse(
                GetResponseAsyncCompleted, state);

        // Indicate busy using dots
        while (
            !asyncResult.AsyncWaitHandle.WaitOne(100))
        {
            Console.Write('.');
        }
```

```csharp
            state.ResetEvent.Wait();
    }


    // Retrieve the results when finished downloading
    private static void GetResponseAsyncCompleted(
        IAsyncResult asyncResult)
    {
        State completedState =
            (WebRequestState)asyncResult.AsyncState;
        HttpWebResponse response =
            (HttpWebResponse)completedState.WebRequest
                .EndGetResponse(asyncResult);
        Stream stream = response.GetResponseStream();
        StreamReader reader = new StreamReader(stream);
        int length = reader.ReadToEnd().Length;

        Console.WriteLine(FormatBytes(length));
        completedState.ResetEvent.Set();
        completedState.Dispose();
    }
    // ...
}
```

```csharp
class WebRequestState : IDisposable
{
  public WebRequestState(WebRequest webRequest)
  {
      WebRequest = webRequest;
  }
  public WebRequest WebRequest { get; private set; }
  private ManualResetEventSlim _ResetEvent =
      new ManualResetEventSlim();
  public ManualResetEventSlim ResetEvent
      { get { return _ResetEvent; } }

  public void Dispose()
  {
      ResetEvent.Dispose();
      GC.SuppressFinalize(this);
  }
}
```

Notice that in Listing 19.15, we pass data for both of the parameters on BeginGetResponse(). The first parameter is a delegate of type System.AsyncCallback that takes a single parameter of type System.AsyncResult. The AsyncCallback identifies the code that will execute once the asynchronous call completes. Registering a callback enables a fire-and-forget calling pattern called **continuation passing style (CPS)** rather than placing the `EndGetResponse()` and `Console.WriteLine()` code sequentially below `BeginGetResponse()`. With CPS we can "register" the code that will execute upon completion of the asynchronous method. Note that it is still necessary to call `EndGetResponse()`, but by placing it in the callback we ensure that it doesn't block the main thread while the asynchronous call completes.

Passing State between APM Methods

In addition to the `AsyncCallback` parameter, there is the `state` parameter, which is used to pass additional data to the callback when it executes. Listing 19.15 includes a `WebRequestState` class for passing additional data into the callback, and it includes the `WebRequest` itself in this case so that we can use it to call `EndGetResponse()`. One alternative to the `WebRequest-State` class itself would be to use an anonymous method (including a lambda expression) with closures for the additional data, as shown in Listing 19.16.

LISTING 19.16: Passing State Using Closure on Anonymous Method

```
using System;
using System.IO;
using System.Net;
using System.Linq;
using System.Threading;

public class Program
{
  public static void Main(string[] args)
  {
      string url = "http://www.intelliTechture.com";
      if (args.Length > 0)
      {
          url = args[0];
      }

      Console.Write(url);
      WebRequest webRequest = WebRequest.Create(url);
      ManualResetEventSlim resetEvent =
          new ManualResetEventSlim();
      IAsyncResult asyncResult =
          webRequest.BeginGetResponse(
```

```
                        (completedAsyncResult) =>
                        {
                            HttpWebResponse response =
                                (HttpWebResponse)webRequest.EndGetResponse(
                                completedAsyncResult);
                        Stream stream =
                            response.GetResponseStream();
                        StreamReader reader =
                            new StreamReader(stream);
                        int length = reader.ReadToEnd().Length;

                        Console.WriteLine(FormatBytes(length));
                        resetEvent.Set();
                        resetEvent.Dispose();
                    },
                    null);

        // Indicate busy using dots
        while (
            !asyncResult.AsyncWaitHandle.WaitOne(100))
        {
            Console.Write('.');
        }
        resetEvent.Wait();
    }

    // ...
}
```

Regardless of whether we pass the state via closures or not, notice that we are using a ManualResetEvent to signal when the AsyncCallback has completed. This is somewhat peculiar because IAsyncResult includes a WaitHandle already. The difference, however, is that the IAsyncResult's WaitHandle is set when the asynchronous method completes but before the AsyncCallback executes. If we only blocked on the IAsyncResult's Wait-Handle we are likely to exit the program before the AsyncCallback has executed. For this reason we use a separate ManualResetEvent.

Resource Cleanup

Another important APM rule is that no resource leaks should occur, even if the EndX method is mistakenly not called. Since WebRequestState owns the ManualResetEvent, it specifically owns a resource that requires such cleanup. To handle this the state object uses the standard IDisposable pattern with the IDispose() method.

Calling the APM Using TPL

Even though TPL simplifies making an asynchronous call on a long-running method significantly, it is generally better to use the API-provided APM methods than to code TPL against the synchronous version. The reason for this is that the API developer best understands the most efficient threading code to write, which data to synchronize, and what type of synchronization to use. Fortunately, there are special methods on TPL's TaskFactory that are designed specifically for invoking the APM methods.

APM with TPL and CPS

TPL includes a set of overloads on FromAsync for invoking the APM. Listing 19.17 provides an example. The same listing expands on the other APM examples to support downloading of multiple URLs; see Output 19.11.

LISTING 19.17: Using TPL to Call the APM

```
using System;
using System.IO;
using System.Net;
using System.Linq;
using System.Threading.Tasks;
using System.Collections.Generic;

public class Program
{
    static private object ConsoleSyncObject =
        new object();

    public static void Main(string[] args)
    {
        string[] urls = args;
        if (args.Length == 0)
        {
            urls = new string[]
                {
                    "http://www.habitat-spokane.org",
                    "http://www.partnersintl.org",
```

```
                    "http://www.iassist.org",
                    "http://www.fh.org",
                    "http://www.worldvision.org"
                };
        }


        int line = 0;
        Task<WebResponse>[] tasksWithState =
            urls.Select(
                url=>DisplayPageSizeAsync(
                    url, line++)).ToArray();


        while (
            !Task.WaitAll(tasksWithState.ToArray(), 50))
        {
            DisplayProgress(tasksWithState);
        }
        Console.SetCursorPosition(0, line);
    }


    private static Task<WebResponse>
        DisplayPageSizeAsync(string url, int line)
    {
        lock (ConsoleSyncObject)
        {
            Console.WriteLine(url);
        }
        WebRequest webRequest = WebRequest.Create(url);
        WebRequestState state =
            new WebRequestState(webRequest, line);
        Task<WebResponse> task =
            Task<WebResponse>.Factory.FromAsync(
                webRequest.BeginGetResponse,
                GetResponseAsyncCompleted, state);


        return task;
    }


    private static WebResponse GetResponseAsyncCompleted(
        IAsyncResult asyncResult)
    {
        WebRequestState completedState =
            (WebRequestState)asyncResult.AsyncState;
        HttpWebResponse response =
            (HttpWebResponse)completedState.WebRequest
                .EndGetResponse(asyncResult);
        Stream stream =
            response.GetResponseStream();
        using (StreamReader reader =
            new StreamReader(stream))
```

```
    {
        int length = reader.ReadToEnd().Length;
        DisplayPageSize(completedState, length);
    }
    return response;
}

private static void DisplayProgress(
    IEnumerable<Task<WebResponse>> tasksWithState)
{
    foreach (
        WebRequestState state in tasksWithState
            .Where(task => !task.IsCompleted)
            .Select(task=>
                (WebRequestState)task.AsyncState))
    {
        DisplayProgress(state);
    }
}

private static void DisplayPageSize(
    WebRequestState completedState, int length)
{
    lock (ConsoleSyncObject)
    {
        Console.SetCursorPosition(
            completedState.ConsoleColumn,
            completedState.ConsoleLine);
        Console.Write(FormatBytes(length));
        completedState.ConsoleColumn +=
            length.ToString().Length;
    }
}

private static void DisplayProgress(
    WebRequestState state)
{
    int left = state.ConsoleColumn;
    int top = state.ConsoleLine;
    lock (ConsoleSyncObject)
    {
        if (left >= Console.BufferWidth -
            int.MaxValue.ToString().Length)
        {
            left = state.Url.Length;
            Console.SetCursorPosition(left, top);
            Console.Write("".PadRight(
                Console.BufferWidth -
                    state.Url.Length));
            state.ConsoleColumn = left;
```

```csharp
            }
            else
            {
                state.ConsoleColumn++;
            }

            Console.SetCursorPosition(left, top);
            Console.Write('.');
        }
    }

    static public string FormatBytes(long bytes)
    {
        string[] magnitudes =
            new string[] { "GB", "MB", "KB", "Bytes" };
        long max =
            (long)Math.Pow(1024, magnitudes.Length);

        return string.Format("{1:##.##} {0}",
            magnitudes.FirstOrDefault(
                magnitude =>
                    bytes > (max /= 1024) )?? "0 Bytes",
                (decimal)bytes / (decimal)max).Trim();
    }
}

class WebRequestState
{
    public WebRequestState(
        WebRequest webRequest, int line)
    {
        WebRequest = webRequest;
        ConsoleLine = line;
        ConsoleColumn = Url.Length + 1;
    }
    public WebRequestState(WebRequest webRequest)
    {
        WebRequest = webRequest;
    }
    public WebRequest WebRequest { get; private set; }
    public string Url
    {
        get
        {
            return WebRequest.RequestUri.ToString();
        }
    }
    public int ConsoleLine { get; set; }
    public int ConsoleColumn { get; set; }
}
```

OUTPUT 19.11:

```
http://www.habitat-spokane.org ..9.18 KB
http://www.partnersintl.org .........14.74 KB
http://www.iassist.org  .17.12 KB
http://www.fh.org ..................35.09 KB
http://www.worldvision.org ...........54.56 KB
```

Connecting a `Task` with the APM method pair is relatively easy. The overload used in Listing 19.17 takes three parameters. First, there is the `BeginX` method delegate (`webRequest.BeginGetResponse`). Next is a delegate that matches the `EndX` method. Although the `EndX` method (`webRequest.End GetResponse`) could be used directly, passing a delegate (`GetResponse-AsyncCompleted`) and using the CPS allows additional completion activity to execute. The last parameter is the state parameter similar to what the `BeginX` method accepts.

One of the advantages of invoking an APM pair of methods using TPL is that we don't have to worry about signaling the conclusion of the `AsyncCallback` method. Instead, we monitor the `Task` for completion. As a result, `WebRequestState` no longer needs to contain a `ManualResetEventSlim`.

Using TPL and `ContinueWith()` to Call the APM

Another option when calling `TaskFactory.FromAsync()` is to pass the `EndX` method directly and then to use `ContinueWith()` for any follow-up code. This approach has the advantage that you can query the continue-with-`Task` parameter (see `continueWithTask` in Listing 19.18) for the result (`continueWithTask.Result`) rather than storing a means to access the `EndX` method via an async-state object or using closure and an anonymous delegate (we store `WebRequest` in Listing 19.17).

LISTING 19.18: Using TPL to Call the APM Using `ContinueWith()`

```
// ...

    private static Tuple<Task<WebResponse>, WebRequestState>
        DisplayPageSizeAsync(string url, int line)
    {
        lock (ConsoleSyncObject)
        {
```

```csharp
        Console.WriteLine(url);
    }
    WebRequest webRequest = WebRequest.Create(url);
    WebRequestState state = new WebRequestState(url, line);
    Task<WebResponse> task =
        Task<WebResponse>.Factory.FromAsync(
            webRequest.BeginGetResponse,
            webRequest.EndGetResponse, state)
        .ContinueWith(continueWithTask =>
        {
            // Optional since state is available
            // with closure
            WebRequestState completedState =

(WebRequestState)continueWithTask.AsyncState;
            Stream stream =
                continueWithTask.Result.
                    GetResponseStream();

            using (StreamReader reader =
                new StreamReader(stream))
            {
                int length =
                    reader.ReadToEnd().Length;
                DisplayPageSize(
                    completedState, length);
            }

            return continueWithTask.Result;
        });

    return new Tuple<
        Task<WebResponse>,WebRequestState>(
            task, state);
}

// ...
```

Unfortunately, the ContinueWith() approach includes a caveat as well. The AsyncState property on a Task returned by ContinueWith() contains null rather than the state specified in the call to FromAsync(). Accessing the state outside ContinueWith() will require saving it into an alternate location. Listing 19.18 achieves this by placing it into a Tuple<T1, T2> and returning that.

▪ BEGINNER TOPIC

Synchronizing `Console` Using `lock`

In Listing 19.17, we repeatedly change the location of the console's cursor and then proceed to write text to the console. Since multiple threads are executing that are also writing to the console, possibly changing the cursor location as well, we need to synchronize changes to the cursor location with write operations so that together they are atomic.

Listing 19.17 includes a `ConsoleSyncObject` of type `object` as the synchronization lock identifier. Using this within a lock construct whenever we are moving the cursor or writing to the console prevents an interim update between move and write operations to the console. Notice that even one-line `Console.WriteLine()` statements are surrounded with `lock`. Although they will be atomic, we don't want them interrupting a different block that is not atomic. Therefore, all console changes require the synchronization as long as there are multiple threads of execution.

Asynchronous Delegate Invocation

There is a derivative APM pattern called Asynchronous Delegate Invocation that leverages special C# compiler-generated code on all delegate data types. Given a delegate instance of `Func<string, int>`, for example, there is an APM pair of methods available on the instance:

```
System.IAsyncResult BeginInvoke(
    string arg, AsyncCallback callback, object @object)
int EndInvoke(IAsyncResult result)
```

The result is that you can call any delegate (and therefore any method) synchronously just by using the C# compiler-generated methods.

Unfortunately, the underlying technology used by the asynchronous delegate invocation pattern is an end-of-further-development technology for distributed programming known as **remoting**. And although Microsoft still supports the use of asynchronous delegate invocation and it will continue to function as it does today for the foreseeable future, the performance characteristics are suboptimal given other approaches—namely `Thread`, `ThreadPool`, and TPL. Therefore, developers should tend to favor one of these alternatives rather than implementing new development using the asynchronous delegate invocation API. Further discussion of the pattern is included in the Advanced Topic text that follows so that developers who encounter it will understand how it works.

▪ADVANCED TOPIC

Asynchronous Delegate Invocation in Detail

With asynchronous delegate invocation, you do not code using an explicit reference to `Task` or `Thread`. Instead, you use delegate instances and the compiler-generated `BeginInvoke()` and `EndInvoke()` methods—whose implementation requests threads from the `ThreadPool`. Consider the code in Listing 19.19.

LISTING 19.19: Asynchronous Delegate Invocation

```csharp
using System;

public class Program
{
  public static void Main(string[] args)
  {
      Console.WriteLine("Application started....");

      Console.WriteLine("Starting thread....");
      Func<int,string> workerMethod =
          PiCalculator.Calculate;
      IAsyncResult asyncResult =
          workerMethod.BeginInvoke(500, null, null);

      // Display periods as progress bar.
      while(!asyncResult.AsyncWaitHandle.WaitOne(
          100, false))
      {
          Console.Write('.');
      }
      Console.WriteLine();

      Console.WriteLine("Thread ending....");
      Console.WriteLine(
          workerMethod.EndInvoke(asyncResult));
```

```
            Console.WriteLine(
                "Application shutting down....");
        }
    }
```

The results of Listing 19.19 appear in Output 19.12.

OUTPUT 19.12:

```
Application started....
Starting thread....
.......................
Thread ending....
3.14159265358979323846264338327950288419716939937510582097494459230781664
0628620899862803482534211706798214808651328230664709384460955058223172535
9408128481117450284102701938521105559644622948954930381964428810975665933
44612847564823378678316527120190914564856692346034861045432664821339360
72602491412737245870066063155881748815209209628292540917153643678925903
60011330530548820466521384146951941511609433057270365759591953092186117
81932611793105118548074462379962749567351885752724891227938183011949120
Application shutting down....
```

Main() begins by assigning a delegate of type Func<string, int> that is pointing to PiCalculator.Calculate(int digits).

Next, the code calls BeginInvoke(). This method will start the PiCalculator.Calculate() method on a thread from the thread pool and then return immediately. This allows other code to run in parallel with the pi calculation. In this example, we print periods while waiting for the PiCalculator.Calculate() method to complete.

We poll the status of the delegate using IAsyncResult.AsyncWaitHandle.WaitOne() on asyncResult—the same mechanism available on APM. As a result, the code prints periods to the screen each second during which the PiCalculator.Calculate() method is executing.

Once the wait handle signals, the code calls EndInvoke(). As with all APM implementations, it is important to pass to EndInvoke() the same IAsyncResult reference returned when calling BeginInvoke(). In this example, EndInvoke() doesn't block because we poll the thread's state in the while loop and call EndInvoke() only after the thread has completed.

Passing Data to and from an Alternate Thread

The example in Listing 19.18 passed an integer and received a string—the signature of Func<int, string>. The key feature of the asynchronous delegate invocation is the fact that passing data in and out of the target invocation is trivial; it just lines up with the synchronous method signature as it did in the APM pattern. Consider a delegate type that includes out and ref parameters, as shown in Figure 19.2. (Although more common, this example intentionally doesn't use Func or Action since generics don't allow ref and out modifiers on type parameters.)

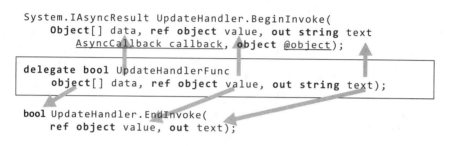

FIGURE 19.2: Delegate Parameter Distribution to BeginInvoke() and EndInvoke()

The BeginInvoke() method matches the delegate signature except for the additional AsyncCallback and object parameters. Like the IAsync-Result return, the additional parameters correspond to the standard APM parameters specifying a callback and passing state object. Similarly, the EndInvoke() method matches the original signature except only outgoing parameters appear. Since object[] data is only incoming, it doesn't appear in the EndInvoke() method. Also, since the EndInvoke() method concludes the asynchronous call, its return matches the original delegate's return as well.

Since all delegates include the C# compiler-generated BeginInvoke() and EndInvoke() methods used by the asynchronous delegate invocation pattern, invoking any method synchronously—especially given Func and Action delegates—becomes relatively easy. Furthermore, it makes it simple for the caller to invoke a method asynchronously regardless of whether the API programmer explicitly implemented it.

And before TPL, the asynchronous delegate invocation pattern was significantly easier than the alternatives, making it a common practice when an API didn't provide explicit asynchronous calling patterns. However, apart from support for .NET 3.5 and earlier frameworks, the advent of TPL diminishes the need for using the asynchronous delegate invocation approach if it occurs at all.

Event-Based Asynchronous Pattern (EAP)[1]

Another pattern more typical of higher-level programming than that of the APM is the **Event-based Asynchronous Pattern** (EAP). As with APM, API developers implement EAP for methods that are long-running.

Implementing the EAP pattern in its simplest form involves duplicating a long-running method signature and appending "Async" to the method name while removing any outgoing parameters and returns. The "Async" suffix indicates to callers that this version of the method will execute synchronously rather than blocking until the work of the method completes. The elimination of the outgoing parameters is required since the method will not necessarily complete by the time the call concludes.

For example, consider the signature of an EAP calling convention `string PiCalculator.Calculate(int digits)` method:

```
void PiCalculator.CalculateAsync(int digits)
```

Unlike APM, the EAP model doesn't require returning an `IAsyncResult` object. However, support for passing arbitrary state is available to the API implementer through the addition of an `object state` parameter:

```
void PiCalculator.CalculateAsync(int digits, object state)
```

or possibly even a generic version

```
void PiCalculator.CalculateAsync<T>(int digits, T state)
```

With .NET Framework 4, a version that takes a `CancellationToken` would also be a welcome edition (see Listing 19.20).

Exposing an "Async" method allows the caller to begin execution but doesn't, on its own, allow for monitoring it or using CPS. To do this requires the addition of a completion event and an appropriate `EventArgs` implementation to pass back the outgoing results (see Listing 19.20).

---

1. *Concurrent Programming on Windows* by Joe Duffy (Addison-Wesley, 2009), pages 421–426.

LISTING 19.20: Event-Based Asynchronous Pattern

```csharp
using System;
using System.ComponentModel;
using System.Threading;
using System.Threading.Tasks;

partial class PiCalculation
{
  public void CalculateAsync(
      int digits)
  {
      CalculateAsync(digits, null);
  }
  public void CalculateAsync(
      int digits, object userState)
  {
      CalculateAsync(
          digits, default(CancellationToken),
          userState);
  }
  public void CalculateAsync<TState>(
      int digits,
      CancellationToken cancelToken,
      TState userState)
  {
      if (SynchronizationContext.Current == null)
      {
          SynchronizationContext.
              SetSynchronizationContext(
                  new SynchronizationContext());
      }
      TaskScheduler scheduler =
          TaskScheduler.
              FromCurrentSynchronizationContext();
      Task<string>.Factory.StartNew(
          () =>
          {
              return PiCalculator.Calculate(digits);
          }, cancelToken)
          .ContinueWith<string>(
              continueTask =>
              {
                  CalculateCompleted(
                      typeof(PiCalculator),
                      new CalculateCompletedEventArgs(
                          continueTask.Result,
                          continueTask.Exception,
                          cancelToken.
                              IsCancellationRequested,
```

```
                userState));
            return continueTask.Result;
        }, scheduler);
    }

    public event
        EventHandler<CalculateCompletedEventArgs>
            CalculateCompleted = delegate { };


    public class CalculateCompletedEventArgs
        : AsyncCompletedEventArgs
    {
        public CalculateCompletedEventArgs(
            string value,
            Exception error,
            bool cancelled,
            object userState) : base(
              error, cancelled, userState)
        {
            Result = value;
        }
        public string Result { get; private set; }
    }


}
```

In Listing 19.20, this support is provided via the `CalculateCompleted` event. Registering for this event will allow the caller to receive a notification when the calculation completes. The value of the calculation will be on the `Result` property of the `CalculateCompletedEventArgs` class (which derives from `AsyncCompletedEventArgs`). This same class will allow the caller to check for an error (via the `Error` property), cancellation (via the `Canceled` property), and user state (via the `UserState` property).

In the past, cancellation support was available in EAP through the addition of a `CancelAsync` method, which optionally took an `object` `objectState` parameter. However, with .NET Framework 4, using a `CancellationToken` would be the preferred approach since it would avoid the need to save the state.

Frequently with multithreaded operations, not only do you want to be notified when the thread completes, but you also want the method to provide an update on the status of the operation. EAP includes support for this by declaring an event of type `ProgressChangedEventHandler` (or a derivative thereof given support for variance in C# 4.0) and naming the event `ProgressChanged`. This, however, would push the EAP class into the saving state. To avoid this, developers could also pass a progress listener into the `Async` method.

Here are a couple of final points to note about Listing 19.20. First, `PiCalculation` is an instance class rather than a static class. Given that the implementation relies on coordinating between events and the initial `Async` member call, using an instance class lends toward a pattern in which the complexity associated with having multiple invocations and multiple listeners to the same events is avoided. Without the instance approach, for example, it would be suboptimal (synchronization would be required at a minimum) to support a `CancelAsync(object state)` member because it would be necessary to look up the `state`–associated invocation. Even worse, progress change notifications (using the standard signature) would be impossible.

Second, `PiCalculation` is thread-safe since it doesn't store any state information. If support for `CancelAsync()` or progress monitoring was added such that state was required, care should be taken to keep the thread-safe nature of the class.

Background Worker Pattern

Another pattern that provides operation status and the possibility of cancellation is the **background worker pattern,** a specific implementation of EAP. The .NET Framework 2.0 (or later) includes a `BackgroundWorker` class for programming this type of pattern.

Listing 19.21 is an example of this pattern—again calculating pi to the number of digits specified.

LISTING 19.21: Using the Background Worker Pattern

```
using System;
using System.Threading;
using System.ComponentModel;
using System.Text;

public class PiCalculator
```

```csharp
{
    public static BackgroundWorker calculationWorker =
        new BackgroundWorker();
    public static AutoResetEvent resetEvent =
        new AutoResetEvent(false);

    public static void Main()
    {
        int digitCount;

        Console.Write(
            "Enter the number of digits to calculate:");
        if (int.TryParse(Console.ReadLine(), out digitCount))
        {
            Console.WriteLine("ENTER to cancel");
            // C# 2.0 Syntax for registering delegates
            calculationWorker.DoWork += CalculatePi;
            // Register the ProgressChanged callback
            calculationWorker.ProgressChanged +=
                UpdateDisplayWithMoreDigits;
            calculationWorker.WorkerReportsProgress =
                true;
            // Register a callback for when the
            // calculation completes
            calculationWorker.RunWorkerCompleted +=
                new RunWorkerCompletedEventHandler(
                    Complete);
            calculationWorker.
                WorkerSupportsCancellation = true;

            // Begin calculating pi for up to
            // digitCount digits
            calculationWorker.RunWorkerAsync(
                digitCount);

            Console.ReadLine();
            // If cancel is called after the calculation
            // has completed it doesn't matter.
            calculationWorker.CancelAsync();
            // Wait for Complete() to run.
            resetEvent.WaitOne();
        }
        else
        {
            Console.WriteLine(
                "The value entered is an invalid integer.");
        }
    }
}
```

```
private static void CalculatePi(
    object sender, DoWorkEventArgs eventArgs)
{

    int digits = (int)eventArgs.Argument;

    StringBuilder pi =
        new StringBuilder("3.", digits + 2);
    calculationWorker.ReportProgress(
        0, pi.ToString());

    // Calculate rest of pi, if required
    if (digits > 0)
    {
        for (int i = 0; i < digits; i += 9)
        {
            // Calculate next i decimal places
            int nextDigit =
                PiDigitCalculator.StartingAt(
                    i + 1);
            int digitCount =
                Math.Min(digits - i, 9);
            string ds =
                string.Format("{0:D9}", nextDigit);
            pi.Append(ds.Substring(0, digitCount));

            // Show current progress
            calculationWorker.ReportProgress(
                0, ds.Substring(0, digitCount));

            // Check for cancellation
            if (
              calculationWorker.CancellationPending)
            {
                // Need to set Cancel if you need to
                // distinguish how a worker thread
                // completed
                // i.e., by checking
                // RunWorkerCompletedEventArgs.Cancelled
                eventArgs.Cancel = true;
                break;
            }
        }
    }

    eventArgs.Result = pi.ToString();
}

private static void UpdateDisplayWithMoreDigits(
    object sender,
    ProgressChangedEventArgs eventArgs)
```

```
    {
        string digits = (string)eventArgs.UserState;

        Console.Write(digits);
    }


    static void Complete(
        object sender,
        RunWorkerCompletedEventArgs eventArgs)
    {
        // ...
    }
}
```

```
public class PiDigitCalculator
{
    // ...
}
```

Establishing the Pattern

The process of hooking up the background worker pattern is as follows:

1. Register the long-running method with the BackgroundWorker. DoWork event. In this example, the long-running task is the call to CalculatePi().

2. To receive progress or status notifications, hook up a listener to BackgroundWorker.ProgressChanged and set Background-Worker.WorkerReportsProgress to true. In Listing 19.8, the UpdateDisplayWithMoreDigits() method takes care of updating the display as more digits become available.

3. Register a method (Complete()) with the BackgroundWorker. RunWorkerCompleted event.

4. Assign the WorkerSupportsCancellation property to support cancellation. Once this property is assigned the value true, a call to BackgroundWorker.CancelAsync will set the DoWorkEventArgs.CancellationPending flag.

5. Within the DoWork-provided method (CalculatePi()), check the DoWorkEventArgs.CancellationPending property and exit the method when it is true.

6. Once everything is set up, you can start the work by calling Back-
groundWorker.RunWorkerAsync() and providing a state parameter
that is passed to the specified DoWork() method.

When you break it into steps, the background worker pattern is relatively easy to follow and, true to EAP, it provides explicit support for progress notification. The drawback is that you cannot use it arbitrarily on any
method. Instead, the DoWork() method has to conform to a System.Compo-
nentModel.DoWorkEventHandler delegate, which takes arguments of type
object and DoWorkEventArgs. If this isn't the case, then a wrapper function
is required—something fairly trivial using anonymous methods. The can-
cellation- and progress-related methods also require specific signatures,
but these are in control of the programmer setting up the background
worker pattern.

Exception Handling

If an unhandled exception occurs while the background worker thread is
executing, then the RunWorkerCompletedEventArgs parameter of the Run-
WorkerCompleted delegate (Completed's eventArgs) will have an Error
property set with the exception. As a result, checking the Error property
within the RunWorkerCompleted callback in Listing 19.22 provides a means
of handling the exception.

LISTING 19.22: Handling Unhandled Exceptions from the Worker Thread

```csharp
// ...
static void Complete(
    object sender, RunWorkerCompletedEventArgs eventArgs)
{
    Console.WriteLine();
    if (eventArgs.Cancelled)
    {
        Console.WriteLine("Cancelled");
    }
    else if (eventArgs.Error != null)
    {
        // IMPORTANT: check error to retrieve any
        // exceptions.
        Console.WriteLine(
            "ERROR: {0}", eventArgs.Error.Message);
    }
```

```
        else
        {
            Console.WriteLine("Finished");
        }
        resetEvent.Set();
    }
    // ...
```

It is important that the code check eventArgs.Error inside the RunWorker-
Completed callback. Otherwise, the exception will go undetected; it won't
even be reported to AppDomain.

Windows UI Programming

One more important threading concept relates to user interface development using the System.Windows.Forms and System.Windows namespaces.
The Microsoft Windows suite of operating systems uses a single-threaded,
message-processing-based user interface. This means that only one thread
at a time should access the user interface, and code should marshal any
alternate thread interaction via the Windows message pump.

Windows Forms

When programming against Windows Forms, the process of checking
whether UI invocation is allowable from a thread involves calling a component's InvokeRequired property to determine whether marshalling is
necessary. If InvokeRequired returns true, then marshalling is necessary
and can be implemented via a call to Invoke(). Internally, Invoke() will
check InvokeRequired anyway, but it can be more efficient to do so beforehand explicitly. Listing 19.23 demonstrates this pattern.

LISTING 19.23: Accessing the User Interface via Invoke()

```
using System;
using System.Drawing;
using System.Threading;
using System.Windows.Forms;

class Program : Form
{
    private System.Windows.Forms.ProgressBar _ProgressBar;
```

```csharp
[STAThread]
static void Main()
{
    Application.Run(new Program());
}

public Program()
{
    InitializeComponent();
    // Prior to TPL use:
    // ThreadPool.QueueUserWorkItem(state=>Increment());
    Task.Factory.StartNew(Increment);
}

void UpdateProgressBar()
{
    if (_ProgressBar.InvokeRequired)
    {
        MethodInvoker updateProgressBar =
            UpdateProgressBar;
        _ProgressBar.BeginInvoke(updateProgressBar);
    }
    else
    {
        _ProgressBar.Increment(1);
    }
}

private void Increment()
{
    for (int i = 0; i < 100; i++)
    {
        UpdateProgressBar();
        Thread.Sleep(100);
    }

    if (InvokeRequired)
    {
        // Close cannot be called directly from
        // a non-UI thread.
        Invoke(new MethodInvoker(Close));
    }
    else
    {
        Close();
    }
}

private void InitializeComponent()
{
```

```
        _ProgressBar = new ProgressBar();
        SuspendLayout();

        _ProgressBar.Location = new Point(13, 17);
        _ProgressBar.Size = new Size(267, 19);

        ClientSize = new Size(292, 53);
        Controls.Add(this._ProgressBar);
        Text = "Multithreading in Windows Forms";
        ResumeLayout(false);
    }
}
```

This program displays a window that contains a progress bar that automatically starts incrementing. Once the progress bar reaches 100 percent, the dialog box closes.

Notice from Listing 19.23 that you have to check InvokeRequired twice, and then the marshal calls across to the user interface thread if it returns true. In both cases, the marshalling involves instantiating a MethodInvoker delegate that is then passed to Invoke(). Since marshalling across to another thread could be relatively slow, an asynchronous invocation of the call is also available via BeginInvoke() and EndInvoke().

Invoke(), BeginInvoke(), EndInvoke(), and InvokeRequired comprise the members of the System.ComponentModel.ISynchronizeInvoke interface which is implemented by System.Windows.Forms.Control, from which Windows Forms controls derive.

Windows Presentation Foundation (WPF)

To achieve the same marshalling check on the **Windows Presentation Foundation (WPF)** platform involves a slightly different approach. WPF includes a static member property called Current of type DispatcherObject on the System.Windows.Application class. Calling CheckAccess() on the dispatcher serves the same function as InvokeRequired on controls in Windows Forms.

Listing 19.24 demonstrates the approach with a static UIAction object. Anytime a developer wants to call a method that might interact with the user interface she simply calls UIAction.Invoke() and passes a delegate for the UI code she wishes to call. This, in turn, checks the dispatcher to see if marshalling is necessary and then responds accordingly.

LISTING 19.24: Safely Invoking User Interface Objects

```csharp
using System;
using System.Windows;
using System.Windows.Threading;

public static class UIAction
{
    public static void Invoke<T>(
        Action<T> action, T parameter)
    {
        Invoke(() => action(parameter));
    }
    public static void Invoke(Action action)
    {
        DispatcherObject dispatcher =
            Application.Current;
        if (dispatcher == null
            || dispatcher.CheckAccess()
            || dispatcher.Dispatcher == null
            )
        {
            action();
        }
        else
        {
            SafeInvoke(action);
        }
    }


    // We want to catch all exceptions here
    // so we can rethrow
    private static void SafeInvoke(Action action)
    {
        Exception exceptionThrown = null;
        Action target = () =>
        {
            try
            {
                action();
            }
            catch (Exception exception)
            {
                exceptionThrown = exception;
            }
        };
        Application.Current.Dispatcher.Invoke(target);
        if (exceptionThrown != null)
        {
            throw exceptionThrown;
```

```
        }
    }
}
```

One additional feature in the `UIAction` of Listing 19.24 is the "marshalling" of any exceptions on the UI thread that may have occurred. `SafeInvoke()` wraps all requested delegate calls in a try/catch block and, if an exception is thrown, it saves the exception off and then rethrows it once context returns back to the calling thread. In this way, `UIAction` avoids throwing unhandled exceptions on the UI thread.

▪ ADVANCED TOPIC

Controlling the COM Threading Model with the `STAThreadAttribute`

With COM, four different apartment-threading models determine the threading rules relating to calls between COM objects. Fortunately, these rules—and the complexity that accompanied them—have disappeared from .NET as long as the program invokes no COM components. The general approach to handling COM Interop is to place all .NET components within the main, single-threaded apartment by decorating a process's `Main` method with the `System.STAThreadAttribute`. In so doing, it is not necessary to cross apartment boundaries to invoke the majority of COM components. Furthermore, apartment initialization does not occur, unless a COM Interop call is made. The caveat to this approach is that all other threads (including those of `Task`) will default to using a Multithreaded Apartment (MTA). The result is that care needs to be taken when invoking COM components from other threads besides the main one.

COM Interop is not necessarily an explicit action by the developer. Microsoft implemented many of the components within the .NET Framework by creating a runtime callable wrapper (RCW) rather than rewriting all the COM functionality within managed code. As a result, COM calls are often made unknowingly. To ensure that these calls are always made from a single-threaded apartment, it is generally a good practice to decorate the main method of all Windows Forms executables with the `System.STAThreadAttribute`.

SUMMARY

We began the chapter with a look at various synchronization mechanisms and how a variety of classes are available to protect against race conditions. Armed with this knowledge, we were able to delve further into a variety of additional multithreading patterns, including the following:

- *Asynchronous Programming Model (APM):* generally exposed by low-level libraries as a way to call long-running methods asynchronously.
- *Event-Based Asynchronous Patter (EAP):* like EAP, but for higher-level programming. EAP exposes an API for asynchronous programming that includes support for cancel and progress notifications.
- *Background Worker Pattern:* An API provided by the `Background-Worker` class that allows callers to impose an asynchronous pattern onto a long-running method even if designers implemented no such pattern.

Given the multitude of patterns available in addition to those provided by TPL, it can be somewhat puzzling to know which one to choose. Generally, it is better to choose an API-provided pattern (APM or EAP, for example) rather than using TPL to execute a method asynchronously. However, in the case of EAP, TPL provides calling support that takes advantage of EAP, so it is advisable to use the combination if TPL is available. The choice to use the background worker pattern rather than TPL is a little subtler. Developer preference would be an acceptable determinant as long as `BackgroundWorker` provides everything you need. As soon as you require additional functionality, TPL is better-suited, however. Also, consider using TPL if all registered listeners (to cancel, progress, and completion) are made through careful use of anonymous methods and closures as TPL would likely prove easier to maintain. However, if this is not the case, consider using `BackgroundWorker` instead as you can easily register members without relying on closure.

The next chapter investigates another complex .NET technology: that of marshalling calls out of .NET and into managed code using P/Invoke. In addition, it introduces a concept known as unsafe code, which C# uses to access memory pointers directly, as in unmanaged code (for example, C++).

■ 20 ■
Platform Interoperability and Unsafe Code

C# HAS GREAT CAPABILITIES, but sometimes it still isn't sufficient and you need to escape out of all the safety it provides and step back into the world of memory addresses and pointers. C# supports this in three ways. The first way is to go through Platform Invoke (P/Invoke) and calls into APIs exposed by unmanaged DLLs. The second is through **unsafe code,** which enables access to memory pointers and addresses. Frequently, code uses these features in combination. The third way, which is not covered in this text, is through COM interoperability.

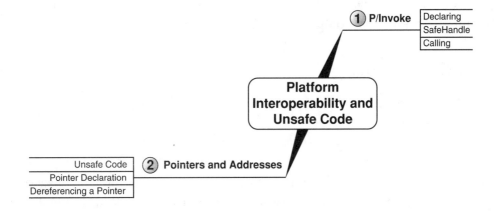

This chapter culminates with a small program that determines whether the computer is a virtual computer. The code requires that you do the following.

1. Call into an operating system DLL and request allocation of a portion of memory for executing instructions.
2. Write some assembler instructions into the allocated area.
3. Inject an address location into the assembler instructions.
4. Execute the assembler code.

Aside from the P/Invoke and unsafe constructs covered here, the final listing demonstrates the full power of C# and the fact that the capabilities of unmanaged code are still accessible from C# and managed code.

■ BEGINNER TOPIC

What Is a Virtual Computer?

A **virtual computer** (or virtual machine), also called a **guest computer,** is virtualized or emulated through software running on the host operating system and interacting with the host computer's hardware. For example, virtual computer software (such as VMware Workstation and Microsoft Virtual PC) can be installed on a computer running a recent version of Windows. Once the software is installed, users can configure a guest computer within the software, boot it, and install an operating system as though it were a real computer, not just one virtualized with software.

Platform Invoke

Whether a developer is trying to call a library of her existing unmanaged code, accessing unmanaged code in the operating system not exposed in any managed API, or trying to achieve maximum performance for a particular algorithm that performs faster by avoiding the runtime overhead of type checking and garbage collection, at some point she must call into unmanaged code. The CLI provides this capability through P/Invoke. With P/Invoke, you can make API calls into exported functions of unmanaged DLLs.

All of the APIs invoked in this section are Windows APIs. Although the same APIs are not available on other platforms, developers can still use P/Invoke for APIs native to their platform, or for calls into their own DLLs. The guidelines and syntax are the same.

Declaring External Functions

Once the target function is identified, the next step of P/Invoke is to declare the function with managed code. Just like all regular methods that belong to a class, you need to declare the targeted API within the context of a class, but by using the extern modifier. Listing 20.1 demonstrates how to do this.

LISTING 20.1: Declaring an External Method

```
using System;
using System.Runtime.InteropServices;
class VirtualMemoryManager
{
  [DllImport("kernel32.dll", EntryPoint="GetCurrentProcess")]
  internal static extern IntPtr GetCurrentProcessHandle();
}
```

In this case, the class is VirtualMemoryManager, because it will contain functions associated with managing memory. (This particular function is available directly off the System.Diagnostics.Processor class, so there is no need to declare it in real code.)

extern methods are always static and don't include any implementation. Instead, the DllImport attribute, which accompanies the method declaration, points to the implementation. At a minimum, the attribute needs the name of the DLL that defines the function. The runtime determines the function name from the method name. However, it is possible to override this default using the EntryPoint named parameter to provide the function name. (The .NET platform will automatically attempt calls to the Unicode [. . .W] or ASCII [. . .A] API version.)

It this case, the external function, GetCurrentProcess(), retrieves a pseudohandle for the current process which you will use in the call for virtual memory allocation. Here's the unmanaged declaration:

```
HANDLE GetCurrentProcess();
```

Parameter Data Types

Assuming the developer has identified the targeted DLL and exported function, the most difficult step is identifying or creating the managed data types that correspond to the unmanaged types in the external function.[1] Listing 20.2 shows a more difficult API.

LISTING 20.2: The `VirtualAllocEx()` API

```
LPVOID VirtualAllocEx(
    HANDLE hProcess,              // The handle to a process. The
                                  // function allocates memory within
                                  // the virtual address space of this
                                  // process.
    LPVOID lpAddress,             // The pointer that specifies a
                                  // desired starting address for the
                                  // region of pages that you want to
                                  // allocate. If lpAddress is NULL,
                                  // the function determines where to
                                  // allocate the region.
    SIZE_T dwSize,                // The size of the region of memory to
                                  // allocate, in bytes. If lpAddress
                                  // is NULL, the function rounds dwSize
                                  // up to the next page boundary.
    DWORD flAllocationType,       // The type of memory allocation.
    DWORD flProtect);             // The type of memory allocation.
```

`VirtualAllocEx()` allocates virtual memory that the operating system specifically designates for execution or data. To call it, you also need corresponding definitions in managed code for each data type; although common in Win32 programming, `HANDLE`, `LPVOID`, `SIZE_T`, and `DWORD` are undefined in the CLI managed code. The declaration in C# for `Virtual-AllocEx()`, therefore, is shown in Listing 20.3.

LISTING 20.3: Declaring the `VirtualAllocEx()` API in C#

```csharp
using System;
using System.Runtime.InteropServices;
class VirtualMemoryManager
{
    [DllImport("kernel32.dll")]
    internal static extern IntPtr GetCurrentProcess();
```

---

1. One particularly helpful resource for declaring Win32 APIs is www.pinvoke.net. This provides a great starting point for many APIs, helping to avoid some of the subtle problems that can arise when coding an external API call from scratch.

```
    [DllImport("kernel32.dll", SetLastError = true)]
    private static extern IntPtr VirtualAllocEx(
        IntPtr hProcess,
        IntPtr lpAddress,
        IntPtr dwSize,
        AllocationType flAllocationType,
        uint flProtect);
}
```

One distinct characteristic of managed code is the fact that primitive data types such as int do not change size based on the processor. Whether the processor is 16, 32, or 64 bits, int is always 32 bits. In unmanaged code, however, memory pointers will vary depending on the processor. Therefore, instead of mapping types such as HANDLE and LPVOID simply to ints, you need to map to System.IntPtr, whose size will vary depending on the processor memory layout. This example also uses an AllocationType enum, which I discuss in the section Simplifying API Calls with Wrappers, later in this chapter.

An interesting point to note about Listing 20.3 is that IntPtr is not just useful for pointers; it is also useful for other things such as quantities. IntPtr does not just mean "pointer stored in an integer"; it also means "integer that is the size of a pointer." An IntPtr need not contain a pointer; it just needs to contain something the size of a pointer. Lots of things are the size of a pointer but are nevertheless not pointers.

Using ref Rather Than Pointers

Frequently, unmanaged code uses pointers for pass-by-reference parameters. In these cases, P/Invoke doesn't require that you map the data type to a pointer in managed code. Instead, you map the corresponding parameters to ref (or out), depending on whether the parameter is in-out or just out. In Listing 20.4, lpflOldProtect, whose data type is PDWORD, is an example that returns the "pointer to a variable that receives the previous access protection of the first page in the specified region of pages."

LISTING 20.4: Using ref and out Rather Than Pointers

```
class VirtualMemoryManager
{
    // ...
    [DllImport("kernel32.dll", SetLastError = true)]
```

```
    static extern bool VirtualProtectEx(
        IntPtr hProcess, IntPtr lpAddress,
        IntPtr dwSize, uint flNewProtect,
        ref uint lpflOldProtect);
}
```

In spite of the fact that lpflOldProtect is documented as [out] (even though the signature doesn't enforce it), the description goes on to mention that the parameter must point to a valid variable and not NULL. The inconsistency is confusing, but common. The guideline is to use ref rather than out for P/Invoke type parameters since the callee can always ignore the data passed with ref, but the converse will not necessarily succeed.

The other parameters are virtually the same as VirtualAllocEx(), except that the lpAddress is the address returned from VirtualAllocEx(). In addition, flNewProtect specifies the exact type of memory protection: page execute, page read-only, and so on.

Using StructLayoutAttribute for Sequential Layout

Some APIs involve types that have no corresponding managed type. To call these requires redeclaration of the type in managed code. You declare the unmanaged COLORREF struct, for example, in managed code (see Listing 20.5).

LISTING 20.5: Declaring Types from Unmanaged Structs

```
[StructLayout(LayoutKind.Sequential)]
struct ColorRef
{
  public byte Red;
  public byte Green;
  public byte Blue;
  // Turn off warning about not accessing Unused.
  #pragma warning disable 414
  private byte Unused;
  #pragma warning restore 414

  public ColorRef(byte red, byte green, byte blue)
  {
      Blue = blue;
      Green = green;
      Red = red;
      Unused = 0;
  }
}
```

Various Microsoft Windows color APIs use COLORREF to represent RGB colors (levels of red, green, and blue).

The key in this declaration is StructLayoutAttribute. By default, managed code can optimize the memory layouts of types, so layouts may not be sequential from one field to the next. To force sequential layouts so that a type maps directly and can be copied bit for bit (blitted) from managed to unmanaged code and vice versa, you add the StructLayoutAttribute with the LayoutKind.Sequential enum value. (This is also useful when writing data to and from filestreams where a sequential layout may be expected.)

Since the unmanaged (C++) definition for struct does not map to the C# definition, there is not a direct mapping of unmanaged struct to managed struct. Instead, developers should follow the usual C# guidelines about whether the type should behave like a value or a reference type, and whether the size is small (approximately less than 16 bytes).

Error Handling

One inconvenient characteristic of Win32 API programming is the fact that it frequently reports errors in inconsistent ways. For example, some APIs return a value (0, 1, false, and so on) to indicate an error, and others set an out parameter in some way. Furthermore, the details of what went wrong require additional calls to the GetLastError() API and then an additional call to FormatMessage() to retrieve an error message corresponding to the error. In summary, Win32 error reporting in unmanaged code seldom occurs via exceptions.

Fortunately, the P/Invoke designers provided a mechanism for handling this. To enable this, given the SetLastError named parameter of the DllImport attribute is true, it is possible to instantiate a System.ComponentModel.Win32Exception() that is automatically initialized with the Win32 error data immediately following the P/Invoke call (see Listing 20.6).

LISTING 20.6: Win32 Error Handling

```
class VirtualMemoryManager
{
  [DllImport("kernel32.dll", ", SetLastError = true)]
  private static extern IntPtr VirtualAllocEx(
      IntPtr hProcess,
      IntPtr lpAddress,
      IntPtr dwSize,
```

```csharp
        AllocationType flAllocationType,
        uint flProtect);

    // ...
    [DllImport("kernel32.dll", SetLastError = true)]
    static extern bool VirtualProtectEx(
        IntPtr hProcess, IntPtr lpAddress,
        IntPtr dwSize, uint flNewProtect,
        ref uint lpflOldProtect);

    [Flags]
    private enum AllocationType : uint
    {
        // ...
    }

    [Flags]
    private enum ProtectionOptions
    {
        // ...
    }

    [Flags]
    private enum MemoryFreeType
    {
        // ...
    }

    public static IntPtr AllocExecutionBlock(
        int size, IntPtr hProcess)
    {
        IntPtr codeBytesPtr;
        codeBytesPtr = VirtualAllocEx(
            hProcess, IntPtr.Zero,
            (IntPtr)size,
            AllocationType.Reserve | AllocationType.Commit,
            (uint)ProtectionOptions.PageExecuteReadWrite);

        if (codeBytesPtr == IntPtr.Zero)
        {
            throw new System.ComponentModel.Win32Exception();
        }

        uint lpflOldProtect = 0;
        if (!VirtualProtectEx(
            hProcess, codeBytesPtr,
            (IntPtr)size,
            (uint)ProtectionOptions.PageExecuteReadWrite,
            ref lpflOldProtect))
        {
            throw new System.ComponentModel.Win32Exception();
```

```
    }
    return codeBytesPtr;
}

public static IntPtr AllocExecutionBlock(int size)
{
    return AllocExecutionBlock(
        size, GetCurrentProcessHandle());
}
}
```

This enables developers to provide the custom error checking that each API uses while still reporting the error in a standard manner.

Listing 20.1 and Listing 20.3 declared the P/Invoke methods as internal or private. Except for the simplest of APIs, wrapping methods in public wrappers that reduce the complexity of the P/Invoke API calls is a good guideline that increases API usability and moves toward object-oriented type structure. The `AllocExecutionBlock()` declaration in Listing 20.6 provides a good example of this.

Using SafeHandle

Frequently, P/Invoke involves a resource, such as a window handle, that code needs to clean up after using it. Instead of requiring developers to remember this and manually code it each time, it is helpful to provide a class that implements `IDisposable` and a finalizer. In Listing 20.7, for example, the address returned after `VirtualAllocEx()` and `VirtualProtectEx()` requires a follow-up call to `VirtualFreeEx()`. To provide built-in support for this, you define a `VirtualMemoryPtr` class that derives from `System.Runtime.InteropServices.SafeHandle` (this is new in .NET 2.0).

LISTING 20.7: Managed Resources Using SafeHandle

```
public class VirtualMemoryPtr :
    System.Runtime.InteropServices.SafeHandle
{
    public VirtualMemoryPtr(int memorySize) :
        base(IntPtr.Zero, true)
    {
        ProcessHandle =
            VirtualMemoryManager.GetCurrentProcessHandle();
        MemorySize = (IntPtr)memorySize;
```

```
        AllocatedPointer =
            VirtualMemoryManager.AllocExecutionBlock(
            memorySize, ProcessHandle);
        Disposed = false;
    }

    public readonly IntPtr AllocatedPointer;
    readonly IntPtr ProcessHandle;
    readonly IntPtr MemorySize;
    bool Disposed;

    public static implicit operator IntPtr(
        VirtualMemoryPtr virtualMemoryPointer)
    {
        return virtualMemoryPointer.AllocatedPointer;
    }

    // SafeHandle abstract member
    public override bool IsInvalid
    {
        get
        {
            return Disposed;
        }
    }

    // SafeHandle abstract member
    protected override bool ReleaseHandle()
    {
        if (!Disposed)
        {
            Disposed = true;
            GC.SuppressFinalize(this);
            VirtualMemoryManager.VirtualFreeEx(ProcessHandle,
                AllocatedPointer, MemorySize);
        }
        return true;
    }
}
```

System.Runtime.InteropServices.SafeHandle includes the abstract members IsInvalid and ReleaseHandle(). In the latter, you place your cleanup code; the former indicates whether the cleanup code has executed yet.

With VirtualMemoryPtr, you can allocate memory simply by instantiating the type and specifying the needed memory allocation.

■ ADVANCED TOPIC

Using IDisposable **Explicitly in Place of** SafeHandle

In C# 1.0, System.Runtime.InteropServices.SafeHandle is not available. Instead, a custom implementation of IDisposable, as shown in Listing 20.8, is necessary.

LISTING 20.8: **Managed Resources without SafeHandle but Using IDisposable**

```csharp
public struct VirtualMemoryPtr : IDisposable
{
  public VirtualMemoryPtr(int memorySize)
  {
      ProcessHandle =
          VirtualMemoryManager.GetCurrentProcessHandle();
      MemorySize = (IntPtr)memorySize;
      AllocatedPointer =
          VirtualMemoryManager.AllocExecutionBlock(
          memorySize, ProcessHandle);
      Disposed = false;
  }

  public readonly IntPtr AllocatedPointer;
  readonly IntPtr ProcessHandle;
  readonly IntPtr MemorySize;
  bool Disposed;

  public static implicit operator IntPtr(
      VirtualMemoryPtr virtualMemoryPointer)
  {
      return virtualMemoryPointer.AllocatedPointer;
  }

  #region IDisposable Members
  public void Dispose()
  {
      if (!Disposed)
      {
          Disposed = true;
          GC.SuppressFinalize(this);
          VirtualMemoryManager.VirtualFreeEx(ProcessHandle,
              AllocatedPointer, MemorySize);
      }
  }
  #endregion
}
```

In order for `VirtualMemoryPtr` to behave with value type semantics, you need to implement it as a `struct`. However, the consequence of this is that there can be no finalizer, since the garbage collector does not manage value types. This means the developer using the type must remember to clean up the code. There is no fallback mechanism if he doesn't.

The second restriction is not to pass or copy the instance outside the method. This is a common guideline of `IDisposable` implementing types. Their scope should be left within a `using` statement and they should not be passed as parameters to other methods that could potentially save them beyond the life of the `using` scope.

Calling External Functions

Once you declare the P/Invoke functions, you invoke them just as you would any other class member. The key, however, is that the imported DLL must be in the path, including the executable directory, so that it can be successfully loaded. Listing 20.6 and Listing 20.7 provide demonstrations of this. However, they rely on some constants.

Since `flAllocationType` and `flProtect` are flags, it is a good practice to provide constants or enums for each. Instead of expecting the caller to define these, encapsulation suggests you provide them as part of the API declaration, as shown in Listing 20.9.

LISTING 20.9: Encapsulating the APIs Together

```
class VirtualMemoryManager
{
  // ...

  /// <summary>
  /// The type of memory allocation. This parameter must
  /// contain one of the following values.
  /// </summary>
  [Flags]
  private enum AllocationType : uint
  {
      /// <summary>
      /// Allocates physical storage in memory or in the
      /// paging file on disk for the specified reserved
      /// memory pages. The function initializes the memory
      /// to zero.
      /// </summary>
```

```
        Commit = 0x1000,
        /// <summary>
        /// Reserves a range of the process's virtual address
        /// space without allocating any actual physical
        /// storage in memory or in the paging file on disk.
        /// </summary>
        Reserve = 0x2000,
        /// <summary>
        /// Indicates that data in the memory range specified by
        /// lpAddress and dwSize is no longer of interest. The
        /// pages should not be read from or written to the
        /// paging file. However, the memory block will be used
        /// again later, so it should not be decommitted. This
        /// value cannot be used with any other value.
        /// </summary>
        Reset = 0x80000,
        /// <summary>
        /// Allocates physical memory with read-write access.
        /// This value is solely for use with Address Windowing
        /// Extensions (AWE) memory.
        /// </summary>
        Physical = 0x400000,
        /// <summary>
        /// Allocates memory at the highest possible address.
        /// </summary>
        TopDown = 0x100000,
    }


    /// <summary>
    /// The memory protection for the region of pages to be
    /// allocated.
    /// </summary>
    [Flags]
    private enum ProtectionOptions : uint
    {
        /// <summary>
        /// Enables execute access to the committed region of
        /// pages. An attempt to read or write to the committed
        /// region results in an access violation.
        /// </summary>
        Execute = 0x10,
        /// <summary>
        /// Enables execute and read access to the committed
        /// region of pages. An attempt to write to the
        /// committed region results in an access violation.
        /// </summary>
        PageExecuteRead = 0x20,
        /// <summary>
        /// Enables execute, read, and write access to the
        /// committed region of pages.
```

```
        /// </summary>
        PageExecuteReadWrite = 0x40,
        // ...
    }


    /// <summary>
    /// The type of free operation
    /// </summary>
    [Flags]
    private enum MemoryFreeType : uint
    {
        /// <summary>
        /// Decommits the specified region of committed pages.
        /// After the operation, the pages are in the reserved
        /// state.
        /// </summary>
        Decommit = 0x4000,
        /// <summary>
        /// Releases the specified region of pages. After this
        /// operation, the pages are in the free state.
        /// </summary>
        Release = 0x8000
    }

    // ...
}
```

The advantage of enums is that they group together each value. Furthermore, they can limit the scope to nothing else besides these values.

Simplifying API Calls with Wrappers

Whether it is error handling, structs, or constant values, one goal of good API developers is to provide a simplified managed API that wraps the underlying Win32 API. For example, Listing 20.10 overloads `Virtual-FreeEx()` with public versions that simplify the call.

LISTING 20.10: Wrapping the Underlying API

```
class VirtualMemoryManager
{
    // ...

    [DllImport("kernel32.dll", SetLastError = true)]
    static extern bool VirtualFreeEx(
        IntPtr hProcess, IntPtr lpAddress,
        IntPtr dwSize, IntPtr dwFreeType);
```

```csharp
public static bool VirtualFreeEx(
    IntPtr hProcess, IntPtr lpAddress,
    IntPtr dwSize)
{
    bool result = VirtualFreeEx(
        hProcess, lpAddress, dwSize,
        (IntPtr)MemoryFreeType.Decommit);
    if (!result)
    {
        throw new System.ComponentModel.Win32Exception();
    }
    return result;
}
public static bool VirtualFreeEx(
    IntPtr lpAddress, IntPtr dwSize)
{
    return VirtualFreeEx(
        GetCurrentProcessHandle(), lpAddress, dwSize);
}

[DllImport("kernel32", SetLastError = true)]
static extern IntPtr VirtualAllocEx(
    IntPtr hProcess,
    IntPtr lpAddress,
    IntPtr dwSize,
    AllocationType flAllocationType,
    uint flProtect);

// ...
}
```

Function Pointers Map to Delegates

One last P/Invoke key is that function pointers in unmanaged code map to delegates in managed code. To set up a Microsoft Windows timer, for example, you would provide a function pointer that the timer could call back on, once it had expired. Specifically, you would pass a delegate instance that matched the signature of the callback.

Guidelines

Given the idiosyncrasies of P/Invoke, there are several guidelines to aid in the process of writing such code.

- Check that no managed classes already expose the APIs.
- Define API external methods as private or, in simple cases, internal.

- Provide public wrapper methods around the external methods that handle the data type conversions and error handling.

- Overload the wrapper methods and provide a reduced number of required parameters by inserting defaults for the extern method call.

- Use enum or `const` to provide constant values for the API as part of the API's declaration.

- For all P/Invoke methods that support `GetLastError()`, be sure to assign the `SetLastError` named attribute to `true`. This allows the reporting of errors via `System.ComponentModel.Win32Exception`.

- Wrap resources such as handles into classes that derive from `System.Runtime.InteropServices.SafeHandle` or that support `IDisposable`.

- Function pointers in unmanaged code map to delegate instances in managed code. Generally, this requires the declaration of a specific delegate type that matches the signature of the unmanaged function pointer.

- Map input/output and output parameters to `ref` parameters instead of relying on pointers.

The last bullet implies C#'s support for pointers, described in the next section.

Pointers and Addresses

On occasion, developers will want to be able to access and work with memory, and with pointers to memory locations, directly. This is necessary for certain operating system interaction as well as with certain types of time-critical algorithms. To support this, C# requires use of the unsafe code construct.

Unsafe Code

One of C#'s great features is the fact that it is strongly typed and supports type checking throughout the runtime execution. What makes this feature especially great is that it is possible to circumvent this support and manipulate memory and addresses directly. You would do this when working with things such as memory-mapped devices, or if you wanted to implement time-critical algorithms. The key is to designate a portion of the code as unsafe.

Unsafe code is an explicit code block and compilation option, as shown in Listing 20.11. The `unsafe` modifier has no effect on the generated CIL code itself. It is only a directive to the compiler to permit pointer and address manipulation within the unsafe block. Furthermore, *unsafe* does not imply *unmanaged*.

LISTING 20.11: Designating a Method for Unsafe Code

```
class Program
{
  unsafe static int Main(string[] args)
  {
      // ...
  }
}
```

You can use `unsafe` as a modifier to the type or to specific members within the type.

In addition, C# allows `unsafe` as a statement that flags a code block to allow unsafe code (see Listing 20.12).

LISTING 20.12: Designating a Code Block for Unsafe Code

```
class Program
{
  static int Main(string[] args)
  {
      unsafe
      {
          // ...
      }
  }
}
```

Code within the `unsafe` block can include unsafe constructs such as pointers.

> **▪ NOTE**
>
> It is important to note that it is necessary to explicitly indicate to the compiler that unsafe code is supported.

From the command line, this requires the /unsafe switch. For example, to compile the preceding code, you need to use the command shown in Output 20.1.

OUTPUT 20.1:

```
csc.exe /unsafe Program.cs
```

With Visual Studio this may be activated by checking the Allow Unsafe Code checkbox from the Build tab of the Project Properties window.

You need to use the /unsafe switch because unsafe code opens up the possibility of buffer overflows and similar possibilities that expose the potential for security holes. The /unsafe switch includes the ability to directly manipulate memory and execute instructions that are unmanaged. Requiring /unsafe, therefore, makes the choice of potential exposure explicit.

Pointer Declaration

Now that you have marked a code block as unsafe, it is time to look at how to write unsafe code. First, unsafe code allows the declaration of a pointer. Consider the following example:

```
byte* pData;
```

Assuming pData is not null, its value points to a location that contains one or more sequential bytes; the value of pData represents the memory address of the bytes. The type specified before the * is the **referent** type, or the type located where the value of the pointer refers. In this example, pData is the pointer and byte is the referent type, as shown in Figure 20.1.

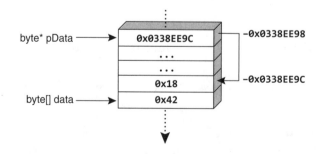

FIGURE 20.1: Pointers Contain the Address of the Data

Because pointers are simply integers that happen to refer to a memory address, they are not subject to garbage collection. C# does not allow referent types other than **unmanaged types,** which are types that are not reference types, are not generics, and do not contain reference types. Therefore, the following is not valid:

```
string* pMessage
```

Neither is this:

```
ServiceStatus* pStatus
```

where `ServiceStatus` is defined as shown in Listing 20.13; the problem again is that `ServiceStatus` includes a `string` field.

LISTING 20.13: Invalid Referent Type Example

```
struct ServiceStatus
{
  int State;
  string Description;  // Description is a reference type
}
```

In addition to custom structs that contain only unmanaged types, valid referent types include enums, predefined value types (`sbyte`, `byte`, `short`, `ushort`, `int`, `uint`, `long`, `ulong`, `char`, `float`, `double`, `decimal`, and `bool`), and pointer types (such as `byte**`). Lastly, valid syntax includes `void*` pointers, which represent pointers to an unknown type.

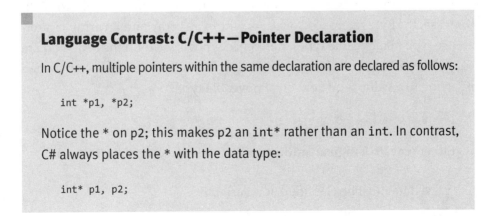

Language Contrast: C/C++—Pointer Declaration

In C/C++, multiple pointers within the same declaration are declared as follows:

```
int *p1, *p2;
```

Notice the * on p2; this makes p2 an `int*` rather than an `int`. In contrast, C# always places the * with the data type:

```
int* p1, p2;
```

The result is two variables of type `int*`. The syntax matches that of declaring multiple arrays in a single statement:

```
int[] array1, array2;
```

Pointers are an entirely new category of type. Unlike structs, enums, and classes, pointers don't ultimately derive from `System.Object` and are not even convertible to `System.Object`. Instead, they are convertible to `System.IntPtr` (which does convert to `System.Object`).

Assigning a Pointer

Once code defines a pointer, it needs to assign a value before accessing it. Just like reference types, pointers can hold the value `null`; this is their default value. The value stored by the pointer is the address of a location. Therefore, in order to assign it, you must first retrieve the address of the data.

You could explicitly cast an integer or a long into a pointer, but this rarely occurs without a means of determining the address of a particular data value at execution time. Instead, you need to use the address operator (&) to retrieve the address of the value type:

```
byte* pData = &bytes[0];  // Compile error
```

The problem is that in a managed environment, data can move, thereby invalidating the address. The error message is "You can only take the address of [an] unfixed expression inside a fixed statement initializer." In this case, the byte referenced appears within an array and an array is a reference type (a moveable type). Reference types appear on the heap and are subject to garbage collection or relocation. A similar problem occurs when referring to a value type field on a moveable type:

```
int* a = &"message".Length;
```

Either way, to assign an address of some data requires the following.

- The data must be classified as a variable.
- The data must be an unmanaged type.
- The variable needs to be classified as fixed, not moveable.

If the data is an unmanaged variable type but is not fixed, then use the fixed statement to fix a moveable variable.

Fixing Data

To retrieve the address of a moveable data item, it is necessary to fix, or pin, the data, as demonstrated in Listing 20.14.

LISTING 20.14: Fixed Statement

```
byte[] bytes = new byte[24];
fixed (byte* pData = &bytes[0])  // pData = bytes also allowed
{
  // ...
}
```

Within the code block of a fixed statement, the assigned data will not move. In this example, bytes will remain at the same address, at least until the end of the fixed statement.

The fixed statement requires the declaration of the pointer variable within its scope. This avoids accessing the variable outside the fixed statement, when the data is no longer fixed. However, it is the programmer's responsibility to ensure that he doesn't assign the pointer to another variable that survives beyond the scope of the fixed statement—possibly in an API call, for example. Similarly, using ref or out parameters will be problematic for data that will not survive beyond the method call.

Since a string is an invalid referent type, it would appear invalid to define pointers to strings. However, as in C++, internally a string is a pointer to the first character of an array of characters, and it is possible to declare pointers to characters using char*. Therefore, C# allows declaring a pointer of type char* and assigning it to a string within a fixed statement. The fixed statement prevents the movement of the string during the life of the pointer. Similarly, it allows any moveable type that supports an implicit conversion to a pointer of another type, given a fixed statement.

You can replace the verbose assignment of &bytes[0] with the abbreviated bytes, as shown in Listing 20.15.

LISTING 20.15: Fixed Statement without Address or Array Indexer

```
byte[] bytes = new byte[24];
fixed (byte* pData = bytes)
{
  // ...
}
```

Depending on the frequency and time to execute, fixed statements have the potential to cause fragmentation in the heap because the garbage collector cannot compact fixed objects. To reduce this problem, the best practice is to pin blocks early in the execution and to pin fewer large blocks rather than many small blocks. Unfortunately, this has to be tempered with pinning as little as possible for as short a time as possible, to minimize the chance that a collection will happen during the time that the data is pinned. To some extent, .NET 2.0 reduces the problem, due to some additional fragmentation-aware code.

Allocating on the Stack

You should use the fixed statement on an array to prevent the garbage collector from moving the data. However, an alternative is to allocate the array on the call stack. Stack allocated data is not subject to garbage collection or to the finalizer patterns that accompany it. Like referent types, the requirement is that the stackalloc data is an array of unmanaged types. For example, instead of allocating an array of bytes on the heap, you can place it onto the call stack, as shown in Listing 20.16.

LISTING 20.16: Allocating Data on the Call Stack

```
byte* bytes = stackalloc byte[42];}
```

Because the data type is an array of unmanaged types, it is possible for the runtime to allocate a fixed buffer size for the array and then to restore that buffer once the pointer goes out of scope. Specifically, it allocates sizeof(T) * E, where E is the array size and T is the referent type. Given the requirement of using stackalloc only on an array of unmanaged types, the runtime restores the buffer back to the system simply by unwinding the stack, eliminating the complexities of iterating over the f-reachable queue (see Garbage Collection and Finalization in Chapter 9) and compacting reachable data. Therefore, there is no way to explicitly free stackalloc data.

Note that the stack is a precious resource and, although small, running out of stack space will result in a program crashing; every effort should be taken to avoid running out. If a program does run out of stack space, the best thing that can happen is for the program to shut down/crash immediately. Generally, programs have less than 1MB of stack space (possibly a lot less). Therefore, take great care to avoid allocating arbitrarily sized buffers on the stack.

Dereferencing a Pointer

Accessing the data stored in a variable of a type referred to by a pointer requires that you dereference the pointer, placing the indirection operator prior to the expression. `byte data = *pData;`, for example, dereferences the location of the `byte` referred to by `pData` and returns the single `byte` at that location.

Using this principle in unsafe code allows the unorthodox behavior of modifying the "immutable" string, as shown in Listing 20.17. In no way is this recommended, but it does expose the potential of low-level memory manipulation.

LISTING 20.17: Modifying an Immutable String

```
string text = "S5280ft";
Console.Write("{0} = ", text);
unsafe  // Requires /unsafe switch.
{
  fixed (char* pText = text)
  {
      char* p = pText;
      *++p = 'm';
      *++p = 'i';
      *++p = 'l';
      *++p = 'e';
      *++p = ' ';
      *++p = ' ';
  }
}
Console.WriteLine(text);
```

The results of Listing 20.17 appear in Output 20.2.

OUTPUT 20.2:

```
S5280ft = Smile
```

In this case, you take the original address and increment it by the size of the referent type (sizeof(char)), using the preincrement operator. Next, you dereference the address using the indirection operator and then assign the location with a different character. Similarly, using the + and – operators on a pointer changes the address by the * sizeof(T) operand, where T is the referent type.

Similarly, the comparison operators (==, !=, <, >, <=, and =>) work to compare pointers translating effectively to the comparison of address location values.

One restriction on the dereferencing operator is the inability to dereference a void*. The void* data type represents a pointer to an unknown type. Since the data type is unknown, it can't be dereferenced to another type. Instead, to access the data referenced by a void*, you must convert it to any other pointer type variable and then dereference the later type, for example.

You can achieve the same behavior as Listing 20.17 by using the index operator rather than the indirection operator (see Listing 20.18).

LISTING 20.18: Modifying an Immutable with the Index Operator in Unsafe Code

```
string text;
text = "S5280ft";
Console.Write("{0} = ", text);

Unsafe  // Requires /unsafe switch.
{
  fixed (char* pText = text)
  {
      pText[1] = 'm';
      pText[2] = 'i';
      pText[3] = 'l';
      pText[4] = 'e';
      pText[5] = ' ';
      pText[6] = ' ';
  }
}
Console.WriteLine(text);
```

The results of Listing 20.18 appear in Output 20.3.

OUTPUT 20.3:

```
S5280ft = Smile
```

Modifications such as those in Listing 20.17 and Listing 20.18 lead to unexpected behavior. For example, if you reassigned text to "S5280ft" following the Console.WriteLine() statement and then redisplayed text, the output would still be Smile because the address of two equal string literals is optimized to one string literal referenced by both variables. In spite of the apparent assignment

```
text = "S5280ft";
```

after the unsafe code in Listing 20.17, the internals of the string assignment are an address assignment of the modified "S5280ft" location, so text is never set to the intended value.

Accessing the Member of a Referent Type

Dereferencing a pointer makes it possible for code to access the members of the referent type. However, this is possible without the indirection operator (&). As Listing 20.19 shows, it is possible to directly access a referent type's members using the -> operator (that is, a->b is shorthand for (*a).b).

LISTING 20.19: Directly Accessing a Referent Type's Members

```
unsafe
{
  Angle angle = new Angle(30, 18, 0);
  Angle* pAngle = &angle;
  System.Console.WriteLine("{0}° {1}' {2}\"",
      pAngle->Hours, pAngle->Minutes, pAngle->Seconds);
}
```

The results of Listing 20.19 appear in Output 20.4.

OUTPUT 20.4:

```
30° 18' 0
```

SUMMARY

This chapter's introduction outlined the low-level access to the underlying operating system that C# exposes. To summarize this, consider the Main()

function listing for determining whether execution is with a virtual computer (see Listing 20.20).

LISTING 20.20: Designating a Block for Unsafe Code

```
using System.Runtime.InteropServices;

class Program
{
  unsafe static int Main(string[] args)
  {
      // Assign redpill
      byte[] redpill = {
          0x0f, 0x01, 0x0d,        // asm SIDT instruction
          0x00, 0x00, 0x00, 0x00,  // placeholder for an address
          0xc3};                   // asm return instruction

      unsafe
      {
          fixed (byte* matrix = new byte[6],
              redpillPtr = redpill)
          {
              // Move the address of matrix immediately
              // following the SIDT instruction of memory.
              *(uint*)&redpillPtr[3] = (uint)&matrix[0];

              using (VirtualMemoryPtr codeBytesPtr =
                  new VirtualMemoryPtr(redpill.Length))
              {
                  Marshal.Copy(
                      redpill, 0,
                      codeBytesPtr, redpill.Length);

                  MethodInvoker method =
                      (MethodInvoker)Marshal.GetDelegateForFunctionPointer(
                      codeBytesPtr, typeof(MethodInvoker));

                  method();
              }
              if (matrix[5] > 0xd0)
              {
                  Console.WriteLine("Inside Matrix!\n");
                  return 1;
              }
              else
              {
                  Console.WriteLine("Not in Matrix.\n");
                  return 0;
              }
          }
```

```
        } // fixed
      } // unsafe
   }
}
```

The results of Listing 20.20 appear in Output 20.5.

OUTPUT 20.5:

```
Inside Matrix!
```

In this case, you use a delegate to trigger execution of the assembler code. The delegate is declared as follows:

```
delegate void MethodInvoker();
```

This book has demonstrated the power, flexibility, consistency, and fantastic structure of C#. This chapter demonstrated the ability, in spite of such high-level programming capabilities, to perform very low-level operations as well.

Before I end the book, the next chapter briefly describes the underlying execution platform and shifts the focus from the C# language to the broader platform in which C# programs execute.

▌21 ▪

The Common Language Infrastructure

O NE OF THE FIRST ITEMS that C# programmers encounter beyond the syntax is the context under which a C# program executes. This chapter discusses the underpinnings of how C# handles memory allocation and deallocation, type checking, interoperability with other languages, cross-platform execution, and support for programming metadata. In other words, this chapter investigates the Common Language Infrastructure (CLI) on which C# relies both at compile time and during execution. It covers the execution engine that governs a C# program at runtime and how C# fits into a broader set of languages that are governed by the same execution

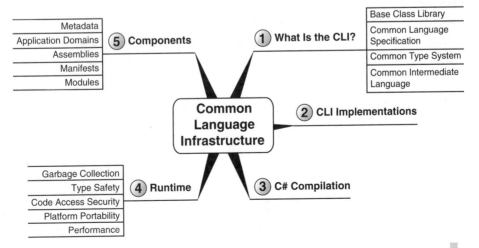

engine. Because of C#'s close ties with this infrastructure, most of the features that come with the infrastructure are made available to C#.

Defining the Common Language Infrastructure (CLI)

Instead of generating instructions that a processor can interpret directly, the C# compiler generates instructions in an intermediate language, the **Common Intermediate Language (CIL).** A second compilation step occurs, generally at execution time, converting the CIL to **machine code** that the processor can understand. Conversion to machine code is still not sufficient for code execution, however. It is also necessary for a C# program to execute under the context of an agent. The agent responsible for managing the execution of a C# program is the **Virtual Execution System (VES),** generally more casually referred to as the **runtime.** (Note that the runtime in this context does not refer to a time, such as execution time; rather, the runtime—the Virtual Execution System—is an agent responsible for managing the execution of a C# program.) The runtime is responsible for loading and running programs and providing additional services (security, garbage collection, and so on) to the program as it executes.

The specification for the CIL and the runtime is contained within an international standard known as the **Common Language Infrastructure (CLI).** This is a key specification for understanding the context in which a C# program executes and how it can seamlessly interact with other programs and libraries, even when they are written in alternate languages. Note that the CLI does not prescribe the implementation for the standard, but rather identifies the requirements for how a CLI platform should behave once it conforms to the standard. This provides CLI implementers with the flexibility to innovate where necessary, while still providing enough structure that programs created by one platform can execute on a different CLI implementation, and even on a different operating system.

■ NOTE

Note the similarity between these two acronyms and the names they stand for. Take care to understand these upfront to avoid confusion later on.

Contained within the CLI standard are specifications for the following:

- The Virtual Execution System (VES, or runtime)
- The Common Intermediate Language (CIL)
- The Common Type System (CTS)
- The Common Language Specification (CLS)
- Metadata
- The framework

This chapter broadens your view of C# to include the CLI, which is critical to how C# programs operate and interact with programs and with the operating system.

CLI Implementations

There are currently seven predominant implementations of the CLI (four of which are from Microsoft), each with an accompanying implementation of a C# compiler. Table 21.1 describes these implementations.

TABLE 21.1: Primary C# Compilers

Compiler	Description
Microsoft Visual C# .NET Compiler	Microsoft's .NET C# compiler is dominant in the industry, but it is limited to running on the Windows family of operating systems. You can download it free as part of the Microsoft .NET Framework SDK from http://msdn.microsoft.com/en-us/netframework/default.aspx.
Microsoft Silverlight	This is a cross-platform implementation of the CLI that runs on both the Windows family of operating systems and the Macintosh. Resources for getting started with development on this platform are available at http://silverlight.net/getstarted.
Microsoft Compact Framework	This is a trimmed-down implementation of the .NET Framework designed to run on PDAs and phones.

Continues

TABLE 21.1: Primary C# Compilers *(Continued)*

Compiler	Description
Microsoft XNA	This is a CLI implementation for game developers targeting Xbox and Windows Vista. For more information, see www.xna.com.
Mono Project	The Mono Project is an open source implementation sponsored by Ximian and designed to provide a Windows-, Linux-, and Unix-compatible version of the CLI specification and C# compiler. Source code and binaries are available at www.go-mono.com.
DotGNU	This is focused on creating platform-portable applications that will run under both the .NET and the DotGNU. Portable.NET implementations of the CLI. This implementation is available from www.dotgnu.org. Supported operating systems include GNU/Linux *BSD, Cygwin/ Mingw32, Mac OS X, Solaris, AIX, and PARISC. DotGNU and Mono have used portions of each other's libraries at various times.
Rotor	The Rotor program, also known as the Shared Source CLI, is an implementation of the CLI that Microsoft developed to run on Windows, Mac OS X, and FreeBSD. Both the implementation and the source code are available free at http://msdn.microsoft.com/en-us/library/ms973880.aspx. Note that although the source code is available for download, Microsoft has not licensed Rotor for developing commercial applications, and instead has targeted it as a learning tool.

Although none of these platforms and compilers would have any problems with the source code shown in Chapter 1, note that each CLI and C# compiler implementation is at a different stage of compliance with the specifications. For example, some implementations will not compile all the newer syntax. All implementations, however, are intended to comply with the ECMA-334 specification for C# 1.0[1] and the ECMA-335 specification for the CLI 1.2.[2] Furthermore, many implementations include prototype features prior to the establishment of those features in standards.

---

1. This is available for free via mail, or via download at www.ecma-international.org/publications/standards/Ecma-334.htm.
2. This is available for free via mail, or via download at www.ecma-international.org/publications/standards/Ecma-335.htm.

C# Compilation to Machine Code

The HelloWorld program listing in Chapter 1 is obviously C# code, and you compiled it for execution using the C# compiler. However, the processor still cannot directly interpret compiled C# code. An additional compilation step is required to convert the result of C# compilation into machine code. Furthermore, the execution requires the involvement of an agent that adds additional services to the C# program, services that it was not necessary to code for explicitly.

All computer languages define syntax and semantics for programming. Since languages such as C and C++ compile to machine code, the platform for these languages is the underlying operating system and machine instruction set, be it Microsoft Windows, Linux, Unix, or others. Languages such as C# are different; the underlying platform is the runtime (or VES).

CIL is what the C# compiler produces after compiling. It is termed a "common intermediate language" (CIL) because an additional step is required to transform the CIL into something that processors can understand. Figure 21.1 shows the process.

In other words, C# compilation requires two steps:

1. Conversion from C# to CIL by the C# compiler
2. Conversion from CIL to instructions that the processor can execute

The runtime is able to understand CIL statements and compile them to machine code. Generally, a **component** within the runtime performs this compilation from CIL to machine code. This component is the **just-in-time (JIT) compiler,** and **jitting** can occur when the program is installed or executed. Most CLI implementations favor execution-time compilation of the CIL, but the CLI does not specify when the compilation needs to occur. In fact, the CLI even allows the CIL to be interpreted rather than compiled, similar to the way many scripting languages work. In addition, .NET includes a tool called NGEN that enables compilation to machine code prior to actually running the program. This preexecution-time compilation needs to take place on the computer on which the program will be executing because it will evaluate the machine characteristics (processor, memory, and so on) in order to generate more efficient code. The advantage of using

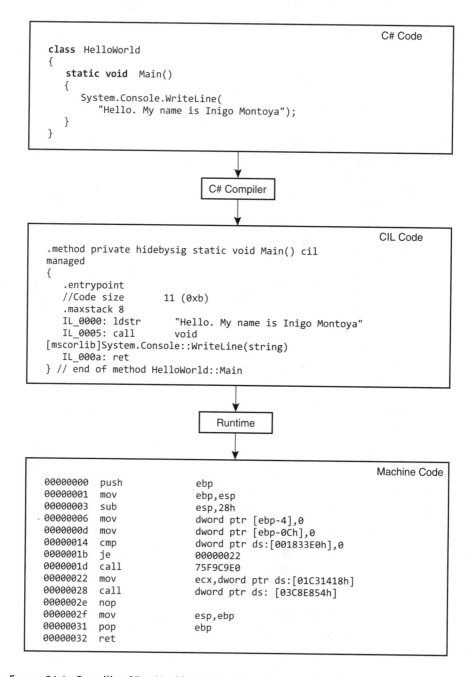

FIGURE 21.1: Compiling C# to Machine Code

NGEN at installation (or at any time prior to execution) is that you can reduce the need for the jitter to run at startup, thereby decreasing startup time.

Runtime

Even after the runtime converts the CIL code to machine code and starts to execute, it continues to maintain control of its execution. The code that executes under the context of an agent such as the runtime is **managed code,** and the process of executing under control of the runtime is **managed execution.** The control over execution transfers to the data; this makes it **managed data** because memory for the data is automatically allocated and de-allocated by the runtime.

Somewhat inconsistently, the term *Common Language Runtime* (CLR) is not technically a generic term that is part of the CLI. Rather, CLR is the Microsoft-specific implementation of the runtime for the .NET platform. Regardless, CLR is casually used as a generic term for *runtime*, and the technically accurate term, *Virtual Execution System,* is seldom used outside the context of the CLI specification.

Because an agent controls program execution, it is possible to inject additional services into a program, even though programmers did not explicitly code for them. Managed code, therefore, provides information to allow these services to be attached. Among other items, managed code enables the location of metadata about a type member, exception handling, access to security information, and the capability to walk the stack. The remainder of this section includes a description of some additional services made available via the runtime and managed execution. The CLI does not explicitly require all of them, but the established CLI platforms have an implementation of each.

Garbage Collection

Garbage collection is the process of automatically de-allocating memory based on the program's needs. This is a significant programming problem for languages that don't have an automated system for doing this. Without the garbage collector, programmers must remember to always free any memory allocations they make. Forgetting to do so, or doing so repeatedly for the same memory allocation, introduces memory leaks or corruption into the program, something exacerbated by long-running programs such as web servers. Because of the runtime's built-in support for garbage collection, programmers targeting runtime execution can focus on adding program features rather than "plumbing" related to memory management.

Language Contrast: C++—Deterministic Destruction

The exact mechanics for how the garbage collector works are not part of the CLI specification; therefore, each implementation can take a slightly different approach. (In fact, garbage collection is one item not explicitly required by the CLI.) One key concept that may take C++ programmers a little getting used to is that garbage-collected objects are not necessarily collected **deterministically** (at well-defined, compile-time-known locations). In fact, objects can be garbage-collected anytime between when they are last accessed and when the program shuts down. This includes collection prior to falling out of scope, or waiting until well after an object instance is accessible by the code.

It should be noted that the garbage collector only takes responsibility for handling memory management. It does not provide an automated system for managing resources unrelated to memory. Therefore, if an explicit action to free a resource (other than memory) is required, programmers using that resource should utilize special CLI-compatible programming patterns that will aid in the cleanup of those resources (see Chapter 9).

Garbage Collection on .NET

The .NET platform implementation of garbage collection uses a generational, compacting, mark-and-sweep-based algorithm. It is generational because objects that have lived for only a short period will be cleaned up sooner than objects that have already survived garbage collection sweeps because they were still in use. This conforms to the general pattern of memory allocation that objects that have been around longer will continue to outlive objects that have only recently been instantiated.

Additionally, the .NET garbage collector uses a mark-and-sweep algorithm. During each garbage collection execution, it marks objects that are to be de-allocated and compacts together the objects that remain so that there is no "dirty" space between them. The use of compression to fill in the space left by de-allocated objects often results in faster instantiation of new objects (than with unmanaged code), because it is not necessary to search through memory to locate space for a new allocation. This also decreases the chance of paging because more objects are located in the same page, which improves performance as well.

The garbage collector takes into consideration the resources on the machine and the demand on those resources at execution time. For example, if memory on the computer is still largely untapped, the garbage collector is less likely to run and take time to clean up those resources. This is an optimization rarely taken by platforms and languages that are not based on garbage collection.

Type Safety

One of the key advantages the runtime offers is checking conversions between types, or **type checking.** Via type checking, the runtime prevents programmers from unintentionally introducing invalid casts that can lead to buffer overrun vulnerabilities. Such vulnerabilities are one of the most common means of breaking into a computer system, and having the runtime automatically prevent these is a significant gain.[3] Type checking provided by the runtime ensures the following.

- Both variables and the data the variables refer to are typed, and the type of the variable is compatible with the data that it refers to.

- It is possible to locally analyze a type (without analyzing all of the code in which the type is used) to determine what permissions will be required to execute that type's members.

- Each type has a compile-time-defined set of methods and the data they contain. The runtime enforces rules about what classes can access those methods and data. Methods marked as "private," for example, are accessible only by the containing type.

---

3. Assuming you are not the unscrupulous type that is looking for such vulnerabilities.

Circumventing Encapsulation and Access Modifiers

Given appropriate permissions, it is possible to circumvent encapsulation and access modifiers via a mechanism known as **reflection.** Reflection provides late binding by enabling support for browsing through a type's members, looking up the names of particular constructs within an object's metadata, and invoking the type's members.

Code Access Security

The runtime can make security checks as the program executes, allowing and disallowing the specific types of operations depending on permissions. Permission to execute a specific function is not restricted to authentication of the user running the program. The runtime also controls execution based on who created the program and whether she is a trusted provider. Similarly, you might want to note that Code Access Security (CAS) also applies security policy based on the location of the code—by default, code installed on the local machine is more trusted than code from the LAN, which is much more trusted than code on the Internet. Permissions can be tuned such that partially trusted providers can read and write files from controlled locations on the disk, but they are prevented from accessing other locations (such as email addresses from an email program) for which the provider has not been granted permission. Identification of a provider is handled by certificates that are embedded into the program when the provider compiles the code.

Platform Portability

One theoretical feature of the runtime is the opportunity it provides for C# code and the resultant programs to be **platform-portable,** capable of running on multiple operating systems and executing on different CLI implementations. Portability in this context is not limited to the source code such that recompiling is necessary. A single CLI module compiled for one platform should run on any CLI-compatible platform without needing to be recompiled. This portability occurs because the work of porting the code lies in the hands of the runtime implementation rather than the application developer.

The restriction is, of course, that no platform-specific APIs are used. Because of this restriction, many developers forgo CLI platform-neutral code in favor of accessing the underlying platform functionality, rather than writing it all from scratch.

The platform portability offered by .NET, DotGNU, Rotor, and Mono varies depending on the goals of the platform developers. For obvious reasons, .NET was targeted to run only on the Microsoft series of operating systems. Rotor, also produced by Microsoft, was primarily designed as a means for teaching and fostering research into future CLI development. Its inclusion of support for FreeBSD proves the portability characteristics of the CLI. Some of the libraries included in .NET (such as WinForms, ASP.NET, ADO.NET, and more) are not available in Rotor.

DotGNU and Mono were initially targeted at Linux but have since been ported to many different operating systems. Furthermore, the goal of these CLIs was to provide a means for porting .NET applications to operating systems in addition to those controlled by Microsoft. In so doing, there is a large overlap between the APIs found in .NET and those available in Mono and DotGNU.

Unfortunately, the variance in the Based Class Library alone (even just within the Microsoft-developed CLI platforms) makes portability difficult at best. Perhaps the best option is for Silverlight development to be compatible with the full .NET Framework (but the reverse is unlikely to work unless development is restricted to the set of compatible APIs).

Performance

Many programmers accustomed to writing unmanaged code will correctly point out that managed environments impose overhead on applications, no matter how simple. The trade-off is one of increased development productivity and reduced bugs in managed code versus runtime performance. The same dichotomy emerged as programming went from assembler to higher-level languages such as C, and from structured programming to object-oriented development. In the vast majority of scenarios, development productivity wins out, especially as the speed and reduced price of hardware surpass the demands of applications. Time spent on architectural design is much more likely to yield big performance gains than the complexities of a low-level development platform. In the climate of security holes caused by buffer overruns, managed execution is even more compelling.

Undoubtedly, certain development scenarios (device drivers, for example) may not yet fit with managed execution. However, as managed execution increases in capability and sophistication, many of these performance considerations will likely vanish. Unmanaged execution will then be reserved for development where precise control or circumvention of the runtime is deemed necessary.[4]

Furthermore, the runtime introduces several factors that can contribute to improved performance over native compilation. For example, because translation to machine code takes place on the destination machine, the resultant compiled code matches the processor and memory layout of that machine, resulting in performance gains generally not leveraged by nonjitted languages. Also, the runtime is able to respond to execution conditions that direct compilation to machine code rarely takes into account. If, for example, there is more memory on the box than is required, unmanaged languages will still de-allocate their memory at deterministic, compile-time-defined execution points in the code. Alternatively, jit-compiled languages will need to de-allocate memory only when it is running low or when the program is shutting down. Even though jitting can add a compile step to the execution process, code efficiencies that a jitter can insert lead to performance rivaling that of programs compiled directly to machine code. Ultimately, CLI programs are not necessarily faster than non-CLI programs, but their performance is competitive.

Application Domains

By introducing a layer between the program and the operating system, it is possible to implement virtual processes or applications known as **application domains (app domains).** An application domain behaves like an operating system process in that it offers a level of isolation between other application domains. For example, an app domain has its own virtual memory allocation, and communication between application domains requires distributed communication paradigms, just as it would between two operating system processes. Similarly, static data is not shared

---

4. Indeed, Microsoft has indicated that managed development will be the predominant means of writing applications for its Windows platform in the future, even those applications that integrate with the operating system.

between application domains, so static constructors run for each application domain, and assuming a single thread per application domain, there is no need to synchronize the static data because each application has its own instance of the data. Furthermore, each application domain has its own threads, and just like with an operating system process, threads cannot cross application domain boundaries.

The point of an application domain is that processes are considered relatively expensive. With application domains, you can avoid this additional expense by running multiple application domains within a single process. For example, you can use a single process to host a series of web sites. However, you can isolate the web sites from each other by placing them in their own application domain. In summary, application domains represent a virtual process on a layer between an operating system process and the threads.

Assemblies, Manifests, and Modules

Included in the CLI is the specification of the CIL output from a source language compiler, usually an assembly. In addition to the CIL instructions themselves, an assembly includes a **manifest** which is made up of the following:

- The types that an assembly defines and imports
- Version information about the assembly itself
- Additional files the assembly depends on
- Security permissions for the assembly

The manifest is essentially a header to the assembly, providing all the information about what an assembly is composed of, along with the information that uniquely identifies it.

Assemblies can be class libraries or the executables themselves, and one assembly can reference other assemblies (which, in turn, can reference more assemblies), thereby establishing an application composed of many components rather than one large, monolithic program. This is an important feature that modern programming platforms take for granted, because it significantly improves maintainability and allows a single component to be shared across multiple programs.

In addition to the manifest, an assembly contains the CIL code within one or more modules. Generally, the assembly and the manifest are combined into a single file, as was the case with `HelloWorld.exe` in Chapter 1. However, it is possible to place modules into their own separate files and then use an assembly linker (`al.exe`) to create an assembly file that includes a manifest that references each module.[5] This not only provides another means of breaking a program into components, but it also enables the development of one assembly using multiple source languages.

Casually, the terms *module* and *assembly* are somewhat interchangeable. However, the term *assembly* is predominant for those talking about CLI-compatible programs or libraries. Figure 21.2 depicts the various component terms.

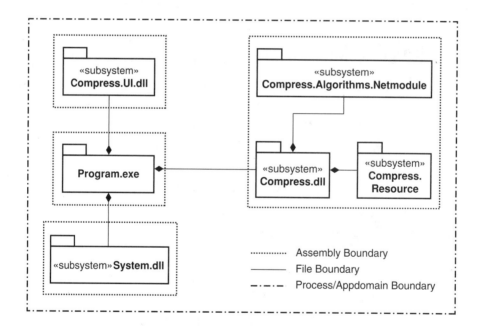

FIGURE 21.2: Assemblies with the Modules and Files They Reference

---

5. This is partly because one of the primary CLI IDEs, Visual Studio .NET, lacks functionality for working with assemblies composed of multiple modules. Current implementations of Visual Studio .NET do not have integrated tools for building multimodule assemblies, and when they use such assemblies, IntelliSense does not fully function.

Note that both assemblies and modules can also reference files such as resource files that have been localized to a particular language. Although it is rare, two different assemblies can reference the same module or file.

In spite of the fact that an assembly can include multiple modules and files, there is only one version number for the entire group of files and it is placed in the assembly manifest. Therefore, the smallest versionable component within an application is the assembly, even if that assembly is composed of multiple files. If you change any of the referenced files—even to release a patch—without updating the assembly manifest, you will violate the integrity of the manifest and the entire assembly itself. As a result, assemblies form the logical construct of a component or unit of deployment.

▪ NOTE

Assemblies form the smallest unit that can be versioned and installed, not the individual modules that comprise them.

Even though an assembly (the logical construct) could consist of multiple modules, most assemblies contain only one. Furthermore, Microsoft now provides an `ILMerge.exe` utility for combining multiple modules and their manifests into a single file assembly.

Because the manifest includes a reference to all the files an assembly depends on, it is possible to use the manifest to determine an assembly's dependencies. Furthermore, at execution time, the runtime needs to examine only the manifest to determine what files it requires. Only tool vendors distributing libraries shared by multiple applications (Microsoft, for example) need to register those files at deployment time. This makes deployment significantly easier. Often, deployment of a CLI-based application is referred to as **xcopy deployment,** after the Windows `xcopy` command that simply copies files to a selected destination.

Language Contrast: COM DLL Registration

Unlike Microsoft's COM files of the past, CLI assemblies rarely require any type of registration. Instead, it is possible to deploy applications by copying all the files that comprise a program into a particular directory, and then executing the program.

Common Intermediate Language (CIL)

Considering the Common Language Infrastructure (CLI) name, another important feature of the CIL and the CLI is to support the interaction of multiple languages within the same application (instead of portability of source code across multiple operating systems). As a result, the CIL is the intermediate language not only for C#, but also for many other languages, including Visual Basic .NET, the Java-like language of J#, some incantations of Smalltalk, C++, and a host of others (more than 20 at the time of this writing, including versions of COBOL and FORTRAN). Languages that compile to the CIL are **source languages** and each has a custom compiler that converts the source language to the CIL. Once compiled to the CIL, the source language is insignificant. This powerful feature enables the development of libraries by different development groups across multiple organizations, without concern for the language choice of a particular group. Thus, the CIL enables programming language interoperability as well as platform portability.

> ### ■ NOTE
>
> A powerful feature of the CLI is support for multiple languages. This enables the creation of programs using multiple languages and the accessibility of libraries written in one language from code written in a different language.

Common Type System (CTS)

Regardless of the programming language, the resultant program operates internally on data types; therefore, the CLI includes the **Common Type System (CTS).** The CTS defines how types are structured and laid out in memory, as well as the concepts and behaviors that surround types. It includes type manipulation directives alongside the information about the data stored within the type. The CTS standard applies to how types appear and behave at the external boundary of a language because the purpose of the CTS is to achieve interoperability between languages. It is the responsibility of the runtime at execution time to enforce the contracts established by the CTS.

Within the CTS, types are broken down into two categories.

- **Values** are bit patterns used to represent basic types, such as integers and characters, as well as more complex data in the form of structures. Each value type corresponds to a separate type designation not stored within the bits themselves. The separate type designation refers to the type definition that provides the meaning of each bit within the value and the operations that the value supports.
- **Objects** contain within them the object's type designation. (This helps in enabling type checking.) Objects have identity that makes each instance unique. Furthermore, objects have slots that can store other types (either values or object references). Unlike values, changing the contents of a slot does not change the identity of the object.

These two categories of types translate directly to C# syntax that provides a means of declaring each type.

Common Language Specification (CLS)

Since the language integration advantages provided by the CTS generally outweigh the costs of implementing it, the majority of source languages support the CTS. However, there is also a subset of CTS language conformance called the **Common Language Specification (CLS).** Its focus is toward library implementations. It targets library developers, providing them with standards for writing libraries that are accessible from the majority of source languages, regardless of whether the source languages using the library are CTS-compliant. It is called the Common Language Specification because it is intended to also encourage CLI languages to provide a means of creating interoperable libraries, or libraries that are accessible from other languages.

For example, although it is perfectly reasonable for a language to provide support for an unsigned integer, such a type is not included as part of the CLS. Therefore, developers implementing a class library should not externally expose unsigned integers because doing so would cause the library to be less accessible from CLS-compliant source languages that do not support unsigned integers. Ideally, therefore, any development of libraries that is to be accessible from multiple languages should conform to the CLS specification. Note that the CLS is not concerned with types that are not exposed externally to the assembly.

Note that it is possible to have the compiler issue a warning when you create an API that is not CLS compliant. To accomplish this, use the assembly attribute System.CLSCompliant and specify a value of true for the parameter.

Base Class Library (BCL)

In addition to providing a platform in which CIL code can execute, the CLI also defines a core set of class libraries that programs may employ, called the **Base Class Library (BCL).** These libraries provide foundational types and APIs, allowing the program to interact with the runtime and underlying operating system in a consistent manner. The BCL includes support for collections, simple file access, some security, fundamental data types (string, and so on), streams, and the like.

Similarly, there is a Microsoft-specific library called the **Framework Class Library (FCL)** that adds to this and includes support for rich client user interfaces, web user interfaces, database access, distributed communication, and more.

Metadata

In addition to execution instructions, CIL code includes **metadata** about the types and files included in a program. The metadata includes the following:

- Descriptions of each type within a program or class library
- The manifest information containing data about the program itself, along with the libraries it depends on

- Custom attributes embedded in the code, providing additional information about the constructs the attributes decorate

The metadata is not a cursory, nonessential add-on to the CIL. Instead, it forms a core part of the CLI implementation. It provides the representation and the behavior information about a type and includes location information about which assembly contains a particular type definition. It serves a key role in saving data from the compiler and making it accessible at execution time to debuggers and the runtime. This data not only is available in the CIL code, but also is accessible during machine code execution so that the runtime can continue to make any necessary type checks.

Metadata provides a mechanism for the runtime to handle a mixture of native and managed code execution. Also, it increases code and execution robustness because it smoothes the migration from one library version to the next, replacing compile-time-defined binding with a load-time implementation.

All header information about a library and its dependencies is in a portion of the metadata known as the manifest. As a result, the manifest portion of the metadata enables developers to determine a module's dependencies, including information about particular versions of the dependencies and signatures of who created the module. At execution time, the runtime uses the manifest to determine what dependent libraries to load, whether the libraries or the main program has been tampered with, and whether assemblies are missing.

The metadata also contains **custom attributes** that may decorate the code. Attributes provide additional metadata about CIL instructions that are accessible via the program at execution time.

Metadata is available at execution time by a mechanism known as **reflection.** With reflection, it is possible to look up a type or its member at execution time and then invoke that member or determine whether a construct is decorated with a particular attribute. This provides **late binding,** determining what code to execute at execution time rather than at compile time. Reflection can even be used for generating documentation by iterating through metadata and copying it into a help document of some kind (see Chapter 17).

SUMMARY

This chapter described many new terms and acronyms that are important to understanding the context under which C# programs run. The preponderance of three-letter acronyms can be confusing. Table 21.2 provides a summary list of the terms and acronyms that are part of the CLI.

TABLE 21.2: Common C#-Related Acronyms

Acronym	Definition	Description
.NET	None	Microsoft's implementation of the entire CLI stack. Includes the CLR, CIL, and various languages, all of which are CLS-compliant.
BCL	Base Class Library	The portion of the CLI specification that defines the collection, threading, console, and other base classes necessary to build virtually all programs.
C#	None	A programming language. Note that separate from the CLI standard there is a C# Language Specification, also ratified by the ECMA and ISO standards bodies.
CIL (IL)	Common Intermediate Language	The language of the CLI specification that defines the instructions for the code executable on implementations of the CLI. This is sometimes also referred to as IL or Microsoft IL (MSIL) to distinguish it from other intermediate languages. (To indicate that it is a standard broader than Microsoft, CIL is preferred over MSIL and even IL.)
CLI	Common Language Infrastructure	The specification that defines the intermediate language, base classes, and behavioral characteristics which enable implementers to create Virtual Execution Systems and compilers in which source languages are interoperable on top of a common execution environment.
CLR	Common Language Runtime	Microsoft's implementation of the runtime, as defined in the CLI specification.

TABLE 21.2: Common C#-Related Acronyms *(Continued)*

Acronym	Definition	Description
CLS	Common Language Specification	The portion of the CLI specification that defines the core subset of features which source languages *must* support in order to be executable on runtimes implemented according to the CLI specification.
CTS	Common Type System	A standard generally implemented by CLI-compliant languages that defines the representation and behavior of types that the language exposes visibly outside a module. It includes concepts for how types can be combined to form new types.
FCL	.NET Framework Class Library	The class library that comprises Microsoft's .NET Framework. It includes Microsoft's implementation of the BCL as well as a large library of classes for such things as web development, distributed communication, database access, rich client user interface development, and a host of others.
VES (runtime)	Virtual Execution System	An agent that manages the execution of a program that is compiled for the CLI.

▌A▪

Downloading and Installing the C# Compiler and the CLI Platform

T O COMPILE AND RUN C# programs, it is necessary to install a version of the compiler and the CLI platform.

Microsoft's .NET

The predominant CLI platform is Microsoft .NET and this is the platform of choice for development on Microsoft Windows.

- The minimum installation that includes the compiler and the .NET Framework with C# 2.0 syntax support is the redistributable package for the .NET Framework 2.0 or higher. This is available at http://msdn.microsoft.com/en-us/netframework/default.aspx.
- For a rich IDE that includes IntelliSense and support for project files, install a version of the Visual Studio IDE. This includes Visual C# Express, which is available free at http://lab.msdn.microsoft.com/express.

For command-line compilation, regardless of a Visual Studio install or only the runtime, you must set the PATH environment variable to include the C# compiler, CSC.EXE.

Setting Up the Compiler Path with Microsoft .NET

If Visual Studio .NET is installed on your computer, open the command prompt from the Start menu by selecting All Programs, Microsoft Visual Studio .NET, Visual Studio Tools, Visual Studio Command Prompt. This command prompt places CSC.EXE in the path to be available for execution from any directory.

Without Visual Studio .NET installed, no special compiler command prompt item appears in the Start menu. Instead, you need to reference the full compiler pathname explicitly or add it to the path. The compiler is located at %Windir%\Microsoft.NET\Framework\<version>, where <version> is the version of the .NET Framework (v1.0.3705, v1.1.4322, v2.0.50727, and so on) and %Windir% is the environment variable that points to the location of the Windows directory. To add this location to the path use Set PATH=%PATH%;%Windir%\Micro-soft.NET\Framework\<version>, again substituting the value of <ver-sion> appropriately. Output A.1 provides an example.

OUTPUT A.1:

```
Set PATH=%PATH%;%Windir%\Microsoft.NET\Framework\v2.0.50727
```

Once the path includes the framework, it is possible to use the .NET C# compiler, CSC.EXE, without providing the full path to its location.

Mono

For CLI development on platforms other than Microsoft Windows, consider Mono, which is a platform you can download at www.mono-project.com. As with the .NET platform, Mono requires the full path to the C# compiler if it is not already in the search path. The default installation path on Linux is /usr/lib/mono/<version> and the compiler is gmcs.exe or mcs.exe, depending on the version. (If Mono is installed on Microsoft Windows, the default path is `%ProgramFiles%\Mono-<version>\lib\mono\<version>\`.)

One option for a Linux version that includes an installation of Mono is Monoppix. This builds on the CD-bootable Linux distribution known as Knoppix and is available for download at www.monoppix.com.

Instead of `CSC.EXE`, the Mono platform's compiler is `MCS.EXE` or `GMCS.EXE`, depending on the compiler version. Therefore, the command for compiling `HelloWorld.cs` is as shown in Output A.2.

OUTPUT A.2:

```
C:\SAMPLES>msc.exe HelloWorld.cs
```

Unfortunately, the Linux environment cannot run the resultant binaries directly; instead, it requires explicit execution of the runtime using `mono.exe`, as shown in Output A.3.

OUTPUT A.3:

```
C:\SAMPLES>mono.exe HelloWorld.exe
Hello. My name is Inigo Montoya.
```

■ B ■
Full Source Code Listings

M ANY OF THE CHAPTERS in this book have source code spread over multiple listings. When listings are large, this makes the code difficult to follow. This appendix includes the code listings as one program, making the individual listings easier to understand as a whole.

Chapters 3 and 4

LISTING B.1: Tic-Tac-Toe

```
#define CSHARP2

using System;

#pragma warning disable 1030 // Disable user-defined warnings

// The TicTacToe class enables two players to
// play tic-tac-toe.
class TicTacToeGame          // Declares the TicTacToeGame class
{
  static void Main()  // Declares the entry point to the program
  {
      // Stores locations each player has moved.
      int[] playerPositions = { 0, 0 };

      // Initially set the currentPlayer to Player 1;
      int currentPlayer = 1;

      // Winning player
```

```csharp
    int winner = 0;

    string input = null;


    // Display the board and
    // prompt the current player
    // for his next move.
    for (int turn = 1; turn <= 10; ++turn)
    {
        DisplayBoard(playerPositions);

        #region Check for End Game
        if (EndGame(winner, turn, input))
        {
            break;
        }
        #endregion Check for End Game

        input = NextMove(playerPositions, currentPlayer);

        winner = DetermineWinner(playerPositions);

        // Switch players
        currentPlayer = (currentPlayer == 2) ? 1 : 2;
    }
}

private static string NextMove(int[] playerPositions,
            int currentPlayer)
{
    string input;

    // Repeatedly prompt the player for a move
    // until a valid move is entered.
    bool validMove;
    do
    {
        // Request a move from the current player.
        System.Console.Write("\nPlayer {0} - Enter move:",
                currentPlayer);
        input = System.Console.ReadLine();
        validMove = ValidateAndMove(playerPositions,
                    currentPlayer, input);
    } while (!validMove);

    return input;
}
```

```csharp
static bool EndGame(int winner, int turn, string input)
{
    bool endGame = false;
    if (winner > 0)
    {
        System.Console.WriteLine("\nPlayer {0} has won!!!!"
                    winner);
        endGame = true;
    }
    else if (turn == 10)
    {
        // After completing the 10th display of the
        // board, exit out rather than prompting the
        // user again.
        System.Console.WriteLine("\nThe game was a tie!");
        endGame = true;
    }
    else if (input == "" || input == "quit")
    {
        // Check if user quit by hitting Enter without
        // any characters or by typing "quit".
        System.Console.WriteLine("The last player quit");
        endGame = true;
    }
    return endGame;
}

static int DetermineWinner(int[] playerPositions)
{
    int winner = 0;

    // Determine if there is a winner
    int[] winningMasks = {
        7, 56, 448, 73, 146, 292, 84, 273};

    foreach (int mask in winningMasks)
    {
        if ((mask & playerPositions[0]) == mask)
        {
            winner = 1;
            break;
        }
        else if ((mask & playerPositions[1]) == mask)
        {
            winner = 2;
            break;
        }
    }
}
```

```csharp
        return winner;
    }

    static bool ValidateAndMove(
      int[] playerPositions, int currentPlayer, string input)
    {
        bool valid = false;

        // Check the current player's input.
        switch (input)
        {
            case "1":
            case "2":
            case "3":
            case "4":
            case "5":
            case "6":
            case "7":
            case "8":
            case "9":
#warning   "Same move allowed multiple times."
                int shifter;  // The number of places to shift
                // over in order to set a bit.
                int position;  // The bit which is to be set.

                // int.Parse() converts "input" to an integer.
                // "int.Parse(input) - 1" because arrays
                // are zero-based.
                shifter = int.Parse(input) - 1;

                // Shift mask of 00000000000000000000000000000001
                // over by cellLocations.
                position = 1 << shifter;

                // Take the current player cells and OR them
                // to set the new position as well.
                // Since currentPlayer is either 1 or 2 you
                // subtract one to use currentPlayer as an
                // index in a 0-based array.
                playerPositions[currentPlayer - 1] |= position;

                valid = true;
                break;

            case "":
            case "quit":
                valid = true;
                break;
```

```csharp
        default:
            // If none of the other case statements
            // is encountered, then the text is invalid.
            System.Console.WriteLine(
                "\nERROR:  Enter a value from 1-9. "
                + "Push ENTER to quit");
            break;
    }

    return valid;
}


static void DisplayBoard(int[] playerPositions)
{
    // This represents the borders between each cell
    // for one row.
    string[] borders = {
"|", "|", "\n---+---+---\n", "|", "|",
"\n---+---+---\n", "|", "|", ""
};

    // Display the current board;
    int border = 0;  // set the first border (border[0] = "|")

#if CSHARP2
    System.Console.Clear();
#endif

    for (int position = 1;
        position <= 256;
        position <<= 1, border++)
    {
        char token = CalculateToken(
            playerPositions, position);

        // Write out a cell value and the border that
        // comes after it.
        System.Console.Write(" {0} {1}",
            token, borders[border]);
    }
}

static char CalculateToken(
    int[] playerPositions, int position)
{
    // Initialize the players to 'X' and 'O'
    char[] players = {'X', 'O'};

    char token;
    // If player has the position set,
```

```csharp
        // then set the token to that player.
        if ((position & playerPositions[0]) == position)
        {
            // Player 1 has that position marked
            token = players[0];
        }
        else if ((position & playerPositions[1]) == position)
        {
            // Player 2 has that position marked
            token = players[1];
        }
        else
        {
            // The position is empty.
            token = ' ';
        }
        return token;
    }


    #line 113 "TicTacToe.cs"
    // Generated code goes here
    #line default
}
```

Chapter 9

LISTING B.2: **ProductSerialNumber**

```csharp
public sealed class ProductSerialNumber
{
    public ProductSerialNumber(
        string productSeries, int model, long id)
    {
        ProductSeries = productSeries;
        Model = model;
        Id = id;
    }

    public readonly string ProductSeries;
    public readonly int Model;
    public readonly long Id;

    public override int GetHashCode()
    {
        int hashCode = ProductSeries.GetHashCode();
        hashCode ^= Model;  // Xor (eXclusive OR)
        hashCode ^= Id.GetHashCode();  // Xor (eXclusive OR)
        return hashCode;
```

```
}

public override bool Equals(object obj)
{
    if (obj == null)
    {
        return false;
    }
    if (ReferenceEquals(this, obj))
    {
        return true;
    }
    if (this.GetType() != obj.GetType())
    {
        return false;
    }
    return Equals((ProductSerialNumber)obj);
}

public bool Equals(ProductSerialNumber obj)
{
    // STEP 3: Possibly check for equivalent hash codes
    // if (this.GetHashCode() != obj.GetHashCode())
    // {
    //     return false;
    // }

    // STEP 4: Check base.Equals if base overrides Equals()
    // System.Diagnostics.Debug.Assert(
    //     base.GetType() != typeof(object));
    // if ( base.Equals(obj) )
    // {
    //     return false;
    // }

    // STEP 1: Check for null
    return ((obj != null)
        // STEP 5: Compare identifying fields for equality.
        && (ProductSeries == obj.ProductSeries) &&
        (Model == obj.Model) &&
        (Id == obj.Id));
}

public static bool operator ==(
    ProductSerialNumber leftHandSide,
    ProductSerialNumber rightHandSide)
{

    // Check if LeftHandSide is null.
    // (operator== would be recursive)
```

```csharp
        if (ReferenceEquals(leftHandSide, null))
        {
            // Return true if rightHandSide is also null
            // but false otherwise.
            return ReferenceEquals(rightHandSide, null);
        }

        return (leftHandSide.Equals(rightHandSide));
    }

    public static bool operator !=(
        ProductSerialNumber leftHandSide,
        ProductSerialNumber rightHandSide)
    {
        return !(leftHandSide == rightHandSide);
    }
}
```

Chapter 12

LISTING B.3: Binary Tree and Pair

```csharp
public enum PairItem
{
    First,
    Second
}
```

```csharp
interface IPair<T>
{
    T First
    {
        get;
        set;
    }

    T Second
    {
        get;
        set;
    }

    T this[PairItem index]
    {
        get;
        set;
```

```
        }
    }
```

```csharp
using System.Collections;
using System.Collections.Generic;

public struct Pair<T> : IPair<T>, IEnumerable<T>
{
    public Pair(T first)
    {
        _First = first;
        _Second = default(T);
    }
    public Pair(T first, T second)
    {
        _First = first;
        _Second = second;
    }
    public T First
    {
        get
        {
            return _First;
        }
        set
        {
            _First = value;
        }
    }
    private T _First;


    public T Second
    {
        get
        {
            return _Second;
        }
        set
        {
            _Second = value;
        }
    }
    private T _Second;

    [System.Runtime.CompilerServices.IndexerName("Entry")]
    public T this[PairItem index]
    {
        get
```

```csharp
        {
            switch (index)
            {
                case PairItem.First:
                    return First;
                case PairItem.Second:
                    return Second;
                default:
                    throw new NotImplementedException(
                        string.Format(
                        "The enum {0} has not been implemented",
                        index.ToString()));
            }
        }
        set
        {
            switch (index)
            {
                case PairItem.First:
                    First = value;
                    break;
                case PairItem.Second:
                    Second = value;
                    break;
                default:
                    throw new NotImplementedException(
                        string.Format(
                        "The enum {0} has not been implemented",
                        index.ToString()));
            }
        }
    }

    #region IEnumerable<T> Members
    public IEnumerator<T> GetEnumerator()
    {
        yield return First;
        yield return Second;
    }
    #endregion

    #region IEnumerable Members
    IEnumerator IEnumerable.GetEnumerator()
    {
        return GetEnumerator();
    }
    #endregion

    public IEnumerable<T> GetReverseEnumerator()
    {
```

```
            yield return Second;
            yield return First;
        }


        // Listing 12.24
        public IEnumerable<T> GetNotNullEnumerator()
        {
            if ((First == null) || (Second == null))
            {
                yield break;
            }
            yield return Second;
            yield return First;
        }
    }
}
```

```
using System.Collections;
using System.Collections.Generic;

public interface IBinaryTree<T>
{
    T Item
    {
        get;
        set;
    }
    Pair<IBinaryTree<T>> SubItems
    {
        get;
        set;
    }
}
public class BinaryTree<T> : IEnumerable<T>
{
    public BinaryTree(T value)
    {
        Value = value;
    }

    public T Value
    {
        get { return _Value; }
        set { _Value = value; }
    }
    private T _Value;

    public Pair<BinaryTree<T>> SubItems
    {
        get { return _SubItems; }
        set
```

```csharp
            {
                IComparable first;
                first = (IComparable)value.First.Value;

                if (first.CompareTo(value.Second.Value) < 0)
                {
                    // first is less than second.
                }
                else
                {
                    // first and second are the same or
                    // second is less than first.
                }
                _SubItems = value;
            }
        }
    private Pair<BinaryTree<T>> _SubItems;

    public T this[params PairItem[] branches]
    {
        get
        {
            BinaryTree<T> currentNode = this;
            int totalLevels =
                (branches == null) ? 0 : branches.Length;
            int currentLevel = 0;

            while (currentLevel < totalLevels)
            {
                currentNode =
                    currentNode.SubItems[branches[currentLevel]];
                if (currentNode == null)
                {
                    // The binary tree at this location is null.
                    throw new IndexOutOfRangeException();
                }
                currentLevel++;
            }

            return currentNode.Value;
        }
    }
    #region IEnumerable<T>
    // Listing 12.22
    public IEnumerator<T> GetEnumerator()
    {
        // Return the item at this node.
        yield return Value;

        // Iterate through each of the elements in the pair.
```

```csharp
            foreach (BinaryTree<T> tree in SubItems)
            {
                if (tree != null)
                {
                    // Since each element in the pair is a tree,
                    // traverse the tree and yield each
                    // element.
                    foreach (T item in tree)
                    {
                        yield return item;
                    }
                }
            }
        }
        #endregion IEnumerable<T>


        #region IEnumerable Members
        IEnumerator IEnumerable.GetEnumerator()
        {
            return GetEnumerator();
        }
        #endregion
    }
```

Chapter 14

LISTING B.4: Command-Line Attributes

```csharp
using System;
using System.Diagnostics;

public partial class Program
{
  public static void Main(string[] args)
  {
      string errorMessage;
      CommandLineInfo commandLine = new CommandLineInfo();
      if (!CommandLineHandler.TryParse(
          args, commandLine, out errorMessage))
      {
          Console.WriteLine(errorMessage);
          DisplayHelp();
      }

      if (commandLine.Help)
      {
          DisplayHelp();
      }
```

```csharp
        else
        {
            if (commandLine.Priority !=
                ProcessPriorityClass.Normal)
            {
                // Change thread priority
            }

        }
        // ...

    }

    private static void DisplayHelp()
    {
            // Display the command-line help.
            Console.WriteLine(
                "Thankyou for contacting the help text");  }
}
```

```csharp
using System;
using System.Diagnostics;

public partial class Program
{
  private class CommandLineInfo
  {
      [CommandLineSwitchAlias("?")]
      public bool Help
      {
          get { return _Help; }
          set { _Help = value; }
      }
      private bool _Help;

      [CommandLineSwitchRequired]
      [CommandLineSwitchAlias("FileName")]
      public string Out
      {
          get { return _Out; }
          set { _Out = value; }
      }
      private string _Out;

      public ProcessPriorityClass Priority
      {
          get { return _Priority; }
          set { _Priority = value; }
      }
```

```
        private ProcessPriorityClass _Priority =
            ProcessPriorityClass.Normal;
    }
}
```

```
using System;
using System.Diagnostics;
using System.Reflection;

public class CommandLineHandler
{
  public static void Parse(string[] args, object commandLine)
  {
      string errorMessage;
      if (!TryParse(args, commandLine, out errorMessage))
      {
          throw new ApplicationException(errorMessage);
      }
  }

  public static bool TryParse(string[] args, object commandLine,
      out string errorMessage)
  {
      bool success = false;
      errorMessage = null;
      foreach (string arg in args)
      {
          string option;
          if (arg[0] == '/' || arg[0] == '-')
          {
              string[] optionParts = arg.Split(
                  new char[] { ':' }, 2);

              // Remove the slash/dash
              option = optionParts[0].Remove(0, 1);
              PropertyInfo property =
                  commandLine.GetType().GetProperty(option,
                      BindingFlags.IgnoreCase |
                      BindingFlags.Instance |
                      BindingFlags.Public);
              if (property != null)
              {
                  if (property.PropertyType == typeof(bool))
                  {
                      // Last parameters for handling indexers
                      property.SetValue(
                          commandLine, true, null);
                      success = true;
                  }
```

```csharp
                else if (
                    property.PropertyType == typeof(string))
                {
                    property.SetValue(
                        commandLine, optionParts[1], null);
                    success = true;
                }
                else if (property.PropertyType.IsEnum)
                {
                    try
                    {
                        property.SetValue(commandLine,
                            Enum.Parse(
                                typeof(ProcessPriorityClass),
                                optionParts[1], true),
                            null);
                        success = true;
                    }
                    catch (ArgumentException )
                    {
                        success = false;
                        errorMessage =
                            string.Format(
                                "The option '{0}' is " +
                                "invalid for '{1}'",
                                optionParts[1], option);
                    }
                }
                else
                {
                    success = false;
                    errorMessage = string.Format(
                        "Data type '{0}' on {1} is not"
                        + " supported.",
                        property.PropertyType.ToString(),
                        commandLine.GetType().ToString());
                }
            }
            else
            {
                success = false;
                errorMessage = string.Format(
                    "Option '{0}' is not supported.",
                    option);
            }
        }
    }
    return success;
```

```
      }
  }
```

```csharp
using System;
using System.Collections.Specialized;
using System.Reflection;

[AttributeUsage(AttributeTargets.Property, AllowMultiple = false)]
public class CommandLineSwitchRequiredAttribute : Attribute
{
  public static string[] GetMissingRequiredOptions(
      object commandLine)
  {
      StringCollection missingOptions = new StringCollection();
      PropertyInfo[] properties =
          commandLine.GetType().GetProperties();

      foreach (PropertyInfo property in properties)
      {
          Attribute[] attributes =
              (Attribute[])property.GetCustomAttributes(
                  typeof(CommandLineSwitchRequiredAttribute),
                  false);
          if ((attributes.Length > 0) &&
              (property.GetValue(commandLine, null) == null))
          {
              if (property.GetValue(commandLine, null) == null)
              {
                  missingOptions.Add(property.Name);
              }
          }
      }
      string[] results = new string[missingOptions.Count];
      missingOptions.CopyTo(results, 0);
      return results;
  }
}
```

```csharp
using System;
using System.Reflection;
using System.Collections.Generic;

[AttributeUsage(AttributeTargets.Property)]
public class CommandLineSwitchAliasAttribute : Attribute
{
  public CommandLineSwitchAliasAttribute(string alias)
  {
```

```csharp
            Alias = alias;
        }


    public string Alias
    {
        get { return _Alias; }
        set { _Alias = value; }
    }
    private string _Alias;

    public static Dictionary<string, PropertyInfo> GetSwitches(
        object commandLine)
    {
        PropertyInfo[] properties = null;
        Dictionary<string, PropertyInfo> options =
            new Dictionary<string, PropertyInfo>();

        properties = commandLine.GetType().GetProperties(
            BindingFlags.Public | BindingFlags.NonPublic |
            BindingFlags.Instance);
        foreach (PropertyInfo property in properties)
        {
            options.Add(property.Name.ToLower(), property);
            foreach (CommandLineSwitchAliasAttribute attribute in
                property.GetCustomAttributes(
                typeof(CommandLineSwitchAliasAttribute), false))
            {
                options.Add(attribute.Alias.ToLower(), property);
            }
        }
        return options;
    }
}
```

```csharp
using System;
using System.Reflection;
using System.Collections.Generic;

public class CommandLineHandler
{
  // ...

  public static bool TryParse(
      string[] args, object commandLine,
      out string errorMessage)
  {
      bool success = false;
      errorMessage = null;
```

```csharp
            Dictionary<string, PropertyInfo> options =
                CommandLineSwitchAliasAttribute.GetSwitches(
                    commandLine);

        foreach (string arg in args)
        {
            PropertyInfo property;
            string option;
            if (arg[0] == '/' || arg[0] == '-')
            {
                string[] optionParts = arg.Split(
                    new char[] { ':' }, 2);
                option = optionParts[0].Remove(0, 1).ToLower();

                if (options.TryGetValue(option, out property))
                {
                    success = SetOption(
                        commandLine, property,
                        optionParts, ref errorMessage);
                }
                else
                {
                    success = false;
                    errorMessage = string.Format(
                        "Option '{0}' is not supported.",
                        option);
                }
            }
        }

        return success;
    }

    private static bool SetOption(
        object commandLine, PropertyInfo property,
        string[] optionParts, ref string errorMessage)
    {
        bool success;

        if (property.PropertyType == typeof(bool))
        {
            // Last parameters for handling indexers
            property.SetValue(
                commandLine, true, null);
            success = true;
        }
        else
        {

            if ((optionParts.Length < 2)
```

```csharp
                    || optionParts[1] == ""
                    || optionParts[1] == ":")
                {
                    // No setting was provided for the switch.
                    success = false;
                    errorMessage = string.Format(
                        "You must specify the value for the {0} option.",
                        property.Name);
                }
                else if (
                    property.PropertyType == typeof(string))
                {
                    property.SetValue(
                        commandLine, optionParts[1], null);
                    success = true;
                }
                else if (property.PropertyType.IsEnum)
                {
                    success = TryParseEnumSwitch(
                        commandLine, optionParts,
                        property, ref errorMessage);
                }
                else
                {
                    success = false;
                    errorMessage = string.Format(
                        "Data type '{0}' on {1} is not supported.",
                        property.PropertyType.ToString(),
                        commandLine.GetType().ToString());
                }
            }
            return success;
        }
    }
```

Chapter 17

LISTING B.5: Virtual Computer Detection Using P/Invoke

```csharp
using System.Runtime.InteropServices;

class Program
{
    delegate void MethodInvoker();

    unsafe static int Main(string[] args)
    {
        // Assign redpill
```

```
    byte[] redpill = {
        0x0f, 0x01, 0x0d,      // asm SIDT instruction
        0x00, 0x00, 0x00, 0x00, // placeholder for an address
        0xc3};                 // asm return instruction

    unsafe
    {
        fixed (byte* matrix = new byte[6],
            redpillPtr = redpill)
        {
            // Move the address of matrix immediately
            // following the SIDT instruction of memory.
            *(uint*)&redpillPtr[3] = (uint)&matrix[0];

            using (VirtualMemoryPtr codeBytesPtr =
                new VirtualMemoryPtr(redpill.Length))
            {
                Marshal.Copy(
                    redpill, 0,
                    codeBytesPtr, redpill.Length);

                MethodInvoker method =
                    (MethodInvoker)Marshal.GetDelegateForFunctionPointer(
                    codeBytesPtr, typeof(MethodInvoker));

                method();
            }
            if (matrix[5] > 0xd0)
            {
                Console.WriteLine("Inside Matrix! \n");
                return 1;
            }
            else
            {
                Console.WriteLine("Not in Matrix. \n");
                return 0;
            }
        } // fixed
    } // unsafe
  }
}


public class VirtualMemoryPtr :
  System.Runtime.InteropServices.SafeHandle
{
  public VirtualMemoryPtr(int memorySize) :
      base(IntPtr.Zero, true)
  {
      ProcessHandle =
```

```csharp
            VirtualMemoryManager.GetCurrentProcessHandle();
        MemorySize = (IntPtr)memorySize;
        AllocatedPointer =
            VirtualMemoryManager.AllocExecutionBlock(
            memorySize, ProcessHandle);
        Disposed = false;
    }

    public readonly IntPtr AllocatedPointer;
    readonly IntPtr ProcessHandle;
    readonly IntPtr MemorySize;
    bool Disposed;

    public static implicit operator IntPtr(
        VirtualMemoryPtr virtualMemoryPointer)
    {
        return virtualMemoryPointer.AllocatedPointer;
    }

    // SafeHandle abstract member
    public override bool IsInvalid
    {
        get
        {
            return Disposed;
        }
    }

    // SafeHandle abstract member
    protected override bool ReleaseHandle()
    {
        if (!Disposed)
        {
            Disposed = true;
            GC.SuppressFinalize(this);
            VirtualMemoryManager.VirtualFreeEx(ProcessHandle,
                AllocatedPointer, MemorySize);
        }
        return true;
    }
}
```

```csharp
class VirtualMemoryManager
{

    /// <summary>
    /// The type of memory allocation. This parameter must
    /// contain one of the following values.
    /// </summary>
```

```
[Flags]
private enum AllocationType : uint
{
    /// <summary>
    /// Allocates physical storage in memory or in the
    /// paging file on disk for the specified reserved
    /// memory pages. The function initializes the memory
    /// to zero.
    /// </summary>
    Commit = 0x1000,
    /// <summary>
    /// Reserves a range of the process's virtual address
    /// space without allocating any actual physical
    /// storage in memory or in the paging file on disk.
    /// </summary>
    Reserve = 0x2000,
    /// <summary>
    /// Indicates that data in the memory range specified by
    /// lpAddress and dwSize is no longer of interest. The
    /// pages should not be read from or written to the
    /// paging file. However, the memory block will be used
    /// again later, so it should not be decommitted. This
    /// value cannot be used with any other value.
    /// </summary>
    Reset = 0x80000,
    /// <summary>
    /// Allocates physical memory with read-write access.
    /// This value is solely for use with Address Windowing
    /// Extensions (AWE) memory.
    /// </summary>
    Physical = 0x400000,
    /// <summary>
    /// Allocates memory at the highest possible address.
    /// </summary>
    TopDown = 0x100000,
}


/// <summary>
/// The memory protection for the region of pages to be
/// allocated.
/// </summary>
[Flags]
private enum ProtectionOptions : uint
{
    /// <summary>
    /// Enables execute access to the committed region of
    /// pages. An attempt to read or write to the committed
    /// region results in an access violation.
    /// </summary>
```

```csharp
    Execute = 0x10,
    /// <summary>
    /// Enables execute and read access to the committed
    /// region of pages. An attempt to write to the
    /// committed region results in an access violation.
    /// </summary>
    PageExecuteRead = 0x20,
    /// <summary>
    /// Enables execute, read, and write access to the
    /// committed region of pages.
    /// </summary>
    PageExecuteReadWrite = 0x40,
    // ...
}


/// <summary>
/// The type of free operation
/// </summary>
[Flags]
private enum MemoryFreeType : uint
{
    /// <summary>
    /// Decommits the specified region of committed pages.
    /// After the operation, the pages are in the reserved
    /// state.
    /// </summary>
    Decommit = 0x4000,
    /// <summary>
    /// Releases the specified region of pages. After this
    /// operation, the pages are in the free state.
    /// </summary>
    Release = 0x8000
}

[DllImport("kernel32.dll", EntryPoint="GetCurrentProcess")]
internal static extern IntPtr GetCurrentProcessHandle();

[DllImport("kernel32.dll")]
internal static extern IntPtr GetCurrentProcess();

[DllImport("kernel32.dll", SetLastError = true)]
private static extern IntPtr VirtualAllocEx(
    IntPtr hProcess,
    IntPtr lpAddress,
    IntPtr dwSize,
    AllocationType flAllocationType,
    uint flProtect);

// ...
[DllImport("kernel32.dll", SetLastError = true)]
```

```csharp
    static extern bool VirtualProtectEx(
        IntPtr hProcess, IntPtr lpAddress,
        IntPtr dwSize, uint flNewProtect,
        ref uint lpflOldProtect);

public static IntPtr AllocExecutionBlock(
    int size, IntPtr hProcess)
{
    IntPtr codeBytesPtr;
    codeBytesPtr = VirtualAllocEx(
        hProcess, IntPtr.Zero,
        (IntPtr)size,
        AllocationType.Reserve | AllocationType.Commit,
        (uint)ProtectionOptions.PageExecuteReadWrite);

    if (codeBytesPtr == IntPtr.Zero)
    {
        throw new System.ComponentModel.Win32Exception();
    }

    uint lpflOldProtect = 0;
    if (!VirtualProtectEx(
        hProcess, codeBytesPtr,
        (IntPtr)size,
        (uint)ProtectionOptions.PageExecuteReadWrite,
        ref lpflOldProtect))
    {
        throw new System.ComponentModel.Win32Exception();
    }
    return codeBytesPtr;
}

public static IntPtr AllocExecutionBlock(int size)
{
    return AllocExecutionBlock(
        size, GetCurrentProcessHandle());
}

[DllImport("kernel32.dll", SetLastError = true)]
static extern bool VirtualFreeEx(
    IntPtr hProcess, IntPtr lpAddress,
    IntPtr dwSize, IntPtr dwFreeType);
public static bool VirtualFreeEx(
    IntPtr hProcess, IntPtr lpAddress,
    IntPtr dwSize)
{
    bool result = VirtualFreeEx(
        hProcess, lpAddress, dwSize,
        (IntPtr)MemoryFreeType.Decommit);
    if (!result)
```

```csharp
        {
            throw new System.ComponentModel.Win32Exception();
        }
        return result;
    }
    public static bool VirtualFreeEx(
        IntPtr lpAddress, IntPtr dwSize)
    {
        return VirtualFreeEx(
            GetCurrentProcessHandle(), lpAddress, dwSize);
    }

}
```

C
Concurrent Classes from System.Collections.Concurrent

THE CONCURRENT CLASSES APPEAR in Figures C.1 through C.6 and are discussed in Chapter 19.

FIGURE C.1: System.Collections.Concurrent.ConcurrentQueue<T>

IProducerConsumerCollection<T>
IEnumerable<T>
ICollection
IEnumerable
ISerializable
IDeserializationCallback

B ConcurrentStack<T>
Generic Class

☐ Properties
  Count
  IsEmpty
☐ Methods
  Clear
  ConcurrentStack (+ 2 overloads)
  CopyTo
  GetEnumerator
  GetObjectData
  OnDeserialization
  Push
  PushRange (+ 1 overload)
  ToArray
  TryPeek
  TryPop
  TryPopRange (+ 1 overload)

FIGURE C.2: System.Collections.Concurrent.ConcurrentStack<T>

IProducerConsumerCollection<T>
IEnumerable<T>
ICollection
IEnumerable
ISerializable
IDeserializationCallback

C ConcurrentBag<T>
Generic Class

☐ Properties
  Count
  IsEmpty
☐ Methods
  Add
  ConcurrentBag (+ 2 overloads)
  CopyTo
  GetEnumerator
  GetObjectData
  OnDeserialization
  ToArray
  TryPeek
  TryTake

FIGURE C.3: System.Collections.Concurrent.ConcurrentBag<T>

FIGURE C.4: System.Collections.Concurrent.ConcurrentLinkedList<T>

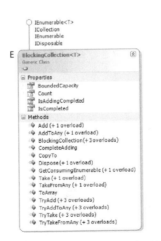

FIGURE C.5: System.Collections.Concurrent.BlockingCollection<T>

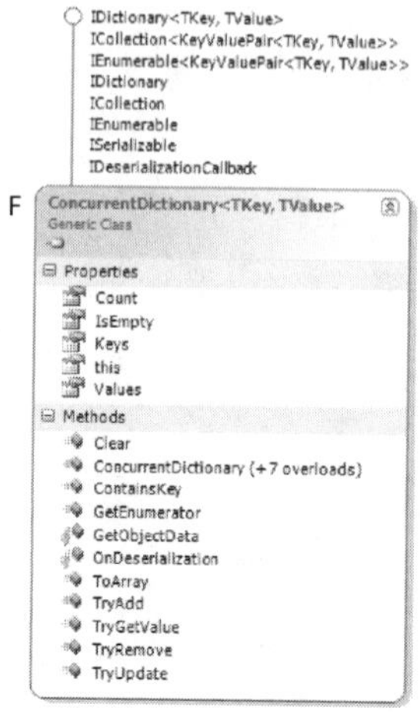

○ IDictionary<TKey, TValue>
ICollection<KeyValuePair<TKey, TValue>>
IEnumerable<KeyValuePair<TKey, TValue>>
IDictionary
ICollection
IEnumerable
ISerializable
IDeserializationCallback

ConcurrentDictionary<TKey, TValue>
Generic Class

□ **Properties**
- Count
- IsEmpty
- Keys
- this
- Values

□ **Methods**
- Clear
- ConcurrentDictionary (+7 overloads)
- ContainsKey
- GetEnumerator
- GetObjectData
- OnDeserialization
- ToArray
- TryAdd
- TryGetValue
- TryRemove
- TryUpdate

FIGURE C.6: System.Collections.Concurrent.ConcurrentDictionary<TKey, TValue>

▪D▪
C# 2.0 Topics

Continues

Topic Title	Page Number
System.Threading.Interlocked class methods	762
System.Threading.Mutex	766
TryParse() method	63–64
turning off warning messages (#pragma)	142–143

7

E

C# 3.0 Topics

▉ F ▪
C# 4.0 Topics

Index

intelliTechture
INTELLIGENT.TECHNICAL.ARCHITECTURE.TRAINING

Mark Michaelis is the founder and chief technical architect of IntelliTechture Corporation, a high-end software architecture and development consulting firm based in Spokane, Washington. The company hires the best and brightest engineers and focuses on providing architecture consulting, software development, and training to enable their customers to solve the most challenging problems. IntelliTechture has principal and senior engineers specializing in the latest Microsoft technologies, including Microsoft .NET (WCF/WPF/WF), Visual Studio VSTS/TFS, SharePoint, and BizTalk Server.

IntelliTechture uses best practice application life-cycle management to deliver quality software solutions on time, on scope, and within budget. It specializes in the following services:

- From the concept phase onwards, IntelliTechture offers and delivers training, consulting, and implementation using state of the art software—**Visual Studio Team System (VSTS)** and **Team Foundation Server (TFS).**

- IntelliTechture enables companies to achieve efficient and effective collaboration, corporate publishing, and enterprise content management (ECM). **SharePoint** services include consulting, training, deployment/upgrading, internet/intranet portals, and application development.

- IntelliTechture conducts software architecture workshops that design service (SOA), security, scope, layout, and deployment blueprints.

- For the integration and migration of large enterprise applications as well as business-to-business transactions, IntelliTechture offerings include **BizTalk** and **SQL Server Integration Services (SSIS)** solutions. BizTalk Integrations include the use of line-of-business adapters and the Enterprise Service Bus (ESB).

IntelliTechture personnel serve on Microsoft's VSTS and Connected Systems Advisory Councils, publish frequently, and present at conferences such as TechEd, DevConnections, and VSLive.

IntelliTechture is committed to devoting a significant portion of its profits to the fight against extreme poverty around the world.

For more information, please visit www.intelliTechture.com or email info@intelliTechture.com.

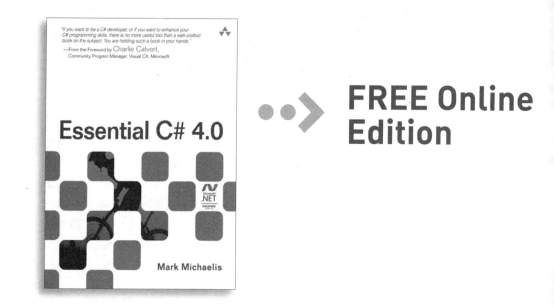

FREE Online Edition

Your purchase of **Essential C# 4.0** includes access to a free online edition for 45 days through the Safari Books Online subscription service. Nearly every Addison-Wesley Professional book is available online through Safari Books Online, along with more than 5,000 other technical books and videos from publishers such as Cisco Press, Exam Cram, IBM Press, O'Reilly, Prentice Hall, Que, and Sams.

SAFARI BOOKS ONLINE allows you to search for a specific answer, cut and paste code, download chapters, and stay current with emerging technologies.

Activate your FREE Online Edition at www.informit.com/safarifree

R.C.L.

NOV. 2010

G

> **STEP 1:** Enter the coupon code ▇▇▇▇▇▇

> **STEP 2:** New Safari users, complete the brief registration form.
> Safari subscribers, just log in.

If you have difficulty registering on Safari or accessing the online edition, please e-mail customer-service@safaribooksonline.com

Safari
Books Online